A Portrait of Mendelssohn

A Portrait of Mendelssohn

Clive Brown

Yale University Press · New Haven and London

Published with assistance from the foundation established in memory of Amasa Stone
Mather of the class of 1907, Yale College.

Set in Adobe Garamond type by Binghamton Valley Composition,
Binghamton, New York.
Printed in the United States of America by Sheridan Books.

Library of Congress Cataloging-in-Publication Data

Brown, Clive, 1947–
  A portrait of mendelssohn / Clive Brown.
      p.   cm.
Includes bibliographical references (p.   ) and index.
  ISBN 0-300-09539-2 (alk. paper)

  1. Mendelssohn-Bartholdy, Felix, 1809–1847.   2.
Composers—Germany—Biography.   I. Title.
  ML410.M5 B76 2003
  780'.92—dc21   2002012154

A catalogue record for this book is available from the British Library.

10   9   8   7   6   5   4   3   2   1

For Felix

(25 SEPTEMBER 1996)

Contents

Preface

Felix Mendelssohn's personality and work have been distorted in the eyes of posterity by extremes of unthinking admiration and ideologically motivated opprobrium, which began to develop during his lifetime and became increasingly exaggerated in the decades after his death. The stereotypical images of Mendelssohn, as man and artist, that crystallized during the first half of the twentieth century, are the product of historical forces that have little to do with the intrinsic qualities of his music or with an objective appraisal of his position and importance in mid-nineteenth-century musical life. They are often based on selective or inaccurate citation of the primary evidence; and they still persist to a considerable degree despite more recent scholarly reassessment.

According to these views Mendelssohn was, at best, Felix by name and *felix* (happy or fortunate) by nature, a rather innocuous composer whose music is essentially skilful and refined but lightweight and emotionally undemanding, or even effeminate, calculated rather to please the senses than to stimulate the intellect or move the passions. At worst, he was a musical magpie, lacking genuine creative ability (a consequence of his Jewish origins, according to Wagner and other racially motivated writers), whose propensity for mawkish sentimentality exerted a seriously deleterious influence on the development of nineteenth-century music. These distorted images are intimately related to the charge of shallowness conventionally levelled against his music. In the early twentieth century, Mendelssohn's reputation paid the price of excessive adulation; his detractors, who regarded it as axiomatic that their taste was superior to that of their forefathers, saw his former popularity and influence as proof, according to their elitist criteria, of the facile and meretricious nature of his music. And after Hitler's rise to power in 1933, the perverted dialectic of Wagner's anti-Semitic tracts reached its absurd culmination in an attempt to write Mendelssohn out of the history of Western music.

The reality is altogether more complex. Mendelssohn was cultivated, intellectually gifted to a remarkable degree, possessed tremendous mental and physical energy, and was motivated in both his life and his art by sincerely and deeply held aesthetic and moral convictions. At the same time, he had a lively sense of fun, was fundamentally kind and considerate, exhibited an extraordinary degree of charm, and aroused deep devotion in many who came into contact with him. Yet he was also capable of moody unsociability, violent fits of rage, abrupt rudeness, long-maintained resentment when he fancied he had been wronged or slighted, boisterous and sometimes insensitive high spirits, firmness bordering on inflexibility where he encountered anything that offended his artistic or moral creed, and even a degree of self-centered arrogance. In addition, his hypersensitive temperament undoubtedly nourished inner tensions, which he rarely revealed but which surely contributed to the emotional and physical exhaustion that hastened his early death.

Growing understanding of the complexity of Mendelssohn's character, and of the aesthetic and racial politics that coloured the reception of his music during the century after his death, is gradually creating a more rounded view. Mendelssohn is beginning to emerge from the reassessment of the past half century not merely as the possessor of phenomenal musical skills but also as an innovative and highly cerebral musician with profoundly held and passionate, though seldom openly articulated, views about the nature and purpose of art. His habit of disciplined and regular composition was combined with an almost morbid concern for perfection, which manifested itself in obsessive revision and led him to withhold major works from publication for decades, while his activity as performer, conductor and musical educator placed him at the forefront of musical developments in the 1830s and 1840s. Furthermore, his musical influence, persistently decried by Wagner and his followers as wholly negative, had powerful ramifications. Numberless imitators during the second half of the nineteenth century testify to the attractions of Mendelssohn's style for lesser talents, but his example also provided more fruitful inspiration for important composers from Schumann through Brahms and Saint-Saëns to Elgar (Ravel even went so far as to dub Elgar "tout à fait Mendelssohn" [Vaughan Williams, *National Music*, 191]); even Wagner himself privately admitted to Mendelssohn's influence on his early development, confessing to Cosima in 1879, for instance, that his *Columbus* Overture was plagiarized from Mendelssohn's *Meeresstille und glückliche Fahrt* (Cosima Wagner, *Diaries*, 2:325).

The task of illuminating Mendelssohn and the reception of his music through his own words and those of his contemporaries is made especially difficult by the sheer quantity of material available. A large number of Mendelssohn's own letters survive, as do the vast bulk of those he received during the years 1833 to 1847; his music was extensively discussed in print during his lifetime, and after his death many of those who had known him published recollections of him. Much of this material has been in the public domain, and in English translation, since the nineteenth century, though not always in reliable forms, because of often unacknowledged censorship. Other material, which was published only in German or French, especially in periodicals, has not been available in English. Where acceptable nineteenth-century English translations exist, I have used them here (with occasional amendments of inaccuracies, as noted) and have given references to the published English versions in order to make it easier for interested readers to locate extracts in their context. All translations are my own unless otherwise attributed. In translating from German, where the original contains long and elaborate sentences, with idiosyncratic vocabulary and grammar typical of much nineteenth-century academic and critical writing (Gottfried Wilhelm Fink and Otto Lange provide particularly good examples), I have generally opted for as literal a translation as possible, retaining the involved and sometimes puzzling complexities of the original language, rather than imposing my own interpretation of what the author might have intended to convey.

Because this study attempts to provide a rounded picture of Mendelssohn's life and works in their historical setting, some relatively well-known accounts have inevitably been included. Where appropriate, however, I have presented less familiar and less easily accessible sources. This is particularly the case with passages from nineteenth-century periodicals, many of which have not been reprinted since their original publication. In dealing with Mendelssohn's career and the reception of his works, I have necessarily been very selective but have tried to include material that represents all important issues, or shades of opinion, and to give as clear an impression as possible of their relative importance.

Acknowledgments

It is with great pleasure that I acknowledge the courteous assistance of the staff of the libraries whose research facilities I have used. Foremost among these are the British Library, the Staatsbibliothek zu Berlin, the Brotherton Library, Leeds, and the Bodleian Library, Oxford. To the head of the music collection at the Bodleian, Peter Ward Jones, a distinguished Mendelssohn scholar in his own right, I owe particular thanks for his ready response to my many queries. For permission to reproduce illustrations I am grateful to the Bodleian Library, Oxford, the Mendelssohn Archiv of the Staatsbibliothek zu Berlin and the Bildarchiv Preußischer Kulturbesitz, Berlin.

I thankfully acknowledge the invaluable information and inspiration that derives from the work of all those scholars who, over recent years, have contributed so notably to our understanding of Mendelssohn and his music. Very many individuals have stimulated and encouraged my work on this book, sometimes perhaps without realizing it, and I hope that those whose names are not included here will pardon the omission. Among those who have most directly contributed assistance and information I should like in particular to thank Baroness Marie Sophie Doblhoff-Dier, Harry Lyth, and Mireille Ribière. Nina Platts has earned my special gratitude for her tireless pursuit of elusive information and for proof reading my typescript. At Yale University Press, Harry Haskell, who first suggested the idea of this book, has been a constant source of support and encouragement, and Otto Bohlmann has been a thorough, sympathetic, and discriminating editor of my typescript. Last, but by no means least, I thank my wife, Dorothea Brown-Doblhoff, for her patience and interest and my son, Felix, for the unwitting motivation he has provided.

A Checklist of Mendelssohn's Life and Principal Works

Posthumous opus numbers are given in parentheses. Works are listed twice where the gap between composition and publication is significant (except songs, which are listed only under their publication dates). Publications are given in capitals. Where there was a significant gap between composition and publication, substantial revision took place in most cases.

Year	*Events and Works*
1776	Abraham Mendelssohn born Berlin
1777	Lea Salomon born Berlin
1786	Moses Mendelssohn dies Berlin
1804	Marriage of Abraham Mendelssohn and Lea Salomon Napoleon proclaimed emperor of the French
1805	Fanny Mendelssohn born Hamburg
1808	Haydn dies
1809	Felix Mendelssohn (FMB) born Hamburg
1811	Family moves to Berlin Rebecka Mendelssohn born Berlin
1813	Paul Mendelssohn born Berlin
1815	FMB begins to study piano with Ludwig Berger Napoleon defeated at Waterloo
1816	FMB takes piano lessons with Marie Bigot and violin lessons with Pierre Baillot in Paris FMB and siblings baptized
1817?	Carl Friedrich Zelter begins instruction in musical theory Violin lessons with Carl Wilhelm Henning
1818	FMB's first public appearance in Friederich Gugel's concert

1819   Carl Wilhelm Ludwig Heyse appointed private tutor
        First extant composition (?)
        Sonata for Two Pianos in D

1820   Joines chorus of Berlin Singakademie as alto
        Earliest dramatic compositions
        Piano Trio in c
        Violin Sonata in F
        Male-voice part-songs
        Solo songs
        Ich J. Mendelssohn
        Die Soldatenliebschaft

1821   First visit to Goethe
        Weber directs *Der Freischütz* in Berlin
        Die beiden Pädagogen
        Piano Sonata in g (op. 105)

1822   Family expedition to Switzerland
        Die wandernden Komödienten
        First six or seven string symphonies
        Piano Concerto in a
        Violin Concerto in d
        Piano Quartet in c, op. 1
        Gloria in E-flat
        Psalm 66
        Magnificat in D
        Last string symphonies (1822–1823)

1823   Short trip with father to Silesia
        Concerto for Violin and Piano in d
        Concerto for two Pianos in E
        String Quartet in E-flat
        Die beiden Neffen
        Piano Quartet in F Minor, op. 2
        PIANO QUARTET IN C, OP. 1

1824   Short trip with father to Doberan
        First critical articles on compositions appear in the press
        Beethoven's Ninth Symphony premières in Vienna
        Concerto for Two Pianos in A-flat
        Symphony no. 1 in c, op. 11
        Sextet in D (op. 110)

Overture for Wind Instruments in C
Viola Sonata in c
Clarinet Sonata in E-flat
Salve Regina in E-flat
PIANO QUARTET IN F MINOR, OP. 2
Die Hochzeit des Camacho (begun)

1825   Journey to Paris; Cherubini endorses him for a musical career
Family moves to 3 Leipziger Straße
PIANO QUARTET IN B, OP. 3
VIOLIN SONATA IN F, OP. 4
Kyrie in d
Die Hochzeit des Camacho (finished)
String Octet in E-flat, op. 20
CAPRICCIO IN F-SHARP, OP. 5

1826   Publication (anonymously) of FMB's metrical translation of Terence's
Andria
Weber dies
Ein Sommernachtstraum Overture, op. 21
Capriccio brillant in b, op. 22
Overture in C (op. 101)
String Quintet in A, op. 18
PIANO SONATA IN E, OP. 6
Te Deum in D

1827   Concert in Stettin: première of *Ein Sommernachtstraum*
Public staging of *Die Hochzeit des Camacho*
Travels in Germany
Meeting with Justus Thibaut
Attends University of Berlin
Beethoven dies
String Quartet in a, op. 13
Two Fugues in E-flat for String Quartet
SIEBEN CHARACTERISTISCHE STÜCKE, OP. 7
Fantasia in E, op. 15
Piano Sonata in B-flat (op. 106)
Fugue in e (piano)
Motet: "Tu es Petrus" (op. 111)
Chorale cantata: "Christ du Lamm Gottes"
Various lieder

1828 Berlin
Schubert dies
ZWÖLF GESÄNGE, OP. 8
DIE HOCHZEIT DES CAMACHO, op. 10 (vocal score)
SYMPHONY NO. 1, OP. 11
Chorale cantata: "Jesu meine Freude"
Meeresstille und glückliche Fahrt Overture, op. 27
Motets: "Ave maris stella" "Hora est"
Grosse Festmusik zum Dürerfest Begrüssung (*Humboldt* Cantata)

1829 April–July: first concerts London
August–September: travels through Scotland and Wales
September–December: sojourn in London
October: Fanny marries painter Wilhelm Hensel
December: returns to Berlin
STRING QUARTET IN E-FLAT, OP. 12
SCHERZO FOR PIANO IN B
TROIS FANTAISIES OU CAPRICES, OP. 16
VARIATIONS CONCERTANTES, OP. 17
Chorale cantata: "Wer nur den lieben Gott"
Die Heimkehr aus der Fremde (op. 89)
Various lieder

1830 Offered, and refuses, chair of music at University of Berlin
May: last visit to Goethe
June–December: journey to Munich, Vienna, Venice, Florence, Rome
Revolutions in Paris, Brussels, Poland, Italy and many German states.
ZWÖLF LIEDER, OP. 9
STRING QUARTET IN A, OP. 13
RONDO CAPRICCIOSO, OP. 14
FANTASIA IN E, OP. 15
Ouvertüre zur einsamen insel (first version of *Die Hebriden*), op. 26
Reformation Symphony (op. 107)
Psalm 115, op. 31
Drei Kirchenmusiken, op. 23
Three Motets, op. 39

1831 January–July: travels in Italy
August–October: journey through Switzerland, Munich, Frankfurt, Bonn, Düsseldorf, to Paris
December: Paris
Piano Concerto no. 1 in g, op. 25

1832   January–April: Paris
        April–June: London
        June–December: Berlin
        Deaths of Goethe, Zelter, Eduard Rietz
        EIN SOMMERNACHTSTRAUM OVERTURE OP. 21
        CAPRICCIO BRILLANT, OP. 22
        DREI KIRCHENMUSIKEN OP. 23
        PIANO CONCERTO NO. I IN G, OP. 25
        ORIGINAL MELODIES FOR THE PIANOFORTE (LIEDER OHNE WORTE BK.
        I), OP. 19B
        Die erste Walpurgisnacht (first version)

1833   January: fails to secure election to succeed Zelter as director of Berlin
        Singakademie
        April–May: London, first performance of *Italian* Symphony
        May: conducts Lower Rhine Music Festival, Düsseldorf; accepts post
        of city music director in Düsseldorf
        June–August: social visit to London with father
        September: takes up duties in Düsseldorf
        STRING QUINTET IN A, OP. 18
        SECHS GESÄNGE, OP. 19A
        STRING OCTET IN E-FLAT, OP. 20
        DIE HEBRIDEN OVERTURE, op. 26
        Responsorium et Hymnus (op. 121)
        Ouvertüre zum Märchen von der schönen Melusine, op. 32

1834   January–August Düsseldorf
        September: Berlin and Leipzig
        October–December: Düsseldorf
        FANTASIA (SONATA *ÉCOSSAISE*), OP. 28
        RONDO BRILLANT, OP. 29
        Concert aria: *Infelice* (first setting)
        St Paul (begun)

1835   January–July: Düsseldorf
        April: accepts directorship of the Gewandhaus concerts in Leipzig
        July–September: Berlin
        September–December: Leipzig
        November: Abraham Mendelssohn-Bartholdy dies
        MEERESSTILLE UND GLÜCKLICHE FAHRT OVERTURE, OP. 27
        LIEDER OHNE WORTE BK. 2, OP. 30
        PSALM 115, OP. 31

1836 May: Premiere of *St Paul* at Lower Rhine Music Festival
Summer: deputizes for Schelble as director of Frankfurt Cäcilienverein
September: engagement to Cécile Jeanrenaud
OUVERTÜRE ZUM MÄRCHEN VON DER SCHÖNEN MELUSINE, OP. 32
TROIS CAPRICES, OP. 33
ST PAUL, OP. 36

1837 March: marriage to Cécile Jeanrenaud
Summer: wedding journey and work on compositions
September: directs *St Paul* at Birmingham Festival and premières Second Piano Concerto
October: begins "historical" concert series at Gewandhaus
SECHS GESÄNGE OP. 34
SIX PRELUDES AND FUGUES (PIANO), OP. 35
THREE PRELUDES AND FUGUES (ORGAN), OP. 37

1838 April: Berlin
July: direction of Lower Rhine Music Festival
Summer: Berlin
THREE MOTETS, OP. 39
PIANO CONCERTO NO. 2 IN D, OP. 40
PART-SONGS: SECHS LIEDER, OP. 41
PSALM 42, OP. 42
Violin Sonata in F
Psalm 95, op. 46

1839 April: Frankfurt
May: direction of Lower Rhine Music Festival
Summer: Frankfurt
September: directs *St Paul* at Brunswick Festival
OVERTURE FOR WIND INSTRUMENTS IN C, OP. 24
SERENADE AND ALLEGRO GIOJOSO OP. 43
STRING QUARTETS OP. 44
CELLO SONATA IN B-FLAT, OP. 45
SECHS LIEDER, OP. 47
Overture *Ruy Blas* (op. 95)
Psalm 114

1840 First attack of fatal illness?
April: submits plan for a Leipzig Music School to the Saxon government
April–June: Berlin

June: Gutenberg festival in Leipzig; accession of Friedrich Wilhelm IV to the Prussian throne

July: directs *St Paul* at North German Music Festival, Schwerin

August: gives concert of organ music to raise funds for Leipzig Bach monument

September: London and Birmingham (*Lobgesang*)

December: beginning of negotiation over a Berlin appointment

PART SONGS: *SECHS LIEDER*, OP. 48

PIANO TRIO IN D, OP. 49

PART-SONGS: *SECHS LIEDER*, OP. 50

PSALM 31 (in English)

1841 January–March: Leipzig

April: conducts *St Paul* at Weimar

April–July: visits Berlin and Dresden

May: moves to Berlin

October: première of *Antigone* in Potsdam

November–December: visits Leipzig to direct Gewandhaus concerts

SYMPHONY-CANTATA *LOBGESANG*, OP. 52

LIEDER OHNE WORTE BK. 3, OP. 53

VARIATIONS SÉRIEUSES, OP. 54

PSALM 114, OP. 51

Piano Duet in A (op. 92)

1842 January–February: directs two performances of *St Paul* in Berlin; visits Leipzig to direct Gewandhaus concerts

March: directs first performance of Third Symphony at Gewandhaus; shares direction of Lower Rhine Music Festival with Julius Rietz

May–September: visits London

October: return to Berlin after conducting first Gewandhaus concert; relinquishes half his Berlin salary and is freed from specific duties, pending the formation of a new cathedral music organization; King Friedrich Wilhelm confers title Generalmusikdirektor

November: interview with King Friedrich August of Saxony, who endorses the foundation of a Leipzig Music School

December: Lea Mendelssohn Bartholdy dies

PSALM 95, OP. 46

SYMPHONY IN A MINOR, OP. 56

1843 April: Leipzig Conservatory opened

September: assumes direction of cathedral choir and symphony concerts in Berlin

October: première of incidental music for *Ein Sommernachtstraum* at Potsdam

October–November: directs concerts in Leipzig

November: moves with family to Berlin

ANTIGONE, OP. 55 (vocal score)

SECHS LIEDER, OP. 57

CELLO SONATA IN D, OP. 58

SECHS LIEDER, OP. 59 (part-songs)

Psalm 2 (Three Psalms [op. 78])

Psalm 98 (op. 91)

Concert aria: *Infelice* (second setting), op. 94

1844 January–March: composing and directing in Berlin

April: returns to Leipzig

May–July: London; conductorship of Philharmonic concerts; begins editing Handel's *Israel in Egypt*

July–September: holiday (and composition) in Soden (directs *St Paul* and *Die erste Walpurgisnacht* at Zweibrücken Music Festival, 31 July–1 August)

September–November: Berlin, extricates himself from bulk of duties in Berlin, retained by king as a composer only

December: takes up residence in Frankfurt

DIE ERSTE WALPURGISNACHT, OP. 60

EIN SOMMERNACHTSTRAUM, OP. 61 (vocal score)

LIEDER OHNE WORTE BK. 5, OP. 62

SECHS ZWEISTIMMIGE LIEDER, OP. 63

Psalms 43 and 22 (*Three Psalms* [op. 78])

1845 January–July: remains in retirement in the Rhineland

August: resumes duties at Gewandhaus, with Gade as deputy

December: completion of work on Handel's *Israel in Egypt*

VIOLIN CONCERTO IN E, OP. 64

SIX SONATAS (ORGAN), OP. 65

LIEDER OHNE WORTE BK. 6, OP. 67

HEAR MY PRAYER

String Quintet in B-flat (op. 87)

Oedipus Coloneus (op. 93)

Athalie (op. 74)

1846 May–June: Lower Rhine Music Festival

June: Liège, Corpus Christi celebration; Cologne, German-Flemish Choral Festival

July: Leipzig

August: Première of *Elijah* at Birmingham Festival

October–December: Leipzig, conducts Gewandhaus concerts

PIANO TRIO NO. 2 IN C, OP. 66

AN DIE KÜNSTLER, OP. 68

Lauda Sion (op. 73)

Sechs Sprüche (op. 79)

1847   January–April: musical activities in Leipzig

April: tenth visit to England, performances of *Elijah* in London, Manchester, and Birmingham

May: Fanny Hensel dies

June: FMB recuperates in Baden-Baden

July–September: vacation in Interlaken

September: Leipzig

October: FMB has mild subarachnoid hemorrhage followed by more serious attacks; dies 4 November

THREE MOTETS, OP. 69

ELIJAH, OP. 70

SECHS LIEDER, OP. 71

String Quartet in f (op. 80)

Christus (unfinished, op. 97)

Die Lorelei (unfinished, op. 98)

Biographical Notes

The following biographical notes indicate FMB's relationship with those whose first-hand comments and accounts are referred to in the literature and in this book. Where the context is made clear in the main text the relevant section is indicated for ease of reference.

Becher, Alfred Julius (1803–1848). German journalist and composer. FMB met Becher for the first time in 1833, in Elbersfeld, which he visited in search of choral repertoire shortly after taking up his post in Düsseldorf. The relationship was cordial: in a letter of 1842 Becher called FMB "dear friend," and in one of 1846 signed himself "Your enthusiastic friend" ("Ihr begeisterte Freund"). They did not, however, use the familiar "Du" form of address. Twenty-seven letters (1833–1847) from Becher to FMB are preserved in the "Green Books," while only four (1841–1847) from FMB to Becher are known.

Benedict, (Sir) Julius (1804–1885). German composer, pianist and conductor (later a naturalized British subject). Benedict first met FMB in 1821, when he accompanied his master, Weber, to Berlin for the premiere of *Der Freischütz;* thereafter they encountered each other periodically. Their third meeting was in Naples in 1831, and in 1844 they spent a fortnight together in Soden. Benedict's letters to FMB in the "Green Books" date from 1842 to 1847.

Bennett, (Sir) William Sterndale (1816–1875). English composer, pianist, conductor and teacher. He was perhaps the closest of FMB's English friends. They first met in Düsseldorf during the Lower Rhine Festival of 1836. FMB's admiration for his musicianship is indicated by his comment in a letter to Klingemann after Bennett had arranged an extended stay in Leipzig: "I am certain to gain as much pleasure and profit from his society, as he from mine" (Bennett, *Life of William Sterndale Bennett*, 42). They remained lifelong friends and corresponded extensively.

Berlioz, Hector (1803–1869). French composer and journalist. Berlioz became acquainted with FMB in Rome in 1831. They were together much at that time, but their relationship was equivocal. FMB evidently found Berlioz good company, though he disliked his music and had little sympathy with his enthusiasms. Berlioz enjoyed teasing FMB but regarded him highly as a musician. In 1843 they met again on friendly terms, when FMB facilitated Berlioz's Leipzig concert despite his continuing distaste for his compositions.

Brendel, Franz (1811–1868). German writer and teacher. Schumann's successor as editor of the *Neue Zeitschrift für Musik*. During FMB's lifetime Brendel's writings displayed a respectful but cool attitude towards his music. After FMB's death Brendel's comments became increasingly negative, and the journal adopted a pro-Wagner stance, publishing Wagner's anonymous *Das Judenthum in der Musik* in 1850.

Brockhaus, Heinrich (1804–1874). Leipzig publisher. He was married to Richard Wagner's sister. FMB became acquainted with Brockhaus on moving to Leipzig in 1836, and they remained on friendly terms. Brockhaus undertook the publication of a collected edition of Moses Mendelssohn's works after discussion with FMB. Brockhaus's diaries show him to have been an admirer but not worshiper of FMB's music.

Chorley, Henry Fothergill (1808–1872). English journalist and writer. From the early 1830s until after FMB's death he was music critic of the *Athenaeum*. He first met FMB at the Brunswick Festival of 1839 and began an acquaintance that was, as he himself expressed it, "soon to be ripened into indulgent friendship on the one side, and faithful regard on the other" (Chorley, *Modern German Music*, 1: 14). Chorley saw FMB for the last time during late August 1847 at Interlaken.

David, Ferdinand (1810–1873). German violinist and composer. While working as a violinist in the orchestra of the Königstadt theatre in Berlin between 1826 and 1829 he became friendly with FMB and his family. At FMB's suggestion he applied for the post of leader of the Gewandhaus Orchestra in 1835. He became and remained one of FMB's closest friends.

Davison, William Henry (1813–1885). English journalist. He was one of the leading English musical journalists of his day as editor of the *Musical World* and music critic of the *Times* from 1845. FMB first encountered him during one of his early visits to England, and their acquaintance was renewed when Davison accompanied Bennett to Düsseldorf in 1836. Davison became one of FMB's most vigorous partisans in the English press; they met periodically during FMB's visits to England and exchanged letters on a number of occasions in the early 1840s.

Devrient, Eduard Philipp (1801–1877). German singer, actor, librettist, and theatre historian. He met FMB in July 1822, and despite their disparity in age they became close friends. Devrient was closely associated in the revival of Bach's *St Matthew Passion* in 1829 and acted as FMB's most vociferous advocate for the directorship of the Berlin Singakademie in 1832. Despite tensions, resulting particularly from FMB's concern about Devrient's artistic integrity and commitment, their friendship endured. Devrient's *Recollections*, published in 1869, are a valuable source of information but must be read with caution; Devrient's citations of FMB's letters are often unreliable and misleading, especially with respect to their relationship. Dorn, however, stated in his *Recollections* of 1870 that he could vouch for the truth of Devrient's account (referring, of course, only to the 1820s). Devrient's association with Wagner after 1849 has been identified as a possible distorting influence on his *Recollections*. It should be noted, nevertheless, that on the book's appearance Wagner's reaction was anything but positive. Cosima commented in her diary: "That Devrient is an uneducated play-actor and Mendelssohn a Jew emerges clearly" (C. Wagner, *Diaries*, 1:49).

Dorn, Heinrich Ludwig Egmont (1804–1892). German composer, conductor and writer. In about 1823, while studying law in Berlin, he became acquainted with FMB and was, in his own words, "quite at home in the Mendelssohns' house" during the winter of 1824–1825. They met again briefly on friendly terms in Leipzig, where Dorn conducted at the theatre from 1829 to 1832, and later during a visit by Dorn to Leipzig in 1843. Their last meeting, a brief encounter in Cologne the following year, was soured by misunderstandings about arrangements for the musical festival.

Fétis, François-Joseph (1784–1871). Belgian writer on music, critic, teacher and composer. See section 46.

Fink, Gottfried Wilhelm (1783–1846). German critic and composer. After a theological training he began writing for the Leipzig *Allgemeine musikalische Zeitung* in 1808 and was editor from 1827 to 1841. He contributed articles to various musical dictionaries, including those of Brockhaus and Schilling. Fink was unsympathetic towards Schumann, Chopin, and other "Romantic" composers of their generation. FMB and Fink were undoubtedly known to each other but seem not to have had more than a passing acquaintance.

Hauptmann, Moritz (1792–1868). German composer, theorist and teacher. Studied violin and composition with Spohr. From 1822 to 1842 he was a violinist in the court orchestra at Kassel under Spohr and taught privately. He initially met FMB in Kassel in October 1834, describing him from the first as "the beloved Felix Mendelssohn" (Hauptmann, *Letters*, 1: 109). FMB thought very highly of him as a teacher and recommended many pupils to him. In 1842 Hauptmann was appointed cantor at the Thomasschule in Leipzig, where he remained for the rest of his life. He became teacher of theory and composition at the Leipzig Conservatorium on its foundation in 1843.

Hensel, Sebastian (1830–1898). Son of Wilhelm and Fanny (née Mendelssohn) Hensel. His book *Die Familie Mendelssohn*, a vital source of information about FMB and the Mendelssohns in general, was originally written as a memoir for the family. It was extensively rewritten and expurgated for publication in 1879. It must be used with care, as, like Devrient's *Recollections*, the citations of letters are not always reliable, and the suppression of information considered unsuitable for publication produces an inevitably distorted impression. It remains a key source of information, however.

Hiller, Ferdinand (1811–1885). German composer, pianist, conductor and teacher. He first met FMB in 1822 in Frankfurt and later became one of his closest friends. They spent much time together in Paris in 1830 and corresponded regularly until 1843. Hiller directed the Gewandhaus concerts for the 1843–1844 season, because of FMB's commitments in Berlin. A misunderstanding at that time put an end to their correspondence and interrupted their association. They retained their esteem for each other, however. Hiller's book is an affectionate but largely unsentimental portrait of his friend, and his citations of letters are generally more accurate than is usual in such memoirs.

Hirschbach, Herrmann (1812–1888). German composer and critic. See section 24.

Horsley, Charles Edward (1822–1876). English composer. See section 31.

Kahlert, (Karl) August Timotheus (1807–1864). German aesthetician and writer on music. Gustav Freytag met Kahlert in 1839 and described him in his *Erinnerungen aus meinem Leben* as an "aesthetician who possessed a good musical education and knowledge of German literature of the eighteenth-century, an honourable and trustworthy man." Kahlert wrote musical reviews for *Caecilia* and the *Allgemeine musikalische Zeitung*. His *System der Aesthetik* was published in Leipzig by Breitkopf und Härtel in 1846. There is no evidence that he knew FMB personally or corresponded with him.

Klingemann, Karl (1798–1862). German poet, musician and diplomat. Despite the disparity in their ages, Klingemann was probably FMB's closest friend (FMB often called him "the only friend"). Klingemann took up a junior post in the Hanoverian embassy in Berlin in 1818. After the Mendelssohn family's move to 3 Leipziger Straße, where the embassy rented accommodation, Klingemann became a part of FMB's intimate circle. In 1827 he moved to the embassy in London, but FMB's visit to England in 1829 renewed their relationship, which ripened into close friendship with their journey to Scotland (on which they adopted the familiar "Du" form of address). From then until FMB's death their friendship was maintained by letter, with periodic meetings, mostly in London. FMB's letters to Klingemann, and some of Klingemann's to FMB, were published in a largely accurate transcription by Klingemann's son in 1909.

Kossak, Ernst (1814–1880). German critic and writer on music. He was described in the Mendel-Reissmann *Lexikon* in 1881 as "one of the most brilliant, versatile and accomplished writers on music and journalists of the present." He contributed to a number of Berlin journals, including the *Neue Berliner Musikzeitung*, and founded the *Berliner Musik-Zeitung Echo* in 1851. There is no evidence of a personal relationship with FMB.

Krüger, Eduard (1807–1885). German critic, writer on music and composer. After writing to Schumann in 1838 Krüger regularly contributed to the *Neue Zeitschrift für Musik*. He also contributed to the *Allgemeine musikalische Zeitung* and the *Neue Berliner Musikzeitung*. He appears never to have made FMB's acquaintance.

Kühne, Gustav (1806–1888). German writer and journalist. From 1835 to 1842 he was editor of the *Zeitung für die elegante Welt* and from 1846 of *Europa Chronik der gebildeten Welt*. He may have been slightly acquainted with FMB.

Lampadius, Wilhelm Adolf (1812–1892). German writer and teacher. He took a doctorate at Leipzig University. After becoming a priest he was attached to the Peterskirche. He regularly participated as a singer in performances under FMB.

Lobe, Johann Christian (1797–1881). German composer, writer on music and flautist. He was among the Weimar court musicians who accompanied FMB in chamber music at Goethe's house in 1821. He later had a cordial relationship with FMB. His earliest surviving correspondence with FMB dates from 1838. In 1846 he moved to Leipzig to become editor of the *Allgemeine musikalische Zeitung*.

Macfarren, (Sir) George Alexander (1813–1887). English composer, writer on music and teacher. He made FMB's acquaintance in 1840 and in that year began an extensive correspondence, much of it concerning the edition of *Israel in Egypt* FMB was to make for the London Handel Society, of which Macfarren was secretary. He dedicated his C-sharp Minor Symphony to FMB.

Marx, Adolf Bernhard (1795–1866). German theorist, critic and composer. From 1824 to 1831 Marx was editor of the *Berliner allgemeine musikalische Zeitung*. He became friendly with the Mendelssohn family in 1826, though Abraham was uneasy about his influence on FMB. Marx undoubtedly stimulated FMB's ideas on programme music, and their relationship was particularly close around 1830. Their friendship cooled during the 1830s (perhaps partly because FMB was disappointed in Marx as a composer, but also because of misgivings, shared by a number of the Mendelssohn circle, about Marx's sincerity). They became estranged after FMB declined to perform Marx's oratorio *Moses* in Leipzig in 1841. Marx's later writings indicate his lasting bitterness.

Meinardus, Ludwig Siegfried (1827–1896). German composer, conductor and writer on music. See section 33.

Moscheles, Ignaz (1794–1870). Bohemian pianist and composer. In 1824, on a visit to Berlin, he was asked to give FMB piano lessons. He quickly became one of FMB's closest musical friends, and their warm relationship was maintained over the years by regular correspondence, meetings and performances together. In 1846 FMB persuaded him to become principal professor of piano at the Leipzig Conservatory. *Aus Moscheles' Leben*, compiled from his diaries by his widow, and *Briefe von Felix Mendelssohn-Bartholdy*, edited by his son (FMB's godchild), are important sources of information.

Polko (née Vogel), Elise (1823–1899). German musical biographer, novelist and singer. From 1840 she studied singing in Leipzig and often performed under FMB. At his recommendation she went to Paris in 1847 to study with Jenny Lind's former teacher, Manuel Garcia. After her marriage in 1849 she gave up the idea of a singing career and turned to writing. Her *Erinnerungen an Felix Mendelssohn Bartholdy* has often been criticized as fanciful, and it must indeed be used with care. It contains valuable first-hand memories, however, and also plausible recollections contributed by other of FMB's friends, especially in Düsseldorf.

Rellstab, Ludwig (1799–1860). German music critic, poet and novelist. He studied piano with FMB's teacher, Berger. In 1824 he began to contribute to the *Berliner allgemeine musikalische Zeitung* and was music critic for the *Vossische Zeitung* between 1826 and 1848. In 1830 he founded *Iris im Gebiete der Tonkunst*. He was personally known to the Mendelssohn family.

Riehl, Wilhelm Heinrich (von) (1823–1897). German writer and journalist. After theological studies Riehl was active as a journalist, particularly in Nassau and Augsburg. His *Musikalische Charakterköpfe*, published in book form from 1853, seem largely to consist of earlier journal articles. From internal evidence the discussion of FMB appears to have been written shortly after the composer's death.

Rockstro (Rackstraw), William Smyth (1823–1895). English music historian, composer and teacher. See section 33.

Rollett, Hermann (1819–1904). Austrian poet and writer. As a boy he heard FMB play the organ in the Stephanskirche in Baden bei Wien. He met him for a second time in Leipzig in spring 1847. Rollett left an account of both encounters in his *Begegnungen*.

Schubring, Julius (1806–1889). German Lutheran pastor. As a theology student in Berlin between 1825 and 1830, he was a frequent guest in the Mendelssohn household and struck up a warm friendship with FMB. After moving to Dessau as a pastor he remained in contact with FMB. His letters to him cover the period 1830 to 1847. Many of the letters exchanged between Schubring and FMB concern the texts of *St Paul* and *Elijah*.

Schumann, Robert (1810–1856). German composer and critic. In his manuscript recollections of Mendelssohn Schumann wrote: "1835 first meeting in the hall of the Gewandhaus. The musicians played him his overture 'Meeresstille.' I said to him that I knew all his compositions well; he answered this with something very modest. The first impression was that he was an unforgettable person." And, on another page: "I saw him for the last time in his apartment on the journey back from Berlin to Dresden, the morning of the 25th March 1847." Although they never used the familiar "Du," they evidently had a very cordial relationship; its nature is indicated by Schumann's account of a meeting on 14 March 1837, where they discussed FMB's interpretation of Beethoven's Ninth Symphony: "When we had finished with the symphony he seized my hand: ['] Schumann don't take it the wrong way now; I feel so comfortable with you; but I have had such sad experiences particularly with those who have something to do with a public journal, that it has left me with an aversion even against those whom he [sic] well knew it was not necessary to fear. He wanted very much to write to me, and really uninhibitedly, what was on his mind. If I promised him also to be discreet with it[.]' This was the sense; I was somewhat embarrassed; but this was quickly overcome" (Schumann, *Erinnerungen*, 62–63, 48–49, 64–65).

Taylor, Bayard (1825–1878). American poet and travel writer. Met FMB in Frankfurt during the winter of 1844 to 1885, and recalled the occasion in his published account of travels in Europe.

Taylor, Edward (1784–1863). English writer on music, lecturer and singer. See section 44.

Varnhagen von Ense, Carl August (1785–1858). German poet and historian.

Varnhagen von Ense, Rahel (née Levin) (1771–1833). Writer and Berlin salon hostess. See section 16.

Wagner, Richard (1813–1883). German composer and writer on music. Wagner first wrote to FMB on 11 April 1836, sending him a copy of his C Major Symphony, asking that he "should glance over it in some idle hour" and hoping "it may serve to give you an indication of my efforts and industry." In a letter to friends of 3 May 1842 he referred to "Mendelssohn (with whom I am on very friendly terms)." His later letters to FMB are friendly to the point of sycophancy. His well-known denigration of FMB, discussed below, dates from after 1847, and many of his comments, especially in *My Life*, can be shown to be disingenuous.

Wauer, Wilhelm (1827–1902). German composer and choral conductor. Wauer was active as a choral conductor and published a small quantity of church music. He had no personal contact with FMB.

Wasielewski, Wilhelm Joseph von (1822–1896). German violinist, conductor and writer on music. See section 33.

Willis, Richard Storrs (1819–1900). American writer on music, journalist and composer. After graduating from Yale in 1841 he went to Europe, where he studied music under Xavier Schnyder and Moritz Hauptmann for six years and made FMB's acquaintance.

Woringen, Ferdinand von (1798–1896). Prussian government official. Biographical details remain elusive. For information on his family's relationship with FMB, see section 18.

ONE · The Man

1 · Appearance and Manner

In the opinion of most of Mendelssohn's contemporaries, none of his portraits succeeded in conveying the mercurial qualities that so frequently made his features fascinating and arresting. The impression he made on observers was strongly conditioned by his relationship to the observer and by his state of mind. One of his closest English musical friends, William Sterndale Bennett, recalled "that Mendelssohn's personal appearance was often insignificant, not such as would attract passers-by in the street—but that, at other times, he had the appearance of an *angel*."[1] Subjective reactions could range from Thackeray's reported comment, "His face is the most beautiful face I ever saw, like what I imagine our Saviour's to have been,"[2] to Wagner's doubtless spiteful recollection, "I saw him after his marriage, and he looked so fat, so unpleasant—an unsavoury fellow!"[3]

The inadequacy of all Mendelssohn's portraits was insisted upon by his English friend, the journalist Henry Fothergill Chorley, who remarked: "Nature had gifted her favourite with one of the brightest and most expressive countenances ever bestowed on Genius. Those who have seen its expression at once brighten and deepen as he sat 'making music' (his own phrase), or watched its wonderful play in society will bear us out, in saying that the best portrait extant is meagre and pedantic as a likeness."[4] And Elise Polko, who often sang under his baton between 1840 and 1847, observed: "I have never hitherto seen any portrait (the one by Hildebrandt I have unfortunately never met with) that represents that artistic head as it lives in my memory; there is something effeminate and sentimental in all the Mendelssohn portraits, which were certainly not the attributes of the living head. A marvellously executed little ivory relief, a profile in the possession of a musical friend of the deceased master, Knaur's statuette, and the large bust alone are exempt from this character, and therefore bear more affinity to the image in my memory."[5]

Mendelssohn's appearance and manner as a child seem to have elicited almost as much attention as his musical gifts. The composer and conductor Julius Benedict recalled his meeting Mendelssohn for the first time in May 1821: "I shall never forget . . . that beautiful youth, with his auburn hair clustering in ringlets round his shoulders, the look of his brilliant clear eyes, and the smile of innocence and candour on his lips;"[6] and he later told the American writer Bayard Taylor that the boy "was a picture of almost supernatural beauty."[7] Eduard Devrient, subsequently one of Mendelssohn's closest friends, remembered encountering him at a musical party at about the same time, where "he took his place amongst the grown-up people, in his child's dress—a tight-fitting jacket, cut very low at the neck, and over which the wide trousers were buttoned; into the slanting pockets of these the little fellow liked to thrust his hands, rocking his curly head from side to side, and shifting restlessly from one foot to the other. With half-closed eyelids, beneath which flashed his bright brown eyes, he would almost defiantly, and with a slight lisp, jerk out his answers to the inquisitive and searching questions that people usually address to young prodigies."[8] Mendelssohn's composition teacher Carl Friedrich Zelter, writing to his friend Goethe on 26 October 1821, described his pupil more objectively, and with typical succinctness, as "good and pretty, lively and obedient."[9]

With maturity Mendelssohn apparently lost none of his physical attractiveness. At twenty he was, according to Devrient,

> Of middle height, slender frame, and of uncommon
> muscle power, a capital gymnast, swimmer, walker, rider,
> and dancer. . . . His features, of the Oriental type, were
> handsome; a high, thoughtful forehead, much depressed
> at the temples; large, expressive dark eyes, with drooping
> lids, and a peculiar veiled glance through the lashes; this,
> however, sometimes flashed distrust or anger, sometimes
> happy dreaming and expectancy. His nose was arched
> and of delicate form, still more so the mouth, with its

short upper and full under lip, which was slightly protruded and hid his teeth, when, with a slight lisp, he pronounced the hissing consonants. An extreme mobility about his mouth betrayed every emotion that passed within.

His bearing retained from his boyhood the slight rocking of the head and upper part of the body, and shifting from foot to foot; his head was much thrown back, especially when playing; it was always easy to see whether he was pleased or otherwise when any new music was going on, by his nods and shakes of the head. In society his manners were even then felt to be distinguished. The shyness that he still retained left him entirely during his subsequent travels, but even now, when he wished to propitiate, he could be most fascinating, and his attentions to young ladies were not without effect.[10]

In youth Mendelssohn evidently took greater care of his appearance than in later years, for when he visited Frankfurt in the autumn of 1827, his boyhood friend the composer Ferdinand Hiller recalled that "his figure had become broad and full, and there was a general air of smartness about him, with none of that careless ease which he sometimes adopted in later life."[11] Devrient's statement about Mendelssohn's loss of shyness during his travels between 1829 and 1832 is corroborated by the Belgian journalist François-Joseph Fétis, who first met him in 1829; writing in 1838, Fétis recalled: "In 1834, I found him again at Aix la Chappelle, where he had gone for the Easter musical festival. He was then twenty-five; his former youthful shyness had given way to the assurance of an established artist, and even to a certain air of haughtiness."[12]

The contrast between Mendelssohn's slight build and his athleticism was commented on by many. The American musician and journalist Richard Storrs Willis, for instance, noted in the 1840s that he was "a man of small frame, delicate and fragile looking; yet possessing a sinewy elasticity, and a power of endurance which you would hardly suppose possible."[13] He retained, in particular, a love of swimming and hiking. In 1837, shortly after his marriage, he almost lost his life when he suffered a cramp while bathing in the Rhine; but the experience did not deter him, for a couple of weeks later his bride, Cécile, recorded in her diary, "Felix went to bathe today just like every other day."[14] Despite well-corroborated reports of physical strain in 1847, Mendelssohn retained his bodily vigor until his final illness; his close friend and colleague Ferdinand David stated that in Switzerland during that summer "he walked uninterruptedly for several days at a time in the mountains and came back to the house very sunburned and exhausted."[15]

Descriptions from the early 1840s emphasize a number of prominent characteristics. Queen Victoria remarked in her diary, after meeting him on 16 June 1842: "He is short, dark, and Jewish looking—delicate, with a fine intellectual forehead."[16] Around the same time Elise Polko, a young girl already predisposed to hero-worship, also saw him for the first time. She recalled that "his grandly modelled head was at once impressed on my memory. . . . His hair was black and curling, the forehead of the highest order of intellectual beauty, the nose somewhat bent, the lips well chiselled, the shape of the face oval, the eyes irresistible, brilliant and spiritual. His slender figure, scarcely attaining to middle size, seemed to increase in height and become imposing as he stood at his director's desk. His hands were of remarkable beauty."[17]

Many descriptions referred to the arresting effect of his eyes. George Grove, in his *Dictionary of Music and Musicians*, summarizing information gathered from those who knew him, reported that his most striking feature was "the large dark-brown eyes. When at rest he often lowered the eyelids as if he were slightly short-sighted—which indeed he was; but when animated they gave an extraordinary brightness and fire to his face and 'were as expressive a pair of eyes as were ever set in a human being's head.' They could also sparkle with rage like a tiger's. When he was playing extempore, or was otherwise much excited, they would dilate and become nearly twice their ordinary size, the brown pupil changing to a vivid black."[18] Willis recalled: "His eye possessed a peculiarity which has been ascribed to the eye of Sir Walter Scott,—a ray of light seemed often to proceed from its pupil to your own, as from a star. But yet, in the eyes of Mendelssohn, there was none of that rapt dreaminess so often seen among men of genius in art. The gaze was rather external than internal: the eye had more outwardness than inwardness of expression."[19]

Mendelssohn's eyes also impressed another American writer, Bayard Taylor, who left an evocative account after encountering him in Frankfurt during the winter of 1844 to 1845. "As we pushed through the crowd," he wrote, "my eyes, which had been wandering idly over the picturesque faces and costumes around us, were suddenly arrested by the face of a man, a little distance in front, approaching us. His head was thrown back; and his eyes, large, dark, and of wonderful brilliancy, were fixed upon the western sky. Long, thin locks of black hair, with here and there a silver streak, fell across his ears. His beard, of two or three days' growth, and his cravat, loosely and awkwardly tied, added to the air of absorption, of self-forgetfulness, which marked his whole appearance. He made his way through the crowd mechanically, evidently but half conscious of its presence."[20] Taylor also recorded a visit to Mendelssohn two days later and, in recalling the appearance of the composer on that occasion, was conscious of the similarity of his description to the fictional idealization of the composer in Elizabeth Sara Sheppard's 1853 novel *Charles Auchester. A Memorial*:

> I sat thus, face to face with him, and again looked into those dark, lustrous, unfathomable eyes. They were black, but without the usual opaqueness of black eyes, shining, not with a surface light, but with a pure, serene, planetary flame. His brow, white and unwrinkled, was high and nobly arched, with great breadth at the temples, strongly resembling that of Poe. His nose had the Jewish prominence, without its usual coarseness: I remember, particularly, that the nostrils were as finely cut and flexible as an Arab's. The lips were thin and rather long, but with an expression of indescribable sweetness in their delicate curves. His face was a long oval in form; and the complexion pale but not pallid. . . . Those who have read the rhapsodical romance of *Charles Auchester*, wherein the character of Seraphael is meant to represent Mendelssohn, will find his personality transfigured by one of his adorers,—yet, having seen that noble head, those glorious eyes, I scarcely wonder at the author's extravagance.[21]

The similarity of descriptions of Seraphael, in Sheppard's novel, to those of the real Mendelssohn is well illustrated by a passage in which Seraphael conducts a performance of *Messiah:* "He raised his eyes to the chorus and let them fall upon the band. Those piercing eyes recalled us. . . . He was slight, so slight that he seemed to have grown out of the air. He was young, so young that he could not have numbered twenty summers;— but the heights of eternity were foreshadowed in the forehead's marble dream. A strange transparency took the place of bloom upon that face of youth, as if from temperament too tender, or blood too rarefied; but the hair betrayed a wondrous strength, clustering in dark curls of excessive richness. The pointed fingers were pale, but they grasped the time-stick with an energy like naked nerve."[22]

Wilhelm Joseph von Wasielewsky, who as a pupil at the Leipzig Conservatorium knew Mendelssohn in the mid-1840s, also referred in particular to his eyes:

> Mendelssohn had a slender, delicately formed figure. His dextrous and agile bodily movements were extraordinarily lively. These matched the facial expressions, which often changed suddenly. The dark eye blazed like lightning. It could just as quickly assume a friendly, benevolent and cheerful expression as a sharply penetrating one or a serious and thoughtful one. In the latter case he also blinked his eyes, with his glance directed at a particular person, which gave him a somewhat questioning look. The high, beautifully domed forehead was framed by black hair, which fell in curls to the sides and behind. The face that tapered towards his chin was bordered by thick sideboards. The moderately curved nose was of the Roman type and betrayed his oriental ancestry. The extremely finely formed mouth made a striking impression. When he opened it in conversation or laughter, two rows of dazzlingly white teeth could be seen. Everything combined in Mendelssohn to make his appearance as a whole attractive and charming. It is thus understandable that he was a highly beloved and admired personality, and all the

more so because his intellectual qualities were irresistibly engaging.[23]

In the last few years of his life Mendelssohn's features and bearing clearly showed signs of strain. This is evident from a number of accounts of his final visit to London. In November 1847, for instance, the English writer Sarah Austin, who had first met him in Berlin in the mid-1820s, described his appearance at a Philharmonic concert the previous April, playing Beethoven's G Major Piano Concerto "with all the playful grace, the ease, and conscious mastery that communicated their peculiar charms to the performance"; but she continued, "such was the promising aspect in which Dr. Mendelssohn appeared in the lighted evening concert-room to his admiring audience. By daylight, and in closer contiguity, the spectator was struck by a certain appearance of premature age which his countenance exhibited; he seemed already to have outstretched the natural term of his existence by at least ten years. No one, judging by the lines in his face, would have guessed his age to be thirty-nine only. The disproportion between his actual age and the character of his face was especially noticed at the morning 'Homage to Mendelssohn,' performed in Harley Street by the Beethoven Quartet Society. Here he was gay and animated, and played delightfully; but, to the surprise of close observers he was no longer a young man."[24] Mrs Austin's observation tallies with that of Chorley, who, after meeting him in Interlaken at the end of August 1847, recalled that "he looked aged and sad;—and stooped more than I had ever seen him do"; but he also remarked that "his smile had never been brighter, nor his welcome more cordial."[25]

2 · Character and Personality

Character reveals itself in different ways to different people, depending on the nature of the relationship. Wasielewsky drew a clear distinction between Mendelssohn's demeanor and behaviour with friends, in general society, and with young musicians: "In his relationship with friends Mendelssohn was uninhibited, cheerful, and comfortable, indeed, when he was in a good mood, extraordinarily merry, in which case he spoke animatedly, lisping a little when he made witticisms. Towards those who were not of his close circle he behaved in an obliging, but somewhat reserved manner. When he spoke with young, striving artists about their achievements, however, he expressed his opinion unreservedly and was not reticent about giving either praise or criticism, though he always expressed the latter in a kindly tone."[26] In the accounts of those for whom Mendelssohn's personal attractions were inseparable from reverence for his genius, there is a marked tendency to idealize him and, in general, to ignore or minimize all those aspects of his personality and behaviour that did not fit the stereotype. Thus Wasielewsky, the admiring pupil, failed to record that Mendelssohn's reserved manner could sometimes be taken for coldness and that, in certain circumstances, his criticism of young musicians was sharp to the point of harshness.

Chorley provides an impression from a different standpoint. He undoubtedly belonged to that outer circle of friends with whom, had Chorley been German, Mendelssohn would have used the formal *Sie* rather than the intimate *Du* form of the second-person pronoun (as he did with Schumann, despite their very cordial relationship), and his account of Mendelssohn's character, written under the immediate impact of his death, vividly conveys the combination of affection and admiration he inspired in many such friends.

> Of the man it is difficult for those who knew him to
> speak in terms which shall not seem exaggerated. To such
> as have been used to distrust or make excuses for Genius,
> as a fever necessarily destructive of sound principles and
> healthy domestic affections—to those who maintain that
> a life of exhibition, fame and adulation must be incompatible with the simplest tastes and the freshest enjoyments, Dr. Mendelssohn may be pointed out as an instance falsifying all their accusations or self-apologies. He
> was an affectionate son and brother; an exemplary and
> devoted husband; a wise and indulgent father. He remained faithful to old friends, with a constancy rare even
> among those who are less brilliantly tempted to fickle-

ness. His wit was ready, his spirit as playful, as his sense was sound. While never was musician more keenly alive to the honour and beauty of his own art, few men have possessed tastes and sympathies embracing so wide a circle of pursuits and objects. He drew from Nature with great fidelity:—he kept close pace with the questions of the day and its literature, solid or ephemeral. Let it never be forgotten that he was intensely and affectionately German; regarding his country and its prospects with an interest impossible to counterfeit or conceal,—and anxious to employ his art as an instrument of peace, brotherly love and progress. The last time we heard him discuss his future plans, he spoke with warm and eager anxiety of the *liedertafel* societies—which, owing to the spell of their political significance, seem, in Germany, gradually displacing the elder mixed musical festivals in which the amateurs of both sexes joined. He had been advised not to write for them, on the plea that the music produced at their meetings was too trivial and popular— "but," said he, in a larger and more liberal spirit, "let us make them as good as we can." Deeply marked, however, as was his nationality—it was neither morbid nor narrowing in its influences. We have never known a foreigner more honest in his love for—more discriminating in his appreciation of—England. He relished our humour—he loved our poetry—he interested himself in our politics—and how heartily and charmingly he gave himself up to all that was best and sincerest in our society, his sorrowing friends have a thousand reasons to remember.[27]

The warmth of Chorley's feeling is scarcely surprising in view of the kindness and thoughtfulness he experienced at an early stage of their acquaintance. During a visit to Leipzig in 1839, while Chorley was confined to his bed at an inn by illness, a piano was unexpectedly delivered to his room, and he relates how a few moments later Mendelssohn arrived, "with that bright cordial smile of his," and played Schubert piano music, about which Chorley had earlier expressed interest, "for hours delighting himself in delighting an obscure stranger."[28]

Mendelssohn evidently won the heart of many an acquaintance by such acts of consideration. Another was recalled by William Rockstro. Having spent a few days in Frankfurt with Mendelssohn, he had just joined Ferdinand David to board the coach for Leipzig.

> A few moments later, Mendelssohn joined us, to say, as
> he was careful to express it in mixed German and En-
> glish, "Not *Leben Sie wohl,* but *Auf Wiedersehn.*" He had
> thought of everything that could help to make the dreary
> diligence journey comfortable. A little basket of early
> fruit, for refreshment during the night; a packet of
> choice cigars for David; and, for ourselves, a quite pater-
> nal scolding for insufficient defences against cold night-
> air. There were many last words to be said; but so much
> confusion had been caused by the hurried arrival of a
> party of outside passengers, that, at the moment of start-
> ing, our kind friend, who had wisely retired from the
> scuffle, was missing. The conductor declared that he
> could wait no longer, and we were just giving up Men-
> delssohn for lost, when he suddenly reappeared, rushing
> round the corner of the street, with a thick woollen scarf
> in his hand. "Let me wrap this round your throat," he
> gasped, quite out of breath with his run; "it will keep
> you warm in the night; and, when you get to Leipzig,
> you can leave it in the coach."[29]

The origin of much mythologizing can be seen in accounts of this kind, yet they are undoubtedly a genuine reflection of Mendelssohn's thoughtful and warm-hearted nature, which so often manifested itself in the evident desire to give pleasure to those with whom he felt a bond of sympathy.

He would sometimes create quite a different impression, however, on those for whom he had little or no sympathy, or of whose character, views, or behaviour he disapproved. His own exacting ethical standards, both in life and in art, often conditioned his conduct towards others; Schumann remarked in his unpublished memoirs of Mendelssohn that he had "the highest moral and artistic maxims; therefore inexorable, apparently sometimes gruff and inhuman."[30] This was undoubtedly a factor in Mendelssohn's relationship with Wagner. Cosima Wagner recorded her husband's comments about Mendelssohn on a number of occasions in her diaries. In 1881, "in reply to a question from Rub[enstein], he had described Mendelssohn's 'daemonic' and impish manner, all the more sinister because of its taciturnity";[31] and in the same year Wagner referred to Mendelssohn as "that uncanny man, silently lying in wait, then suddenly breaking into violent speech."[32] The latter observation recalls a passage in *My Life*, where Wagner described a meeting with Mendelssohn in Leipzig: "While I accompanied him home after the orchestral rehearsal and was expatiating with great warmth about music, this by no means loquacious man interrupted me with sudden agitation to state that the only bad thing about music was its capacity to excite not only the good but also the evil emotions, such as envy for example, more intensely than all the other arts."[33] Wagner interpreted Mendelssohn's remark as a confession that *Rienzi*, part of which he had just heard, aroused feelings of envy in him. Even if Wagner's report of the conversation was broadly accurate (which, in view of his demonstrable disingenuousness elsewhere, seems questionable), this is certainly not a credible interpretation of Mendelssohn's reaction. Mendelssohn's relationship with Wagner, whom he met on a number of occasions, seems to have been coloured as much by his disquiet about Wagner's personality and conduct as by his reservations about his music.[34] In the case of other composers whose music he could not admire, or actively disliked, such as Liszt or Berlioz, Mendelssohn maintained a cordial personal relationship.

When he was in sympathy with a composer's artistic tendency, and especially when his opinion was directly sought, he was frank in apportioning approval and criticism. Where his opinion was not asked he seems to have felt that if he could not react positively he had better show no reaction at all; as Schumann noted: "If he were not asked, then he did not say what he thought (of musical compositions)."[35] In correspondence or discussion with close friends and family, however, especially in early manhood, he made no secret of his dislikes. He expressed his profound antipathy for Berlioz's music to his family and to Ignaz Moscheles on several occasions, though towards Berlioz himself he behaved in a thoroughly friendly manner and facilitated the performance of his music in Leipzig in 1843.[36] Sometimes his uncompromising aesthetic stance could have serious consequences. When his childhood friend Adolf Bernhard Marx pressed him to accept his oratorio *Moses* for performance in Leipzig in 1841, Mendelssohn, judging the work unworthy, refused, which led to a permanent breach.

When Mendelssohn expressed approval or admiration, however, there seems little doubt that it was entirely sincere, despite his English acquaintance G. A. Macfarren's statement in the 1880s: "The foible of his character was his thirst for good opinion, which led him indiscriminately to conciliate everyone whose judgment could receive attention; thus his testimonials are of little credit, and his complimentary letters are not always utterances of his true opinion."[37] It would probably be fairer to say that when the expression of an opinion was unavoidable, Mendelssohn tried to say whatever he could in praise without actually perjuring himself. This is implied, for instance, by his comment about a visit to Alfred Shaw (a painter) and his wife (a singer) in 1837. He recorded in his "honeymoon diary"[38] for 10 September: "Some of Mr Shaw's paintings were shown to me, which I praised as much as I possibly could, which wasn't that much. After dinner, however, his wife sang me the alto aria from my *St Paul*, plus some Handel and other Italian pieces, all so superbly that I was able with a good conscience to furnish all the praise which before dinner I had held back."[39] In this context a passage in Mendelssohn's "confirmation confession," written when he was sixteen, is relevant: "Christ gave the commandment to be strictly truthful, and it is difficult in our times always to follow it precisely, because social convention often requires, if not that we deny the truth, at least that we know how to conceal it elegantly or cloak it. Yet we may well combine the two by speaking the strictest truth to everyone, but without pressing it upon anyone, without seeking to be troublesome to anyone with it."[40] Where he felt it necessary he could be blunt, however, especially with old friends, for, as he wrote to Wilhelm von Boguslawski in 1845, "in a childhood friend . . . everything good seems twice as good, and everything bad hurts twice as much"; thus, in 1832 he considered it his duty to warn Devrient of what he perceived as a tendency to be too self-satisfied.[41]

With his family and his inner circle of friends Mendelssohn could relax completely and would often be uninhibitedly merry. Grove (apparently citing John Horsley, with whose family Mendelssohn spent many happy hours in England) wrote: "His laugh was hearty and frequent; and when especially amused he would quite double up with laughter and shake his hand from the wrist to emphasise his merriment. He would nod his head violently when thoroughly agreeing, so that the hair came down over his face."[42] Moscheles's diary describes how, during the charades arranged to celebrate his birthday in 1847, "Mendelssohn was sitting on a large straw arm-chair which creaked under his weight, as he rocked to and fro, and the room echoed with his peals of laughter."[43] But those to whom he was closest knew his more excitable, nervous nature as well as his deeply felt affection and childlike enjoyment of unsophisticated fun. Devrient, for instance, focused particularly on these characteristics in an unsentimental assessment of his friend's character:

> The leading feature of his outward and inner nature was an extraordinary sensitiveness. Excitement stimulated him to the verge of frenzy, from which he was restored only by his sound, death-like sleep. This restorative he had always had at hand; he assured me that he had but to find himself alone and unoccupied in a room where there was a sofa, to go straightway to sleep. His brain had from childhood been taxed excessively, by the university course, study of modern languages, drawing, and much else, and to these were added the study of music in its profoundest sense. The rapidity with which he mastered a score; his perfect understanding of the requirements of new compositions, the construction and complications of which were at once transparent to him; his marvellous memory, which placed under his hand the entire range of great works; these wondrous gifts filled me with frequent doubts as to whether his nervous power could possibly sustain him through the length of an ordinary life.
>
> Moreover, he would take no repose. The habit of constant occupation, instilled by his mother, made rest intolerable to him. To spend any time in mere talk caused him to look frequently at his watch, by which he often

gave offence; his impatience was only pacified when something was being done, such as music, reading, chess, &c. He was fond of having a leaf of paper and pen at hand when he was conversing, to sketch down whatever occurred to him. . . .

Felix's nature fitted him particularly for friendship; he possessed already then a rich store of intimates, which increased as he advanced in life. To his friends he was frankly devoted, exquisitely tender; it was indeed felicity to be beloved by Felix. At the same time it must be confessed that his affection was exclusive to the utmost; he loved only in the measure as he was loved. This was the solitary dark speck in his sunny disposition. He was the spoilt child of fortune, unused to hardship or opposition; it remains a marvel that egotism did not prevail more than it did over his inborn nobleness and straightforwardness.

The atmosphere of love and appreciation in which he had been nurtured was a condition of life to him; to receive his music with coldness or aversion was to be his enemy, and he was capable of denying genuine merit in any one who did so. A blunder in manners, or an expression that displeased him, could alienate him altogether; he could then be disagreeable, indeed quite intolerable. The capital musician, Bernhard Klein, he could never bear, and simply because—as he himself confessed to me—Klein, sitting beside Felix in a box at the opera when Felix was yet a boy, whose feet when sitting on a chair did not reach the ground, impatiently muttered, "Cannot that boy keep his feet from dangling?" About such small things he could be unforgiving, for he could not use himself to hear what displeased him, and he never had been compelled to conform cheerfully to the whims of any one. I often took him to task about this, and suggested that, like the Venetian, he should keep a book of vengeance, in which to enter a debtor and creditor account for offences. I could venture to speak thus jokingly to him, for he knew that I could never have believed him capable of retaliation, even for unkindness and spite.

But his irritability, his distrustfulness even towards his most intimate friends, were sometimes quite incredible. A casual remark, a stupid jest, that he often accepted from me with perfect good temper, would sometimes suddenly cause him to drop his lids, look at me askance, and ask doubtfully, "What do you mean by that? Now I want to know what you wish me to understand by this?" &c., and it was difficult to restore his good humour. These peculiarities in Mendelssohn caused him, though much beloved, to be often judged unfavourably; but those who knew him intimately accepted these few faults, the natural growth of his exceptional position, and prized none the less all that was excellent in him.

He was exquisitely kind-hearted and benevolent, even towards dumb animals. I recollect him, when a boy of thirteen, ardently pleading for the life and liberty of a small fish which had been given to his brother Paul, who wished to have it fried for himself. Felix in anger said, "If you were anything of a boy, you would put it back in the water directly." Although the mother took the part of her nestling, the father decided the point with, "Paul, put the fish back into the water. You are no fisher, and are not entitled to his life; for pleasure or for daintiness' sake we are not to take the life of any creature." Felix joyfully seized the little fellow's hand, ran with him to the pond, and threw in the struggling fish. I have often since thought of that fish when I have seen Felix take the part of those who were in trouble.[44]

Mendelssohn's own feeling about the relationship that ought to exist between close friends is indicated by his response to Devrient's statement, in a letter of 30 May 1829, that Mendelssohn's last letter from London had been "useful" in reassuring him and his wife that he was not falling into bad ways through too much socializing:

If you were here I might walk up and down your room and vent my vexation about many things; I might, however, possibly spare you the homily which I am going to write now, since you cannot see my angry face. Ought anything to be useful to me with you and your wife? Nothing ought to be either useful or hurtful to me with you, for I thought you knew me. At all events, when I am once convinced that any one is sincere with me, and that I know him, I put down the fellow as firm and true, and life or what you will may tug and change, in my thoughts he still stands firm and true. What would you say to me if I were to implore you not to be carried away by the glitter of Spontini, but to remain true to good music? You would charge me with want of trust, nor would I think of making such an appeal. But life and art are not to be separated; and if you have no fears of my going over to Rossini or to John Bull, you must also have none that life is dragging me down. It will be some time till we meet, and if you have not full reliance on one whom you should know, you will have cause enough hereafter to feel uncomfortable about him. Now I should be sorry for this, and very sorry if anything again were to be useful or hurtful to me in your opinion, or that you thought I could ever change. Upon my word, Devrient, when I improve or deteriorate I shall let you know by express; till then believe it not (of course I mean as to certain things usually called sentiments).

I wish many things at the devil, especially the entire last page, which is good for nothing. But I know what I mean.[45]

Despite Devrient's suggestion that Mendelssohn, as "the spoilt child of fortune, unused to hardship or opposition," was inclined to be wilful, it is clear that he developed the ability to adapt his behaviour to circumstances at an early age. For instance, although with his family and its intimate circle he gave his naturally exuberant spirits free rein, he generally behaved with courteous urbanity in the presence of strangers or in more formal situations. This is nicely illustrated by Ferdinand Hiller's account of his first meeting with Mendelssohn in Frankfurt in 1822 when Mendelssohn was thirteen and Hiller eleven. Hiller's teacher Aloys Schmitt was well acquainted with the Mendelssohn family, for he had performed a double concerto by Dussek with Felix in Berlin earlier in the year and had evidently struck up a friendly relationship with the boy. Hiller recalled that, after watching the door to the courtyard of the house through a window for Mendelssohn's expected arrival, "[I] was rewarded by seeing the door open and my master appear. Behind him was a boy, only a little bigger than myself, who kept leaping up till he contrived to get his hands on to Schmitt's shoulders, so as to hang on his back and be carried along for a few steps, and then slip off again. 'He's jolly enough,' thought I, and ran off to the sitting-room to tell my parents that the eagerly-expected visitor had arrived. But great was my astonishment when I saw this same wild boy enter the room in quite a dignified way, and, though very lively and talkative, yet all the time preserving a certain formality. He himself impressed me even more than the account of his performances had done, and I could not help feeling a little shy during the whole of the visit."[46]

Hiller, who quickly formed a friendly relationship with Mendelssohn, also described an instance of the "mad spirits Mendelssohn was capable of" that took place in Paris in the winter of 1831 and 1832: "One night as we were coming home across the deserted boulevard at a late hour, in earnest conversation, Mendelssohn suddenly stops and calls out: 'We *must* do some of our jumps in Paris! our jumps, I tell you! Now for it! one!—two!—three!—' I don't think my jumps were very brilliant, for I was rather taken aback by the suggestion, but I shall never forget the moment."[47] A similar display of animal spirits is indicated by another incident recounted by Hiller. "When he liked a thing he liked it with his whole heart, but if it did not please him, he would sometimes use the most singular language. One day when I had been playing him some composition of mine, long since destroyed, he threw himself down on the floor and rolled about all over the room."[48]

Mendelssohn retained a propensity to high spirits throughout his life. As late as 1845 he wrote to his sisters: "I came with Schlemmer last night from a musical punch-party, where I first played Beethoven's Sonata 106 in B-flat, and then drank two hundred and twelve glasses of punch *fortissimo*; we then sang the duet from 'Faust' in the Mainz Street, because there was such wonderful moonlight, and today I have rather a head-ache."[49]

Mendelssohn's excitability and emotionality were also described in contemporary private letters by Fanny Horsley, who was far from idealizing him. After visiting him at his lodgings in Great Portland Street in 1833, where he was tending his father, who had suffered an injury to his shin, she wrote: "Felix was very lachrimose and rushed four times in and out of the room in a very phrensied manner. I gazed at him for some time in such deep amaze that I am sure at last he perceived it. What an odd tempered creature he is. But most geniuses are the same they say, and at any rate he is always delightful for he is always original."[50] On another occasion in 1833, she remarked of Felix: "He wants to compose a great deal I believe, and I think he had better at the same time compose himself, for his mind wants a little settling in my opinion."[51] About their final meeting before his departure she reported: "Of all the many times we have seen him this year and last, we unanimously agree that never was he so brilliant, so droll, and so delightfully friendly and intimate as this memorable morning." When the time for parting came "he turned quite as pale as death, though he had been looking as fresh as a great damask rose all the walk, and his eyes filled with tears. . . . His last words almost were 'Oh pray, Mrs. Horsley, pray let me find no changes, let all be the same as ever."[52]

How deep was his longing for the simple companionableness that the Horsley family represented, and how much he disliked pomp and ceremony, is indicated by his account of a visit on 7 September 1837 to the home of Fanny Horsley's sister, Mary, who had married Isambard Kingdom Brunel.

> At seven in the evening to dinner at Brunel's in the Park
> with Klingemann. O what should man request? If friends
> are not well, that causes distress, and if they are well,
> then there is still no lack of distress. For example, as
> here, where everything was so elegant, and aristocratic,
> and befitting a Member of Parliament, that the likes of
> me began to feel quite sick in the stomach. What had
> happened to the Mary Horsley of old? And what to the
> former Isambard Brunel? Flown off into a world of gran-

deur, where there is room for everything, but pleasure for no one and concern for no one. For nothing was forthcoming from the two at dinner, except for plenty of fish, poultry and the like. And beforehand we had to wait a while with the ladies and the baby before the man of the house arrived with his father, and Mr Hawes MP and goodness knows who else, still engrossed in the deepest conversation, and then we proceeded straight to the feast, and immediately after the feast we went into an elegant room, in which stood a small organ, upon which I was expected to play! However, I took my hat, and walked home alone through St James's Park, and there in the dark heard the retreat sounded on trumpets and drums, and could almost have wept, so moved was I. Klingemann stayed on and sought to excuse me, and I resolved that I would not go there again, where a merry, good companion had become twisted into a grand speculator, politician, and man of quality. I know of nothing which I regret more.[53]

Mendelssohn's approach to living and entertaining undoubtedly derived from his parents who, although occupying a palatial house, chose the simplest furnishings and welcomed guests without ceremony. Hiller's description of Mendelssohn's own domestic arrangements in Leipzig in 1840 indicate a style of life which, although consistent with his affluent financial circumstances, was unpretentious and sociable:

Mendelssohn's house was pleasantly situated, with a nice open look-out from the front upon the Leipsic boulevard, and the St Thomas's school and church, once the sphere of the great Bach's labours. The arrangement of the rooms was as follows:—first, a sort of hall, with the dining table and a few chairs: to the right of this a large sitting room and some bedrooms; to the left my friend's study with his piano. Opening out of this was a fine large drawing room, which however was robbed of some of its natural elegance by the bed which had been put there for me, though this was counteracted by a piano also put there for my use.

Our way of life was regular and simple. At about eight we breakfasted on coffee and bread and butter. Butter Felix never eats, but broke his bread into his coffee like any schoolboy, "as he had been accustomed to do." We dined at one, and though he despised butter he always liked a glass of good wine, and we often had to try some special sort, which he would produce with great delight, and swallow with immense satisfaction. We generally made quick work with our dinner, but in the evenings after supper we used often to sit round the table for hours chatting (not smoking), unless we moved to the pianino which had been presented to Madame Mendelssohn by the directors of the Gewandhaus.[54]

Many accounts indicate Mendelssohn's "capriciousness" and "irritability."[55] He seems often to have found it difficult to restrain himself when he felt people were treating music carelessly or insultingly. Writing to Hiller from Berlin in 1838 he remarked, "At the Sing-Akademie they sang me a piece of my own, in such a way that I should have got seriously angry, if Cécile had not sat by me and kept on saying: 'Dear husband, do be calm.' They also played me some quartets, and always bungled the very same passages that they had bungled ten years ago, and which had made me furious ten years ago—another proof of the immortality of the soul."[56] And on 20 January 1841 the Leipzig publisher Heinrich Brockhaus recorded Mendelssohn's reaction to Ole Bull's performance at the Leipzig Gewandhaus: "I sat next to Mendelssohn and it was interesting and characteristic that at every tasteless thing that Bull permitted himself, in order to shine, he became progressively more disturbed and agitated. I said to him that he should not ask that everyone should regard art as holy, to which he very aptly countered: 'but then one should also not act as if it were.'"[57]

Occasionally Mendelssohn was prone to sudden fits of rage, or even exhibited symptoms of violent mental disturbance. Hiller related that during an excursion near Frankfurt in the mid-1830s "the coachman did or said some stupidity or other, upon which Mendelssohn jumped out of the carriage, in a towering rage, and after pouring a torrent of abuse upon the man, declared that nothing should make him get in again. The punishment was on our side, and my mother was quite frightened when we arrived later in the evening hot and exhausted, having had to walk the whole way home. At supper Felix himself could not help laughing, though still stoutly maintaining that he was right."[58] More extreme was Mendelssohn's behaviour in 1829, on the eve of the performance of his liederspiel *Die Heimkehr aus der Fremde*, to celebrate his parents' silver wedding anniversary. When a summons from the crown prince for Devrient to sing at court threatened to disrupt the occasion, Mendelssohn's "excitement increased so fearfully, that when the family was assembled for the evening, he began to talk incoherently, and in English, to the great terror of them all. The stern voice of his father at last checked the wild torrent of words; they took him to bed, and a profound sleep of twelve hours restored him to his normal state."[59]

The same sleep remedy served Mendelssohn well in later years. An entry in the "honeymoon diary" by Cécile on 7 August 1837, for instance, records: "Felix played and became so excited by it that it gave him a headache. . . . Felix went to bed and slept everything off."[60] The efficacy of sleep, along with the relaxation provided by friendship and by artistic and literary activity as an aid to recovering from exhaustion, depression or agitation, was also attested by Hiller in his recollections of his visit to Leipzig during 1839 and 1840:

> In the midst of the manifold occupations and social
> meetings in which he gladly took part, which he graced
> by his talent and brilliant conversation, there would
> come days of exhaustion, even of depression. At such
> times, visits from his friends, foremost among whom
> were David and Dr Schleinitz, would always do him
> good. Sometimes he would amuse himself with doing lit-
> tle water-colour sketches—or he would read some poem
> of Goethe's, such as "Hermann and Dorothea" or "Iphi-
> genie." The first of these he was especially fond of, and
> he would go into raptures over the deep feeling which
> penetrates the most insignificant things in that wonderful
> work. He said one day that the line, "Und es lobte dar-

auf der Apotheker den Knaster," was enough to bring tears into one's eyes. He would also get out Jean Paul sometimes, and revel in his humour; one evening he read aloud to me out of *Siebenkäs* for at least an hour. But sleep was always his best resource. Several times I found him lying on the sofa before dinner, ready dressed, having been asleep for hours, after which he would awake with a capital appetite. A quarter of an hour after he would say with the air of a spoiled child, "I am still quite tired;" would lie down again, saying how delicious it was, stretch himself out, and in a few minutes be fast asleep again. "He can go on in that way for two days," Cécile said to me, "and then he is fresher than ever."[61]

Most accounts indicate Mendelssohn's innate modesty, which led him rather to deprecate his gifts or his status than to flaunt them. Queen Victoria's diary twice comments specifically on his modesty; at their first meeting in 1842 she noted that he was "very pleasing and modest," and on receiving news of his death in 1847, after describing him as "the greatest musical genius since Mozart, . . . the wonderful genius, and the great mind," she added: "With it all he was so modest and simple."[62] Schumann felt that "he was free from every weakness of vanity,"[63] and Moscheles noted in his diary in 1846 that Mendelssohn "earnestly objected to his name standing first in the list [of professors at the Leipzig Conservatorium], instead of following the rest in alphabetical order."[64] A typical example of Mendelssohn's tendency to self-deprecation occurs in a letter to Emil Nauman from 1845, where he wrote: "As I said before, you must *continue* to work: I must also beg you to place the same reliance on me, that you so kindly expressed in your letter. And as you apply Goethe's words to me, and call me a *master*, I can only reply once more in Goethe's words:-

'Learn soon to know wherein he fails;
True Art, and not its type, revere.'

The advice in the first line is not difficult to follow, and the latter is not to be feared with you."[65]

His modesty was also evident in his attitude towards the publication of his portrait, as expressed in a letter from Paris to his sister Rebecka in December 1831. After asserting his scorn for orders and other such distinctions, he wrote: "*Apropos*, shall I be lithographed full length? Answer what you will, I don't intend to do it. One afternoon in Berlin, when I was standing *unter den Linden* before Schenk's shop looking at H——'s and W——'s lithographs, I made a solemn vow to myself, unheard by man, that I would never allow myself to be hung up till I became a great man. The temptation in Munich was strong; there they wished to drape me with a Carbonaro cloak, a stormy sky in the background, and my facsimile underneath, but I happily got off by adhering to my principles. Here again I am rather tempted, for the likenesses are very striking, but I keep my vow; and if, after all, I never do become a great man, though posterity will be deprived of a portrait, it will have an absurdity the less."[66] Four years later he still maintained the same position when the organizers of the Lower Rhine Musical Festival, which he was to conduct in Cologne in May 1835, wanted to produce a portrait of him in connection with the festival. On 3 April he wrote to his father: "They persist that my 'admirable likeness' shall appear and be published by Whitsunday, a project from which I gallantly defend myself, refusing either to sit or stand for the purpose, having a particular objection to such pretensions."[67] And to the secretary of the council in Cologne he explained, "It is now so very much the fashion for obscure or commonplace people to have their likeness given to the public, in order to become more known, and for young beginners to do so at first starting in life, that I have always had a dread of doing so too soon. I do not wish that my likeness should be taken until I have accomplished something to render me more worthy, according to my idea, of such an honour. This, however, not being yet the case, I beg to defer such a compliment till I am more deserving of it; but receive my best thanks for the friendly good nature with which you made me this offer."[68] The success of *St Paul* may have convinced him that he could at last relax his opposition; in January 1837 he was able to supply three different portraits of himself for Aloys Fuchs's collection.[69]

Such reticence might help explain the fact that although Mendelssohn lived for several years after the invention of photography, no photographic image appears to have been preserved.[70] However, the Austrian poet Johannes Nordmann, who met Mendelssohn in Leipzig in 1847, left an account that conflicts with the general impression of his essential modesty. His comments make it clear that he held Mendelssohn in high regard and that he was not motivated by spite or prejudice, but he evidently gained the impression that in society Mendelssohn expected, or even required, to be the center of attention: "In personal intercourse Mendelssohn was very amiable; in larger gatherings, however, he required with striking vanity that one concern oneself exclusively and solely with him, and was really put out if one person or another drew the attention to themselves. One could, however, overlook this small failing in a man who had such great qualities. He still remains in my memory as a beautiful manifestation of humanity."[71] Perhaps Nordmann's impression derived from observing an instance when Mendelssohn showed the impatience with "mere talk" referred to by Devrient. Hiller's comment in a letter to Ferdinand David in 1842 contrasting Mendelssohn's innate modesty with the self-absorption and self-importance of other celebrated musicians, is more typical. "What a difference between him and other so-called great artists!" Hiller wrote, "Since his departure Thalberg and Berlioz (who will come again) have been here, and Döhler is here now. They are really nice people and fine artists, but they are so wrapped up in their own little egos, they require so much and give so little."[72] Characteristic of Mendelssohn's modesty, as Schumann noted,[73] was his refusal to wear the ribbons of any of the orders he received, and his insistence, where possible, on having his name given on title pages without any honorifics.[74]

A particularly vivid account of Mendelssohn's personality in general, as it struck a Leipzig contemporary towards the end of his life, occurs in an obituary written the day after Mendelssohn's death, which, according to Schumann, was "the best that was written about Mendelssohn."[75] The author, Gustav Kühne, was a Leipzig musician and journalist who was evidently personally acquainted with Mendelssohn but did not belong to his inner circle; his appraisal provides a rare example of an entirely unsentimental impression of Mendelssohn by a sympathetic but acutely perceptive contemporary, who could appreciate the magic of his personality but was not overwhelmed by it.

> Mendelssohn's music has not been taken up by his contemporaries without loud approval, not without the deepest fervour of enthusiasm. Even an artist is seldom

celebrated to such an extent, seldom is the talent in the man, and the man in the talent, as greatly loved as in his case. His was one of those finely strung natures that may be likened to the *Noli me tangere* plant.[76] His reserve as a man was erroneously taken for pride, the ease with which he was shocked by every uncouth contact for refined over-sensitivity. He was fundamentally of a refined nature, he was only interested in the finest, only the noblest came up to his expectations. He was testily closed to all that lay outside the bounds of his individuality. Passionately irritated by all that was alien to him, every dissonance that did not belong in his harmony was inimical to him. As if he knew that his stay would not be long, he was jealous of the short span of life, every moment had to serve him and the high seriousness of his profession, and yet in this conscientious seriousness of his nature there lay at the same time so much playful harmlessness, in this strong wilfulness so much love, friendliness and feeling of happiness. He was thankful for all the care that was afforded him, thankful for all assistance to smooth the way for his temperament, to lighten the pressure of his work, the birth hours of his genius. What was taken for niggardliness and moodiness was a wise economy with time and strength. With his acute mind he did not fail to understand the noisy din of the world, but he did not sympathize with it; he was an artistic innocent, with all the self-denial and naturalness, all the cheerful receptiveness, and all the wilfulness of the well-cared-for, softly bedded, grown-up child. So much care was a requirement of his delicately constituted, very fragile nature. As a man he was only accessible to a few, but to these few he was a rare phenomenon, seeming a miracle in his loving, blissful friendship, a miracle in his effects on the circle of close friends, a miracle of inspiriting power in his effects when a work of art was to be called into being.[77]

3 · Relationships with Women

There are abundant indications that Mendelssohn was attractive to young women and that several may have lost their heart to him; but information about his reciprocation of these feelings, other than in a conventionally gallant or charming manner, are scantily documented in currently available sources. In recent years there has been an increasing tendency to believe that creative virility and sexual appetite are intimately connected, and by these criteria Mendelssohn's apparent self-control equates with a presumed lack of emotional depth in his music. This fallacious link is not new, for in 1869, Cosima Wagner recorded in her diary: "I asked R. whether he thought every boy should lead a wild and dissolute life in his youth. He says: 'Yes, if only for the sake of the salutary longing to return to one's senses. This is what always seemed to me questionable about Mendelssohn—that he never lost control of himself.' "[78] An alternative view, however, widely held during Mendelssohn's lifetime, was that sexual restraint was a sign of strength. This quality was widely attributed to Mendelssohn in his day, and, as yet, no persuasive evidence has been advanced to suggest that the attribution was misplaced.

As a youth Mendelssohn was drawn towards Betty Pistor (later Rudorff), and he (privately) dedicated his E-flat String Quartet, op. 12, to her, though his feelings, if romantic, seem to have been unrequited.[79] A number of young women whom he met on his early visits to England undoubtedly fell in love with him, but, whatever his inner feelings, there is no reliable evidence of his returning their affections other than with friendship. We know for certain of only two cases, apart from his relationship with his wife, where his emotional interest seems to have been seriously aroused, and in both instances the women concerned, Delphine von Schauroth and Jenny Lind, were, unlike his wife, fine musicians. Eric Werner has claimed that there is also evidence in the surviving correspondence of a flirtation or affair during Mendelssohn's time in Düsseldorf; this is said to have involved "a widowed aristocratic lady." Werner quotes from an "unpublished letter from Lea to Felix, January 11, 1834," admonishing him to extricate himself from the affair, which his mother seems to have feared might end in an unsatisfactory marriage.[80] Werner also suggests, though he does not reveal his source for the supposition, that it may have been a physical relationship. Werner's reading of the evidence, however, is often unreliable. Elsewhere he states that Cécile was jealous of "every woman who made eyes at her famous husband," adding: "In Berlin, she really had no basis for this attitude, for Felix scarcely bothered to answer the occasional 'propositions' of society ladies. The affair with Miss Louise Bendinen [sic] in London was something else again. Felix took such obvious pleasure in her company that his friend, the critic J. W. Davison, had to warn both parties against too obvious manifestations of their feelings."[81] In fact, Werner's insinuation is entirely unsupported by the source he cites as evidence. The volume of Mendelssohn's correspondence for July to December 1842 contains a letter from Louise Bendixen, couched in formal language, which, though certainly that of an admirer, gives no hint of any amorous attentions on Mendelssohn's part; and the letter from Davison that Werner refers to contains no suggestion of a warning to either party. Davison mentioned her only briefly: "Miss Louise Bendixen (who is eternally talking of you, and eternally playing the song you gave her) brought me your Sinfonia in A Minor," after which he turned to lavishing praise on the symphony.[82]

During Mendelssohn's visit to Munich in June 1830, on his outward journey to Italy, he was deeply impressed artistically, and probably romantically, by Delphine von Schauroth, the daughter of one of Munich's leading families. Although only sixteen years old, she was already a talented pianist and composer, and he inscribed the Rondo Capriccioso, op. 14, to her. Felix praised her playing to Fanny in a letter of 11 June,[83] though he compared Fanny's compositions favourably to Delphine's. In Venice in October, he sketched the "Venetianisches Gondellied" (op. 19b, no. 6) for Delphine. While Mendelssohn was staying in Munich on the return journey in September and October 1831, the relationship developed significantly. He rapidly composed the G Minor Piano Concerto with her in mind, and there seems to have been an expectation of marriage on the part of Delphine's family. The affair even reached the ears of the king, for in a letter to his father on 18 October 1831 Felix reported: "The main thing that the king said to me, though, was that I should marry Fräulein von Schauroth, that would be an excellent match, and why didn't I do it? That, from a king, annoyed me, and somewhat piqued, I was going to answer him, when he, not even waiting for my answer, jumped to something else and then to a third thing."[84]

Evidently the Mendelssohn family were by no means happy with the idea of such a marriage, and Felix, either out of duty or inclination, concurred with their view. A degree of embarrassment on Felix's part resulted from this, as is indicated by a rather unconvincing story in a letter he wrote on 5 September the following year to his Munich friend, the clarinettist Heinrich Baermann: "It would have been a pleasure to hear Delphine play; but no doubt the whole family are highly offended with me, for I have not been able to send a single letter. I began to write in Paris, finished the letter in London, and put it in the post, when two days afterwards, it was returned to me because the postage, it appeared, was not properly paid. Since then I have made no further attempts. No doubt they will be very angry, but I have been all along in the worst humour for writing."[85] The legacy of his feelings for Delphine is suggested in his comment to Baermann in a letter of 7 July 1834, after he had received the news of Delphine's marriage to Hill Handley: "What did you say to Delphine's marriage? and what did I say to it? I said *Donner-wetter!*"[86] Delphine's continuing warmth of feeling is suggested by a letter from Fanny to Felix in 1839. After visiting Delphine in Munich Fanny wrote: "It's utterly indescribable how fondly they remember you in this house. They know every word you spoke and every movement you made."[87]

The woman Mendelssohn married in 1836 could hardly have been more different from Delphine. Cécile had no particular musical gift, though she had a talent for drawing and painting. Fanny described her in a letter to Klingemann as "amiable, childlike, fresh, bright and even-tempered. . . . Her presence produces the effect of a fresh breeze, so light and bright and natural is she."[88] In some sense the death of Abraham Mendelssohn in 1835, which removed a dominating influence on Felix's life, may have enabled Felix seriously to consider marriage, or perhaps impelled him to it as a means of filling the emotional void. It seems clear, however that his marriage to Cécile was a genuine love match. He wrote to his sister Rebecka in July 1836, "I am more desperately in love than I ever was in my life before";[89] and Hiller, referring to this period, recalled: "Lying on the sofa in my room after dinner, or taking long walks in the mild summer nights with Dr S and myself, he would rave about her charm, her grace, and her beauty. There was nothing overstrained in him, either in his life or in his art: he would pour out his heart about her in the most charmingly frank and artless way, often full of fun and gaiety; then again, with deep feeling, but never with any exaggerated sentimentality or uncontrolled passion. It was easy to see what a serious thing it was, for one could hardly get him to talk of anything which did not touch in some way upon her."[90]

The joy and satisfaction that Mendelssohn's marriage brought him springs out of many pages of his letters. On 2 June 1837 he wrote to Ferdinand David, who had been married for about six months: "Listen, if things are going as well with you as with me (and I am very confident they are), then the best thing we ever did in our whole lives was to put the sacred order of bachelorhood on the shelf. I, at least, know for certain that I would not like to exchange the last two months with any year of my past life for any price; I often feel as if I now know for the first time what life is about. But if everything in and about one changes so much, I keep thinking that the whole world must also change at the same time."[91] Mendelssohn's deep feeling for his wife and growing family shines out from a letter to his closest friend, Klingemann, written on 4 January 1841, immediately after the birth of his third child.

> Mother and son are as sound and well as I could wish
> and pray for, and since then it is as if the heaviest stone
> were lifted from my heart, the most oppressive care from
> my breast. In recent weeks I continually thought of only
> one thing and could not drive away a deep and powerful
> fear, and now everything has passed off so happily, since
> my beloved Cécile looks so cheerful and bright and
> happy, and feels strong and unchanged, so that I cannot
> describe to you how good I feel about it. Just now I sat
> for a while by her bed, and watched how peacefully she
> sleeps, and I don't know how I can thank God enough
> for this great joy he has given me. May he preserve it for
> me and make me worthy of it. Such a peaceful, gentle
> sleep at such a time has something magical about it; one
> desires it so often from one's heart and can give it nei-
> ther to oneself or to others, and suddenly there it is all

by itself. You have a part in everything that happens to me, how much more at such important moments—therefore I tell you everything, just as I feel it.[92]

Little is directly known of Mendelssohn's relationship with Cécile over the years of their marriage, for in fulfilment of her wishes, his letters to her were burnt after her death, only one apparently escaping. But this one letter, written to Cécile in Leipzig on her birthday in 1843, when Mendelssohn was in Berlin arranging for the première of the *Sommernachtstraum* music, clearly shows the warm intimacy of their relations at that time: "I can only write to you today, when I should be speaking to you, kissing you and being with you the whole day, so as to rejoice in your looks, the festive day and my happiness, and to wish you happiness! Good, dear Cecile! . . . and if we were together, and I had already kissed you so much and again kissed you, you would still have to notice that I was there; I would not leave you in peace the whole day with my love and my joy over your birthday."[93] It seems clear that their marriage remained stable and happy to the end. In 1846 Charlotte Moscheles commented on her relationship with the family after she and her husband had moved to Leipzig: "We are truly happy in our intercourse with the Mendelssohns; not only he, the amiable, intimate friend, but his wife and their charming children becoming daily more and more attached to us; and what a happy household it is! The abundant means at his command are never squandered upon outward show, but judiciously spent on a well-regulated, comfortable household. Their principles and ideas are entirely in conformity with our own; they, like ourselves, love to welcome friends or interesting guests cordially, but without ceremony."[94]

The only potential threat to the stability of Mendelssohn's marriage seems to have been his close relationship with the great singer Jenny Lind during the last three years of his life. The nature of Mendelssohn's relationship with Lind during the short period of their acquaintance has been a matter of some speculation. There can be no doubt about the extent of his admiration for her musical gifts or about the extent of hers for his, and it is abundantly clear that a rare bond of personal sympathy existed between them. There were those at the time, including Clara Schumann, who believed that she was in love with him. How deeply Mendelssohn's emotional feelings were aroused is unclear. His extant letters to her give no hint of a relationship that overstepped the bounds of friendship (albeit a very strongly motivated friendship), and his comments to others about her, though often extraordinarily warm, always centered upon her great gifts as an artist. There is no doubt that Jenny Lind's combination of supreme artistry and seriousness of artistic purpose inspired the composer. As he explained in a letter to his friend Franz Hauser, "You will never be able to look upon her as a stranger, but as one of ourselves—a member of that invisible Church [that is, the association of those who treat art with true reverence], concerning which you write to me sometimes. She pulls at the same rope with all of us who are really in earnest about that; thinks about it; strives for it; and if all goes well with her in the world, it is as pleasant to me as if it went well with me: for it helps me, and all of us, so well on our road. And to you, as a singer, it must be especially delightful to meet, at last, with the union of such splendid talents, with such profound study, and such heartfelt enthusiasm."[95] The soprano part of *Elijah* was created with Jenny Lind's voice in mind (her beautiful f sharp" was quite deliberately made a prominent feature in "Hear Ye, Israel," the opening number of the second part of the oratorio), and Mendelssohn's almost frenetic efforts to compose an opera at that time were entirely caused by his desire to provide one for her. He wrote on 31 October 1846: "I should indeed be glad if I could soon, in accordance with my most hearty wish write something dramatic—and especially for you," and added prophetically, "I have a secret foreboding which tells me that, if I do not attain to the composition of a fairly good Opera *now*, and *for you*, I shall never accomplish it at all."[96]

The orthodox view of their relationship was expressed by Eric Werner when he wrote: "The master remained faithful to his wife and to his principle 'Art and life are not divisible.' "[95] Suggestions that Mendelssohn's relationship with Jenny Lind may have been more intimate have, however, been fuelled by rumours of papers in possession of the Mendelssohn Society of London, deposited in 1896 by Lind's husband, Otto Goldschmidt (whom she married in 1852), which were to remain sealed for a hundred years. They are said to have been duly opened in 1996, but a conspiracy of silence surrounds the contents; nevertheless, it has been rumoured that the papers tend to substantiate the notion of an affair between Mendelssohn and Lind, though with what degree of reliability must remain highly questionable.

TWO · Multiplicity of Talent

4 · Writing

Nineteenth-century composers were much more likely than their eighteenth-century predecessors to engage actively in wider artistic and intellectual pursuits. Spohr showed talent for painting, Weber, Schumann, Berlioz and Wagner for literature, Brahms became involved in editing older music. In addition, these and other contemporary composers saw themselves, and were seen, as the intellectual equals of the scholars and thinkers of the day. Even among his most cultured colleagues, however, Mendelssohn stood out for the range, depth and quality of his talents. This resulted partly from his exceptionally rigorous and comprehensive education, which was strengthened by the stimulating cultural milieu in which he grew up, partly from the broadening effect of his extensive travels, and partly from his own extraordinary qualities of mind. Schumann, for instance, thought that there was "profound sense in everything that he did and said, from the smallest to the greatest," observing that "in the last years he spoke ever more wisely and profoundly" and that "he was never short of an apt response. If one said something good, significant to him, one could be sure to receive it back two- or threefold." Schumann noted "his enormous knowledge of literature[;] the Bible, Shakespeare, Goethe, J. Paul (also Homer) he knew thoroughly in the principal parts, almost by heart." Schumann also referred to Mendelssohn's less intellectual pastimes, writing laconically at one point of "our chess and billiard playing."[1] Other sources indicate that Mendelssohn was a particularly good chess player; Hiller, for instance, described how he often played chess in Paris in 1831 and 1832, particularly with Dr Hermann Franck, who "would not allow that he was inferior," upon which "Mendelssohn invented a phrase which he relentlessly repeated after every victory: 'We play quite equally well—*quite equally*—only I play a very little better.' "[2]

Summing up his impression of Mendelssohn's acquirements and versatility Schumann remarked: "If all his close friends had been writers, each of them would have had some other extraordinary thing [to relate], each could have written whole volumes about him. Every day he was as if new born."[3] Mendelssohn's family and friends knew him as a gifted poet and translator of poetry, a brilliant writer whose letters conveyed the wit, vivacity and wisdom of his conversation, and an artist whose drawings and paintings would not have disgraced a professional; and to the wider world he displayed his rare discrimination as editor of Handel's *Israel in Egypt*.

Mendelssohn is most widely known as a writer from his letters. Of these the most striking are the ones he sent to family and close friends, from which his character and views emerge with remarkable force and clarity. The immediacy of their style and the liveliness with which he expressed his ideas show his fine feeling for the written word. But also in letters to acquaintances, formal letters and even in many shorter business notes his personality and his gift for the telling phrase is constantly apparent. The letters to his intimate circle, often amusing, idiosyncratic, even impudent, have an almost literary quality, which reveals the influence of one of the favourite authors of his youth, Jean Paul (Richter); a conversation recorded by Schumann "about Jean Paul and the seductiveness of imitating him" hints at Mendelssohn's own awareness of this.[4] When the first volume of Mendelssohn's letters, from 1830 to 1832, was published in 1861, Moritz Hauptmann characterized them as "so clever and original, that it is a delight to read them. . . . Most of the letters published now-a-days depend entirely for their interest on the personality of the writer; Mendelssohn's, characteristic as they are, have something besides. They are full of that genial cultivation, which left its mark on everything that he did."[5]

Of course, even in the best English translation Mendelssohn's letters lose something of their verbal vitality, but their spirit is unmistakable. A few letters written in English, French and Italian show that in a foreign language he was still able to express himself fluently and individually. The quality of the letters, extending also to their beautiful presentation, is even more remarkable when their quantity is taken into account. As Hiller observed: "His correspondence really took up most of his time, and the number of letters he must have written is incredible. But it was a pleasure to him to be in such general requisition, and he never complained of it. Everything he did he strove to do in the most perfect manner possible, down to the smallest details, and it was the same with his correspondence. It was delightful to see the care and evident satisfaction with which he would fold and seal his letters. Anyhow, he could always feel sure of their giving pleasure. Whatever hard work he had before him it never prevented him from occupying himself with something else up to the last minute. How often, when I called for him to go to a concert where he had to play and conduct, I would find him in full dress, sitting quietly at the writing table! It was just because he felt so secure in all that he did."[6] And Schumann remarked that "his handwriting also [was] an image of his harmonious soul!"[7]

Few of Mendelssohn's contemporaries were aware of his poetic gifts, which went beyond mere versification. From an early age he took a lively interest in reading and writing poetry, but very few of his poems were known outside the family circle. Hiller, who was in Leipzig while Mendelssohn was translating some of Dante's sonnets into German verse at the behest of his uncle Joseph,[8] observed in his recollections: "I feel sure that Felix must have written a considerable number of lyrical poems, though I do not know if he told his friends of it. If I am right, we may surely hope that some future time may bring them to light. They would certainly not be without merit."[9] A few of his poems may in fact have been published during his own lifetime, for it seems likely that the J. H. Voss, to whom the texts of songs in the Lieder op. 8 and 9 were attributed, was Mendelssohn himself.[10] His translation of Terence's *Andria*, in the metre of the Latin original, was published anonymously in 1826 by his tutor, Heyse, who observed in his introduction: "The young translator, whose natural calling, and the education appropriate to this, belongs to the art of a different, related Muse, dedicated few hours of study to this work. The editor, after having looked it through and applied careful polishing, considered it not unworthy of publication." Heyse added, "The editor merely wishes that his polishings, which are mostly in connection with the metre, more rarely the meaning and expression, may not, despite all his care, here and there have damaged the original lightness and natural flow."[11] When Goethe received a copy, he replied to Zelter: "Be so good as to give my best thanks to the excellent and industrious Felix for this glorious specimen of his serious aesthetic studies; his work will be a special amusement for the circle of art lovers at Weimar during the coming long winter evenings."[12] Another published poetic translation by Mendelssohn is of Byron's "Sun of the Sleepless," which he used for the German version of his own setting in 1838.

It is believed that Mendelssohn continued to write verse and translate foreign poems into German throughout his life. Max Schneider suggested in 1961 that more than were currently known might emerge from unresearched parts of the Mendelssohn legacy;[13] but this has not, so far, been the case. Apart from the poems and translations already mentioned, only a few occasional pieces are known: *Paphlëis*,[14] a piece written for his mother's birthday in 1826,[15] a few poems connected with his visits to Weimar from about 1830 and a much later acrostic verse, thanking Karl Emil von Webern for a birthday poem, in which the initial letters of the lines spell "Dank Dir Webern" (Thank you, Webern). His unpublished verses include a translation of Dryden's *Alexander's Feast* and the draft of an oratorio text, *Moses*, for A. B. Marx, both of which date from 1833.

5 · Editing Music

Mendelssohn, following the practice of Mozart and others, arranged a number of baroque choral compositions, including Bach's *St Matthew Passion*, for the larger orchestral resources of his own day. In his youth he made several such arrangements of Handel for use by the Berlin Singakademie. A few years later, however, his attitude towards the performance of baroque music had changed. In 1833 he wrote to Devrient asking him to retrieve his arrangements of Handel's *Acis and Galatea* and "Dettingen" Te Deum from the archives of the Singakademie; when the Te Deum did not arrive he again urged Devrient to obtain it, explaining: "In the score of 'Acis' . . . I have found, amongst many good things, several which I could not now endorse, and want to correct before it can pass into other hands, because I consider this matter of re-instrumenting as requiring the utmost conscientiousness. Now it happens that I recollect having done some still more arbitrary things in the 'Te Deum' than in 'Acis,' and I must expunge these faults (as I now regard them), as I cannot annul the score."[16]

Over the years his stance towards these works became increasingly strict, although he still performed them in ways that seem far from "purist" in the sense this term acquired during the twentieth century. Even in his Leipzig period he was not averse to performing a piano accompaniment to Bach's Chaconne for Solo Violin, elaborating the arpeggios in performing Bach's Chromatic Fantasia and Fugue or introducing modifications to suit the circumstances of his 1842 performance of the *St Matthew Passion*. When it came to publishing editions of this music, however, he took a different position. This was demonstrated by his approach to editing *Israel in Egypt* for the London Handel Society in 1844 and 1845. His stated aim, of producing a score in which all editorial intervention was clearly distinguished from the composer's text, was ahead of its time, and his unshakeable insistence on this basic principle occasioned lengthy and often testy correspondence with the committee of the Handel Society. Mendelssohn explained his editorial procedures in the introduction, which he supplied in English:

> The Council of the Handel Society having done me the honor to request me to edit "Israel in Egypt," an Oratorio which I have always viewed as one of the greatest and most lasting musical works, I think it my first duty to lay before the Society the Score as Handel wrote it, without introducing the least alteration, and without mixing up any remarks or notes of my own with those of Handel. In the next place, as there is no doubt that he himself introduced many things at the performance of his works which were not accurately written down, and which even now, when his music is performed, are supplied by a sort of tradition, according to the fancy of the Conductor and the Organist, it becomes my second duty to offer an opinion in all such cases; but I think it of paramount importance that all my remarks should be kept strictly separate from the Original Score, and that the latter should be given in its entire purity, in order to

afford every one an opportunity of resorting to Handel himself, and not to obtrude any suggestions of mine upon those who may differ from me in opinion.

The whole of the Score (excepting my Organ Part and the Pianoforte Arrangement, which are distinguished by being printed in small notes) is therefore printed according to Handel's manuscript in the Queen's Library. I have neither allowed myself to deviate from his authority in describing the movements in the Score, nor in marking pianos and fortes, nor in the figuring of the Bass, because he has frequently done so himself in his manuscripts (for instance the Chorus "The people shall hear" affords a striking instance of the accuracy with which he occasionally did it). Those remarks of mine which I had to offer, are therefore *only* to be found in the Pianoforte Arrangement, and those which are contained in the Score are written by Handel himself.

There are a few instances in this manuscript where Handel evidently omitted an accidental, or wrote a different note in one part from that which he gave to the other, the Council decided that I should alter such notes, and the places where this has been done are the following: [here follows a list].

And the *titles* of the different pieces have also been added by the Council, as also the division of a first and second Part. With these exceptions there is no deviation whatever in the Score from Handel's manuscript, which I found to be more correct and accurate than the printed edition, in spite of the great haste with which Handel used to write down his works.

After much more detailed description of the manuscript, Mendelssohn continued:

I have now only to add a few remarks concerning the Organ Part and Pianoforte Arrangement; for both of

which I am responsible. As for the Organ Part, I have
written it down in the manner in which I would play it,
were I called upon to do so at a performance of this Oratorio. These works ought of course never to be performed without an Organ, as they were done in Germany, where additional wind instruments are introduced
to make up for the defect. In England the Organist plays
usually ad libitum from the Score, as it seems to have
been the custom in Handel's time, whether he played
himself, or merely conducted and had an Organist under
his control. Now as the task of placing the chords in the
fittest manner to bring out all the points to the greatest
advantage, in fact of introducing, as it were, a new part
to Compositions like Handel's, is of extreme difficulty, I
have thought it useful to write down an Organ Part expressly for those who might not prefer to play one of
their own. I must leave it to the Organist to choose the
stops according to the strength and number of the Chorus Singers, to the nature of the instrument, etc.; but I
have indicated six gradations of strength, PP, P, MF, F,
FF, FFF; meaning by the last the whole power of the full
Organ and by the first one soft stop of eight feet alone.
Whenever the word *Bassi* appears in the Organ Part, I
want the Organ *not to play at all*, (the notes being written merely to enable the Organist to follow the performance); and where the word *Organo* comes after it, the
Organist is to resume playing. There are also two Violoncello parts for the accompaniment of the Recitatives
to be found in the Organ Part; I have written them likewise, in order to indicate to the performers (should they
not choose to follow their own fancy) the manner in
which I would place the chords. The description of the
movements, metronomes, pianos and fortes etc., which I
would introduce had I to conduct the Oratorio, are to be
found in the *Pianoforte Arrangement*. Whoever wishes to
adopt them, can easily insert them in the Original Score,

and he who prefers any other is not misled so as to take my directions for those which Handel wrote himself.[17]

Behind such phrases as "the Council decided" lies a long and complex story, preserved in great detail in the exchange of correspondence between Mendelssohn and G. A. Macfarren, secretary to the council. At the beginning of the correspondence, in April 1844, when Macfarren requested Mendelssohn to edit *Messiah*, as "a work worthy [of] your attention," he relayed the council's view of the duties of editors:

> To correct to the best of their ability a copy which shall be furnished them by the Council of the work that shall be entrusted to their respective care—introducing at their discretion such directions of *piano & forte*, other marks of expression, & such descriptions of the movements as they shall deem desirable—& adding suggestions of the Time according to Mälzel's Metronome upon the best traditional authority, or, in the absence of such, upon their own judgment—to compress the instrumental parts for the Pianoforte so as to form an accompaniment to the voices in the absence of the orchestra—to complete the figuring of the Organ part—& to compile a preface embodying any historical particulars of the work that can be collected & pointing out & explaining any variations in the text that exist between this & other Editions— The Editors must submit their corrected scores & and their MSS to the Council, who, when they see that they are uniform with the other productions of the Society, will order them to be engraved—The Editors shall revise the first proof of their respective works which being corrected, the Council will individually and collectively examine a second proof and the Editors must adopt their united decision (made always with deference to the Editors' opinions) upon all questionable points.[18]

On 24 February 1845, after the council had examined the proofs, Macfarren wrote to Mendelssohn telling him that it was "the object of the

Society to produce a *Standard* edition" and asking him, among other things, to add dynamics and to figure the bass. This Mendelssohn declined to do, and his point was conceded. The work then proceeded slowly through the summer, with Mendelssohn insistent upon complete control. On 28 September he wrote (in English): "Pray *be sure* that no more alterations be introduced, and at any rate *not one* with which I am not *previously acquainted,* (may they relate to matters of form or not, to the text of the music or to the Preface)."[19] In the letter as sent he confined himself to this relatively mild statement, but in the draft of the letter (also in English), which is preserved among his papers, this passage is much longer, and it fully reveals his extreme irritation with the council and his attitude towards the edition:

> *But I must be sure* that except these alterations no others are now made, because else I could not give my name to the publication. Indeed I think the Council have no other responsibility than that of entrusting me with the Edition, and I have the responsibility of the Edition itself. Therefore I wish that the Edition might be made exactly according to my corrected proofs, & that no other alteration might be introduced by the Council and no further Correspondence about these things become necessary. Of course I need not tell you that I should consider any alterations, introduced *without my knowledge* into the Edition to which I agreed to give my name as Editor, as *out of the question*; and indeed I should protest against anything of this kind in the most formal and public manner. But I am sure that you would yourself prevent any such thing, without my asking you to do so, and I have to thank you so much for the very great pain you have taken on my account, & for the very great patience you have shown! But pray let the Council now[20]

At that point the draft breaks off. Mendelssohn, having vented his anger, evidently decided upon a less confrontational response.

Nevertheless, the following month, on receipt of a set of very inaccurate proofs, he felt obliged to write again in strong terms.[21] Macfarren replied: "I have the pleasure to say—& it is one of the first, to me, pleasurable things on the subject, that, as the mouth of the Council, I have had the good fortune to utter—at the meeting last night it was unanimously resolved to waive all objection & opposition to your wishes with regard to this edition of Israel—upon the grounds that as you are the Editor & therefore responsible—& that as the Members of the Society have the greatest respect for your name & authority, the Council can with propriety (as regards the Society) give way to you whereas it would be necessary for them to enforce their views in the case of a less eminent person." His letter contained a final bone of contention, however, for he suggested that Mendelssohn might provide trombone parts: "Handel's choruses are never performed in England without the accompaniment of Trombones, & it is thought desirable that (since, according to custom trombones must be played,) our Society should put forth a set of musicianly parts for them rather than leave them as they have heretofore been left, to be arranged by the copyist—or someone worse— this however is, as I have said before, a matter of option to the Editor."[22] Mendelssohn responded tartly to this in his next letter: "I will not write Trombone parts. I wish not to prolong the Correspondence, as I told you, or else I should be tempted to tell you my candid opinion of this "Trombone" decision of the Council, which you now communicated to me. Perhaps I shall do so in a letter which I shall soon write to you, (not to the Secretary, but the musician)."[23] And with that the business was effectively brought to a conclusion in December 1845.

In addition to *Israel*, Mendelssohn also edited a number of Bach's organ works for publication. Had he lived he might well have involved himself with further editorial projects, in which he would have been the guiding spirit. A tantalizing hint of this occurs in Schumann's jottings on Mendelssohn: "1846 Journey to Norderney. the 7th and 8th July saw and spoke to Mendelssohn. Tristan and Isolde. We also spoke somewhat about a collected edition [Gesamtausgabe] of Bach; his principles for it."[24]

6 · Drawing and Painting

No book about Mendelssohn is complete without illustrations of his drawings and paintings. Many of these survive in public collections, but it seems probable that very many more are lost or remain in private hands. Numerous references in his letters and elsewhere suggest that the majority of his finished paintings were given to friends and family. His finest surviving collection of watercolours, painted in Switzerland during the summer of 1847, was probably kept together because his death prevented their being given away.

In his childhood Mendelssohn, like most well-educated children at the time, received instruction in drawing. From at least 1822 he began to draw regularly in bound sketchbooks; the earliest surviving books date from 1822, when he made many drawings during the family's travels in Germany and Switzerland. Many similar books exist for later years, documenting his preoccupation with recording his visual impressions of the places he visited throughout his life. The childish hand of the early sketches becomes rapidly more confident and flexible. It is evident, however, that relatively few of the pencil sketches were meant to be finished pictures; he seems to have regarded most of them as aids to his memory, and he often reverted to sketches made many years before as a basis for finished paintings.

Mendelssohn's perfectionism meant that he was never satisfied with his skill in drawing and painting. In particular, he was dissatisfied with his ability to draw figures and wrote to his mother in September 1829 that the eldest of the Taylor sisters, with whose family he was staying, was "very clever at sketching, and can do men and women in the foreground very well. . . . As I cannot do that, she puts the figures into some of my Scotch landscapes; yesterday, for instance, she put in some exquisite Highlanders."[25] But he determined to remedy this defect and, although he never showed as much ability in drawing the human figure as in delineating landscapes, his later drawings indicate his progress in depicting people. He was also conscious of his deficiency in handling colours, and during his time in Düsseldorf took lessons in painting from Johann Wilhelm Schirmer, writing on 5 February 1834 to Devrient: "He is giving me lessons, and teaching me to use purple for my distances, and how to paint sunlight."[26]

Often when he was upset or irritated, Mendelssohn would turn to drawing and painting as a form of recreation. At the height of his frustration in 1843 over the Prussian government's failure to agree on satisfactory conditions for his position as Generalmusikdirektor for church music, for instance, he wrote to his brother that his head was "bewildered" by "a thousand annoyances. . . . I have not been able to work during these days. To make up for this, I have done the 'Jungfrau' for you in Indian ink; the mountain I think is excellent, but I have again utterly destroyed the pines in the foreground."[27]

The drawings on the following pages are all taken from the collection in the Bodleian Library, Oxford, which possesses the vast majority of Mendelssohn's surviving sketchbooks, dating from 1822 to 1847. Most of them are reproduced here for the first time. The water-colour painting from 1847 (figure 11) is one of the thirteen painted during Mendelssohn's last summer holiday in Switzerland, which are preserved in the Mendelssohn-Archiv at the Staatsbibliothek zu Berlin. These pictures illustrate Mendelssohn's preoccupation with sketching and painting, and the development of his technique over a period of more than twenty years.

During the family's three-month excursion to Switzerland in 1822, Mendelssohn, who had just begun to study with the Berlin painter Rösel,[28] made more than forty sketches of the places they visited. The drawing of Prieuré in the Chamouni valley (figure 1), juxtaposing small rural buildings and a church with towering mountains, is typical of the Alpine scenes that attracted him throughout his life. Whereas the majority of later sketches are in pencil, the thirteen-year-old Mendelssohn here uses pen and ink, rather in the manner of contemporary engraving techniques. Though the execution is stiff and somewhat awkward, the sketch already shows a strong feeling for form, and displays his lasting predilection for intricate detail. The naming of mountain peaks occurs on many of the sketches, indicating their function as an *aide memoire* to places he had visited as much as drawings in their own right.

The pen-and-ink sketch of the twelfth-century brick-built cathedral at Bad Doberan (figure 2) is one of a number of drawings made during a cure that he and his father took at the Baltic spa in July and August 1824. In a letter to Zelter of 9 July Mendelssohn mentioned that the cathedral

FIGURE 1. Prieuré im Chamouny Thale. d. 15 Sept[ember] 1822. Bodleian Library, Oxford, MS MDM c. 5, fol. 26r.

FIGURE 2. Dobberan [cathedral] 13 Aug[ust 1824]. Bodleian Library, Oxford, MS MDM c. 5, fol. 42r.

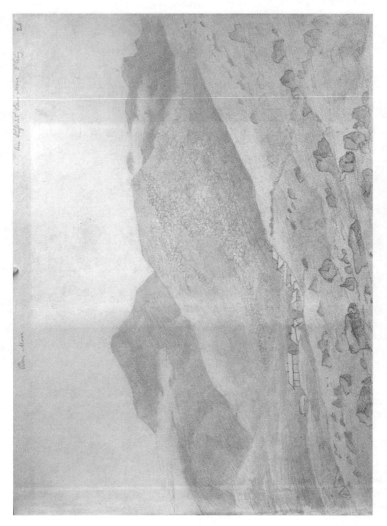

FIGURE 3. Am Fuss des Ben More 5 Aug[ust 1829]. Bodleian Library, Oxford, MS MDM d. 2, fol. 26r.

FIGURE 4. desselbe 29 J[uly] (that is, Blick aufs Zirlerthal von Reit aus). Bodleian Library, Oxford, MS MDM d. 10, fol. 13r.

FIGURE 5. Ischia bei Don Tommaso 21 Mai [1831]. Bodleian Library, Oxford, MS MDM d. 3, fol. 4r.

FIGURE 6. Chamouny d. 30 July [1831]. Bodleian Library, Oxford, MS MDM d. 3, fol. 29r.

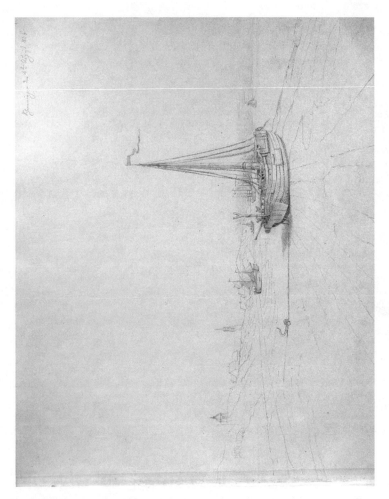

FIGURE 7. Schevingen den 4ten August 1836. Bodleian Library, Oxford, MS MDM d. 11, fol. 4r.

FIGURE 8. Interlaken 20 Aug[ust 1842]. Bodleian Library, Oxford, MS MDM e. 1, fol. 11r.

FIGURE 9. Interlaken d. 20 Aug[ust 1842]. Bodleian Library, Oxford, MS MDM e. 1, fol. 12r.

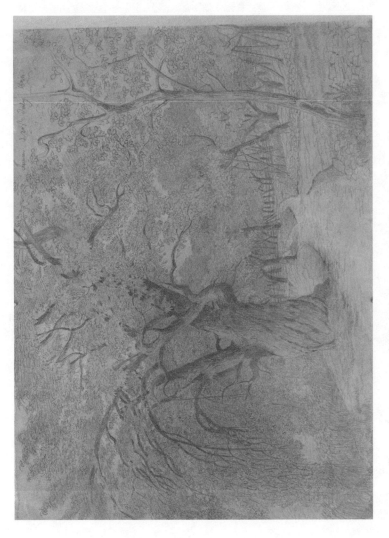

FIGURE 10. Taunus d. 20 July 1844. Bodleian Library, Oxford, MS MDM d. 4, fol. 2v.

FIGURE II. Auf dem Gipfel des Seidelhorns [summer 1847]. Staatsbibliothek zu Berlin, Musikabteilung Mendelssohn--Archiv.

"is both simple and grandiose. I particularly love the exterior view of the sanctuary and of the back end of the church," and he remarked that the building was a "special favourite of Professor Rösel, who recommended it to me very strongly."[29] In this case he seems first to have made a pencil sketch, which he later elaborated in ink. It has many of the same technical characteristics as the Prieuré drawing and is still rather gauche, but it provides an early example of another of Mendelssohn's abiding interests, the forms and textures of trees. The primitive outline of a man with a stick under the second arch from the left testifies to Mendelssohn's self-confessed ineptitude at figure drawing.

At the same time as Mendelssohn acquired mastery in musical composition and performance during the late 1820s, his sketching, at a much more modest level, acquired new confidence and maturity. By the time of his journey to Scotland in 1829, his drawings exhibited more flowing lines, greater command of contrast and more convincing integration of detail into the design as a whole. Some of the Scottish drawings[30] show him experimenting with ways of using a simple medium in a more subtle manner to achieve atmosphere and to capture the emotional impact of a scene. In a letter begun on 3 August, he described how he drew his sketch of Ben More (figure 3) on 5 August: "The weather is discouraging. I have invented my own manner of drawing it, and today I have rubbed in clouds and painted grey mountains with my pencil."[31] Here, as in other Scottish sketches, is a genuine visual counterpart to the musical ideas that these scenes inspired in him.

A rather similar approach to a very different kind of scenery is evident in a highly finished sketch of the Zirlerthal near Reit (figure 4), which he made on 29 July 1830, during a holiday in the Bavarian Alps with A. B. Marx at the beginning of his journey to Italy. Here he combines his love of detail with a well-developed feeling for distance and atmosphere. Whether the picture was completed at the scene or only drawn in outline and completed later is unclear. It is certainly an elaboration of a very rough sketch of the same scene from a slightly different viewpoint, which occurs two folios earlier in the book. From Mendelssohn's letters we may surmise that he did not always complete pictures on site but often finished them from memory later, for he wrote to his mother from Linz less than a fortnight after the date on the sketch: "I took up my pencil, and so entirely destroyed two of my pet sketches, taken in the

Bavarian mountains, that I was obliged to tear them from my book, and to throw them out of the window."[32]

During his stay in Italy, Mendelssohn spent much of his time with German artists and sketched regularly. In May 1831 he made an excursion from Naples with three painter friends, Eduard Bendemann, Theodor Hildebrandt and Carl Sohn. On the island of Ischia, they arrived at the house of a certain Don Tomasso late in the evening of 20 May. His account in a letter home describes the scene and the circumstances, providing an illuminating counterpart to the skilful sketch (figure 5) that he completed the following day:

> The next morning the weather was bad, and the rain in-
> cessant, so we could not ascend the Epomeo, and as we
> seemed little disposed to converse (we did not get on in
> this respect, Heaven knows why!) the affair would have
> become rather a bore, if Don Tomasso had not possessed
> the prettiest poultry-yard and farm in Europe. Right in
> front of the door stands a large leafy orange tree covered
> with ripe fruit, and from under its branches a stair leads
> to the dwelling. Each of the white stones steps is deco-
> rated with a large vase of flowers, these steps leading to a
> spacious open hall, whence, through an archway you
> look down on the whole farmyard, with its orange-trees,
> stairs, thatched roofs, wine casks and pitchers, donkeys
> and peacocks. That a foreground may not be wanting, an
> Indian fig-tree stands under the walled arch, so luxuriant
> that it is fastened to the wall with ropes. The back-
> ground is formed by vineyards with summer-houses, and
> the adjacent heights of Monte Epomeo. Being protected
> from the rain by the archway, the party seated themselves
> there under shelter, and sketched the various objects in
> the farm the best way they could, the whole livelong day.
> I was on no ceremony, and sketched along with them,
> and I think in some degree profited by so doing.[33]

Comparison of Mendelssohn's sketch with Bendemann's pencil and sepia wash drawing of the same scene, which is also in the Bodleian collection,[34] reveals that Bendemann (evidently sitting to Mendelssohn's left) focused more strongly on tone and contrast, while Mendelssohn concerned himself more with capturing the details of the features described in his letter, though not at the expense of the image as a whole. Just as the drawing of Ben More exudes the soft, damp and misty atmosphere of Scotland in the rain, so the sketch of 21 May 1831 evokes the sharp focus and clarity that can characterize southern Italy, even in the rain. Here, unlike in the earliest sketches, detail and composition seem entirely in harmony.

A pencil drawing dated 30 July 1831 (figure 6), which Mendelssohn sketched on his journey northwards through Switzerland, makes fascinating comparison with the pen-and-ink drawing of the same scene, Prieuré in the Chamouni valley, that he had completed almost exactly nine years before. As in the earlier sketch, he used the engraver's technique of drawing fine lines to give texture to his sky and set off the whiteness of the snow, but the whole picture is executed with much greater delicacy, and with a far more effective sense of the topography; by drawing the scene from further away he was able to emphasize the contrast between the tiny village and the towering peaks. As in the case of his drawing at Don Tomasso's, his account of the scene in a letter home throws revealing light on his drawing. He wrote to his parents from Prieuré:

> Fortunately you already know this valley, so there is no
> occasion for me to describe it to you; indeed, how could
> I possibly have done so? But this I may say, that no-
> where has nature in all her glory met my eyes in such
> brightness as here. . . . I have been told that I exaggerated
> the forms of the mountains in my imagination; but yes-
> terday, at the hour of sunset, I was pacing up and down
> in front of the house, and each time I turned my back
> on the mountain, I endeavoured vividly to represent to
> myself these gigantic masses, and each time when I faced
> them, they far exceeded my previous conceptions. . . .
> The snow pure, and sharply defined, and apparently near
> in the dark blue atmosphere; the glaciers thundering un-
> remittingly, as the ice is melting. . . . I have passed the
> whole day here quietly and entirely alone. I wished to

sketch the outlines of the mountains, so I went out and
found an admirable point of view, but when I opened
my book, the paper seemed so very small that I hesitated
about attempting it. I have indeed succeeded in giving
the outlines what is called *correctly*,—but every stroke
looks so formal, when compared with the grace and freedom which everywhere here pervade nature. And then
the splendour of colour![35]

Interestingly, Mendelssohn's picture of this scene corresponds closely
with a pen-and-wash drawing made from near the same viewpoint by
John Ruskin in 1843.[36] Mendelssohn, however, managed more effectively
to convey the immensity of the mountains.

Mendelssohn never lost the fascination with detail and polish that his
drawings and paintings share with his music. Few of the sketches in the
Bodleian collection are completed, but many of them include a highly
finished focal point within lightly sketched surroundings. Sometimes this
is to the advantage of the image as a whole, and more evocative, though
not necessarily better, than some of the sketches that are complete down
to the smallest detail, or virtually so. This is evident from a sketch of
boats made on 4 August 1836 on the beach at Schevingen (figure 7), where
he took a cure with two of his Düsseldorf artist friends, Johann Wilhelm
Schirmer and Wilhelm von Schadow. In fact, he had exiled himself there
to test the strength of his feelings for Cécile Jenrenaud before proposing
marriage, and his emotional state continued much as it had a month
earlier, when he had written from Frankfurt to his sister Rebecka: "Such
is my mood now the whole day: I can neither compose nor write letters,
nor play the piano; the utmost I can do is sketch a little."[37] The juxta-
position of the finely drawn detail of the boat in the foreground, together
with a few simply but delicately executed boats and buildings, with merely
a line to indicate sand, sea and sky, effectively evokes the flat expanse of
the Dutch coast.

It was not only stress, however, that drove Mendelssohn to his sketchbooks in his later years; he also sketched intensively whenever he was fired
by his surroundings. Thus, on August 1842 he wrote to his mother from
Interlaken: "Descriptions of Switzerland are impossible . . . I sketch furi-
ously, and sit in front of a mountain, and try to draw its likeness, and

do not give it up till I have quite spoiled the sketch; but I take care to have at least one new landscape in my book every day."[38] But besides landscapes, his sketches include some that concentrate simply on elaborating a single subject; of these the two included here, which he made on 20 August 1842, are typical. They once again emphasize his fascination with observing and recording detail, often, as in the fencing study (figure 8), in objects that would not conventionally be described as beautiful. The charming drawing of a small boy (figure 9), who apparently signed his name, Heinrich Zumbrunn, in the bottom right-hand corner, shows how much Mendelssohn had learned about figure drawing since he wrote to his family from North Wales in 1829, telling them how he induced Susan Taylor to put figures into some of his Scottish landscapes, while he provided trees for her sketches.[39]

Trees in all their forms remained favourite subjects with Mendelssohn either as the principal focus of a sketch or as part of the design as a whole. A sketch in pencil and brown wash (figure 10), dated 20 July 1844, when he was holidaying in Bad Soden am Taunus, shows his preoccupation with the intricacies of natural forms and textures, and his skill in capturing these details within the context of a pleasing composition.

At times of great stress, drawing and painting sometimes provided Mendelssohn's principal form of relief or distraction, as suggested by his remark to Rebecka in 1836. This was particularly the case after Fanny's sudden and unexpected death in May 1847, and his last summer vacation in Switzerland gave rise to a series of thirteen water-colours as well as the usual pencil sketches. His longing for solace in nature and his desire to get as far from civilization as possible at this time of grief, which led him to undertake long and exhausting hikes into the mountains, is movingly conveyed by his painting of the view from the summit of the Seidelhorn (figure 11).[40]

THREE · Family Background, Childhood
and Education

7 · Moses Mendelssohn

Mendelssohn's genetic inheritance and the circumstantial factors that moulded and developed his character, outlook and abilities were, by any measure, extraordinary. His name, later to be the subject of one of his few differences of opinion with his father, emphasized the association with his grandfather, Moses Mendelssohn, the celebrated Enlightenment philosopher and powerful reforming influence on Judaism in Germany.[1] But his maternal inheritance, too, was exceptional. His mother's grandfather, Daniel Itzig, had been one of the richest men in Prussia and as financier of Friedrich II's wars had been granted privileges, unique for Jews in Prussia before the enactment of the emancipation laws of 1819, that gave his children and grandchildren assured rights of citizenship and residence.[2] Moses Mendelssohn had received the privilege of residence only for himself, though this was posthumously extended to his children. In both these families culture and learning were assiduously fostered; many members of Felix Mendelssohn's immediate family displayed remarkable intellectual attainments and were prominent in philosophy, the arts and the sciences.

The interest and respect that the writings of Moses Mendelssohn aroused among Enlightenment thinkers played an important role in showing that a Jew could stand on an equal intellectual footing with the most distinguished minds of the day, and his efforts helped facilitate the assimilation of a significant portion of German Jewry into gentile culture. Moses, son of Mendel, a poor scribe in Dessau, travelled alone to Berlin in 1743 at the age of fourteen, speaking virtually no German and without any means to support himself, to continue his studies with his old teacher Rabbi David Fränkel, who had recently been appointed chief rabbi in Berlin. At that time German Jews were actively discouraged by their own religious establishment (dominated by Polish Jews) from learning the language of the host nation; but Moses quickly mastered German and acquired proficiency in Latin as well as several modern European languages. In 1750 he obtained the position of tutor to the children of a rich Jewish silk merchant, Isaac Bernhard, and successively became his bookkeeper and business partner.

In his spare time Moses devoted himself to philosophical studies and, having met the dramatist Gotthold Ephraim Lessing over a game of chess in 1754, began to develop connections with the Christian intelligentsia of the Prussian capital and to earn their admiration. Lessing arranged for the publication of Moses's *Philosophische Gespräche* (Philosophical conversations) in 1755 without consulting him. This initial publication was followed by a succession of distinguished philosophical and critical writings, among the most acclaimed of which was *Phädon*, a dialogue on the immortality of the soul, modelled on Plato, which was translated into many languages. Most of his publications appeared under the Germanized form of his name, Moses Mendelssohn.

In 1762 Moses married Fromet Gugenheim, with whom he had eight children, six of whom survived to adulthood. They were, in order of birth, Dorothea (Veit, later Schlegel), Joseph, Abraham (Felix Mendelssohn's father), Henriette, Recha and Nathan. Moses adopted a tolerant and undogmatic stance in religion, which was not typical of traditional Judaism: he considered all the great monotheistic religions to be differing expressions of the one eternal truth. But he remained a member of the Jewish faith, despite the efforts of the Swiss theologian Johann Caspar Lavater to persuade him that he was a Christian in all but name and should take the final step of conversion. Of his children only Joseph and Recha remained Jewish throughout their lives.

Moses devoted careful attention to the education of his children, who were instructed partly by private tutors and partly by their father. His last philosophical work, the *Morgenstunden* (Morning hours), was so called because, according to his eldest son, Joseph, it was the product of "the instruction he gave from 5 o'clock to 9 o'clock in the morning to his son-in-law, his eldest son and the latter's school friend, the later royal kapellmeister Wessely, in philosophical subjects, and then for the most part dictated straight on to the page."[3] Joseph Mendelssohn described his and his surviving siblings' education:

> Six children remained to him, upon whose upbringing he directed great attention and much expense. He put general education, as well as supervision of the children's morality, in the hands of private tutors, and for this purpose chose men whose knowledge he had adequately tested and of whose morality he was convinced. From the letters to [Herz] Homberg, who was earlier one of the private tutors in the Mendelssohn household, one sees how greatly he had prized him as a scholar. Homberg left Mendelssohn's house for Austria, where he was reformer of the Jewish schools, and died as imperial and royal director of studies. After him Mendelssohn took on a scholar called Ensheim, a native of Alsace, as private tutor. This man never had anything printed, out of excessive modesty; but he was a profound thinker, very much initiated into abstract branches of learning and of unsurpassable gentleness and goodness of heart. Under him his pupils were already more in a position than under Homberg to judge the teacher and feel his beneficial effects. Ensheim's memory remained fresh, in thankfulness and love, in the grown-up children for a long time after he left the house. Foreign languages, music and drawing were catered for by private instruction, and Mendelssohn also had his elder children instructed in cutting pens. He himself wrote German, French and Hebrew script extremely beautifully and clearly, and was of the opinion that many people wrote badly because they could not cut a pen to suit their hand, and yet good handwriting was just as much a good recommendation in correspondence as a beautiful face in verbal intercourse. He taught his eldest son the Talmud and the Hebrew language from the age of ten to twelve, later he sent him

to a grammar school [*Gymnasium*]. Out of friendship towards Mendelssohn, Engel undertook to instruct this eldest son in German style.[4]

8 · Abraham, Lea and Fanny Mendelssohn

Abraham, the second son, although he was only nine years old at the time of his father's death and therefore did not enjoy the benefit of more advanced studies with him, perpetuated this educational tradition in his own children's upbringing. His marriage to Lea Salomon, who had received a considerable legacy under her grandfather Daniel Itzig's will, put the family on a sound financial basis, and Abraham's own activities as a banker, in partnership with his brother Joseph, considerably augmented their wealth. This allowed them to engage the best available teachers for specialist studies, and, after Felix had finished at elementary school in the summer of 1818, they employed a private tutor to direct the children's general studies: first, in 1818 and 1819, G. A. H. Stenzel, a history lecturer at the University of Berlin, and then, in 1819, the twenty-two-year-old Carl Ludwig Heyse, later to become professor of philosophy at the University of Berlin, who stayed with the family until 1827. Both Abraham and Lea participated actively in their children's education. Lea gave Felix and his elder sister Fanny their first piano lessons, while Abraham instructed the children in French and mathematics.

Lea's intellectual and artistic acquirements were recalled shortly after her death in 1842 by G. Merkel, an intimate friend of the Salomon family: "Lea was not handsome, but her eloquent black eyes, her sylph-like figure, her gentle, modest behaviour, and the power of her lively conversation, full of accurate judgment and striking but never malicious wit, made her most attractive. She was acquainted with every branch of fashionable information; she played and sang with expression and grace, but seldom, and only for her friends; she drew exquisitely; she spoke and read French, English, Italian, and—secretly—Homer, in the original language. Secretly! How would others have boasted of their knowledge! Her taste, formed by the classic authors of so many languages, was exact and refined, but she seldom ventured to pass a judgment."[5] Hiller, who first met Lea in Frankfurt in 1822, recalled: "I found the whole family assembled in a great room at the 'swan' hotel and was very kindly received. I shall never forget the impression made on me by the mother, whom I was never to see again. She was sitting at work at a little table, and enquired about all that I was doing with an infinite kindness and gentleness that won my childish confidence at once."[6] And of her musical attributes A. B. Marx observed: "In her the traditions or resonances of Kirnberger[7] lived on; she had encountered Sebastian Bach's music and in her home she perpetuated his tradition by continually playing the *Wohltempierte Clavier*."[8]

Abraham's influence on Felix's upbringing in general, and the formation of his ethical outlook in particular, can scarcely be overrated; his musical interests, however, centered mostly on opera, and he regarded instrumental music as his wife's department, although he was always ready to apply his sharp critical mind to his son's compositions. Eduard Devrient, who although eight years older than Felix Mendelssohn remained his lifelong friend after getting to know him in 1822, recalled: "It was easy to perceive that the most remarkable influence upon the son's development was the father. Abraham Mendelssohn was a remarkable man, in whose mental and spiritual being life was reflected with singular clearness. His thoughts and feelings led him to find the highest satisfaction in the intellect. This was natural in the Jewish-born son of the philosopher Moses Mendelssohn, but to me, then in the age of religious effervescence, this did not become clear till later in life, and by degrees; his sound and certain judgement, however, impressed me even then. The conviction that our life is given us for work, for usefulness, and constant striving—this conviction Felix inherited from his father."[9]

Scarcely less important than the influence of his parents during Felix's formative early years was that of his sister Fanny. She was four years older and, being equally precocious musically, she provided him not only with a model to emulate but also with encouragement and guidance. As she observed in 1822: "Thus far I have possessed his full confidence. I have watched his talent develop step by step and have even, to a certain degree, contributed to his musical education. He has no other musical advisor but me. Furthermore, he never puts down an idea on paper until I have considered it. Thus, for instance, I knew his operas from memory before even a single note was written down."[10] Fanny's role as Felix's mentor and musical companion remained strong throughout his childhood and persisted to some extent, though with inevitably decreasing intensity, throughout his life.[11]

9 · The Children's Education

From the age of nine Felix Mendelssohn's régime of instruction was thorough and arduous. The day began at five, except on Sundays, when the children were allowed an extra couple of hours in bed. Devrient recalled their educational environment:

> I had opportunity to notice the rich stores of learning and powerful influences that were brought to bear upon his education. The mother first perceived the musical talent of the two eldest children, and began to teach them. In Berlin they were placed under the excellent but crusty Zelter,[12] for thoroughbass; under the genial, tenderhearted Berger,[13] for pianoforte; and under the accurate Henning,[14] for violin. The droll little Professor Rösel[15] taught them landscape-drawing: Felix profited more from him than his sisters, he learned to free himself from his master's mannerisms. The young Doctor Heyse was tutor to the four children, all of extraordinary capacity; his quiet thoroughness guided Felix's scholastic studies until he was prepared for the University examination. His younger sister, Rebecca, shared the lessons in Greek with Felix, in order to make the study more attractive to him. The mother, a highly-cultivated and intelligent woman as well as an active housewife, ever occupied either in reading or some domestic duty, kept the children to their work with inflexible energy. The unceasing activity of Felix, which became a necessity of life with him, is no doubt to be ascribed to early habit. He must have often wearied of his tasks at the mother's feet, by Rebecca's little table. If I called in the forenoon upon the mother,

and he came with his lunch into the front room, during which he was allowed to quit his work, and we happened to chat longer than the bread-and-butter rendered necessary, the mother's curt exclamation, "Felix, are you doing nothing?" quickly drove him away into the back room.[16]

On 22 March 1820, some two years before the circumstances described by Devrient, Felix Mendelssohn himself wrote a letter to an unidentified doctor in which he gave an account of his studies that confirms the information derived from other sources. The letter also gives us a glimpse of one of his earliest major contributions to the family music making that was to become such an important element in his experience.

Excuse me for having delayed so long in answering your letter. I had so much to do in the evening that I could find no time at all for writing. That is to say, I have composed two operettas; one for father's and the other for mother's birthday. The one for father's birthday [11 December] was the first; we surprised father with it in the evening, and although it was only sung at the piano, it pleased him so much that he determined to give it on 3rd February, my birthday, with all the instruments. At one of the rehearsals of it he went into an adjoining room with Dr Casper,[17] who had freely translated both of them from the French, and after a short time called me in, and father said that Dr Casper wanted to write the second one for me and that I should have it ready for mother's birthday on 15th March. I could not promise it for certain, since the time from 24th January, on which I received the first vocal piece, to 15th March was very short, and I could only employ a few hours in the evenings to it. Nevertheless, I promised to do my best. Dr Casper sent me one vocal piece after another, and that is how I composed them. It has become longer than the previous one, although I had less time for it than for the previous one. On 14th March I was ready, and on

the 15th we sang it at the piano. It went very well, although we had only had three rehearsals, and it has been
determined to perform this one too with instruments.

Herr Stümer[18] is now married. He sang in both operettas and now comes to us frequently.

I have six hours of Latin a week, Caesar twice, Ovid
twice, grammar once and exercises once. I have begun
the second book of Caesar, which I do not find at all
difficult. Each lesson I read two chapters and make no
translation of them. In Ovid, which I find much more
difficult, I am reading the first book, about 14 lines in
each lesson, and I make a translation of them. I am up
to the metamorphosis of Daphne.

In mathematics I am now reading the fifth book of
Euclid, which seems to me more difficult than all the
preceding ones.

In addition, together with Fanny, I have two lessons
in history, two in arithmetic, one in geography and one
in German language.—The violin is going fairly well, I
have lessons twice a week and play studies by Kreutzer.—
Also, on Monday and Tuesday I attend the Singakademie, where I hear very beautiful things. Professor Zelter
is really well, he comes to us twice a week. Herr Rabe[19]
also comes twice a week, his wife is very unwell, and he
therefore has very little time to spare. I have now arranged my working times so that in the evening I always
do the work I have been given in the morning.

Consolation is published by Breitkopf und Härtel, at
least it says *chez Breitkopf et Härtel* underneath it.

I have not been to Schutz's[20] for a long time, since we
now live so far away and since I have had so little time
this winter.

Herr Heise [*sic*] sends you greetings. Stay well.[21]

A further source that throws a particularly personal and vivid light on
the home background and education of the Mendelssohn children is Felix

Mendelssohn's comic-heroic poem *Paphlëis*,[22] which probably originated shortly after that letter.[23] The lengthy poem illustrates the breadth of culture enjoyed by the children. It is evidently a parody of Goethe's *Achillëis* of 1808, both in content and versification, and internal references display the young Felix's knowledge of Shakespeare and of modern and classical languages, as well as showing his skill in versification, of which he continued to give evidence in later life.[24] Like Goethe's *Achillëis*, Mendelssohn's *Paphlëis* is written throughout in classical hexameters: a mixture of dactyls (‾ ˘ ˘) and trochees (‾ ˘) that are interchangeable except in the fifth foot, which should be a dactyl, and the sixth foot, which must be a trochee.[25] Some 460 lines of *Paphlëis* survive (of which 148 are translated here); the last two of the poem's three parts are complete, but the opening section of the first part is lost. The anti-heroic central character of the poem is Felix's younger brother, Paul (whose name is given the Greek form Paphel, or Paphlos in the accusative case), whose childish adventures and foibles furnish the subject matter of the poem. A similar teasing tone towards his younger brother is also encountered frequently in Felix Mendelssohn's letters of this period. The first and third parts of the poem centre on the conflict between two rival gangs of children, one of which is lead by Paphel, who is addressed thus by one of his companions:

Hear! great-grandson of Mendel, you grandson of excellent Mendels-Sohn, whose son took the name of Bartholdy upon him! My general!

The second part focuses on the recreational activities of Paphel and three of his companions, Pinne, Eduard (Ed, or Ede) and Wilhelm. The section translated here comes from this part; it follows an episode in which Paphel has soundly defeated his companions at marbles. (Devrient recalled that in the years before he came to know Mendelssohn personally he "often noticed him . . . busily playing at marbles or touchwood with other boys before the door of his grandmother's house on the new Promenade.")[26] Felix makes Paul describe his daily activities and his personal acquirements, in the manner of a Greek hero recounting the saga of his life. The Mendelssohn household will have derived amusement from the description, in mock-heroic terms, of familiar people and routines, from the good-natured but sometimes rather sharp depiction of the younger brother's less admirable character traits, and from the lively mimicking of the childish and sometimes ungrammatical speech (reflected in this translation). Allowing for the element of dramatization, and some poetic exaggeration of the range of Paul's studies, for instance in the references to Arabic, Syriac, Chaldean and Sanskrit, this episode in *Paphlëis* gives a vivid glimpse into the family life of the children and the pattern of their educational activity.

> Taking their caps they hastened to go. But then up spake
>   Paphel:
> "Don't go yet, o ye youngsters, we wish that a tale be
>   recited."
> "Yes, a story, a story!" responded each of his comrades.
> Then, laying down all their caps once again, they quickly
>   were seated
> Down on the green-grass lawn 'neath a window-box full
>   of flowers.
> "Who will tell us a tale?" quoth Paphel. Said little Pinne:
> "I know none," then said Eddy: "Me neither," then
>   piped up William:
> "I know one I could tell you, yet have not the skill to
>   relate it."
> "Why not attempt?" "I cannot." "Try, do but try," cried
>   the others.
> Then spake the noble Paphel: "With suchlike tales I'm
>   familiar;
> They are mystic and too philosophic, his stories I like
>   not.
> *I* now shall tell a tale that will move and rouse you to
>   wonder.
> My life's saga must very surely kindle your interest."
> One and all then they bid him tell them the tale that he
>   promised.
> So he clearèd his throat and began to address them as
>   follows:

"Hear my reverent prayer, o ye muses of spring and of
   mountain;
Come, fill my soul with fire, and lend me divine
   inspiration.
Hear my lay, o comrades, and take it to be your
   example.
First I shall give you the tally of all my branches of
   learning.
E'en though you know not the names of the numerous
   tongues I have mastered
Or of the arts that I command, 'tis scarcely important.
For you surely know not the names of the subjects I've
   studied.
First, I'm perfectly skilled in Latin; I even read Phaedrus,
And he is truly the hardest of all of the classical poets.
Greek I know like a native and read in the classical
   Ιάχοψ [Iacops].[27]
All the *Arabian Nights* in their native tongue I can
   savour,
Syriac, Chaldean, Sanscrit, these are as easy as winking.
Aristocratic mathematics, geometrical reckoning
I have studied in full, and know all their cardinal
   precepts.
Thus no doubt can remain that my learning is really
   stupendous.—
If at the midday hour you have walked by the front of
   our mansion,
You will have often heard there a mighty roaring above
   you,
As when a lion roars, on the tree-shaded slopes of the
   mountain.
But, friends, that is no lion, that is the violoncello,
Which, with my powerful arm, I sometimes practise. It
   roars and
Yet 'tis a lovely sound. I play many studies by
   Quickrack.[28]

Difficult pieces, but still to me such things are mere
  trifles.
Wonderful too is my sepia painting, drawing and
  sketching.
Soon you will see that my pictures are hung in art
  exhibitions.
Thus it's proved that I'm truly a budding artist of
  genius.
Thus you see in one person artist and scholar united.
Now you have to acknowledge the kind of man who's
  before you.
Hark now, hear all the titles, with which my knowledge
  is honoured.
Firstly I am professor and doctor of Polyheydia;[29]
Then I am private and principal royal courtly flunkey;[30]
Then I'm a leading banker (who makes all the greatest
  transactions);
Then I am lastly your leader, guiding your games and
  your mischief.
Also I have two orders, conferred by the emperor of
  Russia;
One's a golden rabbit, the other's a sloth cast in silver.
Now I shall tell you the various things that I have to do
  daily.
When the clock strikes five I awake, and arise from my
  pillow.
From my bed I look out to see whether Felix has
  wakened.
If he has not then I threaten to spray him straightway
  with water,
And the blankets, the warming covers, to pull from his
  body.
If he still will not waken, again I encourage and call
  him,
Then he gets up, and he clothes himself as quickly as
  maybe.
But I stay in my bed until I'm fetched by Herr Heyse.

Why should I rise so soon? For sleep is healthy and
    pleasant.
And you also should know: my voice is of beauty
    astounding.
Thus I sing like a lark, as soon as Herr Heyse has called
    me,
Sweetly chant my own composition, a song in a key with
Fifteen flats and words with an "eh" that comes very
    often.
But it is hard to keep time, so Herr Heyse must beat me
    the measure.
Then at last I get up, and start with my lessons in Latin.
Pah! bagatelle, bagatelle! At eight we start upon Caesar,
He gives lessons to me in Kalokagathiatugrapein.[31]
("Caesar?" murmured young Pinne, "I thought he taught
    good writing.")
"Breakfast comes then at nine o' clock, and I eat it with
    gusto.
Then I swot Latin a little, and learn some more Greek in
    passing.
But at ten I bake in the oven a garland of apples,[32]
Next comes mathematics with father, that really gives me
    a headache.
Then at eleven I practise my cello, with vigorous
    bowing.
And on certain occasions we strike up a dire
    caterwauling.
Mistress Benicke plays the piano, Flix scratches the
    fiddle,
And I play on the cello; but often there is a fourth one
Takes up his place in the yard, and plays the guitar and
    the whistle.
All of our neighbours now hear our noise, but we do not
    stop it;[33]
For we know our rights and we don't want to lose an
    iota.
Half eleven till one, I'm free to choose my amusement;

But then at one I've studies historical and geographic,
German language and politics, Greek mythology also.
And then at two I study French language, and when that
    is over,
Look thorough the window perhaps, to study human
    behaviour.
When at last we have dinner, I eat my fill till I'm
    bursting.
And at four I go back upstairs, for my studies with
    Strunze.
I am a master of art. I'll soon draw all of your portraits,
From the life, just as soon as I've slicker and masser[34] to
    do it.
Masser, that just consists of tears mixed together with
    moonlight.
Slicker, however, that is—" "For slicker and masser we
    care not
One small tittle," thus cried all the youngsters, "just tell
    us your story."
"Then at five o'clock I have French once again with my
    father."
"Ah, French language," said young Ed, "O speak just a
    little,
I have never even heard it before, but I'll understand it."
"Il n'a point incompréhensible là il lui croule!"
Chanted the learned Paphlos, and wonder o'erwhelmed
    his companions.
None of them knew the arcane meaning hid in this
    puzzle.
Eddy still had not thought what to say, but Pinn' had a
    notion.
"He's no idea what it means, he's just talking nonsense."
Thus he cried to the youngsters, and laughed fit to burst
    like a goblin.
Paphel demanded silence, and then went on with his
    story:

"When the clock strikes six it is time for baked apples
with sugar
Carefully brought from the corner, without disturbing
the garland.
Next I watch for a while, as Felix plays chess with our
father.
And when I notice a pawn in check I straightway tell
Felix,
Then I tell them at once which one of the two will be
victor.
After that I recline on the sofa, and peacefully slumber.
Tireless now I sleep unperturbed eleven full hours there.
Calm, I rest from the troubles, that I endured in the
daytime.
If I'm in bed then, however, I ponder many a matter
And seek to strengthen my soul, with philosophical
musing.
That's the reason my soul is so awesomely strong and
enduring,
Full of power and might; it holds sway o'er the impotent
body,
For I'm stronger than all other men in my firm self-
denial."
"Hm, Hm," murmured the youngsters, "then give us a
worthy example."
"Two for one," quoth Paphel; "I am by nature too
tender,
Pain I hate, and doctors I view with dreadful aversion.
But by my soul I am driven, to take a prescription each
morning,
And I take up the glass unconcerned and drink half its
contents.
Freely, I own I don't like it; Amalie[35] must persuade me;
But at last my all-powerful soul will emerge with the
victory.
That is one; and next: I have broken the habit of crying

Ow! or even o woe! Amalie may torment as
Much as she likes, but I will not let e'en *one* ow escape
    me.
I endure every pain with aplomb and I suffer in silence,
Thus I am a strong—" Then a dreadful sound
    interrupted,
And the window-box began to fall down with a clatter,
Terrible noise ensued, as plant pots, planks and
    carnations,
Stocks and also some roses and compost recently watered
Fell on them all at once; and some had their mouths
    filled with foliage,
Others had sand in eyes and noses, yet all laughed
    together,
But not Paphel, who bellowed and whimpered: "Ow!
    help me I'm choking.
Woe! I'm certain to die, a plank is wedged on my nose
    now."
Anxious then they all rushed to his aid, and tried to
    determine
Where he was wounded, but search as they might they
    could find no abrasions.
Then with rage they were filled, and cried with angry
    derision:
"Woe, o Paphel! You are the greatest of all earthly
    cowards.
What? you try to deceive us with tales of daring yet you
    are
Only a pitiful wretch, who whimpers, while we merely
    chuckle!
Ow and woe you squeal, yet say you scorn pain as
    nothing?
Truly, we've found you out now, you spun us a lot of
    balony,
Shameful! that's what you are! Farewell! you braggardly
    Paphlos!

Find yourself other companions, to credit your fanciful
   stories."
Then they went out of the yard, and slammed the door
   hard behind them.

10 · Social and Intellectual Environment

The picture of Mendelssohn's environment and activities, and the people
who belonged to his close circle during his teenage years in Berlin, is
amplified by a number of first-hand accounts. Devrient emphasised the
beneficial effect on Mendelssohn's development imparted by the regular
intellectual and musical gatherings that "prevailed to perfection in the
Mendelssohns' house, and gave rise to the most unconstrained and sug-
gestive intellectual intercourse. . . . Felix heard much that awoke and stimulated thought. Foreign musicians mostly brought introductions to the
house, and afforded endless entertainment and suggestions to Felix and
Fanny. . . . It would not be but that Felix should receive the most varied
and stirring impressions from coming in contact with so many different
types of power and character." Devrient also described how provision was
made for physical education, especially after the family moved to their
extensive house and grounds at 3 Leipziger Straße in 1825:

> In the new house Felix entered upon his young man-
> hood, with freshly awakened powers and inclinations.
> With his usual energy and ardour he now devoted him-
> self to gymnastic exercises. The father had a small gym-
> nasium fitted up for his sons in the large and beautiful
> garden of the house. Felix attained the greatest perfection
> in these exercises, and was able to keep them up for a
> long time. He took great pleasure, too, in his riding-
> lessons, and used to have much to tell about the horses,
> and of the jokes of the old royal riding-master, which I
> already knew. Swimming was practised during the ensu-
> ing summer with intense enjoyment. A small swimming

society had been formed; Klingemann, who lived at the Hanoverian Embassy, which was in an upper story of the Mendelssohns' house, belonged to this society; he wrote the words of swimming-songs, to which Felix composed the music, and these the members tried to sing as they were swimming about; endless merriment grew out of this, and at the supper-table there was enough to recount of youthful pranks and freaks.

And Devrient remarked how Klingemann (later regarded by Mendelssohn as his closest friend) "aroused his and Fanny's sympathy in Jean Paul, whose infinite tenderness and profound sense of humour exercised great influence on Felix."[36]

Julius Schubring, who studied in Berlin between 1825 and 1830, left an informative account of Mendelssohn's social and intellectual environment during the years immediately before his travels to Britain and Italy. Schubring recalled how "the parents and their four children . . . were harmoniously united to each other by unusual warmth of affection and congeniality of character, and produced a most pleasing impression upon every one who entered their house," and how they were "most partial, after the labours of the day, to spending the evening in familiar intercourse with one another." He added, however, that they were seldom alone, for the Mendelssohns kept open house, and "whoever felt so inclined went, and whoever took a pleasure in going was welcome. Science, Art, and Literature were equally represented." He mentioned that the scientist Alexander von Humboldt and the philosopher Georg W. F. Hegel were among the regular guests. Schubring's account also confirms that Mendelssohn was "a vigorous and skilful gymnast," "a very good swimmer," "a good horseman," "played chess admirably"; but he noted that "anything connected with mathematics . . . appeared to be less in his way."[37]

11 · Musical Activities

Musical activities, of course, played a major part in the education of all the Mendelssohn children, and the period around 1820 saw the beginning of the regular Sunday concerts at which Felix gained so much practical experience by directing and participating in performances of his own compositions with accomplished professional musicians. Felix's gifts also made him a valued guest at musical parties in other houses. A vivid picture of his musical and social circle during the family's last years in his grandmother's house on the Neue Promenade and first years at their later home, 3 Leipziger Straße, was given by Heinrich Dorn, who spent the years 1821 to 1828 in Berlin. He recalled:

> One Friday, at the "at home" evening of my old countryman Abraham Friedländer,[38] as I was in the midst of the well-known duet of Spohr's between Faust and Röschen,[39] with a talented young singer, a commotion arose in the anteroom, which was most unusual, for a profound silence always prevailed when anything was going on. During the pathetic air, "Fort von hier auf schönere Auen," my partner whispered to me, "Felix is come"; and when the duet was finished, I made the acquaintance of Felix Mendelssohn, then a lad of twelve years old, residing with his parents on the Neue Promenade, only a few steps from Friedländer's house. He apologised for having interrupted our song by his entrance, and offered to play the accompaniments for me; "or shall we play them alternately?" he said—a regular Mendelssohn way of putting the question, which, even twenty years later, he made use of to a stranger in a similar position. . . . Young as he was, he even then accompanied singing in a manner only to be met with amongst the older and more thorough musicians who possessed that especial gift. At Königsberg the orchestral management of the piano was an unknown thing, and even in Berlin I had as yet had no opportunity of admiring this skill and facility in any one. That man was considered a very respectable musician who played from the printed copy *con amore*, and thus helped the singer now and then; but he who was able to enrich the slender pianoforte accompaniment with octave basses and full chords, of course stood in a much higher position. Such a gifted being was

Felix even at that time and in the duet between Flores-
tan and Leonora, which he accompanied, he astonished
me in the passage "Du wieder nun in meinen Armen, o
Gott!" by the way in which he represented the violoncello and the contre-basso parts on the piano, playing
them two octaves apart. I afterwards asked him why he
had chosen this striking way of rendering the passage,
and he explained all to me in the kindest manner.

Dorn recalled that he "very seldom missed one of those interesting
gatherings at the Neue Promenade, where, besides the greater compositions, which were henceforth studied under Berger's guidance, the newest
works of the wonderful boy Felix were regularly played over—mostly sets
of symphonies for stringed instruments with pianoforte accompaniment—
by a small number selected from the royal chamber-musicians." And he
described how "Professor Zelter, with whom Felix had studied counterpoint, was his most eager auditor, and at the same time his most severe
censor. More than once after the performance, I myself have heard Zelter
call out in a loud voice to his pupil that several alterations were necessary,
whereupon, without saying a word, Felix would quietly fold up the score,
and before the next Sunday he would go over it, and then play the
composition with the desired corrections."

Dorn's recollections contain the earliest account of the incident, also
described in Sebastian Hensel's book on the family, that occurred in connection with a domestic performance of Mendelssohn's opera *Der Onkel
aus Boston oder Die beiden Neffen*, in which Dorn sang in the chorus.
After it had been given with "all the characters being apportioned and
the dialogue read out at the piano," while refreshments were being handed
out "Zelter's voice resounded through the room: 'Felix, come here.' The
old gentleman stood in the middle of the room with a brimming glass
in his hand, and whilst every one was listening intently, he said: 'Felix,
you have hitherto only been an apprentice; from today you are an assistant, and now work on till you become a master.'[40] Therewith he gave
him a tap on the cheek, as if he were dubbing him a knight, and then
the whole party pressed forward to congratulate the affected and astonished parents, as well as Felix, who pressed his old master's hand warmly

more than once. This is one of those scenes that can never be effaced from one's memory."[41]

Further revealing glimpses of Mendelssohn's musical activities in Berlin have been left by two of his older musical contemporaries, who later became his friends, the composer, conductor and pianist Julius Benedict and the pianist and composer Ignaz Moscheles. Benedict, then a pupil of Weber, met Mendelssohn for the first time when he accompanied Weber to Berlin to superintend the first production there of *Der Freischütz* in 1821. Benedict gave an account of this meeting in a lecture delivered to the Camberwell Literary Institution in London, which was first published in 1850:

> My first meeting with Felix took place under such peculiar circumstances, that I may, perhaps, be permitted to enter into some particulars about it. It was in the beginning of May 1821, when, walking in the streets of Berlin with my master and friend, Carl Maria Von Weber, he directed my attention to a boy, apparently about eleven or twelve years old, who, on perceiving the author of Freyschütz, ran towards him, giving him a most hearty and friendly greeting. "Tis Felix Mendelssohn," said Weber; introducing me at once to the prodigious child, of whose marvellous talent and execution I had already heard so much at Dresden. I shall never forget the impression of that day on beholding that beautiful youth, with his auburn hair clustering in ringlets round his shoulders, the look of his brilliant clear eyes, and the smile of innocence and candour on his lips. He would have it that we should go with him at once to his father's house; but as Weber had to attend a rehearsal, he took me by the hand, and made me run a race till we reached his home. Up he went briskly to the drawing-room, where, finding his mother, he exclaimed, "Here is a pupil of Weber's, who knows a great deal of his music of the new opera. Pray, mamma, ask him to play it for us"; and so, with an irresistible impetuosity, he pushed

me to the pianoforte, and made me remain there until I had exhausted all of the store of my recollections. When I then begged of him to let me hear some of his own compositions, he refused, but played from MEMORY such of Bach's fugues or Cramer's exercises as I could name. At last we parted—not without a promise to meet again. On my very next visit I found him seated on a footstool, before a small table, writing with great earnestness some music. On my asking what he was about, he replied, gravely, "I am finishing my new Quartet for piano and stringed instruments."

I could not resist my own boyish curiosity to examine this composition, and, looking over his shoulder, saw as beautiful a score as if it had been written by the most skilful copyist. It was his first Quarter in C minor, published afterwards as Opus 1.

But whilst I was lost in admiration and astonishment at beholding the work of a master written by the hand of a boy, all at once he sprang up from his seat, and, in his playful manner, ran to the pianoforte, performing note for note all the music from Freyschütz, which three or four days previously he had heard me play, and asking, "How do you like this chorus?" "What do you think of this air?" "Do you not admire this overture?" and so on. Then, forgetting quartets and Weber, down we went into the garden, he clearing high hedges with a leap, running, singing or climbing up the trees like a squirrel—the very image of health and happiness.[42]

Moscheles's first encounter with Mendelssohn occurred three years later. It is described, with extensive quotations from Moscheles's contemporaneous diaries, in the biography written after his death by his wife, Charlotte.

On the 31st October, Moscheles and his brother arrived at Berlin. His notes on his stay here are more cursory than usual. He seems to consider all else unimportant as compared with his relations to the family of Mendelssohn. It is incidentally mentioned that he gave three brilliant concerts for the sufferers from inundation, for the blind, and for other charitable institutions, also that he played for some personal friends. We read, too, that the *haute finance*, the poets, the statesmen, were glad to welcome him. Spontini's operas, with their brilliant scenery and pageantry, the admirable singers Bader, Blum, Frau Milder-Hauptmann, and Frau Seidler-Wranitzky, even the charming actress Fräulein Bauer, are merely alluded to, and the great political event, the marriage of the King with the Princess Leignitz is referred to in a few passing words. He writes, however, whole pages about Felix Mendelssohn's home and his family. We quote his impressions after a first visit: "This is a family the like of which I have never known. Felix, a boy of fifteen, is a phenomenon. What are all prodigies as compared with him? Gifted children, but nothing else. This Felix Mendelssohn is already a mature artist, and yet but fifteen years old! We at once settled down together for several hours, for I was obliged to play a great deal when really I wanted to hear him and see his compositions, for Felix had to show me a Concerto in C minor, a double Concerto, and several motets; and all so full of genius, and at the same time so correct and thorough! His elder sister Fanny, also extraordinarily gifted, played by heart, and with admirable precision, Fugues and Passacailles by Bach. I think one may well call her a thorough "Mus. Doc." (guter Musiker). Both parents give one the impression of being people of the highest refinement. They are far from overrating their children's talents; in fact, they are anxious about Felix's future, and to know whether his gift will prove sufficient to lead to a noble and truly great career. Will he not, like so many other brilliant children, suddenly collapse? I asserted my conscientious conviction that Felix would ultimately become a great master, that I had not the slightest doubt of his genius; but again and again I had to insist on my opinion before they believed me. These two are not specimens of the genus prodigy-parents (Wunderkinds-Eltern), such as I must frequently endure."[43]

At about the same time, the song composer Wilhelm Speyer visited Berlin and reported in a letter of 19 November 1824 to his friend Spohr: "Karl Arnold, a childhood friend of mine, gave a concert. In this I heard a symphony by the little Felix Mendelssohn, which moved me to astonishment. This boy is a phenomenon such as nature seldom produces. This, his thirteenth symphony [revised and published as his First Symphony, op. 11], is so excellent that it might be attributed to the leading masters. Fantasy, originality, symmetry of forms, outstanding melodies, combined with the strictest style of writing, the purest harmony and contrapuntal art. At his house I heard a double concerto for two pianos, quartets, sonatas etc. etc., all masterpieces. And how splendidly, how expressively this boy plays."[44]

Mendelssohn's education in Berlin concluded with a period of study, beginning in May 1826, at the university, where he attended Hegel's lectures in philosophy and Ritter's in geography. His matriculation essay, a translation of Terence's *Andria*, was published in July of that year.[45] At the same time, his musical development continued with astonishing rapidity; the first version of the Octet was completed in 1826, and the high points of the next two years were the overture *Ein Sommernachtstraum*, the A Minor String Quartet, op. 13, and the overture *Meeresstille und glückliche Fahrt*. In the winter of 1827 he began practising Bach's *St Matthew Passion* privately with a small choir, and Zelter was finally persuaded to permit its public performance with the Singakademie. The two performances of the *Passion* that Mendelssohn conducted in March 1829 were his last important musical engagements in Berlin before his years of travel began with his departure for England on 10 April.

FOUR · Religion and Race

12 · Moses Mendelssohn's Legacy

There can be no doubt that Mendelssohn's Jewish background, like his sincere, if undemonstrative, Christian faith, was a significant factor in his upbringing, his outlook, his social relationships, his relationships with contemporary musicians, and the critical reception of his music in Germany. It is also impossible to understand Mendelssohn's own moral and religious views except in the context of his family's experience. Conversion to Christianity, which Heine acerbically called "the ticket of admission into European culture," may have ostensibly put the Mendelssohns on the same footing as their fellows, yet their racial origins continued to set them apart from those with whom they appeared to mix on socially equal terms. However much Felix Mendelssohn may have identified himself with Germany, and felt himself to be German, he was not seen in this light by many contemporaries. Even those who admired him sincerely and profoundly always remained conscious of his Jewish origins, while those who did not sympathize with his musical tendency, or were jealous of his talent or achievements, could cite his Jewish blood as a justification for their antagonism.

The two generations of Felix Mendelssohn's family that preceded him faced a variety of problems with respect to their relationship with ethnic Germans, which were determined by changing social and legal conditions. The experiences of individual members of both these generations played an important part in determining how Felix, his brother and his sisters approached and were affected by the situation in which they found themselves.

Moses Mendelssohn's achievements and eminence were an inescapable inheritance. Felix was especially proud of his relationship with the Jewish philosopher and in 1840 played a key role in facilitating the collected edition of Moses Mendelssohn's works published in Leipzig by Brockhaus between 1843 and 1845. On 20 February 1840 he wrote to his uncle Joseph:

> The first occasion for today's letter is Brockhaus, who asked me last week why should there not be a proper collected edition of grandfather's works, since the Vienna edition is, firstly, only a reprint in one volume, full of printing errors, and then also, as he suggested, not properly compiled, and with respect to the correspondence and particularly the appended biographical account leaves very much to be desired. He suggested that it would not be difficult to come to an understanding about it with the publishers who own the rights to the individual works. Since I now know nothing of the closer relationships, I said to him that I would write to you and in due course relay your answer to him. In any case it will make you happy to see from his inquiry the lively and increased interest that people now take in grandfather's works; and if a proper handsome edition of them, in several volumes, perhaps (as Brockhaus gave out) edited by Lachmann,[1] but above all really exact and faithful, came about, I suppose it would give us all pleasure. If you think so too, perhaps you will give me your opinion soon, and then I shall have a still more frequent opportunity to write to you about it.[2]

Joseph Mendelssohn presumably replied promptly, for on 28 March Heinrich Brockhaus wrote in his diary: "In the evening Mendelssohn and his wife here, entirely *en famille*. I thought that it would not be a bad thing to compile a proper edition of Moses Mendelssohn's writings, since there is no good, critical edition. The family shares this view, and we shall now take a closer look at the undertaking. Mendelssohn was very merry and amiable."[3]

Mixed with Mendelssohn's pride in his grandfather was an awareness of the obstacles Moses had had to overcome to gain respect from his

Christian contemporaries and the extent to which, despite his intellectual eminence, he remained an outsider. Joseph reminded him of this in a letter of 27 January 1843: "Paul brings you the picture of your grandfather—a lithograph, which will be included in the new edition of Mendelssohn's works, and I enclose his biography, you are *the first* to receive both of them, and it is due to you in several respects. You gave the first impulse towards the new edition and you are the first to give new life to the brilliance of your grandfather's name. The picture will, I hope, have your approval, and that it is perfectly like him I can assure you. About the biography I can only say to you, *it is true*, the gulf between the conditions of the grandfather's life and that of the grandson will astonish you. If the moral world were always to make such giant steps, it would be inconceivable that it has not progressed further in 5,000 years. Backward steps seem therefore to belong to the order of the world and as such one must look upon them calmly."[4]

The aspects of his grandfather's life that Felix must have seen as particularly remote from his own were the poverty in which his childhood was spent and, above all, the legal disabilities that arose directly from his Jewishness. Despite the respect Moses Mendelssohn's personal and intellectual qualities elicited, he was, as a Jew, subject to laws that seriously limited his civil rights. In the sketch of his father's life, referred to in his letter to Felix, Joseph Mendelssohn, leaning heavily on the account given by Moses Mendelssohn's friend Nicolai, described the manner in which being Jewish affected Moses.

> Mendelssohn and his wife were not born in Prussian territories, therefore according to the regulations relating to the Jews that were in force at that time they could only remain in the country under the protection of a resident Jew. The silk manufacturer Bernhard, whose accountant Mendelssohn was, guaranteed this protection. Nicolai relates: "The Marquis d'Argens, who, as a philosophical companion of Friedrich II, lived in Potsdam, and who knew Mendelssohn very well and was often in his company, discovered by chance that foreign Jews were not able to remain in the country.—'But,' he said, [']surely this does not affect *notre cher Moise*?' 'Oh yes'

came the answer, [']he is merely tolerated because he is
employed by the manufacturer Bernhard.[5] If the latter
discharged him from his service today and he did not
find another protected Jew who would take him into his
service, the police would compel him to leave the country today.' The marquis was beside himself about it, he
did not want to believe that such a wise and learned
man, whom every right-thinking person ought to esteem
highly, should be daily in peril of seeing himself treated
in such a base manner. He talked about it with Mendelssohn. The latter corroborated it and said: 'Socrates
showed his friend Criton that the wise man is obliged to
die if the laws of the state require it, thus I must account
the laws of the state in which I live mild, in that they
merely drive me out if, failing any other protected Jew,
even a pedlar Jew will not declare me to be his servant.'
The marquis was extremely concerned about this state of
affairs and wanted to write immediately to the king
about it. He was dissuaded from it with difficulty, since
it was foreseen that now—it was in the year 1762, during
the war—was not the right time. After the ensuing peace
the marquis thought about it again and requested Mendelssohn to prepare a petition which he wished to pass
on personally, although normally this was something in
which he never involved himself. At first Mendelssohn
did not want to comply. He said: 'It pains me that I
should have to plead for the right to exist, which is the
right of every human being who lives as a peaceful citizen. If, however, the state has pressing reasons for only
taking in a certain number of people of my nation, what
priority can I have over my other brethren to request
that I be made an exception?' Nevertheless, Mendelssohn's friends put it to him that he should do it for the
sake of his family, and so he wrote the following petition
(taken from the archives): 'From my childhood I have
lived constantly in Your Majesty's dominions and would
like to be able to settle in them permanently. But since I

was born abroad and do not have the property required by law, your most humble subject makes so bold as to beg that Your Majesty might be most graciously moved to grant me and my descendants your most gracious protection together with the freedoms enjoyed by your subjects, in consideration of the fact that my lack of property may be offset by my efforts in the field of learning, which enjoys Your Majesty's protection.'

The marquis himself gave this petition to the king in April 1763, but Moses received no answer. We (Nicolai relates) were all concerned about this, and the otherwise so gentle Moses was rather sensitive about it, and to a certain extent blamed us, who had induced him to write it. There the matter rested, for Moses made no further move of any kind, and did not even want to let the marquis know anything about it. By chance the latter discovered during the year 1763 that Mendelssohn's petition had led to no result and that the king had not answered. The marquis was extremely indignant about it, and when he went to the king the same evening he began to rebuke him as soon as he entered the room. The king, who did not know what he wanted, looked surprised. 'Ah!' the marquis cried, 'Sire! You were always accustomed to keep your word. Now I have for once asked something of you, not for me, but for the most worthy, most upright man, you promise me to grant it but then you do not do it. No! that is too bad!'

The king insisted that Mendelssohn had received the privilege of protection, but the marquis insisted that Mendelssohn had received no answer to his petition. Finally it transpired that there was simply a misunderstanding. The king insisted that the petition must have gone astray through a peculiar accident; Moses should merely present another petition and he would order the privilege to be made out. 'Good,' said the marquis, 'I shall make one myself for you, but do not lose it again.' At the marquis's reiterated request Moses wrote the petition once more on 12 July 1763, and the marquis added to it under his own name:

> *Un Philosophe mauvais catholique supplie un Philosophe mauvais protestant de donner le privilège à un Philosophe mauvais juif. Il y a trop de philosophie dans tout ceçi pour que la raison ne soit pas du côté de la demande.*

Moses received the privilege dated 26 October. In accordance with the regulations the finance office required a thousand thalers from him, which the king waived in the year 1764. In 1779, out of love for his children, Moses directly petitioned the king that his privilege should be extended to his children of both sexes. This Friedrich II declined. Under his successor, Friedrich Wilhelm II, his widow received a privilege of this kind in 1787.["] So much according to Nicolai. We add to it that this privilege contained the expression: "On account of the well-known merits of your husband and father" and that the conferring of such a universal privilege was an extraordinary favour that few enjoyed.[6]

Although Moses Mendelssohn's personality and writings aroused affection and admiration in cultured circles, he and his family did not escape the obloquy in daily life that was the common lot of the Jewish community in that period. In a letter to his friend Winkopp Moses wrote: "I sometimes go out in the evening with my wife and children. 'Papa,' inquires one of them in innocent simplicity, 'what is it those lads call out after us? Why do they throw stones at us? What have we done to them?' 'Yes, dear papa,' says another, 'they always run after us in the streets and shout, "Jew-boy! Jew-boy!" Is it a disgrace in the eyes of these people to be a Jew? What is that to them?' I cast down my eyes and sigh to myself, Poor humanity! To what a point have things come!"[7] The effect of such experiences on Moses's children cannot be underestimated. At the very least it was made clear to them that their Jewishness set them apart. Each dealt with this in his or her own way. The eldest son, Joseph, out of respect for his father's memory, remained a Jew throughout his life, though in his later years he was not an observant one. Of his two sons the elder, Benjamin, converted to Christianity; the other, Alexander, was the only one of Moses Mendelssohn's grandsons to remain Jewish. Joseph's youngest sister, Recha, also remained Jewish, and her daughter, Betty, was the only Jewish granddaughter. Moses's other two sons, Abraham and Nathan, converted relatively late in life to Lutheran Christianity. Of the daughters, Dorothea first became a Lutheran and then a Roman Catholic, and Henriette converted directly to Roman Catholicism. These decisions were taken partly as a matter of conviction and partly as a response to the changing relationship between Judaism and the law. The initial effect upon the two eldest sons, Joseph and Abraham, of their Jewish religion was to limit to medicine and commerce the professions they could legally follow in Prussia; both, despite their undoubted intellectual gifts and inclinations chose to become bankers.

13 · Abraham Mendelssohn's Dilemma

At the time Abraham's three eldest children, Fanny, Felix and Rebecka, were born, he was faced by a particular dilemma. As Joseph's account makes clear, the privilege obtained by his father, Moses, applied solely to him and his wife. The posthumously awarded privilege applied only to Moses's children, not to any future grandchildren. The more generous privilege given by King Friedrich Wilhelm II to Daniel Itzig, grandfather of Abraham's wife, Lea, granting him "all the rights of a Christian citizen in all our states and lands,"[8] extended only to his grandchildren, not to Abraham and Lea's children. In the event, the 1812 Prussian Edict of Emancipation removed this problem, but Abraham and Lea, along with many other Jews of their class, came to the conclusion that, regardless of the legal position, assimilation into the Christian majority was the right thing for their children. Such a decision was not essentially in conflict with Moses Mendelssohn's philosophical and theological stance, for as Joseph implied in his biography, Moses's adherence to Judaism was less a matter of religious conviction than of rational choice, reinforced by personal sentiment, which led him to conclude that he could confer the greatest benefit on his fellows by remaining within his inherited faith. Joseph's considered view was that careful perusal of his father's writings would lead to the following conclusion:

One would be convinced that Mendelssohn had a love of mankind in his heart, which did not inquire about religious creed, but rather in his spirit reason as opposed to faith was dominant. Therefore he could not profess the Christian religion without being a hypocrite—and that he did not want!

However, even if Mendelssohn had not felt himself bound to observe the Jewish ceremonies, he certainly would have, so as not to become estranged from the Jews, to retain their trust and through this the possibility of influencing them morally. Already at an earlier stage he used his knowledge to this end, in order to enlighten his fellow religionists. We have seen that as early as 1750 he edited a weekly moral newspaper in Hebrew, which through no fault of his was soon given up; that in addition he prepared a book on logic in Hebrew, which was published in 1761, though not under his name. After Lavater's challenge,[9] however, and after the pressure of so many uncalled-for successors who sought to convert Mendelssohn to Christianity by any means, it became clear to him that he must go further and do more to instruct the Jews and kindle the light of knowledge for them. It was Mendelssohn's opinion, founded on unshakeable conviction, that the variety of religious viewpoints among mankind must not be suppressed and that the world would fall into terrible barbarism if it were possible to make a single religion the sole one.[10]

There is little evidence to suggest that Abraham ever felt himself temperamentally a Jew in the religious sense; he clearly inclined towards the part of his father's teaching that maintained that all the great monotheistic religions were, in essence, manifestations of the one fundamental truth, and that different ages favoured one form over another. These considerations, combined with an awareness of the practical advantages to his children of belonging to the Christian majority, led him to have all four of them baptised on 21 March 1816 in the Neue Kirche in Berlin, when Felix was seven years old. Abraham's thinking about these issues is made

clear by the letter he wrote to Fanny from Paris on her confirmation four
years later.

> You have taken an important step, and in sending you
> my best wishes for the day and for your future happi-
> ness, I have it at heart to speak seriously to you on sub-
> jects hitherto not touched upon.
>
> Does God exist? What is God? Is He a part of our-
> selves, and does He continue to live after the other part
> has ceased to be? And where? And how? All this I do not
> know, and therefore I have never taught you anything
> about it. But I know that there exists in me and in you
> and in all human beings an everlasting inclination to-
> wards all that is good, true, and right, and a conscience
> which warns and guides us when we go astray. I know it,
> believe it, I live in this faith, and this is my religion.
> This I could not teach you, and nobody can learn it; but
> everybody has it who does not intentionally and know-
> ingly cast it away. The example of your mother, the best
> and noblest of mothers, whose whole life is devotion,
> love, and charity, is like a bond to me that you will *not*
> cast it away. You have grown up under her guidance,
> ever intuitively receiving and adopting what alone gives
> real worth to mankind. Your mother has been, and is,
> and I trust will long remain to you, to your sister and
> brothers, and to all of us, a providential leading star on
> our path of life. When you look at her and turn over in
> your thoughts all the immeasurable good she has lavished
> upon you by her constant self-sacrificing devotion as
> long as you live, and when that reflection makes your
> heart and eyes overflow with gratitude, love, and venera-
> tion, then you feel God and are godly.
>
> This is all I can tell you about religion, all I know
> about it; but this will remain true, as long as one man
> will exist in the creation, as it has been true since the
> first man was created.
>
> The outward form of religion your teacher has given

you is historical, and changeable like all human ordi-
nances. Some thousands of years ago the Jewish form
was the reigning one, then the heathen form, and now it
is the Christian. We, your mother and I, were born and
brought up by our parents as Jews, and without being
obliged to change the form of our religion have been
able to follow the divine instinct in us and in our conscience. We have educated you and your brothers and
sister in the Christian faith, because it is the creed of
most civilised people, and contains nothing that can lead
you away from what is good, and much that guides you
to love, obedience, tolerance, and resignation, even if it
offered nothing but the example of its Founder, understood by so few, and followed by still fewer.

By pronouncing your confession of faith you have fulfilled the claims of *society* on you, and obtained the *name*
of a Christian. Now *be* what your duty as a human being demands of you, *true, faithful, good*; obedient and devoted till death to your mother, and I may also say to
your father, unremittingly attentive to the voice of your
conscience, which may be suppressed but never silenced,
and you will gain the highest happiness that is to be
found on earth, harmony and contentedness with yourself.

I embrace you with fatherly tenderness, and hope always to find in you a daughter worthy of your, of our,
mother. Farewell, and remember my words.[11]

14 · Felix Mendelssohn's Faith

How deeply rooted Fanny's Christian faith may have been, in view of
her relatively recent baptism, remains uncertain. Felix's Christian instruction, however, began at an earlier age, and there is no reason to doubt
the sincerity of the convictions expressed in the "confirmation confession"
he wrote for his religious instructor, Pastor Wilmsen, in September 1825.

The confession undoubtedly represents the kind of statement that would have been expected of a candidate for confirmation and to that extent may be seen as conventional; but at the same time, in view of everything that is known about Felix's moral integrity and his intellectual maturity at this stage in his life, it seems inconceivable that the confession does not reflect his sincerely held views. It is, in many respects, the most important surviving document for understanding the basis of Mendelssohn's religious and ethical thinking, for in later life these remained very private matters about which he rarely talked and even more rarely wrote.

Answer to questions as preparation for confirmation
["]For God so loved the world, that he gave his only
begotten Son, that whosoever believeth in him should
not perish, but have everlasting life.["] [John 3:16][12] Thus
Christ is, according to his own revelation, the only begotten Son of God; he is directly furnished by God with
divine strength. He came down to earth with the dignity
of a saviour of sinful mankind in order to accomplish
the reconciliation of mankind with God. Through his
teaching, his example and his death he saved mankind.
His teaching illuminates our inmost self for us, and our
fate and our relationship to God, it shows us the right
way to obtain bliss; but how could it have found acceptance when mankind is so deeply submerged in superstition and darkness, how could it have penetrated through
the mass of prejudices with which it had to battle, how,
despite its divine truth, could it have been recognized
and understood if Christ's example had not gone hand in
hand with his teaching? Now he bore witness through
his pure and holy life to the truth of his teaching,
through his example people felt themselves drawn to his
teaching, recognized it, seized upon it, and sought to be
true to Christ's teaching, to follow his example. His
death finally completed his divine work, and crowned his
merit in reconciling mankind with God. For a sacrifice
had to be made to God for the sins of the world, and
Christ took our misdeeds upon himself, so that we might

have peace, and died for our salvation. Thus he reconciled us with God; this reconciliation was necessary, for mankind could make no just claim to God's forgiveness, not even through repentance and amendment; for repentance is never, or at least very rarely, sincere and unalloyed with feelings of ambition or of shame or of self-interest; the amendment is rarely lasting, and so we require reconciliation with God. But that alone cannot gain us God's forgiveness and blessedness. It is written: ["]Be ye reconciled to God [2 Corinthians 5: 20], ["] that is, do everything to make yourselves as worthy as possible of God's grace, thus God will forgive you and be a loving father to you.

But in order to gain acceptance for his teaching in the face of the superstition and darkness that prevailed at that time Christ also required divine acknowledgment. God acknowledged his only begotten Son through the divine power that he bestowed on him, and through miracles, so that mankind might have a visible sign by which to believe in him and his divine mission. But if we adopt Christ's teaching and follow it, we shall certainly soon recognize in our hearts that Christ's teaching is from God and that he did not speak on his own account, for we see how Christianity provides light, power and consolation at decisive moments. It provides us with light where we need enlightenment about the most important subjects and still waver back and forth doubtfully, where everything is against us, and where our human power is insufficient. We would have to succumb if religion did not give us power to persevere and overcome evil with good. Finally, religion gives us consolation, either if, feeling the burden of our sins, we become fearful and timid, or if at the approach of death we fear God's judgment seat and his eye that shines through[13] us. Then religion comes to us with its consolation and lifts us up if, as sinners or in the face of death, our courage forsakes us.

Through his holy life Christ also presented us with an uplifting and moving example, rich in traits of purest virtue. His imperturbable and joyful courage, because of which he did not even shun death, indeed, the most dishonourable death, but rather delivered himself up willingly to his enemies, his gentle unselfish goodness (he did not look for reward, or thankfulness, or even recognition of his good deeds, and did good only for God's sake, not for mankind's), his frank truthfulness (never, and to no-one, did he deny the truth, and he told it even to the governor on the throne), his faithfulness, his imperturbable steadfastness—truly these are all excellent, uplifting examples, which all people should aspire to, even if they can never realize these virtues as Christ possessed them. For God looks only into the heart and Christ recognized his own in their self-denial, their meekness and humility. We must practise self-denial at every moment of our lives; what should we learn in our youth without sacrifice, without shunning pleasures, however enticingly they beckon us, and without persevering in work?[14] What could we carry out and achieve in our mature years without renouncing things in order to remain true to our duty? Would not the most dreadful egotism ensue, for if we were unwilling to refuse any benefit, how could we bestow one on others? And there can be no self-denial, no love without meekness and humility, which allow us to recognize our weaknesses and reveal God to us as our refuge. And again Providence commands men to deny themselves, for man only shows humility, reverence and submission to God's will when he offers the most difficult sacrifice. Thus these three Christian virtues are bound together in the closest manner.

If man wants to give himself sufficient reasons for everything that he does, if he wants to retain the strength to undertake all trials, even the most difficult, and to obey the commandments, if he does not want, like wavering grass,[15] to be driven to and fro by the slightest wind or trodden down by the lightest step, he must proceed according to principles, i.e., according to set rules from which he never deviates. As a Christian, too, he must therefore have fixed principles by which he lets himself be guided and ruled, which he never denies or infringes: *Reverence before God*.[16] One must obey God more than man, says the apostle. *Undaunted candour* "And fear not them which kill the body, but are not able to kill the soul: but rather fear him which is able to destroy both soul and body in hell." [Matthew 10:20] How can one bring anything great to fruition without undaunted candour? Never has a great man not been true to this principle, and also the greatest improvements in the Christian church have been carried out in this manner by men who were to the greatest degree undaunted and likewise candid; we need only think of Thomas, who first and fearlessly combated the superstition that imagined every old woman to be a witch or an evil sorceress, or of Wiklef [Wycliffe], who tirelessly preached Christianity in England and sought to spread it, or of Huss, who became a martyr and preferred the stake to recantation, or of his friend Hieronymus of Prague and so many more;—in all these cases we see that they only prevailed and achieved great things by means of undaunted candour. A third principle should be *humility*. "And I seek not my own glory: there is one that seeketh and judgeth [John 8:50]," says Christ, and wishes by this means to warn against ambition and selfishness everyone who has lost humility from his heart and has therefore made room for those vices. Further, *Unselfishness*. "Look not every man on his own things, but every man also upon the things of others.["] [Philippians 2:4] *Love*, and indeed love without hope of return. Thus the Christian should love without hoping for reward, thanks, or even indeed acknowledgment, even if he should be paid for his love with ingratitude and mockery, for Christ says: "Love your enemies, do good to them that hate you, for if ye love them which love you what reward have ye, thus your reward will be great and you will be children of the Almighty, for he maketh the sun to rise on the evil and the good." [Matthew 5:44–46][17] *Truthfulness*, "But let your communication be, Yea, yea; Nay, nay: for whatsoever is more than these cometh of evil." [Matthew 5:37] Here Christ gave the commandment to be strictly truthful, and it is difficult in our times always to follow it precisely, because social convention often requires, if not that we deny the truth, at least that we know how to conceal it elegantly or cloak it. Yet we may well combine the two by speaking the strictest truth to everyone, but without pressing it upon anyone, without seeking to be troublesome to anyone with it, and thus we shall fulfil Jesus Christ's commandment.—Finally, *Piety* [Gottesfurcht]. "And whatsoever ye do, do it heartily, as to the Lord, and not unto man" [Colossians 3:23], i.e., do nothing out of avarice or ambition, do good not for the praise of men, for fame, for the sake of gratitude, do good for the sake of your conscience, for the conscience is the voice of God. And then you will turn to the Lord and have piety, which is a principle for Christians.

Christianity requires from us the worship of God in spirit and truth, and on the other hand repudiates empty ceremonial and hypocrisy. We should now[18] elevate ourselves to this worship of God in the Christian church, i.e., in the institution concerned with the maintenance, diffusion and propagation of Christianity. These three things are unavoidably necessary. Since we believe that Christianity is the best of all religions, we must work for its maintenance in its purity; if, however, we acknowledge it as the only true and divine religion, we must be concerned about its diffusion, for it cannot possibly be a matter of indifference to us whether our neighbour possesses and acknowledges the true religion or not. It would be the greatest egotism if one were to retain its light for oneself alone, without sharing it with one's brothers.[19] If at last we are convinced of the truth of our religion, then we must also think about passing it on to our descendants, and therefore ought not to neglect the propagation of Christianity. How, therefore, can we be indifferent to the institutions that further such important aims as maintenance, diffusion and propagation of Christianity, which have such a beneficial influence on our life. For the influence of the church community on our domestic and public life is undeniable. In domestic life too much that is earthly happens, so much care, so much pleasure occupies man, he finds so many disturbances that it must certainly do him good to put aside one peaceful day in the week to occupy himself with serious thoughts of his Creator, so that he is then able, reinvigorated, courageously to get to grips again with his work. And how necessary must it indeed be to he who has to superintend public business to bring his duties very vividly before his eyes at least once in the week, and to take stock of his subjective feelings, and to test his conscientiousness, and to let heavenly thoughts take the place of earthly ones.[20]

Christ, in saying "Go ye therefore, and teach all heathens[21] baptizing them," established baptism as one sacrament of the Christian church. In endowing the celebration of his memory he established the second sacrament, Communion, and since the apostles were given the power not only to baptise the heathen but also, by laying on of hands, to inspire them with the Holy Spirit, and thus to make them teachers of Christianity, the office of preacher came about. Baptism should symbolically show[22] that through Christianity the soul will be freed from every blemish, just as the water makes every stain on the body disappear without trace, and by Communion the wine signifies Christ's blood and the bread Christ's body. At all times, and particularly at the time of the Reformation, there was much disputation over the question of whether the wine and the bread were really Christ's blood and body, or only signified them. But how could we think that without a miracle the real body and the real blood should be present? In any case it is of little importance.[23] If we know only that Christ's divine spirit is present why then presuppose that the human body which he assumed exalts us? His spirit supports us, and that is life.

In the celebration of Communion a Christian should make a threefold vow, so that it is really a reunion for him. He should pledge: *submission to the divine will.* (Christ said: "O my Father, if it be possible, let this cup pass from me, nevertheless not as I will but thou wilt.") [Matthew 26:39–40] Then *love*, the sincerest love, that does not even shun death, for Christ says: "This is my commandment, that ye love one another, as I have loved you. Greater love hath no man than this, that a man lay down his life for his friends." [John 15:12–13]—*Truthful-ness*, for to Pilate's question: "Art thou a king then?" Christ answered: "Thou sayest that I am a king. To this end was I born, and for this cause came I into the world, that I should bear witness unto the truth. Every one that is of the truth heareth my voice" [John 18:37]; and we should emulate Christ. And finally *obedience*, for it is said, "He humbled himself and became obedient unto death, even the death of the cross. Wherefore God also hath highly exalted him, and given him a name which is above every name." [Philippians 2:8–9]

Through its divine power and its divine truth the Church of Jesus Christ has survived the dangers of eclipse, oppression, degeneration and schism, which affect it more frequently than all other religions. For men usu-ally seek most to oppress the greatest[24] truth, because it commands them to control themselves and deny them-selves. The small number of its followers, the great mi-grations of peoples, the hatred[25] of so many Roman em-perors, were all against the Christian religion at first. And nevertheless in a period of 300 years it became the dominant one,[26] and spread over the world the blessing of enlightenment and a spirit of love and inquiry.

Yet even now many dangers threaten it: the Pietists and Mystics again begin to lift their heads, and in this respect we live in a time of transition, since it is not yet decided which side will be victorious. But we do have Christ's consoling words: "Heaven and earth shall pass away but my words shall not pass away [Matthew 24: 35]," and our duty therefore is to heed his exhortation: "Watch ye therefore, and pray always, that ye may be accounted worthy to escape all these things that shall come to pass and stand before the Son of men." [Luke 21:36]

How should we bring to fruition the commandment that Jesus Christ calls the chiefest and greatest? Through *compassion* (the story of the Samaritan), *charity* (the widow with the mite, of whom Christ says, she has given more than all the others), *forbearance and leniency* (the exhortation: "And why beholdest thou the mote that is in thy brother's eye, but considerest not the beam that is in thine own eye?" [Matthew 7:3]), *gentleness* (story of the adulteress: "Whosoever among you is without sin let him cast the first stone upon her"), *meekness and peaceableness, forgiveness* (we think of Jesus's moving words when he saw Judas coming to betray him: "Friend wherefore art thou come?" [Matthew 26:50]), *magnanimity* and *generosity* (when Peter asks, "Lord, how oft shall my brother sin against me and I forgive him? Till seven times?" [Matthew 18:21], and Christ answers: "I say not unto thee: Until seven times: But, until seventy times seven["] [Matthew 18:22]), *self-denial* and *self-sacrifice* (Jesus answered his Peter, who asked him to save himself: "Get thee behind me, Satan: thou art an offence to me: for thou savourest not the things that be of God, but those that be of man" [Matthew 16:23]), *humility* (for Christ says: "But he that is greatest among you, let him be as the younger; and he that is chief, as he that doth serve["] [Luke 22:26]).

Entry to the Church is by means of confirmation, and for that is required: familiarity with the duties of a Christian, with the teaching of Christ and the intention to remain true to it and to control and deny oneself.— The essential difference between the Catholic and the Protestant Church consists principally of the fact that the Catholic sets the word of man on a level with the Word of God, and the Protestant sets Holy Writ above everything.

Since at first Christianity had to withstand innumerable dangers, it is no wonder that it did not remain so pure that many should not have turned aside from the true religion, and thus step by step founded their own sects. Others sought to bring them back to true religion, and (since they may well have gone too far in their zeal) they founded new sects, and thus it happened that almost the whole of Christendom was divided into sects. But the spirit of sectarianism is not a good spirit. For their adherents generally go too far in one way or another, be it in strictness, or in the desire to segregate and distinguish themselves, or through something else. Thus we do not want to deviate from our religion, and thus we want to fulfil through our whole life the exhortation: "Be ye reconciled to God." [2 Corinthians 5:20] Reconcile yourselves with your brothers, reconcile yourselves with everyone with whom you are angry and who is angry with you if you want to be reconciled with God. Do good and do charitable works, without hesitation, without timidity, without boasting; deny yourselves, control yourselves and you will be reconciled with God. Whatever difficult tests of faith we have to undergo as a result of ridicule, pressing occupation and unprecedented supplications, we trust in God's infinite goodness, we pray: Embodiment of all goodness let Thy blessings rest upon us, let us follow Thy way, and teach us Thyself to do according to Thy pleasure, and to stand firm, trusting in God's grace and his all-governing mercy.

To this confession, written down by the sixteen-year-old in what Carl Klingemann Jr. describes as "his well-known, beautiful, almost fully developed handwriting," Wilmsen added a lengthy homily, admonishing Mendelssohn to remain faithful to the "spirit of truth," because the Christian "abhors every injury against truth, especially hypocrisy, dissimulation and falsehood," to cherish "a spirit of love and faithfulness" and to be a "benefactor, friend and saviour of his unfortunate bretheren." Wilmsen also exhorted him to remember that the "immortal soul is destined for a higher life, it has dispositions that are capable of endless development," and to "acquire the spirit of wisdom . . . which in blessed partnership with the Redeemer spreads truth and love among mankind, and does homage to all that is truly beautiful and good." He went on to add, "May everything that you do, that you strive for, that you enjoy and feel, lead to an undisturbed harmony of the soul that may protect you against the onslaught of bad temper and of internal discord. It is written: To whom much is given, from him much will be expected." And he concluded with a direct reference to Mendelssohn's chosen career: "May the Lord illuminate and strengthen your soul and let you live to be a joy to your father and your mother, and to bear witness to the world so that art, exalted and sanctified through religion, makes the soul strong and free, noble and great."[27]

The reminsicences of Pastor Julius Schubring cast further light on Mendelssohn's religious standpoint and on his relationship with Wilmsen, broadly confirming the impression made by the "confirmation confession."

> Mendelssohn's character had a deep feeling of religion for
> its basis. That this wanted the specifically church colour-
> ing is a fact on which we disputed a great deal in our
> earlier years. As an unconditional Schleiermacherite,[28] I
> was then almost incapable of recognizing Christianity in
> any other shape, and, consequently, wronged Felix.
> Wilmsen, who had instructed and confirmed Mendels-
> sohn, and his brothers [sic] and sisters, struck me as a
> man of no great capacity, and I let fall some hint or
> other to the effect that it would have been better had
> they gone to Schleiermacher. Felix was seriously angry,

and gave me to understand that he would not allow anyone to attack his spiritual adviser, for whom he entertained a feeling of affectionate reverence. It is true that
he did not go very often to hear him perform Divine
Service. When I recollect, however, with what a serious
religious feeling he pursued his art, the exercise of it always being, as it were, a sacred duty; how the first page
of every one of his compositions bears impressed on it
the initial letter of a prayer;[29] how he devoted the time,
as he watched through the night by the bed of his dying
friend, Hanstein, to marking in the first fugue, composed
here, of the six he afterwards published[30]—in E minor—
the progress of the disease as it gradually destroyed the
sufferer, until he made it culminate in the choral[e] of
release in E major; how the very best touches in his oratorios result from his delicate tact—for instance, the
words for the air of Paul during the days of his blind-
ness, when he had just been converted before Damascus,
for which Mendelssohn, dissatisfied with everything proposed to him, himself hit upon the 51st Psalm, that seems
as though it had been written on purpose; moreover,
when I call to mind everything connected with my beloved friend, as regards his views and opinions on art
and artists—whether he was standing at the conductor's
desk, sitting at the piano, or taking his tenor-part in a
quartet—religion and veneration were enthroned in his
countenance; this was why his music possessed such a
magic charm. On one occasion, he expressly said that sacred music, as such, did not stand higher in his estimation than any other, because every kind of music ought,
in its peculiar way, to tend to the glory of God.[31]

Felix Mendelssohn's "confirmation confession" was written three years
after Abraham and his wife had also adopted Christianity, in a conversion
that undoubtedly did not represent a change of theological outlook for
them. It seems likely that Lea had been disposed to convert at an early
stage, though she would undoubtedly have felt obliged to leave any such

decision to her husband. Abraham took longer to convince himself; he was evidently inhibited from taking the final step by a sense of loyalty to his father's memory, as the surviving fragment of a letter to him from his brother-in-law Jacob Lewin Bartholdy suggests. This letter also indicates the background to Abraham's decision to accompany his conversion with a change in the family name from Mendelssohn to Mendelssohn Bartholdy, and it illustrates the extent to which these moves were dictated by Abraham's concern to distance his family from its Jewish roots. (His brother-in-law had changed his name from Salomon to Bartholdy, the name of a former owner of an estate he had inherited, at the time of his own conversion.) Bartholdy wrote, apparently in reply to a letter from Abraham:

> I was not at all convinced by your arguments for loyalty
> to your name and faith. These arguments have become
> invalid in our era, for reasons internal as well as external.
> You say you owe it to the memory of your father; but
> do you think you have done something bad in giving
> your children the religion that appears to you to be the
> best? It is the justest homage you or any of us could pay
> to the efforts of your father in promoting true light and
> knowledge, and he would have acted like you for his
> children, and perhaps like me for himself. You may re-
> main faithful to an oppressed, persecuted religion; you
> may leave it to your children as a prospect of lifelong
> martyrdom, as long as you believe it to be absolute
> truth. But when you have ceased to believe that, it is
> barbarism. I advise you to adopt the name of Mendels-
> sohn Bartholdy as a distinction from the other Mendels-
> sohns. At the same time, you would please me very
> much, because it would be the means of preserving my
> memory in the family. Thus you would gain your point,
> without doing anything unusual, for in France and else-
> where it is the custom to add the name of one's wife's
> relations as a distinction.[32]

15 · The Family Name

In the period immediately following his conversion, Abraham Mendelssohn's ideas about the family name developed and became, if not a matter of open dispute between him and his children, at least a matter of passive resistance on their part. In London in 1829 Felix quietly dropped the Bartholdy. That he did this consciously is indicated by a letter that Fanny dispatched to him on 8 July, after Abraham had become aware of the situation from the English newspapers: "I know and approve of your intention to lay aside someday this name that we all dislike, but you can't do it yet because you're a minor, and it's not necessary to make you aware of the unpleasant consequences it could have for you. Suffice it to say that you distress Father by your actions. If questioned you could easily make it seem like a mistake, and carry out your plan later."[33] A letter Abraham sent to his son gives a clear indication of his thinking about the matter.

> Today's family sheet will run full without my contribution . . . I will, therefore, write to you separately because I have to discuss with you a most serious matter.
>
> The suspicion has come to me that you have suppressed or neglected or allowed others to suppress or neglect the name which I have taken as the name of our family, the name Bartholdy.
>
> In the concert programmes you have sent me, likewise in newspaper articles, your name is given as Mendelssohn. I can account for this only on the supposition that you have been the cause.
>
> Now, I am greatly dissatisfied about this. If you are to blame, you have committed a huge wrong.
>
> After all, a name is only a name, neither more nor less. Still, so long as you are under your father's jurisdiction, you have the plain and indisputable duty to be called by your father's name. Moreover it is your ineffaceable, as well as reasonable, duty to take for granted

that, whatever your father does, he does on valid grounds and with due deliberation.

On our journey to Paris after that neck-breaking night,[34] you asked me the reasons why our name was changed. I gave you those reasons at length. If you have forgotten them, you could have asked me about them again. If my reasons seemed unconvincing, you should have countered with better reasons. I prefer to believe the former, because I am unable to think of any reasons countervailing. I will here repeat my arguments and my views.

My grandfather was named Mendel Dessau. When my father, his son, went forth into the world and began to win notice and when he undertook the project which can not be too highly praised, that noble project of lifting his brethren out of the vast degradation into which they had sunk, and to do this by disseminating among them a better education, my father felt that the name Moses ben Mendel Dessau, would handicap him in gaining the needed access to those who had the better education at their disposal. Without any fear that his own father would take offence, my father assumed the name Mendelssohn.[35] The change, though a small one, was decisive. As Mendelssohn, he became irrevocably detached from an entire class, the best of whom he raised to his own level. By that name he identified himself with a different group. Through the influence which wisely and worthily he exerted by word and pen and deed,—an influence which, ever growing, persists to this day,—that name Mendelssohn acquired a Messianic import and a significance which defies extinction. This, considering that you were reared a Christian, you can hardly understand. A Christian Mendelssohn is an impossibility. A Christian Mendelssohn the world would never recognize. Nor should there be a Christian Mendelssohn; for my father himself did not want to be a Christian. "Mendelssohn" does and always will stand for a Judaism in transition, when Judaism, just because it is seeking to transmute itself spiritually, clings to its ancient form all the more stubbornly and tenaciously, by way of protest against the novel form that so arrogantly and tyrannically declared itself to be the one and only path to the good.

The viewpoint, to which my father and then my own generation committed me, imposes on me other duties toward you, my children, and puts other means of discharging them into my hands. I have learnt and will not, until my dying breath, forget that, while truth is one and eternal, its forms are many and transient. That is why, as long as it was permitted by the government under which we lived, I reared you without religion in any form.[36] I wanted you to profess whatever your convictions might favour, or, if you prefer, whatever expediency might dictate. But it was not so to be. I was obligated to do the choosing for you. Naturally, when you consider what scant value I placed on any form in particular, I felt no urge to choose the form known as Judaism, that most antiquated, distorted, and self-defeating form of all. Therefore I reared you as Christians, Christianity being the more purified form and the one most accepted by the majority of civilized people. Eventually, I myself adopted Christianity, because I felt it my duty to do for myself that which I recognized as best for you. Even as my father found it necessary to adjust his name to conditions, filial devotion, as well as discretion, impelled me to adjust similarly.

Here I must reproach myself for a weakness, even if a pardonable one. I should have done decisively and thoroughly that which I deemed right. I should have discarded the name Mendelssohn completely, I should have adhered to the new name exclusively. I owed that to my father. My reason for not doing so was my long established habit of sparing those near to me and of forestalling perverted and venomous judgments. I did wrong. My purpose was merely to prepare for you a path of transition, making it easier for you that have no one to spare and nothing to care about. In Paris, when you, Felix, were about to step into the world and make a name for yourself, I deliberately had your cards engraved: Felix M. Bartholdy. You did not accept my way of thinking. Weakly enough I failed to persist. Now I only wish, though I neither expect nor deserve it, that my present intervention may not have arrived too late.

You can not, you must not carry the name Mendelssohn. Felix Mendelssohn Bartholdy is too long; it is unsuited for daily use. You must go by the name of Felix Bartholdy. A name is like a garment; it has to be appropriate for the time, the use, and the rank, if it is not to become a hindrance and a laughing-stock. Englishmen, otherwise a most formal lot, change their names frequently. Seldom is anyone renowned under the name conferred at baptism. And that is as it should be. I repeat: There can no more be a Christian Mendelssohn than there can be a Jewish Confucius. If Mendelssohn is your name, you are ipso facto a Jew. And this, if for no other reason than because it is contrary to fact, can be to you of no benefit.

Dear Felix, take this to heart and act accordingly,
Your Father and Friend.[37]

It is a testimony to Abraham's influence that the letter permanently dissuaded Felix from discarding the name Bartholdy. A few weeks later Felix wrote to Fanny: "It would never in my life occur to me to want to oppose Father's will, and over such a trifle! No, believe me, it doesn't enter my mind."[38] His father's letter did not, as was intended, persuade him to give up the name Mendelssohn entirely, however. For the rest of his life he was invariably to sign himself Felix Mendelssohn Bartholdy, though he continued generally to be known simply as Mendelssohn.[39]

16 · Early Nineteenth-Century Anti-Semitism

Ten years earlier, at the time of the racially motivated disturbances known as the *Judensturm*, Felix Mendelssohn will have observed, if he had not done so earlier, what it could mean to be a Jew in Prussia, and he cannot have failed to become aware of the deep-seated prejudice, not merely against his ancestors' religion but also against their race, that pervaded much of German society, a prejudice that may well have been sharpened by the growth of nationalist feeling during the Napoleonic Wars. The only explicit mention of Felix Mendelssohn's having been touched by the 1819 *Judensturm* occurs in Carl August Varnhagen von Ense's *Denkwür-digkeiten*, which, despite the doubts expressed by Felix Gilbert,[40] seems clearly to refer to an actual incident. Varnhagen and his wife, Rahel, were in close contact with the Mendelssohn family during the early 1820s, and any such incident is likely to have been known to them. Furthermore, the version of Varnhagen's account given by Eric Werner, to which Gilbert refers, is grossly misleading, not to say inaccurate. Werner begins his chapter with the sentence "On a bright spring day in 1819 a royal prince of Prussia stopped Felix Mendelssohn, then ten years old, on the street, spat at his feet, and exclaimed: 'Hep hep, Jew-boy.' "[41] And Leon Botstein, too, incorrectly states that Varnhagen reported that Mendelssohn was "spat upon."[42] The following extract from Varnhagen makes clear, however, that the reality of the incident was very different. As Varnhagen related it, it seems rather to have been a tasteless joke on the part of a prince who was, in all probability, personally acquainted with the family. Nevertheless, Varnhagen's account, which vividly illustrates the feelings roused by this event, underscores the inevitability of Mendelssohn's consciousness that he was in some sense marked out by his Jewishness.

> At the end of August [1819] a movement arose in Germany which cast ugly stains on the German people's reputation for being good natured, civilised and of the best character, but which also showed that they had an inner association with and common receptivity for incitement and emotion, to an extent that had not previously been suspected. Suddenly, in a middle-sized town, I no longer

remember in which, there occurred without particular cause a wild outcry against the Jews. With the wild cry Hep, Hep! individuals were assailed and followed in the street, their homes attacked and to some extent plundered, insults and assaults of all kinds were practised against them; however, no blood was shed; this was as far as the courage or the malice of the malefactors would go.

As quickly as the rumours of these excesses spread, so they themselves spread like wildfire, like an infectious St. Vitus' Dance. In all the towns of Germany, large and small, in those that were best supplied with troops and police as much as in the less well policed ones, in royal residences and at the seat of the Federal Diet[43] as much as in the Hanseatic towns, the same scene was repeated in an identical manner as if directed by one and the same invisible hand. Hep, Hep! resounded throughout the whole of Germany, from one end to the other, as an incitement to assault, as a warning to flight or defence for the outlaws. As if it were a banner of Germanness, the persecution of the Jews also arose in such towns that, although they were not German and did not want to be German, could still not deny an element in them that was German—unfortunately in the worst sense; in Straßburg and Amsterdam, in Copenhagen and Riga, they cried Hep, Hep! Irresponsible banter, an inclination to waggishness, was mixed with the assaults; a royal prince called out Hep, Hep! in the street to the boy Felix Mendelssohn, not everything was intended to be malicious, some of those who were shouting would, if it had gone further, have come to the aid of the Jews if necessary; but the rough high spirits did not take account of the fact that wantonness knows no bounds, that scorn and insult may give rise to pillage and murder and that these could then spread from the Jews to engulf themselves too! In fact no-one knew where this suddenly ignited excitement might lead, and the persecuted could not but see themselves threatened, with respect both to goods and life. . . . After a comparatively long time, considering the substantial police force that was available everywhere, the shameful mischief gradually petered out on its own, and no real enmity was left behind, but there merely remained on the one side the deep feeling of having been wronged, and on the other shamefaced denial,[44] for no-one wished any longer to have taken part in the rough outburst.[45]

Werner gives an account of an abusive attack on Felix and Fanny Mendelssohn during a stay in Doberan in 1824, based on a quotation from a document by the children's tutor, J. L. Heyse, but typically without a bibliographical reference.[46] The reliability of the account is called into question too, by the fact that neither Fanny nor Heyse accompanied Felix and Abraham to Doberan. No other recorded incidents of Mendelssohn's having been faced with openly anti-Semitic behaviour are known. There is, however, evidence that he continued to be regarded, pejoratively, as a Jew by many contemporaries. The memoires of Ernst Rudorff suggest that much of the awkwardness between Mendelssohn and Betty Pistor arose from the anti-Semitism of some branches of her family, who "looked askance at Betty because of her relationship with the Mendelssohn family and mockingly called her 'the music- and Jew-loving cousin.' "[47] Mendelssohn's Jewish origins may also have played a significant part in his being rejected for the directorship of the Berlin Singakademie in 1832. It is hardly surprising that there were those like Wagner who, disliking Mendelssohn or jealous of him for other reasons, used his race as a means of denigrating him; but it is also clear that even those who in general admired and liked him could not escape the common prejudice of their period. The anti-Semitic remarks made by Zelter in his correspondence with Goethe, though undoubtedly casual rather than malicious, caused considerable pain to the Mendelssohn family when they were published in 1834, and it has even been suggested that distress over this published correspondence may have been a direct contributory cause of Abraham Mendelssohn's death.[48] More surprising, perhaps, are comments in the diary of Robert and Clara Schumann. On 14 and 15 November 1840 they wrote:

Saturday 14 November 1840

[RS:] Clara said to me that I seemed altered towards Mendelssohn; towards him as an artist certainly not— you know that—after all, I have contributed so much to promoting him, as hardly anyone else. Nevertheless—let's not forget ourselves too much in the meanwhile. Jews remain Jews; first they secure their own positions tenfold, and perhaps then comes the Christian.[49] The stones that we add to their temple of fame they then use to throw at us when the occasion arises. So not too much, in my opinion. We also must act and work for ourselves. Above all, let us now always approach more closely to the beautiful and true in art.

Sunday 15 November

[CS:] First, my dear husband, I must say to you regarding what you have written above, that I absolutely agree with you, and I have also often silently thought something similar, but out of great respect for *Mendelssohn's* art I have time and again adopted the old excessive consideration towards him. I shall follow your counsel and not humble myself too much before him as I have so often done.[50]

Such sentiments, however, remained private and do not appear to have disturbed the Schumanns' relationship with Mendelssohn; indeed, Mendelssohn's consideration and attentiveness in his dealings with both of them strengthened their attachment to him over the years. Not until after Mendelssohn's death was his Jewish origin openly used as a means of undermining his artistic stature, most notably by Wagner, whose article *Das Judenthum in der Musik* (1850) may be seen as the first in a line of racially orientated critiques that link directly with the Nazi excesses of the 1930s and 1940s.[51]

FIVE · Professional Career

17 · The Singakademie

The family's financial circumstances would have made it feasible for Mendelssohn, like Meyerbeer, to have concentrated on composition without unduly concerning himself with pecuniary considerations. It had always been Abraham Mendelssohn's firm intention, however, that if his son were to devote his life to music he should not do so from a position of complete financial independence but should have proper professional appointments, thus putting his gifts at the service of society. Felix Mendelssohn undoubtedly shared his father's belief that his talents and material advantages laid him under an obligation towards his fellows, which he should not shirk for the sake of his own comfort or convenience. He believed, furthermore, that his motivation always had to be the achievement not of worldly acclaim or material success but of the best of which he was capable in whatever sphere he applied himself.

Eventually, the tension between his sense of duty and his own physical and emotional capacity proved self-defeating, and it undoubtedly contributed to his early death. Yet his iron self-discipline and capacity for hard work made his thirteen-year professional career exceptionally productive and influential. He never lost his conviction that the pursuit of a public career was a moral obligation: it affected the decision to apply, against his own inclinations, for the directorship of the Berlin Singakademie after Zelter's death; it was a decisive influence on his acceptance of a post in Düsseldorf in 1833; it was still a factor in his move to Leipzig in 1835; it led to his reluctant agreement to accept, at least partially, King Friedrich Wilhelm IV's call to participate in his schemes for the regeneration of music in Prussia; and it determined his return to Leipzig during the last two years of his life, despite the attractions of remaining in the Rhineland to devote himself full-time to composition.

The subject of a professional career recurs several times in Mendelssohn's correspondence with his family during his travels from 1830 to 1832. He aired the matter at length in a letter to his father from Milan on 7 July 1831;[1] and writing from Paris on 21 February 1832 he gave him a detailed account of his views.

It is now high time, dear father, to write you a few words with regard to my travelling plans, and on this occasion in a more serious strain than usual, for many reasons. I must first, in taking a general view of the past, refer to what you designed to be the chief object of my journey; desiring me strictly to adhere to it. I was closely to examine the various countries, and to fix on the one where I wished to live and work; I was further to make known my name and capabilities, in order that the people, among whom I resolved to settle, should receive me well, and not be wholly ignorant of my career; and finally, I was to take advantage of my own good fortune, and your kindness, to press forward in my subsequent efforts. It is a happy feeling to be able to say, that I believe this has been the case.

Always excepting those mistakes which are not discovered till too late, I think I have fulfilled the appointed object. People now know that I exist, and that I have a purpose, and any talent that I display, they are ready to approve and accept. They have *made advances* to me here, and *proposed* to take my music, which they seldom do; as all the others, even Onslow, have been obliged to *offer* their compositions. The London Philharmonic have requested me to perform something new of my own there on the 10th of March. I also got the commission from Munich without taking any step whatever to obtain it, and indeed not till *after* my concert. It is my intention to give a concert here (if possible) and certainly in London in April, if the cholera does not prevent my going there; and this on my own account in order to make money; I hope, therefore, I may say that I have also fulfilled this part of your wish—that I should make myself known to the public before returning to you. Your injunction, too, to make choice of the country that I preferred to live in, I have equally performed, at least in a general point of view. That country is Germany. This is a point on which I have now quite made up my mind. I cannot yet, however, decide on the particular city, for the most important of all, which for various reasons has so many attractions for me, I have not yet thought of in this light—I allude to Berlin. On my return therefore I must ascertain whether I can remain and establish myself there, according to my views and wishes, after having seen and enjoyed other places.

This is also why I do not endeavour to get the commission for an opera here. If I compose really good music, which in these days is indispensable, it will both be understood and valued in Germany. (This has been the case with all the good operas there.) If I compose indifferent music, it will be quickly forgotten in Germany, but here it would be often performed and extolled, and sent to Germany, and given there on the authority of Paris, as we daily see. But I do not choose this; and if I am not capable of composing good music, I have no wish to be praised for it. So I shall first try Germany; and if things go so badly that I can no longer live there, I can then have recourse to some foreign country. Besides, few German theatres are so bad or in so dilapidated a condition as the Opéra Comique here. One bankruptcy succeeds another. When Cherubini is asked why he does not allow his operas to be given there, he replies, "Je ne sais pas donner des opéras, sans chœur, sans orchestre, sans chanteurs, et sans décorations." The

Grand Opéra has bespoken operas for years to come, so there is no chance of anything being accepted by it for the next three or four years.

In the meantime therefore I intend to return to you to write my "Tempest,"[2] and see how it succeeds. The plan, therefore, dear Father, that I wish to lay before you is this—to remain here till the end of March, or the beginning of April, (the invitation to the Philharmonic for the 10th of March, I have of course declined, or rather postponed,) then to go to London for a couple of months. If the Rhenish musical festival takes place, to which I am summoned, I shall go to Düsseldorf; and if not, return direct to you by the shortest road, and be by your side in the garden soon after Whitsunday.[3]

In the event, Mendelssohn went from Paris to London in April 1832 and stayed there longer than anticipated, missing the Lower Rhine Festival in Cologne and returning directly to Berlin in late June. He now faced the momentous decision of whether to choose Berlin or some other city as the forum for his future activities. Family ties pulled him strongly towards Berlin, but he seems all along to have had grave doubts about whether a career there would be practicable. During his time in London family letters had repeatedly pressed him to seek a position with the Berlin Singakademie, first as the ailing Zelter's substitute and then, after his death on 15 May, as his successor. Filial duty would not permit Felix to reject outright a proposal that stemmed from his father, though his letters, especially to Fanny,[4] make his reluctance to solicit a position abundantly clear. As Devrient reported, Felix "would take no other view than that expressed in his letters from London of the 25th of May, and the 1st of June. He was ready to assume the conductorship (as he had already stated to Councillor Lichtenstein) as soon as he was distinctly chosen, but he would not apply for it or take any steps to obtain it."[5]

On returning to Berlin Mendelssohn initially maintained his resolve not to declare his candidature in opposition to Carl Friedrich Rungenhagen, who had been Zelter's vice-director since 1815. Deverient continued: "I placed my hopes in what Felix had already conceded to Lichtenstein, that he would conduct the society in conjunction with

Rungenhagen. I repeatedly urged this plan upon Felix, and though the father shook his head, Felix entered upon it cheerfully, nor did he seem to mind that in the eyes of the public he would appear as second in command. He only stipulated that leave of absence for travel should be granted to him."[6] On 4 August Mendelssohn could write quite complacently to Klingemann about the situation: "I live happily at home; where it is quite like before, only quieter; since you left it has never really been so cheerful. But every evening we are all together and get along with each other. Besides, I read much, draw a little and see no-one. Rungenhagen will probably get or, more to the point, retain the [Sing]akademie post. Perhaps the matter will just be quietly forgotten; I shan't take it on in any case without brilliant terms, a good salary, complete authority and leave for travelling, as for instance in 1833 for a Swiss and an English journey."[7]

At a meeting of the male members of the society on 17 August it became evident that most were in favour, according to Devrient, "of a conductor who was personally popular amongst them. Such a one was Rungenhagen, from pleasant old association; such a one, however, Mendelssohn was not, for many reasons, of which his youth was a prominent one; for it was not decorous that so many highly-born gentlemen and women advanced in years should be dictated to by a young fellow." In fact, though Devrient did not say so directly, it must have seemed perfectly proper and just to many of the members that Rungenhagen, who had given many years of efficient service to the Singakademie, should not be unceremoniously displaced. Devrient also indicated, however, that there were more prejudiced feelings at work: "I heard said near me, in an animated knot of talkers, that the Vocal Academy, from its almost exclusive devotion to sacred music, was a Christian institution, and on this account it was an unheard-of thing to try to thrust a Jewish lad upon them for their conductor."[8] Lampadius, writing shortly after Mendelssohn's death, relayed a view, presumably current in Leipzig, that "the opposition seems to have been headed by the more elderly ladies of the Sing-Akademie, though the failure of 'Camacho's Wedding' seems to have left a lasting prejudice against Mendelssohn."[9]

Whatever the combination of factors that worked against Mendelssohn, it is clear that the unpleasantness of the contest weighed heavily upon him. On 3 September he wrote a very dispirited letter to Charlotte

Moscheles, ending "But oh! how I should like you to lecture me as you used to do! For how to overcome these fits of intense depression, I really do not know"; two days later he complained to Klingemann of "the business of the [Sing]akademie, about which they torment me more than is proper, when, in the end, they will still choose their Rungenhagen or God knows whom."[10] Mendelssohn himself clearly believed that Berlin society had a very equivocal attitude towards him, for in the aftermath of the affair, when he was being regularly featured in Berlin concerts as performer and composer, he observed to Klingemann: "I tell you I am all the fashion in Berlin, but they take me for an arrogant oddity."[11]

An attempt to establish a compromise solution, by which Rungenhagen would be chief authority in business matters and performances while Mendelssohn would have primacy in purely musical affairs, met with agreement even from the majority of Rungenhagen's supporters. But Rungenhagen himself rejected it, feeling that "he had a right to the post on the conditions under which it was held by Zelter."[12] Rungenhagen's decision was announced to a meeting of the members on 2 October, but Mendelssohn's family and close friends nevertheless persuaded him to let his name go forward, and an election became inevitable. From this point on Mendelssohn seems to have become even more distraught. As he could not bring himself to blame his family directly for their role in the matter, he sublimated his resentment in a diatribe to Klingemann against Berlin and Berliners, particularly Devrient, who had played the leading role in brokering his candidature:

> Every step outside the house reminds me of how the
> whole city has remained stagnant and has therefore re-
> gressed. The music is bad; the people have become even
> dryer, the best have died, the others who still had fine
> plans have become happy philistines and still speak often
> of their memories of youth. Devrient, for example, from
> whom I really expected something worthwhile for the
> stage, has become a common actor and a bad poet, and
> that's all there is to it. He has written an opera in one
> act *Die Kirkmess*, every aspect, every good idea of which
> is copied from your liederspiel [*Die Heimkehr aus der
> Fremde*], but so crude, so Berlinish, so dammed naïve

that such a trampling on delicate threads immediately put me out of humour; what is more, he no longer sings well, is concerned about how much he is applauded in the opera house, is occasionally called for, gets upset when this doesn't happen, in short he is a philistine, and even when his genuine good intentions, his serious desire for progress still occasionally breaks through, I still feel like weeping every time, although it is only natural."[13]

Later in the letter he addressed the matter of the election directly: "About the Singakademie? Ask Moscheles about it.[14] Things are just the same as when he was here; no-one believes it. They still waver between Rungenhagen and me, and four months ago I was stupid enough not to beg them right away to be kind enough to leave me unshorn. Now they shear me thoroughly and spoil my wool in the process; everyone who meets me knows a new bit of gossip."[15]

Mendelssohn could not even take pleasure in the success of the three charity concerts that he had planned and conducted in November, December and January. Berlin's leading critic, Ludwig Rellstab, described them as "more significant for art than a whole year of the usual concerts,"[16] while the reviewer for the Leipzig *Allgemeine musikalische Zeitung* thought that "through these highly interesting musical performances, which he organized, he revealed himself not only as an outstanding piano virtuoso of the first rank, an instrumental composer of genius and diligence and a skilful conductor, but also earned twofold thanks for his achievements on behalf of art and the charitable aims of his concerts."[17] The concerts were to some extent perhaps consciously designed to remind the members of the Singakademie of Mendelssohn's practical capabilities, but successful though they may have been, they did not affect the outcome.

On 22 January a formal election was held, in which 148 votes were cast for Rungenhagen, eighty-eight for Mendelssohn and four for Eduard August Grell. The formalities of the matter were finally laid to rest in February, shortly after Mendelssohn's twenty-fourth birthday. As he informed Klingemann: "My birthday was nice, but I must tell you that the letter I received from you was one of the best presents; Heinrich Beer,[18] whom I treat in a shamefully off-hand manner, gave me the manuscript of Beethoven's C Major Trio and an almost touching letter of Mozart's in which he applies to the Vienna city authorities for an unpaid post, adding that his musical talents are known abroad and that his name is worthy of consideration. At the same time, I had to write to the Singakademie, which had offered me the post of vice-director, after choosing Rungenhagen, with trumpets and drums, as director. I think my answer would have turned out rather blunt, but the letter [of Mozart's] made me feel humble, and so I merely told them with polite expressions that they could go hang themselves."[19] The position of vice-director was then offered to Grell, who had already acted as such during the interregnum after Zelter's death; he occupied the position until 1853, when he succeeded Rungenhagen as director.

Although this was materially the end of the matter, its effects on Mendelssohn were enduring. It was not so much that he was deeply disappointed at his failure to obtain the post, for it seems clear that he had never really considered it as the goal of his ambition, but rather that he had been exposed to the unpleasantness and humiliation attendant upon the contest with Rungenhagen. Coming on top of earlier disappointments (most notably the disagreeable circumstances surrounding the production of his opera *Die Hochzeit des Camacho* in 1827) and the refusal of the Royal Orchestra to perform under his direction in 1828,[20] the experience left him with a lasting distaste for Berlin, which even his later appointment as Generalmusikdirektor and the other distinctions bestowed on him in the city could not wholly efface. The expressions of disgust about Berlin that appear several times in his letters to Klingemann during the Singakademie affair are mirrored over and over again in his later correspondence with those close to him. It is evident from his comments to Klingemann in February 1833 that he had convinced himself that his feelings about Berlin were objectively sound and not merely a manifestation of his own discontent: "This is really a dump; I am not against it in a partisan way, believe me, but at times it makes one despair, I don't think China can be much worse, and less conscious, more natural. The whole city is just as it was when I left it three years ago; and 1830[21] lies between, incredible times, 'deplorable revolutions' as our countrymen say, but as yet nothing has penetrated here, we have not woken up or gone to sleep, it is as if time stood still. Formerly I attributed all this to my bad mood, not my mood to all this, but now when I feel I am free, now

I see that it is not my fault. The social gatherings are boring, they are neither sociable nor outward-looking. One can only be comfortable when one retreats behind one's own walls; that I am now doing vigorously."[22] On the other hand, the affair provided him with an object lesson in human relations, and it may help to explain the anxious concern he showed, especially in connection with his appointment to Leipzig, not to be put in the position of displacing anyone from a position that he might reasonably be seen to have a claim to occupy.

18 · Düsseldorf

The circumstances in which Mendelssohn obtained his first professional post are not wholly clear. Some sort of connection with the Lower Rhine Music Festival seems to have been established in 1832, as the letter written from Paris to his father on 21 February 1832 (quoted above) implies. The 1832 festival, in Cologne, was conducted by Ferdinand Ries, but it is possible that Mendelssohn had received some sort of invitation to participate, which in the end he was unable to accept. Ferdinand von Woringen's account (quoted below) indicates that it was Ries who, after meeting Mendelssohn in Berlin in the autumn of 1832, was instrumental in securing the invitation for him to conduct the festival in 1833. There were however, other forces at work, for in February 1833 Mendelssohn also received a commission to write instrumental music for a production of *Der standhafte Prinz* (a German version of Calderon's *El principe constante*), which was to be produced under Immermann at the Düsseldorf theatre, and to direct its performance. This was, as he informed Klingemann, in connection with "a society for the improvement of the theatre there, which under Immermann, Uetritz, etc., will bring classical works to performance as perfectly as possible."[23] The official invitation to conduct the 1833 festival was conveyed to Mendelssohn by a committee including Otto von Woringen (1760–1838), head of the civic authority in Düsseldorf (Regierungspräsident). A close and enduring relationship quickly developed between Mendelssohn and the Woringen family, especially Otto's son Ferdinand, with whom he was already on friendly terms.

The intimacy of Mendelssohn's relationship with the Woringen family, attested by many letters he received from them,[24] gives particular interest to an account of his two years in Düsseldorf, signed "v. W.," which was written for the *Neue Berliner Musikzeitung* on 16 November 1847 under the immediate impact of his death. The author was undoubtedly Ferdinand von Woringen, who was resident in Berlin at the time. Although the account is written in a partisan spirit, it gives a vivid impression of the impact those who were personally attached to Mendelssohn felt he had made on the musical life of the region, and it provides information, particularly about Ferdinand Ries's involvement in Mendelssohn's appointment, that is not mentioned elsewhere. As the article appears to have received little or no attention in the Mendelssohn literature, it is given here in full.

> A gifted, rich human life is ended. The beautiful hopes,
> for whose fulfilment the present and the future could still
> believe they had a well-founded claim, rest in the grave.
> They were justified by the splendid gifts that the genius,
> who has been parted from us too early, offered to his
> contemporaries in a brief period, in rich abundance, in
> the most varied directions and in the beauty of great per-
> fection. We dedicate our lives to his true memory and
> live in continual enjoyment of his works, whose number
> and range, whose maturity and individual abundance of
> beauty might richly stand as the work of a much longer
> lifetime. Its significance for art and its progress in our
> time calls for a comprehensive, serious evaluation, and it
> may well soon receive this from a more competent hand.
> Simply let the author of such a document be given ac-
> cess to every source that, apart from revealing the artistic
> impact and greatness of the departed, may facilitate the
> perception and portrayal of what Felix Mendelssohn-
> Bartholdy was as boy, youth and man, what he was as a
> thinker, who in the academic field had rare and wide-
> ranging intellectual knowledge at his disposal, and what
> he was as friend and father of a family. We believe, since
> we had the advantage of his affection and friendship—

and such a statement is justified by a life shared over several years—that we can unhesitatingly say that the gifts of his spirit in that respect were just as great as his artistic activities; that we consider him no less perfect in that aspect of his human existence, in his intellectual cultivation and in the rich possession of a noble, true heart, and, in consequence, that we consider the depiction of his inner and outer life all the more important a task, because from this the artist and creative genius received the initial consecration, for which he was able to derive his gifts just as much from the depth of a full, feeling heart as from the clarity of bright understanding and testing thought and similarly from an inexhaustible spring of talents. We were privileged to share with Felix Mendelssohn-Bartholdy the time when, at the beginning of his public activity in Germany, he was civic music director in Düsseldorf, and the love that we cherished for the deceased may justify us in considering ourselves called to cast a glance back to that time that can, as an episode, offer a contribution to our Felix's biography, in which the time of his first activity in the Rhineland had a significance that was all the greater because it undoubtedly remained not without influence for his later work and for the direction of his artistic activity.

Since 1818[25] the Lower Rhine Music Festival had been an annual event in the Rhineland at Whitsuntide. From comparatively small beginnings, furthered and sustained as a result of many battles by true friends of art, an institution was established, which, from the year 1824, gained the significance of a national Rhenish music festival. At that time the best German musicians: Spohr, Schneider of Dessau, above all F. Ries devoted their participation,[26] their activity, to the Lower Rhine Music Festival; composers and artists came from far and wide to take part in these festivals. As they gained further significance they worked in return on the spirit that was particularly important for the love of art. The more serious direction, the predilection for oratorio, predominated in the Rhineland, even in smaller places. Where one annually found delight in Handel's larger works, the preference for such worthy artistic creations could only grow and remain dominant, and we believe we do not exaggerate when we attribute to the Lower Rhine Music Festivals—in particular to the solicitude which F. Ries devoted to them at that time—the fact that the shallow type of music that is nowadays already widespread found a lasting place in the Rhineland only to a restricted extent.

As a supporter of the Lower Rhine Music Festival he [Ries] had come to know Felix Mendelssohn-Bartholdy in Berlin in the Autumn of 1832, soon after his return from his several years of travelling in France, Italy, etc. From the first moment of this acquaintance Ries became warmly attached to the richly gifted one, and when the Lower Rhine Music Festival was due to be held in Düsseldorf at Whitsuntide 1833, this resulted in a proposal to transfer the direction of the festival to Felix Mendelssohn-Bartholdy, since F. Ries, the native born and resident conductor of the festival in previous years, was at that time away in England.[27] Felix Mendelssohn-Bartholdy was happy to accept the offer that was made to him. He came a good while before Whitsuntide to Düsseldorf and directed the choral rehearsals for the festival, at which *Israel in Egypt* was given for the first time under his direction, the performance being glorified by the participation of a celebrated female artist still living in Berlin.[28] This music festival was like no earlier one in its successful realization, through being blessed with the most universal lively participation, the latter being chiefly called forth by the invigorating, inspiring direction of the young man who was at that time in his 25th year, by whose acknowledged mastery even the oldest participants felt themselves happily swept along. Whoever at that time attended the orchestral rehearsals of *Israel*, the "Pastoral Symphony" of Beethoven and his overture to *Leonore*, whoever felt the simple but inspired manner with which Felix knew how to bind into a whole the musical forces that had hurried together from all around, and how to gain the accomplishment of a breath of perfection that had previously remained unattainable, was also won over by him. Felix later celebrated greater triumphs in larger circles and for more important achievements, but earlier, perhaps, hardly such a great one, issuing so purely from the first impressions of his personality, which won all hearts, and from his other well-known more excellent artistic abilities. We must particularly consider one circumstance. The earlier conductors of the music festivals, recognizing the difficulties of moulding such a large mass of singers and instrumentalists, who had streamed together from far and wide, into a polished whole that was also sensitive to detail, had always divided the orchestra into solo and tutti groups,[29] and putting the best forces into the former, had sought to heighten the effect of the performance by the alternation of the *piano* of the solo orchestra with the *forte* of the total body. Felix Mendelssohn-Bartholdy did not agree with that. It did not make sense to him that since everyone had hastened to the festival with the greatest desire for joyful involvement, not everyone was also just as able to follow his indication for *piano* as for *forte*. He maintained: "Everyone has come to sing and play, not partly to rest [pausieren: i.e., in the musical sense]," and lo, it was almost miraculous how quickly, with what success and with how few and unstressful rehearsals the total effect was reached and in such a manner greatly enhanced. Previously the orchestral rehearsals, which began two days before Whitsunday, had often lasted into the late afternoon even on the festival days. F. M-B. knew how to make them altogether less extensive and less tiring, and even dispensed with the rehearsal on the morning of the first festival day. All the participants joyfully knew how much the excellence of the achievements had gained thereby. Everyone, particularly the former tutti players, who for the most part were not inferior to the solo players in accomplishment, were heartily thankful for this essential alteration of Mendelssohn's, and the listeners had gained a degree of effectiveness in the performance that was foreign to us until then. The earlier arrangement could not be re-established at any later Rhenish music festival.

The musical festival of 1833 was over. The music had died away, and the mass had melted into the distance. But nearer to hand the festival and the enthusiastic love for Felix had a lasting effect. Already, during the days of the festival, a music society had formed in Düsseldorf that set itself the goal of fostering serious music for public performance. A constitution was drawn up, and under the patronage of HRH Prince Friedrich of Prussia, the society came immediately into being and chose Felix Mendelssohn-Bartholdy as musical director. He was charged with:

a) The direction of the vocal and instrumental music societies, two separate institutions, which had long existed and now obtained a conductor in Felix on condition that they took part in the public activities that were to be undertaken by the newly established society;

b) The establishment of these activities in at least 8 yearly musical performances in concert as well as in church music, of which the number, apart from the musical masses that took place on high feast days, were fixed at four yearly; and finally

c) The direction of the Lower Rhine Music Festival, if that were to occur in Düsseldorf, where in a rotating sequence with Cologne and Aachen, the festival was produced every three years.

Soon after the festival Felix Mendelssohn-Bartholdy entered upon his new duties as civic music director.

At the same time as the Music Society, there came into being a joint-stock company for the founding of a permanent civic theatre under Immerman's direction, and

Mendelssohn had undertaken to take part as a co-director of the opera, for the immediate direction of which an outstanding artist, Julius Rietz from Berlin, was called to Düsseldorf. At first Felix Mendelssohn-Bartholdy had also dedicated his participation to this institution with the same keenness that he always devoted to every task that he chose and undertook. However, the insufficient success of the opera within an institution that had set itself the fine goal of spoken theatre, which was capable of being attained with great success under Immermann, and also perhaps the perception that the very time-consuming cares occasioned by this aspect of his activity would narrowly constrict the achievement of the initially proposed intentions and leave him little time for creative work, caused Felix Mendelssohn to distance himself from the theatre, especially since he knew that its musical interests were completely safe in his friend Julius Rietz's hands.[30]

On the other hand his artistic direction of the Choral Society provides us with a fruitful area for consideration. The achievements of the Music Society in the concert performances and particularly in the church-music performances that were organized during the years 1833–1835 have given telling evidence of the manner in which Felix knew how to put his intentions into practice and breathe life into the musical activities of Düsseldorf. At present we unfortunately lack the material that is carefully preserved on the spot, which would be necessary to go into detail in this article about that time and to give evidence of the influence that Felix gained with the public for the musical achievements of Düsseldorf. We shall gladly be willing to offer these details to his biographer. This article is only intended to provide an indication for the latter and a reminiscence of that time, from faithful memories, for Mendelssohn's friends. We have therefore still the following to say.

That was the time in which artistic life in Düsseldorf

was also stimulated to the most felicitous developments by its Academy [of art]. Under Schadow, and together with him Lessing, Hübner, Sohn, Hildebrandt, Bendemann, Schirmer, Schrödter, Nerenz and many others, had at that time unfolded their artistic gifts to reveal the most beautiful blossom. With all these, with the inspiring influence that Immermann and Schnaase in general, and von Wuhtritz and others in particular, in constant partnership with the artists and their friends, must have exercised, Felix worked and lived in his circle, to which all these belonged, here too co-operating or happily participating in the inspiring creations of the honoured and beloved friend. Who, among those of the above-mentioned who are still living, will not think with delight about the artistic achievements that the co-operation of all the united artistic forces called forth? We recall the depiction of living tableaux from *Israel in Egypt*, accompanied by the choruses that they illustrated, performed by the Choral Society under F. M-B.'s direction on the occasion of the presence of His Majesty the present king when he was crown prince in the year 1833; in addition we recall the church music in Holy Week when Mendelssohn performed the choral music from the Sistine Chapel and had the Lamentations sung by a single voice in the original, simple plainsong without any accompaniment in the dark church, with deeply moving effect on all the hearers, and he even provided soul-stirring organ playing in the pauses; finally we remember the performances which took place in the more restricted circles of the members of the Choral Society under Felix's leadership, and which led to perfection of the highest kind, thus *The Seasons* of Haydn, for which Mendelssohn with Ed. Franck accompanied on two pianos and through their brilliant treatment of this accompaniment sent all the participants into transports of delight, which did not cause one to miss the orchestra; the motets of [J.] S. Bach, the Marcello Psalms, the grand Passion Music, etc., then again the performances from *Euryanthe, Ali Baba* [Cherubini], the Mozart and Cherubini Requiems, etc. It may specially be remarked that Felix was extremely sparing with the performance of his own works, so that only the most persistent requests could induce him to include one of his own works in the repertoire, while on the other hand he was very willing to play publicly, and the concert bills of that period also provide frequent evidence of his own performances, with which he adorned the concerts in the best manner and ignited zeal for emulation in the artists. If on such occasions Julius Rietz and his excellent cello appeared with him, or if other artists, who for Mendelssohn's sake never neglected to include Düsseldorf on their route at that time, were stimulated in their aims by joint efforts—it was everywhere his inspiring, productive activity that brought the artistic and musical life of Düsseldorf at that time to that point which will be remembered there as long as contemporaries are able to recall these efforts and their fine results. Just as, in the concert activities, Felix Mendelssohn accustomed the public to only the best in music and gave a hearing to the excellent works of Handel, *Messiah, Samson, Israel, Judas Maccabaeus,* etc., of Seb. Bach, Beethoven, Mozart, Haydn, Cherubini, C. M. von Weber and the old Italian composers always in precisely calculated alternation, so he also brought the church music to the dignified level where the service was genuinely edifying and uplifting. He was responsible for dispensing with the practice of interpolating overtures from operas during the Mass, and everyone approved his choice of music appropriate to the place and more worthy of the purpose.

Mendelssohn's effect on the furtherance of public music in Düsseldorf would have been accompanied by complete success, quite in accordance with his expectations, if the musical forces, particularly the orchestra, could have been brought into a better, more satisfactory condition.

Good voices and also sound musical education among individuals were not lacking, and what the town itself could not provide could be found at the right time elsewhere. It was only for the instrumental parts that there was less adequate provision. The available means did not allow the establishment of a permanent orchestra. At the time this consisted of the members of the former Town Music [Stadtmusik], to which others from among the military musicians of the garrison were added. There were accomplished people among them; however, a closer personal relationship with the music director was scarcely possible for them, since to them music remained primarily a milch cow, but only a few were able to recognize what the master was able to offer them. Thus occasionally conflict and annoyance were unavoidable, which, in such a partnership, necessitated *rapprochement*.[31] Everything was done to keep the unpleasantnesses that arose from the situation from impinging upon the friend and master; yet it was impossible to shield him entirely from them, and it is most probable that these drawbacks, which it was impossible to remove in the brief period of 2 1/2 years, contributed to Mendelssohn's willingness to hark to the call to Leipzig and leave the Rhineland and his true friends, as he was no longer able to cherish the hope that better means of attaining happier, freer performance of his own and other works, removed from the influence of inhibiting personalities, could be provided for him in Düsseldorf.

If we here hint at the motives that took him away from Düsseldorf and the Rhineland sooner than his own inclinations, dependent on numerous bonds of friendship, might have done, we must not forget the more pleasing retrospect, which takes account, in addition to his public activity, of the quieter influences that had promoted and blessed his sociable relationships. F. M-B. was loved by everyone for the sake of his affable personality and honoured for the gifts that he was able to give with a liberal hand. Everyone sought him out, everyone wanted to be near him; and if, indeed, he only selectively found himself inclined to allow his wonderful talent to give way to the common desire of every society, his friends and the families with which he was intimate were nevertheless not allowed to go without his readiness to brighten and enliven the domestic circle through his playing and his participation in musical entertainments. Many of his smaller compositions, the little duets for female voices, individual choruses, songs for male voices, Songs without Words, etc. owe their existence to this participation, and if he guided the performers along the proper path concurrently by his leadership and advice, without letting himself be tempted merely to give instruction, he thus gained all the more credit with many and by this means also laid the foundations of a faithful remembrance. But it was not merely in the field of music that Felix's comrades learned to honour and love him. Advancement in every respect, where the good, the beautiful and the cheerful were concerned, was a necessity for him. Thus there were his activities among the painters, the poets and artists among his companions. We think here particularly of the time when Seydelmann was in Düsseldorf; we point to F. M-B.'s occupation with painting, which he pursued seriously and successfully under Schirmer's guidance, and to the merry activities among the friends, which Stockkämpfcher or Grafenberg organized, to which F. M-B.'s small chestnut [horse] trotted out with him. His creative work inspired every activity of the others, whether he would compose, or busy himself with the translation of poems by Byron, or perhaps with the translation of sonnets by Dante into the metre of the original and with critical commentary thereon; everywhere F. M-B.'s brilliant endeavours came to light and also the often highly amusing games among the young companions could not deny the origin of their witty, unrestrained, merry exuberance.

It was a wonderful time for the unfolding of many fresh, youthful powers, which spirit, head and heart developed in united effort towards the most joyful goal.

Around autumn 1835 Mendelssohn left Düsseldorf in order to assume the direction of the Gewandhaus concerts in Leipzig. In Düsseldorf there remained an unfillable void, and one could only be grateful to him that in his successor Jul. Rietz he left behind a friend who was able to sustain and further the framework that he had created. The Music Society that was founded for Mendelssohn's sake remained in existence, and it must certainly be seen as a sign of the preservation of that which Felix created that after J. Rietz the direction of Düsseldorf's musical life was committed to F. Hiller's care. Mendelssohn's participation and care remained dedicated to his friends on the Rhine even from afar. In 1835 he had directed the Lower Rhine Music Festival in Cologne and committed himself to the 1836 festival that was to take place in Düsseldorf. Who would deny that the character of these music festivals continued to have a decided effect on the course that Felix Mendelssohn had chosen to follow in his works initially, and subsequently with growing interest? In these festivals sacred music, the oratorio, the symphony, and solemn, serious music in general, were allotted their place. Here, where only large-scale works succeeded in being performed and solo performances were not permitted, such works were assured of the appropriate, dignified performance. We do not deny that our Felix's spiritual and artistic course would have led him in any case to the predestined field of activity. Whether *St Paul*, however, would already have succeeded in coming to performance by Whitsuntide 1836 if the Düsseldorf relationships and connections had not enlivened him is certainly open to question. Unfortunately, a deplorable situation for some time threatened danger to the work that had been begun in 1835 for the 1836 Düsseldorf Music Festival. Mendelssohn's father, to whom F. M-B., in a circle of friends in Düsseldorf after the Cologne Music Festival in the summer of 1835, gave a first hearing of the already finished scene of Stephen from *St Paul*, and who, moved to tears by what he had heard, thanked Felix with the words to which the son had already become accustomed in his earliest years: "Thank you, Felix. But you must make it even better!", suddenly died in Berlin. The son had wanted to perform his work for his beloved father at the 1836 festival in Düsseldorf. As this had become impossible, he did not want to hear anything of the festival or of *St Paul* for a long time. Finally genius triumphed over sorrow and the music festival of 1836 provided Felix Mendelssohn with a triumph that was transplanted from the Rhine throughout the whole musical world and out over the broad ocean. It was in Düsseldorf that F. M-B. heard his work for the first time in its entirety; many choruses had been brought there almost as soon as they had been written, for he sent the individual numbers of part two from Leipzig in a great hurry, one after another, as soon as they were completed. It was only in the days immediately before the festival that the tenor Cavatina was first composed. We shall never forget how, after his arrival in Düsseldorf, where J. Rietz directed the choral rehearsals, Felix made them sing the choruses "Mache dich auf, werde Licht" and the chorale "Wachet auf" for the first time, declaring beforehand that he had not yet heard either of them. At that time the singers had long finished rehearsing the first part, and that which inspiration and the most sincere devotion to the master and friend was able to achieve now showed itself in the liveliest manner. F. M-B., himself uplifted, sat at the piano accompanying with all his might and, as he was quite accustomed to do when he was in such a mood, rocked his body back and forth while playing. His eyes shone with light and finally tears of joy trickled down his cheeks. When the chorus came to an end, F. M-B. rose with the words: "Thank you. You will feel the composer's joy if he sees his work sung and felt like that. Thank you." He did not play any more that evening. Jul. Rietz had to continue the rehearsal and Felix sat at the back of the room in the corner, saying little and deep in his own thoughts.

And yet in the following rehearsal he was once again ready with the most apposite observations and with a hundred suggestions, which indicated how to render what had been heard in a more effective manner and made their desired effect on everyone concerned. It was, in fact, a distinct individual characteristic of his acute understanding and correct feeling that he knew how to indicate the most essential aspects of the interpretation and presentation of every musical composition, suggestively, simply and tellingly in few words. His words were like the highlights which the painter applies to complete his picture and which suddenly, like lightning, give the picture spirit, life and real truthfulness. Thus with little hints he wafted these fine nuances, a breath of perfection, into a musical performance that otherwise the best performance may well lack, and we should be delighted to praise and honour anyone among his successors who may have picked up this secret from him, by which his direction, which in its composure and sober calmness remained scarcely perceptible, appeared to be perfect. The brief, clear suggestions, in the simplest words, which he gave in the rehearsals, were paralleled in the performance by a lightning glance of his brilliant sparkling eye or a gesture of his gently raised hand.

Thus we knew him on the Rhine and thus he always lived in the memory of his contemporaries. The oratorio *St Paul* was a phenomenon there, the effect of which continues today and beyond. Mendelssohn's influence on the Rhine, despite his distance from it, grew ever greater. From then he directed the Lower Rhine Music Festival almost every year and always returned gladly to the place in Germany where the most flowery garlands were bestowed on him as director and as the creator of a fresh musical life.

A letter from Düsseldorf said: "Down to the lowest classes everything here seems as if it were stunned by the sudden, irreplaceable loss. Everyone knew him, everyone loved him; with his death everyone has lost a friend, a relation." Today a memorial celebration is being prepared, and just as it may not lack true memories and heartfelt tears for his untimely death, so may it retain the most heartfelt love for him and dedicate an everlasting reverence to his works.[32]

Woringen glossed over one of the less successful aspects of Mendelssohn's time in Düsseldorf: his relationship with Immermann and his withdrawal from involvement with the direction of the opera. From an early stage, albeit cautiously, Mendelssohn had allowed himself to be drawn into plans for the revitalization of the Düsseldorf theatre. During the winter of 1833 and 1834 he conducted a number of carefully prepared performances, beginning with *Don Giovanni*. In December he informed his parents that although he would not conduct all the operas ("for almost every week two operas are given, and the performers consider themselves absolved by one rehearsal"), he would undertake "six or eight classical performances every year" under the auspices of the projected Theatrical Association. Then, reporting Immermann's determination to devote himself full time to the theatre project, he continued: "I hear that most of the shareholders have only given their signatures on condition that *he* should undertake the plays, and *I* the operas; how this may be, lies close hidden as yet in the womb of time, but in any event I will not entirely withdraw from the affair."[33] The Theatrical Association was formally constituted on 10 March 1834, and Mendelssohn agreed to assume responsibility for the operas, which were to begin in the autumn. His continuing ambivalence, however, is indicated by his letter home on 28 March:

The matter has been very sensibly begun, and may turn out well; but I keep out of the way, because in spite of the pleasure that the opera, for instance, lately caused me, I can feel no sympathy for actual theatrical life, or the squabbles of the actors and the incessant striving after effect; it also estranges me too much from my own chief purpose in Düsseldorf, which is to work for myself. I am the chief superintendent of the musical performances, the arrangements of the orchestra, and the engagement of the singers, and about every month I have an opera to conduct (but even this is to depend on my own convenience); of course I still have my three months vacation: in short, I wish to be entirely independent of the theatre, and only to be considered a friend, but with no official duties; on this account I have given up all claim to any salary, which is to be transferred to a second conductor, on whom the chief trouble will devolve."[34]

The assistant conductor, Mendelssohn's friend Julius Rietz, came to Düsseldorf in September, but within a few weeks he was left as principal conductor, for after a rapid decline in Mendelssohn's relations with Immermann, resulting in an ill-tempered exchange of letters during October, Mendelssohn relinquished his responsibilities, having conducted only Weber's *Oberon*.[35] To his mother he wrote on 4 November 1834:

You always take me at once back home, and while I am reading your letters I am there once more. . . . To be thus transported home is most pleasant to me just at this time, when during the last few weeks I have been fuming and fretting in a rare fashion at Düsseldorf and its art doings, and Rhenish *soaring impulses*, and new efforts! I had fallen into a terrible state of confusion and excitement, and felt worse than during my busiest time in London. When I sat down to my work in the morning, at every bar there was a ringing at the bell: then came grumbling choristers to be snubbed, stupid singers to be taught, seedy musicians to be engaged; and when this had gone on the whole day, and I felt that all these things were for the sole benefit and advantage of the Düsseldorf theatre, I was provoked; at last, two days ago, I made a "salto mortale," and beat a retreat out of the

whole affair, and once more feel myself a man. This resignation was a very unpleasant piece of intelligence for
our theatrical autocrat, *alias* stage mufti; he compressed
his lips viciously, as if he would fain eat me up; however,
I made a short and very eloquent speech to the Director,
in which I spoke of my avocations as being of more consequence to me than the Düsseldorf theatre, much as I
etc.: in short, they let me off, on condition that I would
occasionally conduct; this I promised, and this I will certainly perform. I began a letter to Rebecca long ago,
containing the details of three weeks in the life of a Düsseldorf Intendant, which I have not yet finished, and I
upbraid myself for it.[36]

In his letter of 23 November to Rebecka he went into further detail:

We exchanged desperately uncivil letters, in which I was
obliged to be very circumspect in my style, in order to
leave no point unanswered, and to maintain my independent ground and basis; but I think I did credit to Herr
Heyse. We came to an agreement after this, but quarrelled again immediately, for he required me to go to
Aix, to hear and to engage a singer there, and this I did
not choose to do. Then I was desired to engage an orchestra,—that is, prepare two contracts for each member
and previously fight to the death about a dollar [thaler]
more or less of their monthly salary; then they went
away, then they came back and signed all the same, then
they all objected to sit at the second music desk, then
came the aunt of a very wretched performer, whom I
could not engage, and the wife and two little children of
another miserable musician, to intercede with the Director; then I allowed three fellows to play on trial, and
they played so utterly beneath contempt, that I really
could not agree to take any of them; then they looked
very humble, and went quietly away, very miserable,
having lost their daily bread; then came the wife again,

and wept. Out of thirty persons there was only one who said at once, "I am satisfied," and signed his contract; all the others bargained and haggled for an hour at least, before I could make them understand that I had a *prix fixe*. The whole day I was reminded of my father's proverb, "Asking and bidding make the sale"; but they were four of the most disagreeable days I ever passed. On the fourth, Klingemann arrived in the morning, saw the state of things, and was horrified. In the mean time Rietz studied the "Templar," morning and evening; the choruses got drunk, and I was forced to speak with authority; then they rebelled against the manager, and I was obliged to shout at them like Boots at an inn; then Madame Beutler became hoarse, and I was very anxious on her account (a new sort of anxiety for me, and a most odious one); then I conducted Cherubini's "Requiem" in the church, and this was followed by the first concert. In short I made up my mind to abdicate my intendant throne three weeks after the reopening of the theatre. The affair goes on quite as well as we could expect in Düsseldorf: Rietz's playing is admirable,—he is studious, accurate, and artistic, so that he is praised and liked by every one. The operas we have given hitherto are, the "Templar" twice, "Oberon" twice, which I conducted, "Fra Diavolo," and yesterday the "Freischütz." We are about to perform the "Entführung," the "Zauberflöte," the "Ochsenmenuett," the "Dorf Barbier," and the "Wasserträger." The operas are well attended but not the plays, so that the shareholders are sometimes rather uneasy; five of the company up to this time have actually run away, two of them being members of the orchestra.

The Committee gave a supper to the company, which was very dull, and cost each member of the Council (including myself) eleven dollars [thalers]; but pray refrain from all tokens of sympathy, in case of causing my tears to flow afresh. But since I have withdrawn from this sphere, I feel as if I were a fish thrown back into the water; my forenoons are once more at my own disposal, and in the evenings I can sit at home and read.[37]

Mendelssohn wrote in similar terms a few days later to his theatrical friend Eduard Devrient, concluding his account of the affair with the remark, "I did think of you much when I threw it up, and how you would growl over me; but suppose a year and a day went by, and I had accomplished nothing save official dignity and somewhat better performances in the Düsseldorf opera, would you not growl then? and so it is better thus. I go no more to sea, to sea. You might hand me Spontini's diploma upon a salver at this minute, I should not touch it; but to be musical conductor or Kapellmeister I have no objection, in Kyritz or where you like." Devrient, however, having quoted Mendelssohn's letter, claimed that this version of events did not tell the whole story.

> I could read through the lines of this letter that it was an exaggerated, and not ingenuous account of the rupture. The excellent letter of his father [see below] speaks of it in general terms, disapprovingly. I afterwards heard the particulars and am bound, in the interests of justice, to say that Felix was entirely in the wrong. It was unfortunate that he implicated himself in some of the business responsibilities, entirely unfitted as he was for them; but this fault is rather to be ascribed to the business-like Immermann, who ought to have known better, than to Mendelssohn, who, in his zeal for the cause, too hastily pledged himself. The radical error of incorporating a joint administration of opera and drama in the management of the theatre, Immermann was also answerable for. It was impossible that Felix should remain in so false a position; but he should have modified it, withdrawn into his functions as Kapellmeister, and if his resignation were inevitable, it should have taken place without acrimony. The breach was not brought about by the theatrical worries, as he represents, but by a personal quarrel with Immermann, in which Felix showed a hasty and snappish temper that one would hardly have suspected in him.[38]

Abraham Mendelssohn's letter to his son mentioned by Devrient, which was written a short while after the events, was undoubtedly salutary. Abraham, although himself given to excessive irritability, was an experienced man of the world and, as far as his son's character and career were concerned, a perceptive observer.

> With regard to the administrative career, it gives rise to another series of reflections, which I wish to impress upon you. Those who have the opportunity and the inclination to become more closely and intimately acquainted with you, as well as those to whom you have the opportunity and the inclination to reveal yourself more fully, cannot fail to love and respect you. But this is really far from being sufficient to enable a man to enter on life with active efficiency; on the contrary, as you advance in years, and opportunity and inclination fail, both in others and yourself, it is much more likely to lead to isolation and misanthropy. Even what we consider faults will be respected, or at least treated with forbearance, when once firmly and thoroughly established in the world, while the individual himself disappears. He has least of all arrived at the ideal of virtue who exacts it most inexorably from others. The sternest moral principle is a citadel, the outworks of which may well be relinquished if by doing so we can fix ourselves more firmly in the centre, and defend that with our very life.
>
> Hitherto it is undeniable that you have never been able to divest yourself of a tendency to austerity and irascibility, suddenly grasping an object and as suddenly relinquishing it, and thus creating for yourself many obstacles in a practical point of view. For example I must confess that though I approve of your withdrawing from any active participation in the management of the details of the Düsseldorf theatre, I by no means approve of the manner in which you accomplished your object, since you undertook it voluntarily, and, to speak candidly, rather heedlessly. From the beginning you, most wisely,

declined any positive contract, and only agreed to undertake the study and conducting of particular operas, and,
in accordance with this resolution, very properly insisted
on the appointment of another music-director. When
you came here some time ago with the object of engaging your rank and file, I did not at all like the idea; I
thought, however, that as you were to be here at all
events, you could not with politeness decline this service.
But on your return to Düsseldorf, after wisely refusing to
undertake another journey for the purpose of making engagements for the theatre, instead of persevering in this
intention and getting rid of all annoyances, you allowed
yourself to be overwhelmed by them; and as they naturally became very obnoxious to you, instead of quietly
striving to remedy them, and thus gradually get rid of
them, you at one leap extricated yourself, and by doing
so undeniably subjected yourself to the imputation of
fickleness and unsteadiness, made a decided enemy of a
man whom at all events policy should have taught you
not to displease, and most probably lost the friendship of
many members of the committee, among whom there
are no doubt most respectable people. If my view of this
matter is incorrect, then teach me a better one.[39]

The lesson was not lost on Mendelssohn; indeed, it may be seen as
one of the most important formative experiences of his time in Düsseldorf. In his private relations and subsequent correspondence his continuing dislike of the distractions and restrictions imposed by official appointments is clearly apparent, but he showed more circumspection about
the responsibilities he was prepared to assume and took care not to act
so impulsively in public affairs thereafter. In fact, this was all part of the
process of becoming an effective practical musician, which he had consciously chosen to further by accepting the post in Düsseldorf. As he
wrote to Friedrich Kistner in January 1835: "Little by little I have set
myself the goal of being a practical musician and not a theoretical one.
I have sacrificed my independence to that goal here, since I could easily
live anywhere, in larger cities and ones more preferable to me, whether

employed or not; since it occurred to me that I would learn a few practical things here and then be able to make use of some abilities which until then I had lacked." By such means, he believed, he could more effectually accomplish his aim of exerting a beneficial influence on music and musical culture. That this was a conscious aim is apparent from many sources—for instance, at another point in the letter to Kistner he remarked: "For me the only motive for holding any sort of post lies in its sphere of influence, and as gladly as I would set aside my personal pleasure and well-being and all other considerations, so it is impossible to set aside, particularly with regard to this point, all of the plans and resolutions which I have made for my continued progress in music."[40]

Although Mendelssohn's time in Düsseldorf was fruitful for the region's music and for his own personal development, it was increasingly evident that the resources which he desired and required for the further evolution of his vision were not available to him there; and it seems likely that the theatre debacle had soured his feelings about the city to some extent. For his work as a composer, too, it had been a frustrating time. The two years he spent in Düsseldorf were among the most unproductive in his career. Although much of *St Paul* was written during this time, and the *Meeresstille* Overture and the "Italian" Symphony revised, the only substantial works he seems to have completed were the concert aria *Infelice*, a couple of short sacred compositions and a few other small pieces. A letter to Hiller of 14 March 1835, by which time he had determined to exchange his Düsseldorf post for one in Leipzig, provides a glimpse of his feelings at that time. After a few opening remarks he continued:

> There is no thought of my leaving Germany and going
> to England; who can have told you such a thing?
> Whether I stay at Düsseldorf longer than I am bound by
> my contract, which comes to an end next October, is an-
> other question; for there is simply nothing to be done
> here in the way of music, and I long for a better orches-
> tra, and shall probably accept another offer that I have
> had. I wanted to be quite free for a few years, and go on
> a sort of art-journey, and snap my fingers at musical di-
> rectorships and the like; but my father does not wish it,

and in this I follow him unconditionally. You know that from the very beginning all I wanted here was a really quiet time for writing some larger works, which will be finished by October; and so I hope to have made use of my stay. Besides it is very pleasant, for the painters are capital fellows, and lead a jolly life; and there is plenty of taste and feeling for music; only the means are so limited that it is unprofitable in the long run, and all one's trouble goes for nothing. I assure you that at the beat, they all come in separately, not one with any decision, and in the *pianos* the flute is always too high, and not a single Düsseldorfer can play a triplet clearly, but all play a quaver and two semi-quavers instead, and every *Allegro* leaves off twice as fast as it began, and the oboe plays E natural in C minor, and they carry their fiddles under their coats when it rains, and when it is fine they don't cover them at all—and if you once heard me conduct this orchestra, not even four horses could bring you there a second time. And yet there are one or two musicians among them, who would do credit to any orchestra, even to your [Paris] conservatoire; but that is just the misery in Germany—the bass trombones and the drum and the double bass excellent, and everything else quite abominable. There is also a choral society of 120 members, which I have to coach once a week, and they sing Handel very well and correctly, and in the winter there are six subscription concerts, and in the summer every month a couple of masses, and all the *dilettanti* fight to the death, and nobody will sing the solos, or rather everybody wants to, and they hate putting themselves forward, though they are always doing it; but you know what music is in a small German town—Heaven help us![41]

19 · Leipzig

Mendelssohn's dissatisfaction with the situation in Düsseldorf led him to consider a number of moves during the latter part of 1834. From Munich came a proposal that he should become director of the opera, which he rejected. From Leipzig several propositions were made. There was talk of instituting a professorship of music for him at the university (that was the matter about which he wrote to Kistner in January 1835), but he turned that down just as firmly as he had rejected a similar suggestion in Berlin several years earlier. He also declined to consider the post of cantor at the Thomasschule but did enter into correspondence about a proposition that he should become civic music director and director of the Gewandhaus concerts. His letter of 16 April 1835 to Conrad Schleinitz,[42] later to become one of his most intimate friends and an unqualified admirer of his genius, nicely reveals his feelings about the balance between the official responsibility required of him as a professional musician and the independence that his financial position made possible.

> I thank you cordially for your last letter, and for the friendly interest which you take in me, and in my coming to Leipzig. As I perceive by the Herr Stadtrath Porsche's letter, as well as by that of the Superintendent of the concerts, that my going there does not interfere with any other person, one great difficulty is thus obviated.[43] But another has now arisen, as the letter of the Superintendent contains different views with regard to the situation from yours. The direction of twenty concerts and extra concerts is named as among the duties, but a benefit concert (about which you wrote to me) is not mentioned. I have consequently said in my reply what I formerly wrote to you, that, in order to induce me to consent to the exchange, I wish to see the same pecuniary advantages secured to me that I enjoy here. If a benefit concert, as you say, would bring from two to three hundred [thalers], this sum would certainly be a considerable increase to my salary: but I must say that I never

made such a proposal, and indeed would not have accepted it had it been made to me. It would be a different thing if the association chose to give an additional concert, and to devote a share of the profits towards the increase of my established salary. During my musical career, I have always resolved never to give a concert for myself (for my benefit). You probably are aware that, personally, pecuniary considerations would be of less importance to me, were it not that my parents (and I think rightly) exact from me that I should follow my art as a profession and gain my livelihood by means of it. I, however, reserved the power of declining certain things which, in reference to my favoured position in this respect, I will never do; for example, giving concerts or lessons. But I quite acknowledge the propriety of what my parents insist on so strongly, that in all other relations I shall gladly consider myself as a musician who lives by his profession. Thus, before giving up my present situation, I must ascertain that one equally advantageous is secured to me. I do not consider that what I require is at all presumptuous, as it has been offered to me here, and on this account I trust that a similar course may be pursued in Leipzig. An association was at that time formed here, who intrusted to me the duty of conducting the Vocal Association, concerts, etc., and made up my salary partly in common with the Vocal Association and partly by the profits of the concerts. Whether anything of this kind be possible with you, or whether it could be equalized by an additional concert, or whether the execution of particular duties is to be imposed on me, I cannot, of course, pretend to decide. I only wish that, in one way or another, a definite position should be assured to me, like the one I enjoy here; and if your idea about the benefit concert could be modified and carried out, there would then be a good hope for me that the affair might turn out according to my wish.

If you can induce the directors to fulfil the wishes I

have expressed, you will exceedingly oblige me, for you know how welcome a residence and active employment in your city would be to me. In any event, continue your friendly feelings to me, and accept my thanks for them.[44]

At the time Mendelssohn moved to Leipzig in August 1835 his reputation with the general concert-going public as a composer was still fairly slight, and the music journals paid relatively little attention to his works. The production of his oratorio *St Paul*, which was to bring his name to the attention of a much larger public and to mark him out decisively as the leading German composer of his generation, was still a year away; but his travels to England and to various important German cities had already made him familiar to musicians and cognoscenti as an exceptional composer and practical musician. He had also gained the reputation of animating and enlivening the musical culture of any place or organization with which he was associated. In Leipzig his qualities in this respect were to be brilliantly demonstrated. Half way through his first season there the *Allgemeine musikalische Zeitung* observed: "How justly we report first on our chief musical institution, subscription [Gewandhaus] concerts, which have been extraordinarily frequented this year, under the direction of Herr F. Mendelssohn-Bartholdy, about whose ability the enthusiasm of the town was already very great before his arrival, and has now even grown."[45]

For the majority of these townsfolk, the enthusiasm that preceded and greeted Mendelssohn continued throughout the next twelve years. In 1840, for instance, a reviewer of the Gewandhaus concert of 1 January remarked: "How great the interest of the public is for these concerts as a whole was proved yet again on this day by the concert hall being truly filled to bursting by auditors, and particularly by the voluntary participation of a significant number of artistically accomplished amateurs in the performance of the vocal pieces."[46] Lampadius, who observed Mendelssohn's Leipzig career at first hand, summed up his time there as "an epoch full of the richest, most varied, most untiring activity for himself, and one of such splendor in the musical life of Leipzig as can hardly be expected to come again," and continued:

He directed the Gewandhaus concerts personally from 1835 to 1841; producing during this time a great number of master-pieces of enduring excellence, yet compelled to earn his way into public favor step by step. He knew how to command the resources of the place perfectly in orchestra, dilettanti, and chorus singers; to bear with them with the greatest patience; to stimulate them all into activity; and thus to obtain effects almost unequalled until then. For he did not confine himself to the almost purely classical training necessary for the Gewandhaus concerts, but improved every opportunity to influence the public taste; so that it may be truly said, that, in the practice of one art, he developed an appreciation of all, and gave to the life of the cultivated people of Leipzig a higher ideal by the pure moral and truly aesthetic influence which he exercised over them. He did this not only by an always admirable selection of the music to be performed at the concerts, but also by awakening, through his superb direction of the orchestra, a taste on the part of the public for the works of the later great masters; as, for example, the "Ninth Symphony" of Beethoven. He not only cultivated a relish for the historical development of music, but he summoned the mighty spirits of the past to the help and delight of the present age, and often combined the entire musical resources of Leipzig in rendering some of their master-pieces.[47]

Lampadius also commented upon the major change in the method of directing the Gewandhaus concerts, which Mendelssohn had immediately implemented: the substitution of baton conducting for direction by the leader.[48]

Although Mendelssohn may have raised the Gewandhaus orchestra to a new peak of excellence, he started from a position that was much better than the one with which he had been faced in Düsseldorf. The Leipzig orchestra was well established and had enjoyed a succession of strong leaders in Bartolomeo Campagnoli (1797–1816), and Heinrich August Matthai (1817–1835). Under Matthai, who directed all instrumental pieces from the leader's desk (only choral works being directed by a time beater), the standard of performance had kept pace with the increasing difficulty of the repertoire. Mendelssohn himself described his first encounter with the orchestra in positive terms to his family, and he outlined his determination to enhance its standard still further: "I cannot tell you how satisfied I am with this beginning, and with the whole aspect of my position here. It is a quiet, regular, official business. That the Institute [the Gewandhaus concerts] has been established for fifty-six years is very perceptible, and moreover, the people seem most friendly and well-disposed towards me and my music. The orchestra is very good, and thoroughly musical; and I think that six months hence it will be much improved, for the sympathy and attention with which these people receive my suggestions, and instantly adopt them, were really touching in both the rehearsals we have hitherto had; there was as great a difference as if another orchestra had been playing. There are still some deficiencies in the orchestra, but these will be supplied by degrees; and I look forward to a succession of pleasant evenings and good performances."[49]

Throughout his time in Leipzig Mendelssohn continually strove to raise the quality of performance by improving the conditions of the players and by engaging the best talent available whenever a vacancy occurred. He was also among the first important German musicians to exert himself strenuously on behalf of rank-and-file musicians and, like his older contemporary Spohr, was motivated just as much by the conviction that music was an honourable profession, and that its practitioners deserved fair financial recompense and security, as by the recognition that a well-paid and contented orchestra is likely to attract and retain better musicians. Until Mendelssohn arrived in Leipzig, the members of the orchestra had been obliged to supplement their incomes by the demeaning activity of playing in coffee-and-cake gardens, to the accompaniment of conversations and clattering crockery during the summer season.[50] Matthai's illness and death in 1835 may fortuitously have eased Mendelssohn's task, for it meant not only that he could more easily assume sole control over the performances but also that he was able to secure the appointment of his old friend, the twenty-five-year-old Ferdinand David, to the vacant post of leader, after a successful trial period, in December 1835. Over the next few years, with David's energetic support, the standard of performance was slowly raised by careful rehearsal, good new appointments and every means that could be employed to get the best out of the existing players.

In 1838 Mendelssohn achieved a small increase in the number of string players, from 8 first violins, 8 second violins, 4 violas, 3 'cellos, 3 basses to 9, 8, 5, 5, 4. At the same time, he also worked hard to improve the members' employment conditions. As he informed Moscheles in November 1839, "My present hobby is the improvement of our poor orchestra. After no end of letter-writing, soliciting, and importuning, I have succeeded in getting their salaries raised by five hundred thalers; and before I leave them I mean to get them double that amount. If this is granted, I won't mind their setting a monument to Sebastian Bach in front of the Saint Thomas school; but first, mind you, the grant. You see I am a regular small-beer Leipziger. But really you would be touched if you could see and hear for yourself how my good fellows put heart and soul into their work, and strive to do their best."[51] He was also able to establish a formal pension fund in place of the occasional benefit concerts that had previously provided aid in cases of serious need.

The results of Mendelssohn's efforts on the quality of performances are attested by many contemporary accounts. Some, doubtless exaggerating, hailed the Gewandhaus orchestra under Mendelssohn's direction and David's leadership as the finest in Europe, but all seem to have agreed that, although inferior to some of the most celebrated orchestras in particular qualities, it deserved to be numbered among the best in respect of its overall achievement. Hiller, who went to stay with Mendelssohn in Leipzig for the first time in 1839, recorded a balanced judgment of the orchestra's achievements at that time, noting that though it could not compete with the Paris Conservatoire orchestra in terms of excellent players, this was counterbalanced "by the spirit and life which Mendelssohn instilled into the orchestra."[52]

Henry Chorley, who visited Leipzig during the same season as Hiller, took a similar view of the relationship between the Leipzig and Paris orchestras. He contrasted the technical efficiency of the Conservatoire orchestra with the spiritual exaltation of the Leipzig ensemble, which emanated from Mendelssohn's leadership. "Never, indeed," he wrote, "did I hear the symphonies of Beethoven so intensely enjoyed as at Leipzig, and never so admirably performed. As regards those works of the Shakespeare of music, I felt, for the first time in my life, richly and thoroughly satisfied beyond reserve or question. There was a breadth of freedom in their outlines, a thorough proportion in all their parts, a poetical development of all their choice and picturesque ideas, which fully compensated for the occasional want of the hyper-brilliancy, and the hyper-delicacy, on the possession of which my friends in Paris boast themselves so vaingloriously." Chorley referred in particular to "those small aggravations of emphasis, those slight retardations of time, neither finically careful, nor fatiguingly numerous,—for which imagination thirsts so eagerly, so rarely to be gratified." He considered them "no holiday effort, got up for once, but the staple mode of interpretation and execution belonging to the place. Till, indeed, I heard the Leipsic orchestra . . . I felt I had no right to say, 'Now I am indeed in the musical Germany of which I have so long dreamed.' " He later returned to the subject, adding that without having heard the Leipzig orchestra he would "not have ventured to print the strictures upon that marvel of mechanical perfection, the orchestra of the Conservatoire, which are recorded in a former page of these journals."[53]

Schumann's reviews of music in Leipzig at this time confirm the impression of an orchestra devoted to music, inspired by its conductor and well drilled by its leader. In his comments on the 1836 to 1837 season Schumann observed: "First, as all know, Mendelssohn conducted the principal events at the head of his faithful orchestra, with the power that is peculiarly his own, and with a zeal which must be partly inspired by the kindliness that greets him on all sides. If ever an orchestra, without a single exception, believed in and depended upon its director, ours thoroughly deserves praise for doing so. Of intrigues and cabals we have not heard a word; and the result of this harmony has been most favourable to art and artists."[54] After the next concert series, he wrote "Before we take leave of the Gewandhaus Concerts for half a year, we must award a crown of merit to its forty or fifty orchestral members. We have no solo-players like Brod in Paris, or Harper in London; but even these cities can scarcely boast such fine, united symphony playing. And this results from the nature of circumstances. Our musicians here form a family; they see each other and practise together daily; they are always the same, so that they are able to play a Beethoven symphony without notes. Add to these a concert-master who can conduct such scores from memory, a director who knows them by and reveres them at heart, and the crown is complete."[55]

Schumann's review of the 1839 to 1840 season, written after he had spent most of the previous year in Vienna, seems to acknowledge the continual development of the orchestra, both in the quality of its personnel and of its performances overall: "It is well known that a worthy home for German music has been secured in the now fifty-year-old Gewandhaus Concerts, and that this institution accomplishes more at present than it ever did before. With a famous composer at its head, the orchestra has brought its virtuosity to still greater perfection during the last few years. It has probably no German equal in its performance of symphonies, while among its members many finished masters of the several instruments are to be found."[56] Two years later, however, Moritz Hauptmann, newly arrived in Leipzig from Cassel, still contrasted the lack of really fine players with the musical effectiveness of the orchestra, writing to Spohr that "our wind-instrument players, though some are first-rate fellows, cut a poor figure as soloists, but the *ensemble* is very satisfactory, and the rhythmical *nuances* are as animated as those of good Quartet players."[57]

The mutual devotion that existed between the members of the Leipzig orchestra and their conductor is nicely illustrated by an exchange of letters in 1841, when Mendelssohn moved to Berlin in connection with King Friedrich Wilhelm IV's plans. On 9 August Mendelssohn sent Ferdinand David a letter to pass on to the orchestra. David replied: "Your letter to the orchestra will circulate tomorrow; it is as kind and heartfelt as we have come to expect from you (if there are no blunders). I shall put it into Grenser's head that he should answer you in the name of the orchestra."[58] Later in the month Grenser, one of the longest-standing members of the orchestra, composed the following response, which was signed by the whole orchestra.

> Your letter from Berlin, dated 9 August, with which you
> have honoured us, the members of the Leipzig orchestra,
> has aroused such lively feelings of joy and thankfulness
> in us that we could no longer keep them to ourselves in
> Leipzig. When you stepped into our midst as music di-
> rector six years ago, we loudly showed you our joy over
> your decision to place yourself at our head in order to
> lead us forward victoriously on the path of fame. How
> beautiful in their fulfilment are the happy hopes initiated

at that time, how greatly, indeed, have they even been exceeded. The Leipzig orchestra holds an honoured place among the other institutions of the city and is gloriously inscribed in the history of German music.

And how did you achieve this? How else but by the same means that a great general employs to secure victory for himself and his army: through the example of his own daring, adequate weapon training, maintenance of order and discipline, the proper distribution and greatest possible readiness of forces, apportionment of just praise and blame, care that the army does not suffer want, and by inspiring confidence in the wisdom of his plans. You unfolded all these special virtues before us in the ever unforgettable time of your activity here; it is no wonder, therefore, if our respect and love for you should have risen to the highest level, to absolute devotion. With such a devoted orchestra you have secured the victory here for German music, and have exhibited a distinguished model before all regions of Germany. The Fatherland will thank you for it!

We, however, rejoice in your thanks and your satisfaction with our collaboration and thank you heartily for this greatly rewarding joy. Also your parting words: Auf wiedersehen! [till we meet again] give us consolation and lift our spirits, which have been deeply afflicted by your separation from us. More uplifting for us, though, would be the hope of a possible renewal of our activities under your masterly direction. Yet this hope immediately appears conceited, when we consider that a great king, who knows how to value art and artists, has chained you to him and that he does not lack any of the means to preserve the treasure he has acquired.

So we must comport ourselves patiently in the unavoidable separation from you. We vow not to slacken in the artistic ardour that you have kindled, so that when you return your eyes will shine with satisfaction on your most devoted servants, the members of the grand concert orchestra.[59]

Mendelssohn's genuine pleasure is evident from his response to David on 3 September: "The orchestra's letter has delighted me enormously, and I would have written again and thanked them for it if that would not have been like the inn upon the inn sign, etc. But I had a good mind to; for it is really too friendly and kind of you all: the many signatures and the whole letter. If I only deserved half of the many compliments in it and could believe them without vanity! But I gave it to mother to read, and I beg you, give my very best, most heartfelt thanks to Grenser for the composition of it and to all the rest for their friendly participation."[60]

During the first six years of Mendelssohn's association with Leipzig his achievements were considerable not only in enhancing the standard of performance of the Gewandhaus concerts but also in stimulating public interest by broadening and developing the repertoire. He strove to present a judicious mixture of music, including classic masterpieces, such as works by Mozart and Beethoven and, to a lesser extent, Haydn, Gluck and Weber, works by acknowledged contemporary masters like Cherubini, Spohr and Marschner, works by lesser-known as well as more established younger composers like Gade, Bennett, Rosenhain, Kalliwoda, Schumann and Hiller. Furthermore, he also included unfamiliar music from the past, some of which was to become a standard part of the nineteenth- and twentieth-century concert repertoire, most notably by Bach, Handel and Schubert as well as some of Beethoven's lesser-known works. The series of so-called historical concerts, arranged in roughly chronological order, which he gave in 1838 and 1841, also included works by Viotti, Righini, Naumann, Cimarosa, Salieri, Romberg and Méhul. Chorley, in 1840, commented both on the balance and variety of the repertoire performed under Mendelssohn's leadership:

> Exclusive of benefit and charitable concerts, the winter series of these entertainments extends to twenty perform- ances. Nowhere in Germany is the *cramming* system of five consecutive hours of music resorted to; and I have

seen our monstrous London *programmes* hoarded up and spelt over like curiosities from Nootka Sound or Ceylon; but still, to provide variety for a score of evenings, in the present dearth of compositions of the highest order, requires no ordinary measure of intellectual energy. Yet this was done at Leipsic, in 1839 and 1840, without parade or without charlatanry. The directors of these concerts, a committee of gentlemen,—among whom are not to be forgotten Herr Rochlitz, the patriarch of German critics, and Dr. Härtel, whose name is historical among all those caring for continental music,—seconding Dr. Mendelssohn, opened their doors liberally to every new instrumental work of promise; taking good care, however, in cases of experiment, to assure the interest of the evening's performance by the repetition of some favourite and well-known production. In the four concerts which I attended during my two first visits to Leipsic—besides two Symphonies by Beethoven, two Symphonies by Mozart, two Overtures by Weber, and one by Spohr—and *Concertos* for the pianoforte, violin, trombone, and flute—I fell in with the whole of one act and the overture of M. Chelard's opera, "Die Hermannschlacht," and a grand manuscript concert *cantata* by Herr Marschner, including an overture, songs, and choruses. Neither M. Chelard's nor Herr Marschner's effort was worth the labour bestowed upon it; but the want in London of such catholicity and enterprise as brought this music forward has gone far, by permitting audiences to remain within one unchanging and narrow circle, to destroy more than one of our musical establishments of high renown. These very trials and hearings of all that rising contemporary talent can do, instead of seducing the love of an audience from its old objects of reverence, should tend, by contrast, to make what is sterling more sterling, and what is grand, grander; and to send listeners back to the unfading masterpieces of Music with a sharpened relish.[61]

Besides the Gewandhaus concert series, which took place each season between October and February, Mendelssohn organized and directed a range of other occasional concerts and large choral performances, and in these too the same concern for the quality and variety of repertoire is evident. He performed choral works by Handel and Bach with large forces, including *Israel in Egypt* (1836), *Messiah* (1837), and the *St Matthew Passion* (1841), as well as classical and contemporary oratorios and cantatas. In addition he organized and took part in extra concerts for visiting virtuosos, such as Liszt in 1840. From 1839 Mendelssohn also enriched the musical life of Leipzig by participating regularly in David's annual series of chamber music concerts;[62]"They are really lovely evenings," he told Klingemann, "and we amuse ourselves with them almost more than the [orchestral] subscription concerts."[63] Hiller recalled:

> The interest of the Quartet-Evenings, which Ferdinand
> David had carried on for some years past, was greatly
> heightened this winter by Mendelssohn's co-operation.
> He often played at them, and his renderings of Mozart
> and Beethoven were incomparably beautiful. He and I
> also occasionally played four-hand things, and made a
> great sensation with Mozart's Variations in G. But what I
> remember most distinctly was his performance of Bach's
> Chromatic Fantasia; it was quite overwhelming, and the
> applause was so great he was obliged to go back to the
> piano. He then improvised, combining in the cleverest
> way a theme of Bach's with his own well-known Song
> without Words in E (No. 1 Book 1)—thus uniting the
> past and present into something new and difficult to de-
> scribe. David was no less many-sided in *his* way; in addi-
> tion to the three great quartet writers he favoured us
> with Spohr, Onslow and Mendelssohn and also Schubert,
> then little known as a quartet composer. I must not for-
> get to mention the fact that this winter he brought be-
> fore the public the Chaconne of Bach, since so much
> played. Mendelssohn accompanied *ad libitum* on the pi-
> ano, and it was a great success.[64] The public were also

much delighted one evening to see Mendelssohn and Kalliwoda playing the violas in Spohr's double quartet and Mendelssohn's octet.[65] Mendelssohn never touched a stringed instrument the whole year round, but if wanted he could do it—as he could most other things.[66]

Heinrich Brockhaus's diary entry for 29 February 1840, when he attended one of the concerts mentioned above by Hiller, gives a fascinatingly different slant on the impression made by the performance of Bach's Chromatic Fantasia, and at the same time indicates just how greatly Mendelssohn was admired in Leipzig. Recording his impression of the concert, Brockhaus mentioned "an excellent sonata for piano and violin by Beethoven, from his most beautiful, healthiest period, played in a masterly manner by Mendelssohn and David. Also interesting was a so-called chromatic fantasia by the old Bach and a fugue, which Mendelssohn performed excellently; because the masses, however, do not grasp the significance of that kind of thing, only the Mendelssohn mania [*Mendelssohnomanie*] which rules here can explain why the public was so electrified that it was loudly encored. No-one can value Mendelssohn's genius higher than I, and acknowledge his great significance, especially for Leipzig; but they practise a real idolatry with him."[67]

Schumann, who, however much he may have admired Mendelssohn, was certainly not a victim of the Mendelssohn mania, was undoubtedly one of those who were electrified by this performance of music by his favourite old master. He recorded, simply but enthusiastically: "Mendelssohn also played, with his ever fresh mastership, Bach's chromatic fantasia and fugue as well as his five-part fugue in C sharp minor; and, accompanied by Mendelssohn, Concert-master David gave us, in the most admirable manner, two pieces—priceless as compositions—from Bach's sonata for violin alone,—the same of which it has been said that 'no other part could ever be imagined to it,' a declaration which Mendelssohn contradicted in the finest manner by surrounding the original with many parts, so that it was a delight to listen."[68] Schumann was well aware of the charge that the Leipzig public was increasingly idolizing Mendelssohn, and at one point in his overview of the 1839 to 1840 season he took the opportunity, while discussing a performance of Mendelssohn's new setting of Psalm 114, to address this directly, citing the fact that most listeners expressed their preference for the earlier Psalm 42 "as a proof that our public here, in spite of its admiration for the composer, does not blindly admire him."[69]

Mendelssohn's own contentment with his work in Leipzig, and his professional activity in general during this period, is succinctly expressed in a letter he wrote in October 1839, inviting Eduard Devrient to visit him.

> Here you would hear a great deal of music, and much of it, I believe, you would like; the finished way in which we play the symphonies of Mozart and Beethoven, I know would please you. We have not very much music during the summer; it begins with the autumn, and from now to November is at its height, when all are assembled, and both executants and listeners have gathered fresh love and power in the long recess. By New Year's day there is almost too much of it, and when spring returns one feels quite exhausted and surfeited with music, so that a stop is very welcome. These conditions have by degrees moulded my arrangements. During the six winter months I am overwhelmed with concerts, visitors, and no end of worldly concerns, so that only seldom, when the impulse is quite irresistible, I can steal any time for my natural work. But in the summer months I have delightful leisure; a musical festival or two makes but a short interruption, and gives pleasant occasion for travel. So long as God spares me wife, child, and self, in health as hitherto, there is not a wish I could form, only gratitude for the great happiness that is accorded to me.[70]

20 · The Genesis of the Leipzig Conservatorium

Towards the end of Mendelssohn's first period in Leipzig a bequest of 20,000 thalers for "the founding of a new, or the support of an existing all-purpose national institution for the arts or science" in the will of the

Leipzig lawyer Heinrich Blümner, who died on 13 February 1839, provided the impetus for the establishment of the Leipzig Conservatorium. Blümner left his bequest to be disposed of by the king of Saxony, to whom, through his minister Baron Johann Paul von Falkenstein, Mendelssohn addressed a formal petition on 8 April 1840 that the money should be used for a music school. In it he explained why he thought that "Leipzig is peculiarly entitled to aspire" to such an institution, observing that "the sense of what is true and genuine . . . has at all times struck its roots deep into the soil." The fact that music was not merely a "passing enjoyment" but rather an "elevated and intellectual" necessity could not, he maintained, be "without influential results on general cultivation." And he argued that an institution in which "all the various branches of this art" were taught "from one sole point of view, as only the means to a higher end," would help to preserve "a genuine sense of art," counterbalancing the meretricious focus on technique and material success, which was "so prevalent at the present day." He believed that "as the extension of sound instruction is the best mode of promoting every species of moral improvement, so it is with music also," and that only through the establishment of "a good music academy", might the bad example of many influential artists "be effectually checked."

The need for a school was all the more urgent, Mendelssohn stated, because of changing social conditions, which made it increasingly difficult for gifted young musicians from poor backgrounds to obtain training. He claimed that "a public institution would, at this moment, be of the most vital importance to teachers as well as to pupils; and the latter would thus acquire the means of improving capabilities which otherwise must often remain undeveloped and wasted; while, for the teachers of music, such a standard of combined action from *one* point of view, and for the attainment of *one* purpose, would also be advantageous, as the best remedy against lukewarmness and isolation, the unfruitfulness of which, in these days, is but too apt to exercise a ruinous influence on the mind."

Mendelssohn devoted the rest of the petition primarily to demonstrating why Leipzig, which, "by its numerous concerts and oratorios, possesses the means of cultivating the taste of young artists to an extent that few other German cities can offer," was a particularly suitable place for a music school, and why a school would be an appropriate use for Blümner's legacy. He also enclosed "some general outlines for the arrangement of such a musical academy," which, however, appear not to have been preserved.[71] The king was favourably disposed towards the suggestion, but it took another three years for the scheme to come to fruition.

21 · Between Berlin and Leipzig, 1841–1844

Shortly after the beginning of the 1840 to 1841 season it looked as if Leipzig was about to lose its cherished music director. Within a few months of the death of King Friedrich Wilhelm III of Prussia in July 1840, his successor, Friedrich Wilhelm IV, who as crown prince had taken a close interest in Mendelssohn's activity in Düsseldorf, initiated moves to bring him to Berlin. A process of negotiation began in December that led to a succession of ultimately abortive attempts to secure Mendelssohn's services in realizing the new king's ambitious but ill-thought-out plans for revivifying the musical life of his capital and kingdom. Advised by Christian Karl Josias von Bunsen and Wilhelm von Humboldt, both of whom knew Mendelssohn personally, Friedrich Wilhelm was persuaded that Mendelssohn was the only person who could be entrusted with the directorship of the musical division of the Academy of Arts, one of four sections (the others being painting, sculpture, and architecture) into which the Prussian Academy was to be divided.[72]

Around the beginning of December, at the request of the king's undersecretary Ludwig von Massow, Paul Mendelssohn travelled from Berlin to Leipzig to broach the idea with his brother in general terms, and a few days later he followed this up with a letter conveying more detailed propositions. Mendelssohn's reply clearly demonstrates his ambivalent attitude. On the one hand, he focused on the desirability of living in close contact with his family again: "Even if the affair leads to nothing further than to show me (what is the fact) that you participate in my wish once more to pass a portion of our lives together, that you, too, feel there is something wanting when we are not all united in one spot, this is to me invaluable, and more gratifying than I can express. Whether it be attended with a happy result or not, I would not give up such a conviction for anything in the world." On the other hand, he did not feel happy to accept the terms as he understood them. At this stage he believed that he was essentially being offered a combined post as director of the music section of the academy (without any clear specification of what that entailed) and director of concerts. As he explained to Paul, "Either of these situations would suit me, but not the two combined." With regard to the latter he was specially concerned about his authority over the orchestra: "I must be quite as much their real chief there as I am here"; and he added that his appointment must be "despotic as regards the musicians, and consequently imposing in outward position (not merely brilliant in a pecuniary point of view), otherwise, according to my ideas, it would be fatal to my authority after the very first rehearsal."[73]

Once negotiations began directly with Berlin, it became apparent to Mendelssohn that, as he wrote to Paul on 2 January 1841, "It all sounds so different from what they commissioned you to say to me when you came here; and if it begins in such a way, no doubt the sequel will be worse."[74] To his closest Leipzig friends, Conrad Schleinitz and Ferdinand David, he had explained the situation immediately,[75] and in January he also discussed it confidentially with the Saxon minister Falkenstein insofar as it might affect his proposals for the establishment of a music school in Leipzig. His letters make it plain that at this stage he considered it more than likely that he would exchange Leipzig, with all its attractions, for a post in Berlin, which potentially offered a much more influential sphere of activity. Perhaps, too, he was influenced by the feeling that the offer, in such pressing terms, from the Prussian king compensated for the slights he felt he had previously experienced in Berlin, for in February he wrote to his brother: "The Berlin affair is much in my thoughts, and is a subject for serious consideration. I doubt whether it will ever lead to *that* result which we both (I believe) would prefer; for I still have misgivings as to Berlin being a soil where a person of my profession could feel even tolerably at home, in spite of all honours and money; but the mere offer in itself gives me an inward impulse, a certain satisfaction, which is of infinite value to me, even if I were never to speak of it to any one; in a word, I feel that an honour has been done me, and I rejoice in it." Indeed, another factor had entered the equation during the early part of 1841, as a direct result of a highly successful concert that King Friedrich August II of Saxony had attended at the Gewandhaus in October 1840. The standard of the concert and especially the performance of Mendelssohn's recently premièred *Lobgesang* forcibly impressed the king. Mendelssohn informed Paul in the same letter: "You cannot think what a good impulse the mere visit of the King, and his really cordial and kind approbation, has imparted to our concerts here. . . . By his demeanour here, as well as by the way in which he has sounded forth our praises in Dresden, he has facilitated a number of things for us which were not thought of formerly. Since that time, we have strangers from Dresden at every concert, and the female singers there vie with each other in their efforts to appear in public here. The grant, too, of the legacy bequeathed two years ago, will now probably be entirely devoted to musical purposes, and perhaps be finally decided this month."[76]

Leipzig, therefore, looked increasingly attractive. In March, however, Mendelssohn wrote from Leipzig to Klingemann about attractions and counter-attractions to the Berlin offer.

> A few months ago the new Prussian king offered me the most brilliant and advantageous position in Berlin. He wants to reorganize the Academy of Arts and make it into a lively institution; to this end he has put Cornelius at the head of the painting section, and Rauch of the sculpture section, and wants me as director of the music section, to which a proper music school, and annual concerts, could be connected, with a salary of 3,000 thalers, holiday, etc., everything one could wish for. You will probably see straight away what appeals to me about it: mother, siblings and the parental home. But now there is something against it, and it is not unimportant: I feel happy and live contentedly here; for me the external show of the post is and remains a secondary matter, I am really not concerned with what people call honourable distinction, which is what the invitation to Berlin actually signifies; I feel like composing many different new things, and, note well, I know that an annoying external situation, bickering with the public, musicians and authorities can very much disturb me in this, my principal aim, if not completely make it impossible for me for a long time. Here I have not had any of these kinds of distractions, there I have them all to fear; is it wise then

to go away with wife and children when a return (here) would be impossible? [77]

The negotiations with Berlin continued, nevertheless, and by May 1841 Massow could report to the king of Prussia that "Herr Mendelssohn, according to his promise, recently came here, and he adheres to his resolution not to accept any *fixed situation* in your Majesty's service till he is previously informed what duties he is expected to undertake." Massow then explained that the scale of the proposed reorganization of the Academy of Arts prevented the ministry from preparing sufficiently detailed plans "to lay these proposals before your Majesty, and also render it impossible to define the situation for Herr Mendelssohn, or to prescribe the duties which, as Director of the musical class [section], he must undertake to fulfil." But he added that since Mendelssohn had to "declare, in the course of a few weeks, whether it is his intention to give up his situation in Leipzig or not: he therefore presses for a decision." In the circumstances Massow made the following proposal to Mendelssohn: "That for the present he should only for a certain period fix his residence in Berlin,—say, a year,—*placing himself at your Majesty's disposal*, in return for which your Majesty should confer on him the title of *Capellmeister*, but without imposing on him the performance of the duties of this office in the Royal Opera; likewise the previously-named salary of three thousand *Thalers pro anno* to be bestowed on him; during this time, however, he is neither to hold *any* office, nor to undertake any *definite duties*, unless in the course of this period Herr Eichhorn [the minister responsible] should furnish him with the long-wished-for details, and he should declare himself satisfied with them, in which case the reserved consent as to a definitive nomination should ensue." Massow later added: "From the well-known honourable character of Herr Mendelssohn, it may be confidently anticipated that in this kind of interim relation he will be the more anxious to devote all his powers to your Majesty, from the very fact of his duties not being more closely defined. If, contrary to expectation, the reorganization of the musical class of the Academy and the establishment of a musical institute be not so carried out as to cause Herr Mendelssohn the conviction of finding a field of activity for his bent and his vocation, or if the claims on him should prevent his acceptance, or, lastly,—which I subjoin at the express desire of Herr Mendelssohn,—should the expec-

tations now entertained by your Majesty with regard to him not be fulfilled, then the relation now formed shall be dissolved at the end of the
appointed period on the above conditions, and, therefore, in an honourable manner."[78]

At the same time, Mendelssohn submitted a memorandum outlining
ideas for the reorganization of the academy. This memorandum illustrates
the consistent guiding principles that, despite his increasing desire to devote himself more fully to composition, continued to motivate his commitment to a public career: the education of musicians to compose and
perform music with the highest of artistic aims, and the improvement of
public taste through technically excellent performances of the finest music. Given the political importance of Berlin, he evidently saw this as an
opportunity to establish a German institution more significant than the
proposed Leipzig music school that, attracting the services of the finest
German musicians, could effectively counterbalance the Paris Conservatoire by focusing not merely on technical brilliance but also on the most
elevated aesthetic values. His artistic credo is clearly expressed in the opening and closing paragraphs, the implicit subtext once more being that the
refinement of public taste equates with the improvement of public ethics.
Significantly, he expected tuition to be free of charge.

> It is proposed to establish a German Music Academy in
> Berlin, to concentrate in one common focus the now
> isolated efforts in the sphere of instruction in art, in or-
> der to guide rising artists in a solid and earnest direction,
> thus imparting to the musical sense of the nation a new
> and more energetic impetus; for this purpose, on one
> side, the already existing institutes and their members
> must be concentrated, and on the other, the aid of new
> ones must be called in.
>
> Among the former may be reckoned the various Royal
> Academies for musical instruction, which must be united
> with this Musical Academy, and carried on as branches
> of the same, with greater or less modifications, in *one*
> sense and in *one* direction. In these are included, for ex-
> ample, the Institute for Élèves of the Royal Orchestra;
> the Organ Institute; that of the Theatre (limited to the

theatre alone) for instruction in singing, declamation, etc. Further, the members of the Royal *Capelle* must be required to give instruction on their various instruments. A suitable locality can no doubt be found among the royal buildings, and also a library, with the requisite old and new musical works, scores, and books.

The new appointments to consist of—

1. A head teacher of composition; the best that can be found in Germany, to give regular instruction in theory, thorough-bass, counterpoint, and fugues.

2. A head teacher of solo singing; also the best to be had in Germany.

3. A head teacher of choral singing, who should strive to acquire personal influence over the scholars under his care, by good pianoforte-playing and steady direction.

4. A head teacher of pianoforte-playing for which office a man of the most unquestionable talent and reputation must alone be selected. The other teachers for these departments could be found in Berlin itself; nor would there be any difficulty in procuring teachers of Æsthetics, the history of music, etc. The complete course to last three years; the scholars, after previous examination, to be instructed *gratis*; no prize works to be admitted but at stated periods; all the works of the scholars, from the time of their admission, to be collected and criticized in connection with each other, and subsequently a prize (probably consisting of a sum sufficient for a long journey through Germany, Italy, France, and England) to be adjudged accordingly. Every winter a certain number of concerts to take place, in which all the teachers (including the above-named members of the Royal *Capelle*) must co-operate, and by which, through the selection of the music, as well as by its execution, direct influence may be gained over the majority of the public.

The following principle must serve as a basis for the whole Institute; that every sphere of art can only elevate itself above a mere handicraft, by being devoted to the expression of lofty thought, along with the utmost possible technical finish, and a pure intellectual aim; that also solidity, precision, and strict discipline in teaching and learning should be considered the first law, thus not falling short in this respect of any handicraft; that in every department, all teaching and learning should be exclusively devoted to the thoughts intended to be expressed, and to that more elevated mood, to which technical perfection in art must ever be subordinate.[79]

The negotiations almost foundered several times over the next couple of months. Devrient, apparently referring to the beginning of June, recalled that after "his second official conference" Mendelssohn was "quite beside himself" and told him that "he would not stay here, but from Leipzig, wither he was called immediately for the adjustment of sundry affairs, he would send in his resignation. He felt he was not the man for Berlin, for people wanted to have him without being able to make use of him."[80] Another crisis point occurred over a disinclination to grant Mendelssohn the title of kapellmeister before the academy affair was settled. This he considered essential, as he explained to his brother Paul on 9 July, first, because he disliked the idea of accepting the position on less advantageous terms than those to which he had agreed, second, because he considered the title essential to establish his authority to "give the desired concerts and performances in the course of the winter," and, third, as "a public proof of the king's confidence." He added that people could not accuse him of a love of titles for their own sake, as he had just been granted the title of kapellmeister by the king of Saxony.[81]

Despite these drawbacks, Mendelssohn moved to Berlin at the end of July, but at the same time the possibility of a return to Leipzig was kept open by the establishment of a temporary arrangement according to which David should direct the 1841 to 1842 Gewandhaus concerts. On the eve of his move to Berlin, however, he revealed the ambivalence of his feelings to Klingemann. He expressed all the old detestation of Berlin, which his deep misgivings about the situation revived, describing his imminent move there as "one of the sourest apples a man can eat, and yet eaten it must be. . . . That I am to become a sort of schoolmaster to a Conservatorium, is what I can scarcely understand, after my excellent vigorous orchestra here. I might perhaps do so if I were to really enjoy an entirely private life in retirement; but the mongrel Berlin doings interfere,—the vast projects, the petty execution, the admirable criticism, the indifferent musicians, the liberal ideas, the Court officials in the streets, the Museum and the Academy, and the sand!" Yet his overriding commitment to productive activity quickly reasserted itself in the statement, "I shall of course do all in my power not to allow this time to pass without some profit to myself and others."[82] But at no point does he seem to have felt that there was the slightest chance of the academy affair itself leading to anything positive. As he wrote to Erich Heinrich Wilhelm Verkenius in August, even with the best efforts of all concerned the benefits of the proposed reforms "could not be anticipated till *after* a succession of years had elapsed; yet they are expected first and foremost. The soil must be entirely ploughed and turned up before it can bring forth fruit, at least so it seems to me in my department; the musicians work, each for himself, and no two agree; the amateurs are divided and absorbed into thousands of small circles; besides all the music one hears is, at the best, only indifferent; criticism alone is keen, close and well-studied. These are no very flattering prospects, I think, for the approaching period, and to 'organize this from the foundation' is not my affair, for I am deficient both in talent and inclination for the purpose."[83]

As it turned out, the most productive aspect of Mendelssohn's appointment in Berlin was the opportunity it provided him for composition. The lack of gainful public employment meant, at least, that he had more time for his own creative work. He acknowledged this in the autumn of 1841, when he informed Franz Hauser: "In the mean while I write music, and when asked a question I answer it."[84] As Massow had predicted to the king, Mendelssohn's dislike of receiving a salary without fixed duties made him all the more anxious to give something in return, and when the king presented him with the idea of writing instrumental music for Sophocles's *Antigone* he seized it with enthusiasm, finishing the score within a few weeks, in time for its performance at Potsdam on 22 October. Apart from completing this commission, and responding to questions, his only other obligation in Berlin was to direct a series of concerts, beginning in January, which included his own *St Paul* and *Lobgesang* as well as a repertoire of classical works. But the public remained cool; according to Devrient they had "no ears for earnest music." It is clear, too, that despite all his attempts to ensure that he had the necessary authority over the orchestra, he never established anything like the close relationship with the Berlin players that he had with the Leipzig musicians. Devrient continued: "Some disagreeables had also occurred at the rehearsals, such as had already shown themselves in the orchestra during the rehearsals of 'Antigone.' Sarcastic jokes and observations were made, even Felix's instructions were questioned, which drove him to be angry and hasty."[85] Although contemporaries commented on Mendelssohn's beneficial influence on the standard of orchestral performance in Berlin, he never felt that he was able to achieve the same artistic level, despite the undeniable technical superiority of the Berlin musicians, because he remained unconvinced of their commitment to his own high aesthetic aims.[86]

Mendelssohn's relatively undemanding, if irksome, duties in Berlin meant that he did not, in fact, need to sever his ties with the Gewandhaus orchestra in 1841. Although David was officially director for the season, Mendelssohn returned from time to time to conduct before Christmas 1841, and again during the latter part of the season, notably for the première of his A Minor Symphony on 3 March 1842. After a summer spent in England, the Rhineland and Switzerland, he was in Leipzig to conduct the first concert of the new season on 2 October 1842. The succession of grand proposals, but continuing lack of gainful employment, in Berlin was becoming increasingly intolerable; the latest proposal, put to him by Minister Eichhorn, was to undertake the superintendence of all the Lutheran church music. Unwilling to accept such a massive and ill-defined task, and convinced that the academy scheme had foundered, he wrote to Massow on 23 October, asking for an interview with the king to tender his resignation, explaining: "Thus the case now occurs which your Excellency may remember I always anticipated, much to my regret, at the very beginning of our correspondence in December, 1840,—there is no opportunity on my side for a practical, influential, musical efficiency in Berlin . . . it would not be responding properly on my part to the confidence the king has placed in me, if I were not at once to employ my energies in fulfilling what your Excellency at that time told me, in the name of the King, were his designs; if, instead of at least making the attempt to animate and ennoble my art in this country (as your Excellency was pleased to say), I were to continue to work for myself personally; if I were to wait instead of to act. . . . My wish is that his Majesty would permit me in the mean time to reside and to work and to await his commands in some other place, where I could for the moment be useful and efficient."[87]

Contrary to expectations that his request would be badly received and that he would leave Berlin under the cloud of royal displeasure, the interview with the king resulted in a new proposal—and at the same time allowed Mendelssohn to resume his position in Leipzig for the forthcoming season. Mendelssohn gave a detailed account of the meeting and its consequences to Klingemann in a letter of 23 November.

> We are now again settled in Leipzig, and fairly established here for this winter and till late in the spring. The old localities where we passed so many happy days so pleasantly are now rearranged with all possible comfort, and we can live here in great comfort. I could no longer endure the state of suspense in Berlin; there was in fact nothing certain there, but that I was to receive a certain sum of money, and that alone should not suffice for the vocation of a musician; at least I felt more oppressed by it from day to day, and I requested either to be told plainly I should do *nothing* (with which I should have been quite contented, for then I could have worked with an easy mind at whatever I chose), or be told plainly what I was to do. As I was again assured that the results would almost certainly insure my having employment, I wrote to Herr von Massow begging him to procure me an audience of the King, that I might thank him verbally, and endeavour to obtain my dismissal on such and such grounds, requesting him to communicate the contents of this letter to his Majesty; this he did, and appointed a day for the audience, at the same time saying that the affair was now at an end, the King was very much displeased with me, and that it was his intention to take leave of me in very few words. He had made me some proposals in the name of the King to which I could not altogether agree, and with which I do not now

detain you, as they led to nothing, and could lead to nothing. So I was quite prepared to take my leave of Berlin in very bad odour, however painful this might be to me. I was at length obliged also to speak to my mother on the subject, and to break to her that in the course of eight days I must return to Leipzig; I could not have believed that this would have affected her so terribly as it actually did. You know how calm my mother usually is, and how seldom she allows any one to have a glimpse of the feelings in her heart; and therefore it was doubly and trebly painful to me to cause her such a pang of sorrow, and yet I could not act otherwise; so next day I went to the King with Massow,—the most zealous friend I have in Berlin—and who first took a final leave of me in his own house. The King must have been in an especial good humour, for, instead of finding him angry with me, I never saw him so amiable and so really confidential. To my farewell speech he replied: he could not indeed compel me to remain, but he did not hesitate to say that it would cause him heartfelt regret if I left him; that, by doing so, all the plans which he had formed from my presence in Berlin would be frustrated, and that I should leave a void which he could never fill up. As I did not admit this, he said if I would name any one capable of carrying such and such plans into execution as well as he believed I could do, then he would intrust them to the person I selected, but he felt sure I should be unable to name one whom he could approve of. The following are the plans which he detailed at full length; first of all, to form a kind of real *capelle*, that is, a select choir of about thirty very first-rate singers, and a small orchestra (to consist of the élite of the theatrical orchestra); their duties to consist in church music on Sundays and at festivals, and, besides this, in performing oratorios and so forth; that I was to direct these, and compose music for them, etc. etc. "Certainly," said I, "if there were any chance of such a thing here, if this were only accomplished"; it was the very point at issue on which I had so much insisted. On which he replied, again, that he knew perfectly well I must have an instrument to make music on, and that it should be *his* care to procure such an instrument of singers and players; but when he had procured it, he must know that I was prepared to play on it; till then I might do as I liked, return to Leipzig, or go to Italy,—in short, be entirely unfettered; but he must have the certainty that he might depend on me when he *required* me, and this could only be acquired by my remaining in his service. Such was at least the essential substance of the whole long conversation; we then separated. He said I was not to give him my decision *immediately*, because all difficulties could not be for the moment entirely obviated; I was to take time to consider, and to send my answer to Massow, who was present during the whole of this conversation of an hour and a quarter. He was quite flushed with excitement when we left the room, repeating over and over again, "Surely you can never *now* think of going away!" and, to tell you the truth, I thought more of my dear mother than of all the rest. In short, two days afterwards I wrote to the King, and said that after his words to me I could no longer think of leaving his service, but that, on the contrary, my best abilities should be at his command so long as I lived.[88] He had mentioned so and so (and I repeated the substance of our conversation), that I would take advantage of the liberty he had granted me, and remain in Leipzig *until* I was appointed to some *definite* sphere of work; on which account I begged to relinquish one-half of my salary, so long as I was not really engaged in active work. This proposal he accepted, and I am now here again with my wife and child.[89]

To Moscheles, on 18 November, he had expressed his feelings about the new situation succinctly, but revealingly, when he wrote: "It is decided that I am to have nothing to do with the Berlin public, but only with the King, whose qualities of head and heart I value so highly that they weigh heavier in the scale than half a dozen Berlin publics."[90]

As a result of his interview with the Prussian king, Mendelssohn immediately arranged a meeting with the king of Saxony to make it clear that, having accepted the Prussian proposals, he could no longer retain his official appointment as kapellmeister or consider other propositions that had been made to him from Dresden. While politely declining a formal post, however, he finally secured the king's agreement to devote Blümner's legacy to setting up the music school in Leipzig for which he had petitioned more than two years earlier. He informed Klingemann in his 23 November letter, two days after receiving official confirmation of the king's decision: "This music school is to be organized next winter, at least in its chief features; when it is established, I may well say that I have been the means of procuring a permanent advantage for music here. If they begin anything solid in Berlin, I can settle there with a clear conscience; it they allow the matter to stand over, it is probable that I may go on with my half-salary and my situation here for more than a year, and my duties be confined, as now, to executing particular commands of the King: for instance, I am to supply him with music for the 'Midsummer Night's Dream,' the 'Tempest,' and 'Oedipus Coloneus.' Such, then, is the desired conclusion of this long, long transaction."[91]

During the following months Mendelssohn threw himself into his Leipzig duties with the usual vigour, though the death of his mother in December affected him deeply and caused him to lose interest in musical activities for more than a month. In the immediate aftermath of the shock, he found consolation in completing the revised score of *Die erste Walpurgisnacht* and doing other more or less mechanical musical tasks. On 19 January 1843, as he began to emerge from the worst of his grief, he wrote to Hiller: "Thank God, my wife and children are well, and I really ought never to do anything but thank Heaven on my knees for such happiness. When I am alone with them drawing windmills for the children, putting the oboes and violas into the score, or correcting tiresome proof-sheets, I sometimes feel quite cheerful and happy again; but when I begin to think of other things, or have to see people, and look after the rehearsals or concerts which I have to go on conducting directly afterwards, it is as bad as ever." The death of his mother had also affected his feelings about his professional future. In the same letter to Hiller, having explained the situation in Berlin, he concluded: "In a word I am only awaiting here what I was at first to have awaited in Berlin, namely, that I should be indispensably needed there. I still doubt whether that will ever be the case, and hope (more than ever now, as you may imagine) that the King of Prussia will allow the present state of things to continue. What made me specially cling to Berlin, what in fact produced that consultation, or rather combination, no longer exists now." It was not, however, just the severing of this close personal tie with Berlin that motivated Mendelssohn, for he clearly also felt a commitment to seeing through the plans for the new music school in Leipzig. In the next paragraph of his letter he informed Hiller about the imminent establishment of the school, adding, "I shall have to go to the Gewandhaus three or four times a week and talk about 6-4 chords in the small hall there. I am quite willing to do this for love of the cause, because I believe it to be a good cause."[92] Two days earlier he had written to Klingemann in much the same terms: "I have my half-salary and have begun music for the Midsummer Night's Dream, Oedipus and other things for the king. My private notion is that he will decide to leave it permanently as it is now. In the meanwhile I have established the music school here, about which you will probably read an official announcement in the newspapers; it is under the direction of 5 gentlemen from the city, 5 of our best musicians have, together with me, offered to take teaching posts.[93] There is much to do."[94]

Not the least of Mendelssohn's tasks was his involvement as conductor or facilitator in a busy succession of Gewandhaus performances that season. The repertoire included the new version of his own *Walpurgisnacht* (2 February 1843), Berlioz's overtures *King Lear* and *Les francs juges*, the *Symphonie fantastique* and other works of his conducted by the composer (4 February), Gade's First Symphony in C Minor (2 March), music by Leipzig composers past and present, together with Beethoven's Ninth Symphony, to celebrate the centenary of the Leipzig subscription concerts (9 March), and a number of Bach's works in a special concert for the dedication of the Bach memorial (23 April). In the midst of all this the city of Leipzig named Mendelssohn an honorary citizen, and the music school, for which preparations had been going on throughout the winter, was formally opened on 3 April.

For much of this time, still affected by the depression that followed his mother's death, Mendelssohn performed his public duties conscientiously but without enthusiasm. Although he successfully kept up appearances in public, as demonstrated for instance by his warm reception of Berlioz in February, this clearly cost him a great effort, and he continuously longed for the end of the season at Easter. He confessed to Klingemann in mid-March: "I still can't mix with people at all, in half an hour I have to get away again, only work helps. But because of the excessive amount of music making here, because of the incessant time-beating of the last three weeks, this is also impossible until more peaceful times arrive. Amid all this I always have a single dominant thought: if only God will mercifully help me over the end of this month and the beginning of the next!"[95]

22 · The Establishment of the Leipzig Conservatorium

A succinct sketch of the foundation of the Conservatorium and Mendelssohn's role in it was given by Lampadius five years later, shortly after Mendelssohn's death; this account undoubtedly reflects contemporary, pro-Mendelssohn, Leipzig opinion.

> On 16th of January [1843] appeared the general programme of the new school for music at Leipzig, announcing that instruction would be given in composition; in violin, piano-forte, and organ playing, and in singing; with scientific lectures on the history of music, aesthetics, and exercises in combination [ensemble] playing and chorus singing. The chief professors were Mendelssohn, Hauptmann, Robert Schumann, David, Pohlenz, and Becker. Those who wished to enter the school were requested to give in their names before the 23rd of March. The number of applications up to this time was forty-six; by July there were sixty-eight; forty-two candidates were accepted,—among them two Dutchmen, one Englishman, and one American. On the 3rd of April, the Con-

servatorium was solemnly opened by Minister Falkenstein, in the name of his majesty the King of Saxony. In
the middle of this month, the full programme of instruction was given. Mendelssohn was to instruct in solo singing, in instrumental music and composition; Hauptmann, in harmony and counterpoint; Schumann, in
piano-forte playing and in musical composition. David
taught the violin, and Becker the organ. In the place of
Pohlenz, the accomplished teacher of singing, who died
suddenly, Madame Grabau-Bünau and Herr Böhme undertook the direction of that department. Other accomplished subordinate teachers were added; instruction was
given in Italian, and lectures were delivered on the history of music. Many munificent gifts were made to the
institution, to establish it on the foundation where it
ought to be: one gentleman gave five hundred rix-dollars
[Reichsthaler]; another, a valuable piano; another, the free
use of his circulating library, for the use of the students
of the Conservatorium. We are especially interested now,
however, to see the active interest which Mendelssohn
took in this object of his pride. He was not only its
founder, but its lasting benefactor. He not only entered
into the matter with the greatest ardour, but showed a
much greater degree of talent in instruction than his
friends had expected to see in a man of his genius. How
rich in suggestion the merest hint in reviewing musical
compositions, how valuable the hours spent in the more
difficult departments of piano-forte playing, and solo
singing, all his scholars know, and thankfully confess.
The private examinations of special classes, as well as the
semi-annual public examinations, he conducted, whenever he was in Leipzig, with the greatest care. Even in
the lower classes, he made every pupil show with what
facility he could modulate from one key to another: his
keen eye, his fine ear, were everywhere; the timid ones,
who wanted to be sheltered by the great crowd, he
would draw out; and at times, when the conduct of a

pupil did not please him, he knew how to be severe. At an early stage he once sat up half the night, in order to write an appropriate report on the performance of every single student.[96] Of course, his large and varied interests did not permit him to continue this close supervision of details; but, so long as he remained in Leipzig, he gave himself uninterruptedly to the work of instruction, and with his whole heart. He always conducted the general examinations when it was possible for him to be in the city; and he was always ready to assist the institution by deed and word, and to distribute praise and blame whenever and wherever they were needed. Yet, with beautiful modesty, he waived the distinction of being the leader in all things: he always spoke of himself as one of the six instructors. As it was a darling wish of Mendelssohn to live and labor by the side of Moscheles, he pressed upon the latter the plan of leaving England, transferring his school to the Conservatorium at Leipzig, and joining the corps of teachers already gathered there. Through Mendelssohn's efforts, the directors came to satisfactory terms with Moscheles, who did indeed transfer the scene of his labors to Leipzig [in 1846], where he reaped new honors, and added new strength to the youthful institution.[97]

In fact Mendelssohn had written to Moscheles as early as November 1842 about joining the Conservatorium. Responding to Moscheles's expressed interest in returning permanently to Germany from England, he discussed the possibility of a suitable position in Berlin, but added: "Suppose, now, that the thing you thought feasible in Berlin should take place in Leipzig! Not that I should think of offering you the post I have held here, merely as conductor of the Subscription Concerts; but there is every reason to believe that that office may be supplemented by the directorship of a musical school, which will probably be started within the next twelvemonth. . . . The principal outlines of the scheme are to be settled before the end of the year. I am bound up with it, heart and soul. But then the first and most important question arises, Who is to be at the head of it? Now, just see how all difficulties would at once be solved if, in answer to that question, we could put your name!"[98] Several months later he returned to the subject in a letter of 15 April 1843, which clearly demonstrates that he himself had no intention or desire to be seen as the head of the institution:[99]

Three years ago I endeavored to found a music-school in Leipzig; and after endless interviews and exchanges of letters with some prominent men here, and also with the King, I felt, on my return from Berlin, that there was no time to be lost, and that it was a case of now or never. My engagements in Berlin did not allow of my accepting a permanent appointment here; but I took the matter in hand last November, and, having got the necessary funds, the school was opened, and I engaged to act as one of the teachers during the time I should remain here. I wrote to you then, and expressed my ardent desire to see you eventually at the head of the institution. Nothing has changed my desire since; only, what was then a long-cherished plan became four weeks ago a reality, and promises to bear good fruit.

Now, if we could only persuade you to come! Whether I am here or not, it would be equally desirable to have you at the head of the institution. So far the Board of Directors is composed of only five gentlemen, none of whom are musicians. The six teachers are subordinate to them, but amongst themselves they are on an equal footing. But I believe that later on, when the institution develops, as seems very likely to be the case, a change will be necessary, and a musical man will have to join the Directors, or even to take the lead independently. And that is the position which, in connection with the Subscription Concerts, would be worthy of your acceptance.[100]

Yet not everyone, even in Leipzig, was as convinced as Mendelssohn and his collaborators of the value of the institution by now referred to as the Conservatorium. The editor of the *Musikalisch-Kritisches Repertorium*, Herrmann Hirschbach, observed in 1844:

> The music school, incorrectly called Conservatorium,
> since up till now it has neither its own premises nor
> fixed teachers of its own, is still an embryonic, wholly
> undeveloped institution. At present there are only Herren
> Hauptmann (theory), C. F. Becker (organ and piano
> playing and general music), David (violin), Madame
> Bünau (singing), (Herr Böhme has resigned), as well as a
> teacher of Italian and several assistants in post. I am no
> friend of class teaching, for the pupil can learn more on
> his own in a single hour than in 10 together with five
> others, for time is squandered so uselessly, and great, in-
> dividual talents never prosper in such institutions, not to
> mention that the instruction in these places is somewhat
> expensive for the students. Therefore, I do not think that
> an outstanding creative spirit will emerge at the moment
> from the Leipzig music school. Of the students who are
> there at present I even prophesy, however much people
> who are there may glorify things, that there will be nei-
> ther a significant player nor singer. Social distractions
> have a particularly deleterious influence on the female
> students, for talent grows strong only with study and se-
> clusion. Furthermore, the path that German singers are
> accustomed to pursue is a much more practical one, in
> that, if only they have some sort of basic voice, they go
> on the stage and thus further both means and end at the
> same time. As things stand at the moment the music
> school is not capable of arousing sympathy. But we await
> the future. Even great things often had small begin-
> nings.[101]

By the time Hirschbach wrote this critique, Mendelssohn had once again moved to Berlin, hence the absence of his name from the list of teachers. But, as we shall see, an even more negative opinion of the Conservatorium was given in a satirical article about Leipzig music, published in the same journal the following year, after Mendelssohn resumed his activities there.[102]

23 · Generalmusikdirektor in Berlin

Mendelssohn's scepticism, expressed to Klingemann, Hiller, and many and others in the early months of 1843, about the likelihood of King Friedrich Wilhelm's latest scheme being implemented in any form that he could accept, was misplaced. Although the project ultimately proved abortive, the conditions upon which his provisional acceptance of the appointment had depended were in the end sufficiently fulfilled for it to be impossible for him to withdraw. But this situation was not achieved without the usual bureaucratic obstacles having to be overcome. A new cathedral choir had already been established in May, but the other elements of the scheme, especially the provision of orchestral forces, proved more difficult and almost caused Mendelssohn to retract his agreement.

On 16 July Massow dispatched to him a contract containing a whole series of conditions that differed from those to which he had orally agreed in a meeting six days earlier.[103] On 21 July Mendelssohn wrote to his brother: "Herr von Massow has sent me a communication connected with that tedious everlasting affair, which irritated me so much that it almost made me ill, and I do not feel right yet. In my first feeling of anger, I wished to go to Berlin to speak to you and break off the whole affair." Towards the end of the letter, having explained the situation in detail, he added: "It is really too provoking that in all and everything the same spirit prevails; in this case too, all might be smoothed over and set to rights by a few words, and every moment I expect to hear them spoken, and then there would be a possibility of something good and new; but they are not spoken, and they are replaced by a thousand annoyances, and my head at last is so bewildered that I think I almost become as perverted and unnatural as the whole affair is at last likely to turn out."[104] After he had travelled to Berlin for direct discussions around the beginning of August, however, the difficulties were smoothed over. In addition to completing and directing the incidental music for *Ein Sommernacht-*

straum and *Athalie*, and the choruses in *Oedipus*, for the king's performances at Potsdam, Mendelssohn agreed to undertake two oratorio performances and a series of orchestral concerts during the winter, as well as
direct choral and orchestral performances in the cathedral on festival days,
for which he would also supply compositions. This was ratified in a
cabinet order on 2 September.

Mendelssohn was predisposed to find fault with Berlin music, musicians and musical conditions, and his expectations were quickly fulfilled.
At the otherwise highly successful première of *Ein Sommernachtstraum* in
October he was seriously put out of humour by an unscheduled delay at
the end of the second act for refreshments to be served to the royal party
and the clattering of tea cups during the introduction to Act III, to the
extent that, as Fanny informed Rebecka, "Felix was called for with immense applause, but did not come forward, and Mlle. Hagen [Puck]
apologised for him."[105] Hiller recalled that after the performance "this
disregard of artistic considerations, as well as common civility, so enraged
Mendelssohn that he hardly took any notice of all the fine things that
we had to say to him."[106] Artistically, however, the performance was a
great success, and the orchestral playing was notably fine. Fanny remarked
that she had never heard an orchestra play so *pianissimo*,[107] and Hiller
observed that "the band played to perfection; Felix had had eleven rehearsals, and the result showed what was possible with means like these
under the direction of such a conductor."[108]

The weekly subscription concerts began on 30 November, with Mendelssohn and Wilhelm Taubert conducting alternate concerts. Writing to
Ferdinand David in December, Mendelssohn frankly expressed his feelings, referring obliquely to the pronouncement by Berlin's leading critic,
Rellstab, that under Mendelssohn's direction the orchestra already played
as well as the celebrated Paris Conservatoire Orchestra:

> In many respects these concerts are very creditable in-
> deed, but in some they merit criticism; they also lack
> one little requirement, which is completely overlooked
> here, but which I would not willingly give up: inner
> freshness and lively enthusiasm. People live, listen, per-
> form irreproachably, but also without joy. I can never
> take very much pleasure in that. There is no lack of

good will, but each and every basic quality, genuine feeling, genuine sentiment is lacking. At the same time,
technique is not cultivated to the level of the real techni-
cians in Paris, and what they permit themselves to dream
about the Conservatoire Orchestra will probably remain a
dream for ever. But that would upset me least of all, if it
were compensated for by that in which our German musicians so infinitely surpass them, you can call it what
you will, profundity, or honesty, or musical feeling, or
geniality, or philistinism, or whatever you like—but since
they fail to reach either goal, they are, in this respect as
in so many others, falling between two stools; they want
to be French and cannot, nor are they German. What
pleases me most is the basses, because that is something I
am not accustomed to; the eight cellos and four good
double basses sometimes give me much pleasure with
their powerful tone.[109]

Mendelssohn was no more positive about the prospects for music in the
cathedral: "Next Sunday we have a big musical service, which, however,
consists of little pieces, namely, an eight-part psalm without orchestra by
me (composed expressly for this occasion),[110] a chorus out of *Messiah*,
and three chorales with 'trombones etc.' Precisely according to the king's
decree about which there was so much trouble before;[111] for now we can
have all sorts of wind instruments, so I have orchestrated it in my own
manner and the oboes etc. will probably now remain. Here, therefore,
we at last get as far, with great difficulties, as you get elsewhere with none
at all, and in the end the grand, much vaunted church music is diminished to the point where it has shrivelled away to a piece of music before
the beginning of the service, and that is where you got to long ago."
Earlier in the letter he had described to David that he and his family "live
in extraordinary retirement, and there are few places in which I have lived
for any time, where my circle of acquaintances is so small as here."[112]

In fact, despite all the irritations of his public situation, Mendelssohn
seems to have taken great pleasure in living quietly within his family circle.
Fanny wrote to Rebecka on 11 December 1843, "Felix is as amiable, in as
good spirits, and as delightful as you know he can be in his best days. I

admire him afresh every day, for this quiet life together is new to me, and his mind is so many-sided, and so unique and interesting in every respect, that one never gets accustomed to him. I do believe that he gets more lovable, too, as he increases in years."[113] Although the concerts did not give Mendelssohn unalloyed pleasure, and the situation in the cathedral was uncomfortable, especially because of increasing tensions with the court chaplain Friedrich Adolf Strauss, he seems to have been able to enjoy himself in private. At the end of January 1844 Fanny informed Rebecka: "On Sunday week my music begins again, at Felix's request, for he has heard that the gossips are saying he does not like our having musical parties. His position at the cathedral is but so-so, but how is it possible for him to get on with Strauss! You would not believe, however, how little these vexations affect him now."[114]

By this stage Mendelssohn had probably come to the conclusion that his appointment in Berlin must be brought to an end. He wrote music for the cathedral for only four services, Christmas, New Year, Passion Sunday and Good Friday, and when presented with the list of introits for the services between Good Friday and the Fifth Sunday after Pentecost, he suggested that other composers should be commissioned to set them to music. In the meanwhile, he had also decided to accept the invitation, conveyed to him by William Sterndale Bennett in November 1843,[115] to conduct the 1844 London Philharmonic season, and arranged to leave Berlin as soon after Easter as possible. In Frankfurt, on the way to England, he received a letter from Bunsen, which, if he had not already made up his mind to relinquish his duties in Berlin, undoubtedly pushed him further in that direction. The letter concerned Mendelssohn's unwillingness to set the choruses of Aeschylus's *Eumenides* as requested by the king. Bunsen informed Mendelssohn: "You have *hurt* the feelings of the King by your refusal to compose music for the 'Eumenides' " and he added: "The affair, too, is very much talked of *here*, and minutely discussed. In this good town it is thought 'very wrong' in you to go to England instead of composing for the King."[116] Nothing could have been calculated to upset Mendelssohn more. He ended his dignified, but uncompromising, reply with the statement:

> I will always obey the commands of a sovereign so beloved by me, even at the sacrifice of my personal wishes

and advantage. If I find I cannot do so with a *good artistic conscience*, I must endeavour candidly to state my scruples or my incapacity, and if that does not suffice, then I must go. This may sound absurd in the mouth of a musician, but shall I not feel duty as much in *my* position as others do in *theirs*? In an occurrence so personally important to me, shall I not follow the dictates of integrity and truth, as I have striven to do all my life? After this fresh experience, I fear even what I verbally mentioned to your Excellency already,—that my stay on such slippery ground, and under such perplexing circumstances is impossible. By this mode of acting, and this *alone*, can I hope, independently of momentary impressions, to preserve the good opinion of his Majesty, which is more important to me than all the rest; indeed, it is only thus that I can hope *really* to serve the King and his ideas. I cannot be an indifferent, doubtful, or secretly discontented servant to such a monarch; he could not employ me *thus*, and *thus* I would not only be useless to him, but sacrifice myself.[117]

During his stay in England, further correspondence with Bunsen prepared the way for his withdrawal from his duties at the cathedral, and on his return Mendelssohn travelled alone to Berlin for an audience with the king on 30 September. It was agreed that in future he should continue to receive a reduced stipend of 1,000 thalers and would fulfil only the king's individual commissions. At the end of November he left for Frankfurt "amid regret and good wishes," though according to the cellist Alfredo Piatti, who was in Berlin at that time, "the coldness of the ordinary musical circles towards him was but too evident."[118] Sebastian Hensel expressed it slightly differently, remarking sardonically that after Mendelssohn's final performance in November (of *St Paul*), everybody was "in a state of distress at Mendelssohn's going away, though they had all, or nearly all, contributed to make him go."[119] This was not quite the end of Berlin matters, however, for in March 1845, Mendelssohn received further overtures, from Minister Eichhorn, about participating in the establishment of a music academy, and in response to a renewed request from the king for the composition of choruses for the whole of the Aeschylus trilogy he was once more obliged to make a diplomatic refusal, pointing out that he had completed Sophocles's *Oedipus Coloneus* and Racine's *Athalie* and had fully sketched the music for the final part of the Sophocles trilogy, *Oedipus Rex*.[120] His residual duties in Berlin amounted to little more than conducting the performances of *Oedipus Coloneus* and *Athalie* in 1846; *Oedipus Rex* was never completed.

24 · The Final Years in Leipzig

Throughout Mendelssohn's involvement with Berlin the prospect of a return to Leipzig was seldom absent from his thoughts. When it had become evident, however, that he would be fully occupied as Prussian Generalmusikdirektor, the temporary arrangements put in place in 1842 were deemed inadequate, and Ferdinand Hiller was appointed to take over the conductorship of the Gewandhaus concerts for the 1843 to 1844 season. Mendelssohn eased his friend into the post by playing his G Minor Piano Concerto under Hiller's direction at the first concert, and he later returned to play Bach's Triple Concerto with Hiller and Clara Schumann. But, as Hiller recorded, citing the testimony of Ferdinand David and Cécile Mendelssohn, Mendelssohn "had felt rather a pang at seeing the person who was to fill the place he so loved and gave up so unwillingly," and their relationship became strained to the point where correspondence between them ceased.[121] Hiller's tenure of the post was not successful; as the *Musical World* observed in 1846, "Though less severe than Mendelssohn, Hiller was not liked half as much by the band, and by the subscribers he was not liked at all."[122] At Mendelssohn's suggestion, the young Danish composer Niels Gade, whose First Symphony had impressed Mendelssohn in January 1843, was appointed conductor for the 1844 to 1845 season. Mendelssohn spent this time mainly in Frankfurt and the Rhineland, where he occupied himself intensively with composition and resisted inducements to participate in musical activities elsewhere. In June 1845, however, he was approached by Falkenstein, who relayed the king of Saxony's request that he resume his position in Leipzig, and towards the end of July he somewhat reluctantly assented. Gade was retained as assistant conductor to lighten his load.

Even while preparing to give up his Leipzig post to Hiller, in October 1843, Mendelssohn had shown his continuing concern for the welfare of the Leipzig orchestral musicians by writing a long letter to the city corporation strongly supporting a petition by the members of the theatre orchestra (which consisted largely of the same players as the Gewandhaus orchestra) for better terms and conditions. In the course of his letter, having compared their salaries to the much higher ones in Frankfurt, he expressed his own high estimation of the qualities of the Leipzig orchestra: "The performances of our orchestra are not only equal to that of Frankfurt, but to those of every other German city; indeed, undeniably superior to most of those with which I am acquainted! The favourable and widespread musical reputation which Leipzig enjoys throughout the whole of Germany, it owes entirely and solely to this orchestra, the members of which must get on as they best can, in the most sparing and scanty manner."[123] His continuing care for their interests as well as his inspiring musical presence ensured that his return filled the orchestra with renewed enthusiasm. A review of the first concert of the 1845 to 1846 season in Hirschbach's journal, now retitled the *Repertorium für Musik*, which was not normally complimentary towards Mendelssohn, indicates that this enthusiasm was immediately evident in the quality of performance: "Mendelssohn had taken over the direction of this concert and really gave fresh and brilliant evidence of his mastery in conducting. The orchestra made the greatest of efforts; one could read in the expressions of every single member the eagerness to give thanks to their master, and thus it came about that the overture and the symphonies were executed with a degree of excellence that we have not heard for years."[124] (This review, signed N., was evidently not by Hirschbach himself.) A similar view of the orchestra during Mendelssohn's last two seasons was expressed by the correspondent of the *Musical World*, who considered the Gewandhaus concerts "one of the principal attractions of Leipsic to the lovers of music. . . . There you have the finest instrumental music executed by an orchestra equal in number and far superior in discipline to that of the London Philharmonic. . . . The life and soul of these concerts is Mendelssohn, the conductor in chief, who, by severe drilling, has brought the orchestra to a high state of perfection."[125]

In the *Repertorium für Musik*, Herrmann Hirschbach's own assessment of Mendelssohn's effect on Leipzig music was generally much less sympathetic. His views, and those of most of the "association of artists" who contributed to the journal, may be seen partly as an early manifestation of the aesthetic stance of the protagonists of the movement later identified as "Young Germany" or "the music of the future," their principal aim at that stage being to promote Schumann's music in opposition to Mendelssohn's.[126] But they clearly represented a minority opinion at that time, and seem not to have been entirely uninfluenced by less disinterested motives. Hirschbach himself may well have had a personal grudge against Mendelssohn, for among Mendelssohn's surviving correspondence there are two letters from Hirschbach and a short note from Mendelssohn which indicate that in 1838 Hirschbach sent a symphony to Mendelssohn for performance at the Gewandhaus concerts, which Mendelssohn rejected. The extent of Hirschbach's chagrin is suggested by the contrast in tone and appearance of the letter offering the work and the letter requesting the return of the score.[127]

Hirschbach's contributions to the *Repertorium*, which seem not to have been noted in the Mendelssohn literature, act as a striking counterbalance to the tone of most other accounts. In the first volume he reviewed the state of music in Leipzig.

> Next to the music publishers it is the Gewandhaus concerts that distinguish Leipzig. There are also yearly subscription concerts in other German towns, but they perform little or absolutely nothing new, while here many new talents first appear in public. Certainly the latter must be keen on Leipzig on account of its publishing houses. The spirit in which these performances, which in any case are recognized for their excellence, are directed has been repeatedly criticized, and people think that they represent too exclusively the outlook of the beloved master who for a period of years has stood at the head of musical life here. In fact the tendency of the Gewand-

haus concerts may be described as a purely Mendelssohnian one. His music is prized above all other, his views are
worshipped, they turn up their noses at everything that is
not in sympathy with the smooth forms of this composer, or that breathes a deeper inwardness than his creations, and seek to make it seem ridiculous. Nowhere
more than in the letters about Leipzig did Hector Berlioz
fail to recognize his friends and enemies. Perhaps deliberately.—We shall look more closely at the roots of the
matter. A board of directors, consisting of a lawyer, some
music publishers and various other persons, stands at the
head of the institution. The first of these is well known
to be devoted body and soul to Mendelssohn and is one
of those who write: it would be sacrilege against art to
criticize a work of Mendelssohn, for this tremendous,
unattainable master is above all criticism.—It is he that
sets everything in motion for Mendelssohn and orders,
for instance, festive receptions, etc.[128] The two music
publishers[129] are tied by their publishing interests to
Mendelssohn, as far as the other persons are concerned,
however, they gladly cling to such a smooth and clever
artist as Mendelssohn. So the matter proceeds comforta-
bly along its chosen path. One can only be thankful that
it is nevertheless a Mendelssohn who is deified here;
much lowlier spirits rule in other towns. For seen from
the other side there are not a few who are unpleasant
about Mendelssohn on account of his good fortune
(since indeed every great man is envied and must endure
the blunt arrows of attempted libel). Even men who, on
account of their cultivation, should be above such cheap
intentions, may be counted among these, not to mention
the great press of musicians and other people who, in
their lowly positions, that are often, however, also wholly
appropriate to their accomplishments, are, out of base
envy, unwilling to recognize anything good about Mendelssohn. It is true that Mendelssohn's career has been
easier for him than for any other composer. But who

would reject good fortune if it came to him, or once it had been acquired, if only through artificial means, would not gladly keep it?—You false accusers, who demand greatness of spirit, practise it first yourselves! If, however, one inquires how Mendelssohn has used his position, can anyone deny that he has brought forward and fostered much excellent talent, if also admittedly only that which follows his example?—We do not sympathize with Mendelssohn, his tendency appears to us too superficial, avoiding warmth of feeling, nevertheless we have never wavered in recognizing his great talent, which is all the greater for having to seek where genius already finds. Who can now tell how many of his works will survive him? For the present one must content oneself with the fact that he is an artist whose merits are worthy of the greatest respect of all his contemporaries. We have described the circumstances without being coy, for the applause and hatred of mankind are all one to us.[130]

After the first year Whistling seems to have declined to continue publication of the journal. The second volume with its modified title, had a different publisher (acting merely as printer), and thereafter Hirschbach no longer made any attempt to conceal his implacable antipathy towards Mendelssohn and his supporters. A distinguishing feature of his writing was the use of heavy-handed irony, of which an extended example occurs in a bogus contribution to the journal (undoubtedly by Hirschbach himself) reviewing the state of music in Leipzig in 1845.

"No novelties—no Repertorium! Where there is nothing, even the emperor has lost his rights, and the critic, who is no emperor, but rather a species of fisherman whose hook waits fruitlessly for a big catch, is silent.—Ah, it really causes pain if one seizes hold of such little creatures at the moment when they dare to raise themselves above the surface of the water and puts them on dry land." So I said to myself after I had long waited in vain for novelties—when a manuscript was brought to me

that got me right out of my dilemma. We may now
hope that people will willingly grant the Repertorium the
honour of being an unpartisan paper. For this article
contains, for the most part, the opposite of that which
the Repertorium believes. At least it teaches us how people in certain circles think about certain things, and how
sharply views are divided. We print the article una-
mended, as it came to us.

The State of Music in Leipzig

Leipzig has been famous for the state of its music since
the establishment of its precedence over all other towns
in respect of music selling. But it never gained such fame
from it as it has since the great composer and conductor
Felix Mendelssohn Bartholdy has stood at the head of
the Gewandhaus concerts and, whether he is absent or
present, has directed musical events with his all-
embracing genius. Certainly many will wish to know that
in earlier times the exciting concerts were no less outstanding, but the supremely excellent man needed to
bring such things to people's attention was lacking, and
therefore the greatness of this musical hero may be taken
for granted, since everything has improved through his
efforts. What novelties have we not got to know through
him! Not merely the Franz Schubert and Gade symphonies but also Rosenhain's and many other of the latter's
similar creations. How could we have gained the enjoyment of these things if they had not been obtained for
us through the personal friendship of the powerful musical master, of whom an intimate admirer once rightly
said in the famous *Allgemeine musikalische Zeitung* that to
criticize him would be a sin, and if he were not always
so willing to give preference to the works of those who
are devoted to him, i.e., therefore those who are worthy
of it? Must it not in general be an uplifting feeling for
the young artist to seek the favour of such a great genius?—Can he choose a more exalted model, not only in

purely musical matters, but also in all the qualities that can adorn a great artist, in justice and condescension towards every talent, particularly towards every new development? Naturally, only a tone poet who remains so unreachable for all time as He[131] can take it upon himself to dispense such condescension. Yet even such merit may not deflect slander, and the tiny proportion of novelties in the repertoire for several years gives occasion for it. What can He do about it? Has his genius not already inspired many other, more imitative talents to similar achievements, and could He then fail to have these performed?—People have charged him with one-sided preference for mere form, but is not form everything?—Is not form the thing that predominantly strikes one? Among true worshippers of the Mendelssohnian muse, therefore, a work of Beethoven, e.g., a symphony such as his third or ninth, has, for a long time, not been received as kindly as one of Mendelssohn's, however much connoisseurs may reproach the latter with lack of content. In order to understand Mendelssohn one must believe in him. Faith is the beginning of knowledge. To understand this, one need only remind oneself of the sublime, divinely inspired church compositions of Mendelssohn, who has thus soared to the heights of humanity and of the century.[132] And the three famous overtures! And the gigantic Symphony in A Minor, played one after the other? ———— But our pen is too weak to describe these miracle works of the world and of the human spirit, and what would be the point of it anyway?— Have they not already penetrated into the hearts of all? Have they not conquered the souls of all?—The world knows how great Mendelssohn is as a conductor. Even the most recalcitrant orchestra must submit to the magic of his baton. And with what amiable modesty does He achieve such great and incomparable things?—When has anyone ever seen or heard that He has got a tempo wrong? particularly in his own works? Thus, therefore, the enthusiasm for our musical master that is shown by all orchestras that have ever had the honour of being directed by him is explicable. Leader, bassoonist, trumpeter, timpanist play, blow and strike once again with such joy when He conducts. Although Mendelssohn stands at the summit of human perfection as tone poet and conductor, and Leipzig can thank him in such a manner for all pleasures that the genius of mankind can offer, he has nevertheless earned very particular merit with our town, namely, through the erection of the Bach monument and through his work for the foundation of the Conservatorium for music. Concerning the former, it is known to ornament our town. Even if it is a failure in respect of its form and a really dreadful eyesore, it is nevertheless conceived wholly in the spirit of its originator—Mendelssohn, and whoever absorbs himself in it will eventually cry enthusiastically with us: only a Mendelssohn could suggest something like that!—It is only a pity that this beautiful work, like our town's other monuments, has to be shut up in a box for half the year, that is to say, in winter, so as not to suffer damage. Thus, the many who journey to Leipzig specifically to see the Bach monument are often painfully disappointed, and therefore a plan has already been made to erect a large building around the monument. Yet another charitable foundation will be connected with this. That is to say, every week in this building a performance entirely of works by Mendelssohn (the three overtures every time) will take place, to which, however, access will only be for needy musicians, who will receive pecuniary support at each assembly. Certainly this plan will be received with enthusiasm by those concerned. If we consider further Mendelssohn's merits with respect to the Conservatorium— I nearly said Music School[133]—we find them to be immeasurable. To whom, apart from him, does it owe its fame? Is not his name, therefore, always mentioned in the programme of every semester, even when he has ab-

solutely no intention of coming to Leipzig? So indispensable is his participation, yea even the enlivening breath
of his presence, to every undertaking that is to thrive.—
It is of no account if the great talents that the institution
has already educated have nevertheless remained unknown to the world, and have only revealed themselves
to the teachers of the school. If only the initiate is convinced of it. One certainly wants to have evidence that
with private tuition someone has made further progress
in a quarter of a year than with the Conservatorium in
triple as much time, but what does that signify?—Is it,
then, a matter of knowledge and understanding? Is any
lack of that not entirely outweighed by the protection
and recommendation of men such as those who stand at
the head of it? In any case private instruction not only
remains available but is even necessary for the students of
the exalted Leipzig Music School, if they really intend to
gain an education; for the course itself is only there to
prepare the pupil for private instruction and make him
capable of benefiting from it. Anyone who has been in
the Leipzig Conservatorium will be in a far better position to appreciate the worth of conscientious and capable
private instruction than someone who has not been so
fortunate. The private teachers who at first looked upon
the institute with such jaundiced eyes, therefore, really
had no justification. As is well known, the institute also
has female students. Since the humane board of directors
is not concerned with greater or lesser talent, parents will
with pleasure grasp the opportunity to let their daughters
share here in the harmonious education. The board of
directors of the Conservatorium is in part the same as
that of the Gewandhaus concerts, at least the leading
members are the same. The most well known among
these are the artistic friends, a learned lawyer, just as
great in his judicial achievements as in his musical and
literary ones,[134] and a music dealer, who unfortunately
died a year ago.[135] The latter's amiable personality and

intelligent savoir faire will remain unforgettable to his friends and to artists. Such strong spirits are also required to form a phalanx that is able to keep out everything outlandish from the halls of the Gewandhaus, which Mendelssohn's music has consecrated. The tide of every advance breaks against this armoured spiritual power, for everything that does not derive from Him is, quite rightly, little valued. May the remaining members of the board of concert directors carry on operating in this spirit. They will thereby earn themselves incalculable merit in the matter, and the history of art will immortalize their names. After this all too weak description, it remains to praise the work of a man whose greatness as an artist equals his most amiable, most charming openness of behaviour. Our leader Ferdinand David rightly enjoys the reputation of being Mendelssohn's right-hand man. And with that everything, i.e., the greatest praise that can be given to a leader, is said. Who has ever heard a wrong note from him in the most powerful and most fatiguing tutti? Few equal his greatness as a violinist. A bowstroke that cuts deeply into the heart, a tone that is the proper mean between thin and thick, and comprehension ditto, are the main characteristics of his playing. The romantic is his particular genre, and no-one has been seen who is as enthusiastic as he in compositions of Schubert and Schumann, but particularly in those of Berlioz. The exertion that he devoted to the latter was so great that the directors, so anxiously concerned about the health of the irreplaceable leader, have not since then brought any more of Berlioz's things to performance. But our David agrees entirely with his sublime friend Mendelssohn in this aspect of taste.[136]—As a composer David is no less great than as a violinist, and if one places Mendelssohn higher than Mozart, then one can quite rightly place David above Haydn. The style of both is extraordinarily similar. Unfortunately, the modest artist holds back his work too much, so that no-one knows anything about it.

However, what has so far appeared from him can serve to enable the connoisseur, by means of diligent study, to draw himself gradually up the steps that David takes, and his most recent pieces in particular give a foretaste of what one can expect from this eminent composer. Apart from these two chief personalities in our blooming, continually growing musical circumstances, there are still some who certainly fade in comparison with these stars of the first rank, whose existence, however, can nevertheless not be denied. The name of Gade is best known among them. Indeed, he was dignified in Mendelssohn's absence by being permitted to take the latter's place on the conductor's podium. It goes without saying that no independent influence or any kind of value ought thereby to be conceded to the young man. With sufficient further study of Mendelssohn and true knowledge of him he will not, under the protection of his master, lack more exalted positions and progress. He is still young and has time to learn. Apart from Gade we mention Hauptmann, a man just as distinguished by energy as he is as composer and teacher. Here we encounter, which is rare with musicians, a decisive personality, an independence and liberality of opinion that must make a grand impression on everyone, and could only thrive in intercourse with Spohr. He is one of the worthiest representatives of our art, and we proudly call him our own.[137]

All the efforts of these chosen men for the benefit of the matter find their meeting point in the famous *Allgemeine musikalische Zeitung*. This has made a noteworthy advance in recent years, in that it has thrown off the burden of a specific editor and is now merely edited by the publishing house. It competes worthily in this respect with the *Berliner musikalische Zeitung* and Schuberth's *Hamburger musikalische Blättern*. Our Leipzig institution offers weekly the deepest essays about music, the most veracious correspondence, the most unbiased reviews. It is the only one of all the musical papers that appear in Leipzig that also enjoys an established reputation elsewhere, and particularly the articles on the Italian opera and on the Leipzig Gewandhaus concerts are greatly admired. Apart from this most worthy representative of musical literature there is only the *Signale* [*für die musikalische Welt*] to mention, an outstanding paper that, scorning all entertaining wit and merely attending to that which is useful, devotes itself more to a purely scientific investigation of music, and in this way chiefly exerts a valuable influence on the female students of the Conservatorium.[138] In fact these students owe a great part of their musical culture, or at least its consolidation, to reading the *Signale*, and the directors of the Conservatorium rightly treasure the paper highly and make it the basis of the teaching.

That good music will be protected in our distinguished circles is self-evident, for good music is identical with Mendelssohnian music. Its zealous cult is indeed most suitable for cultivating nobility. We hope that such happy circumstances will long delight us, and above all that we may keep the One whom we have to thank for all this.[139]

According to Ludwig Meinardus, Hirschbach's journal "had attacked Mendelssohn and his followers with outrageous virulence and cheekiness, and made such an extended group of wounded opponents bitter against it that it had to close down after completing its second year of publication."[140] Not until after Mendelssohn's death did his critics in Leipzig again have the opportunity to express themselves so publicly. A passage in Heinrich Brockhaus's journal suggests that in the ferment accompanying the political disturbances of 1848, many of those who had so recently been enthralled by Mendelssohn and his music quickly changed their allegiances. Brockhaus remarked after hearing a performance of *Elijah* on 21 April 1848: "I often have to think about dear Mendelssohn when the confused and uncertain times trouble me so much. He really did die at the right time; he stood at the height of his artistic fame, and would have felt very unhappy in the unharmonious times in which we have to live. Only a few friends remember him still with real feeling; those who considered him merely as a fashionable object have long forgotten him and follow other gods."[141] Under the editorship of Franz Brendel, the *Neue Zeitschrift für Musik* adopted a more critical tone within weeks of Mendelssohn's death, and it soon became closely associated with the forces in German music that most strongly opposed what Mendelssohn was perceived to have stood for. The extent of that opposition was shown most notably through the publication of Wagner's anonymous *Das Judenthum in der Musik* in the journal in 1850.

Nevertheless, Mendelssohn's impact in Leipzig was enduring in many respects. In the autumn of 1846, at the beginning of his last season there, he summed up his feelings about the city quite simply to Moscheles, whom he had finally persuaded to join the staff of the Conservatorium. Moscheles recorded in his diary: "I took another long walk with Felix, and, in the course of our confidential talk, asked him why he preferred Leipzig as a residence, whilst the greatest cities in Europe were ready to do him homage. He explained his preference by saying that the art atmosphere and tendencies of Leipzig had special attractions for him, and that the Conservatoire was a subject so near his heart that, even during the composition of his last oratorio, he had not neglected his pupils."[142] The continuing vitality of the Gewandhaus orchestra at the center of Leipzig's thriving musical life was a living legacy. Until the end of the century, too, the Conservatorium remained, to a large extent, identified with the cause for which Mendelssohn had striven, although in doing so it became increasingly open to the charge of inflexible conservatism. In their attempt to preserve what they saw as Mendelssohn's precepts, his heirs undoubtedly offended against his spirit.

six · The Practical Musician

25 · Keyboard Playing

When Wagner, in conversation, referred to Mendelssohn as the "greatest specifically musical genius that appeared in the world since Mozart"[1] and remarked to Cosima, "Such an enormous talent as Mendelssohn's is frightening, it has no place in the development of our music,"[2] he was merely giving voice to a feeling, almost of awe, that appears to have affected virtually all musicians who came into direct contact with Mendelssohn. Whatever view might be taken of the significance of Mendelssohn's compositions, his extraordinary abilities as an executant musician invariably made an indelible impression on those who had the opportunity to witness them. There were even some among his admirers who rated his influence and attainments as a practical musician as high as, or even higher than, his achievements as a composer. Thus Benedict remarked: "It would be a matter of difficulty to decide in which quality Mendelssohn excelled the most—whether as composer, pianist, organist, or conductor."[3] And the author of an obituary in the *Atlas* opined:

We lament more that Mendelssohn's presence, example, opinion, and delightful execution will now be withdrawn, than at the silence of his muse, charming as that was and is. There was a warmth, a gusto, a geniality, in his extemporaneous effusions, which we may not soon hope to reach. In his extempore cadences his countenance flushed with the passion of the moment, and the powers of his hands redoubled with every great occasion. Never since Beethoven took the pianoforte under his protection have such cadences been heard. It was said by a great composer in our hearing that Mendelssohn was compounded of Beethoven and Bach; and admitting a due colouring of his own, the description is just. We could have wished from him more oratorios, more symphonies, more of his delightful choruses to the Greek drama; but most we regret the musical head and prompt fingers that dealt unpremeditated delights on any genial opportunity. First and chiefest we esteem his pianoforte playing, with its amazing elasticity of touch, rapidity, and power; next his scientific and vigorous organ playing. He was the first to disabuse the public of the notion that the arts of playing the organ and pianoforte were incompatible. He himself was a living instance of the perfection of both. His triumphs on these instruments are fresh in public recollection. In private society he displayed more varied powers; he extemporized canons with the learned; he played the tenor [viola] with quartet players, or combined the songs of ladies at a party in an effective pianoforte fantasia;—often making the two go together. The spectacle of such readiness as this is absolutely necessary from time to time to support the idea of genius which languishes under constantly prepared composition. The poetic fire struck out by collision in an unpremeditated effort has magical power, and no musical performance equals the effect of improvisation which is at once enthusiastic and regular.

We cannot trust ourselves to speak of the memory of the master which retained the store of an ancient and modern library—and pursued a symphony or an opera on the instant through its minutest details. The elaborate concertos he has played in public give but a faint picture of his faculty of memory. No musician of the present century has equalled Mendelssohn in the variety and perfection of his *personal* endowments as an artist. This was the active principle of his influence on music, and rendered him in some sort the soul of the art. The respect inspired by such acquirements, by such devotion to an *ideal,* such intellectual power and modesty of demeanour, elevated the standard of music and was a constant lesson to the young. "Who being dead yet speaketh" may certainly be affirmed of Mendelssohn during the present generation.[4]

It was said by Clara Schumann, Ferdinand Hiller, and others that Mendelssohn, in his mature years, scarcely practised the keyboard; indeed, Chorley reported Mendelssohn's own avowal that under all his early tutors "he laboured *well*,—but under his pianoforte masters, he has assured us again and again, never *hard*. Besides great aptitude to acquire, Nature had given him a singular vivacity and willingness of finger, which made all the combination of keyed instruments easy to him. We remember hearing his sister tell how, on a visit of Kalkbrenner to Berlin, he caught and executed after a single hearing, a famous left-hand passage in the 'Effusio Musica,' which in those days was thought the *ne plus ultra* of pianism."[5]

Reports like these contributed to the notion that Mendelssohn's immense abilities were somehow inborn, and that his apparently flawless technique was acquired without effort. Chorley may well have inferred from Mendelssohn's own casual words that the acquirement of his keyboard skills cost him little effort, but this is contradicted by other sources. As a young man Mendelssohn evidently practised assiduously. Henry Heinke (the son of Mendelssohn's landlord in London in 1829) recalled that "Mendelssohn had two grand pianofortes in his room. He was constantly practising, and often after returning home late at night he would sit down to play; moreover he used to practise on a dumb keyboard while sitting up in bed!"[6] To William Sterndale Bennett, Mendelssohn made no secret of the hard work he had put into acquiring his skill on the organ. As Bennett's son remembered, "When relating how his surprise at Mendelssohn's organ-playing had led him to enquire by what means it had been attained, Bennett would always give [Mendelssohn's] answer, 'By working like a horse,' in the tone of a tart rebuke."[7] That Mendelssohn could and did practise hard when necessary is demonstrated in a letter to his mother, where, referring humorously to the strenuous régime to which he subjected himself in preparation for an organ recital in Leipzig on 6 August 1840, he wrote: "I gave it *solissimo*, and played nine pieces, winding up with an extempore fantasia. . . . I practised hard for eight days previously, till I could really scarcely stand upright, and executed nothing but organ passages along the street in my gait when I walked out."[8]

In later years Mendelssohn clearly did not maintain his keyboard skills by means of regular practice, yet he was acknowledged throughout his life, by almost all those who recorded their impressions, as one of the finest pianists and organists in Europe. Descriptions of his playing range in tone from extravagant hero-worship to coolly professional appreciation; but, as a whole, these accounts indicate that his technique seemed effortless, his sight-reading was astonishing, his interpretations were frequently revelatory, his musical memory was apparently inexhaustible, and his powers of improvisation little short of miraculous.

Mendelssohn's practical skill developed at an early age. Among the earliest published references to his keyboard ability is a review in the Leipzig *Allgemeine musikalische Zeitung* of a concert by the horn player Gugel and his eleven-year-old son in Berlin on 28 October 1818: "The Trio for Pianoforte and 2 Waldhorns by Wölfl, performed by the 9-year-old son of the banker Mendelssohn (a pupil of Herr Berger), and Herr Gugel and son, received much applause."[9] A few years later the same journal carried a report of a more ambitious performance on 3 March 1822: "A remarkable feature was a double concerto by Dussek, performed by the talented 13-year-old Felix Mendelssohn (grandson of the celebrated philosopher Moses, and pupil of Herr Louis Berger) with Herr Schmidt [*sic*];[10] his playing revealed him as a master, and through his dexterity, precision and purity gained universal applause."[11] And on 5 December of the same year, at Anna Milder's Berlin concert the journal observed: "The young Felix Mendelssohn also graced the evening by a piano concerto composed and played by himself,"[12] though the reviewer did not comment on the performance or the piece. Revealing glimpses of his piano playing in private society at this time occur in memoirs by Dorn and by Benedict,[13] and a first-hand account by Rellstab of Mendelssohn's visit to Goethe in 1821 contains many short references to the boy's capacity in improvisation, sight-reading and playing from memory,[14] as does the description of the same occasion by J. C. Lobe, one of the Weimar court musicians.[15]

By the time Mendelssohn was fifteen years old, his command of the piano was such that he could be acknowledged as a master by leading virtuosos of the day. When Ignaz Moscheles, then at the zenith of his fame, visited Berlin in 1824, Lea Mendelssohn asked him to give lessons to her elder children. Moscheles wrote in his diary: "Felix has no need of lessons; if he wishes to take a hint as to anything new to him, from hearing me play, he can easily do so." But, responding to repeated requests, he finally agreed; his diary contains the following entry for 22 November 1824: "This afternoon from two to three o'clock, I gave Felix Mendelssohn his first lesson, without losing sight for a moment of the fact that I was sitting next to a master, not a pupil. I feel proud that after so short an acquaintance with me his distinguished parents entrust me with their son, and congratulate myself on being permitted to give him some hints, which he seizes on and works out with that genius peculiar to himself." And six days later he wrote: "Felix Mendelssohn's lessons are repeated every second day; to me they are of ever increasing interest; he has already played with me my Allegri di Bravoura, my concertos, and other things, and how played! The slightest hint from me, and he guesses at my conception."[16] Shortly after this, during Mendelssohn's visit to Paris between March and May 1825, a journal report of pianists then resident in the French capital noted that, although Mendelssohn did not play in public, "all artists and connoisseurs who heard his fine pianoforte quartets, in which he took a part in several private parties, are of unanimous opinion that he is deeply founded in his art, and holds forth the finest promise of future excellence. His style as a performer is brilliant and exact, and full of the same energy which his compositions display."[17]

Over the next few years Mendelssohn performed publicly from time to time, but the majority of his piano playing occurred in private or semi-private gatherings; he never contemplated a professional career as a pianist. However, a review in the *Berliner allgemeine musikalische Zeitung* of a public concert in Stettin in 1827, where he performed his Double Piano Concert in E Major with Carl Loewe[18] and played Weber's *Konzertstück* in F Minor (without orchestral accompaniment), leaves no doubt about the exceptional quality of his performance. The reviewer reported:

> It is not customary in our concerts for people to show
> their satisfaction by applauding, for which reason the
> brilliant overture and the double concerto found little
> audible approval, though, as experience later convinced

me, all the greater recognition; indeed, some cold-blooded genteel people chided their enthusiastic friends, who could not restrain themselves from noisy approbation, for such neglect of good manners. However, even the genteel people forgot good manners and gentility, and everyone broke into rousing applause when, in the Weber Sonata [*sic*], which he played from memory, Mr Mendelssohn convinced the public through the most distinguished technical polish in the most brilliant passages, through inflections of tone from the most tender, scarcely audible whispers to the wildest outburst, and through the masterly calm, by which he seemed not to expend any more effort on the most difficult passages than on the easy ones, that they had before them a pianist who at 18 years old need not be ashamed of comparison with the greatest masters.[19]

When Mendelssohn again played Weber's *Konzertstück*, in London in 1829, the *Times* noted that "It is full of the chromatic difficulties peculiar to Weber's pianoforte compositions, and was executed with indescribable brilliance by M. Mendelssohn. The *crescendo* in the march movement was very ably managed, and produced a powerful effect. It may be added, that M. Mendelssohn had no music before him while he played, but executed the whole piece from recollection."[20] Describing his keyboard skills in general, another London reviewer in 1829 observed that he was "a pianoforte player of almost transcendent talent" and added: "His abilities are quite first-rate. In the act of playing he is lost to everything besides the instrument before him; and, indeed, in the most ordinary affairs of life, this musical enthusiasm is always present, and directs his thoughts and actions into one universal channel. His memory is represented as being the most wonderful of his faculties. After playing through one of Beethoven's most intricate symphonies, he can close the book and repeat it accurately by rote."[21]

Much less is recorded about the early development of Mendelssohn's organ playing than about his piano playing, but it is evident that it was equally striking; he particularly excelled in organ improvisation. One of the earliest organ performances of which a description has come down to us took place in Baden bei Wien, where he stayed for a while in 1830, during his journey to Italy. The author of this little-known account, the Austrian writer Hermann Rollett, committed his recollection to paper many years after the event.

In the autumn of the year 1829 the twenty-year-old Felix Mendelssohn-Bartholdy, staying in Vienna on the return from his first visit to England, also came to the neighbouring town of Baden. There he wanted to visit the Ephraims, who were already known to him from Berlin. The interesting young musician, whom I—then a ten-year-old boy—saw by chance on his arrival, was greeted with joy by the old lady and her lively, versatile daughter. He was well known to be an excellent organist. It was immediately arranged that, if possible, a small circle of friends should hear him. The Baden parish priest and Dechant, whose good will had been obtained, willingly offered the use of the parish church for this purpose, and it thus happened that in the Catholic house of God on a September day of that year, at midday, a number of Israelites—as well as invited friends—assembled to listen in reverent state of mind to the playing of the genial young man of the same racial descent [Stammesgenossen] who had already made a celebrated name for himself. I too, already having a lively interest in everything significant at an early age, found myself among the listeners, as a youth favoured by the intelligent old lady, and I retain an indelible impression of it. Accompanied by the choirmaster, the pale, black-haired young composer and virtuoso, who had his first flush of whiskers, ascended the steps of the gothic spiral staircase with merry naturalness, and after a few minutes of deepest silence a long sustained note, which in its mighty swelling penetrated to the innermost soul, began to waver, trembling through the three-aisled nave of the church. I had never heard anything of the kind, although I had already often heard organ playing. I could not grasp how a single note could make such an effect. Now followed all kinds of the most gripping feelings: whispering, rustling, roaring, rolling, storming, begging and demanding, lament and jubilation— as I can describe it from the most lively recollection— everything, however, in the most exalted spirit, in the noblest execution and style. Everyone there was pro- foundly moved, as the performance died away, and prob- ably none of them ever forgot it.[22]

In the winter of 1831 and 1832 Mendelssohn completed his travels with a sojourn in Paris. Ferdinand Hiller was often with him during his stay and described the phenomenon, noted by others, that Mendelssohn often seemed more constrained when performing his own music in private than when he played the works of other composers: "The first time I heard Mendelssohn really at his best was one evening at the house of the Leo-Valentinis, in Beethoven's D major Trio. It was a peculiarity of his, that when he played new things of his own to intimate friends, he always did it with a certain reticence, which was evidently founded on a wish not to allow his playing to increase the impression made by the actual work itself. It was only in orchestral works, where his attention was fully oc- cupied, that he allowed himself to be carried away. But in the music of the great masters he was all fire and glow."[23] After the fourth Conserva- toire concert on 18 March 1832, at which Mendelssohn gave the first Paris performance of Beethoven's Fourth Piano Concerto, a writer in the *Revue Musicale* observed that he displayed a "refinement, technical finish and sensibility that deserved the greatest praise," and, referring to the Adagio, remarked: "I have heard it said to pianists that there is no piano music there: God be praised! I hope these gentlemen always obtain success as flattering, as genuine with all their notes, as that which M. Mendelssohn obtained with these passages so simple and so well delivered."[24]

It seems probable that Mendelssohn's years of travel, with their inev- itable enrichment of his experience, may have deepened his interpretative powers, for Devrient, referring to the winter of 1833 and 1834, observed: "About this time Felix's pianoforte playing must have reached its highest point of perfection and individuality. It was not his prodigious and precise mechanism, the sustained energy of his performance, that fascinated his hearers—these were means, and were forgotten; it was his interpretation of the thoughts of the composer (on which account, too, he only played intellectual music). In short, he gave musical revelations; through him spirit spoke with spirit. . . . His playing made a profound and enthusiastic impression in Berlin, but yet not what it made in other towns. There was also the circumstance that Liszt had shortly before intoxicated the public with admiration of his dazzling powers, so different in kind."[25] In referring here to the spiritual dimension of Mendelssohn's playing, Devrient articulated a view that became widely held during the 1830s. Anton Schindler, for instance, in his 1840 *Biographie von Ludwig van Beethoven*, asked rhetorically: "Has there been a piano virtuoso since the death of Hummel, apart from F. Mendelssohn-Bartholdy (to speak only of Germans), who, even to a significant extent, has set himself the honourable aim of raising his listeners forthwith to his own level: demands that art makes equally on all its votaries, whether professional or amateur?"[26]

Mendelssohn's own estimation of his playing at this time was typically modest. He briefly compared it to that of Chopin and Hiller in a letter to his mother of 23 May 1834, written after attending the musical festival at Aix a week earlier, where Hiller's arrangement of Handel's *Deborah* had been performed.

> [Hiller] had come from Paris to hear the oratorio, and Chopin had cut his lessons to come with him, and so we met once more. I could now thoroughly enjoy the festival, for we three stayed together, and got a box for ourselves in the theatre where the performances took place; and the next morning of course we were all at the piano, and that was a great delight to me. They have both improved in execution, and as a pianoforte player Chopin is now one of the very first; quite a second Paganini, doing entirely new things, and all sorts of impossibilities which one never thought could be done. Hiller also is a capital player, with plenty of power, and knows how to please. They both labour a little under the Parisian love for effect and strong contrasts, and often sadly lose sight of time and calmness and real musical feeling; perhaps I go too far the other way, so we mutually supply our deficiencies, and all three learn from each other, I think;

meanwhile I felt rather like a schoolmaster, and they seemed rather like *mirliflores* or *incroyables*.[27]

The qualities hinted at in this letter find confirmation in other accounts. This is how Chorley characterized Mendelssohn's performance of his own D Minor Piano Concerto, op. 40, and his Serenade and Allegro Giojoso for Piano and Orchestra, op. 43, at the Brunswick Festival of 1839:

> The pianoforte playing, then, was the chief treat. It is rarely that I have been so delighted without novelty or surprise having some share in the delight. It would have been absurd to expect much *pianism*, as distinct from music, in the performance of one writing so straightforwardly, and without the coquetries of embroidery, as Mendelssohn. Accordingly, his performance had none of the exquisite *finesses* of Moscheles, on the score of which it has been elsewhere said, that "there is wit in his playing"; none of the delicate and plaintive and spiritual seductions of Chopin, who swept the keys with so insinuating and gossamer a touch, that the crudest and most chromatic harmonies of his music floated away under his hand, indistinct, yet not unpleasing, like the wild and softened discords of the Æolian harp; none of the brilliant extravagances of Liszt, by which he illuminates every composition he undertakes, with a living but lightening fire, and imparts to it a soul of passion, or a dazzling vivacity, the interpretation never contradicting the author's intention, but more poignant, more intense, more glowing than ever the author dreamed of. And yet, no one that ever heard Mendelssohn's pianoforte-playing could find it dry—could fail to be excited and fascinated by it, despite its want of all the caprices and colourings of his contemporaries. Solidity, in which the organ touch is given to the piano without the organ ponderosity—spirit (witness his execution to the *finale* of the D minor *Concerto*) animating, but never intoxicating the ear—expres-

sion, which, making every tone sink deep, required not the garnishing of trills and *appoggiaturi*, or the aid of changes of time, were among its outward and salient characteristics. Within, and beyond all these, though hard to be conveyed in words, there was to be felt a mind clear and deep; an appreciation of character and form referring to the inner spirit rather than the outward details: the same which gives so exquisitely southern a character to barcarole, and gondola tune in the composer's "Lieder ohne Worte," and its fresh, Ossianic, sea-wildness to his overture to the "Hebriden," ("Isles of Fingal"); the same which enabled him, when little more than a boy, in the happiest piece of descriptive music of our time, to illustrate Shakespeare's exquisite fairy scenes neither feebly nor unworthily. Demanding, as it does, execution without grimace; fancy, cheerful and excursive, but never morbid; and feeling under the control of a serene, not sluggish spirit—Mendelssohn's is eminently manly music; and loses effect, beyond that of almost any other of his contemporaries, when attempted by female hands.[28]

Mendelssohn's organ playing, too, seems to have reached a peak of excellence during the 1830s, when he became a persuasive advocate of some of Bach's greatest organ works, which he generally played from memory. Although admired in Germany, his organ playing made, perhaps, its most powerful impact in England, where its influence on future developments was immense. His command of the pedal board, which was as striking as his manual dexterity, was a particular revelation in England, where full pedal boards were still almost unknown at that time (though they were by no means universal in Germany). The most interesting and extensive account of Mendelssohn as an organist appeared in the *Musical World* in 1838. It is particularly valuable, since its author, H. J. Gauntlett, was himself an accomplished organist who played a significant part in fostering the repertoire and technique of organ playing in England. Gauntlett's qualifications to judge are attested by the fact that Mendelssohn chose him to play the organ for the Birmingham première of *Elijah* in 1846.

On the organ the real artist, the musician, triumphs: there genius, however, fascinating and extraordinary, invests itself with a loftiness and purity of sentiment—a luxuriance of fancy—a picturesque conception—a power as touching as it is extensive and irresistible. A grand instrument excites grand ideas, and nothing can be more interesting than to witness a highly gifted performer grapple with his thoughts when he sits down unpremeditatedly to a large organ, on which however astonishing his fertility of invention, unbounded his command of harmony, or dexterous and precise his finger, there is a clear and unencumbered arena for his display. As a pianist, M. Mendelssohn has been listened to with mingled emotions of delight and astonishment; as a composer he occupies a position of such acknowledged excellence as challenges and almost defies competition; the pupil of Zelter, the worshipper of Sebastian Bach, as an organist, becomes therefore an object of great and absorbing interest. During the present week he has twice touched the organ; on Sunday afternoon at St. Paul's Cathedral, and on Tuesday morning at Christchurch, Newgate Street. On both occasions the large auditories who assembled to listen to his efforts, testified how high they held in estimation the composer of the oratorio of "St. Paul." The first ten minutes is a trying situation for the popular organist, closely pressed on all sides, as he generally is, surrounded by persons not less excited than himself, by the promise of no ordinary intellectual gratification, and often by friends whose good opinions he is well assured he has had unreservedly surrendered to him. Genius, however mighty, is ever modest, and even the mind of a Mendelssohn does not instantaneously escape from the scene: hence his opening movements are distinguished for seriousness and solemnity: the perfect purity of his harmonies, the natural manner in which they follow each other, the rigid exclusion of every note not exclusively belonging to them, and their perfect unity one with the other, however, proclaim the refined and accomplished scholar, with whom art has become second nature; and as his thoughts thicken and the spirit retires to commune within itself, the themes break forth one by one, and a warmth and energy, a freedom and fluency diffuse a life, and spread a charm over his performance, that at once rivet the undivided attention of his auditors. Such was his first voluntary at St. Paul's: but his performance was interrupted ere he could give those memorable instances of his extraordinary abilities, by a ridiculous accident. He had played extemporaneously for some time, and had commenced the noble fugue in A minor, the first of the six grand pedal fugues of Sebastian Bach, when the gentlemen who walk about in bombazeen gowns and plated sticks, became annoyed at the want of respect displayed by the audience to their energetic injunctions. "Service is over," had been universally announced, followed by the command "you must go out, Sir." The party addressed moved away, but the crowd got no less; the star of Sebastian was in the ascendant. The vergers of St. Paul's are not without guile, and they possessed sufficient knowledge of organ performance to know that the bellows--blower was not the least important personage engaged in that interesting ceremony. Their blandishments conquered, and just as Mendelssohn had executed a storm of pedal passages with transcendent skill and energy, the blower was seduced from his post and a farther supply of wind forbidden, and the composer was left to exhibit the glorious ideas of Bach in all the dignity of dumb action. The entreaties of friends, the reproofs of minor canons, the outraged dignity of the organists, were of no avail; the vergers conquered, and all retired in dismay and disappointment. We had never previously heard Bach executed with such fire and energy—never witnessed a composition listened to with greater interest and gratification; and consoling ourselves with the hope that on Tuesday all might re-unite in a place where vergers are not, and under more fortunate auspices, we were hurried out of the cathedral.

Our hope was realised, and a scene of more unmingled delight we never participated in. The organ, through the spirited exertions of the parishioners, (their liberality joined to that of the Dean and Chapter of Westminster, and the Governors of St. Bartholomew's Hospital,) has been made a truly magnificent instrument, containing no fewer than ten diapasons and eight reed stops. M. Mendelssohn placed it before that in St. Paul's, and considered it the finest instrument he had yet played on in this country.[29]

It is the highest boast of genius, that its strains are not too high for the low and simple, nor yet too low for the wise and the learned. Many who were present on the Tuesday morning at Christchurch, were probably attracted there more by the desire to see the lion of the town, than from an earnest attachment to classical music: but all were charmed into the most unbroken silence, and at the conclusion only a sense of the sacred character of the building prevented a simultaneous burst of the most genuine applause. M. Mendelssohn performed six extempore fantasias, and the pedal fugue he was not allowed to go through with at St. Paul's. Those who know the wide range of passages for the pedals with which this fugue abounds, may conceive how perfectly cool and collected must have been the organist who could on a sudden emergency transpose them to suit the scale of an ordinary English pedal board. His mind has become so assimilated to Bach's compositions, that at one point in the prelude, either by accident or design, he amplified and extended the idea of the author, in a manner so in keeping and natural, that those unacquainted with its details could not by any possibility have discovered the departure from the text. His execution of Bach's music is transcendently great, and so easy, that we presume he has every feature of this author engraven in his memory. His touch is so even and firm, so delicate and *volant,* that no difficulties, however appalling, either impede or disturb his equanimity.

His extempore playing is very diversified—the soft movements full of tenderness and expression, exquisitely beautiful and impassioned—and yet so regular and methodical, that they appear the productions of long thought and meditation, from the lovely and continued streams of melody which so uninterruptedly glide onwards in one calm and peaceful flow. In his loud preludes there are an endless variety of new ideas totally different from those usually in vogue; and the pedal passages so novel and independent, so solemn and impressive, so grand and dignified, as to take his auditor quite by surprise. His last performance, on a subject given him at the moment, was the most extraordinary of his efforts. The theme was followed with an intenseness and ardour surpassing belief, but in the eagerness of pursuit was never deprived of its dignity or importance. There were no wild eccentricities, no excursive digressions, no ineffective displays of erudition: it was as if whilst anxiously untwisting the subtleties of counterpoint,—

> "Something within would still be shadowing out
> All possibilities: with thoughts unsought
> His mind held dalliance, to which his hand
> Gave substance and reality."

The enthusiasm, the fire and energy, with which the whole was carried on, was perfectly marvellous; he sat at the keys as one inspired, casting forth one gorgeous jewel after the other, sparking in all the radiance of light— throwing out a succession of bright passages, any one of which would have made the reputation of an ordinary performer. His invention never failed him for a moment; there was no return to any phrases or expressions used at an earlier part of his performance, and his genius appeared less unwearied and more boundless than during the first half hour.

Mr. Samuel Wesley, the father of English organists, was present and remained not the least gratified auditor, and expressed his delight in terms of unmeasured approbation. At the expressed desire of M. Mendelssohn, who wished that he could hereafter say he had heard Wesley play, the veteran took his seat at the instrument and extemporised with a purity and originality of thought for which he has rendered his name ever illustrious. The touch of the instrument, however, requires a strong and vigorous finger, and Mr. Wesley, who is at present an invalid, was unable to satisfy himself although he could gratify those around him.[30]

Mendelssohn's comment on the incident in St Paul's Cathedral, in a letter to Klingemann of 5 October 1837, indicates the difficulties he had continually faced in practising the organ. Responding to the statements of German friends that such an incident could only happen in an "unmusical land," he remarked: "They would talk differently if they only knew how I had to beg, pay and entertain the organists in Berlin so that I could play the organ for an hour, and how I had to stop ten times during such an hour for one reason or another." And he added with typical humility: "This time I have decided, since they take me for an organist, to practise the organ here assiduously so that I will actually become one."[31]

Mendelssohn gave his most notable public organ recital in 1840, in support of the erection of the Bach monument in Leipzig. Once again he impressed contemporaries by the extraordinary manner in which he seemed to enter into the spirit of the works he was playing. His programme consisted entirely of music by Bach but opened with an improvised prelude and concluded with an improvisation in which, according to Schumann, "he displayed the fullest glory of his art"; this was based on the chorale "O Haupt voll Blut und Wunden," "into which he introduced the name Bach[32] and a fugued movement, rounded to such a clear and masterly whole, that if printed, it would have appeared a finished work of art." For Schumann the whole concert was an experience that he wanted to record in "golden letters." He asserted that one should not analyze the greatness of Bach: "The best illustration and explanation of his works will always be found in the music itself; and by whom can we expect to find this warmly and truthfully performed, if not by the artist who yesterday delighted us, he who has devoted the greatest part of his life to precisely this master; who was the first to refresh, with all the strength of his own enthusiasm, the memory of Bach in Germany."[33]

During his years in Leipzig, Mendelssohn continued to play the piano regularly, though not frequently, in public. In private society or in select gatherings where music was treated seriously he needed little persuasion to play. Many ear-witness accounts of both public and private performances and improvisations from these years have survived. Some have a distinct flavour of the effusive enthusiasm that gripped many people in both Germany and England, but it is hard to escape the impression that there really was something bewitching about his playing that made it difficult even for the most phlegmatic listeners to retain their objectivity. An enthusiastic but balanced judgment is indicated by a remark made, late in life, by William Sterndale Bennett and recorded by W. Crowther Alwyn, a pupil at the Royal Academy of Music: "On discussing one morning, during the Composition class, an impromptu characterization of Mendelssohn's pianoforte-playing, with which he was in profound disagreement, he said, speaking very earnestly and with deep feeling: 'It was not playing that *could* be criticized. At times it seemed to send a thrill through every fibre of my body—but he did not always play alike, for, after all, he was human.' "[34]

Some of the most telling responses to Mendelssohn's playing are those that were not intended for publication. The diaries of Robert and Clara Schumann contain a number of illuminating references. Robert, recording a performance of an aria from Mozart's *Don Giovanni* by Clara Novello and Mendelssohn in 1837, ignored the singer's contribution entirely, merely commenting, "Mendelssohn accompanied like a god." Clara's testimony, coming from one of the leading pianists of the age, is particularly valuable. She was not always uncritical, remarking of a performance of Beethoven's *Kreutzer* Sonata in 1840, for instance, "He played this like he plays everything—in a masterly manner, brilliantly, yet not, to my mind, grandly enough, on the whole too hurried." But after hearing him play his D Minor Trio and several of his *Lieder ohne Worte* the following year she wrote: "I know no player whose playing might make me feel so good, and one really does not know in what *genre* one most likes to hear him, he plays everything in an equally masterly manner." Then, later in 1841, she recorded an instance that reveals both her own and Robert's profound admiration: "On Saturday 27th [March] *Mendelssohn* brought the Duo[35] he composed for my concert. We played it, he did not like it, and he got himself into a comical fury, because he had thought some things more beautiful. He played us some Lieder ohne Worte, among them a uniquely beautiful Volkslied. His playing made me melancholy, I did not like to think of mine anymore; I saw Robert's look of radiant joy, and it was so painful to me to have to feel that I could never do that for him. Later, I was ashamed of the tears that I shed in *Mendelssohn's* presence, but could not help myself—sometimes one's heart overflows like that!" Again, in 1843, after hearing Mendelssohn perform Bach's D Minor Concerto, she referred to his "accustomed and yet always once more astonishing mastery."[36]

With the growth of a Mendelssohn mania, especially in England and in Leipzig during the 1840s, the idea of Mendelssohn as a uniquely gifted performer, whose total absorption in the spirit of the music he played gave his interpretations unparalleled authority, became almost an article of faith. Some, while acknowledging the stature of his compositions, even rated him more highly as a pianist than as a composer. Thus, after his performance of Beethoven's Fourth Piano Concerto at a London Philharmonic Concert on 24 June 1844, a reviewer commented:

> Of the playing of this extraordinary master we can never have enough: he is simply the greatest pianist of the day by having the advantage over the parade-players of an intense devotion to music—whatever he does is not only worth hearing, but worth remembering. If this one circumstance alone would account for his superiority, how much more clearly is his position defined when we remember the faculties natural and acquired that he brings to music—the fine extemporaneous power, the extraordinary memory, the deep reading, the poetic fire and vivacity! When we combine with all these qualifications his powerful and refined mechanism, that serves to produce

any idea however fantastic with roundness and beauty, we see not only Mendelssohn, but why he stands alone. As an executive artist his position is even higher than as a composer; because we are always in hearing him under the influence of the past, and thinking thus did Bach, Mozart, Handel, or Beethoven. The career of Mendelssohn recalls the true view of the life of a musician—in which habit has made many err: it elevates the art, and renders its honours more difficult and more enviable. The Concerto of Beethoven was played by him from memory, that comprised evidently not only his own part but the entire instrumentation. His delivery of the work was characterized by truth and simplicity: and in the first and last movements he made extempore cadences which had each its own peculiar character and degree of excellence. The first was full and powerful; combined Bach with Beethoven, and treated the subject in a profusion of grand sequences and imposing harmonies. The second, in which the phrases to be worked were not obvious, fixed attention by its extraordinary ingenuity and science. We believe that the whole audience listened to these cadences as the most interesting parts of the fine concerto; and this, indeed, the warmth of character inseparable from genuine improvisation rendered them.[37]

The kind of hero-worship that grew out of such experiences is reflected in Elise Polko's *Reminiscences*. This book was not published until some twenty years after Mendelssohn's death, and its excess of enthusiasm, which is generally seen as a posthumous development, even caused so strong an admirer of Mendelssohn as George Grove to describe it as "a poor gushing book." But comparison of Polko's prose with numerous articles written during Mendelssohn's lifetime, especially in England, reveals many similarities. At the time of the book's publication a reviewer remarked in the *Musical World* that it was only "by those persons who have been in intimate communication with Mendelssohn that his true mental photograph can be handed down to posterity. It is with this feeling that we welcome these reminiscences of Madame Polko; for in them we find so many little incidents connected not only with the artistic, but with the domestic daily life of the composer, that we seem actually to be living in close companionship with him."[38] And the reviewer approvingly cited part of the following extract from her description of Mendelssohn's playing, based on her own first-hand experience. This clearly reflects the powerful impression it made on many contemporaries. She referred to "the magic of his touch, which could only be felt, and not defined," and to "his finished technical powers," but, like so many others, she thought that "it was his absolute and unqualified devotion to the master whose work he was executing that imparted to his playing a character of perfection that probably never was heard before and never will be heard again. In rendering the creations of others, he introduced nothing of himself; he was entirely absorbed in the soul and spirit of the composer." She continued: "When I recall the impression Mendelssohn's playing made on my own young heart, I can only say that other virtuosos have often enchanted and enraptured me, such as Liszt, Klara Schumann, Ferdinand Hiller, &c.; but not one of these ever inspired me with the feeling which came over me when listening to Mendelssohn. I always then felt as if I must seek out the most profound solitude, that I might continue to hear the echoes of those tones that had scarcely died away in my ear." After recalling that her brother Edward "had precisely the same feeling," she concluded: "Even now, in some compositions that I had the good fortune to hear played by Mendelssohn, my spirit seems, when others are playing them to me, to hear distinctly him and him alone, for no other hand can efface the impression I received from his execution of particular melodies, and more especially some of his 'songs without words'; so at length my physical ear seems to hear those very tones once more."[39]

George Grove tried to assemble a more objective picture of Mendelssohn's keyboard playing by means of recollections specially collected from eminent contemporary musicians who had experienced it at first hand. Although his estimation of Mendelssohn appeared exaggeratedly high to later generations,[40] it was, by the standards of the day, a sober one. He described Mendelssohn's manner at the keyboard: "His hands were small, with taper fingers. On the keys they behaved almost like 'living and intelligent creatures, full of life and sympathy.'[41] His action at the piano was as free from affectation as everything else he did, and very interesting. At times, especially at the organ, he leant very much over the keys, as if watching for the strains as they came out of his finger tips. He sometimes swayed from side to side, but usually his whole performance was quiet and absorbed."

The recollection of Mendelssohn's playing with which Clara Schumann supplied Grove is wholly consistent with her diary entries. She described it as "among the most delightful things in my artistic life," and continued: "It was to me a shining ideal, full of genius and life, united with technical perfection. He would sometimes take the *tempi* very quick, but never to the prejudice of the music. It never occurred to me to compare him with virtuosi. Of mere effects of performance he knew nothing—he was always the great musician, and in hearing him one forgot the player and only revelled in the full enjoyment of the music. He could carry one with him in the most incredible manner, and his playing was always stamped with beauty and nobility. In his early days he had acquired perfection of technique; but latterly, as he often told me, he hardly ever practised and yet he surpassed every one. I have heard him in Bach, and Beethoven, and in his own compositions, and shall never forget the impression he made upon me." Hiller agreed that Mendelssohn "possessed great skill, certainty, power and rapidity of execution, a lovely full tone—all in fact that a virtuoso could desire," but he felt that "these qualities were forgotten while he was playing, and one almost overlooked even those more spiritual gifts which we call fire, invention, soul, apprehension, etc. When he sat down to the instrument music streamed from him with all the fullness of his inborn genius,—he was a centaur, and his horse was the piano. What he played, how he played it, and that he was the player—all were equally riveting, and it was impossible to separate the execution, the music and the executant." He felt that Bach, Mozart, Beethoven "had become his spiritual property." Hiller, too, believed that Mendelssohn "never practised" but added that "he once told me that in his Leipzig time he had played a shake (I think with the second and third fingers) several minutes every day for some months, till he was perfect in it." Joseph Joachim, who played chamber music regularly with Mendelssohn towards the end of his life, described his staccato as "the most extraordinary thing possible for life and crispness" and thought that his playing as a whole "was extraordinarily full of fire, which could hardly be controlled, and yet was controlled, and combined with the greatest delicacy." Rockstro, too, felt that "though lightness of touch and a delicious liquid pearliness of tone were prominent characteristics, yet his power in *fortes* was immense." Otto Goldschmidt, a pupil at the Leipzig Conservatorium during Mendelssohn's last years, and later Jenny Lind's husband, recalled: "His mechanism was extremely subtle, and developed with the lightest of wrist (never from the arm); he therefore never strained the instrument or hammered. His chord-playing was beautiful, and based on a special theory of his own. His use of the pedal was very sparing, clearly defined and therefore effective; his phrasing beautifully clear. The performances in which I derived the most lasting impressions from him were the Thirty-two Variations and last sonata (op. III) of Beethoven, in which latter the variations of the final movement came out more clearly in their structure and beauty than I have ever heard them before or since."[42]

Very few contemporaries indeed seem to have advanced contrary opinions about Mendelssohn's powers as an interpreter of his favourite composers. One of these, however, was Adolf Bernard Marx, who went far beyond Clara Schumann's mild reservations about Mendelssohn's performance of the *Kreutzer* Sonata by deprecating his interpretation of Beethoven in general; he remarked in his memoirs that Fanny's performances of Beethoven surpassed Felix's in "tenderness and sensitivity" and that, "as much as I admired and loved his playing, his interpretation of Beethoven was seldom able to satisfy me."[43] But Marx's remarks may well have been conditioned by the breakdown of his personal relationship with Mendelssohn. Also, Marx had his own highly individual theories about Beethoven interpretation, and the denial of Mendelssohn's ability to comprehend the composer whom Marx revered above all was consistent with his claim that Mendelssohn's own music lacked depth. Hiller, in contrast, believed that Mendelssohn was less successful in performing the music of other contemporary composers than that of the great masters: "The music of other composers he knew, but could not produce it as he did theirs. I do not think, for instance, that his execution of Chopin was at all to be compared to his execution of the masters just mentioned; he did not care particularly for it, though when alone he played everything good with interest."[44]

26 · Improvisation

Inseparable from Mendelssohn's performance of his own and other composers' music was his improvisation, which has been mentioned in a number of passages already quoted. In a period in which fidelity to the composer's notation implied something quite different from what it has meant since the early twentieth century, the performance of finished compositions and improvisation were not so far apart. Even though Mendelssohn may have told the young Joachim that in playing the music of the great masters "it is inartistic, nay barbaric, to alter anything they have ever written, even by a single note,"[45] it is clear that his own practice did not correspond with any modern interpretation of that statement (nor indeed did Joachim's, as his 1903 recordings testify).[46] He was willing to improvise an accompaniment to Bach's Chaconne for Solo Violin,[47] or to alter the arpeggiation in the Chromatic Fantasia and Fugue.[48] Although we can only speculate, it seems highly probable that in many respects his performances, though strict by the standards of the day, would have struck a modern listener as very free. The statements that Mendelssohn liked "nice strict tempo" and that "he never himself interpolated a *ritardando*, or suffered it in any one else,"[49] must be balanced by Joachim's assertion that Mendelssohn "perfectly understood the management of time as a subtle means of expression,"[50] and by other accounts, such as Chorley's.[51] Even Grove, having remarked that "his adherence to his author's meaning, and to the indications given in the music, was absolute," acknowledged instances where Mendelssohn had adopted his own reading and explained this by saying: "Still, in intimating this it should be remembered how thoroughly he knew these great masters, and how perfect his sympathy with them was."[52]

Mendelssohn's skill in extemporizing developed at an early stage. He was apparently at the age of twelve already an intrepid improviser. On his first visit to Goethe he extemporized on a simple tune given to him by Zelter. "Felix played it through after him, and the next minute went off into the wildest allegro, transforming the simple melody into a passionate figure, which he took now in the bass, now in the upper part, weaving all manner of new and beautiful thoughts into it in the boldest style. Everyone was in astonishment, as the small childish fingers worked away at the great chords, mastering the most difficult combinations, and evolving the most surprising contrapuntal passages out of a stream of harmonies, though certainly without paying much regard to the melody."[53] His ability to make given material the binding feature of his improvisation seems to have developed rapidly. Devrient recalled an occasion in Frankfurt in 1822:

> The music-seller and composer André of Offenbach, a stout man, with loud speech and noisy laugh, came also to make acquaintance with Felix, and showed some of his new songs. He requested Felix to extemporize on the piano. An art that, since the precedent of Hummel, was much thought of and looked upon as the true test of a first-rate pianist and musician,—Felix, who had already given tokens of remarkable power for this task, had a quiet bit of fun on this occasion. He ingeniously wove an air of André, that had just been sung, into his improvisation, together with one of my humble attempts, that had lain in his all-retaining memory, though I had only shown it him once, and elaborated them. He laughed about it afterwards, and recalled with amusement how the big André, sitting close to the piano, greeted his air at each recurrence with a loud chuckle, whilst I, standing behind Felix's chair, acknowledged my little theme with a purr, and how he made us repeat these accomplishments again and again. But at the Cecilia Society, where Felix also extemporized, at the request of the Director Schelble, he treated the matter more seriously. Taking his subjects from the motets of Bach that had just been sung, he fairly amazed all hearers with his wealth of invention, his complete command of counterpoint, as well as by his astounding execution and sustained energy. This hour secured for the boy Schelble's friendship, and convinced me of his great vocation.[54]

Shortly after this, on another visit to Frankfurt during the spring of 1825, Mendelssohn improvised again at the Caecilienverein, and Hiller, who had already met him in 1822, recounted how this was the first time Mendelssohn's playing "made a full and permanent impression" on him: "We had been singing choruses from *Judas Maccabaeus*. He took some of the principal melodies—specially 'See the Conquering Hero'—and began to extemporise on them. I hardly know which was most wonderful—the skilful counterpoint, the flow and continuity of the thoughts, or the fire, expression and extraordinary execution which characterised his playing. He must have been very full of Handel at that time, for the figures which he used were thoroughly Handelian, and the power and clearness of his passages in thirds, sixths and octaves, were really grand; and yet it all belonged to the subject-matter, with no pretension to display, and was thoroughly true, genuine, living music."[55]

A few years later, during his return journey from Italy, Mendelssohn himself wrote a detailed account, in a letter home, of one of his organ improvisations, which occurred in the monastery of Engelberg in Switzerland on 24 August 1831. He described his participation in a "grand fête-day" in the monastery, for which the monks had asked him to play the organ, following this with an account of his private improvisations for the monks.

> This afternoon I played again alone to the monks, who gave me the finest subjects in the world—the "Credo" among others—a *fantasia* on the latter was very successful; it is the only one that in my life I ever wished I could have written down, but now I can only remember its general purport, and must ask permission to send Fanny, in this letter, a passage that I do not wish to forget. By degrees various counter subjects were introduced in opposition to the *canto fermo*; first dotted notes, then triplets, at last rapid semiquavers, through which the "Credo" was to work its way; quite at the close, the semiquavers became very wild, and arpeggios followed on the whole organ in G minor. I proceeded to take up the theme on the pedal in long notes (during the continued arpeggios), so that it ended with A. On the A, I made a pedal point in arpeggios, and then it suddenly occurred to me to play the arpeggios with the left hand alone, so

that the right hand could introduce the "Credo" again in the treble with A . . . This was followed by a fermata on the last note, and a rest,[56] and then it concluded. I wish you had heard it, for I am sure you would have been pleased.[57]

Throughout his life improvisation remained central to Mendelssohn's keyboard playing and to his creative activity in general. Devrient recalled the compelling fascination of his improvisations when inspired, indicating, perhaps, that his most profound expression of personal feeling in music may have occurred in this context rather than in finished compositions. He described an occasion in 1832: "In sad moments also he opened his heart to us, so far as this lay in his nature. Thus he told us, the first evening he spent with us, that he had been that day to the house of his friend Eduard Rietz, and followed the traces of his last moments. We spoke of the excellent qualities of the deceased, when Felix suddenly broke off, took a turn through the room, and stopped before the piano, saying he wanted to hear the well-known sound once again. He preludised, spoke of the touch and tone of the instrument, and gradually got absorbed in an improvisation that lasted above an hour. We sat motionless, devoutly listening to this revelation of profound sorrow, wild despair, and heavenly consolation. It was a glorious memorial of faith and love built into our hearts. Never before or since has music affected me like that."[58]

Another such moving improvisation, at the house of his friends the Woringens in Düsseldorf in the early 1840s, is related by Polko, probably quoting or paraphrasing the account of someone who was present: "After supper," she wrote, "Mendelssohn seated himself, as formerly at the piano, and took his little son Karl on his knee. At first he played in subdued tones, as if in a dream, while the child sat motionless, his eyes fixed on his father's hands. He then gently put him down, though the handsome boy continued to stand beside him, and Mendelssohn played on and on, every moment more beautifully, more touchingly, until all those around were in tears; and when he ceased, sighs and low sobs alone betrayed the overwhelming impression he had made. Then Cécile rose, and going up to him softly, she seized the hand that was hanging down, kissed it, and gently retreated. He raised his eyes to hers—it was a wonderful look;—well might she esteem herself happy to whom it was directed!"[59]

An account of Mendelssohn's powers as an improviser from an English source occurs in a short biography of the composer published in the *Musical World* in 1837:

> Mendelssohn's talent in Improvisation partakes of the
> same great character with his other extraordinary gifts
> from Heaven. His ideas do not flow in a thin, if uninter-
> rupted stream; but in a torrent; and not in jets or rush-
> ings of thought, but in a sustained volume of elaborated,
> and grandly constructed design, with amazing logical
> consistency—if such a term may be applied to a theme
> and argument in music. We once heard him in a private
> party—and what a night that was! After Malibran, at his
> request, had sung three or four of her own little melo-
> dies, she drew him *nolens volens*, in her own irresistible
> way, to the instrument, exclaiming all the time: "No, no,
> Mr. Mendelssohn, I never do nothing for nothing!" And
> he soon cleared off the amount of his debt, with a cent.
> per cent. interest superadded. He took the subjects of her
> melodies one after the other, and as his thoughts thick-
> ened, and the capabilities of each developed in the work-
> ing of them, he contrived, before he finished, to bring
> three of the subjects together. It was like a tornado. He
> appeared to require four pairs of hands to answer the
> throng of ideas that were struggling for development.
> The countenances of his audience were a curiosity during
> this exhibition.[60]

Another graphic English appraisal was printed in the *Spectator* in 1844, in a review of one of Dando's Quartet Concerts where, after Mozart's Quintet in G Minor, Spohr's Quartet in C, and Mendelssohn's Octet had been played, Mendelssohn also performed as a solo pianist.

> The opportunity of hearing Mendelssohn on the piano-
> forte, alone and unaccompanied, seemed to be eagerly

coveted. His performance of the *Lieder* was confined to some two or three pieces, from books not yet in general circulation in England. But, while his audience waited in expectation of more, he broke bounds into a free fantasia on the music performed; taking for his principal subjects the leading features of the G minor Quintet. The promptitude with which this matter was arranged and combined with that invented by himself, in the form of a regular composition replete with character and effects, was one of the marvels of improvisation, to which we can hardly find anything comparable without recurring to the golden days of Hummel and Wesley. The *aplomb* of the playing, the new character given to the subjects, the pleasing episodes, the well-imagined climax, and satisfactory conclusion, rendered this exemplary performance of the highest interest; and we wish the musical public at large better acquainted with this feature of the great artist's talent.[61]

An account by Rockstro of Mendelssohn's ability to thrill an audience with his powers of improvisation also illustrates the way in which, as in the case of the organ recital for the Bach memorial in 1840, he combined improvisation with the performance of finished pieces, in this case two of his own songs without words. It occurred during a charity concert in the Gewandhaus on 5 December 1845, one of his last major public performances in Leipzig. Jenny Lind, who had sung for the first time in Leipzig the previous evening, also took part, and it seems possible that Mendelssohn was inspired by her presence to give of his best. Rockstro left two descriptions of the occasion, which vary slightly. The following version is primarily from his *Mendelssohn*, but it includes a few additional details (given in parentheses), from the version in *Jenny Lind the Artist*.

Mendelssohn's own contributions to this performance were his First Concerto in G minor, and a *Solo für Pianoforte*, which consisted of two *Lieder ohne Worte*—No. 1. Book VI. And No 6. Book V.—both evidently chosen on the spur of the moment, and rendered intensely interesting by a prelude and interlude such as he alone could have improvised. (Beginning with a characteristic prelude in E flat, Mendelssohn played, as only he could play it, his own *Lied ohne Worte*, No. 1, Book VI. Then,) during the course of a long and masterly modulation from the key of E flat to that of A major he carried on the quiet semiquaver accompaniment of the first *lied* for some considerable time, without interruption, treating it with new and unexpected harmonies so contrived as to permit the continuance of the bell-like B flat in the form of an inverted pedal-point, and always presenting the reiterated note in some novel and captivating position. As the modulation proceeded, the B flat gave place to other notes, treated in like manner; and presently these were relieved by a new figure, which rapidly developed into the well-known feathery arpeggio of the famous *Frühlingslied*. Every one thus knew what was coming: but no one was prepared for the fiery treatment which first worked up this arpeggio-form into a stormy climax carrying all before it, and then as it gradually approached the long-expected chord of A major, died gently away, in a long-drawn *diminuendo*, so artfully managed, that, when the delicious melody was at last fairly introduced, it sent an electric thrill through every heart in the room. (The recollection of it returns as vividly as if it had been played but yesterday. It was, we believe, the last time that Mendelssohn ever played this delicious movement—now, alas! so remorselessly hackneyed!—in public; and all present agreed that he had never before been heard to play it with such magical effect.)[62]

Mendelssohn's feats of sight-reading and memory were widely talked about by the mid-1830s. The author of a biographical account published at that time reported: "With respect to technique, and particularly security in sight-reading, probably no living player surpasses him. Similarly, the power of his memory is developed to an incredibly high degree. He does not only play publicly the most difficult pieces of Bach, Beethoven, Hummel, etc. without music, but he also has almost all larger-scale works, such as the operas of Gluck, Mozart, Beethoven, Weber, etc., so firmly in his memory that he accompanies them from memory on the piano with complete security, which he has even done already several times in public, where only the slightest mistake could have overturned the whole performance."[63]

With respect to Mendelssohn's sight-reading, Hiller informed Grove: "In playing at sight his skill and rapidity of comprehension were astonishing and that not with pianoforte music only, but with the most complicated compositions."[64] Berlioz, several of whose works Mendelssohn played from manuscript during his stay in Rome in 1830, described his reading from score as "incomparable,"[65] and Macfarren stated that "in playing at sight from a MS. score he characterised every incident by the peculiar tone by which he represented the instrument for which it was written."[66] Dorn, too, commented on Mendelssohn's extraordinary gift for evoking the sounds of various orchestral instruments,[67] and Joachim recalled hearing him play Beethoven's *Coriolan* Overture on the piano "when he brought out the effects of the orchestral score in a most astonishing manner."[68]

That the "skill and rapidity of comprehension" described by Hiller was present from an early age is indicated by accounts of Mendelssohn's visit to Goethe in 1821:

> Goethe became more and more genial and lively, and
> tried all sorts of tricks and jokes on his little guest. "So
> far," said he, "you have only played me what you knew
> before; now we will see if you can play something that
> you don't know." He went out, and returned with several

sheets of written music. "Here," said he, "are some things out of my collection of manuscripts. Now we will put you to the test; see if you can play that": and he placed on the desk a sheet of music, in clear but very small writing. It was an autograph of Mozart's. The boy solved the task as readily as if he had known the piece by heart for years. "That's nothing," said Goethe, as everybody was applauding loudly; "other people can read that too; but now I am going to give you something in which you will break down. So take care!" And with this joking threat he got out another manuscript and put it on the desk. This one did indeed look strange. It was difficult to say whether it was music at all, or merely a sheet of ruled paper bespattered with ink and smudged all over. Felix burst out laughing, and exclaimed, "What writing! how is it possible to read that?" But suddenly he became serious: for when Goethe asked, "Now guess *who* wrote that!" Zelter, looking over the boy's shoulder as he sat at the piano, called out: "Why, it's Beethoven's writing; one can see that a mile off. He always writes as if he used a broomstick, and then wiped his sleeve over the wet ink. I have several manuscripts of his; they are soon recognized."

Felix kept his eyes reverently fixed on the paper; and his whole face glowed with excitement, as out of the chaos of words and notes, scratched out, smudged, interlined, and written over one another, he brought to light some lofty thought of beauty, or some deep noble sentiment. But Goethe, anxious to make the test a really severe one, left him no time to consider, but kept urging him on:—"You see; didn't I tell you that you would break down? Now try, and show what you can do." Felix began to play at once. It was a simple song, but to distinguish the right notes, among those that had been scratched out and half smeared out, required a rare quickness and sharpness of perception. At the first reading Felix had often pointed laughingly with his finger to the right note, which was to be found in quite another place; and many a mistake had to be corrected with a hurried No, that's it." But at the end he said, "Now I will play it to you," and the second time there was not a single wrong note. "That's Beethoven," he exclaimed once he came upon a phrase which seemed to him to bear the stamp of the composer; "that is quite Beethoven: I should have known him by that."[69]

With regard to Mendelssohn's sight-reading of demanding piano music Moscheles noted in his diary on 13 December 1824: "Returned to Felix his album, in which I yesterday wrote the Impromptu op. 77. He played it admirably at sight."[70] Hiller recalled another characteristic instance, which occurred during a visit to Frankfurt in 1836: "One day, after dinner, Mendelssohn found my Studies lying on the piano, and instantly sat down and played off the whole four-and-twenty one after the other in the most splendid style. My mother was in ecstasy. 'He is a wonderful man, that Felix,' she said to me, beaming with delight. He, meanwhile, was in the greatest spirits at having given us pleasure, but so hot and excited that he went off at once to my room, to the leathern sofa on which he was so fond of rolling about."[71]

There is also impressive evidence of the early development of Mendelssohn's musical memory in Julius Benedict's recollection of his first encounter with him in 1821.[72] Among the many other accounts of this remarkable gift are two characteristic instances recalled by Hiller, which occurred during Mendelssohn's sojourn in Paris in 1831 and 1832:

> Felix's wonderful musical memory was a great source of enjoyment to us all as well as to himself. It was not learning by heart, so much as retention—and to what an extent! When we were together, a small party of musical people, and the conversation flagged, he would sit down to the piano, play some out-of-the-way piece, and make us guess the composer. On one occasion he played an air from Haydn's *Seasons*—"The trav'ller stands perplexed, Uncertain and forlorn"—in which not a note of the elaborate violin accompaniment was wanting. It sounded

like a regular pianoforte piece, and we stood there a long time as "perplexed" as the traveller himself.

The Abbé Bardin, a great musical amateur, used to get together a number of musicians and amateurs at his house once a week in the afternoons, and a great deal of music was gone through very seriously and thoroughly, even without rehearsals. I had just been playing Beethoven's E flat Concerto in public, and they asked for it again on one of these afternoons. The parts were all there, and the string quartet too, but no players for the wind. "I will do the wind," said Mendelssohn, and sitting down to a small piano which stood near the grand one, he filled in the wind parts from memory, so completely, that I don't believe even a note of the second horn was wanting, and all as simply and naturally done as if it were nothing.[73]

Many accounts corroborate Mendelssohn's exceptional ability to retain compositions in his mind, sometimes after a single hearing, even many years after he had heard them. The completeness with which he was able to grasp musical ideas at first hearing is finely illustrated by F. Max Müller's reminiscence of a curious incident that occurred in 1840 when Mendelssohn gave a matinée for Liszt:

Liszt appeared in his Hungarian costume, wild and magnificent. He told Mendelssohn that he had written something special for him. He sat down, and swaying right and left on his music-stool, played first a Hungarian Melody, and then three or four variations, one more incredible than the other.

We stood amazed, and after everybody had paid his compliments to the hero of the day, some of Mendelssohn's friends gathered round him, and said: "Ah Felix, now we can pack up (jetzt können wir einpacken). No one can do that; it is over with us!" Mendelssohn smiled; and when Liszt came up to him asking him to play something in turn, he laughed and said that he never played now; and this, to a certain extent, was true. He did not give much time to practising then, but worked chiefly at composing and directing his concerts. However, Liszt would take no refusal, and so at last little Mendelssohn, with his own charming playfulness, said: "Well, I'll play, but you must promise me not to be angry." And what did he play? He sat down and played first all of Liszt's Hungarian Melody, and then one variation after another, so that no one but Liszt himself could have told the difference. We all trembled lest Liszt should be offended, for Mendelssohn could not keep himself from slightly imitating Liszt's movements and raptures. However, Mendelssohn managed never to offend man, woman, or child. Liszt laughed and applauded, and admitted that no one, not he himself, could have performed such a *bravura*.[74]

Mendelssohn gave another demonstration of this capacity at a musical party attended by Wagner. On 18 August 1878 Cosima Wagner recorded: "Then he [Wagner] remembers that when, after a concert in Leipzig given by Frau Schröder's daughter Wilhelmine, he had played the Venusberg theme at the Brockhauses', Mendelssohn had asked eagerly, 'What is that?' R[ichard]: 'Do you think I am going to reveal it to you?,' and Mendelssohn immediately sat down and played it himself."[75]

Dorn, who renewed his acquaintance with Mendelssohn in Leipzig in 1843, after an interval of thirteen years, recorded an incident that illustrates the longevity of Mendelssohn's musical memory:

> My third and last day at Leipzig was devoted to my friend Petschke, who had assembled a little party in honour of Mendelssohn, who seemed to be as much at his ease as he had formerly been as a young man in the house of Johanna Zimmermann. Petschke had asked me to bring some of my own compositions with me, and I found some attentive listeners to my "schöffen von Paris." Mendelssohn, however, greatly surprised me by declaring he already knew one of the airs I had played,

and seating himself at the piano, went through ten or twelve bars, where certainly the harmonies of my air occurred, although I failed to recognise where I had heard them before. "Why, you do not know your own composition again?" said Mendelssohn; "that is the final chorus to 'The Magician and Monster.' " That was a melodrama for which I had written the music, and which Mendelssohn had liked at the time, and of which now, sixteen years later, he could remember chords, that had long since passed from my mind. When I expressed astonishment at his memory, he said, in a very gratifying manner, "It is only good melodies we should endeavour to retain."[76]

28 · String Playing

No extensive references to Mendelssohn's violin or viola playing have come to light, but a number of short allusions to his string playing have survived. Among the earliest is his own self-effacing comment, in *Paphleïs*,[77] "Flix scratches the fiddle" [Flix kratzt die Geige]. Nevertheless, Mendelssohn had considerable ability on the violin. In 1823, in a letter to Goethe, Zelter had remarked of his fifteen-year-old pupil: "His wonderful pianoforte playing I may consider as quite a thing apart. He might also become a great violin player."[78] Hiller reported an occasion in 1822 on which the thirteen-year-old Mendelssohn sight-read the violin part of a sonata: "At his second visit he astonished me immensely. I was showing him a violin sonata of Aloys Schmitt's when he at once took up a violin which lay on the piano and asked me to play the sonata with him; he got through his part very cleverly and well, though the brilliant passages were naturally somewhat sketchy."[79] A review of the concert in which Mendelssohn participated in Stettin in 1827 provides another tantalizing glimpse of his violin playing: "The second part of the concert comprised Beethoven's newest grand Symphony in D Minor, in which Mr Mendelssohn, as a combatant in the first violins, compelled the respect of his neighbours."[80]

A recollection of Mendelssohn's visit to the Taylor family in North Wales in 1829, by one of the three sisters with whom he spent much of his time, though it tells little about his violin playing *per se* merits inclusion as a charming vignette.

> Mr. Mendelssohn was not a bit "sentimental," though he had so much sentiment. Nobody enjoyed fun more than he, and his laughing was the most joyous that could be. One evening in hot summer we stayed in the wood above our house later than usual. We had been building a house of fir branches in Susan's garden up in the wood. We made a fire a little way off it in a thicket among the trees, Mendelssohn helping with the utmost zeal, dragging up more and more wood; we tired ourselves with our merry work; we sat down round our fire, the smoke went off, the ashes were glowing, it began to get dark, but we could not like to leave our bonfire. "If we had but some music." Mendelssohn said, "Could anybody get something to play on?" Then my brother recollected that we were near the gardener's cottage, and that the gardener had a fiddle. Off rushed our boys to get the fiddle. When it came it was the wretchedest thing in the world, and it had but one string. Mendelssohn took the instrument into his hands, and fell into fits of laughter over it when he heard the sounds it made. His laughter was very catching, he put us all into peals of merriment. But he somehow afterwards brought beautiful music out of the poor old fiddle, and we sat listening to one strain after another, till the darkness sent us home.[81]

In later years Mendelssohn scarcely touched a string instrument unless he had to perform. At a private musical party during his period in Düsseldorf, however, he reportedly played the extremely taxing violin part in Beethoven's *Kreutzer* Sonata with his pupil Eduard Franck at the piano.[82] Generally, however, he confined himself to the viola and on several occasions played it publicly in his own Octet.[83] In private, during his Leipzig years, he quite often played viola and, more rarely, violin in chamber music,[84] and, according to Karl Emil von Webern, during Mendelssohn's residence in Berlin in 1844 there were frequent Saturday-evening quartet parties with either Hubert Ries, Leopold Gans, Heinrich Wilhelm Ernst or Ferdinand David (when he could manage to travel from Leipzig to Berlin) as first violinist, Webern as second violinist, Felix Mendelssohn as violist and Paul Mendelssohn as cellist.[85]

One of Mendelssohn's last documented performances as a violist was in Spohr's E Minor Double Quartet at a party in honour of Spohr in June 1846.[86] Of his viola playing in later life, an anonymous writer observed: "Not very much has been recorded of Mendelssohn's viola playing, doubtless because of its private nature. At the house of Mr. Alsager, of the *Times*, in Queen Square, he used to play the viola in his Quintet in A (Op. 18), having as his colleague the late Mr. J. H. B. Dando, who communicated to the present writer the following affectionate tribute to the composer: 'When dear Mendelssohn,' writes Mr. Dando, 'played tenor with me, I used to play *first* tenor; but if difficulties arose which he thought I could execute better, he used quietly to *change the books*, and I knew my duty. It was always so. He knew quite well how I loved him and his music.' "[87]

29 · Other Instruments

There is little documentation of Mendelssohn's ability to play other instruments, though according to F. Max Müller, who as a student in Berlin was often present at "many a private concert given in the large room overlooking the garden" at Leipzigerstraße 3 (probably around 1843), "Mendelssohn played almost every instrument in the orchestra, and had generally to play the instrument which he was supposed to play worst. When he played the pianoforte, he was handicapped by being made to play with his arms crossed."[88] Hiller described an occasion on which Mendelssohn demonstrated unexpected technical facility on the timpani at a rehearsal for his *Sommernachtstraum* Overture at the Paris Conservatoire in the winter of 1831 and 1832: "I was present at the first rehearsal. The second oboe was missing—which might have been overcome; but just as they were about to begin, the drummer's place was also discovered to be empty. Upon which, to everyone's amusement, Mendelssohn jumped up on to the orchestra, seized the drumsticks and beat as good a roll as any drummer in the Old Guard."[89]

30 · Conducting

The art of conducting was still very much in its infancy during Mendelssohn's lifetime, and his personal contribution to its development was considerable. The necessity for a time beater in orchestral music was not universally accepted in the 1830s, and the notion of a conductor rehearsing a work in detail had by no means gained currency. Mendelssohn was in the forefront of developments in conducting in Germany and England, and his example was undoubtedly stimulating. By a combination of exceptional musicianship, a discreet but effective baton technique, force of character and personal charm he achieved, in many instances, a significantly enhanced standard of performance. His effectiveness as a conductor is attested by many accounts, but there was also considerable criticism of one aspect of his conducting: his choice of tempo. Schumann found fault with the rapidity with which he took the first movement of Beethoven's Ninth Symphony,[90] and Wagner stigmatized him as someone who routinely hurried through pieces to the detriment of the music.[91] Many other contemporaries commented on his liking for fast tempos, both in conducting and piano playing.

Mendelssohn acquired his practical skill in directing ensembles at an early age through participation in the private performances, involving members of the Royal Orchestra, which took place regularly in the family home. Eduard Devrient recalled how "he used to stand on a stool before his music-desk, and look amongst the sedate musicians, especially near the giant double-bass, a wonder-child indeed, in his boy's suit, shaking back his long curls, and looking over the heads of the musicians like a little general; then stoutly waving his *bâton*, firmly and quietly conducted his piece to the end, meanwhile noting and listening to every little detail as it passed."[92] However, Julius Schubring, who knew the family well from 1825, said that until 1829 Mendelssohn did not direct with a baton but "modestly stated his opinion from the piano or the desk of the tenor [viola]." Whatever the truth, it is clear that during those years Mendelssohn's acute musical mind was already absorbing the knowledge and experience that was to make him one of the most effective conductors of his generation. Schubring described the impact of Weber's direction of the Berlin performances of *Euryanthe* in 1825: "The amount of delicacy, and the nice fine gradations Mendelssohn introduced into the orchestra are things so well known, that there is no necessity for me to say aught upon the subject. I think, that, on this particular, he learned a great deal from Weber. When the latter was in Berlin getting up his *Euryanthe*, Mendelssohn frequently attended the rehearsals, and used to speak with astonishment of what the man did with a strange orchestra. It is true that he as little took as a model Weber's charming rudeness as his exaggerated wavering in the *tempo*. In this last particular, he rather preserved an equality, with tolerable strictness, and strove to attain effect more by clever gradations of light and shade than by changes of the time."[93]

It is not clear whether Mendelssohn directed with a baton or from the piano at his first documented public appearance as a conductor, when his First Symphony was performed at one of Kapellmeister Möser's concerts in Berlin in 1825. Adolf Bernard Marx merely remarked: "The young composer conducted his work with the ardour that is, as a rule, given only to the creative artist."[94] However, Mendelssohn certainly employed a baton in connection with the 1829 revival of Bach's *St Matthew Passion*, for the direction of which he was entirely responsible. Devrient, who worked closely with him in facilitating the performances and sang the role of Christ, has left an informative account of the manner in which it was rehearsed and directed.

> Felix's share in making the splendid properties of this
> work felt and known is as memorable as the undertaking
> itself. His perfect mastery of all its details was only half
> his merit. His energy, perseverance, tact, and clever calcu-
> lation of the resources at hand, made this masterpiece
> modern, intelligible, and life-like once more. Those who
> did not witness this, his first and greatest achievement in
> conductorship, can scarcely realise or appreciate the mag-
> nificent powers of this youth of twenty. The revered
> presence of Zelter gave still greater importance to the or-

chestral rehearsals. Until these took place, Felix had both
to accompany and to conduct, a difficult matter with the
rapid alternations of chorus and solos in ever-changing
rhythms: here he used to play the accompaniment with
the left hand and conduct with the right.

When we had an orchestra, the piano was placed
across the platform, between the two choirs; it was then
not yet customary for the conductor to turn his back to
the audience, except at the opera. By this means, though
the first choir was behind Felix, he faced the second and
the orchestra. This latter consisted mainly of amateurs,
only the leaders of the string and principal wind instruments belonged to the royal chapel. The wind instruments were placed at the back, above the semicircular
platform and extended towards the small concert-room
through three open doors. The task of keeping steady
this waving mass devolved upon Eduard Rietz.

Felix was as calm and collected in his difficult post as
though he had already conducted a dozen Festivals. The
quiet and simple way in which he by a look, a movement of the head or hand, reminded us of the inflections
agreed upon, and thus ruled every phrase; the confidence
with which he would drop his *bâton* during the longer
movements, when he knew that they were safe, with a
little nod as much as to say, "This will go very well without me,"—listen with radiant countenance, occasionally
glancing towards me,—in all he was as great as lovable.

We had had many discussions about the best way of
conducting. The continued beating throughout a movement, that must necessarily become mechanical, vexed
me, and does so still. Compositions are really whipped
through sometimes by this process. It always appeared to
me that the conductor ought to beat time only when the
difficulty of certain passages, or unsteadiness of the performers, renders it necessary. Surely the aim of every
conductor should be to influence without intruding him-

self. Felix determined on this occasion to show me how far this could be done, and he succeeded to perfection.

I recall these circumstances with peculiar satisfaction, as of late years the extraordinary gesticulations of conductors have been made a feature of in musical performances.[95]

Mendelssohn's father wrote an evocative, if scarcely impartial, account of his son's approach to conducting the Lower Rhine Musical Festival of 1833. It indicates how successfully the twenty-five-year-old conductor was able to enforce discipline and thus achieve an enhanced level of performance that reinforced his authority. The success of the festival led directly to the offer of Mendelssohn's first professional post as music director in Düsseldorf.[96]

As a musical festival comprehends a conductor, I suppose I must say something about the conductor for this year—Mr. Felix—he is hardly called anything else here. Dear wife, this young man gives us much joy, and I often say to myself, Three cheers for Marten's Mill![97] He has indeed got an immense piece of work to do, but he does it with a spirit, energy, seriousness, and cleverness actually miraculous in its effect. To me at least it does appear like a miracle that 400 persons of all sexes, classes, and ages, blown together like snow before the wind, should let themselves be conducted and governed like children by one of the youngest of them all, too young almost to be a friend for any of them, and with no title or dignity whatever. For instance, by one strict injunction (and but for his pronunciation, which he may yet improve, he speaks well) he has brought about what no other conductor to my knowledge has been able to do, the abolition of that disgusting practice of tuning. On the first rehearsal day this charivari was quite maddening; that same afternoon he addressed them and forbade it, and when several of the players attempted to disobey he

once more forbade it very seriously, and I have not heard
them tune a single note since. Another abuse arose from
the successive arrival of strangers from all directions, who
met for the first time on the orchestra, and found their
friends there. It had become the fashion to use the orchestra as a kind of parlour, where a great deal of talking
and gossiping went on, of course highly detrimental to
the rehearsal, the conductor having to shout with all his
might, and even then without being heard; and since
new-comers dropped in up to the very beginning, the
disturbance was intolerable. The same kind of thing began this time on the first rehearsal day, and then Felix
represented to them that he could not submit to it, that
he neither could nor would shout to enable them to hear
him, and that he must insist and rely on the most absolute silence and quiet in the orchestra every time he had
to speak. He said this for a second time very decidedly
and earnestly, and then I assure you that I never saw an
order so strictly obeyed. They see that it is right and
necessary, and as soon as he knocks and is about to
speak, a general pst is heard, and all is dead silence.

By this means he has produced really fine *nuances*
both in chorus and orchestra, which all assure me were
wanting before, and which of course gratify the performers and must raise the credit of their execution in their
own eyes and ears.[98]

That Mendelssohn did not always achieve his aims by means of cour-
tesy, humour or even firmness is attested by a number of accounts of his
sometimes volatile temper. He alluded to one such instance himself during his Düsseldorf period, in a letter of 16 February 1834: "I have just
come from a rehearsal of 'Egmont,' where, for the first time in my life,
I tore up a score from rage at the stupidity of the *musici*, whom I feed
with 6/8 time in due form, though they are more fit for babes' milk; then
they like to belabour each other in the orchestra. This I don't choose they
should do in my presence: so furious scenes sometimes occur. At the air,
'Glücklich allein ist die Seele die liebt' I fairly tore the music in two, on

which they played with much more expression."[99] Such occasions were the exception, however, and a recollection by Benedict of Mendelssohn's conducting at the Cologne Festival in the spring of 1835 conveys the more familiar picture.

Nobody certainly ever knew better how to communicate, as if by an electric fluid, his own conception of a work to a large body of performers. It was highly interesting, on this occasion, to contemplate the anxious attention manifested by a body of more than five hundred singers and performers, watching every glance of Mendelssohn's eye, and following, like obedient spirits, the magic wand of this musical *Prospero*. The admirable allegretto, in B flat, of this symphony, not going, at first, to his liking, he remarked, smilingly, that "he knew every one of the gentlemen engaged was capable of performing and even of composing a scherzo of his own; but that *just now* he wanted to hear Beethoven's, which he thought had some merits." It was cheerfully repeated.—"Beautiful, charming!" cried Mendelssohn, "but still too loud in two or three instances. Let us take it again from the middle. "No, no," was the general reply of the band; "the whole piece over again for our satisfaction"; and then they played it with the utmost delicacy and finish; Mendelssohn, laying aside his baton, and listening with evident delight to the more perfect execution. "What would I have given," he exclaimed, "if Beethoven could have heard his own composition so well understood, and so magnificently performed!" By thus giving alternately praise and blame as required, spurring the slow, checking the too ardent, he obtained orchestral effects seldom equalled in our days. Need I add, that he was able to detect at once, even among a phalanx of performers, the slightest error either of note or accent?[100]

In Leipzig Mendelssohn's gifts as a conductor were fully realized in the establishment of the Gewandhaus orchestra as a model for its time. Even at his first concert with the orchestra on 4 October 1835 Lampadius recalled that Beethoven's B-flat Major Symphony "was given with a precision till then unknown in Leipzig." He continued: "Mendelssohn had carefully studied the piece, and directed it in person,—an arrangement new to us, but of eminent propriety. There had been no lack of excellence in former days, when the concert-master and the first violin had the direction of Beethoven's symphonies; yet of that nice shading, that exact adaptation of each instrument, that perfect harmony of all instruments, attained under Mendelssohn's direction, there had been no conception. The performance of the B-flat Symphony—that ethereal, soulful music—was one of the master effects gained by Mendelssohn as a director. Every new rendering threw new light upon it; so that the listeners were compelled to say, 'So perfectly performed we never heard it before.' "[101]

Hiller, in his recollections of a Leipzig visit in 1840, when Mendelssohn's methods and influence had had four years to bear fruit, appraised the situation as follows:

> Musical life in Leipsic, which has always been extremely
> active, had certainly acquired an extraordinary impetus
> through Mendelssohn's personal influence and energy.
> His eminent talent as a conductor was especially favour-
> able to the performance of orchestral works. Vigorous
> leaders had managed, before his time, by the help of
> their fiddling, to put plenty of spirit and precision into
> them, but no one had ever imagined so deep a concep-
> tion or such artistic finish in the performances of the
> great symphonies. It was altogether a capital orchestra,
> though the only example of extraordinary talent in it was
> Ferdinand David, who followed the conductor with his
> whole soul, and carried the whole of the strings along
> with him. Having for many years attended the . . . Con-
> servatoire Concerts in Paris, I was naturally at first much
> struck by the contrast, especially in the wind, and the
> general tone and effect. At that time the Leipsic Conser-
> vatorium was not yet founded, and it was only after-
> wards that the Gewendhaus Orchestra gained such mate-
> rial and brilliant reinforcements from David's pupils. But

all the little imperfections in individual execution were thrown into the background by the spirit and life which Mendelssohn instilled into the orchestra, his complete devotion to the cause, and the delight which lit up his expressive features at every successful achievement, and acted like electricity upon the public. When I speak of his conducting thus influencing the audience, it must not be supposed that he in any way courted notice by his behaviour at the desk. His movements were short and decided, and generally hardly visible, for he turned his right side to the orchestra. A mere glance at the first fiddle, a slight look one way or the other, was sufficient. It was the sympathy in the cause, which gathered strength from the sympathy brought to bear on it by so wonderful a man.[102]

Elise Polko, too, confirmed the lack of demonstrativeness in his conducting: "A very graceful movement of the head was peculiar to him, and when he carelessly threw it back, while his rapid glance, like that of a general, passed in array his musical forces, there was not one among them who did not at that moment silently vow to do his duty to the uttermost. He appeared elegant and calm while directing, no peculiarities attracted the attention of the audience, not a vestige of embarrassment, and yet entire security."[103]

Even in the years when his reputation was at its height, Mendelssohn did not have the kind of warm relationship with Berlin orchestral players that he enjoyed in Leipzig, which is so graphically illustrated by the Leipzig orchestra's farewell to its conductor in 1841.[104] What was freely given in Leipzig, out of affection and admiration, was extorted in Berlin by severity and coercion. This is illustrated by Mendelssohn's letter to David and Schleinitz of 29 October 1841, written during rehearsals for *Antigone*, though whether his obvious antipathy for the Berlin musicians was wholly justified, or had deeper psychological roots, may perhaps be questioned. He complained: "In the first rehearsal the orchestra wanted to play fast and loose with me, and there was such disorder and chattering that I could hardly believe my eyes and ears. I therefore turned the tables in the second rehearsal, was unpleasantly coarse, punished six of them,[105] and since then they have taken me for Spontini. None of them has budged since then, as soon as I appear, they take care, play well, and instead of putting on airs all the players have taken to fawning and obsequiousness, which is just as bad as the former. In the meanwhile they are obedient, and I knew beforehand that I could not improve them; this is just further proof of it. You have no idea of the creeping, servile nature of these stuck-up people. Both these things usually go together; and I have not found more than four out of all forty of them with whom I would really like to make music."[106] According to Devrient this was not the end of Mendelssohn's difficulties with the Berlin orchestral players;[107] but he seems to have achieved results, for in 1843 Rellstab asserted in print that in the symphony concerts that Mendelssohn directed in Berlin, the orchestra already played as well as the Conservatoire orchestra in Paris.[108]

It is noteworthy that even in England, where admiration for Mendelssohn was widespread and where he evidently felt comfortable, there were difficulties with orchestral musicians, who were reluctant to surrender the autonomy they had hitherto enjoyed. There was a widely publicized incident of insubordination when he unavoidably arrived late for a Philharmonic rehearsal in 1844.[109] But, as in Berlin, Mendelssohn persisted in enforcing his will. The following year, when Moscheles conducted Mendelssohn's A Minor Symphony with the Philharmonic Society orchestra, a reviewer noted:

> Having heard Mendelssohn's A minor symphony last season under its composer's guidance, we looked to its repetition at the concert of Monday evening with considerable interest. The Philharmonic band have never been celebrated as the most docile assemblage in the world; they were at small pains to conceal their opinion that even Mendelssohn was, as a conductor, officious and trouble-giving beyond the warranty of his years and experience as compared with theirs. He might be the greatest musician of the age, but they needed no teaching of his as to the performance of Beethoven's symphonies:—a few hints with regard to *his own* compositions, to be sure, might not be inadmissible, but even these might be

carried too far for Philharmonic tolerance. Mendelssohn was a very clever fellow, beyond all doubt; but he was very young and very troublesome. Still Mendelssohn, during last season, *was obeyed*. He brought with him somepositional title to command attention, and, moreover, he has, by nature, a manner of enforcing his wishes which most orchestras—and that of the Philharmonic included—find it somewhat difficult to resist. They grumbled and criticised in secret, but publicly they obeyed orders, and, as a necessary result, achieved a measure of success to which we remember no parallel in the society's annals. But even this state of unloving subjection—incomplete and unsatisfactory as it is when compared with that feeling of deference and admiration and hearty enthusiastic co-operation with which, *in every other country*, a great composer has power to inspire a great orchestra—even this compulsory habit of well-doing seems to have taken flight with the opening of the present season. Common sense and all experience point out that if, besides a regiment of soldiers and a ship's crew, there be one other assemblage in the world in which general liberty of opinion on matters of duty should be strictly prohibited, that assemblage is an orchestra. Mendelssohn knew this and enforced it;—Mr. Moscheles, its seems, cannot arrive at the same result.[110]

Many testimonies to the effectiveness of Mendelssohn's conducting at the Philharmonic during the 1844 season appeared in the London press. In the *Spectator*, for instance, a reviewer remarked of the Fourth Philharmonic Concert on 13 May 1844, at which Mendelssohn had directed the performance of his A Minor Symphony mentioned in the previous quotation,

> The effect of Mendelssohn's presence as conductor on
> the music of the evening is scarcely conceivable, except
> by those who experienced it. A man who has as it were
> lived in an orchestra—whose habitual duties as director

have enabled him to detect individual errors amid the densest mass of performers—to guide them when hesitating at new rhythm or unaccustomed effects, and to infuse one spirit into them—above all, who occupies this post as a distinguished composer—stands altogether in a different light from those who have hitherto filled it as a temporary distinction, and who if they have not wanted the talent for such an office have certainly wanted the necessary education for it. The influence of good conductorship, and the propriety of making that appointment permanent, are beginning to be better understood. The general commentaries of hearers on the excellent instrumental performance on Monday all tended to this effect: so obvious was the renewed vigour, animation, and attention of the orchestra. Mozart's Symphony—which contains of all his works the finest feat of pedal points—was performed in a manner differing in many respects from the tradition of the Philharmonic Society, but with no loss of effect. . . . Mendelssohn's Symphony was beautifully performed, and seemed to be better understood by the orchestra and the audience than it ever yet has been. It shows off the instruments in detail with peculiarly fine effect; has a most admirably-designed adagio, and a scherzo that can only be heard to be encored, as it was on this occasion. The playing on all hands was *con amore*.[111]

Mendelssohn's appointment in Berlin curtailed for a while, but did not sever, his connections with the Gewandhaus. He returned to conduct in Leipzig occasionally during the years 1842 to 1844, before taking up the conductorship again on a more regular basis with Gade as his deputy. Moritz Hauptmann referred to one of these occasions, and to Mendelssohn's negative view of Berlin, in a letter of 7 October to his old master and friend Spohr. He observed that "yielding to eager solicitation [Mendelssohn] agreed to conduct the first *Gewandhaus* Concert on the 2nd, and returned here for that purpose. The orchestral performance of Symphonies under his *bâton* is quite first-rate; such crispness and elasticity are rare. Mendelssohn, gratified as he is, will take none of the credit; he insists upon it, that with the many fine players under his command at Berlin, and any amount of zeal and hard work on his part, he cannot get the same result there."[112] Wilhelm von Wasielewski, who was a pupil at the Leipzig Conservatorium between 1843 and 1845, observed Mendelssohn's conducting at close quarters during those years (he acted as page turner when Mendelssohn played from music at a Gewandhaus concert). His account closely confirms the impressions of others.

> Mendelssohn raised the Gewandhaus concerts to a position of authoritative standing for the musical world, not only because the achievements of the orchestra which he obtained won the significance of a model, but also because creative and performing artists found an opportunity of coming before the public with their achievements under favourable circumstances such as they would not easily have encountered elsewhere. What distinguished Mendelssohn's efficacy were not only his pre-eminent qualities as a conductor but also the spiritual force of his winning personality. All participants felt the self-sacrificing seriousness and conscientiousness of this man, and thus everyone gladly and willingly subordinated themselves to him, so that model discipline reigned in the Gewandhaus orchestra. Every individual made it a matter of honour to work for the good of the whole. They did not merely do their duty but approached the matter with eagerness and love.
>
> Mendelssohn's fiery eye surveyed and ruled the whole orchestra. From the other point of view, however, all gazes were fixed upon the tip of his baton. At any moment therefore he was able, with sovereign freedom, to sway the mass as he wanted. If, in the performances, he permitted small modifications of tempo, by means of improvised ritardandos or accelerandos, these occurred in such a fashion that one could have believed they had been practised in rehearsal.
>
> As a rule, Mendelssohn gave his instructions to the

members of the orchestra in a friendly manner, often jokingly. He could, however, also be indignant about blunders and then expressed himself accordingly. Such an instance occurred when, at the end of the first movement of Schumann's B-flat Symphony, a second violinist in his eagerness made the mistake of coming in loudly in a rest. At this Mendelssohn immediately went white as a corpse with vexation, and when the piece finished he went up to the player concerned and said angrily, though only in a subdued voice, that such a thing ought not to occur in a Gewandhaus concert.

Mendelssohn's behaviour in a rehearsal where a new piece was being tried provides a contrast to this scene. The timpanist Pfundt, a musically very reliable member of the orchestra, had miscounted a rest, but when Mendelssohn spoke to him about it he did not want to admit it. When the questionable passage was repeated, however, it was evident that Pfundt really had made a mistake, at which the master, referring to the first scene in *Freischütz* where Kilian beats Max in the "master shot," said with a smile: "See my dear Pfundt, there once again the peasant has surpassed the hunter." The delicate irony that lay in this quotation was naturally noticed and aroused general merriment.

Mendelssohn possessed the finest sense of rhythm. The slightest wavering was admonished with the call: "Tempo, tempo, gentlemen!" In a tutti no fault escaped him, nor any wrong note, and he adhered with great strictness to the punctilious observation of the performance instructions that the composer had written down. His manner of preparing a piece for performance was wholly to the point. First he simply let it be played through, after which he went through the particular passages that required improvement. By means of this proceeding, in contrast to those conductors who repeat the piece over and again from beginning to end in order to make their observations, he was able to achieve a great deal in a comparatively short time. The performers were grateful for every repetition that was avoided and exerted themselves all the more to satisfy their director.

Mendelssohn's conscientiousness as a conductor is shown by the fact that before every rehearsal he had the orchestra servant bring the score of the work that was to be performed to his house, so that he could study it thoroughly, even though he was entirely familiar with its content.[113]

Another eye-witness, who observed Mendelssohn at close quarters during the last year of his life, was Ludwig Meinardus, whose attitude towards Mendelssohn as a man was equivocal, to say the least,[114] but who described his conducting in a wholly positive manner: "He directed the Gewandhaus concerts in the spirit of joyful delight at the beauty of serious art and its pursuit, and through their excellent achievements raised them to one of the best and most high ranking of all musical institutions. How well Mendelssohn knew, as a conductor, how to rouse enthusiasm, when, at particularly beautiful passages in the composition, he laid down his bâton on the music desk, let the experienced orchestra play alone and turned his shining eye on the audience! Now the listeners were sure that the piece must be beautiful, since it was able to lend such a blissful brilliance to Mendelssohn's features. Even today, 40 years after Mendelssohn's death, his influence is decidedly felt on the performance style of distinguished German orchestras."[115]

The question of tempo and tempo variation in Mendelssohn's orchestral performances has been a matter of controversy ever since Wagner's biased critique, in *Ueber das Dirigieren*. He accused Mendelssohn of ill-chosen tempi, lack of flexibility and insufficient attention to dynamics:

> *Robert Schumann* once complained to me at Dresden that he could not enjoy the Ninth Symphony at the Leipzig Gewandhaus concerts because of the quick tempi *Mendelssohn* chose to take, particularly in the first movement. I have, myself, only once been present at a rehearsal of one of Beethoven's Symphonies, when Mendelssohn conducted; the rehearsal took place at Berlin,

and the Symphony was No. 8 (in F major). I noticed that he chose a detail here and there—almost at random—and worked at it with a certain obstinacy, until it stood forth clearly. This was so manifestly to the advantage of the detail that I could not but wonder why he did not take similar pains with other *nuances*. For the rest, this incomparably bright symphony was rendered in a remarkably smooth and genial manner. Mendelssohn once remarked to me, with regard to conducting, that he thought most harm was done by taking a tempo too slow; and that on the contrary, he always recommended quick tempi as being less detrimental. Really good execution, he thought, was at all times a rare thing, but shortcomings might be disguised if care was taken that they should not appear very prominent; and the best way to do this was "to get over the ground quickly." This can hardly have been a casual view, accidentally mentioned in conversation. The master's pupils must have received further and more detailed instruction; for, subsequently, I have, on various occasions, noticed the consequences of that maxim "take quick tempi," and have, I think, discovered the reasons which may have led to its adoption.

I remember it well, when I came to lead the orchestra of the Philharmonic Society in London, 1855. Mendelssohn had conducted the concerts during several seasons, and the tradition of his readings was carefully preserved. It appears likely that the habits and peculiarities of the Philharmonic Society suggested to Mendelssohn his favourite style of performance (Vortragweise)—certainly it was admirably adapted to meet their wants. An unusual amount of instrumental music is consumed at these concerts; but, as a rule, each piece is rehearsed once only. Thus in many instances, I could not avoid letting the orchestra follow its traditions, and so I became acquainted with a style of performance which called up a lively recollection of Mendelssohn's remarks.

The music gushed forth like water from a fountain;

there was no arresting it, and every Allegro ended as an undeniable Presto. It was troublesome and difficult to interfere; for when correct tempi and proper modifications of these were taken the defects of style which the flood had carried along or concealed became painfully apparent. The orchestra generally played *mezzoforte*; no real *forte*, no real *piano* was attained. . . .

I have often been astonished at the singularly slight sense for tempo and execution evinced by leading musicians. I found it impossible to communicate to Mendelssohn what I felt to be a perverse piece of negligence with regard to the tempo of the third movement in Beethoven's Symphony in F major, No. 8. This is one of the instances I have chosen out of many to throw light upon certain dubious aspects of music amongst us.

Wagner then expounded his view about the stately tempo required for classical menuets and continued:

Now, the late Capellmeister Reissiger, of Dresden, once conducted this symphony [Beethoven's Eighth] there, and I happened to be present at the performance together with Mendelssohn; we talked about the dilemma just described, and its proper solution; concerning which I told Mendelssohn that I believed I had convinced Reissiger, who had promised that he would take the tempo slower than usual. Mendelssohn perfectly agreed with me. We listened. The third movement began and I was terrified on hearing precisely the old Ländler tempo; but before I could give vent to my annoyance Mendelssohn smiled, and pleasantly nodded his head, as if to say "Now it's all right! Bravo!" So my terror changed to astonishment. Reissiger, for reasons which I shall discuss presently, may not have been so very much to blame for persisting in the old tempo; but Mendelssohn's indifference, with regard to this queer artistic *contretemps*, raised doubts in my mind whether he saw any distinction and difference in the case at all. I fancied myself standing before an abyss of superficiality, a veritable void.[116]

While Wagner's assertions about other musicians, particularly Mendelssohn, should scarcely ever be accepted at face value, independent evidence of Schumann's distress at the tempo of the first movement of Beethoven's Ninth Symphony exists in a review and in his manuscript memoirs of Mendelssohn.[117] There are also other contemporary references to Mendelssohn's liking for brisk tempi. But with respect to both the first movement of the Ninth Symphony and the Tempo di Minuetto of the Eighth Symphony it is scarcely feasible that Mendelssohn, or other contemporary conductors could have exceeded the tempi indicated by Beethoven's metronome marks in these movements by much, if at all, for technical reasons (for example, the thirty second notes at b. 132ff. in op. 125 and the triplets for violoncelli in the trio in op. 93). The evidence seems much more plausibly to point to a conflict between early nineteenth-century performing traditions and the growing predilection for more expansive and flexible tempi that was shown by Wagner, Liszt and other musicians of that generation.[118] That Mendelssohn's conducting was not without nuances of tempo, albeit subtle ones, is suggested by a significant number of references in reviews and recollections, some of which I have quoted above. Another occurs in a notice of Mendelssohn's performance of Beethoven's *Eroica* Symphony with the London Philharmonic in 1844: "He gave readings of various passages which had remained hidden among the complications of Beethoven's gigantic score. The boldness and vigour with which points were taken up—the effects produced by accelerating and retarding the time—and the delicate shades and gradations of tone—gave the whole composition quite a new character, and produced an extraordinary impression on the audience."[119] Though no extended account of this aspect of his conducting appears to have survived, it seems clear that Mendelssohn was comparatively sparing with larger modifications of tempo, such as evident *ritardando* where none was indicated by the composer (something it was claimed he avoided in his keyboard performances). Grove transmits Kellow Pye's recollection that "after introducing some *ritardandos* in conducting the introduction to Beethoven's second symphony, he excused himself by saying that 'one could not always be good,' and that he had felt the inclination too strongly to resist it."[120] But, as indicated earlier, this does not by any means imply that he performed the music in an inflexible manner.

Wilhelm Lampadius, on the basis of first-hand knowledge, provides a good summary of Mendelssohn's conducting. It vividly conveys the enthusiastic response of those who felt the full force of Mendelssohn's influence:

> What gave Mendelssohn so great a compass to his musical activities was the union, in the highest perfection, of three gifts which are usually granted only singly to men in the measure with which he commanded them. He was as great as a conductor, as he was a virtuoso and composer. His fame as a conductor is now world-wide. When once his fine, firm hand grasped the *bâton,* the electric fire of Mendelssohn's nature seemed to stream out through it, and be felt at once by singers, orchestra, and audience. We often thought that the flames which streamed from the heads of Castor and Pollux must play around his forehead, and break from the conductor's staff which he held, to account for the wonderful manner with which he dissipated the slightest trace of phlegm in the singers or players under his direction. But Mendelssohn conducted not only with his *bâton,* but with his whole body. At the outset, when he took his place at the music-stand, his countenance was wrapped in deep and almost solemn earnestness. You could see at a glance that the temple of music was a holy place to him. As soon as he had given the first beat, his face lighted up, every feature was aflame, and the play of countenance was the best commentary on the piece. Often the spectator could anticipate from his face what was to come. The fortes and crescendos he accompanied with an energetic play of features and the most forcible action; while the decrescendos and pianos he used to modulate with a motion of both hands, till they slowly sank to almost perfect silence. He glanced at the most distant performers, when they should strike in, and often designated the instant

when they should pause, by a characteristic movement of the hand, which will not be forgotten by those who ever saw it. He had no patience with performers who did not keep good time. His wondrously accurate ear made him detect the least deviation from the correct tone, in the very largest number of singers and players. He not only heard it, but knew whence it came. Once, during a grand performance, when there were about three hundred singers and over two hundred instruments, all in chorus, in the midst of the music, he addressed a young lady who stood not far from him, and said to her, in a kindly way, "F, not F sharp" (*F, liebes Fräulein, nicht Fis*). To singers, his rehearsals were a constant enjoyment. His praise was always delightfully stimulating; his criticism, not chilling nor disheartening. By throwing in all kinds of bright and merry words, he knew how to rouse the most indifferent and idle to the best performance they were capable of, and to keep the weary in good-humor. Repeated and perverse carelessness would provoke him, but never to a coarse or harsh word: he had too much knowledge of the world, and too much grace of character, for that; the farthest he went was to a dash of sarcasm. "Gentlemen," he once said to a number of men who insisted on talking together after the signal to begin had been given, "I have no doubt that you have something very valuable to talk about; but I beg you to postpone it now: this is the place to sing." This was the strongest reproof that I ever heard him give. Especially kindly was he when he praised the singing of the ladies. "Really," said he once, when a chorus went passably well at the first singing, "very good, for the first time exceedingly good; but, because it is the first time, let us try it once again": on which the whole body broke into a merry peal of laughter, and the second time they sang with great spirit. All prolonging of the tones beyond the time designated by the written notes, he would not suffer, not even at the close of the chorus. "Why do you linger so long on this note, gentlemen? it is only an eighth." He was just as averse to all monotonous singing. "Gentlemen," he once said at a rehearsal, "remember this even when you sing at home; do not sing so as to put any one to sleep, even if it be a cradle-song." The pianos could not be sung too softly for him. Did the chorus only sink in a piano passage to a mezzo-forte, he would cry out, as if in pain, "Piano, piano, I hear no piano at all!" It was one of the remarkable features of his leading, to hear the largest choir sink at the right places into the faintest breath of sound. Mendelssohn's unwearied patience at rehearsals was all the more remarkable, as his frame was so delicate and his ear so sensitive; but it made the result, when *he* was satisfied with it, as perfect as any work can be in the hands of human performers.[121]

SEVEN · The Teacher

31 · Charles Edward Horsley

Mendelssohn, if not quite a reluctant teacher, was certainly not an enthusiastic one. As with so much else in his life, he saw teaching as a task that, although not really congenial, he felt himself duty bound to undertake, for the sake of his art. Nevertheless, there is every indication that he was successful in stimulating and guiding the composition and performance studies of talented musicians, always encouraging them to strive for self-development, and that he derived satisfaction from their progress. It may be taken for granted that, whatever misgivings he may have entertained about his aptitude as a teacher, Mendelssohn applied himself to this task with the conscientiousness that he regarded as a moral obligation in all his occupations. His success in conveying his aesthetic and artistic principles to most of his pupils is evident from their accounts.

It is unclear when Mendelssohn first began to take private pupils in either composition or piano playing, but from a very young age he was willing and able to offer critical guidance in composition. Even at the age of twelve his abilities evidently inspired confidence, for in a letter of 30 September 1823 to Wilhelm von Boguslawski he preceded his detailed criticism of a symphony that the twenty-year-old Boguslawsky had sent him with the comment: "Since you demanded an expert opinion from me, I guess I have to give it."[1] Ten years later, a letter to Karl Klingemann mentions his giving a weekly piano lesson to his cousin Arnold Mendelssohn.[2] During his time in Düsseldorf he attracted young musicians to study with him in a more or less informal manner, and his teaching activity increased when he moved to Leipzig in 1835. There is a hint of this in a letter written jointly by him and his sister Rebecka to Klingemann on 7 October 1836. In her portion of the letter Rebecka remarked: "His music school is also flourishing; a young Frenchman has just signed up with him, a pupil of the Conservatoire and of Kalkbrenner called Stamáty,[3] who, however, is not coming forward with his piano playing here, but wants to learn German music; Walter Goethe,[4] a friendly red-cheeked, phlegmatic little man, the little Franck[5] well or not well known to you; but where is your Bennett whose enrolment gave me very particular pleasure. There has not yet been an English musical genius, I believe, and it is specially satisfying to me that Felix, who was first acknowledged in England, should have him to educate."[6]

Bennett, who had made Mendelssohn's acquaintance at the Lower Rhine Musical Festival at Düsseldorf earlier in the year, in fact arrived in Leipzig on 29 October 1836. The relationship was more that of a friend and colleague than of a pupil. As Mendelssohn had written to Attwood from Düsseldorf on 28 May 1836 (in English),

> He [Bennett] told me that you wanted him to stay some
> time on the continent and with me. I really do think it
> impossible to give him (advanced as he is in his art) any
> advice which he was not able to give himself as well, and
> I am sure if he goes on in the same way as he did till
> now, without losing his modesty and zeal, he will always
> be perfectly right and develope his talents as his friends
> and all the friends of music may desire; if however, he
> should like to live on the continent for a while, and if he
> should stay at Leipzig, I need not say that I should feel
> most happy to spend some time with such a musician as
> he is, and that at all events I shall always consider it as
> my duty to do everything in my power to assist him in
> his musical projects, and in the course of his career,
> which promises to be a happy and blissful one.[7]

And on 20 June Mendelssohn informed Klingemann that Bennett "wants to come to Leipzig, although I have told him that there is no question any longer of teaching in his case; but he wants to nevertheless, and you can hardly imagine how pleased I should be to get to know him more closely and for a longer time. Therefore, however, I cannot take any money from him, otherwise I would be a music Judas. Also, I will certainly gain as much pleasure and advantage from his presence as he will from mine."[8] In fact, Mendelssohn seems never to have accepted payment for teaching and thus never saw himself formally in the role of a teacher, but rather as a guide and mentor to those who were advanced enough and dedicated enough to benefit from his advice.

One young English musician whom Mendelssohn consented to instruct privately was Charles Horsley, with whose family he was on intimate terms. Mrs Horsley first raised the question of Charles's musical education in a letter of 1 January 1839, asking whether he endorsed the suggestion that Charles should study with Moritz Hauptmann in Kassel. In his reply (in English) on 17 January 1839 Mendelssohn observed that Hauptmann was "certainly the best man whom you could find for your purpose in Germany, as he combines a deep science and a thoroughly musical mind to a very amiable temper and the most honourable character. . . . As for learning I hardly think he could find his equal anywhere, and several of his pupils assured me that his method is as clear and simple as the instructions it conveys are deep and impressive. I have had several opportunities of seeing him, and if uniformity of feelings and taste gives a right to such a title I may call him my friend;[9] at least I have met with few musicians with whom I so entirely agreed in matters of art as well as all others. Perhaps your son will find him rather severe in the beginning, and he has the reputation of being colder than German musicians usually are, but I like him the better for it, as this coldness is only in his exterior, not at all in his soul, and as his warmth is therefore the more sincere."[10]

After more than a year with Hauptmann in Kassel, Charles Horsley went to Leipzig early in 1841 to join Mendelssohn's circle, and apart from spending the second half of 1841 in London, he remained in Leipzig until 1843. From Mendelssohn he received a certain amount of direct tuition and a great deal more informal advice. This is evident from Mendelssohn's report (in English) to William Horsley on his son's progress in a letter dated 15 March 1841:

> I need not tell you that I have few musical friends in
> whom I take a warmer and more cordial interest than in
> your son Charles; the time I can be with him gives me

always a true pleasure. According to the advice in your letter I try to direct his attention more to execution than to composition, and find it the more necessary as it is evident that his own inclination induces him already not to neglect his talent for composition and will never allow him to become careless in that department of his art. I am sure you will be happy to see how perfectly he has developed his talent for composition in Mr. Hauptmann's school, how completely he has fulfilled the object you had in view when you sent him to this master. He writes purely and fluently, without any difficulty and embarrassment, and his ideas follow each other naturally and well; while there is never an attempt at those unmusical and frivolous harmonies (unharmonic [?enharmonic]) which are now considered modern and lovely, his music is equally free from stiffness and commonplaces. A new Capriccio, a Trio, and several other pieces for the Piano have pleased me very much, and he is continually busy in writing something new, trying to do better and to improve with every new attempt. As this desire seems to make part of the talent which nature has given him, I think it the more indispensable to induce him to cultivate also those other branches of art to which he seems not driven by his natural inclinations, I mean execution, and particularly his playing the Pianoforte. It is indeed very important for his future career, and he plays too well not to do better than he does. It was therefore to this that I particularly directed his attention; I found his fingers a little stiff, and not independent enough: he used to go over difficult passages in great haste in order to arrive sooner in smooth water, in short it was the playing of a young composer who had hardly thought of anything but counterpoint, harmony and fugues in the last year. This is not to be changed in the course of a few months, there is hardly anything to be done in the limited time of his residence but a beginning; but yet I think some progress may already be remarked in his touch, which was rather hard, as well as in the independence of his fingers. On the organ he has not been able to practise; our churches are so very cold that a very plain chorale is all that our best organists can perform during the service, and ornaments are out of the question (which makes our Cathedral service sound better in winter than in summer). Let me now also add to this musical report that Charles has gained the esteem and friendship of all those who know him, that his frankness and perfect good-nature soon made him a favourite with our society, and that his character as well as his talent seem to me certain proofs of his future welfare.[11]

The nature of Mendelssohn's guidance is made clear in Charles Horsley's own recollections of his time in Leipzig:

When those who had the right to call themselves pupils of Mendelssohn assert the fact, it must not be thought that he gave lessons in the ordinary acceptation of the word. In the first place I do not believe there is a single instance in which he received pecuniary recompense for his advice. Next, his instruction was not imparted in a formal manner. Speaking of myself as an example of the course he followed with others, I generally went to him three times a week. Previous to fixing an hour he would advise me to practice certain pieces, generally by Bach or Beethoven, and when I played them to him he would either criticize the performance, or more frequently play them to me. His favourite mode of giving advice was, however, by taking a walk, during which he would invariably talk on musical subjects. One of his favourite haunts was a little Inn in a small forest near Leipzig called the Rosenthal. I have frequently walked with him there, and during our wanderings he would invariably select for consideration a Symphony by Beethoven, an Opera of Mozart, or an Oratorio of Handel, or a Fugue of Bach. He would analyze these, point out the various beauties of their ideas, the ingenuity of their instrumentation, or the subtleness of their counterpoint in a most masterly manner. At the rehearsals of the Gewandhaus, to which all his pupils were free, he would always provide us with the scores of the larger works, and we had generally afterwards to undergo a pretty keen examination as to the construction and peculiarities of each.[12]

32 · Emil Naumann

Shortly after the Horsleys first sought his advice about Charles's musical education Mendessohn was approached by Emil Naumann's parents with the request that he directly supervise their son's studies. Naumann, however, was just twelve years old at that time, and Mendelssohn's response shows his concern not merely for the musical education but for the total development of the child. His description of what he considered a desirable education for the boy, in a letter of 19 September 1839, has unmistakable echoes of his feelings about his own upbringing.

> Pray accept my thanks for the great proof of confidence you show me, by the purport of your esteemed letter of the 12th of this month. Believe me, I thoroughly appreciate it, and can indeed feel how important to you must be the development and future destiny of a child so beloved and talented. My sole wish is, like your own, that *those* steps should be taken, best calculated to reward his assiduity and to cultivate his talents. As an artist, I consider this to be my duty, but in this case it would cause me peculiar pleasure from its recalling an early and happy period of my life.
>
> But I should unworthily respond to your confidence, did I not communicate frankly to you the many and great scruples which prevent my *immediately* accepting your proposal. In the first place, I am convinced, from

repeated experience, that I am totally deficient in the talent requisite for a practical teacher, and for giving regular progressive instruction; whether it be that I take too little pleasure in tuition, or have not sufficient patience for it, I cannot tell, but, in short, I do not succeed in it. Occasionally, indeed, young people have stayed with me, but any improvement they have derived was solely from our studying music together, from unreserved intercourse, or casual conversation on various subjects, and also from discussions; and none of these things are compatible with actual teaching. Now the question is, whether in such early youth a consecutive, unremitting, strict course of discipline be not of more value than all the rest? It also appears to me that the estrangement of your son from the paternal roof just at his age forms a second, and not less important objection. Where the rudiments of education are not wholly wanting (and the talents of your wife alone are a security against this), then I consider that the vicinity of his parents, and the prosecution of the usual elements of study, the acquirement of languages, and the various branches of scholarship and science, are of more value to the boy than a one-sided, even though more perfect cultivation of his genius. In any event such genius is sure to force its way to the light, and to shape its course accordingly, and in riper years will submit to no other permanent vocation, so that the early acquired treasures of interest, and the hours enjoyed in early youth under the roof of a parent become doubly dear.

I speak in this strain from my own experience, for I can well remember that in my fifteenth year there was a question of my studying with Cherubini in Paris, and I know how grateful I was to my father at the time, and often since, that he at last gave up the idea, and kept me with himself. It would of course be very different if there were no means in Bonn, of obtaining good and solid instruction in thorough-bass and the piano; but this I cannot believe, and whether that instruction be rather better or more intellectual (provided it be not positively objectionable) is of less moment when compared with the advantages of a longer stay in his own home. Further, my life hitherto has been so unsettled, that no summer has passed without my taking considerable journeys, and next year I shall probably be absent from here for five or six months; this change of association would only be prejudicial to youthful talent. The young man, therefore, must either remain here alone all summer or travel with me; and neither of these is advisable for him.

I state all these disadvantages because I am myself so well aware of them, and fully estimate the importance of the subject. If you do not participate in my views on mature consideration, and are still of the opinion that *I* alone can assist your boy in the attainment of his wish, then I repeat that in any case (irrespective of this) I should esteem it my duty to be useful and serviceable, so far as my ability goes, to a youthful genius, and to contribute to his development by the exercise of my own powers; but, even in this event, a personal interview is indispensable, if only for a few hours, in order to arrange everything clearly, and until then I cannot give an unqualified consent.

Were you to bring the lad to me at Easter, I fear I should already have set off on my summer excursion. Indeed, the only period when I am certain to be in Leipzig is from autumn till Easter. I quite agree with Madam Naumann, that it is most essential to cultivate pianoforteplaying at present as much as possible, and not to fail in studying Cramer's exercises assiduously and steadily; but along with this daily training on the piano, two hours a week devoted to thorough-bass might be useful, as such variety would be a pleasant change, rather than an interruption. The latter study indeed ought to be pursued in an easy and almost playful manner, and chiefly the practical part, that of deciphering and playing figured bass; these are the main points, and can be entirely mastered in a short time; but the sooner it is begun, the sooner it is got quit of, and this is always a relief with such dry things. And now once more accept my thanks for the trust you have reposed in me, which I thought I could only adequately respond to by entire sincerity.[13]

As in Horsley's case, Mendelssohn later recommended a course of instruction with Moritz Hauptmann before he would agree to supervise more advanced studies in composition. Naumann, therefore, came to Leipzig in autumn 1842 to study with Hauptmann, who had just moved there from Kassel. The Leipzig Conservatorium was founded the following year, and it was primarily as a pupil in this institution that Naumann received tuition from Mendelssohn. Naumann's own account of his studies indicates the continuing interest Mendelssohn took in his progress, even after he left the Conservatorium, for personal reasons, the following year.

Although the letters of Felix Mendelssohn that have appeared in recent years give us many glimpses of the character and life of the highly honourable and amiable artist, they could not provide us with an exhaustive depiction of his personality. The necessity for an ordered survey of the course of his artistic and personal development, in which respect even those letters ought only to be regarded as valuable material, becomes an increasingly palpable necessity. For an author to be in a position to proceed with a biography of Mendelssohn, however, it seems to us that much that is indispensably necessary to the completeness of a picture of his amiable character is lacking in the way of documents, reports and testimonies from contemporaries of the master who are still living. From this point of view it seems to us to be the duty of anyone who had the fortune to have been in close personal contact with the deceased, to prepare for the future biography by means of relevant information.

We intend therefore, in the following lines and documents to let a few side-lights fall on an aspect of Mendelssohn that has not been significantly illuminated in the letters that have been printed so far. We refer to his individuality as a teacher. Those of the printed letters that reveal the master to us in such relationships show him to us almost exclusively in relation to finished pupils. The present writer already had the fortune to enjoy Mendelssohn's tuition in his boyhood, and precisely for this reason believes that he can communicate some traits that, in their originality and charm, add new fascination to the picture of the artist which already dwells so pleasantly within us. If it is thereby necessary for him to speak of his own course of development this occurs only insofar as is required by the depiction of the master. Who should delineate the teacher for us, however, if not the student.

From his earliest years the boy was determined that he should be dedicated to music. But before his family gave their consent to this it was considered advisable to seek Mendelssohn's opinion. This can be found in the second part of the published letters under the date: Leipzig 19th September 1839 [given above]. A later letter on this matter from Berlin on 13 October 1841 reads:

HONOURED SIR:

I received your previous letter amidst the press of such diverse work and business that it was impossible for me to answer it immediately, which I would otherwise gladly have done. I was very grateful therefore that Professor Gerhard, who recently talked to you, promised to give you the gist of my answer. If the question is with which teacher of theory, thoroughbass and counterpoint your son can learn most completely and surely, with whom he can learn to lay the firmest grounding and develop inner sense as well as outer skill in the most masterly manner, I must answer according to my heartfelt conviction: with Hauptmann in Cassel. Not only because, on account of his work and his extraordinarily fine musical cultivation, I consider him the most capable person in our Fatherland to do this, but also because I have come to know several of his pupils very well (among others, last winter, a young Englishman, who studied with him for two years)[14] who provide the clearest evidence of the great excellence of his instruction in these important areas. If other circumstances now permit you to send your son to this teacher I am convinced that with respect to musical matters you will subsequently have reason to rejoice over it. With the request ——— etc.

    Your most respectful servant,
    Felix Mendelssohn-Bartholdy.

    The opportunity for a personal trial of the boy, which was mentioned as an indispensable prerequisite to giving a final verdict on his artistic calling, first became possible in 1842 at the Lower Rhine Music Festival, which that year took place in Düsseldorf. Mendelssohn, although he had already been resident in Leipzig for a long time, retained a never extinguished preference for the Rhine and the Rhineland and had therefore kindly undertaken the proffered direction of the above-mentioned as he later did so many other Rhenish music festivals that were honoured by his presence.

    We found him in Schadow's house, which at that time rightly counted as the focus of all artistic and intellectual life in Düsseldorf. Here, surrounded by old friends, among whom, apart from Schadow, we may mention Hildebrandt, he allowed himself to be entirely uninhibited, and just as in the concert hall his high artistic seriousness came to the fore, so in sociable intercourse his fundamentally so cheerful and ingeniously humorous character was enchantingly in evidence.—The boy, who had always revered the master in his heart only from afar as one of the unapproachable divine beings, did not trust his eyes when he saw him, reminiscing about adventures which he had shared with Hildebrand in Italy, fall into an exuberance and hilarity that infected and electrified the whole company.

The musical beginner's trial consisted of adding three upper parts to a figured bass given to him by Mendelssohn, but chiefly in the scrutiny and performance of a range of his own still very childish compositions. The inspection of the latter had the beneficial effect that the boy's desire to dedicate himself to music was now definitely conceded. Since Mendelssohn had declared himself willing to undertake the whole musical education of the young pupil, though only to participate in the teaching himself when the pupil was more mature, my removal to Leipzig for the time being was decided upon. I went there in Autumn 1842 and had the pleasure of instruction from Moritz Hauptmann who had in the meanwhile become cantor of the Thomasschule. Soon afterwards, Mendelssohn founded the Conservatorium for Music in Leipzig, which still exists and flourishes today, among whose teachers, apart from himself, shone the names of Ferdinand David, Niels Gade, Moritz Hauptmann, Ignaz Moscheles and, at a later date, Ferdinand Hiller. At the same time these men constituted the circle of friends which Mendelssohn gradually gathered around him to work together with him in Leipzig.

He retained for himself the teaching of advanced composition, and to this end selected six students from among the others. Twice weekly we gathered ourselves about him, and the memory of those lessons belongs among the most unforgettable things in my life. He sat in our midst at a simple table and went through with us the compositions which we supplied from one session to the next; this was done to a certain extent "publicly" in that praise or criticism, error or merit was tackled and discussed not with the individual but in participation with fellow students. If one of us had written a passage for an instrument that was not appropriate to its character and technical capabilities he would ask, for instance, the viola player among us whether he would gladly perform the passage in question and if the latter would not, he had to explain his reasons. In this way we learned from each other.

Although seriousness and artistic rigour predominated on the whole in these lessons, the amiable master could nevertheless occasionally be extremely humorous and merry. Thus I once brought him an Adagio from a string quartet about which he initially expressed his unreserved approval. Suddenly, however, he broke off reading and exclaimed to me: "But what have you done there, I cannot answer for that with Herr Wittmann" (as one of the most excellent of the Leipzig cellists was called). "At the beginning of your thirty bars rest he will very gently put down his cello, go into Auerbach's Cellar, eat oysters and when he returns the thirty bars will be far from over."— Thus his criticism, that in a quartet movement the four-part texture slipped through my fingers and resolved itself into a trio, was cloaked in a witticism that made us all laugh, and yet it permanently remained a decisive hint for me.

He would not tolerate anything that looked at all like pretension, and he knew how to chastise it soundly. There was one of our number who gave a symphonic menuet the title "First attempt!", only, as I am now convinced, to excuse the deficiency of his work.—"You must think us astonishingly stupid" said Mendelssohn, after he had let him play his composition on the piano that was available in the room, "to have given the thing a title that is uttered by every bar in it. Spare me anything of the kind in future; you will produce many more first attempts in your life and should thank God if, even after the end of your studies, you recognize your compositions only as attempts in comparison with the ideas that swim before you at the beginning of your work."

Mendelssohn had the kindness to encourage me to

seek him out in his house as well as in the Conservatorium. Out of respect and shyness I availed myself of this permission all too infrequently, and when I did, in order not to bother him, I customarily chose his designated afternoon conversation hour from 2 to 3 o'clock. I most often found him reading the score of a Mozart or Beethoven symphony or occasionally a favourite book. Thus, once it was *Don Quixote*, of which he spoke with delight; another time it was Tieck's *Puss in Boots*. He chided me repeatedly, in a touching manner, that I so seldom let him see me. Also, I was not cheerful and high-spirited enough for him. "You should not brood so much with me, but you should also sometimes go for a country walk with friends and cheerfully order a glass of beer." The following lines, which he gave me in the vacation as a report for my parents, can best demonstrate how well he meant this, and how much his noble sympathetic mind was able to enter into the soul of his pupil in order to help him where he needed it:

HONOURED SIR,

Your son asks for a few lines from me, before his vacation, as a testimony of his good conduct and advancement in the Music School here. I gladly give him such a testimony, for I have much praise to bestow on him, especially of late. His natural abilities and inborn talent will not remain hidden to anyone who knows him well; his diligence, too, was unmistakable, and if he goes on in this way I have every hope that, for himself and for you, his efforts will soon result in joy and achievements. But this progress, this diligent, unceasing application, this dedicated, honest striving is an unavoidable requirement. I say this here because I am convinced that it is the main thing that your son still needs. While he is staying with you could you advise him, could you impress upon him that for him the years of study and honest diligence are now here, not those of attainment and reflection, indeed that he might ask Heaven not to let him emerge from these years of study throughout the whole of his life, because only in that way can the proper modest and yet proud artistic feeling come about, thus you would have done him the greatest benefit and have helped him forward as much as anyone can now do. He lacks nothing in natural abilities, in this respect he excels most of the others, that is given to him by Heaven; in addition to that he needs a fresh, powerful will, and that he must provide for himself.

I beg to give your wife my best thanks for the friendly lines that were sent to me a while ago. With the greatest respect I remain always your servant

Felix Mendelssohn-Bartholdy

Leipzig, 7 July, 1843.

I was unfortunately not yet able at that time to fulfil the dear master's wishes. In the child who had grown up in the beautiful Rhineland, and who was not yet mature enough to be satisfied by art alone, the broad plains of Leipzig aroused a longing for the far mountains and verdant streams of his homeland, which soon grew to an irresistible homesickness and robbed him of all joy in his further musical studies. In these circumstances a temporary return home was counselled. It was only later, when Mendelssohn had long given up his personal teaching at the Conservatorium, and in any case only stayed now and then in Leipzig, where Ferdinand Hiller, in the first place, and then Niels Gade took over the direction of the Gewandhaus concerts, that I was again fortunate enough to be allowed to approach him, and this time, indeed, it was really as one favoured by fate, for at that time he also did not want to have anything to do with private pupils.

At this time, Mendelssohn had, if one excepts his periodic journeys to Berlin, England and Leipzig, fixed his real residence in Frankfurt am Main, and spent the winter in the old imperial city, but the summer in the neighbouring Taunus mountains.—By this time it had become a matter of honour to prove to him by my progress that I was beginning to become worthy of the renewed good fortune of laying my work before him. The master's following lines may demonstrate to what extent I was successful:

Soden in Taunus 23 July 1845.

HONOURED LADY,

I can only deserve all the friendly things in your letter of yesterday insofar as I have always had the desire, certainly, to be useful and beneficial to your son. But you believe that this desire has become a fact, and there, to be sure, you overrate what I was in a position to do for your Emil. I lacked the time, the leisure, even the proximity to be able to have a really genuine effect on his studies; it gives me all the more pleasure to be able to give a good and satisfying answer to your queries about these studies—indeed, what I have to say to you today about Emil is better and more hopeful than what I ever said or wrote about him previously. The talent given to him by Heaven, to which neither he himself nor anyone else can add or take away anything, I leave, as ever, out of consideration. Since he apparently lacks nothing that ought not to be lacking in a true and capable artist, it is not in his case, as generally, a question of more or of less, but of the seriousness, the stamina, the real, sincere, unfeigned love of the thing, the greater or lesser depth of feeling, even in preparatory work, that is the question about which others too can comment, and for that reason, as you know, I was not without concern about your Emil. In the last six months, however, he has done as much as anyone could to dissipate this concern, and precisely in the matter of serious diligence I must give him the best of testimonials. His work becomes better and more mature with every week, he even seems to find more and more joy in the fulfilment of these duties of his, and in equal proportion as he works better and more confidently, he seems inwardly to have become better and more confident. If he holds steadfastly to this new course, which there is all probability that he will, since he once more feels so good about it and seems a new man, he and everyone who has his interests at heart can certainly look into the future with full and joyful confidence. His whole personality as well as his works are more capable, are more worthy of a striving artist, also his is not one of those more defective natures that must first proceed painfully step by step. I did not conceal from you and your husband last winter that it seemed to me that it was now high time to push forward the study of art with all strength and all seriousness; if there had once again been failure in this respect I would never again have trusted in a successful outcome. Since, however, on the contrary, everything that even the most demanding person could require and expect is there, since it is there at the right time, I am convinced that Emil is called to something good and considerable in art and life, and firmly hope that you and all your family will experience real joy in him. He has the endowment, and now also the will and the ambition, so may Heaven grant you that he is sustained in this!

Unfortunately I cannot hope to greet you personally in the near future; within a few days I must leave this area, much as I regret it. But I can never survive long without visiting the Rhine, and I therefore also hope it will not be so very long before I once again

come to Bonn. Keep me in your friendly remem-
brances until then, and with the warmest greetings to
your husband I remain

Your most respectful servant

Felix Mendelssohn-Bartholdy

At that time I walked twice a week from Kronenthal,
charmingly situated in a wood of nut trees and fruit trees
at the foot of the mountains, to the friendly spa of Soden, where Mendelssohn spent most hours of the day
with his family in the open air or on walks. My work
now and then gave him occasion for characteristic remarks. Thus he once said to me, when I brought him a
composition that was conceived and executed without
the right feeling: "The mere external physiognomy of this
piece does not allow me to expect much good from it.
Good music looks different on the paper; even before
one has read it this page shows a uniformity as flat as
Berlin people and Berlin surroundings."

Whoever remembers certain events of Mendelssohn's
youth, which seem to prove the saying that a prophet is
not without honour save in his own country, and the
fact that, despite subsequent effusive recognition in his
homeland, the master still tasted these dregs of bitterness,
will find this remark excusable.

If Mendelssohn was satisfied with a piece of work that
was laid before him, he began to nod, to sway and generally to smile happily as he went through it. If the flow or
the musical progress of the whole faltered anywhere, then
the alterations that he scribbled, mostly in pencil, into the
pupil's manuscript were marvellous, and substantiated the
well-known saying that the master perfects with a few
strokes what the apprentice vainly strove to do with great
expenditure of means. I preserve as relics those pieces of
work, in which the increasingly faded and blurred traces
of that long-stilled hand are still recognizable.

Mendelssohn once said to me, among other things:

"When a musical thought comes to us, we do not have to ask whether it is original or not.[15] If the musical motif does not result from a conscious desire or reflection, but from an inspiration and inner revelation, then we are not able, in any case, either to add or to rob anything from its originality. Such inspirations are therefore only to be thankfully received, like a pure gift from Heaven. We sin against them and drain them of their freshness and simplicity if we chip away at them and find fault with them out of vain striving after originality. To be sure, what we begin to do later, in the course of musical working-out, with these ideas that have been bestowed on us without our volition, how we organically refine them further and develop them into the most perfect artistic form—that is our business, the business of our will, our energy and perseverance. In this respect, therefore, we cannot be hard-enough upon ourselves. Yet in the hours when we should only feel thankfulness and good fortune there should be no reflection or criticism. Had I let myself be induced constantly to inquire after the originality of my ideas by the remarks others made about me I would certainly not have been able to achieve anything further. Whoever does not on the whole firmly believe that his life's work is to be found only in art and in honest, true persever-ance and activity as an artist, whoever is still dependent on the approval of others, or on immediate public suc-cess, should rather give it up at once. This is not a mat-ter of overestimating oneself, but the belief that what moves us inwardly most deeply, and most enduringly spurs us on to exertion must also be our God-given call-ing. So you should take note that there are two kinds of thing a man should not let himself be talked into, and two things which no-one but himself can choose for him, these are: his calling and his wife."

When Mendelssohn again exchanged Frankfurt for Leipzig, since I continued, by his desire, with more spe-cialized study with Franz Messer in Frankfurt, he permitted me henceforth to communicate with him in writing and to send him my further works. The second part of the published letters contains one of his letters of reply sent to me from Leipzig at the beginning of 1846.[16]

33 · The Leipzig Conservatorium (Wasielewski, Rockstro, Meinardus)

Naumann's article offered an impression of the activity of the Leipzig Conservatorium in its first year. The foundation of the institution, which was very largely the result of Mendelssohn's personal efforts, may be seen as a logical extension of his concern not only to exercise the moral obligation of making his knowledge and understanding accessible to those who possessed the gifts to appreciate them, but also to provide a broader base for the propagation of the aesthetic creed that he believed was essential to secure the moral health of music in the future.

Particularly valuable accounts of Mendelssohn's activity at the Conservatorium have been left by two of the full-time students, Wilhelm von Wasielewski and William Smith Rockstro (Rackstraw). Wasielewski was in the first intake of pupils in 1843, and he remained until Easter 1845. Rockstro drew a picture of the Conservatorium in 1845 and 1846, when Mendelssohn had resumed his position there after his unsettled period of some two years' residence in Berlin. Both these musicians may be regarded as unreserved admirers of Mendelssohn. Wasielewski recalled:

> A surprise that greatly delighted me was that, along with a few other students, I was allowed to attend the lessons in composition, as well as those in ensemble playing, that were given by Mendelssohn. In those there was an opportunity to learn much, in a certain sense the best of all that was taught in the institution. Every word spoken by the master, founded on rich experience, deep insight and observation, was worth its weight in gold. Mendelssohn had a rare gift of expressing himself concisely, clearly and precisely, without circumlocution, on all the points that

came into question during the instruction, and since he combined the purest taste with an unfailingly apposite opinion, his teaching was certainly stimulating. After more than 50 years I still remember well what demands he made on the interpretation and performance of a piece of classical music, and how, without wasting time, he guided the student towards it with a short observation or even only with a hint. Since it was apparent from the beginning that I was the only one of my fellow scholars who was acquainted with the viola the part of this instrument fell to my lot when necessary. Mendelssohn called me his personal violist [*Leibbratschist*][17] from then on, of which I was rather proud.

For one of the lessons in ensemble playing I had asked permission to be allowed to perform the B Minor [Violin] Sonata No. 1 by Bach with my piano-playing fellow student, the later Berlin music director Hermann Kriegar. Each of us strove to perform his part as well as he could. When the first Allegro came to an end, however, Mendelssohn said to my fellow performer: "Please let me come to the piano, I can play that better." The thought of accompanying the revered master made me feel somewhat ill at ease. However, I pulled myself firmly together. In addition, Mendelssohn carried me with him in the Andante and tore me along with him in the Allegro of the final movement, and thus I played my part enthusiastically. It certainly helped me that I knew the work, and in particular my part, thoroughly before.

Of the composition students Theodore Kirchner was very definitely the most gifted. At that time he inclined towards the Schumannesque tendency, to which he also remained true. The first task that Mendelssohn set us was a four-part vocal piece of the motet type. Afterwards we had first to produce an Andante for string quartet, then the other movements to go with it. There was no lack of amusing incidents connected with this. Thus a pupil, through ignorance of string instruments, had written double stops for the C string of the viola. When Mendelssohn saw this he merely said to the person concerned: "Just ask my personal violist whether that's playable." On another occasion a pupil had written concealed fifths in his work; to which Mendelssohn remarked that although they might be wreathed in garlands of flowers they were none the better for it, for they sounded bad.

Mendelssohn always looked on the spot through the work that was presented at the next lesson, as far we had reached with it, and corrected it in pencil, while at the same time commenting on the errors and deficiencies. In his perplexity one of the pupils asked the master how one should set about composing a quartet movement. To this he said: "Take a quartet of Haydn and model the form on it. That is how my master Zelter treated me too." If any passage in our work pleased him, he praised it with the words: "Very charming [*Recht hübsch*]." On the whole, however, not much came of the attempts at composition; with the exception of Kirchner we still had too little practice at composing in several parts. Nevertheless, for the sake of encouragement, Mendelssohn allowed an Allegro by Kirchner and an Andante by me to be given a hearing by David and his quartet colleagues in front of the assembled teaching staff. There the matter rested, particularly since Mendelssohn's teaching ended with the close of the summer term, because the master, at the behest of the king of Prussia, went to Berlin for the whole winter. Although he later came back to Leipzig again, full of the best will to work at the Conservatorium once more, he was nevertheless unable to return to wholly regular activity. He never resumed composition teaching at all, which in the meanwhile was disposed of elsewhere. On the other hand he participated in instruction in playing from score, in which I took part, and in solo piano playing. Moreover, he directed exercises in counterpoint, but, as already suggested, with interruptions, since he was often away from Leipzig.[18]

FIGURE 12. Moses Mendelssohn. Engraving of a painting by Frisch. In *Moses Mendelssohns gesammelte Schriften* (Leipzig, 1843), 1: frontispiece.

FIGURE 13. Abraham Mendelssohn Bartholdy. Pencil drawing by Wilhelm Hensel in Sebastian Hensel, *The Mendelssohn Family,* 3rd ed., trans. Carl Klingemann et al. (London, 1882), frontispiece.

FIGURE 14. Lea Mendelssohn Bartholdy. Pencil drawing by Wilhelm Hensel in Sebastian Hensel, *The Mendelssohn Family,* 3rd ed., trans. Carl Klingemann et al. (London, 1882), 1: 67.

FIGURE 15. Felix Mendelssohn in about 1820. Pencil drawing by Wilhelm Hensel in Karl Mendelssohn Bartholdy, *Goethe and Mendelssohn*, trans. M. E. von Glehn (London, 1872), 16.

FIGURE 16. *Das Rad* (The wheel). Drawing by Wilhelm Hensel, 1829, depicting members of the Mendelssohn siblings' circle. Felix is in the centre, in Scottish kilt, and again among the other figures, as a shadow (with an F above his head). The remaining figures, identified around the circumference of the wheel by the initial letters of their names, are further identified in a letter from Fanny to Felix dated 15 August 1829 (Citron, *Letters*, 73–75); apart from "Paul M. B.," the names added to the drawing do not correctly identify the figures nearest to them. The entwined figures with B and F above their heads are Felix's sisters Rebecka (Beckchen) and Fanny, referred to by Felix as the "fish-otters"; H is Albert Heydemann; A is Albertine Heine; P, facing her, is her future husband, Paul Mendelssohn Bartholdy; C is Caroline Heine; A, dancing with Felix's shadow, is Auguste Wilmsen; D is Johann Gustav Droysen; M is Minna Heydemann; Wilhelm Hensel depicted himself being drawn into the wheel by his fiancée, Fanny. Reproduced by permission of the Bildarchiv Preuβischer Kulturbesitz.

FIGURE 17. Felix Mendelssohn Bartholdy in 1834. Pencil drawing by Wilhelm Schadow. Staatsbilbliothek zu Berlin, Musikabteilung mit Mendelssohn Archiv, MA BA 135. Reproduced by permission.

FIGURE 18. Felix Mendelssohn Bartholdy in 1835. Oil painting by Theodor Hildebrandt. Staatsbilbliothek zu Berlin, Musikabteilung mit Mendelssohn Archiv MA BA 136. Reproduced by permission.

FIGURE 19. Cécile Mendelssohn Bartholdy (née Jeanrenaud). Pencil drawing by Wilhelm Hensel in Sebastian Hensel, *The Mendelssohn Family,* 3rd ed., trans. Carl Klingemann et al. (London, 1882), 2: 29.

FIGURE 20. Felix Mendelssohn Bartholdy in 1842. Pencil drawing by Carl Müller. According to Ferdinand Hiller (*Mendelssohn*, 183) "Carl Müller, a clever painter, whose acquaintance we had made in Rome, happening to be in Frankfort just at this time, promised to do us a pencil sketch of Mendelssohn if we could only get him to sit. At my wife's request he consented to put himself into the painter's hands on condition that she would sing to him during the time. Sixteen songs of various lengths completed the sitting, and this sketch, with his autograph and the date of the 15th September, 1842, is one of our greatest treasures." F. Hiller, *Mendelssohn. Letters and Recollections*, trans. M. E. von Glehn (London, 1874), frontispiece.

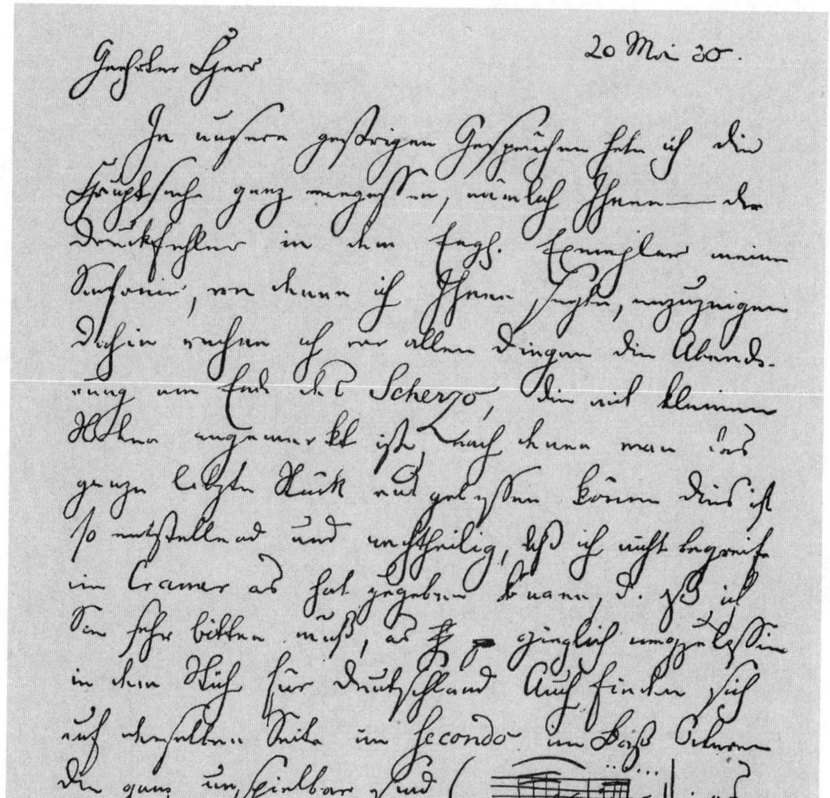

FIGURE 21. Letter of 20 May 1830 from Felix Mendelssohn Bartholdy to an unidentified recipient (probably the publisher H. A. Probst). This hurriedly written note (Mendelssohn added the word *Eilig* [in haste] at the bottom of the page) concerns a possible German edition of his First Symphony in piano duet arrangement. He specifies corrections to the already published English edition, in which the scherzo from the Octet was substituted for the original menuetto. In *Famous Composers and Their Works*, ed. John K. Paine and Leo R. Lewis (London, c. 1895), vol. 2.

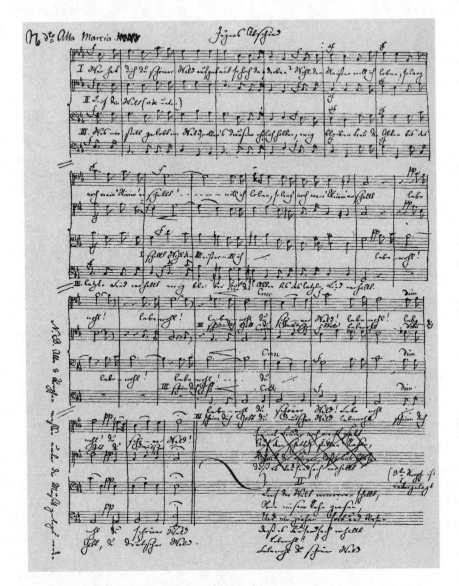

FIGURE 22. Mendelssohn's autograph score of the male-voice part-song *Jägers Abschied* ("Wer hat dich du schöner Wald"), composed in 1840; published as *Der Jäger Abschied*, op. 50, no. 2, with accompaniment for four horns and bass trombone. In *Famous Composers and Their Works,* ed. John K. Paine and Leo R. Lewis (London, c. 1895), vol. 2.

Rockstro, who first met Mendelssohn as a nineteen-year-old youth in London in 1842, approached him in 1845 for guidance about his future training and on his advice entered the Leipzig Conservatorium. Mendelssohn resumed his activities there early in the following year.

On the 3rd January, 1846, he entered upon a course of active service at the Conservatorium; assuming the sole command of two pianoforte classes, and one for composition, and in the management of both fulfilling the duties of a hard-working professor with no less enthusiasm than that which he had so long displayed in his character of conductor at the older institution. Now that the Royal College of Music is attracting so much, and such well-merited attention in our own country, our readers may perhaps be glad to know something of the method of teaching pursued by the founder of the most important music school in Germany, on the authority of one who was fortunate enough to participate in its advantages. We shall therefore devote the remainder of our present chapter to a brief sketch of his mode of proceeding in the class-room, based on our own personal recollections, and corroborated by the contents of a MS. notebook in which we were careful to record the subjects of the various lessons, and the manner of their discussion.

Among the members of the upper classes for the study of the pianoforte and composition were, Mr. Otto Goldschmidt, Mons. Michel de Sentis, Herren Tausch, Kalliwoda, Kahlan, and Wettich, and one or two other pupils, who all met regularly, for instruction on Wednesday and Saturday afternoons, each lasting two hours. The first pianoforte piece selected for study was Hummel's Septett in D minor: and we well remember the look of blank dismay depicted upon more than one excitable countenance, as each pupil in his turn after playing the first chord, and receiving an instantaneous reproof for its want of sonority, was invited to resign his seat in favour of an equally unfortunate successor. Mendelssohn's own manner of playing grand chords, both in *forte* and *piano* passages, was peculiarly impressive;[19] and now, when all present had tried, and failed, he himself sat down to the instrument, and explained the causes of his dissatisfaction with such microscopic minuteness, and clearness of expression, that the lesson was simply priceless. He never gave a learner the chance of mistaking his meaning; and though the vehemence with which he sometimes expressed it made timid pupils desperately afraid of him, he was so perfectly just, so sternly impartial in awarding praise, on the one hand, and blame on the other, that consternation soon gave place to confidence, and confidence to boundless affection. Carelessness infuriated him. Irreverence for the composer he could never forgive. "*Es steht nicht da!*" [it is not there] he almost shrieked one day to a pupil who had added a note to a certain chord. To another, who had scrambled through a difficult passage, he cried with withering contempt, "*So spielen die Katzen!*" [that's how cats play] But, where he saw an earnest desire to do justice to the work in hand, he would give direction after direction, with a lucidity which we have never heard equalled. He never left a piece until he was satisfied that the majority of the class understood it thoroughly. Hummel's Septett formed the chief part of each lesson, until the 25th of February. After that it was relieved, occasionally, by one of Chopin's studies, or a Fugue from the *Wohltemperirte Klavier*. But it was not until the 21st of March that it was finally set aside, to make room for Weber's *Concert-Stück*, the master's reading of which was superb. He would make each pupil play a portion of this great work in his own way, comment upon its delivery with the most perfect frankness, and, if he thought the player deserved encouragement, would himself supply the orchestral passages on a second pianoforte. But he never played through the piece which formed the subject of the lesson in a connected form. On a few rare occasions—we can only remember two or three—he invited the whole class to his house; and, on one of these happy days, he played an entire Sonata— but not that which the members of the class were studying. And the reason of this reticence was obvious. He wished his pupils to understand the principles by which he himself was guided in his interpretation of the works of the great masters, and at the same time to discourage servile imitation of his rendering of any individual composition. In fact, with regard to special forms of expression, one of his most frequently reiterated maxims was, "If you want to play with true feeling, you must listen to good singers. You will learn far more from them than from any players you are likely to meet with."

Upon questions of simple *technique* he rarely touched, except—as in the case of our first precious lesson upon the chord of D minor—with regard to the rendering of certain special passages. But the members of his pianoforte classes were expected to study these matters, on other days of the week, under Herren Plaidy, or Wenzel, professors of high repute, who had made the training of the fingers, and wrist, their speciality. It would be impossible to over-estimate the value of this arrangement, which provided for the acquirement of a pure touch, and facile execution, on the one hand, while, on the other, it left Mendelssohn free to direct the undivided attention of his pupils to the higher branches of Art. An analogous plan was adopted with regard to the class for composition. The members of this simultaneously studied the technicalities of harmony under Herr F. Richter; those of counterpoint, and fugue, under Herr Hauptmann, the Kantor of the Thomas-Schule, and the most learned contrapuntist in Europe; and those of form, and instrumentation, under Herr Niels-W. Gade.

Mendelssohn himself took all of these subjects into consideration, by turns, though only in their higher aspect. For counterpoint, he employed a large black-board, with eight red staves drawn across it. On one of these staves he would write a *Canto fermo*; always using the soprano clef for the soprano part.[20] Then, offering the chalk to one of his pupils, he would bid him write a counterpoint, above, or below, the given subject. This done, he would invite the whole class to criticise the tyro's work; discussing its merits with the closest possible attention to every detail. Having corrected this, to his satisfaction, or, at least, made the best of it, he would pass on the chalk to some one else—generally, to the student who had been the most severe in his criticism— bidding him add a third part to the two already written. And this process he would carry on, until the whole of the eight staves were filled. The difficulty of adding a sixth, seventh, or eighth part, to an exercise already complete in three, four, or five, and not always written with the freedom of an experienced contrapuntist, will be best understood by those who have most frequently attempted the process. It was often quite impossible to supply an additional part, or even an additional note; but Mendelssohn would never sanction the employment of a rest, as a means of escape from the gravest difficulty, until every available resource had been tried, in vain.

One day, when it fell to our own lot to write the eighth part, a certain bar presented so hopeless a deadlock, that we confessed ourselves utterly vanquished. "Cannot you find a note?" asked Mendelssohn. "Not one that could be made to fit in, without breaking a rule," said we. "I am very glad," said he, in English, and laughing heartily, "for I could not find one myself." It was, in fact, a case of inevitable check-mate.

We never knew, beforehand, what form the lessons in this class would assume. Sometimes he would give out the words of a song, to be set to music, by each member of the class, before its next meeting; or a few verses of a psalm, to be set in the form of a Motet. When summoned, towards the end of May, 1846, to direct the Lower Rhine Festival, at Aix-la-Chapelle, the task he left for completion during his absence was a Quartett for stringed instruments. When any trial compositions of this kind pleased him, he had them played by the orchestral class; and would even play the viola himself, or ask Herr Gade to play it, in the chamber music;[21] striving, by every means of encouragement within his power, to promote a wholesome spirit of emulation among his pupils. It was not often that his kindly spirit met with an unworthy response; but the least appearance of ingratitude wounded him, cruelly. When the Quartetts we have mentioned were sent to him for examination, he found one of them headed "Charivari." At the next meeting of the class, he asked for an explanation of the title. "The time was so short," stammered the composer, "that I found it impossible to write anything worthy of a better name. I called it 'Charivari,' to show that I knew it was rubbish." We could see that Mendelssohn felt deeply hurt; but he kept his temper nobly. "I am a very busy man,"[22] he said, "and am, just now, overwhelmed with work. Do you think you were justified in expecting me to waste my time upon a piece which you yourself knew to be 'rubbish'?[23] If you are not in earnest, I can have nothing to say to you." Nevertheless, he analysed the Quartett with quite as much care as the rest, while the culprit stood by, as white as a sheet; well knowing that not a member of the class would speak to him, for many a long day to come. In pleasant contrast to this, we cannot refrain from giving publicity to a very different story. One of the best pianoforte players in the class was a handsome young Pole, with a profusion of jet-black hair, which in true Polish fashion, he allowed to hang half-way down his back. While playing the brilliant passages which form the climax of the *Concert-Stück*, the good fellow shook his head, one day, in such sort as to throw his rich locks over his shoulder, in a tempest of "*Kohlpechrabenschwarze Haare*." "You must have your hair cut," said Mendelssohn, in German, with a merry laugh. The Pole was very proud of his *chevelure*; but, at the next meeting, his hair was the shortest in the class—and there was not a student then present who would not gladly have had his head shaved, could he thereby have purchased the smile with which the happy student was rewarded for his devotion.

More than once, the lesson was devoted to extemporisation upon given subjects; during the course of which Mendelssohn would sit beside the improvisatore, and, without interrupting the performance, suggest, from time to time, certain modes of treatment which occurred to him at the moment.[24] On other occasions, he would take two well-defined motives, and work them up into a model of the Sonata-form, in order to show how much might be accomplished by very simple means. He insisted strongly upon the importance of a natural and carefully arranged system of modulation; and would frequently call up one pupil after another to pass from a given key to some exceedingly remote one, with the least possible amount of apparent effort. On one occasion, when the writer had failed to satisfy him, in an attempt of this kind, he said, in English, "I call that modulation very ungentlemanlike."

When the lesson went well, it was easy to see that he thoroughly enjoyed it. But the work was too hard for him, in addition to his other laborious duties; and the acceptance, by Moscheles, of a pianoforte professorship at the Conservatorium, gave him unmixed satisfaction. But for this, the institution must have suffered terribly, when Mendelssohn's health broke down so suddenly, after the completion of *Elijah*. But, when the new professor entered upon his duties, in October, 1846, after sacrificing his splendid position in London for the sole purpose of doing the best he could for the interests of Art, all anxiety on this point was at an end; and the history of the Conservatorium, during the next twenty years, sufficiently proves the wisdom of the offer Moscheles so generously accepted.[25]

These personal accounts uniformly depict Mendelssohn as a generous and committed but strict and occasionally harsh teacher. The latter qualities are conveyed, from the point of view of a victim of Mendelssohn's irritability, in Charles Villiers Stanford's retelling of the experiences of one of his piano teachers, Miss Flynn, who "had been a pupil of Moscheles at Leipzig and had studied, but with many tears under Mendelssohn, who was a most impatient teacher." Stanford added in a footnote: "The Bishop of Limerick told me that in the course of a walk at Interlarken in 1847 Felix confided in him his deep regret at this failing." He gave an account of an occasion on which Miss Flynn, when a pupil at the Conservatorium, was due to perform a piano solo at one of the students' evening concerts: "There was an inexorable rule that all pieces should be played from notes and not by heart. Miss F. being I suppose a little proud of her memory, left her music at home and arrived at the hall without it. Mendelssohn descended upon her, as she described it, like a hawk; sent her home to fetch it, and told her that the audience should be kept waiting till she came back. On her return she found to her relief that the public was not in the least impatient or resentful. After the concert she found out the reason. Moscheles had immediately gone up on to the platform, struck a chord or two on the pianoforte, made a wry face and sent for the tuner."[26] Moscheles's diary confirms this account in its essentials, though he states that she was to play in a piece by Czerny for eight hands on two pianos, and gives Mendelsslohn's words as, "What, forget your music for a public performance, as if it were a mere trifle! this is too bad. There sits the public, and has to wait because you have forgotten your music! etc. etc."[27]

One source, hitherto apparently unremarked in the Mendelssohn literature, presents a vivid picture of how Mendelssohn's sharp reactions to anything he thought slipshod or unsatisfactory could have a profound and counterproductive effect on an oversensitive student. Ludwig Siegfried Meinardus, encouraged by Schumann's positive opinion of some of his compositions, applied to enter the Leipzig Conservatorium in January 1847. His father wrote to Mendelssohn on 13 December 1846: "Through the kindness of Dr R. Schumann I have learned that through your influential mediation I may hope that the fee associated with entry to the musical institute there may be delayed for a year." He went on to explain that only in these circumstances could he afford to support his son's studies, adding: "And if my son were to be robbed of this prospect his most cherished hopes would be dashed, and the path along which his life is directed, which he sees as the highest goal of his desires, would be closed to him." Furthermore, he said that he had taken the liberty of assuming Mendelssohn's support and was now letting his son depart for Leipzig, so that he would be there early in the new year.[28]

Meinardus's preliminary interview with Mendelssohn and his subsequent, dispiriting experiences of both Mendelssohn and the Conservatorium, were recalled in his curious, novel-like autobiography, *Ein Jugendleben* (published in Gotha in 1874). The incidents described have a ring of authenticity about them, even if they are coloured by the evident unhappiness that lay behind Meinardus's recollections of Leipzig. Mendelssohn's disheartening reception of Meinardus may have resulted from any number of causes, but it is worth remembering that the encounters described by Meinardus occurred at a period when Mendelssohn was under even greater stress than usual. His distress over the death on 23 November 1846 of his servant Johann Krebs, to whom he was deeply attached, had made it impossible for him to work creatively for a while (he occupied himself with collating his score of Bach's B Minor Mass with the performance material from Dresden). Only in December was he able to resume the demanding task of completing his revisions to *Elijah*, and it was probably on this that he was engaged at the time of Meinardus's first visit to him.

Meinardus's account provides not only an unfamiliar picture of Mendelssohn's involvement with the Conservatorium but also an unusually vivid glimpse of the atmosphere and procedures of the institution at that time. The book begins with an introduction that clarifies the nature of Meinardus's treatment of his autobiography, which is narrated in the third person and in which he calls himself Sigfrid (*sic*). It seems possible from this that the letters to his family included in the book may substantially be direct transcriptions of letters written in 1847, for Meinardus stated that "all the retailed facts are taken partly from reliable oral information and are partly borrowed from first-hand written records. Also, in isolated cases, reminiscences that have been acquired by the narrator through personal observation have been included, but only if they had been verified as unobjectionable by the most scrupulous examination." Having arrived in Leipzig, Sigfrid obtained an apartment.

> No less an advantage of his apartment . . . appeared to lie in the fact that part of the first floor had as its tenant no less a person than Felix Mendelssohn-Bartholdy, the sole ruler of the musical taste of the whole of the then civilized world. Mendelssohn's apartment had a special entrance by which one got to it from the garden that lay behind the large building. . . .

THE CONSERVATORIUM

> On one of the first days after having arranged his apartment, [Sigfrid] took the first step towards securing his entry to the Conservatorium. To this end he did not neglect to go to the apartment of the most important person, namely Mendelssohn-Bartholdy, and introduce himself. The report of this visit, in a letter home "to the loved ones," ran as follows:
> "Mendelssohn lives at the back some 70 steps lower than I. Now listen please!—Rather excited, I came to his floor and pulled the shining brass bell. A man in a black tail-coat with white tie and waistcoat opened the door. You are mistaken if you are inclined to think that this elegant man was Mendelssohn. It was only his valet or rather his major domo.—By Jove!—The fellow elegantly wrinkled his nose and condescended to announce me.
> A thick soft carpet fitting exactly in all directions, in true oriental splendour!—to the right, in the middle against the wall a Streicher concert grand, no longer too young; to the left a bookcase and sofa with matching armchairs; heavy silk curtains, which almost made the beloved *chiaroscuro* of fashionable taste too *obscure*:—that was my immediate impression of the room into which I was lead. In the middle of the room, but nearer to the wall with the window, stood a peculiarly designed writing-

desk, apparently light enough to be moved hither and thither without great effort. I remained standing respectfully at the door and observed with satisfaction the back of the small man who sat on a high throne at the desk and who was the real owner of the name that was lauded with enthusiasm by the tongues of countless thousands throughout the musical world. The whole of the man who had his back to me occupied, bodily, a hardly measurable minimum of room compared with the extent of the land mass that was dominated by his widespread fame. His extremely simple house-coat, too, which was suspiciously like a dressing-gown, was in sharp contrast to the choice furnishing of his surroundings. He did not give me the opportunity for further observation but hopped down, none too nimbly, from his high work stool to me on the floor, greeted me briefly and as he took his seat on an ordinary chair he politely directed me, to my not inconsiderable embarrassment, to sit on a large leather-covered armchair. How much famous flesh and blood may already have rested on it!—'You have been very warmly recommended to me by Herr Dr. Schumann,' Mendelssohn then began the conversation in the softness and pitch of a tenor voice. At the same time he looked at me with his finely etched but immobile, detached face, which remained unaltered throughout the almost twenty minute long discussion. He asked after my accomplishments as a musician. I responded truthfully that I still hoped to become a musician and had not yet accomplished anything as such. 'But Herr Dr. Schumann explained to me that he had seen compositions by you that ought to indicate talent.'—He never mentioned Schumann's name without prefacing it with 'Herr doctor.'—I explained how that work had come about; how Schumann came by it; how he kindly looked over all the deficiencies and mistakes and, among other things, made it clear to me that I still lacked every kind of musical training, which I myself never doubted. Mendelssohn appeared hardly to listen as I said all this and asked me to play him something of my work on his piano. You can imagine my horror. I tried to excuse myself—to no purpose. Since my things had not yet come, I had put on Wilhelm Bauer's jacket [*Schniepel*]. This piece of clothing, uncomfortable in itself, since it was designed for a smaller build, was so tight for me that I could only stretch out my arms with difficulty and the blood pressed into the fingers as if I had five fat black puddings on each hand. I asked to be allowed to play on another occasion since I had got out of practice on the journey and my hands had suffered through the winter drive, both of which were more than an excuse.—All that did not help at all. The strict man stuck inexorably to his dry request that I play him something, so I had to do it. I got up and sat down at the piano, on which I played a few chords.—The piano reacted not at all easily and was somewhat worn out. What should I play though?—Mendelssohn, his hands behind his back, started to pace easily from one end of the room to the other; always moving like a pendulum back and forth along the diagonal from the corner to the piano. I chose the 'Song without Words' in E-flat that you know, which Karl thinks sounds Mendelssohnian. My eyes swam as I began and every time Mendelssohn neared the piano I feared that my composure would completely desert me. Luckily I got through to the end without a hitch or even a breakdown. The gods may judge the rest of my performance. A kind of feeling like a hangover told me enough. As I ended, however, Mendelssohn positioned himself by the piano, gave me a penetrating look and with the same detached manner, yet, as it seemed to me, with a somewhat doubtful tone asked: 'Is that by you?'—The imputation against my honesty piqued me and I answered curtly: 'Certainly!—I was supposed to play one of my own attempts.'—He replied: 'Hm—I can already hear [*kann schon hören*].'—This oracular statement was very contradictory. It could mean 'I can already hear that you have talent' or the awful opposite. Fortunately he added some kind of clarification: 'I will write to Hofrat Keil so as to spare you unnecessary bother. Come to me again on Monday to collect the answer."—

Thus the obscure expression "I can already hear" could scarcely be meant as a rejection. Sigfrid rather thought that he could derive hope from it, but he did not entirely give himself up to it, since the memory of his deficient playing and even more deficient concoction troubled him. So on the appointed day it was not without anxious apprehension that he returned to Mendelssohn's threshold.

But this gave way to the greatest joy as Mendelssohn informed him that he was going to be taken as a pupil of the Conservatorium, without having to submit to the usual examination. Now Sigfrid understood the puzzling "I can already hear" and would have happily fallen thankfully on the neck of the conveyor of the gladsome tidings, if a respectful instinct and the unaltered detached nobly etched face had not kept him in seemly bounds.— He was now sent to Hofrat Keil, at that time chairman of the committee of the institute, bringing the request that the fees might be paid later on, which on Mendelssohn's recommendation—as he supposed—would be accepted, and received the instruction to come back again in order to receive the usual papers for his acceptance and more of the like.

In the joyful certainty to which, as a result of this explanation, he gave himself up without thinking, he was, however, suddenly astonished by an invitation to an examination, which was signed by the directorate of the Conservatorium. By whom the change in Mendelssohn's decision, which Hofrat Keil appeared tacitly to confirm, might have been initiated, he, who was so unexpectedly terrified out of his scarcely tasted feelings of happiness, never found out. Mendelssohn, who could best have explained it, did not condescend to do so. It seemed probable therefore that he had not been able to fulfil his promise to write a letter to Hofrat Keil and did not feel obliged to enlighten Sigfrid about it.—

"What else could I have done," the latter wrote to his parents, "than immediately throw all unfounded joy out of the window and be seized by the most terrible anxiety, which had more than 24 hours to torture me."

A future co-scholar of the Conservatorium, whom he got to know at midday in the Gambrinus [restaurant], calmed him to some extent over his painful trouble, as Mendelssohn, on subsequent, more mature consideration may not have found his accomplishments satisfactory enough to excuse him the examination. This examination was described by that pupil of the Conservatorium as purely an outward formality required by the rules, which chiefly had the purpose of introducing the new pupil to his future teachers. Otherwise it had nothing to do with a decision about acceptance, since it hardly ever happened that a pupil was rejected; it was rather to assess his abilities superficially so as to know to which of the teachers he should be assigned. Sigfrid, whose horror at playing before Mendelssohn still made his limbs tremble, who in any case—under the influence of his accustomed isolation, suffered from crippling shyness, was only slightly comforted by that calming disclosure and made his way to the Conservatorium on the appointed day with a heavy heart.

The servant of the institute, "Herr Quasdorf," encouraged him and led him—like a sacrificial lamb to the slaughter—into the hall where the dreadful act was to take place. The directorate and teaching staff, Mendelssohn at their head, were assembled almost in their entirety, probably over 20 men with more or less famous names. Without any further introduction Mendelssohn signified to the examinee, who was almost suffocating with anxiety, that he should play something he had prepared. Several pianos from Breitkopf und Härtel's work-shop stood on the podium. On one of these he played, as well or as badly as may be, a prelude and fugue by Sebastian Bach. In the prelude his fingers threatened to defy him. But he overcame his embarrassment to the extent that he was able to play the fugue with greater care than the prelude. The listeners, who kept rather quiet, did not particularly disturb him any more. As the last chord died away a general murmur of conversation arose among the panel, in the exchanges of which Sigfrid, who remained sitting at the piano, was unable to distinguish any distinct words. He believed he could derive hope from the expressions on some of their faces and was already congratulating himself that this part of the examination seemed to have gone well enough for him, when to his not inconsiderable horror Mendelssohn emerged from the throng, came to the podium and asked him to play the very "Lied ohne Worte" that, several days earlier, he had had to force himself to play before the famous ears of this indulgent master. Here and now there was no way out and this time he even played the piece more calmly and not without satisfaction. What effect it made on those present was not conveyed to him.—Now followed an examination of his harmonic knowledge, which, as our tale has made clear, he had independently acquired with nothing but the guidance of several insufficient textbooks. The examination in this discipline now took place by means of the following procedure:

One of those present went to the lined blackboard, which stood on an easel, and wrote notes in allabreve value and in the bass clef with chalk on one of the staves, leaving three empty ones above, so that he exactly covered the width of the board. The notes were provided with figures. Now the examiner thrust the chalk into the candidate's hand and retired, without giving him a word of explanation about what he should add with the chalk.

The latter looked doubtfully around the assembled company as if he expected instructions.

"Can you not read the figured bass?" the examiner asked him rather brusquely. Sigfrid knew how to do that with tolerable certainty.

"So then, will you write out the chords?"—he was told, and, only slightly enlightened about the real intention, he now set about a task for which he had never previously had any notion of the procedures, and even now had gained none. Over every bass note he wrote the chord indicated by the figures from the tenor upwards to the soprano, putting the notes that formed the harmony as close together as possible. The task was made more difficult by having to write the chords in the form of a score with four different clefs. He certainly knew of the unfamiliar C clef, but had difficulty in reading it. Universal peals of laughter from the high tribunal was the judgment on his work, when it was complete on the board. Sigfrid really could not understand the cause of this merriment.—He checked his chords and did not think he had got any of them wrong. Undeserved humiliation always roused his obstinacy, and since he could see absolutely no reason for the not exactly tactful laughter, he eventually declared, in a raised voice, that he did not understand the reason why his work had given rise to it and begged to be given to understand it.

Now his taskmaster, a small man with loose black hair, which he wore in a manner similar to Mendelssohn, asked whether what was on the board constituted singable parts?—Although Sigfrid had not believed that the given bass had implied that he should write his chords as singable parts, he immediately grasped the meaning of the question that had been put to him.

"Why did you not rather say to me straight away that I should add singable parts to the bass?"—he replied crossly and reminded him that it was only supposed to have been a matter of chords. He then fulfilled the task so much to the satisfaction of his examiner that the latter pardoned a pair of consecutive fifths, about the illegitimacy of which the novice had never had a clear grasp.

Thus the examination ended and the fifths-delinquent was handed over to the castellan "Herr Quasdorf," who led him into a smaller room, where he had to wait until further notice for the decision. He had not been left alone to his own thoughts for long when a gentleman rushed in and, with a brief, silent greeting, hurried to one of the tables, of which there were several, and without saying a word began to occupy himself with volumes of music that lay on it. Sigfrid had not noticed this apparition, which looked like the very image of Mendelssohn, among those who were gathered for the examination. He later discovered that it was one of the piano teachers. Striking as his exterior appeared, Sigfrid was little inclined to observation. He felt something like anger at the manner of a treatment that he had never before experienced from his former teachers. Having retired into a corner of the room he waited a fairly long time for what was to come. Then the door was thrust open and in came Mendelssohn. Without noticing Sigfrid's presence, he hurried up to the unknown gentleman in a lively fashion, laughing loudly, and cried: "What a shame that you were not there; we had extraordinary fun."

The recipient of this remark, indicating the corner where Sigfrid was hardly able to hold himself upright for shamefaced despair, made a sign for silence and the two jolly men, now whispering and chuckling, carried on for a while with their entertainment, the object of which, its dumb witness, could easily be perceived. The victim was released from this painful situation by "Herr Quasdorf," who required him to follow him. He was led into the hall again and there received a number of printed and filled-out forms that dealt with his acceptance into the institution, the teaching plan, a book of disciplinary rules, a bond for the fee, which was only allowed to be paid later to the extent of a half for a foreigner [someone who was not a native of Saxony], and other such things. He had to sign these papers and swear with a solemn handshake to observe the disciplinary rules. With this he was released and formally accepted into the institution as an examined student of the Conservatorium. The painful scene had certainly dampened his enthusiasm for the teaching institution somewhat, and the opinions he received from his new musical acquaintances of the life and work of the institution may also have contributed to this. None of them displayed confidence in it, and with the exception of one individual none had wanted to entrust his studies to it. However, this individual, whose personality in any case appeared decidedly disagreeable to Sigfrid, maintained that no-one learned anything useful at the Conservatorium who had not already made considerable strides and had therefore managed to attract the attention of the excellent teachers to him, so that he was instructed by one of them exactly like a private pupil.—Despite all these unpropitious initial impressions he remained in good spirits at first and hoped that through diligence, and stimulation on the part of the teacher, he could obtain the desired success. Yet this hope soon began to waver and dwindled more and more the longer he attended the prescribed lessons and was able to compare the achievements of the institution with his own personal expectations, demands, and slow progress. . . .

The thing he found most painful was that the enthusiasm he always dedicated to Mendelssohn's music stood in contrast to the impression he obtained from the various personal encounters with the great man who was universally praised as the most amiable of all masters. Two more meetings with Mendelssohn gave even more cause than the already described encounters for the touchy sensitivity of the young artist to be shaken in its devoted love for this no less touchy musical master.

Mendelssohn required to see precisely the same work that, through Schumann's indirect mediation, had decided Sigfrid's fate in such a desired direction. Sigfrid allowed himself to make the very justified remonstrance against this requirement, that that advanced schoolboy's[29] work had been laboriously achieved without artistic training in a purely instinctive or amateurish way, and remarked in addition that Schumann's judgment of it had only been given with the understanding that he should first go through a suitable course of study before once again making his own attempts. Mendelssohn did not let himself be deflected from his requirement by objections and designated the day and hour when he would expect him personally with the work in the familiar private apartment. A cursory glance through the copybooks convinced Sigfrid of his already advanced view of the great and manifold deficiencies of his uncouth work, and he could not conceive how these might have led Schumann to hope that through future studies he could have the possibility of more capable achievements. Nevertheless, remembering Mendelssohn's strict order, he packed several books of songs together and was punctually in his apartment, as the latter liked, at the specified time. This time Mendelssohn received his visitor in another, somewhat smaller room, where a well-maintained Silbermann square piano drew his attention by its narrow black lower keys. Mendelssohn stood not far from the door by a large tiled stove and did not remove himself from this warming friend while he leafed through Sigfrid's books. The latter followed the play of his features, which were rather livelier in their varying shades than before, with anxious expectation. Suddenly the lights on his rather spacious countenance darkened; the book was brought closer to the eyelids, which were drawn together in order to see the unbelievable more precisely:—a storm was brewing, called forth by a wholly illegitimate succession of fifths and octaves that, what is more, had a very unpleasant sounding effect. Three serious transgressions against purity of part-writing in one heap!

"How can one write something like that!" cried the indignant master of pure style, who evidently sustained an acutely violent attack on the ears through the agency of his sight.

Sigfrid pleaded apologetically that at the time when he committed this *crimen laessae majestatis*, his ear was not yet developed enough to adapt itself to his wholly deficient knowledge of musical grammar.

"In the whole of my life I never committed such a barbaric attack on music, not even as a little boy," replied the severe judge, not without exasperation.

"Someone who is so fortunate to have such teachers as Zelter and Louis Berger from infancy"—the condemned one dared timidly to remark, but he got no further; for Mendelssohn received the comment with angry irritation, and as he gave back the book he left his place by the stove with the hastily spoken, memorable words:

"Even in Kamchatka people write more correct counterpoint than you.—Adieu!"—

After such an experience Sigfrid wished very much that he should not have any further cause to cross this threshold of his unlucky fate again. He had hoped that Mendelssohn would encourage him in a friendly manner as Schumann had done, in order not to scare him with the tremendous difficulties of the thorny path; that he would at most admonish him not to waste his years of study; that he might well invite him to call upon him for advice if necessary: instead of all that, deeply dispirited by Mendelssohn's crushing verdict, he found himself cast back into the old doubts; found his none too great confidence in a sufficient quantity of natural aptitude almost annihilated, and as a result reeled for days on the dangerous verge of crippling despair, until finally by means of the resurgence of proud defiance he came to the praiseworthy decision to refute Mendelssohn's unfavourable opinion through redoubled fervour; certainly the most correct path he could take. But his personal feeling against him remained very aggravated for a long time. In consequence of this he tried to make Mendelssohn's individuality and artistic mission clear to himself by making a detailed parallel between him and Gottsched[30] in the "green book." For the better elucidation of the greatly deluded one's state of mind at that time, the concluding sentences of this bold attempt may follow here: . . .

"Gottsched finally came to the most tragic end that one who was formerly fêted can experience: he outlived his fame. The time that he had led onwards and developed further rushed on past him and, sneering and laughing up its sleeve, left him in the lurch. And Mendelssohn?—did he not already take longer paces in order to be able to follow his time, the thankless daughter?—Is it not as if, precisely in our day, she stood still, so as to wait for him, to call to him: 'Run! run! I cannot wait any longer, I cannot stay; I am driven forwards, always forwards!—make haste so that you advance with me!' Before her, however, just as formerly, another Lessing[31] hurries with giant strides. For his beloved, Time, he makes new shoes, because the soles on the old ones are rent and in them she does not advance as quickly as he. Gottsched had only ever caught sight of Lessing from a distance. He was never able to reach him."

In a later addition to this bold parallel, with its concealed allusion to Schumann, it was explicitly brought to the fore that Mendelssohn's personality, as it had emerged in the last conversation, had provided the immediate impulse for that attempt, the audacity of which the author himself freely concedes. Sigfrid was once more, and for the last time, to have a personal encounter with Mendelssohn, which almost took on the character of an insoluble conflict. The Easter examination of all the pupils of the Conservatorium, established by the rules, was the occasion for this.

They sat in rows on benches in the largest room of the institution, the same in which Sigfrid's entrance examination had taken place, and in which his high-flying expectations had first been painfully curtailed. The podium, on which were various grand pianos and music stands, was opposite the benches. To the left a large table was set up at which the remaining and, incidentally, rather numerous portion of the directorate and teaching staff who were present were accommodated.

As Sigfrid had seated himself at a respectful distance from that table he soon noticed conspicuous merriment there, which was to all appearances connected with the performances of the anxious students. Mendelssohn, seeming to be busily engaged with paper and pen, was without doubt the liveliest of the high tribunal and, in the midst of an external setting designed to produce solemnity for the event that was as serious as it was painful for the examinees, managed to abandon himself to the most unconstrained merriment and also carry along with him his colleagues at the judges' table, which on account of his authority coupled with the well-known overpowering amiability of his personality was very easy to do.—At first Sigfrid excused this phenomenon to himself: he thought to find an explanation for it in the fact that a man of Mendelssohn's high artistic stature could not possibly be anything other than amused by frequently repeated, self-conscious performances of the same studies and the like. Meanwhile, as the merriment also began to spread to the pupils sitting immediately next to the bench of judges and to spread ever further through the audience, that explanation could no longer be supported and another reason had to be advanced. This then came to light in the form of several pages that, in clever ink sketches from Mendelssohn's master hand, which was also practised in this art, depicted, with a few lines, easily recognizable cartoons[32] and caricatures of some of those students who had just performed their practised examination pieces. The page that seemed to provoke the most laughter unluckily came into the hands of one of these poor fellows sitting near Sigfrid, who was conspicuous, besides, by a bodily deformity. It contained a cartoon of the deformed student himself and there was not the slightest doubt about the identity of the person who was caricatured. Deeply flushed with anger, the victim crumpled the wounding page in his hand, let it fall on the floor, covered it with his shoe—and covered his eyes with his handkerchief. Sigfrid observed everything with growing indignation and was just about to leave his seat to escape the same fate, when Moscheles was made aware of him by this movement and called upon him to play.—His reverence for this honourable man so far overcame his agitation that he began to treat with him to effect a withdrawal of the request. In vain!—Moscheles became more urgent, but without success. Sigfrid assured him that it would be absolutely impossible for him to play today. He trembled with an inner upsurge of rage, of sympathy and of defiance that was awakened in its old force.—The scene aroused more general attention. Mendelssohn had no sooner discovered what it was about than he sprang vehemently from his seat, placed himself opposite the distant seat where the recalcitrant one sat and, with blazing glance, cried rather than spoke:

"You do not want to play?"—

"No!"—Sigfrid answered loud and clear.

"You are going to play!"—

"I will not play."—

"You want to disobey me?"—

"Yes! I have a reason."

"What—a reason!—As long as you are a pupil of the institution, you must be obedient:—You swore it with a handshake."—

This lucky phrase worked.—"I must keep my word at any rate"—said Sigfrid, trembling in every limb. The pupils, who followed the scene, not without secret astonishment at the courage he had so boldly displayed towards Mendelssohn, made way as the subdued pupil reluctantly betook himself towards the podium. He played only a few bars with a partly deliberate and partly involuntary exaggeration of dynamic force; and said to a pupil loudly enough for all those present to hear: "We have not sworn to provide material for ink sketches; I am sorry that I let myself be taken unawares."—At that he left the room unhindered in the company of that pupil, who praised him greatly for his bold resistance, but at the same time predicted very serious consequences; a prophecy that was not fulfilled: perhaps because from then on Sigfrid attended the lessons more rarely, but perhaps also because Mendelssohn did not want to punish what he himself had occasioned by a mischievous joke. Apart from carefully avoiding meeting Mendelssohn, that scene had no direct consequences of an unpleasant nature for the antagonist.—Long afterwards, however, he discovered that the bold deed was still retained in the memories of later generations of pupils, and had decked Sigfrid's name with the nimbus with which the legends loved to decorate their heroes.

Meinardus later discussed his experiences with Schumann: "As I explained to him that Mendelssohn had delivered such a deeply dispiriting judgment, with rough words, of the very same musical attempts that I had sent to Norderney the previous year, Schumann smiled, removed his hand further from his mouth than usual and said with a somewhat bowed head, and, as it appeared to me, with brightly shining glance: "Oh don't let that discourage you; not everyone can boast of having heard an incivility from Mendelssohn; never forget his remark."—How ashamed I was of my sensitive vexation against Mendelssohn!"[33]

Schumann's own very high estimation of Mendelssohn's judgment in musical matters is evident from his *Erinnerungen*, where he noted: "His opinion in musical matters, particularly about compositions—the most apposite, getting to the innermost core of the matter, that one can imagine. Everywhere and immediately he recognized the fault and its cause and effect"; and: "For me his praise always counted as the highest—he was the highest court of appeal."[34] In his notebook for October 1842, too, Schumann described Mendelssohn as "the highest critic, with the clearest eye of all living musicians."[35]

The contrast between Mendelssohn's and Schumann's attitudes towards teaching as illustrated by Meinardus's account is corroborated by Carl Reinecke's observation: "While Felix Mendelssohn Bartholdy was very free with his comments and had a knack of giving clear expression to sharp but accurate criticism, so that in a quarter of an hour one could glean enough hints and musical rules of wisdom for an entire lifetime, Schumann proved, in general, to be rather uncommunicative. In his personal dealings with the eager disciples of his art, however, he was more confidential and encouraging than Mendelssohn, who, admittedly, may have been forced to adopt a certain reserve on account of the unbelievable crowd of people who sought him out. Robert Schumann expressed more friendly recognition and encouragement than criticism."[36] Meinardus's reference to Mendelssohn and the Leipzig Conservatorium in his later book, *Die deutsche Tonkunst*, suggests that perhaps Schumann's comments and his own more mature reflection may have modified his attitude. He remarked that Mendelssohn "raised Leipzig gradually to the capital of the public musical life of his time, and one can say to his credit that by his influence he directed the music of the whole civilized world of his epoch, namely that of Germany, to a definite goal with respect to taste. He also led the young who were enthusiastic about music to the study of the old classical masters, and to this end he made himself a tool with the Leipzig Conservatorium, which, opening in 1843, soon became a nursery for the classical ideal of beauty." And he added that "Mendelssohn wanted to form the pupils of the Conservatorium into a body of artists who would understand the important connection of free, beautiful art with life, and who might be guided by the conviction that the highest responsibilities of both art and life come together in their ultimate goals. For that reason the artistic education was organized in the spirit of Schiller's admonition to artists: 'The dignity of mankind is given into your hands. Take care of it!' "[37]

34 · Joseph Joachim

Despite Mendelssohn's commitment to the Conservatorium after 1843, he did not necessarily consider it appropriate for the education of all aspiring musicians. In the case of the exceptionally talented twelve-year-old violinist Joseph Joachim, who came to his attention at the time the Conservatorium opened, Mendelssohn once again assumed personal responsibility. The following extracts, from Moser's authorized biography of Joachim, which appeared in 1901, six years before Joachim's death, were based closely on letters and on Joachim's own recollections. After interviewing Joachim with a view to his admission to the Conservatorium Mendelssohn wrote to the boy's relations in Leipzig, who had suggested the idea: "The Cherub [der Posaunenengel] no longer needs the training of a Conservatoire for his instrument, indeed, no teacher of violin-playing is necessary for him at all: let him work by himself, and play occasionally to David for the benefit of his criticism and advice. I myself will often and regularly play with him and be his adviser in artistic matters; the boy has also worked out his tests in harmony without hesitation or fault, and therefore I strongly advise him to continue this study under Hauptmann, in order that he may learn all that is required of a true artist. I consider it, however, of the greatest importance that the boy should receive a thoroughly sound general education, and I myself will undertake to find him a competent teacher." Moser continued:

> Nearly every Sunday Mendelssohn played with the boy,
> whom he designated as "*Teufelsbraten*" whenever he did
> anything particularly well. These Sundays were the occa-
> sion of many a talk on art, the memory of which is ever
> fresh in Joachim's mind, and he is wont to quote the
> wise sayings of the master when speaking of bygone days.
> Above all, Mendelssohn advised him in the choice of
> works for study, his favourite motto being—"a true artist
> should only play the best." He accustomed Joachim to
> think first of the music itself, and then of his instrument,
> and never to sacrifice the intention of the composer in
> order to simplify the execution of any passage. Especially

did he exhort his protégé to honour the old masters. "It is inartistic, nay barbaric, to alter anything they have ever written, even by a single note."

Joachim's inimitable "*rubato*" may be traced to the example of Mendelssohn, who understood perfectly how to blend one subject with another without forcing the passage in the smallest degree. He also freed him from certain prejudices to which violinists are prone,—for example that the use of the springing bow is not permissible in classical compositions. "Always use it, my boy, where it is suitable, or where it sounds well," was Mendelssohn's opinion.

But he did not stop here: he also often accompanied the boy on the pianoforte when he played in private, and almost always when he played in public.

Referring to 1845 or 1846 Moser observed: "Whilst Mendelssohn was absent from Leipzig, Joachim industriously occupied his time in attempts at composition, and on Mendelssohn's return, the work would be laid before him to be thoroughly criticised and commented upon. One day Joachim brought two sonatas for piano and violin for Mendelssohn's judgment. With a smile of satisfaction the master said, 'Ah! you already write a good hand!' The scholar replied that he had not written his work out himself, but had had it copied. 'You duffer, I don't mean that," retorted Mendelssohn, laughing, "but that your style has grown easy and flowing!' "

Reporting Joachim's reaction to Mendelssohn's death, Moser wrote: "The sudden death of his revered and honoured master was the most deeply felt loss that Joachim has ever experienced during the whole of his long and eventful artistic career. He honours Mendelssohn as much for his manly qualities as for his artistic gifts, and expresses his heartfelt gratitude for all that he owes to him. In the words, 'Who knows what I might not have become had I not lost Mendelssohn so early in life?' he shows how keenly he then felt, and still feels, his loss in connection with his own creative talent."[38]

EIGHT · The Composer

35 · Aesthetics and Aspirations

Unlike his younger contemporary Wagner, Mendelssohn showed little interest in speculating about the nature and purpose of music. In his view musicians would be better writing and playing music than talking about it. His letters to family and intimate friends, however, and the comments of his contemporaries provide many indications of his aesthetic attitudes and convictions. He was motivated by what Schumann characterized as "ambition in the noblest sense,"[1] and his guiding principle was a determination always to achieve the finest of which he was capable. Thus he was unwilling to release for wider circulation anything that did not meet his own exacting standards. Mendelssohn's abiding concern never to be satisfied with what he had achieved and always to strive for something better undoubtedly derived from the influence of his father, who, after hearing parts of the as yet incomplete *St Paul* in 1835, shortly before his death, praised the music warmly but added characteristically that it had to be made still better.[2] How completely Mendelssohn had absorbed this attitude is shown by numerous remarks by and about him. He constantly urged it on others as well. To Devrient, for instance, he wrote from Paris on 5 January 1832 (a passage suppressed in the version of the letter published in Devrient's *Recollections*): "This trait of self-satisfaction was a point about which I long wished to write to you because it occurred to me at times that even you are not entirely free of it—naturally not as though you were satisfied with what you have done, or achieved or are capable of—but occasionally it seemed to me as though you were quite content and comfortable with your endeavours and direction, and even that probably should not be the case."[3]

A prerequisite in all of Mendelssohn's work was the utmost attainable technical perfection. To a large extent Mendelssohn seems to have felt that technical skill was not only the fundamental requirement for a composer but also the only quality that could be acquired by individual effort. As he wrote to Moscheles shortly after the founding of the Leipzig Conservatorium in 1843, "The pupils all want to compose and to theorize, whilst I believe that the principal thing that can and ought to be taught is sound practical work,—sound playing and keeping time, sound knowledge of sound music, etc. Out of that, all other knowledge grows of itself; and what is beyond is not a matter of teaching, but must come as a gift from above. Don't you agree with me? That I am not the man to turn art into mere mechanism, I need not say."[4] He himself would often expend immense effort in finding the best technical means of expressing his conception. Hiller described a characteristic instance in 1840: "In the course of that winter I witnessed a curious example of Mendelssohn's almost morbid conscientiousness with regard to the possible perfection of his compositions. One evening I came into his room, and found him looking so heated, and in such a feverish state of excitement, that I was frightened. 'What's the matter with you?' I called out. 'There I have been sitting for the last four hours,' he said, 'trying to alter a few bars in a song (it was a quartet for men's voices) and can't do it.' He had made twenty different versions, the greater number of which would have satisfied most people."[5]

Mendelssohn's concern with finding the perfect formal and technical expression of his ideas made him frequently reluctant to take the irrevocable step of publication. He wrote to Klingemann in June 1843: "I am about to send 4 manuscripts out into the world at the same time, to different publishers: the Walpurgisnacht, a sonata for piano and violoncello, six lieder for a single voice and six lieder to be sung in the open air for 4 mixed voices. As long as they stay here with me they torment me dreadfully, because I am all too unwilling to see such a clean manuscript get into the dirty hands of the engraver, the music seller and the public, and I continue to touch it up a bit here and polish it a bit there and improve it merely so that it stays here. Once the proofs are there it is as foreign and indifferent to me as if it were someone else's."[6] In fact, he sometimes continued to make extensive alterations in the proofs. In several instances, including *St Paul*, the *Lobgesang* and *Elijah*, he made so many changes that whole pages had to be re-engraved. In this context Devrient reported Mendelssohn as saying: "I have an awful reverence for print, and must go on improving my things until I feel sure they are all I can make them."[7] And, referring to *Elijah*, Schumann made a note about Mendelssohn's "troublesome corrections in the printed proofs—and the malicious remark of the engraver, 'That proceeds like a game of chess' and his unyielding attitude towards it."[8] This almost pathological obsession with revising his scores, about which his sister Fanny chided him repeatedly, resulted in his withholding major compositions from publication for many years and in some cases suppressing them entirely. He definitively abandoned the *Reformation* Symphony as irremediable in the 1830s, and many other apparently completed works were laid aside and never published because of his continuing dissatisfaction with them, including the *Italian* Symphony (which he attempted several times to revise), the F Major Violin Sonata of 1838 and the B-flat String Quintet. Other works, for instance the "Infelice" concert arias, the scena "On Lena's Gloomy Heath" and many smaller pieces, which were written for particular people or particular occasions, he was willing to have performed by their recipients or in private but did not consider ripe for publication.

Mendelssohn's earnest striving for the highest technical polish and most faithful representation of his artistic conception was determined by his notion of the meaning and function of art. Unlike those who saw themselves as musical progressives, he maintained (reflecting the Enlightenment views of his grandfather Moses) that the principles of art were universal and immutable. This is illustrated by his views about the question of progress in music; he remarked to J. C. Lobe: "This composer has opened a new road?—Well, I ask, what do they mean by such an assertion? Do they merely intend to say that he has proceeded upon a road which no one else had traversed before him, or does the assertion not rather imply that the composer has opened a track which leads to a new and more charming region of art? For, every one capable of wielding a shovel and moving his legs can open a path for himself; but if we employ the expression in the higher sense, I deny its applicability altogether. *There is no such thing as a new road*, simply because there is no new region of art to which it could lead. They have all been explored long since.—New roads! That artist is sure to be led astray who gives himself up to this cursed demon!"[9]

Mendelssohn's attitude towards the emotional content of his music was powerfully conditioned by his conviction that art has a moral dimension. He consciously avoided exaggerated or distorted feelings and eroticism; as he wrote from Paris in December 1831, deploring what he saw as the calculated sensationalism of Meyerbeer's *Robert le Diable* and another French opera, "All this produces effect, but I have no music for such things," and he concluded prophetically: "I consider it ignoble, so if the present epoch exacts this style, and considers it indispensable, then I will write oratorios."[10] Mendelssohn, like Schumann (whose stance is clearly illustrated by his review contrasting Meyerbeer's *Les Huguenots* with Mendelssohn's *St Paul*),[11] Fink[12] and many other contemporary musicians and critics, undoubtedly recognized an ethical dimension in music and felt that it was capable of exercising moral influence. He believed that this influence could be either beneficial or harmful, as a conversation reported by Wagner indicates.[13] Since he steadfastly maintained that there could be no separation between life and art, Mendelssohn's personality and moral convictions inevitably determined the character of his music. This was at the root of his dislike for the work of Meyerbeer and several other contemporary composers; Schumann approvingly noted Mendelssohn's fundamental criticism of Meyerbeer: "That a composition should actually be part of an artist's life, a necessity—of that he knew nothing."[14] Thus, in his compositions, Mendelssohn aimed to convey all those qualities or feelings that he felt to be healthy and life-enhancing, from noble profundity, heartfelt grief and tender yearning, through passionate enthusiasm to simple merriment and *joie de vivre*. These qualities found a ready response among the substantial portion of the cultivated public of the day who accepted the notion that the beneficial influence of art was a crucial factor in the moral improvement upon which the progress of civilization depended.

Nevertheless, Mendelssohn repeatedly stressed that he never consciously aimed for popular success but wrote simply what was in his heart, though certainly with the hope that it might communicate to others. In 1831 he informed Devrient, who had teased him with the lines "Two and twenty years, and nothing done for immortality" from Schiller's *Don Carlos*: "I compose as little with a view to becoming famous as of becoming a Kapellmeister. It would be delightful to be both, but as long as I am not positively starving, I look upon it as my duty to compose just how and what my heart indites, and to leave the effect it will make to Him who takes heed of greater and better things. As time goes on I think more deeply and sincerely of that,—to write only as I feel, to have less regard than ever to outward results, and when I have produced a piece that has flowed from my heart—whether it is afterwards to bring me fame, honours, orders, or snuff-boxes, does not concern me."[15]

Mendelssohn expressed this explicitly again in July 1838 when responding to Ferdinand David's inquiry about his progress in composing a symphony:

> My symphony ought certainly to be as good as I can make it; but whether popular, whether for the hurdy-gurdy, that indeed I do not know. I feel that with every piece I get closer to learning how to write what is in my heart, and that after all is the only criterion I know. If I am not made for popularity I do not want to learn how to gain it or strive for it. For I really cannot do it, nor do I want to be able to. What comes out thus from within makes me glad, also in its external effect, and therefore I would certainly be very glad if, for your and my friends' sake, I could fulfil the desire you express to me—but I really do not know how to or what to do about it. Much has already happened to me on my journey through life without my having thought about it, and without diverting me from my path, and so too perhaps will this—and if not I shall not complain and shall console myself that I have done what, with my best efforts and my best judgment, I can. Yet I have your sympathy and your joy in my things, and those of other dear friends; one could hardly ask for more.[16]

And in 1843, once again writing to Devrient, who had sent him an opera libretto, he repeated his avowal that his attitude to composition was not determined by external considerations: "Ever since I began to compose, I have remained true to my guiding principle: not to write a page because this or that public, or pretty girl wanted it to be thus or thus; but to write solely as I myself thought best, and as it gave me pleasure. I will not depart from this principle in writing an opera, and this makes it so very hard, since most people, as well as most poets, look upon opera merely as a thing to be popular. Moreover, I consider popularity of secondary importance provided that the work is a good one, and that is never achieved with an eye to popularity or unpopularity."[17]

There can be no doubt that in common with the vast majority of his contemporaries Mendelssohn saw music as an expressive art that communicates directly to the performer's and listener's feelings. But he was notably wary of all attempts to explain the meaning of music in words; indeed, he declared the impossibility of doing so adequately. Perhaps his most explicit explanation of his ideas about this occurs in a letter of 15 October 1842 to his relative by marriage Marc-André Souchay, who had sent him a list of suggested descriptive titles for the *Lieder ohne Worte*. Mendelssohn responded:

> There is so much talk about music, and yet so little really said. For my part I believe that words do not suffice for such a purpose, and if I found they did suffice, then I certainly would have nothing more to do with music. People often complain that music is ambiguous, that their ideas on the subject always seem so vague, whereas every one understands words; with me it is exactly the reverse,—not merely with regard to entire sentences, but also as to individual words; these, too, seem to me so ambiguous, so vague, so unintelligible when compared with genuine music, which fills the soul with a thousand things better than words. What the music I love expresses to me, is not thought too *indefinite* to be put into words, but, on the contrary, too *definite*. I therefore consider every effort to express such thoughts commendable; but still there is something unsatisfactory too in them all, and so it is with yours also. This, however, is not your fault, but that of the poetry, which does not enable you to do better. If you ask me what *my* idea is, I say—just the song as it stands; and if I have in my mind a definite term or terms with regard to one or more of these songs, I will disclose them to no one, because the

words of one person assume a totally different meaning in the mind of another person, because the music of the song alone can awaken the same ideas and the same feelings in one mind as in another,—a feeling which is not, however, expressed by the same words. Resignation, melancholy, the praise of God, a hunting-song,—one person does not form the same conception from these that another does. Resignation is to the one what melancholy is to the other; the third can form no lively idea of either. To any man who is by nature a very keen sportsman, a hunting-song and the praise of God would come pretty much to the same thing, and to such a one the sound of the hunting-horn would really and truly be the praise of God, while we hear nothing in it but a mere hunting-song; and if we were to discuss it ever so often with him, we should get no further. Words have many meanings, and yet music we could both understand correctly. Will you allow this to serve as an answer to your question? At all events, it is the only one I can give,—although these too are nothing, after all, but ambiguous words![18]

Mendelssohn's reluctance to engage in philosophical speculation about music and its effect is also apparent in his disinclination to discuss directly its ethical qualities. In his expression of dislike for other composers' music it is seldom clear whether the grounds of his criticism are merely technical or whether his distaste is motivated by a deeper concern about the potentially corrupting effects of what he considered to be bad music. Some of his most outspoken criticisms were directed against Berlioz, whose whole tendency he was unable to understand. He first expressed his misgivings in 1831, in a letter to his family from Rome, where he had a tense but stimulating personal relationship with Berlioz. He reported that Berlioz "distorts everything, without a spark of talent, always groping in the dark, but esteeming himself the creator of a new world; writing moreover the most frightful things, and yet dreaming and thinking of nothing but Beethoven, Schiller, Goethe; a victim at the same time of the most boundless vanity, and looking down on Mozart and Haydn, so that all his enthusiasm seems to me very doubtful."[19] Later, after playing through

Liszt's arrangement of Berlioz's *Symphonie fantastique*, he remarked: "I cannot conceive anything more insipid, wearisome, and Philistine, for with all his endeavours to go stark mad, he never once succeeds."[20] But perhaps his most revealing outburst concerned the Overture to *Les francs-juges*, about which, responding to Moscheles's criticism of it, he wrote in April 1834:

> It is a chaotic, prosaic piece, and yet more humanly conceived than some of his others. I always felt inclined to say with Faust,—
>
> > "He ran around, he ran about,
> > His thirst in puddles laving;
> > He gnawed and scratched the house throughout,
> > But nothing cured his raving;
> > And driven at last, in open day,
> > He ran into the kitchen."
>
> For his orchestration is such a frightful muddle, such an incongruous mess, that one ought to wash one's hands after handling one of his scores. Besides, it really is a shame to set nothing but murder, misery, and wailing to music; even if it were well done, it would simply give us a record of atrocities. At first he made me quite melan- choly, because his judgments on others are so clever, so cool, and correct, he seems so thoroughly sensible, and yet he does not perceive that his own works are such rubbishy nonsense.[21]

To suggest, however, as Mendelssohn's later detractors did, that his own music was overrefined and "effeminate" misrepresents the nature of his objections to Berlioz. Mendelssohn's lack of appreciation for Berlioz may well indicate an irreconcilable aesthetic standpoint, but it does not imply that he was repelled by the portrayal of strong emotion in music; it was not the strength of the feeling that was important, but its genu- ineness. Shortly after his first strictures on Berlioz in 1831, for instance, he wrote to Devrient about the young Wilhelm Taubert's songs: "There is character and soul in every one, and some phrase, some trait, which clearly tells that it is the thought of a true musician. . . . But he must write other things besides songs, and of these not such sweet ones, but fiery ones, rough, uncouth, wild ones; he must burn and rave a little, I think, until he comes to himself."[22] For Mendelssohn it was a question of degree and balance. He made this clear to Julius Rietz, a decade later: "Just as the French, by conjuring tricks and overwrought sentiment, endeavour to make their style harrowing and exciting, so I believe it possible to fall into the other extreme, and so greatly to dread all that is *piquant* or sensuous, that at last the musical idea does not remain sufficiently bold or interesting; that instead of a tumour there is a wasting away: it is the contrast between the Jesuit churches, and their thousand glittering objects, and the Calvinists, with their four white walls; true piety may exist in both, but still the right path lies between the two."[23]

Further insight into Mendelssohn's attitude towards the relationship between workmanship, inspiration and sincerity in composition is provided by his characterization of music by Sigismund Neukomm and Cherubini, in a letter to Moscheles in 1834:

> I quite agree with you in all you say about Neukomm's music. Isn't it wonderful that a man of such taste and refinement should not be able to transfer those qualities to his music? To say nothing of the fundamental ideas of his compositions, the working out seems so careless and commonplace. The Fantasia is probably an example of that kind of thing; and had I come as the most favourably predisposed of listeners, the very title would have scared me away. Then, again, that constant use of the brass! As a matter of sheer calculation it should be sparingly employed, let alone the question of Art! That's where I admire Handel's glorious style; when he brings up his kettledrums and trumpets towards the end, and thumps and batters about to his heart's content, as if he meant to knock you down—no mortal man can remain unmoved. I really believe it is far better to imitate such work, than to overstrain the nerves of your audience, who, after all, will at last get accustomed to Cayenne pepper. There is Cherubini's new Opera, "Ali Baba," for

instance, which I have just been looking through. I was delighted with some parts, but in others it grieved me to find him chiming in with that perverted new fad of the Parisians, winding up pieces, in themselves calm and dignified, with thunder-clap effects, scoring as if instruments were nothing and effect everything, three or four trombones blasting away at you as if the human ear could stand anything. Then the finales with their uncouth harmonies, tearing and dashing about, enough to make an end of you. How bright and sparkling, on the other hand, are some of the pieces in his former manner; between Faniska and Lodoiska, for instance, and this there really is as wide a difference as between a man and a scarecrow,—no wonder the Opera was a failure. To an admirer of old Cherubini's it really is annoying that he should write such miserable stuff, and not have the pluck to resist the so-called taste of the day and the public, (as if you and I were not part of the public, and didn't live in these times as well, and didn't want music adapted to *our* digestive capacities!) As for those who are not admirers of old Cherubini, they will not be satisfied anyhow, do what he may; for them he is too much himself in "Ali Baba," and after the first three notes they spot their man and put him down as a "vieille perruque," "rococo," etc.[24]

Although Mendelssohn often referred to writing what was in his heart, as though composition were an essentially subconscious process, it is clear from many sources that, from an early age, he pursued a deliberate agenda to reform public taste, not by writing or talking about music but by making it. His sister Fanny showed her awareness of this when she wrote to Klingemann in December 1828: "On the whole, I feel no doubt that with every new work he makes an advance in clearness and depth. His ideas take more and more a fixed direction, and he steadily advances towards the aim he has set himself, and of which he is clearly conscious. I know not how to define this aim, perhaps because an idea in art cannot altogether be well expressed in words—otherwise poetry would be the only art—perhaps also because I only watch his progress with loving eyes, and not on the wings of thought lead the way and foresee his aim. He has full command over all his talents, and day by day enlarges his domain, ruling like a general over all the means of development art can offer him."[25] A few years later, writing to Alfred Baur, Mendelssohn himself hinted at his own sense of mission. Commenting on a recent publication, which lamented the perceived stagnation and degradation of music, he observed: "It is always to be deplored when any but genuine artists attempt to purify and restore the public taste. On such a subject words are only pernicious; deeds alone are efficient. For even if people do really feel this antipathy towards the present, they cannot as yet give anything better to replace it, and therefore they had best let it alone. Palestrina effected a reformation during his life; he could not do so now any more than Sebastian Bach or Luther. The men are yet to come who will *advance* on the straight road, and who will lead others onwards, or back to the ancient and right path, which ought, in fact, to be termed the onward path; but they will write no books on the subject."[26]

Mendelssohn's consistent intention to "purify and restore the public taste" by composing, performing and actively fostering appreciation of what he considered to be good music is frequently indicated in his letters. In 1830, for instance, he wrote to Klingemann from Munich: "I was very content and merry here, for people enjoyed my music more than I could have expected and were friendlier than anywhere else on the journey; but you once wrote me a 'prophecy' that closed with the words 'when you have gone, the strange phenomenon will remain strange, just as before' and I almost fear something similar will occur. The ladies here, who were sunk in Herz and Kalkbrenner and considered Moscheles and Hummel to belong with the old classical composers (literally), have become wild about Beethoven and Weber, weep and go into raptures and play Beethoven. But I really think that I will not have been long gone before they are back to Herz."[27]

In his compositions Mendelssohn strove to adhere as closely as possible to the ideals represented by the great composers of the past, whose music he promoted through performance. With time this created a tension that, in his short life, he was never able to resolve. This is illustrated in a letter to his brother Paul in 1837:

The more I find what are termed encouragement and recognition in my vocation, the more restless and unsettled does it become in my hands, and I cannot deny that I often long for that rest of which you complain. So few traces remain of performances and musical festivals, and all that is personal; the people indeed shout and applaud, but that quickly passes away, without leaving a vestige behind, and yet it absorbs as much of one's life and strength as *better* things, or perhaps even more; and the evil of this is, that it is impracticable to come half out, when you are once in; you must either go on the whole way or not at all. I dare not even attempt to withdraw, or the cause which I have undertaken will suffer, and yet I would gladly see that it was not merely *my* cause, but considered a good and universal one. But this is the very point where people are wanting to pursue the same path,— not an approving public (for that is a matter of indifference), but fellow-workers (and they are indispensable). So in *this* sense I long for a less busy life, in order to be able to devote myself to my peculiar province, composition of music, and to leave the execution of it to others. It seems, however, that this is not to be; and I should be ungrateful were I dissatisfied with my life as it is.[28]

The irony of Mendelssohn's career as a composer was that he began by representing a challenge to trivial and commonplace music, which depended for its effect on empty bravura or thoughtless reiteration of well-worn patterns, and played a large part in cultivating a popular taste for "high art," but was later seen by posterity, influenced by the self-seeking propaganda of mid-nineteenth-century apostles of musical progress, as shallow and meretricious.

NINE · Critical Reception

36 · The Early Years, 1818–1829

Between 1818 and 1823 the Leipzig *Allgemeine musikalische Zeitung*, at that time the most widely circulated and influential music journal in Germany, contained several brief references to Mendelssohn's public appearances as a performer.[1] Its first mention of any of his compositions occurred in connection with Carl Möser's concert on 26 April 1823: "A symphony[2] by the gifted young Mendelssohn Bartholdy deserves notice; its rich invention, unity of design, and attentive study of effect promises much for his future works."[3] Reviews of his early publications in the *Berliner allgemeine musikalische Zeitung* (founded in 1824) were scarcely enthusiastic, however, despite the personal connection of its editor, Adolf Bernhard Marx, with the Mendelssohn family. Zelter observed to Goethe in a letter of 18 June 1825, "They have reviewed his quartetts and symphonies somewhat coldly in the musical paper, but it won't hurt him; for these reviewers are but young fellows looking for the very hat they hold in their hands."[4]

Zelter was probably thinking in particular of a review of the Piano Quartet op. 1, the condescending tone of which is unmistakable. Having introduced Mendelssohn to the reader as a piano pupil of Berger and "a promising theory student of Zelter," the reviewer continued: "To be brief, we shall merely remark in general that the composer has chosen Mozart for his model." The three aspects of Mozart's procedures by which he believed Mendelssohn to have been guided were: (1) "the strict form of the individual movements"; (2) balanced phrases, with "an initial phrase answered by a responding phrase" (which the reviewer contrasted with Beethoven); and (3) the simplicity of Mozart's ideas, which "eternally beautiful, flow forth naturally, with all noble elegance, in simple unpretentious clothes" and which were therefore, according to the reviewer, "so easily imitated." He followed this with a general assessment of Mendelssohn's success in emulating his model, commenting: "It redounds to his honour that in (1) he has not failed with respect to the outward form; it is good and unexceptionable. Also with respect to (2) the correspondence and repetition of ideas occurs, though we miss that irresistible attractiveness in them. Indeed, even (3), the simplicity, is not to be denied (the piano part is easy to play and the string instruments are handled with expertise)—but Mozart's vivifying freshness is lacking." The reviewer continued with a cool assessment of the individual movements, in which he remarked that although the first movement "as a whole made the deep impression that appears to be intended," the Adagio seemed "somewhat tedious and only gained in interest towards the end," that although the Scherzo was "better" its Trio was "insignificant"; but he conceded that "the Finale is well worked out and is unquestionably the most successful movement." In conclusion he remarked:

It is self-evident from what has been said that this quartet deserves to be seen as the work of a young man who is certainly very talented, and it contains much that is charming; but it lacks originality. This was not yet to be expected from a young man of that age. Good tuition can lead very well to everything that the composer of this quartet has done; it can teach how to work, teach how others have done it,—but it cannot supply the warming and igniting spark that brings forth and enlivens original pieces of music. It is more likely that understanding will come before its years than that feeling which the heart can no longer contain and which unfolds its fairest blossoms through genius in music. The reviewer must say, however, that he has silently rejoiced over the lack of that spark. For untimely blossoms and fruits of that kind generally wither just when they ought to become something. We may, however, cherish the hope that such a praiseworthy talent, which already handles the technical and formal aspects of music so happily while still so young, may subsequently achieve something significant and will also exert itself to produce something new that will further the art.[5]

A much more sympathetic review of the same work appeared shortly afterwards in the *Allgemeine musikalische Zeitung*. Its author, Johann Philipp (Samuel) Schmidt, whose singspiel *Das Fischermädchen* had earned Weber's praise in 1818, probably had a personal connection with the Mendelssohn circle, and the discussion of Mendelssohn's background and abilities in the introductory paragraphs of this review is perhaps the first extended account of this kind to have appeared in print; it was certainly the first significant introduction of the young composer to the wider German-speaking world. Schmidt's final comment indicates a recognition of the standpoint that was to be Mendelssohn's guiding principle throughout his career.

> It is probably among the rarest of cases that a young composer comes forward with such a substantial, independent first work as the present piano quartet must appear to the unbiased judge. A rare genius for performance as well as for the creative aspect of music developed in Felix M.B. at an early age. He was endowed by generous mother nature with bodily health and pure childlike mind, and the development of his exceptional mental capacities benefited from the sound tuition of acknowledged masters of harmony and piano playing, such as Zelter and L. Berger and Hummel, among others, combined with the opportunity to hear the leading artists of every type and, through mixing in cultivated society, to acquire aesthetic understanding of manifold kinds.
>
> Felix M.B. showed himself to be a virtuoso on the pianoforte at a very early age. However, among the busily pursued studies in academic subjects and with Professor Zelter in double counterpoint, he displayed at an early stage a striving for the expression of individual musical ideas, at the root of which lay, particularly, a deep, seri-

ous intention; a spiritual fire enlivened the young artist's fantasy, which found expression in such varied works as fugues, symphonies for string instruments only, and for full orchestra, in piano concertos, sonatas, comic operettas, songs, etc. By means of a generous arrangement the young composer often had the opportunity to hear his works in the paternal home and thus to acquire the necessary experience at an early stage. The boy has now matured into a youth; the years of more tender feelings approach, which will lend his intellectual works the colouring that is necessary for their full effect.

Thus prepared, the appearance of the first published work was not premature, and this itself speaks most clearly for the genius of the young composer, on whom one is justified in making the greatest demands, if the eager expectations of contemporaries are to be satisfied.

Schmidt's appraisal of the individual movements is entirely positive. He says of the first movement that its theme develops in "a fiery and artistic manner," that "from time to time enharmonic changes give the harmony new appeal, but they are only sparing and therefore employed with increased effect," that it is full of "beautiful, singing melodies," and that "the flow is natural and pleasant, without reminiscences." His description of the Adagio ends with the comment that in this movement "so much expression of feeling and grace rules, that the pure innocence of the composer reveals itself in it as in a clear stream whose ripples are only rarely put into restless movement by a strong gust of wind." The Scherzo he characterizes as "an ingenious, original piece, full of youthful fire," and remarks that "naturally introduced imitations in the accompaniment show how unconstrainedly the young composer knows how to use his fundamental studies of counterpoint." And he praises the last movement for the manner in which it "artistically develops a melancholy, highly attractive theme." In conclusion he writes:

May this first, early ripened fruit of the spirit soon be followed by beautiful blossoms of inspired fantasy, which the blessed genius's path indicates, to the benefit of art, for the joy of parents and contemporaries as well as for the future fame of the composer. Felix M.B. has chosen an excellent model; this brilliant constellation outshines all subsidiary suns. Mozart always remains the example of the talent that develops itself by means of its own power of spirit right up to the attainment of the distant hidden goal.

To that purpose all benevolent people will certainly join the undersigned in wishing the young artist sincere joy and success. May he never be deflected from the road to truth and beauty in art, by vain thirst for glory and flattery, to worship at the altar of fashionable taste![6]

The following year (1825) an anonymous reviewer published a similarly positive, if brief, notice of Mendelssohn's Violin Sonata op. 4 in the *Allgemeine musikalische Zeitung*, which again begins with a reference to his background, referring to him as the "grandson of Moses Mendelssohn." The writer praised the piece as demonstrating "splendidly" that its composer is, "by nature and through excellent education, a brilliant youth in general and a true musician in particular. He has something to say for head and heart that deserves to be publicly said and really listened to; he is able to express it in a worthy, beautiful, perfectly proportioned manner." He then acknowledged the expressive content of the sonata as "a picture of the state of a soul, deserving of sympathy, that moves in a definite direction," and highly commended the composition as a whole, because "it keeps itself in well-measured bounds and also never gives offence in the technical aspects of its construction." These qualities, he thought, made it worthy to "be recommended just as heartily to the connoisseur as to the amateur."[7]

A longer notice of the same work in the Berlin journal, however, contrasts strongly. Its patronizing tone can hardly have failed to upset the sixteen-year-old composer. The review, published under the pseudonym Lukas van Leyden, was headed "Sonata for Pianoforte and Violin, composed and dedicated to his friend Eduard Ritz [*sic*] by Felix Mendelssohn-Bartholdy," and it began with a bit of facetious scene-setting: "Two young gentlemen come and want to play some music for us, and an old man like me is supposed to review it. Ah, but I'd rather fiddle along with them! But here for once it is unnecessary; for the friend, Herr Ritzius, is supposed to be a really first-rate fiddler, a pupil of young Rode—but he too is already old!—in the good old style with a full, broad bowstroke and a fat, juicy tone. . . . And the other, he is also a decent fellow—with due respect." The reviewer then made a back-handed compliment about the fugal section in the last movement of Mendelssohn's unpublished C minor symphony, which he "recently saw": "Many will be confused by it and will probably opine at the end that the work is confused—but I really enjoyed it." Bringing himself back to the subject he remarked that the sonata too "really pleased me," praised the composer for not calling it a "Grand Sonata," or something similar, and then, after much more about fashionable titles, added: "If I were Herr Laue [the publisher of the sonata] I would not take anything on without a grand title. . . . If, however, I were a composer, which, if I may be permitted to say, I am, then I would call everything by the right name. The title must only be French, or Latin, or Italian. Then people see that one is a German and an educated one. But I have wandered from the subject again and I shall now turn to the sonata itself." His lengthy discussion of the work continued in the same fatuous vein; patronizing praise of the first movement was interspersed with comments like "And then, my dear Mr. Mendelssohn, what sort of transition between the first and second subject is that!" With regard to the Adagio in A-flat, the reviewer avowed that he was "probably not young and modern enough" to appreciate it and wagged his finger at the composer for floating through "an up-to-date mist of feeling, he knows not how, to B major." He considered the last movement to possess "fire and flow and thorough working out spiced with plenty of sauciness!" but the continually ironic tone belies his apparent approval. His concluding words match the character of the rest:

> Now, my dear young gentlemen, once again no offence
> if I have stated my opinion so frankly. Whoever cannot
> endure criticism is not worth praising; you can find exam-
> ples of that everywhere. Those who are most soured when
> they encounter criticism are the weakest in character and
> in art. Whoever, on the other hand, feels right in himself
> says to himself without arrogance that he will not die of
> criticism and sees that in the end every judgment bears

fruit with him or with others, or is able to make seeds
germinate. If, however, I have picked out this and that
from your[8] sonata, I could nevertheless wish that many
had the ability to make these mistakes. But everyone must
be valued according to his capacity and in your case I
have to censure what would be alright for others.

But I don't really say all this to you; for you don't
look that weak to me, but to many another who listens
to us and cries treachery at every shake of the head and
would gladly respond to every free word with poison and
dagger.[9]

It was this kind of review that undoubtedly prompted the poem Mendelssohn wrote for his mother's birthday in 1826:

Schreibt der Komponiste ernst,	If the artist gravely writes,
Schläfert er uns ein;	To sleep it will beguile.
Schreibt der Komponiste froh	If the artist gaily writes,
Ist er zu gemein.	It is a vulgar style.
Schreibt der Komponiste lang,	If the artist writes at length,
Ist er zum Erbarmen;	How sad his hearers' lot!
Schreibt der Komponiste kurz,	If the artist briefly writes,
Kann man nicht erwarmen.	No man will care one jot.
Schreibt ein Komponiste klar,	If an artist simply writes,
Ist's ein armer Tropf;	A fool he's said to be.
Schreibt ein Komponiste tief,	If an artist deeply writes,
Rappelt's ihn am Kopf.	He's mad; 'tis plain to see.
Schreib' er also wie er will,	In whatsoever way he writes
Keinem steht es an.	He can't please every man;
Darum schreib' ein Komponist	Therefore let an artist write
Wie er will und kann.	How he likes and can.[10]

Mendelssohn's deep-seated distaste for all musical journalism is manifest in many later reported and written comments. Schumann, for in-

stance, recorded a conversation on 15 March 1837: "When we had finished discussing the symphony [Beethoven's Ninth] he seized my hand: ['] Schumann, don't take it the wrong way now; I feel so comfortable with you; but I have had such sad experiences, particularly with those who have something to do with a public journal, that it has left me with an aversion even against those whom he [*sic*] well knew it was not necessary to fear. He wanted very much to write to me, and really uninhibitedly, what was on his mind. If I promised him also to be discreet with it[.]' This was the sense; I was somewhat embarrassed; but this was quickly overcome."[11]

Other reviews in the *Berliner allgemeine musikalische Zeitung*, though less flippant, were, in general, cool towards Mendelssohn's works. The journal's editor, Marx, however, wrote one of the most positive notices at this time, about a performance of the First Symphony in Möser's concert series in 1825. He began: "It is written in a truly tragic burst of enthusiasm, and, especially in the first, third and last movements, a fervour glows in it that is certainly not the fruit of instruction but unmistakably reveals the true artist. At the same time, there is everywhere such a clarity and sureness of manner as may rarely be found in a seventeen-year-old composer." And he added in conclusion that those "who have the inner impulse and opportunity to concern themselves deeply with music and to equip themselves intellectually and emotionally to understand it, will already have taken in the beautiful whole after the first hearing, and will not be restrained by the youth of the composer from acknowledging his deserved rank as an artist. If it was really a matter of seniority in matters of art, many kapellmeisters and cymbal players would have to be ranked above Mozart and Spontini."[12]

Mendelssohn also received appreciative mention at the end of an article entitled "Berlin in 1825" in the Mainz journal *Caecilia*, where the writer briefly catalogued the younger Berlin composers whose achievements were "more solid than deceptive,"[13] and in whom "lie our hopes for future days"; he referred briefly to Ludwig Berger, Bernhard Klein, Ludwig Grell (described as "next to Felix Mendelssohn, Zelter's most excellent student") and Carl Arnold, before concluding: "At last I mention with pride and joy the young Felix Mendelssohn, Zelter's and Berger's most excellent pupil, who in his sixteenth year has already achieved more than many in their sixtieth, from whom a year ago we already heard publicly a grand symphony, which was greeted with the most glorious applause, and from whom (if an unconfirmed rumour is to be believed) we will soon expect a new, his third, opera to be staged. [Original footnote:] The first ones, like most of his symphonies were performed in an intimate family circle, with the inclusion of a few artists and lovers of art. Up to now only four works by this rare young man have been published: 2 quartets, by Schlessinger, and 1 quartet and 1 sonata with violin accompaniment by F. Laue in Berlin."[14]

When the C Minor Symphony was given its Leipzig première early in 1827, the *Allgemeine musikalische Zeitung* was again enthusiastic, treating it as the principal novelty of the season. The reviewer still stressed the composer's youth, however:

> We turn our attention to a new symphony by Felix Mendelssohn-Bartholdy of Berlin, heard here for the first time on the first of February. If one considers the instrumentation of the work, in which area our times have made such great advances, one would think that it came from a practised composer with long experience; the young man has shown such ingenuity in the handling of individual instruments and in his command of the whole orchestra. The spirit that animates the whole, however, speaks unmistakably of that youthful power that also captures hearts by its robust health and plenitude of bubbling life, even if it often roams quickly from one to the other with a lack of restraint natural to youth, and therefore all the more pleasant. We do not mean to pronounce this as any kind of reproach, however, but rather as praise; for if the youth stepped forward already like a man, wholly rounded and steady, the overripe nature would hardly be able to promise really solid achievements in the future, which we may confidently expect. If we judge from the whole, therefore, that, with respect to what one designates style, he is still evidently wavering and seeking his individual manner, holding now to this and now to that honoured master, this is not different from saying that we rejoice over the very lively receptive-

ness of a young man whom, on account of his great inherent talent and the rich skill he has already acquired, we bid welcome to a path, which, although it is a particularly difficult one because of the great predecessors, is so splendidly replete with fame for us Germans. Straightaway, the first movement is full of youthful power, and the glowing ardour of his youthful, tender feelings is unable to control itself in an excess of tension, which is something for only the finished master. Nevertheless, although it is, to our mind, the weakest in respect of its content, one already hears this movement with real joy on account of its liveliness. The following Andante is not only orchestrated but also devised in Mozart's manner, and indeed very successful. In the same way the Menuet has something so evidently imitated about it that Beethoven is not to be mistaken as the model. The last movement, just as fiery as the first, but far more self-controlled, sets the crown on the praiseworthy whole. Entirely individual and highly effective is, in particular, a pizzicato passage, on the repetition of which a single clarinet plays such an original melody that one feels very joyfully exalted by it. May the author proceed with joyful courage along his path, which is made extremely difficult by such great predecessors as Haydn, Mozart and Beethoven, who in their way are not to be surpassed, and may he let us very soon hear something more of his work.[15]

Mendelssohn's first important public appearance as composer and performer outside his native city was at a concert in Stettin in 1827. The programme included the public premières of his first real orchestral masterpiece, the recently composed *Ein Sommernachtstraum* Overture, and of his A-flat major Double Piano Concerto, in which he and Carl Loewe were soloists; in addition, he performed Weber's *Konzertstück* (as a piano solo).[16] The account of the concert, apparently by a local journalist, conveys a much more straightforwardly enthusiastic reaction, free from condescension in respect of the composer's youth, than any of the Berlin reviews.

On 20 February the second grand winter concert took place here, which this time in many respects even outdid the achievements already celebrated in this journal, and most especially gained an entirely individual value through the presence of the able musical artist Herr Mendelssohn. The concert opened with his overture to Shakespeare's *Midsummer Night's Dream*, with a well-stocked orchestra of twelve first violins, etc., under the direction of our Löwe [sic], with which our valiant Liebert, famously known as an excellent violinist, took preliminary rehearsals with inexhaustible enthusiasm and stirring artistic skill. The orchestra has previously been accustomed to overtures by the brilliant and fiery masters Spontini and Beethoven; it immediately says all the more for this young artist's work that the orchestra performed it with love and fire, particularly after Herr Mendelssohn saw that, in the final rehearsal, his even more finely shaded nuances were performed to his complete satisfaction. An excellent effect was created by the whisper of divided violins, which an artistic and witty lady compared, certainly not inappropriately, to a swarm of gnats that raise a delightful tumult of life in the last rays of the evening sun. The whole thing moves forward lightly and daringly, swells at various points to gigantic power, and is, at the same time, shot through with noble, pleasing melodies. The rough-toned English bass horn,[17] and the bassoon, which insinuate themselves marvellously enough into the theme like a pair of big donkey's ears in refined society (see Shakespeare), have a comical effect. Enough, the thoughtful work gave us great pleasure throughout. The directorate of the local Music Society has received permission from the composer to keep a copy of the overture here, and thus it may well be heard again frequently. After this Mendelssohn and Löwe performed a double concerto for two pianofortes, composed by the former, in which the former especially displayed brilliant technical skill and a very cultivated style of performance, and both gave extraordinary pleasure by the precise manner in which they seized ensemble passages and rounded them off. Also, with respect to composition, this concerto shows genius, taste, charm and, above all, the cultivated composer's good school, which does not let a striving after pianistic effect make him forget his rich, delicious orchestral forces, but, on the contrary, always permits the participating feelings of the wind instruments to sing out at the appropriate time, reveals rich treatment of the part-writing in the strings, and thus binds together to good effect all available resources, including even the timpani. Furthermore, the two solo pianos also depict different characters, so that each player can sufficiently develop his individuality. In the first movement both seem to display alternating brilliance. The sections of passage work, however, were always of a kind which necessarily required that they could not have been performed merely by a technical wizard, for they rather co-operated and vied appropriately with and against one another. But already in the Andante they separated, each to its own individuality. Pianoforte 2 (Mendelssohn) hung its head in tender femininity, coquetting here and there. Pianoforte 1 (Löwe) strode forth in manly power and sunk in feeling, noble supplication; both melted at the end into that holy unison that reminds one of Solomon when he says "See, how fine and pleasant it is if brothers live harmoniously together." Also, in the finale, 2 was wanton and continuously amusing, while 1 aimed for nobility and constraint right up to the united brilliant final passages with melodies superimposed on them. . . .

The 18-year-old young artist does not promise extraordinary things, he achieves them. How his worthy teacher of theory Professor Zelter must rejoice over such a student! How very respectfully the young man spoke of his master and his method, which never got in the way in a constraining manner but always only stimulated and guided. How seldom one hears that from students. Equally, the young artist's respect for Mr. Berger speaks for itself.[18]

37 · *Die Hochzeit des Camacho*

The positive and heartening experience of Mendelssohn's visit to Stettin was soon overshadowed by irritations, frustrations and disappointments, engendered by the production of his opera *Die Hochzeit des Camacho* at the Königliches Schauspielhaus in April 1827. In Sebastian Hensel's *Die Familie Mendelssohn*, the event is summarized in one sentence: "The narrow-mindedness of the manager, the intrigues behind the curtain, the business, often annoying, with the actors and rehearsals, all this, even if at first amusing, soon became very tedious."[19] This brief reference conceals far more than it reveals; for the experience seems to have had a profound and long-lasting effect on Mendelssohn, deepening his dislike of Berlin, and sharpening his fastidiousness in the matter of opera to a point where it took him another twenty years seriously to undertake composing another for public consumption.[20] Whenever he referred to *Camacho* in the future, it was with a trace of bitterness that is scarcely encountered elsewhere in relation to his published works.

The reviews were far from unkind, but their identification of weaknesses may have confirmed Mendelssohn's own self-doubts. Ludwig Rellstab wrote a generous notice on the première, which, although well disposed, made no secret of his feeling that the opera was the work of an inexperienced composer. His review clearly conveys the equivocal nature of the opera's reception.

> On Sunday we heard the première of the first opera by
> Mr Felix Mendelssohn-Bartholdy, entitled Die Hochzeit
> des Gamacho [*sic*]. This event is certainly of uncommon
> interest for the art, and you will forgive me if on this
> occasion I expand somewhat beyond the space normally
> allowed to the reporter. I shall therefore give you
> now only the sparsest preliminary account of the re-

ception. With regard to its musical treatment the work found not so much tumultuous as very encouraging applause, which must be all the more pleasing to the composer, as it appeared to come from the more discerning part of the audience. The libretto pleased less, and we too, in fact, thought that we detected many weaknesses and prolixities in it. The performance was very successful; one could see (and this shows a praiseworthy zeal on the part of our artists that really deserves acknowledgment) that they had gained a lively interest in the work and wanted to perform it as well as the composer must wish to hear it. Mme. Seidler, excellent as ever, was very charming.—Thus the young man's first work found a very good reception, though we shall not blame him if he says in private: God protect me from my friends, I shall deal with my enemies myself! For it was at least lacking in foresight (even if the composer had not modestly considered his work only to be a generally successful essay that had been undertaken competently) that, prompted by a well-meaning but certainly damaging zeal, they wanted to boost the reception to a level that only ardent enthusiasm can produce. Such applause must prompt opposition, whereas if it had been moderate and encouraging, everyone would naturally have shared it or at least gone along with it. The young artist is therefore much to be commended that, with a proper appreciation of the situation, he did not appear. After a repeated hearing of the work we shall with pleasure engage in a closer analysis in a forthcoming issue, and attempt as well as we can to distinguish the better from that which is less successful. At the moment we may remark that it appears to us that beneficial revisions might be undertaken, upon which we forbear for the moment to elaborate.[21]

The *Allgemeine musikalische Zeitung* carried a more detailed and critical review from its Berlin correspondent, which once again had a distinct tone of condescension.

On 29 April, as announced in advance in our last report, *Die Hochzeit des Gamacho* [*sic*], the first comic opera of the very promising Felix Mendelssohn-Bartholdy, richly endowed by nature with talent, intelligence and diligence, was given in the Königliche Schauspielhaus with thunderous applause, though towards the end with partial opposition to the exaggerated displays of perpetual clapping and calls for the composer. Although Mr F. Mendelssohn distinguished himself already as an eleven-year-old boy through highly skilful, particularly fiery and energetic piano playing and skilful score reading, he occupied himself earlier on mainly with school work in double counterpoint under his worthy teacher Professor Zelter and to that end wrote symphonies in the Bachian style for strings alone, which earlier on were performed in the house of his finely cultivated parents, but then the boy's fiery spirit progressed to composition for his instrument, sonatas, concertos, trios and quartets and he finally attempted operettas too, which revealed much facility of invention and natural melody. Having grown into a youth, however, F. Mendelssohn inclined predominantly to deep, thoughtful seriousness in his instrumental compositions; his first public debut with a comic opera was therefore surprising and appeared to give notice of a new, till now unknown side of this genius. Meanwhile the uselessness of the chosen libretto aroused concern, on account of which, after the composition was completed, it required a complete reworking for the purpose of the production. . . . The composer has certainly conceived the style of the opera in a very brilliant but almost too lofty manner, and particularly demonstrated a striving after effect that should have remained foreign to uninhibited youthful feelings. The ensembles in particular do not lack traits of genius; the arias want melodic fluency to some extent, and the instrumentation seems too prominent. . . . As a whole, the young composer, whose models seem to be Mozart, Beethoven and C. M. v. Weber, has

laid before us a decided example, if not yet a masterpiece, of his prominent talent, which is cultivated in so
many respects that it will certainly bear beautiful fruits if
the incense of praise and the vanity of a young man with
rich parents does not lift him too early to a dizzying
height from which the return to evenly paved paths is
very difficult. We particularly warn against striving to be
original.[22]

The illness of Blume, who sang the part of Don Quixote, prevented
further performances, and it seems probable that Mendelssohn's own unhappiness with the work, at least in the form in which it had been produced, dissuaded him from seeking to revive it. How far the extensive
changes between the version of the opera in Mendelssohn's autograph
score of 1825 and the staged version of 1827 were made of his own volition,
and how far they were pressed upon him by others, cannot now be
determined, but some indication of his dissatisfaction with them may be
seen in his published vocal score of 1829, where there are important modifications of form and content, often reverting substantially to material
from the original version. The vocal score too, however, received a mixed
reception in the *Allgemeine musikalische Zeitung*. The reviewer, having
remarked of the opera that "everyone attributed its fate primarily to the
libretto," also observed that many did not consider the music "light
enough for the situation, or not appealing enough for the public at large,"
or felt that "as a result of an excess of elaborate instrumental music" it
was "not favourable enough to the singers." After much more about the
difference between production in a theatre and the use of a vocal score
in the home, the reviewer explained his view that

> for an opera of this type Mr M. has provided too much
> music in general and in particular too many large-scale
> numbers, also these are not infrequently too long drawn
> out for theatrical effect, even where the treatment should
> only have been light, lively and fleeting. This is the case
> with nearly all young theatre composers who really have
> something to say, particularly the Germans: just like al-

most all young writers for the theatre with their rhetorical perorations, tirades, monologues, etc. Only through direct experiences of the stage does one learn to recognize the right economy and symmetry: only through struggles against oneself and through sacrifices, on account of these experiences, does one learn to use and control this economy and symmetry. . . . But we should not omit to mention that between these larger-scale numbers there are not a few light, pleasant, shorter serious or comic ones for one or for several voices, which give variety to the enjoyment and which, in themselves, everyone will gladly hear or sing. The genuinely comic, however, appears to agree less with Mr M's native ability. One easily sees that he understands how to achieve it; he also manages it in fact, and from time to time very prettily: but that elusive thing, of which one says: whoever has it has it and whoever doesn't won't get it—the humour and the natural liveliness, as well as its sparkle— this he does not seem to have, or he does not move freely and easily enough in it, or he wants to make more out of it and he smothers it. Apart from this, taking his music as a whole into account, we should not know how better to give the reader a short characterization of his taste and his manner of writing, than to say that he seems primarily to have taken Mozart, in his operas, particularly *Figaro* and *Così fan tutte*, as his pattern and model. With spirit, talent, insight, diligence and skill he has followed him successfully in much and excellently in some things: but—apart from that which we mentioned earlier—in the crucial intrinsic characteristics of the genre, the manner and the characters, as well as the charm, tenderness, fluency and appeal of the melody (especially in *Figaro*), and in the uninterrupted flexibility, serenity, plenitude of ideas and life (especially in *Così fan tutte*), he cannot stand beside him. But who can stand beside him in this respect.[23]

Mendelssohn himself may well have largely agreed with much of this criticism. When William Bartholemew suggested translating it into English in 1843, he very decidedly refused, exclaiming: "For God's sake do not let my old sin of 'Camacho's Wedding' be stirred up again!"[24]

38 · Piano Music and Songs, 1825–1829

By the end of the 1820s reviewers were beginning to focus more on Mendelssohn's compositions than on their composer's precocity. In reviews from this period, therefore, appreciation of the music was, on the whole, less strongly characterized by the patronizing tone of earlier notices; yet criticism, where it occurred, tended to have a sharper note. Although some reviewers were receptive to the more individual style of the works that Mendelssohn began to write from 1826 onwards, in which the predominantly Mozartian language of the First Piano Quartet was increasingly enriched by a distinctive synthesis of influences as diverse as Bach, Handel, late Beethoven, Spohr and Weber, more conservative critics saw his style as eccentric, academic or even subversive.

Two notices from the *Allgemeine musikalische Zeitung* nicely illustrate the polarities of enthusiasm and censure at this time. A reviewer of Mendelssohn's Beethovenian Piano Sonata, op. 6, preceded his detailed comments on the individual movements with the remark, "An excellent piano sonata, which will earn credit with truly skilled pianists and serious music lovers for the inspired and artistic author, whose name everywhere has (as Tell says) a good sound in the land, but which will also give pleasure. Mr M. certainly cannot be counted among those composers who allow everything that runs from head and finger to be printed, certain that, on account of their valued name, there will be no lack of customers; he allows little to be printed; what he does issue, however, really deserves to be made known to the world. The reviewer knows his five earlier works and regards them all as valuable. He does not regard this sixth as at all inferior to any of them; in respect of fundamental workmanship and careful and also effective voice leading, he even considers it superior to them; yes, there are very few piano composers, even among the celebrated, who could be compared with him in this respect." The reviewer then went on to state that the work added these new qualities to the best of the old: "youthful freshness; often very original invention; a preference for the melodic and the expressive, and a highly appropriate employment of all the advantages of the instrument." He concluded his review by characterizing the four individual movements appreciatively: the first as "very melodious" and "cheerfully amicable," the second as "powerful, passionate and effective," the third as a movement that even great players would have to practise before playing it in front of others because of its "intrinsic sense and coherence of feeling," and the finale as "fast and fiery."[25]

A review of the *Sieben Characterstücke*, op. 7, from the next volume of the same journal, however, stands in sharp contrast. Although, like the preceding review, it acknowledges the "careful workmanship, well-managed figuration, voice leading, imitation of all kinds, and everything that one understands by the term workmanship," it goes on to suggest that the music contains little beyond this: "If, however, we consider the compositions lying before us as art, not as artificiality, then they deserve manifold censure. Above all we miss melody, facility, truth of feeling, taste; instead we find everywhere rigidity of school and, in most of the pieces, the most unendurable length." The reviewer made it clear that he considered the inexperienced composer, in consciously seeking to avoid triviality, to have fallen into the opposite error; he advised him "not to exclude the Graces" in his future compositions, and ended by admonishing Mendelssohn, in the old condescending tone, to "remember that there is a world of difference between superficiality and school exercises, and that such works as these will be tedious even for the initiated, while for the layman they will always be unpalatable."[26]

Further critical remarks, focusing in particular upon a tendency to eccentricity, with an oblique reference to the baneful influence of Beethoven, occur in a lengthy review of the second volume of the op. 8 songs. Towards the end the reviewer commented, "We know the author of these songs from his larger-scale compositions as a man whom we believe we are justified in observing with hope, of which, we trust, the fulfilment is not far off, if he will abandon himself more to his indwelling spirit than to a quest for originality, which is now, admittedly, made fashionable here and there by celebrated predecessors." He did however, conclude: "At least half these songs will furnish greater pleasure than many of those by acclaimed but less gifted composers."[27]

The schoolmasterly attitude of earlier reviews appears positively generous when compared with the dismissive and sarcastic comments on opp. 1, 5 and 8 by a certain Dr Grosheim in *Caecilia* in 1828. Following a highly critical review of Loewe's *Sechs hebräische Gesänge*, Grosheim dismissed the music of Mendelssohn's *Zwölf Gesänge*, op. 8, with the remark: "The sympathetic, friendly hints that were conveyed to the author of the first work may just as well be recommended to Herr Mendelssohn-Bartholdy; and it would also be beneficial for him, since he is dealing with Christian songs, to take to heart the article 'Lied' in Herr Koch's musical dictionary. And, with that, enough of our author's otherwise so charming music!" Mendelssohn's choice of texts elicited the remark "Herr M. recognizes the beauty of poetry less than that of music." Of the Capriccio op. 5 he simply observed: "It is only designed for the private practice of certain figurations and can be of some use to the beginner in piano playing." Then, bundling together Mendelssohn's Piano Quartet op. 1 with Ferdinand Ries's Sextet op. 142, he confined himself to the comment: "An op. 1 and an op. 142! According to the laws of nature the first fruit of a sapling are of little value. If, however, it has grown into a tree and has produced fruits to 142, that is to say, one hundred and forty-two times, no matter whether they are particular or not particular, then it is again the law of nature that it is worn out."[28]

Such reviews as this were merely insulting and could be relatively easily ignored, but those that took Mendelssohn to task for failing to adhere to tried and tested models must have been more troubling, since even his own father was displeased with the remarkable A Minor String Quartet, op.13, and the influence of Beethoven in general. To what extent criticism of this kind may have encouraged stylistic retrenchment at this period, which has sometimes been identified (by, for instance, Eric Werner) as a retreat into more conventional paths, is questionable. Mendelssohn's own self-critical faculties were strong and largely self-contained. His resentment of such adverse criticism in the musical press, however, made all the stronger by the necessity to project onto it his chagrin at his father's disapproval, which he would have found it difficult to articulate, may well have remained with him for the rest of his life. Schumann's remark about the "nonsensical jabber of the narrow-minded" and Mendelssohn's early "struggle" in his 1840 review of the D Minor Piano Trio, op. 49 (quoted below), may well reflect impressions that Schumann had gathered directly from Mendelssohn.

39 · The Initial Impact of Mendelssohn's Music in England

The earliest references to Mendelssohn in the British press were a couple of brief mentions in articles translated from German journals, which appeared in the *Quarterly Musical Magazine and Review* in 1823[29] and 1825,[30] and a few comments on his early publications in the *Harmonicon* between 1825 and 1827. Interest in Mendelssohn and his music began to grow rapidly in Britain after his visit to London in 1829, during which he made his debut at the Philharmonic Society on 25 May with his Symphony in C Minor (with an orchestral version of the Scherzo from the Octet substituted for the original Menuetto).

The review of the symphony in the *Harmonicon* contrasts with all the earlier German reviews in its bold assertion of Mendelssohn's place as one of Europe's leading composers. After a few words about his background, the reviewer commented: "Though only about one or two-and-twenty years of age, he has already produced several works of magnitude, which, if at all to be compared with the present, ought, without such additional claim, to rank him with the first composers of the age. It is not venturing too far to assert, that his latest labour, the symphony of which we now speak, shews a genius for this species of composition that is exceeded only by the three great writers; and it is a fair presumption, that, if he persevere in his pursuit, he will in a few years be considered as the fourth of that line which has done such immortal honour to the most musical nation in Europe."[31] the *Athenaeum*, too, hailed him as "a musical genius of the very first class" and summed up its remarks on the symphony with the comment that it was "sensible, clear, striking, and yet original, and a new sinfonia has never before been so eminently successful at the Philharmonic," adding that it "exhibited great originality, without that incoherent eccentricity, which Beethoven unfortunately had recourse to."[32] A reviewer in the *Atlas* agreed broadly with the opinions expressed in the other journals, and though he was more cautious about pronouncing it an unqualified masterpiece, did not deny that it was exceptional: "We look upon the new sinfonia of Mendelssohn more as a *study* of great promise than as a finished picture. Still we have heard no composition by any of the rising generation of musicians which throughout kept the attention equally alert, or so often gave us pleasure." He also voiced, more explicitly, the attitude hinted at in the final remark of the *Athenaeum's* review when he observed: "A composer who has the good sense and talent to imitate the great masters well at twenty-two, is likely himself to become a model at forty. We detest the *original* music, as it is so called, for which young composers are often foolishly lauded."[33] Such comments may go a long way to explain the readiness with which English audiences (with their down-to-earth liking for clarity and order) were to embrace Mendelssohn's music.

After the condescending or niggardly criticism of so many German critics, the disappointment with *Camacho* and his growing feeling of alienation from Berlin musical circles, the open-hearted attitude of English musicians and society provided a welcome antidote. Mendelssohn expressed his view of the difference between London and Berlin musicians in a letter to Devrient on 29 October 1829: "When I think of the musicians of Berlin I overflow with gall and wormwood; they are miserable shams, with their sentimentality and devotion to art. I have no intention to sing the praises of English musicians, but when they eat an apple-pie, at all events they do not talk about the abstract nature of a pie, and of the affinities of its constituent crust and apple, but they heartily eat it down."[34] When, in 1836, a writer in the *Allgemeine musikalische Zeitung* stated that "the [London] Philharmonic Society gave him the first public recognition of his merits as a composer, making him an honorary member after the performance of his First Symphony,"[35] he undoubtedly reflected Mendelssohn's own feelings. Many years later, consciously or unconsciously suppressing the memory of earlier public performances of his music, Mendelssohn wrote to Jenny Lind about this visit to England: "It was the first time that I had left the shelter of the parental roof, or had produced anything in public; and it had gone well, and a stone had been lifted from my heart."[36]

When Mendelssohn returned to Berlin from England in December 1829 he left behind the seeds of an interest that during the next two decades was to grow almost into idolatry. An article, "Notes of a Musical Tourist," by John Thomson, who had met Mendelssohn in Edinburgh in 1829 and soon afterwards visited the rest of the family in Berlin,[37] which appeared in the *Harmonicon* in 1830, began the process of acquainting the British public more fully with Mendelssohn and his works. Thomson ended his long article, which included a detailed and highly enthusiastic account of the String Quartet in A Minor (published shortly afterwards), with a paragraph that clearly presaged the growth of Mendelssohn's reputation in England:

> Here, then, is a youth, who at the age of thirteen—an age when the faculties of most men are only about to appear—produced work in the highest classes of composition, instrumental and vocal, exhibiting the most original and felicitous conceptions, impassioned feeling, and scientific knowledge, not surpassed by any one in the prime of manhood:—who, before his sixteenth year, produced Grand Symphonies and Overtures, pronounced by competent judges to be worthy of a place beside those of the three greatest masters:—and who now (in his twenty-second year) is soaring into the regions of fancy with a strengthened wing, and even with a bolder flight. Is it too much, then, to anticipate for him the proudest niche in the temple of Apollo? Haydn's early works have been lost, perhaps deservedly, in oblivion. With those of Mozart all are acquainted; but lovely though they be, it were ridiculous to put them forward as the germ of that genius which afterwards burst forth with so much splendour. And the opere prime of Beethoven were produced at a period of life much later than those of Mendelssohn. What, then, may not be expected from one who, in his first works, has not only surpassed those of the great names just mentioned, but in his later productions has equalled the elaborate compositions of their riper years.[38]

40 · The Years of Widening Recognition, 1831–1836

During Mendelssohn's years of travel between May 1830 and his return to Berlin in June 1832, he and his works were scarcely mentioned in German periodicals. This partly reflected his own strategy, for he had remarked to Ludwig Ganz in October 1828: "It is a very long time since the public has had anything of importance from me (a couple of hastily written cantatas[39] cannot be taken into account), nor have I played the piano, or showed myself as a composer, and so I have gently slipped into forgetfulness, in which I wish to remain until after my great journey."[40] No new compositions were published during 1831, and the two most important works that had appeared in print to date, the String Quartets opp. 12 and 13, aroused no critical interest except, in the case of the latter, Thomson's contribution to the *Harmonicon*. The virtual silence of continental papers contrasts with references to Mendelssohn in the *Harmonicon* during the 1830 and 1831 seasons. Whereas Thomson had furnished the journal with most of its material in 1830, the following year saw several reviews of Mendelssohn's piano works, issued by English publishers, in successive numbers from February to May.

Mendelssohn's visits to Munich, Paris and London between September 1831 and June 1832 stimulated renewed critical interest. His reception in Munich was enthusiastic; he gave a highly successful concert there on 17 October 1831, including the first performance of his newly composed Piano Concerto in G Minor, the Symphony in C Minor (as in London, with the orchestrated version of the Scherzo from the Octet substituted for the Menuetto) and the *Sommernachtstraum* Overture. The local reviewer for the *Allgemeine musikalische Zeitung* wrote enthusiastically: "Herr Bartholdy Mendelssohn [*sic*], who does not know him? A hero in the art of performance; great, master of all difficulties, fiery and yet comprehensible. His concert pieces in the first half, his improvised fantasia at the end reveal the skilled master of his instrument. But the poet of sound also drew our whole attention to him. The grand symphony in C minor, which opened the concert, deserves the fullest, most glorious recognition." Then, after unmixed praise for the symphony, he continued, uncertain whether the *Sommernachtstraum* Overture was a self-contained piece or the overture to an opera: "Just one more step—or perhaps it is already taken and we have missed it—and Germany also has won a dramatic composer in and for its language."[41] He thought that the piece displayed "imagination, character and a musical-romantic spirit throughout," and he concluded with the statement: "We do not need to remind his and our friends in the north that Herr Bartholdy does not play for himself, has not composed for himself."[42]

In Paris, however where Mendelssohn remained for four months and was actively involved in private and public music making, critical notice was confined to brief discussion of his participation in the Conservatoire concerts, focusing in particular on his performance of the Beethoven G Major Piano Concerto.[43] His *Sommernachtstraum* Overture was "much applauded"[44] but seems to have made no lasting impression; his *Reformation* Symphony was quietly shelved because, according to Hiller, it was "much too learned, too much *fugato*, too little melody."[45] Mendelssohn's reception in England immediately afterwards was quite different; once again his works elicited widespread enthusiasm from audiences and reviewers.

Returning home from his travels in June 1832, therefore, Mendelssohn was on the verge of wider recognition as a composer, but appreciation of his music was still confined to a few major centres and to a relatively restricted musical public. After the dearth of publications in 1831, however, a succession of important works appeared during 1832 and 1833; he promoted his music in Berlin through performance either as conductor or soloist, and his publications and activities began to gain more regular acknowledgment in the German press.

The works of greatest importance for Mendelssohn's critical reputation during these years were undoubtedly the G Minor Piano Concerto, the first three concert overtures, *Ein Sommernachtstraum*, *Die Hebriden*, and *Meeresstille und glückliche Fahrt*, issued together in score by Breitkopf und Härtel in 1835,[46] and the fourth concert overture, *Die schöne Melusine*, published in 1836.

41 · The Piano Concerto in G Minor, Op. 25

Mendelssohn performed the G Minor Piano Concerto at every suitable opportunity during 1832 and 1833, and always with great success. His own advocacy as soloist seems to have made the piece irresistible. After its performance at the Philharmonic Society on 28 May 1832 the *Harmonicon* observed: "The great novelty and high treat of the evening was M. Mendelssohn's concerto, never before performed in public. He is a composer who spurns at imitation, for he is original almost to overflowing, and to the very last note of the piece is inexhaustible in new effects. The first movement of this is in G minor, and glides, without any break, into an adagio in E major, a composition of surpassing beauty, in which the violoncellos are more than vocal: they sing better than most of those to whom vocal powers are said to be given. The finale in G major is all gaiety; the composer seems to have been hardly able to keep his spirits within moderate bounds; they flow over, and half intoxicate his hearers, till the close arrives, which is all calmness—a pianissimo! Such an ending is without example, and exceedingly delightful it was admitted to be by universal consent."[47] The critic of the *Athenaeum* too was entirely positive about the work. He thought that the first movement "from the character and novel style of its treatment, might be described as a 'dramatic scena for the pianoforte,' with orchestral accompaniment"; and after praising the slow movement, with its "beautiful melody," he expressed astonishment at the brilliant finale with its "difficulties which none but the author could master!" Impressed as much by the performance as by the composition, he concluded: "This performance throughout was loudly applauded, and, as an exhibition of pianoforte playing, we unhesitatingly pronounce it, more astonishing than any we have yet witnessed."[48] The success of the piece was such that it had to be repeated in a later concert.

Whatever lack of enthusiasm Mendelssohn himself may have felt for the concerts he gave in Berlin during the winter of 1832 to 1833,[49] his concerto certainly roused the enthusiasm of a critic in the *Allgemeine musikalische Zeitung*, who wrote in January 1833, after reviewing the *Reformation* Symphony respectfully but unenthusiastically, "More pleasing to the majority was a piano concerto in a completely new form; the usual three movements are naturally connected, and also in the alternation of the powerful orchestral tutti with the piano solo sections it is completely free of conventionality, following its own path. If the first movement was almost too powerfully accompanied, and the character of the composition, for a piano concerto, very passionate and serious, though from the harmonic point of view very interesting, the expressive, tender Andante in E major soothed the excited spirit again; and the concluding Rondo universally ignited sparks of the most stirring enthusiasm, through the inspired invention of its charming theme, which mostly recalled Beethoven's genius, as well as through the extraordinary rapidity, precision, delicacy and fine taste with which the composer himself performed the exceedingly difficult piano part."[50]

The following year the published edition of the G Minor Piano Concerto was reviewed by August Kahlert in *Caecilia*, along with the solo piano pieces opp. 14, 15 and 19. Kahlert preceded his consideration of the individual works with a general appraisal of Mendelssohn's significance, in which he too drew parallels with Beethoven:

> F. Mendelssohn-Bartholdy is one of those contemporary
> musicians who stand out, no less for their command over
> all means of their art, than for their striving for a higher,
> universal goal, who have not lost the conviction that a
> deeper significance than merely that of sensual charm
> may lie hidden in music, among the mass of coloratura
> and the diminished-seventh chords of the brass instru-
> ments. He is not content with mere form, he strives to
> unite it inextricably with the individual content of the
> matter that he wants to present. Although he does not
> carry this out with that unconscious boldness, that free-
> dom of spirit which characterizes Beethoven, he is never-
> theless to be included among those who have most effec-
> tively continued working on the path that Beethoven
> opened up. Instrumental music easily leads to that insig-
> nificance which quickly causes the most well-ordered,
> most mellifluous musical figures to become outmoded;
> Mendelssohn successfully resists such an aberration. His
> music, even when it is not linked to words, is spiritually
> animated.

Then, having reviewed the solo piano works appreciatively, he turned to the concerto:

> At last, from among the many concert pieces that every fair brings us, we once more have one that stands out from the common wares that are brought there, and demonstrates individuality in form and content. Our familiar digitally dextrous heroes, with their artistic efforts, have in fact already become suspect to the more discerning. Always a long encyclopaedic tutti, in which we get the essentials of the lengthy porridge we have to endure; then passage work that leads to a luscious motif in the dominant, ritardando, grand bravura passages with several rough modulations, tutti, apparently learned development, and the whole saga lands up in the tonic again. The Adagio is only employed as a matter of decency, in order to stimulate the dull senses like caviar after the soup, and then we have a really frivolous rondo, which provokes applause like the wanton leaps of a superannuated ballerina. The concerto is over, we clap, the player mops his brow, and we go home tired and empty in heart and spirit.
>
> We apologize for this effusion. We need it in order to indicate how different *Mendelssohn* is from the host of modern fashionable musicians. Already *C. M. v. Weber* extended, in a brilliant manner, the form of the so-called concertino (in which, as a rule, all the movements are shortened by half) in his excellent Concertstück in F Minor, as Beethoven had already done long before in his unsurpassable fantasia with chorus [op. 80]. Hummel tried something similar in the fantasia "Oberon's Horn."
>
> In the present work *Mendelssohn* provides a whole concerto in three movements, of which the individual parts, although carefully abbreviated, cohere, the second and third being joined by a cadenza-like intermezzo. The *Allegro* in G minor begins, fiery, hurrying rapidly for-

ward, of decisive character, with eight bars of gradual crescendo, tutti, upon which the pianoforte, as it were, improvises, until it reaches the main theme of almost Handelian character, which is once again taken over by the orchestra. This character is also maintained by the pianoforte until it comes to a calm, amiable melodious theme (B-flat major), from which on all sides colourful figures develop, which carry it forward until, at last, instead of a close in B-flat, the main theme comes in again. The cantabile also repeats itself in G minor, but almost merely hinted at, everything is compressed and the movement appears to come to an end, when the trumpets interrupt with B-natural; the restless drive fades away; we arrive at E major; and then a gentle *Andante*, 3/4 glides by, in which the cellos play with the pianoforte in a concertante manner; a connecting orchestral movement (E minor, *Presto*, continually growing), leads us to a *Molto Allegro* in G major, a very cheerful, merry rondino (almost reminding one of Weber), in which a principal figure is firmly maintained, which supports a charming melody in the wind instruments. Here too the form is abbreviated and only a slight reminiscence of the second theme of the first Allegro emerges merely to be suppressed by the ever-increasing jubilation that lasts until the end.—This is the course of the very charming work, so full of life, which delighted on closer study as it had in performance. In the present state of technique it might almost be described as easy, but we know virtuosos who would find it difficult to play it well. Comprehension requires a poetic life.[51]

It seems likely that few other pianists in Germany took up the G minor concerto for a while after its publication. The *Allgemeine musikalische Zeitung* contains no further reviews of performances before 1835, and its relative obscurity is suggested by Gottfried Wilhelm Fink's review of it together with Ferdinand Ries's Ninth Concerto, op. 177, in the same year.

For a long time, and particularly recently, we have often heard the complaint of the virtuosos that they no longer know what to choose! Acknowledged gems are so often performed that they will no longer do for a celebrity concert: and we have no novelties, or rarely any, that can be depended upon to please. The complaint is groundless, but perhaps there are grounds for it.[52] Some derive from the public, others from the virtuosos. Here is not the place to measure the height or breadth of the mountainous stumbling block; it is not one of the most difficult undertakings, everyone can do it: therefore let him do it if he wants; we particularly recommend it to the virtuosos. Here, however, we have Ries and Mendelssohn-Bartholdy, each with a concerto and the latter also with a brilliant Rondo. Are these not serviceable? Or have the virtuosos already made so much use of them that they can judge of their success? Not at all! In most places they have not even been heard. Probably most players do not yet possess them. It would be good, therefore, for them to purchase them. The two men are different; and so it should be: so too are the situations and sensitivities of the listeners. Both have rightly won friends, each according to his type. Both know how to orchestrate; everyone knows that. And judging from the individual parts, as far as one can, the orchestra should significantly increase the charm of the music.[53] And yet we ourselves have still never heard any of these works with the instruments; we have only heard the solo part of all three: otherwise we would not say a word about them, for bravura pieces above all are the least susceptible to judgment on the basis of mere perusal. Thus these works might proffer something new, either not yet heard or only very rarely heard, by significant men and of different types.

Having discussed Ries's concerto, remarking that it appears "well calculated for a mixed public" and "does not plumb greater depths than people like in such a gathering," Fink turned to Mendelssohn's.

[This concerto] is not at all calculated; it is a piece of music produced by the author's mind to express itself at this moment. It is a character piece that requires not only competent players in respect of finger dexterity and easy mastery of distinctive rapid passages but also those who do not make the orchestra's particular expression impossible, nay rather, know how to unite themselves intimately with it where necessary. When we heard it played by the composer himself without the instrumental accompaniment, it sounded extremely brilliant and altogether it made a wholly beautiful impression in its totality, and apart from that one had to admire the dexterity. Since the orchestra often participates powerfully in the solo passages and all movements of the work are bound closely to one another, a good performance also requires power and endurance, in addition to what has already been indicated. Because of this arrangement there may well also be virtuosos who, like many actors, always sigh only for so-called good exits. We consider it better to look at the whole, to take up the work and learn something from it.[54]

42 · The Concert Overtures

As with the G Minor Piano Concerto, Mendelssohn performed his overtures on many occasions prior to their publication, and the earliest extant reviews precede publication, in some cases by several years. The *Sommernachtstraum* Overture had been performed regularly since 1826, *Meeresstille und glückliche Fahrt* was first performed in 1828 but then laid aside for revision. On 14 May 1832, his latest overture, *Die Hebriden*, was performed by the Philharmonic Society in London, when the *Harmonicon* enthused that "unity of invention is no less remarkable in this than in the author's overture to *A Midsummer Night's Dream*, and indeed is a prominent feature in all he has produced. Whatever a vivid imagination could suggest, and a great musical knowledge supply, has contributed to this, the latest work of M. Mendelssohn, one of the finest and most original geniuses of the age; and it will be but an act of justice to him, and a great boon to the frequenters of these Concerts, to repeat the present composition before the conclusion of the season. Works such as this are like 'angel visits,' and should be made the most of."[55] But not every English critic was quite so enthusiastic; the implied programme of the work seems to have caused difficulties for some, including the critic of the *Athenaeum*, who observed: "The burthen of the composition strongly reminded us of Beethoven. Towards the end it was well worked with figurative passages for violins, the subject being sustained by the wind instruments—but as descriptive music, it was decidedly a failure."[56] When it was performed in Berlin the following year, in a revised version, the programmatic implications caused no difficulties for the local reviewer for the *Allgemeine musikalische Zeitung*, who remarked merely that it shared "the wild romantic character" of the Hebrides islands, which had "inspired Ossian's poetry."[57]

Fink was particularly exercised by the relationship of the music in the concert overtures to the ideas that lay behind it, touching upon the issue in his reviews of the four overtures at the time each first appeared, either as orchestral parts, piano arrangement or score. In his review of the *Ouvertüre zu den Hebriden (Fingals-Höhle)* in 1834, he began with the statement: "Musical productions that are tied to particular objects, whose musical manifestation was generated from seeing or contemplating these objects, require at least a general knowledge of the thing that inspired them, so that the listener can be put in a mood, which to some extent approaches that in which the composer was when he conceived his work." He went on to describe Fingal's Cave and its Ossianic associations and then, before considering the quality of the music in greater detail, commented: "Therefore, in hearing this music one must think of Staffa and the celebrated cave. The music manifests this simple grandeur throughout. It gives a waving and flowing to long-held, simple, powerful, and unmoving, solid masses of sound. And that is entirely right here; it would be wrong if it were otherwise. This therefore counters the thoughtless demands of some, who would like this overture to have the lightly moving mutations of the overture to the fantastic transformations of the Midsummer Night's Dream, with which they group this, indeed, in which they seek and find reminiscences. A different object requires a different treatment. Here the immutably solid, the simply grand, the unaffectedly elevated is the firm foundation."[58]

Fink returned to the subject the following year, when the first three overtures were published in full score. He devoted most of his review to a consideration of the legitimacy of the composer's programmatic intentions and the manner in which he sought to relate his music to the external object.

> We discussed these three concert overtures sufficiently at the time of their appearance before the public, as well as after hearing repeated performances, and after their arrangement for piano, and we have therefore nothing more to say about the essential qualities of each and the differences among them; it is much rather a case of referring to what we remarked earlier, for during the brief intervening period our view of these artworks has not changed, unless, that is, we acknowledge the even greater sense of pleasure we have gained from studying the score and regard this increased recognition of their worth as a change. We definitely number these three works among the most significant that the composer has so far brought out, indeed, among the most significant of their kind that have appeared in recent times, and on closer inspection of these beautiful and clearly printed scores we feel such renewed delight that, for the reasons explained earlier, we have to place them among the most pleasing productions of recent years. It must be apparent from our remarks, to which we wish to add an observation from another direction, that we do not separate the exciting from the pleasurable, we see it rather as a necessary adjunct: thus the examples given here will only bring out the latter requirement more strongly, for there is so much that is exciting, and so much often unexpected variety, chiefly in the first and last overtures, that many have been inclined to find their descriptive expression too colourful, in our opinion entirely unjustifiably, which makes them tend to give precedence to the second

because, as they say, of its greater unity. Looking at the three different pieces themselves, it is evident that the different treatment—here a more vivid, there a more uniform colouring of the tone painting—arises from and is justified by the nature of the thing itself, indeed, the overall pleasurableness of all these tone pictures comes wholly from their intrinsic coherence, from their true grasp of the respective objects; and this clarity, together with the way in which an image is naturally evoked, will cause a lively feeling of empathy in the listener. Would one not expect a midsummer night's dream to express itself in sound more fantastically and vividly than a musical expression of the simple grandeur of Fingal's Cave? The pleasurable sensation that still sounds forth and resounds when the music has long since faded away lives and is bound up solely and precisely with this appropriate execution and conception,[59] which is true to the nature of the piece. That is the merit of these tone pictures, that they leave something behind which fills us with residual enjoyment, so that through hearing them we become more enthusiastic and fond of the pieces themselves; we continue to learn something from them, probably because we derive not merely mental but also spiritual enjoyment from them.—However, the claim that music should not imitate these and similar things from other arts, or from nature, would be correct if music forgot its nature and sought to make pictures for our minds, as if with words or colours or engraved lines, which it is not able to do. But this is definitely not attempted here. A knowledge of the images themselves is taken for granted, just as it would be by every cultivated person; the content itself is therefore not conveyed by the music, it does not need to be, since it stands before the mind's eye, but the notes merely express, in an appropriate manner, the feeling that the images create in the mind; thus to the spiritual delight provided by the gifts of others is added the sensual feeling of music, by which means the inner world feels expanded and more universally, more comprehensibly beautified.[60]—And thus it only remains to hope that all friends of music who are able should provide themselves with this inwardly and outwardly beautiful edition in score and find as much delight in it as we ourselves.[61]

In his long analytical review of *Die schöne Melusine* the following year Fink repeated almost verbatim a substantial portion of the preceding passage then articulated what he saw as the parameters of Mendelssohn's programmatic intentions in the new overture: "As far as this tone poem is concerned, it is what it sets out to be, an overture for a particular object, for the tale of the beautiful Melusine, that is to say, introductory music that makes us more receptive to the course of the story and its emotional excitements, thus preparing our feelings, by means of the powerfully effective sense of hearing, to absorb even more. It follows therefore that it does not try to translate the whole tale into musical language, which is not feasible, but only to conjure up for us from the dreamworld of harmonic power, the happiness and unhappiness of two beings, which through the language of the verbal poetry become a mermaid and a knight and are therefore more distinct pictures. These doubled circumstances of both manifestations of the imagination are therefore beautifully portrayed here in the particular emotional language of music."[62]

By the time Mendelssohn took up his post in Leipzig the concert overtures were widely regarded as representing a peak of contemporary instrumental music, so that the writer of Mendelssohn's biography in a *Conversations-Lexicon* in 1836, for instance, could maintain that they were "perhaps the most beautiful overtures that, so far, the Germans possess."[63]

43 · *Songs without Words*

Although successful performances of Mendelssohn's orchestral works during the early 1830s singled him out in critical circles as a composer of increasing stature and importance, it was his chamber and piano music (including arrangements of the overtures for piano solo or duet) that would have made his work accessible to a wider audience. Evidence of the extent to which these compositions and arrangements aroused more general interest is scanty, however. Indeed, in the case of the *Original Melodies for the Pianoforte* (the English title of the first book of *Lieder ohne Worte*, op. 19), issued by Novello in 1832, we know that sales were extremely slow; by June 1833 only forty-eight copies had been sold. Similarly, with respect to the Rondo brillant, op. 29, Mori implied in 1834 that no more than fifty copies had been sold in England.[64] Mendelssohn's only sacred music published during these years, the *Drei Kirchenmusiken*, op. 23 (1833) and the setting of Psalm 115 (1835), went virtually unnoticed. The chamber music published between 1830 and 1836—the String Quartets opp. 12 and 13, the String Quintet op. 18, the Variations concertantes for Piano and Cello, op. 17, and the Octet op. 20—also aroused minimal critical attention at the time of publication; the string chamber works were issued only in parts, not in score, at this stage (though the Octet also appeared in a piano duet arrangement), and there was little occasion for the public performance of such pieces. The most important notices of any of these chamber works were Thomson's discussion of the Quartet op. 13 in the *Harmonicon* in 1829 (prior to the work's publication) and a review of the Octet op. 20 in the *Allgemeine musikalische Zeitung* in 1833.

Although the *Lieder ohne Worte* began to achieve widespread popularity within Mendelssohn's lifetime and were, according to the entry on Mendelssohn in Brockhaus's *Encyclopädie* in 1846, the works "that already gave him access to the larger public at an early stage,"[65] they received little critical attention before the later 1830. Apart from a few reviews in the English press, August Kahlert's discussion of them, in *Caecilia* in 1834, seems to have been the most significant critical notice at this period. Kahlert observed:

> Songs without words are a genre of music that has
> long been indigenous and popular in England. Little can-
> tabile pieces for an instrument may well be given that ti-
> tle if a verse-like structure is to some extent apparent in
> them. In the present works *Mendelssohn* carries out his
> task, which, as is usual in his case, is no common one,
> with imagination and poetic intention. The volume con-
> tains six different character pieces, which are only to be

played by those who have the desire and the ability to grasp poetic states.

It is worth the effort of considering the individual numbers;—No. 1. E major 3/4 *Andante con moto* is quite calm, inwardly moved. The melody, like the imitative bass, with which it plays a duet, must be played in a very vocal style. The accompaniment, providing the inner voices in broken chords, is to be performed in a very legato manner.—No. 2. *Andante espressivo*, 3/8 A minor, is deeply elegiac and loses itself at last as if in gentle tears. It appears to us to be the jewel of the set.—No. 3. *Molto Allegro e vivace* 6/8, E major; evidently a lively, happy hunting scene. Horn calls, hunting cries, the tumultuous dash of the hunters are all to be heard in it if it is well played with its intentions clearly brought out. No. 4. The smallest of all, A major 4/4 *Moderato*, is a genuine song. After a short ritornello (which finally concludes the piece), one gets a peaceful, sweet, trust-inducing style of music, which only reminds one clearly of *Beethoven's* "Seufzend flüstert" in "Adelaide" in two bars.—No. 5. *Piano Agitato* [*sic*] F-sharp minor, 6/4, can no longer be called a song. It is almost a sonata movement. The character of the whole, uneasy, gloomy restlessness, comes out sharply.—No. 6. *Andante sostenuto*, 6/8, G minor would, even without the title, be recognized for what it is by someone who had once lived in the *Hotel d'Europe* on the *Grand Canal* in Venice, that is to say, for one of those melting gondola songs that drift up on warm summer evenings from the dark waters. It is excellent; furthermore, if our memory does not deceive us, it appears to employ a national melody.

We earnestly recommend the volume to every friend of art who does not know it.[66]

The decisive stage in the establishment of Mendelssohn's reputation was reached with the appearance of the oratorio *St Paul* (*Paulus*, premièred at Düsseldorf in 1836 and published the following year), which set the seal upon his recognition within the German- and English-speaking worlds as the leading young composer of the day. The importance of this work was acknowledged in the entry on Mendelssohn in Brockhaus's *Conversations-Lexikon* in 1846, where it was observed that "he achieved universal recognition as a master through his oratorio *St Paul*."[67]

Oratorio was, for a significant number of musicians and music lovers in the Teutonic sphere of influence, the highest form of music. The lively hopes, which many had cherished, of a German school of opera that would offer a serious and uplifting musical experience, in contrast to the melodious inanity of Italian opera and the sensational bombast of French opera, had been dampened by 1830. The rosy dawn that seemed about to break in the early 1820s, with the triumphant receptions of Weber's *Der Freischütz* and Spohr's *Jessonda*, had proved illusory; Weber's and Spohr's later works achieved little more than a *succès d'estime*, and Marschner's early promise was gainsaid by a series of unsuccessful operas after 1833. It was in this context that Wagner's first article, *Die deutsche Oper* (1834), pondered the spiritual bankruptcy of contemporary German opera. Oratorio, on the other hand, seemed to many to offer a genre of large-scale composition, involving the full resources of orchestra, chorus and solo voices, which was more in tune with the Germanic temperament; it also had the advantage of appealing directly to a broader spectrum of the population through the flourishing choral associations and musical festivals that, reflecting the increasing economic significance of the middle classes, had become widely established during the second and third decades of the nineteenth century. In this genre, too, Spohr had enjoyed extraordinary success with *Die letzten Dinge* at the Lower Rhine Music Festival in 1825 and at the Norwich Festival (where it was given as *The Last Judgment*) in 1830. But despite the moderate success of other oratorios by composers like Friedrich Schneider, both before and after the establishment of Spohr's ascendancy in the field, no other contemporary work made a similar impact before the mid-1830s. Until then, the key works in Germany were Haydn's *Die Schöpfung* and, increasingly, the oratorios of Handel (which had enjoyed a continuous performance tradition in England). Mendelssohn himself played an important role in establishing Handel's oratorios at the heart of the German repertoire; and in *St Paul* he created a powerful musical counterpart to the archaizing movement in art, represented especially by the Düsseldorf painters with whom he was so closely associated, drawing as much on his understanding of Bach's *Matthaeus Passion* as upon Handel to produce a work that, without pandering to popular taste, triumphantly captured the popular imagination.

Press response to *St Paul* during the first few years after the 1836 première was considerable, in terms both of the quantity of articles and the extensiveness of discussion, and in 1842 it elicited a twenty-six-page booklet from Otto Jahn. From the first, the vast majority of journal reports echoed the enthusiasm of audiences and performers for the new work: the most sustained criticism of the oratorio was levelled against its text. One of the earliest reflective critiques of *St Paul* was the fourteen-page discussion by Fink in the *Allgemeine musikalische Zeitung* at the time of the oratorio's publication in the summer of 1837; he began with a general survey of its reception and an examination of its significance:

> Wherever this oratorio has been performed, such as Düs-
> seldorf, Leipzig, Zwickau, England, it has been worthily
> honoured with the lively participation of a numerous au-
> dience. In several places a performance of it is being en-
> thusiastically prepared, in Halle a. d. Saale, in Eberfeldt,
> and for the grand music festival in Birmingham from 19–
> 22 September of the present year, where it will be per-
> formed under the composer's own direction.—Such a
> testimonial for any work of art can only indicate, accord-
> ing to the essence of the matter, that in a successful per-
> formance it appeals to the taste, or, in a higher sense, as
> in the present case, that it has decisively satisfied the
> lively demands of the age for a longed-for novelty, for a
> novelty that derives from that which has obtained so far
> but has become commonplace through long familiarity,
> which ranges itself with the familiar and at the same
> time separates itself from it, being both close enough to

it and yet far enough from it, so that it can appeal to
the public without making undue demands on it, but
can be palpably acknowledged as something different
from that which already exists.

Having discussed the desirability of public recognition, even if the
artist did not actively seek it by consciously designing his work to appeal
to the masses, Fink continued:

The esteemed composer has experienced, to the greatest
extent, this joy in the most approving recognition, and
has deserved it; not for nothing did he devote himself to
the difficult genre of oratorio; he could be almost certain
that his work would be taken up in Germany and the
most important towns in England, that it would
therefore have the desired opportunity to speak for itself
everywhere.

But man is not here merely to feel and to express an
indistinct pleasure according to the impression things
make on his feelings, but also so that he becomes aware
of what he feels, so that the feeling becomes sensibility,
and this as spiritualized as possible. This consideration is
all the more necessary because there have already been a
hundred instances, not only in the art world but also in
general, where that which is damaging has been found
just as enjoyable and perhaps even more attractive than
the nourishing and the sanctifying. And this only too well-
-founded experience must make every right-thinking person see the importance of the consideration itself and the
benefit, in every respect, of that which is genuine, that is
to say, everyone who puts the blessing of art and its
flourishing, and the succouring law of truth above everything, however little it may appear at first to satisfy the
kindling of feeling, which only makes poetry but does
not reflect upon things. A poem about a poem falls far
short of a clear examination and educated appraisal of it,
which encapsulate the poem, but which must subordi-

nate contemplation and give more room to circumspection than can be pleasant to the observer, not to speak of
the mere lover of sentiment. Therefore we have also until
now, as far as I know, had several subjective descriptions
of the oratorio *Paulus*, but still no critique. If it were
easy we would have had it long since; also, many to
whom I proposed it would not have rejected the proposal. But this oratorio is not like a fashionable work by
which people are delighted to be entertained and which
today is green grass and tomorrow is cast into the fur-
nace—one can calmly and silently leave such a work
alone, for its flowering is soon over and nothing remains.
With *Paulus* it is different; it is worth the contemplation
and demands it forthwith for its own sake and for that
of art. The voice of informed criticism should let itself
be heard: and since it is silent I must be the first who
pronounces upon the significant work in a considered
manner, in order, where necessary, to arouse others if not
to concurrence in everything, at least to well-founded
contradiction. For one voice, whosesoever it might be,
does not constitute the voice of informed criticism, but
rather brings its personal view, which, to the benefit of
art, one may agree with if it deserves it, or set right with
powerful arguments.—About one thing, I know, we are
all agreed: that this composition must undoubtedly be
counted as one of the most engaging and important
works of our most recent period in music, and that it
must in consequence justify the effort of examining its
essence as precisely as possible in order to appraise it independently as it deserves, for which calm consideration,
rather than exaltation, is necessary for those who want to
find not merely enjoyment but also understanding in art.
This conviction, that there is a general consensus, is
among the most fortunate things for the composer of the
work and for the reviewer of it, for it also secures for the
latter the sympathy of the reader, to whom the words of
the reviewer about a work that is important to him are

all the more welcome the more passionate and judicious they are.

Fink next engaged in a wide-ranging, and historically questionable, digression, which reveals his early training as a theologian, referring to former treatments of the St Paul material in music, discussing the spiritual significance of the subject and glancing at the relationship between opera and oratorio. Before tackling the proposition that *St Paul* should be seen as a Protestant oratorio, which had been advanced by an earlier commentator, he concluded his digression with a colourful diatribe against the pollution of good old German artistic values by degenerate foreign influences and touched upon the issue of Mendelssohn's pursuit of the new through reverence for the old.

> Who does not see that in our times the free movement
> of the secular in long, overweening dominion has risen
> all the way to the summit of impertinence? Arbitrariness
> has for a long time flourished its Furies' sceptre and
> whipped us with infernal torches, as if we had murdered
> the mother of all refreshment; the audacious, inflated
> vanity of wild self-seeking hurls, from one side to the
> other, the impoverished human feelings that receive new
> wounds with every desired recovery, or are made drunk
> out of the cup of confusion.—The German, who will-
> ingly inclines his head to foreigners, has got this from
> abroad. Oh, he gladly gives his money for thinly plated
> wares, which he imports with difficulty to his towns
> from abroad, so that he might have that which will turn
> to rust in his hands. What have we not done in order to
> rob art of that which refreshes it! Art has become superfi-
> cial in many respects, a shimmer of vanity. We all feel
> that we live in a period of transition, in a fluctuation be-
> tween what is in command here and now and what
> should be in command. The noble, the exalted in art
> will win the battle, even if there must still be a few vic-
> tims in the struggle for truth. That is understood and
> does not require further comment. Paul stands as a re-

minder of the more elevated.—But that which is created for the present should not be too alien to it. Therefore the form of the oratorio *St Paul* has one foot in the old and the other in the new period that is here; but the eyes look towards that which is past so that it can become new. And it is this position in its era that makes a clear criticism of this oratorio not insignificantly more difficult. It is new and it is old, and must be both, for the sake of the era and for its own sake. Both are evident at the same time, for every worthy work of the era makes apparent, in its creator's own particular way, an idealized image of the era for the benefit of the next generation and, at the same time, has to satisfy the requirements necessary to give pleasure to the present. All this is to be noted, but it can hardly be noted by mere differences of feeling, which always consider themselves and their ways of feeling to be the only true ones, they therefore also produce ideas, which owe their existence not to insight into the reality of the object but to the tendency and mood of their individual sentiment. Up to now I have encountered only one remark about this extremely admirable oratorio, which for the sake of the work and with respect to the matter of oratorio itself I may not pass over.

Someone has called it a Protestant one, indeed, the first that can be deemed to be Protestant, and has given the expression a significance that, in itself, is as empty as any that can be found in the new world of passionate partisan Christianity. It has been explained as synonymous with "unenthusiastic" [*"unbegeistert"*] and yet the reason that it pleases has been sought therein!—We can only be astonished by the sort of oddity in which people take pleasure for the sake of a whim, and we have to lament that people dissipate their powers in developing striking but actually pointless ideas when, if these powers were directed towards truth, they would produce benefits with less effort. A Protestant oratorio!—Is that an expres-

sion that can be used of oratorio? That seems like an
idea, but it is a vain illusion. An oratorio is not liturgical, it is part neither of the Catholic nor the Protestant
ritual.

After further examination of these issues, Fink observed: "I can only
find one circumstance, which, however, the anonymous man in his extraordinary remarks did not even mention, which could perhaps have
given him that idea. . . . It was probably the interwoven Protestant chorales, which are admittedly rather novel in the oratorio genre, about which
we shall say more below." After explaining that this did not make the
oratorio Protestant, he continued: "What sort of oratorio is it then? It is
a concert oratorio in mixed form, not merely as the result of a whim,
even less by coincidence, but as he planned it after consideration, and
out of love for the old models." Fink then proceeded to a detailed examination of the overture, focusing in particular on the use of the chorale,
and indicating that its use here is not merely arbitrary but, as the whole
oratorio demonstrates, "has a much more laudable basis in the composer's
soul, which can even communicate itself to the listener." He then concluded the first part of his article by outlining his intentions for its sequel,
explaining that he did not believe "further lengthy analysis of the individual numbers is necessary," and that he would rather focus upon the
chief features of the work, which would provide "a more thoughtful dis-
course for those who understand art and be more stimulating to the
benefit of art itself."

In the second part of his article, Fink discussed the text and its structure in great detail (cols. 513–19), concluding that "the plan of the whole
is too extensive . . . there are, fundamentally, two oratorios; the first Stephen, the other Paul. And yet because of that the second oratorio, Paul,
is too constricted." He then turned his attention to the use of chorales,
remarking that "the chorale is evidently suited to the ecclesiastical liturgy,
and can only be used occasionally and exceptionally in the genre of oratorio, when it is not integral to the story itself but functions rather like
the chorus in Greek tragedy." He rightly observed that Mendelssohn's use
of the chorale derived from "the composer's love of the unsurpassable
Sebastian [Bach], whose masterpiece, the *St Matthew*, hovers before him
and which he strives to emulate, his desire to demonstrate his reverence

giving him enthusiasm and courage; and this love not only deserves every recognition and respect but has also been requited by the splendid effect of the chorales that are woven in, out of love for Bach's *Passion*. In other respects, too, this exalted *Passion* of the great old master has acted as a pattern and model for him, and indeed not less, but rather more even than Handel, the hero of oratorio, whose example cannot be avoided as long as oratorio, whose leading spirit he will remain, exists." In an extensive discussion of the work's orchestration (cols. 520–22), Fink alluded to the changes that had occurred since the time of Bach and Handel, and the advantages gained: "These advantages are made the most of in *St Paul*, with a brilliance that contributes greatly to its successful effect." But in the use of the orchestra too he identified the direct influence of the old masters, detecting Handel's "treatment and instrumentation," though with "richly augmented wind instruments," in the first chorus of Christians (no. 2), and observing that "Bach's economy of instrumentation is basic throughout the whole work." With respect to the form and character of the individual numbers (cols. 522–27), he again alluded to the inspiration behind the oratorio: "The composer has expressed his reverence for the two father figures of German sacred music so strongly that he wishes it to be acknowledged, not denied, in his work. The work is so deliberately a Handel-Bach-Mendelssohnian one, that it actually seems as if it were really there in order to make it easier for our contemporaries to be receptive to the depths of the aforementioned musical heroes and to give them an inclination for them."

In the final paragraph of the article, Fink criticized the oratorio for the lack of unity caused by its fluctuation between dramatic and non-dramatic treatment, but he continued:

> And yet it is a truly distinguished, estimable work, not only in very many really excellent movements (which have been cited) but also through its undeniable inclination towards the two aforementioned models, which, because of their excellence, the composer, in his devotion, wants to revive in the present day, which will bring him the thanks and acknowledgment of all friends of serious music, even though some among them might wish it to be a less mixed, more Mendelssohnian work. But then,

too, it would not be such an evident testimony to the great attachment to those heroes of pious music, to the high estimation of which, in a time in which our art is lacerated from without, the composer would like to lead us back, and to help us to turn to that which is more profound, for which we all long, namely, to the victory of the genuine and sincere over frivolity and merely sensual triviality, by which Germany too allows itself to be afflicted, against its better nature, which sustains the victory, like everything that is good, which has previously been, to some extent, crucified or stoned.[68]

While Fink, despite his equivocal feelings about the oratorio's reliance on its eighteenth-century models, couched his review in an appreciative, even enthusiastic tone, a review written at almost the same time in England judged Mendelssohn's homage to Bach and Handel much more harshly. This review, in the *Spectator*, of the Birmingham performance of *St Paul*, which Mendelssohn conducted in October 1837, provides an exceptional example of a strongly adverse critical reaction to the oratorio at that time. The other London papers were, as the reviewer confessed, "full of praises, and not measured [ones]." The tone of the review may, however, largely be explained by the stance of its author, Edward Taylor, who was the translator and enthusiastic promoter of Spohr's oratorios in England. Taylor undoubtedly resented the exclusion of Spohr's works from the Birmingham Festival and saw Mendelssohn's ascendancy in general as a threat to Spohr's pre-eminence. Furthermore, there was a distinctly cool personal relationship between Mendelssohn and Taylor, as indicated by Mendelssohn's description of him, after a meeting prior to the festival in 1837, as "altogether a loathsome, underhand, servile Jesuit."[69] Taylor was undoubtedly at the bottom of what Mendelssohn referred to in a letter to Moscheles in 1841 as the "comparisons between Spohr and myself, or the petty cock-fights in which, for some inconceivable reason and much to my regret, we have been pitted against each other in England."[70] At an early point in his review of the festival as a whole Taylor observed: "The first and most striking feature of the Birmingham Festival is the—not second, but third and fourth rate character of the materials which principally compose it, and the absence of any work, the *Messiah* alone excepted, of known and acknowledged eminence." He later turned to *St Paul*, commenting:

> The principle with which Mendelssohn starts is, that he
> who would write an oratorio must transport himself in
> imagination to the time of Bach and Handel—must
> speak their musical language—must copy their style—
> must discard as heterodox and inadmissible all that sub-
> sequent composers have done to enlarge the sphere of
> musical action and capability. It is upon this principle
> that we join issue with him, and contend that the effort
> were a vain one if not impossible, and if possible, not
> expedient. Our opinion is confirmed by the practice of
> all the great modern masters,—Haydn, Beethoven,
> Spohr, (Mozart wrote no oratorio,) each of whom,
> though thoroughly conversant with the writings of his il-
> lustrious predecessors, spoke in his own musical lan-
> guage. It is easier to talk of writing in the style of the
> old masters than to practise it. Among moderns, mod-
> ernisms will be constantly peeping out; and the attempt
> thus to write, will of necessity impose on the copyist re-
> straints and shackles which his original, writing without
> them, never felt. No great writer ever implicitly copied
> any other however great.

Then, having produced examples of the independent paths pursued by Purcell and Burns, Taylor continued:

> In *St Paul* Mendelssohn has evidently endeavoured to
> place himself in the *same* phasis with some of his prede-
> cessors—to see as they saw, and no further—to hear as
> they heard, and no otherwise: and hence, of necessity,
> the want of "originality of thought" in what he has pro-
> duced. After hearing some of the compositions of the old
> masters,—such a chorus as "See the proud chief," for ex-
> ample,—we are apt to impute its merit rather to the ac-
> cidental form in which its author saw fit to clothe his

thoughts, than to the genius which inspired them—to admire the chariot rather than the mind which impels and guides it. Now there is no abstract merit in any style or form of writing—no inherent excellence in vocal fugue or canon. Like all the powers of art, musical or other, their sole use and value (except as mere exercises) consists in their peculiar applicability to the purpose for which they are used: and Handel sometimes blundered as egregiously in the employment of these means as he was surpassingly successful in others. Every resource which the improved state of musical performance offers to the musician, he should gladly adopt, if he means to interest the feelings as well as to satisfy the critical expectations of his auditors. Language, whether it find expression in poetry or in music, must gush freely from the heart, if it be intended to find its way thither; and not proceed by a constant recurrence to authorities and passages of a certain and remote age.

Like Fink, though for different reasons, Taylor suggested that Mendelssohn's oratorio might prompt the revival of Handel's and Bach's works, for he remarked: "If we stick to Handel and Bach, resolved to advance no further,—if we are to discard Haydn, Beethoven and Spohr, (to which the admission of this principle will compel us)—let us rub the dust off our Handel's scores, and let us also hear (which we never have yet heard) some of Sebastian Bach's church-music." He concluded:

Our objections to *St. Paul*, it will be seen, regard the principle on which its accomplished author has chosen to construct it. We should differ from an authority so high with hesitation, had we not still higher authority on our side; and we venture to urge those considerations upon him, in the hope that, by inspiring him with more self-reliance, he will in future works of the same kind write down his own thoughts and clothe them with his own language, instead of hunting for precedents and phrases of other authorities and past times. Thoroughly master as

he is of all that musical science can impart—endowed
with a genius in which brilliant and beautiful thoughts
are contending for utterance—it is in his power to give
us in his next oratorio a composition "after the manner
of Mendelssohn."[71]

More typical of English opinion were the many laudatory descriptions
of the oratorio, which contained little in the way of systematic appraisal,
to which Taylor alluded. A reference in the *Musical World*, in a short
biographical article on Mendelssohn in 1837, reflects the tone of many.
The author remarked simply that *St Paul* was "a work that will gain
ground with the increase of musical knowledge, for its epic sublimity,
and perfect CONSISTENCY of construction. The strongest test of the high
classical character of this work, is, that we have never yet heard a *musician*
speak of it, but he has coupled his opinion with the observation, that 'it
grows upon him.' One of the soundest theorists of our country expressed
himself in the first instance somewhat coldly respecting this great work;
he now constantly recurs to it, and after the inefficient performance at
Exeter Hall, he could not sleep the whole night."[72] And after a performance at Exeter Hall Henry Chorley, not yet a personal friend of Mendelssohn, wrote in the *Athenaeum*:

> [Mendelssohn] was in the gallery; *he* must, we think,
> have been as much gratified by the enthusiasm with
> which his whole work was received, as we were by the
> spontaneous out-break at the end of the first act, when
> his presence was acknowledged with a storm of applause.
> For his Oratorio, it would be difficult for us to say too
> much in its praise—simple, massive—every note of it
> full of expression: written in the spirit of the great an-
> cients, but not according to their letter. We should be
> disposed, unhesitatingly, to rank it next to the immortal
> works of Handel, being persuaded that every subsequent
> hearing must bring its truth increasingly home to every
> listener. It includes no difficulties crowded together for
> the production of great effects, (the resource of second-
> best genius); the airs are as easy, as they must be delight-

ful to sing; and the orchestra, though, when it is required, as rich and figurative as a master's hand, guided
by a master's mind, can make it—is kept in its proper
place—that is, working together with the vocal parts,
neither predominating over them, nor lagging behind.
For these general characteristics, we could easily add an
extended analysis of a work, whose effectiveness, as well
as its excellence, was proved by the number of *encores* it
commanded; but we are so cramped in space, by science,[73] as not to have room to ride our hobby as far as
we could wish: and perhaps our sober and unmusical
readers will not regret this.[74]

The success of *St Paul* was as decisive in establishing Mendelssohn's
reputation in England, beyond a narrow circle of metropolitan musicians
and amateurs centred upon the Philharmonic Society, as it was in spread-
ing his fame in Germany. According to Henry Hugh Pearson, writing in
German in the *Wiener allgemeine Musik-Zeitung* in 1843, "Before the performance of his *St Paul* Mendelssohn was relatively little known in England,—but as a result of this his name spread with tremendous rapidity."[75]

In Germany, after the oratorio's publication, Fink's lengthy review was
followed by others. *Caecilia*, like the *Allgemeine musikalische Zeitung*, acknowledged the work's major importance by devoting fifteen pages to the
subject. Here, too, weaknesses in the dramatic structure were identified,
but, like Fink, the author stressed that the extraordinary qualities of the
music far outweighed any such criticism. He began:

On the appearance of a significant work it is the obligation of the friends of art to indicate its good qualities in
order to make it known in ever wider circles. If, however, the victory of such a production has already been
decided and everything has been done to praise it—and
this has certainly been the case with the work in question since its first performance at the Lower Rhine Festival in Düsseldorf at Whitsuntide 1836, to which others in
Leipzig, Frankfurt, Elberfeld and Düsseldorf were later

added—then all that is left to the critic is the task, admittedly always more attractive, of explaining more precisely its character as a whole and in particulars, as well as its relationship to the other works of the master as well as to others of a similar kind. Only on this path will the standpoint of the new with respect to that which came earlier, as well as the whole development of art in the course of time, become clearly and instructively evident.

After outlining the story, he continued:

The treatment of this straightforward content is entirely clear and only departs from the biblical text in the periodically introduced chorales, which represent the voice of the congregation. The story is told and advanced by the recitatives, and the lyrical element motivates the choruses. It is never, as is only reasonable, a matter of dramatic build-up or even of plot. The power of Christian conviction is all the more decisively conveyed by the choruses of the faithful, just as hate and rage are by those of the Jews, and blind zeal by those of the heathen. Here we encounter characterfulness and peculiar freshness, even if, at the same time, the recurrence of similar situations in the first and second parts leads to a certain uniformity, which cannot wholly be counteracted, even by the powerfulness of Paul's recitative and aria. This uniformity derives from the plan of the oratorio. If, perhaps by means of a slight deviation from the basic text of the gospel, the second part had contained a new character or a motif that had not yet appeared, the composer would certainly not have had his task made easier, but the success would have been significantly increased. Yet even the scorn for such artistic expedients, the most intimate penetration of the fundamental feeling of the whole, the most firm connection of every particular with the main intention, mark out this *St Paul*, and one would not be far wrong if one recognized in it the same elements as in the great works of J. S. Bach, of which one is also reminded throughout by the character of the choruses and recitatives, as well as the entry of the chorales.

Far from wishing to reproach the composer with this dependency,—(it goes without saying that this may be decisively refuted)—we shall now give an account of the principal moments of the work, which in any case possesses a very decided individuality.

After an extensive number-by-number discussion (pp. 204–15), the author concluded his article with a summary in which he again examined the significance of the work's relationship to the models that had inspired and influenced it, drawing attention to the similarity of Mendelssohn's outlook to that of contemporary visual artists and architects, and concluding that such inspiration did not necessarily detract from the artist's originality.

If we look back from here at the whole of this oratorio, its connection with the masterpieces of Handel and J. S. Bach immediately strike one. Content, treatment, even the rhythmical and harmonic traits have derived from these models.

Effects of a modern kind have been deliberately neglected, and only antique, powerful rhythms and harmonies have, with good reason, been used for the ultimately powerful words of the Bible. Just as people have recently become concerned to recall a pious past in churches and pictures, to conjure up for us, as it were, the spirit of better days, so the musician has the indisputable right to take possession of the past style that most accurately reflects his basic feelings and thought. His individuality will always remain the same, indeed, as long as he is someone who strives he will, in taking on foreign forms, soon bring forth something independent and new. Thus, in *St Paul*, the recitative is handled energetically throughout, having no trace of the old-fashioned figures from Handel arias,[76] while the instrumentation throughout, as appropriate in modern high art, is rich and really gripping.

Thus we most clearly express our opinion of the character of Mendelssohn's *St Paul*. After the most varied essays in almost all branches of his art, of which none remained unsuccessful and uncelebrated, a highly gifted master who already, in early youth, was full of reverence for the great models of the past, takes an apparently backwards step to an earlier manifestation, because he recognized that it was the highest aim of his artistic mission to give back vitality to these supposedly outmoded forms. He armed himself for the task with all the love and spiritual force that the finest talents afforded him, and in his fresh youth he achieved what had long been the silent desire of others. For even if this work might still leave something to be desired, there can be no doubt, that we can call it a success. This is precisely why it may be seen as an important step for the future of the master, who has already given evidence in so many instrumental works how he had more than followed the freest developments of modern practice. Who can fear anything old-fashioned from the composer of the Overture to *A Midsummer Night's Dream*, to name but one of these works?

But who, too, would dare to predict in advance the future path of such a brilliant rising star?[77]

Among the most revealing German endorsements of *St Paul* was Schumann's, in the *Neue Zeitschrift für Musik*, for it indicates not only how close, in many respects, the aesthetic aims of the two composers were but also the extent to which Schumann acknowledged Mendelssohn's leading role in the struggle for victory over the artistic philistines. He was no blind admirer of Mendelssohn's works—indeed, few of his reviews are free of an element of gentle criticism, and in this case he drew attention to many of the problematic aspects that had been discussed elsewhere. But the extent to which Schumann regarded Mendelssohn as a brother-in-arms, in the struggle that he had espoused both as composer and writer, is unmistakable, and he undoubtedly saw *St Paul* as a powerful, if not flawless, manifestation of the best in contemporary art. In this instance, the exposition of his views was made all the more forceful by the starkness of the contrast that he drew between *St Paul* and Meyerbeer's contemporaneous opera *Les Huguenots*, which was then making its triumphant progress across the European stage.

The tone of Schumann's review of *Les Huguenots* is indicated by statements like " 'To startle or to tickle,' is Meyerbeer's maxim, and he succeeds in it with the rabble," and "Some *esprit* he possesses, we cannot deny; but time will not allow us to go through every detail of Meyerbeer's outward tendency; his extreme non-originality and want of style are as well known as his talent in dramatic treatment, preparation, polish, brilliancy, instrumental cleverness, as well as his very considerable variety in forms." Finally, after acknowledging the effectiveness of some features of the opera, he concluded: "—but what is all this compared to the commonness, distortion, unnaturalness, immorality, unmusical character of the whole? Thank heaven, we are at the goal, for nothing worse is to come after this, unless we transform the stage into a scaffold; and in such a case, the last agonised cry of a talent tortured by the spirit of our day will be followed by the immediate hope that matters *must* now take a turn for the better." Schumann continued:

> And now we turn to a nobler subject. Here we are
> again attuned to hope and faith; here we learn to love
> mankind once more; here we rest, after a weary search,
> under the palm-trees, while a flowery landscape lies at
> our feet. "Paulus" is a work of pure art, the creation of
> peace and love. We should injure ourselves and grieve
> the poet if we sought to compare it, even distantly with
> a Bach or Handel work. In certain traits, all church-
> music, all temples of religion, all painted Madonnas, re-
> semble each other, as do the works of the masters in
> question; but Bach and Handel were men when they
> wrote their oratorios, while Mendelssohn was yet little
> more than a youth. So "St. Paul" is the work of a young
> master, with whose senses the Graces sport, who is yet

inspired with delight in life and the future; and it ought not to be compared to those of a more severe day; by any one of those divine masters, whose long and almost holy life lay in a great measure behind him, while his glance already reached beyond the clouds.

We have spoken before, in our paper, of the manner of treatment, the resumption of the chorale, as we find it in old oratorios, the division of choruses and solos into active and passive masses and persons, the character of these, &c. It has already been correctly observed, that the principal events lie, to the injury of the general effect, in the first part; that the character of St. Stephen, if not of more consequence than St. Paul, at any rate lessens our interest in the latter; that, in the music, Saul is more effective as a convert than as a converter; and that the oratorio is very long, and might easily have been divided into two. Mendelssohn's conception of the appearance of the Lord invites artistic discussion;[78] but I think that a subject is sometimes spoiled by harping on it; and one could not offend the composer more than here, in one of his finest inventions. I believe that the Lord God speaks in many tongues, and that He unveils His will to His chosen ones by angel choruses. I think that a painter can express the near presence of the Highest more poetically by means of cherub heads looking out from the edge of the picture, than by the form of an old man, the symbol of the Trinity, and so on. I know not that beauty could offend where truth cannot be attained. It has also been remarked, that the simplicity of certain chorales in *St Paul* has been sacrificed to the rare decorations with which Mendelssohn has surrounded them. As if choral music were not as good a symbol of joyful trust in God as of supplicating prayer; as if there were no possible difference between "Sleepers, wake!" and "Out of the depths"; as if a work of art were not intended to satisfy other demands than those of a singing congregation! And, finally, they have tried to classify *St Paul*, not as a

Protestant, but as a concert-oratorio, though one clever person has struck on the middle path, and baptized it a "Protestant concert-oratorio." We see objections made,—and the zeal of true criticism must be acknowledged. But at the same time, we must acknowledge those qualities which no criticism can take away from the oratorio,—its masterly musical perfection, its noble melodies, the union of word and tone, of speech and music, that cause us to gaze into the whole as into a living depth,—the charming grouping of personages, the grace that seems to have been breathed over the work, the freshness, the inextinguishable colour of instrumentation, the perfectly formed style, its masterly sporting with every form of composition, besides its inward heart, the deeply religious feeling which is expressed throughout it,—and we ought to be satisfied, I think. One observation I will venture on, however. The music of *St Paul* is sustained in so clear and popular a tone, impresses so instantaneously yet lastingly, that it seems as if the composer had intended, while writing, to be effective among the people. Fine as this aim may be, it will certainly deprive future compositions of something of that power and inspiration which we find in the works of those who yield themselves, regardless of consequences, without aim or limit, to their grand subjects. Let us reflect that Beethoven wrote a "Christ on the Mount of Olives," and also a "Missa solemnis"; and let us believe that, as the youth Mendelssohn has written one oratorio, the man will perfect another. Until then, we will be satisfied with, and learn from, and enjoy this.

And now to arrive at a conclusive judgment on the works of two men who, in those works, most sharply point the tendency and confusion of our day. The noise made about Meyerbeer seems to me contemptible in its cause; for in his "Huguenots" we simply find the collective type of all the errors, and some few of the excellencies, of the time. But the Mendelssohnian *St Paul* ought to be honoured and loved, for it is the prophet of a finer future, in which his works, and not the narrow applause of his contemporaries, will ennoble the artist. This road leads to good, the other is the path to evil.[79]

Interest in *St Paul* remained intense during the next few years, and the oratorio continued to attract significant attention in the press. Fétis, in his article on Mendelssohn in volume 6 of the *Biographie universelle*, published in 1838, remarked: "Mr Mendelssohn shows productivity and, at the same time, care in the construction of his works. *St Paul* appears to me to be the one that shows most hope for the future. In it are combined the classical qualities of many masters of the German school with a degree of audacity that augurs well."[80] The following year a performance of *St Paul* by the Dresden Hofkapelle in Weimar called forth a long article, very different from the usual critical notices, entitled "Fleeting Remarks of an Unmusical Music Lover," by Jeanette von Haza (under the pseudonym Heinrich Paris). This gets closer, perhaps, than any other extended German account to conveying the feelings of a cultivated but non-specialist listener. She began: "I do not provide you with a report on the success or failure of the performance, because this can only be done by a musician. . . . Even less do I give you a criticism of the work itself; for without doubt it has already been sufficiently dissected and criticized by well-known and unknown critics. . . . Nevertheless, I, ignorant, write to you about it, and even in a manner that may sometimes seem critical; in this work, therefore, there must be an invisible animating power, which jolts a person of feeling out of his accustomed passivity, but there is also, however, something else, which disturbs the harmony of this uplifting impression to some extent, and involuntarily stimulates one to attempt to make clear to oneself, by means of a more precise analysis of the work of art, the roots of this phenomenon."

Haza recounted her own and others' entirely subjective feelings:

In order to sum up the total impression of the music in short, I can say nothing but: "I am enraptured!" ["ich bin entzückt!"] just as was exclaimed to me on the evening of the performance by a gifted foreign composer who was there (who, like all truly gifted people delighted in the gifted works of others). In order to express my own feeling I need only repeat him word for word when he said: "How it is worked out! Here at last is another work that will endure! It will not be easy for anyone to make another like it!" and when the next day, instead of any other greeting, he merely repeated: "What a piece of work this *St Paul* is! How could such a young man create this!" and on the third day: "I am still with *St Paul* the whole time; I cannot get the duet of the apostle and 'Steinigt ihn' out of my mind!"

I know no better judgment on the latter delicious chorus than the apt words of the most musical lady I know: "I see the stones fly and strike one another!"; and overall the basic character of the whole is probably not better expressed than in the correct remark of the same lady: "In the whole oratorio there is not a single profane note!"

Not a single profane note! In this, in fact, the true worth of the excellent work appears to me to be most strikingly expressed; for while even in the case of the greatest masters, even in Haydn's or Beethoven's sacred music, there are places that are only too worldly, in *St Paul* the integrity of the religious character is not disturbed even once. The whole is in one mould; I would like to say in a single pious mould, if in our time the word pious were not so widely impiously misused that a good Christian can scarcely bear to utter it.

After further comments on the nature of piety in music, she continued:

If, as it is thought, Mozart really said, "as he wrote his Requiem, he felt he was Catholic," I could similarly declare about *St Paul*: that was evidently created by a Protestant! Or if I were French: *voilà bien de la bonne et belle musique puritaine!* So completely unmistakably does one feel the serious,—strict northern type, which does not penetrate the soul so much by imagination and sense as by spirit and intellect, yet nevertheless in the end touches the soul just as well as the moving southern church style of the Sistine Chapel. One sees that the work is born out of the conscientious, respectable, but at the same time somewhat stiff and fusty faith of Bach and Handel; only for that reason is it also thoroughly dignified, noble, sublimely restrained; it does not violate pure ecclesiastical principle at all; it is at once sacred and spiritual, truly Christian music;—"there is no profane note in it!" Therefore it must and certainly will always and everywhere make an effect on all pious souls of all faiths.

The only thing that I would perhaps, individually, object to in the music is: here and there rather too powerful orchestration. But that is unfortunately nowadays the taste of the age. Therefore one must at least always be thankful if, as here, the instruments do not simply drown the voices. On the other side, however, this very orchestration is so highly characteristically blended with the vocal parts that, at the same time, one cannot sufficiently admire the tremendous work that makes such a rounded whole out of such multifarious elements.

In what a dignified and grand manner the whole is introduced immediately by the overture and the first chorus, and how beautifully the chorale, so familiar to all the faithful, "Allein Gott in der Höh' sei Ehr," concludes this introduction, expressing, as it were, the quintessence of the text of the whole work! Also, the Old Testament–like accompaniment of wind instruments to the later chorale in the second half, which calls to mind the service of the Jewish temple, makes a splendid effect.

In general the choruses seem to me pre-eminently to be laid out in a masterly manner appropriate to each situation, especially where they convey the passion of the enraged people against the martyr Stephen and later the preacher Paul. "Steinigt ihn!" and "Hier ist des Herrn Tempel" may well remain classic for all time; quite splendidly worked out, too, is the exchange between the false witnesses against Stephen and, in the second part, the people's question: "Ist das nicht der zu Jerusalem ver- störte?" Imposing and devout at the same time are the concluding choruses of each part of the oratorio, truly heart-lifting in the meanwhile is the chorus of triumph and jubilation, announcing salvation: "Der Herr wird die Thränen von allen Angesichtern abwischen." Then the movement, truly resplendent in its ample richness of sound: "O welche eine Tiefe des Reichtums" in which, in addition, the composer succeeds in the wonderful task of making the most beautiful music one could hear to the most unmusical words one could imagine; further- more, the excellent introduction to the second part: "Der Erdkreis ist nun des Herrn."

If everything of a triumphant and imposing character that the artfully interwoven tone masses can portray is offered here, so the most amiable, almost idyllic joyful- ness and delightfulness contrast with it: "Wie lieblich sind die Boten, die den Frieden verkündigen," and yet at the same time also the most moving anguish, the deepest tenderness in the prayer of the faithful to the pursued apostle: "Schone doch deiner selbst," in which the female voices in particular are of the most completely pleasing effect.

However, I must call the chorus of heathen: "Seid uns gnädig, hohe Götter" a true masterstroke. This is one of those happy inspirations that are given only to genius. Just as the heathens think that, in Paul and Barnabas, they recognize and worship their Jupiter and Mercury, the whole style of the music changes in melody and ac- companiment. We no longer hear the simple and serious gospel of the invisible and sole God, who wants only to be worshipped in spirit and truth; rather, the composer transports us, at a stroke, from the Bible straight into the sensual, cheerful temple service of polytheism, amid joy- ful hymns, flattering flutes and sacred dances. I cannot describe what a highly poetic impression this really happy inspired conception of that moment made on me. Such things always give the listener straightaway the comfortable feeling that he is dealing with a true artist, with a thinking and cultivated composer, who does not merely make music instinctively but has learned other things apart from his music, and is capable of comprehending other things.

Of the solo pieces the duet of Paul and Barnabas is probably indisputably the most outstanding; in the performance here this was also benefited by two quite excellent, beautiful and appreciated voices. The tenor solo, very well performed here, as well as the soprano aria "Jerusalem! Jerusalem!" is also extremely beautiful. . . .

If I now mention Paul's grand aria with the splendid text "Und tilge meine Sünden" as particularly appealing to me, I must nevertheless add, for truth's sake, that in the first "Vertilge sie, Herr Zabaoth!" which Saul sings while he is still bent on persecution, one might wish that the passion of the fanatic might have been somewhat more energetically expressed, although in itself the music here is also beautiful and characteristic.

But I now ask myself: how is it, although I acknowledge so greatly the excellence of the whole work, although the individual parts delighted me so much, that I cannot conceal that, at the same time, it fatigued me, that at the end I did not carry home the total consciousness of my enjoyment as much as, for example, after Handel's *Messiah* or Bach's *Passion*?

And I cannot answer this except by saying: the composer had chosen a text that was not wholly grateful; or rather he had not compiled the text in a really grateful manner. For in itself a subject such as Saul's conversion is certainly a well-chosen one, for it offers such multifarious vacillations of feeling for musical characterization; but there is a certain lack of clarity in the manner in which this material is handled, and this is known to be a stumbling block for every artwork of every type.

I shall try to expand somewhat on this drawback.

Every work of art in which the traditional genres are too mixed always remains more or less incomprehensible to the appreciator; and thus his pleasure will be more or less marred.

We are now on the whole rather accustomed to see our oratorios handled by librettist and composer to some extent as a sacred play, or at least to see the dramatic principle predominating in them.

In *St Paul*, however, not only narrative and active depiction, epic and drama, but also lyrical outflow of feeling fluctuate in such rapid and frequent succession that the listener has difficulty in following the thread and without the libretto would be hard pressed to grasp the coherence; this, then, is what tires him. Thus, for example, I cannot come to terms with the means, however beautiful these individual passages are, by which the composer (and certainly not as a continuous norm but only arbitrarily from time to time) in the middle of the narrative, after an "and he said" or something of the sort, has the words that were spoken sung by a chorus or a second voice; for then the listener is led astray, since he inevitably expects the same individual to be sung by the same voice and as a result he does not properly grasp why, for example, the Godhead, speaking, can suddenly sing with the same voice that he previously used as the medium of human speech.

In accordance with nature, in my view, something that happens should merely be explained or merely be depicted; therefore, I feel that the whole narrative should either always be sung here by the same voice as recitative, or always performed as a dramatic scene.

What chiefly disturbs the beautiful impression of the whole, for the uninitiated such as I who do not have sufficient technical knowledge of composition to appreciate the qualities of such a work as a connoisseur, is the endless quantity of recitatives, which this predominance of the narrative form makes necessary, and which, however beautiful and artistic they may be individually, eventually make the work monotonous and too long for the un-trained ear.

Even the most devout heart cannot be uninterruptedly devout for three hours; and twenty-five recitatives, among which some are of considerable length, is cer-tainly too much of a good thing, for the laity at least.[82]

Having continued her discussion of the recitatives and of the text in general at some length, she concluded her article with the observation: "Those who know about such matters may judge whether these personal objections of mine are right or not; but in any case, even if I were right, the matters concerned are only to be seen as, at most, like spots on the sun. As far as the principal matter is concerned all the initiated and uninitiated are certainly at one in the judgment that, as I already said above, *St Paul* is a work that will last."[83]

This was broadly endorsed, with varying shades of emphasis, by nu-merous other contemporary writers. Schumann reported that after the first Viennese performance in 1839 the veteran Adalbert Gyrowetz de-clared that "according to his judgment this was the greatest work of modern times," and that Ignaz von Seyfried said, "I did not hope to experience such an event in my latter days."[84] No other work by Men-delssohn called forth so many words in his lifetime. Among the most significant later appraisals was Otto Jahn's pamphlet, which gave *St Paul* a very exalted status among contemporary oratorios. An unnamed reviewer of the pamphlet summed up Jahn's standpoint in his first two sentences: "The author speaks about Mendelssohn's oratorio with un-common understanding of art. It appears to him as a truly Protestant piece of church music, and he seeks to explain the impression that *St Paul* has made everywhere by the fact that it is thoroughly dignified, simple and noble in all its elements, in which we fully agree with him."[85] And the author of a long article, which appeared in instalments in seven successive issues in the *Wiener allgemeine Musik-Zeitung* in 1846, began with the unequivocal statement that he considered Men-delssohn's *St Paul* "the sole genuine and true oratorio that has appeared in modern times, that is to say since Bach's time."[86] The oratorio was not, however, without its trenchant critics in Germany during the mid 1840s. But this was part of a broader critical reaction to Mendelssohn's sacred music that began to make itself increasingly felt during Mendelssohn's last years.

45 · The Years of Mastery, 1836–1847

In the years immediately following the production of *St Paul*, Mendelssohn consolidated the position its success had gained for him. Not every new work was received with acclaim, enthusiasm or even, in some cases, appreciation; but, especially in the early 1840s, the general tone in reviews of individual works and in appraisals of Mendelssohn's stature was, with a few notable exceptions, positive, and sometimes eulogistic. The statement or implication that he was the greatest composer of the age was frequent at that time. Among a significant proportion of the European and North American musical public his reputation undoubtedly rose to a very high level during this period; published reviews and assessments often reflect this, yet an estimation of his position based solely on printed sources, which were inevitably seen as providing an opportunity for critical appraisal, would almost certainly misrepresent the level of enthusiasm generated by his music. Of course, attitudes varied widely on a geographical basis. Mendelssohn's reputation was perhaps highest in the English-speaking world, where commentators seemed less inhibited about expressing fulsome admiration, or simply echoing the reactions of the audience, and many writers did not hesitate to name him as a worthy successor to Haydn, Mozart and Beethoven in the canon of great composers.

In Germany, and the Teutonic world in general (which included parts of Eastern Europe and North America), the level of admiration was also high, and by the 1840s he was, in the eyes of many, the undisputed leader among German composers; yet there seems to have been a more significant undercurrent of criticism than in England, perhaps because of the greater tendency of German reviewers to favor quasi-philosophical and ideological dissection and scrutiny. From the mid-1830s writers had begun to speculate whether Mendelssohn would really be able to realize the promise of his remarkable early achievements, and towards the end of his life a number of critics, especially in North Germany where the nationalistic agenda of the "young Germans" was most aggressively advanced, were questioning the enduring value of substantial portions of his output, especially in the context of a self-consciously German agenda, and openly challenging those who wished to rank him with the greatest composers. In Austria and its empire it had taken some time for his music to enter the repertoire, but by the mid-1840s he was acknowledged there too as a major composer. It took longer for his works to make their mark in Russia, though *St Paul* was heard in St Petersburg and Moscow in 1838, and a number of performances of his music, including *Elijah*, took place in St Petersburg in 1848. On the other hand, in the Romance countries, France, Italy and the Iberian Peninsula, very little attention was paid to Mendelssohn's music during his lifetime and in the years immediately following his death. In Paris his only major work to be performed publicly with any regularity was the Symphony in A Minor, given annually from 1844 to 1847; but interest was confined to limited circles, and not until several decades after Mendelssohn's death, perhaps influenced by a growing taste for instrumental music, was there a late flowering of enthusiasm for his music in France.

46 · General Appraisals during Mendelssohn's Lifetime

General appraisals of Mendelssohn and his works, which began to appear with increasing regularity in biographical encyclopaedias and journals during the last ten years of his life, articulated a number of issues that were to remain factors in later critical assessments; they also expressed views that are less commonly associated with his posthumous reputation. Many of these contemporary biographical and critical appraisals drew upon common sources for their material.

Among the most widely circulated specifically musical accounts of Mendelssohn's career published in German during the second half of the 1830s were those in Rudolf Hirsch's *Gallerie lebender Tondichter* (1836) and in Schilling's *Encyclopädie der gesammten musikalischen Wissenschaften* (1837), both of which relied heavily on a common source that has not, so far, been identified.[87] The *Encyclopädie* article, although it takes Mendelssohn's career up to the winter of 1837, was possibly written somewhat earlier and only partially updated before publication; it refers to Mendelssohn as "now only 28 years old" but makes no mention of *St Paul* and does not name any work later than the overture *Die Hebriden*, op. 26 (published in 1833). This anonymous article begins with the statement: "However we view him, and from whatever standpoint, he remains a remarkable phenomenon in the present-day artistic world, and is in any case a very talented, significant musician." In subject matter and phraseology, the biographical section of Schilling's article closely parallels Hirsch's account, but it also includes a significant additional statement. After a comment about Mendelssohn's early precocity having aroused hope of his becoming a second Mozart, which is shared with the other accounts, it continued: "That he has not as yet realized this hope is certainly a consequence partly of Zelter's method of teaching, which held his eminent talent, his genius, with, so to speak, iron tongs, firmly on the practical side of art, yet partly also perhaps of the direction that art in general as well as musical composition in particular appears to have taken, just at that time when his development was in its most powerfully expanding stage. From the exceptionally rapid advances he made, and from the manner in which he made them, one might rightly at that time have inferred such great expectations for the future." In the final section of the article, in which an assessment of his qualities and significance as a composer is attempted, the author elaborated on the view expressed above. After indicating the range and quantity of Mendelssohn's compositions, he began his next section with a sentence common to the other accounts: "Considering his youth, perhaps no currently living composer equals his productivity." He then continued differently, but included a passage (given here in italics) that is taken almost verbatim from August Kahlert's review of Mendelssohn's piano music in *Caecilia* in 1834 (see section 41 above), in which, however, the differences, reflected in this translation, alter the tone of the assessment; the difference in the last sentence is especially noteworthy in its qualification, which is entirely absent from the 1834 review:

> On the other hand, however, from the same point of
> view, an opinion on his achievements can only be prof-

fered with the greatest caution. What he has written will
certainly last, of that we are absolutely certain. But the
artist is now only 28 years old, and at this age perhaps
no-one had wholly realized what was in him. Yet if we
look merely at his latest achievements in the field of
composition, we must take a step back to make our
judgment. In respect of poetic invention they clearly do
not fulfil the expectations that his earlier extraordinary
aptitudes, which were not less than those of the boy Mozart, aroused. We have already referred to that above.
*However, Mendelssohn's place among modern composers is
still with those who stand out no less for their command overall the resources of their art than for their striving for a
higher, universal goal; who have not lost the conviction that
a deeper significance than merely that of sensual charm lies
hidden in music among the numerous lifeless coloraturas,
etc. At least, he is not content with mere form, but strives to
bind this inextricably with the individual content of the
matter. If this is not always achieved with that instinctive
boldness, that freedom of spirit which we marvel at in Beethoven among others, he is nevertheless to be reckoned
among those who have most effectively, and with the most
sincere will, pursued the path opened up by Beethoven. And
there are truly not many of these. Instrumental music easily
leads to that insignificance, which quickly causes the most
well-ordered, most mellifluous musical figures to become outmoded. Even though Mendelssohn may not always resist
such aberrations with consistent success, his music is always
spiritually animated.* He is a complete musical artist,
through nature and education. He has something to say
to both head and heart and is able to express it in a worthy, beautiful manner. He is at his best, certainly, in the
practical and technical. Here he may measure himself
against every master. In his works as a whole careful
workmanship, nicely managed phrasing, voice leading,
imitation of all kinds and everything else one understands by workmanship predominates. Were music a sci-

ence we might perhaps place him at the peak of all phenomena in this field. Yet since it is an art, which springs clear and deep from the heart, created from the most sacred precincts of the soul, we may almost believe that the prevalent cast of mind, which we observe in the composer's individuality as well as in his works, and its predominance is—as we said—perhaps a result of his inflexible schooling, for his genius shows itself, where no exterior influences could yet dominate or rule him, to be unleashed in a higher, more beautiful sphere,—that this prevalent cast of mind may have damaged the pure development of those pristine artistic blossoms and might further damage them in the future. It would be a joy to us, immeasurably valuable, if we were one day constrained to recognize that we had too hastily and erroneously formulated and expressed this view.[88]

Hirsch's account, which largely parallels Schilling's, up to and including the first sentence of the preceding quotation, concluded at that point with a comment upon knowledge of Mendelssohn's music in Vienna at that time:

With us (in Vienna) Mendelssohn's compositions are almost completely unknown. It is quite remarkable: no non-native composers, Herz, Hummel, Kalkbrenner to some extent excepted, have really found acceptance here, in any-meaningful sense of the word. In the case of opera the theatre directors are to blame; for only very rarely does a German opera enter the repertoire. In public concerts we hear nothing but old well-known works; the new ones are mostly Herz and Czerny. This selection is really pitiful, but it remains more or less the same. Of a Parisian Berlioz we know absolutely nothing! Of Mendelssohn not a single piece of music has been publicly performed as far as I know.—At last the piano maestros, who, in planting destroy the plants themselves. Nothing but Herz

and Czerny!—So where should real musical meaning
come from?—I answer my question quite easily.[89]

The author of the biographical sketch in the *Musical World*, who
openly confessed to deriving much of his information directly from
Hirsch, did not qualify his opinion of Mendelssohn's achievements with
any such reservations as those expressed in Schilling's *Encyclopädie*. He
preceded the biographical part of the article with the statement: "Among
the poets of sound, as the Germans in their richly expressive language,
are wont to designate the master-spirits of musical art, the subject of the
present memoir takes an exalted position," and his account continues in
a similarly positive vein. By this date *St Paul* had been performed several
times in England, and the tone of enthusiastic admiration, which coloured
so much later writing about Mendelssohn in England, predominates
throughout. It is evident, too, that some of the information in the article
derived from local knowledge,[90] and a description of Mendelssohn's im-
provising records the author's first-hand experience.[91] The tone of the
article is aptly illustrated by the author's reference to the Overture to *A
Midsummer Night's Dream* as "full of originality, of invention, and indication of the highest genius."[92]

For French readers, a biographical and critical account of Mendelssohn's career up to 1838 was provided by Fétis in his *Biographie universelle
des musiciens*. Much of the information in this account reflects the same
common source used by Schilling, Hirsch and the *Musical World*, but it
was supplemented by material derived from Fétis's own direct encounters
with Mendelssohn. Regarding the 1829 visit to London, for instance, he
remarked: "I found him in this city in April, and at the Philharmonic
Concert I heard a symphony that he performed there. His exterior pleas-
antness, his cultured intellect and his independent position led to his
being received with distinction, and laid the foundations for his success
in the world." Then after mentioning a meeting with him in Aix-la-
Chapelle in 1834, relaying gossip about Mendelssohn's strained relationship with Ferdinand Ries,[93] and providing further biographical details,
Fétis attempted an appraisal of Mendelssohn's artistic importance. Some
of this was more or less paraphrased from earlier German articles, but he
also included his own observations. One comment clearly reflects the

general attitudes of French musicians and foreshadows the view that predominated in France for decades: "There may well already, in 1830, have been tendencies towards originality in his productions, particularly in the Overture to *A Midsummer Night's Dream*, which I heard in Paris; but it was easy to see that it was more the product of research and labour than of inspiration."[94] The contrast between this statement and the *Musical World's* reaction to the same overture could not more forcibly illustrate the difference between English and French responses to Mendelssohn. There were, however, important critics in France during Mendelssohn's lifetime who took a different view. Berlioz, for example, genuinely admired much of Mendelssohn's music, and Henri Blanchard, writing about *St Paul* in the mid-1840s, echoed Schumann's review of the D Minor Piano Trio (see below): "With regard to the music, it demonstrates that Mendelssohn has rightly been designated the modern Mozart. His oratorio *St Paul* is just as inspired and correct a work as the Requiem or *Don Giovanni*."[95] The problem was rather that genuine interest in instrumental music and in Protestant sacred music was narrowly circumscribed in France.

One of the most striking and individual contemporary appraisals of Mendelssohn's position as a composer was published in the *Wiener allgemeine Musik-Zeitung* in 1845; it takes the form of a comparison between Mendelssohn and Berlioz. Although the article was ostensibly about Berlioz, the author, Alfred Julius Becher, who knew and admired both composers,[96] seems to have felt that Berlioz's importance entitled him to be measured against the musician whom he evidently believed to be the leading composer of the day.

> It would be out of place here to provide a closer illustration and appraisal of Mendelssohn's genius; but for the sake of comparison the following observations may be appropriate.—Apart from the expression of smooth, homogeneous sensations, which play no small part with him, Mendelssohn has obviously concerned himself more with perceiving the life of the soul in the reflexes of the external world, and with depicting an organically developed state of mind, than with portraying a fermenting turmoil of different kinds of feelings. Certainly he

seemed at first to want to go down this Beethovenian
path, but he soon abandoned it again; his inborn preference for proportional dimensions and architectonic symmetry in form, nurtured by his uncommonly early occupation with J. S. Bach, together with a preponderating
sense of external (acoustic) beauty, which is related to
Cherubini's, led him to shun a path on which he could
not have helped now and then damaging this [sense of
beauty], albeit with every justification and even to intrinsic poetic advantage. Indeed, for the same reason he
chose almost entirely peaceful, charming material for his
descriptive music, and he depicted for us calm seas and
prosperous voyages rather than storm and shipwreck,
elves rather than gnomes. Purity, tenderness and sincerity
of feeling, nobility and clarity of intention, distinctness
of plan, even amid the most intricate complications,
fresh, spirited but always tightly controlled imagination, a
peacefulness and smoothness in exterior and well as inte-
rior form, deep learning, which is evident everywhere but
never flaunted, palpable piety and a wholly individual,
witty, even teasing but always harmless humour, appear
to me to be the chief characteristics of this most noble,
most chaste, most rounded, most substantial, and most
versatile composer of the present generation, in this context it is important to note that in his work, where the
intention is serious or pleasant, the humour referred to
above is only very rarely interwoven as an ironic element,
but mostly appears as a separate piece or at least as an
independent developed episode. Finally, it may be noted
here that in Mendelssohn's case (similarly in Goethe's)
the effervescent daring that characterizes the works of his
youth has, till now, given way increasingly to a cautious
moderation; for the only work from a later time that appears to contradict this assertion, the *Walpurgisnacht*, was
drafted and even partially elaborated at a very early period of his work. One should not take me to mean by
this, however, that this intellect, which is just as amiable

as it is dignified,[97] has become a lesser one than we might have expected from his first appearance; certainly not,—in many respects rather the opposite; but I believe that every perceptive and attentive critic will concede to me that he is now other than we might have expected from his romantic youthful compositions. Yet have we already reached his final period?—

Becher then turned to Berlioz, whom he described as presenting "an almost complete contrast to this picture." He referred to Berlioz's "audacious, far-reaching imagination," observing that "no colour is too garish for him, no truth too bitter" and that he "seeks out the sharpest contrasts." Finally, he attempted a comparison of the two composers:

> Berlioz has written no work that has as its content that aforementioned organic development of a state of mind, such as Beethoven's Fifth and Ninth Symphonies, which are concerned with inner exultation of the soul, and Mendelssohn's Symphony-Cantata [*Lobgesang*], which is concerned with religious confidence. Rather, in the depiction of feelings that are wildly storming and self-displacing, harsh, conflicting and anxiously piled up, and multifarious, he even crosses the boundaries within which Beethoven keeps; he has undertaken to portray confused feelings that are more entangled and made up of more heterogeneous elements than the boldest creations of that master on this path down which he was the first to travel; in short, Berlioz has taken a step forward here. Backwards say (quite consistently) the enthusiasts for the old musical republic, who entirely reject that Beethovenian path as turning away from the inner sanctum of art.—
> Here the fundamentally different natures of Berlioz and Mendelssohn are very clearly and decidedly set forth. For whereas the latter, in the peaceful fields of organic development, offers a worthy complement to the original creations of the powerful master, the former remains in this respect wholly inactive; and whereas, in reverse, in

the territory of agitated and heart-stirring feelings Mendelssohn retired from the field right at the beginning of his career, Berlioz stormed straight on to this road ahead of his leader.[98]

Whereas Becher does not seem to have regarded Mendelssohn's classic restraint and technical polish as evidence of a fettered imagination, and therefore as a weakness, other German critics clearly did take this view. Among these was Franz Brendel, who, in a comparison of Mendelssohn and Schumann, also published in 1845, contrasted the objectivity of the former with the subjectivity of the latter. He regarded Mendelssohn as "a representative of classicism in our time" and "not an expression of the present time in its entirety, least of all of future trends." He obliquely denigrated Mendelssohn in the statement that his followers "would work for the future even less than their master . . . and, in accordance with the whole movement, would degenerate into superficiality and formalism."[99] The author of the article on Mendelssohn that appeared in the ninth edition of the Brockhaus *Conversations-Lexikon*, the year after Becher's and Brendel's articles, was also among those who considered Mendelssohn's achievements as falling short of the greatness claimed for them by his more enthusiastic admirers. In the following extract from the Brockhaus article, the opinion expressed in the passage beginning "Were music a science" echoes that in Schilling's *Encyclopädie*. After the usual biographical details, the author remarked:

> As far as Mendelssohn's artistic individuality is concerned, we note above all that his most characteristic feature, in contrast to so many present-day artists who serve the moment and its requirements, is the conscious striving for the highest in art, and at the same time he has a musical as well as general cultivation that is truly excellent and only given, to this extent, to few musicians. Even at an early stage he attempted the most noble and difficult forms and genres; single-mindedly and energetically he worked to reach a high ideal; and he remained true to this striving right up to the present. Even at an early stage he stood out for his fine taste and clear, con-

scious recognition of the problems that the artist of the present had to solve. If, despite this excellent endeavour and the possession of all requirements that derive from diligence and study, the critic is obliged to deny M. the certificate of a master of the first rank, this is because of his lack of originality and abundance of imagination, lack of elemental power and immediacy of creativity, excess of reflectiveness, a characteristic that he shares with his native city,[100] and which in this context at least has not been without influence on him. Everything that the noblest and richest education can provide, everything that the artist can acquire through his own activity, we see realized in Mendelssohn, but the natural foundation, the other side of the artistic spirit, which must be present to the same degree if harmonious creations are to be brought forth, is not quite the same as those qualities, and so in his case the activity of the intellect comes forth at the expense of the imagination; the abstract thought and coldness of the north predominates, not the warm, sensual and imaginative life of the south. Were music a science, Mendelssohn would be the greatest musician; but in art the natural power of the spirit is primary and the activity of the intellect secondary. As far as the marked outlook of his works is concerned, we have to remark that the fortunate circumstances in which he lived kept him far from the abysses of pain, far from the vicissitudes of daily life and its pain and struggle; untroubled serenity, smiles of fortune, reconciliation, which artists enjoyed before the year 1830, are therefore the basic traits of his being; at the same time, his attention was directed primarily to the past by the comprehensive education he received at an early stage.[101]

The comments in the final sentence indicate that opinions of Mendelssohn may have been influenced, in "progressive" circles, by the changing mood of the 1840s, with a growing emphasis on the need for struggle and self-sacrifice in the service of nationalistic goals.

47 · Critical Responses to Individual Works and Genres, 1837–1847

Reviews of individual compositions provide a broader context for these opinions. In the period up to *St Paul* Mendelssohn had primarily published instrumental music, but after 1837 vocal and choral music assumed a much larger place in his public output, especially music to religious texts. His development as a composer of sacred music, therefore, became a matter of considerable critical interest. On the other hand, there was speculation about his future as a dramatic composer. His *Walpurgisnacht* cantata, his incidental music to *A Midsummer Night's Dream*, *Antigone*, *Oedipus*, and *Athalie* roused expectation of a future opera, while his focus on oratorio was regarded in some quarters as a sublimation of his dramatic urge, or even, especially in the case of *Elijah*, as a preparatory step towards opera. Only a few of Mendelssohn's contemporaries, such as August Kahlert and Eduard Krüger, seem to have anticipated later writers in seeing his purely instrumental compositions as his most enduring legacy; some, who regarded Mendelssohn's influence on younger composers as the principal impediment to progress in German music, denigrated his works in general. Herrmann Hirschbach, for instance, damned the Piano Trio op. 66 as "stale, like a dish made out of leftovers,"[102] and was sufficiently biased to judge even the Violin Concerto a weak and ephemeral work (see below).

Instrumental Music

During the last decade of his life, Mendelssohn published only one major work for orchestra alone, the Symphony in A Minor. Although he did not publish or sanction the title *Scottish* (or *Scotch*), and even replaced the original descriptive tempo designation "Allegro guerriero," for the fourth movement, with the neutral "Allegro vivacissimo" in the printed edition, contemporaries immediately recognized that the symphony was inspired by an unstated programme, and that it constituted a logical development of the direction taken in his earlier concert overtures. Schumann famously confused the A minor symphony with the unpublished Symphony in A Major and, in his review of the piano-duet arrangement, based his discussion on the belief that it "places us under the heaven of

Italy." Nevertheless, his review contains many typical insights. He referred to the "original folk tone [that] breathes from this symphony" and noted the "inward connection of all its four movements," remarking: "More than any other symphony it forms a closely interwoven whole." Commenting specifically on the music, he observed: "No one will think of doubting its perfect finish. It stands beside his overtures in tenderness and beauty of construction as a whole, and in the detail of the numbers that unite it; nor is it less rich than these in charming instrumental effects. And every page of the score proves how well Mendelssohn understands how to return to his former ideas, how finely he ornaments a return to the theme, so that it comes to us as in a new light, how rich and interesting he can render his details, without overloading them or making a display of pedantic learning." Then, having discussed the orchestration, and the brilliance of the scherzo, he concluded: "The close of the whole symphony will excite contending opinions. Many will expect it to be in the style of the last movement, while actually, rounding the circle of the work, it reminds us of the beginning of the first. We consider it very poetic; it is like an evening that promises a fine morning."[103]

In another review of the piano-duet arrangement of the A minor symphony, August Kahlert showed sensitive understanding of Mendelssohn's conception of the programmatic element in music. He began with a reference to symphonic writing as a distinctively German genre, asserting that France and Italy "do not understand this dreamworld of sound, which the Germans have created, where no words are necessary to lead the imagination of the listener by means of specific ideas, but in which the free forms of the tonal structure constitute themselves lawgivers." After implying the limitations of musical analysis as a way of understanding the meaning of such music, he continued: "Every really musical person knows how poor words are in these circumstances. Serious, cheerful, angry, yearning, playful, all these words suggest only a generalized description of mood that could imply any number of things, at best stimulating curiosity, but always offering only the most incomplete picture. It is precisely the element in music that cannot be conveyed verbally that should not be stolen from it, for this would mean restricting it. Thus the kind of criticism that attributes specific pictures and ideas to an instrumental piece that powerfully stirs the listener seems the most perilous, easily descending into capriciousness and frequently striking the composer as laughable." He pointed out, however, that it was a different matter when the composer, as in Mendelssohn's *Meeresstille* Overture, had provided the key himself, for "it would be just as laughable not to recognize the signal for landing in the trumpet fanfare at the end of that overture."

Kahlert then turned directly to Mendelssohn: "The greater proportion of German music lovers look upon F. Mendelssohn with trust and hope, for those with insight have joyfully awarded him the certificate of mastery, which they are obliged to deny to so many popular composers. The style he has acquired is distinctive, it betrays a personality, it makes whatever the master creates recognizable, but it is handled with freedom, which reveals the master hand, otherwise it would become mannered.[104] The branch of music that most unrestrictedly belongs to him is the instrumental genre. However excellent and masterly his writing for voices may be, no-one will fail to appreciate that he handles the human voice with less freedom than he handles instruments, thus Italian singers are rather shy of *St Paul*, just as they are of *Fidelio*. May he never turn away from the symphony, the crown of all instrumental music, its bounds are far from delineated, its form is still based on many wholly arbitrary precedents; here, in our opinion, he finds the most grateful field for activity."

After a detailed and appreciative description of Mendelssohn's symphony, with music examples, in which he focused particularly on its thematic unity, Kahlert concluded:

> It is not possible here to go into the many refinements of instrumentation that strike us. How happily Mendelssohn knows how to use some favourite ones, e.g., violoncello and horn, has often been remarked. In order to keep symmetry of colouring all the more firmly in mind, he does not use trombones and piccolos. He also uses four horns instead of two only on account of the keys,[105] not to make noise. An account of that charming variety which he knows how to use in part-writing and imitation of all kinds is probably just as unnecessary here. The whole work is characterized by inner symmetry, fine imaginative cohesion of all ideas, surely delineated forms. We may not expect that it will be set above the master's earlier works in respect of inventiveness, or that it will

triumph irresistibly and awaken noisy enthusiasm. But
we may prophesy that it will rouse pure feeling of pleasure everywhere, especially where people are practised at
taking in a piece of music that is made up of so many
sections and yet not broken up by long breaks. It is another question whether the stamina required for the task,
because of the lack of breaks, does not make it too demanding for the orchestra, particularly the wind instruments.[106]

Comparison of German and English reviews again overwhelmingly
reveals the tendency of English critics to praise unreservedly on the basis
of an overall impression, whereas German ones tended to favour a degree
of critical detachment. Many leading musicians and critics in England
saw each new work by Mendelssohn as further confirmation of his pre-
eminence in contemporary music. Thus, after the first English performance of the Symphony in A Minor at the Philharmonic Society in 1842,
G. A. Macfarren began his review:

There is a sense of exultation in an artist who witnesses the glorification of his art. From this feeling there
must have been many a one proud of being a musician
who was present at the first performance of Mendelssohn's new symphony—a work to raise the author to the
highest pinnacle of musical repute—to raise the art
which it adorns and honours—and to raise the present
generation in the chronicles of intellectual progress as being contemporary with such an author, coeval with such
a work. It is this pride at being, how unworthy soever, a
fellow-worshipper with Mendelssohn of the same God-
dess, that gives me confidence to approach him, the high
priest of her temple, with a tribute to his excellence in
the avowal of the feelings which his work has given me;
and, besides the pleasure that there is in being the voice
of a manifold opinion, I feel a satisfaction in thus breaking through our country's custom of anonymous criticism, from supposing that, years hence, when the present

occasion shall be quite forgotten, when this new star in the firmament of genius shall be no longer contemplated as an individual shining, but massed in men's consideration among the galaxy of splendour which illuminates the world, which quickens our purest feelings, and which gives to everyone that loves his art, or hopes to be an artist, the moth-like emulation to exalt himself into the sphere of radiance, and flutter in the light which *may* destroy him—when it shall be that this work, then no more a new one, *is*, and cannot be remembered to have *not been;* I may look out this record of my first impressions, and feel gratified in secret to be reminded I was *one* of those who could and did at first appreciate this wondrous work; who saw and felt the light when new and strange, which shall be then familiar. If Mendelssohn— (I cannot call a being whom Genius makes impersonal, and whom superiority to all cotemporary [*sic*] association raises above society, by the conventional appellatives which living men use to each other)—if Mendelssohn should see this paper, which the common course of things may easily bring before him, he will, I hope, forgive this ostentation of a capacity to feel his merit, for the sake of the sincerity which induces it.

Despite the flowery language of its introduction, however, Macfarren's review was not merely an effusion. In his long discussion of the individual movements he revealed his own preoccupations as a serious composer, explaining his admiration with detailed reference to particular points of construction, orchestration and harmonic procedure. For Macfarren the symphony provided many specific proofs of Mendelssohn's transcendent genius in its achievement of expressive power through innovative treatment of musical techniques. Referring to the beginning of the development section of the first movement, for instance, he observed that it "begins with a most daring, powerful, and unlooked-for start in C sharp minor; and a train of modulation follows, ending in C natural minor, that is one of the most striking and original passages, as to the harmony, the phraseology, and the instrumentation, that I ever heard." His percep-

tion of the music's emotional force, apparent throughout, may be illustrated by his characterization of the beginning of the third movement:

> The slow movement (in A major) opens abruptly, but
> still connectedly with what has just concluded, on a 6th
> upon F natural, which sinks into a chord of E, and
> sounds to me as though a sudden earthquake rent the
> joyous feeling which had filled a loving bosom, and in
> the chasm which it made, revealed the depths of fathom-
> less despair. But then we find this momentary anguish is
> no other than the fear that it must cease, which is the
> tremulous brink of happiness, the incertitude that makes
> delight an ecstasy, which refines mere joy to transport;
> for, after what may be supposed a prelude, or what in a
> song we should call the symphony, there comes a stream
> of broad, grand flowing melody, so full of lovely tender-
> ness, so replete with passion, and so fervent in the heart-
> fulness of its expression, that it seems to say all that
> words, or looks, or pressure of the hand could ever sig-
> nify—almost all heart could ever feel.

Finally, having apologized to the reader for what "may be to some an air
of ostentation, even of bombast, in this vociferation of my feelings on
this subject," Macfarren concluded:

> To me the symphony is, on the whole, the most pathetic
> composition of the kind, and of the length, I ever heard;
> and by pathetic, I must not be thought to mean that
> morbid melancholy quality which some critics, but few
> poets, would set up as the essential of sublimity: by pa-
> thetic, let be understood to signify that deep, intense,
> and soulful feeling which dives down to the bottom of
> the human heart, and there enthrones itself the emperor
> of passion. And these are words, how vague and how in-
> adequate to tell the thoughts which prompt them. But
> when the time shall come, which cannot be remote,
> when all the world shall own this generation has added

one to the great Trinity of Genius that has stood alone
in instrumental music, I shall exult to have been one
who could appreciate the merit, and has, however worthless, paid his tribute of acknowledgement to the original
identity of style, the grandeur of conception, and the
powers of development which this symphony displays,
and which, in aftermen's esteem, shall place as equals,
Haydn, Mozart, Beethoven, and Mendelssohn.[107]

Apart from this work for orchestra alone, Mendelssohn published three
compositions for solo instrument and orchestra during these years: the
Second Piano Concerto, op. 40, the Serenade and Allegro Giojoso, op.
43, and the Violin Concerto, op. 64. The first two were acknowledged
as lightweight, though polished works. Few would have disagreed with
Schumann's judgment concerning the Second Piano Concerto: "If Mendelssohn deserves the praise that he always gives us such musical music,
we cannot, however, deny that in some of his works this character is less,
in others more observable. This concerto is one of those in which it is
least impressive. I err greatly, if he did not write it in a few days, perhaps
even in a few hours. It reminds one of a tree from which, when it is
shaken, the sweet, ripe fruit falls without further trouble." Schumann's
comments about the Serenade and Allegro Giojoso make it plain that
although he thought that charm and polish predominated over depth, he
appreciated the work on its own terms, and he took issue with those who
saw in such casual productions evidence of Mendelssohn's inventive inadequacy: "But why so many words about such music? What avails it to
dissect the Graces, to weigh moonshine? He who comprehends the poet's
language will also understand this; and though we have lately been informed, by someone in Jena [the composer and critic Karl Banck] that
Mendelssohn's imagination often fails to attain the proper height, why,
go hang thyself hop-o'-my-thumb from Jena, if this lovely earth seems to
thee too lowly!"[108]

The Violin Concerto was rather a different matter, since at this date
composers rarely attempted concertos for instruments on which they were
not themselves virtuosos. In these circumstances, critics looked for something more than a brilliant work for violin and orchestra. Many believed
they had found it in Mendelssohn's Violin Concerto. The initial reaction

of the *Allgemeine musikalische Zeitung*, after the première in 1845, was typically respectful: "Mendelssohn's as yet unpublished Violin Concerto struck us immediately on first hearing as a dignified and attractive work, such as we are accustomed to expect from the pen of the revered master. It is again principally the grace and dignity of the motifs that are brilliantly brought out, the sharply characterized individual movements and the clever individuality with which the soloist and orchestra are united, which seizes the interest in a lively manner and holds it to the end."[109] Later in the year, when David performed the concerto in Berlin, Rellstab, hearing the work for the second time, referred more enthusiastically to "Mendelssohn's wonderfully beautiful Violin Concerto . . . which this time made a more lively and decided impression, creating a degree of pleasure that is in fact seldom proffered."[110]

The *Allgemeine musikalische Zeitung* review of the published edition was prefaced by a substantial introduction in which the author lamented the dearth of "musically worthwhile solo compositions for the violin," singling out Spohr's concertos as the only really musically substantial ones and Paganini's as representing a new treatment of the instrument. He observed that the composer of a concerto for an instrument on which he is not a virtuoso is in a good position to treat the work "in a freer and more poetic manner than the composing virtuoso, who more or less always thinks primarily of what will be most effective for the instrument and most grateful in respect of the individuality of his performing style"; thus he would be able to create a piece "in which the solo part certainly dominated the other parts, but not the composition." He then turned to the Beethoven concerto, which had recently been performed in Leipzig by the young Joachim, and observed that for a virtuoso to perform such a work "requires a kind of self denial—from the virtuoso only, not the musician—since the former with fewer means could easily make a greater effect and earn greater applause." He stated that Mendelssohn's Violin Concerto was the sole successor of Beethoven's in this respect but observed that it was hardly necessary to detail the qualities "of this interesting composition," as the composer's name vouched for its significance. After a brief description of the concerto, in which he commented that the first movement overall was "rather in the style of the quartet and the symphony than that of the concerto" and noted, but did not discuss, the connections between the movements, he summed up the work's importance with the remark: "A composition of this kind is to be very gratefully treasured not only for itself, but also because, by departing from the very narrow tracks of convention, it gives the genre itself an impulse and can help to lead it to a revivified existence."[111]

A very different tone was adopted by Herrmann Hirschbach in the *Repertorium für Musik*. His review, given here in full, illustrates his own lack of appreciation of Mendelssohn's music in general and also reflects a minority strand of opinion that was gaining strength during these years. His comments about Mendelssohn's externally fortunate circumstances, and their deleterious effects on his art, were echoed in the Brockhaus *Conversations-Lexikon* in 1846, and his criticism of Mendelssohn's lack of inventiveness and emotional depth were to become stock charges of later detractors.

> Mendelssohn!—fortunate name, which can loosen the purse of even the most hard-hearted publisher—that is all that need be said. I shall not get into a long discussion about a man who has already, a thousand times, been the subject of lengthy articles. Mendelssohn is one of those lucky people who has never suffered an interruption, a disturbance or even a break in their creative activity through external circumstances, to whom were given opportunity and means peacefully to pursue his career without having to seek protection, like poor talent, without at an early stage having experienced the miseries that have afflicted many a more profound spirit than Mendelssohn.—Therefore it comes about, however, that Mendelssohn has rather too little human pain in his pieces; they are mostly music for those who are as fortunate as he, therefore for that circle where the outer man is more important than the inner man, where delicacy is a substitute for genuine feeling. But can one blame him if he is not able to descend to the level of that class of condemned mankind who know nothing of good fortune but the name? It might appear, and I have often heard it said, that Mendelssohn has already reached the peak of his productive power; without wishing to express myself

categorically about it, I nevertheless believe that I can assert that in the future he will still appear more significant than Fr[iedrich] Schneider of Dessau, who has now more or less sunk into obscurity.—This concerto is a work on a declining trajectory. Admittedly my expectations of a violin concerto are entirely different, much higher than those that musicians are accustomed to hold; I require that it should be a work of art in which the vocal powers of the violin unite appropriate depth of feeling and sublimity of melody with continuous characterization and beautiful interweaving, and in this respect the present violin concerto pleases me just as little as every other one. Yes, Spohr has written more beautiful concertos than this, which is a well-made and not very difficult piece in E in three movements (the first movement is in the minor, the second in C, the third in E major), but which in respect of invention presents me with nothing impressive. The ideas are too superficial; straightaway, with the theme of the first movement, one feels that the composer is not serious about seriousness, the theme of the Andante is uninteresting, and that of the last movement displays only contrived cheerfulness. But although for me the whole concerto will merely be a threepenny bit while others, more easily satisfied, will find it to be a gold sovereign, and although the composer may be far from reflecting and bringing out the deep, intrinsic individuality of the instrument in his composition, nevertheless at a time when, for the violin, only miserable fashionable pieces such as fantasias and the like are being produced, a work of this kind is to be seen as a noteworthy, prominent phenomenon, which, proceeding from such a celebrated name, will certainly be able to find numerous purchasers.[112]

Among Mendelssohn's chamber works, the one that undoubtedly made the greatest impression during these years was the Piano Trio in D Minor, op. 49. It elicited Schumann's celebrated accolade that it was "the master trio of to-day, as in their day were those of Beethoven in B flat and D, as was that of Schubert in E flat."[113] Schumann's review is too well-known and too accessible to require quotation in full, but one passage, which clearly reveals his view of Mendelssohn's position in the music of the period, merits repetition (in a clearer translation than Ritter's): "The storm of the last few years is gradually beginning to subside, and—let us confess it—has already cast many a pearl upon the beach. Though Mendelssohn was perhaps less shaken by it than others, he nonetheless remains a child of his epoch. He also had to struggle; also had to listen to the nonsensical jabber of the narrow minded: 'The real springtime of music lies behind us'; and he has raised himself so high that we can indeed say he is the Mozart of the nineteenth century; the most brilliant among musicians; the one who has most clearly recognized the contradictions of the time, and the first to reconcile them. Nor will he be the last composer. After Mozart came Beethoven; this modern Mozart will be followed by a newer Beethoven. Indeed, he may already have been born."[114] Perhaps Schumann saw himself as the newer Beethoven, or perhaps, six years after Mendelssohn's death, he eventually recognized him in Brahms.

Fink's response to the work was more straightforwardly enthusiastic, but he too awarded it a high place in the composer's oeuvre, preceding his discussion of the music itself with the comment:

> If any of this celebrated composer's instrumental
> works, especially of those written chiefly for piano, has
> roused enthusiasm, it is this trio above all. There are not
> a few who immediately declare it to be the best work for
> piano and strings that the composer has ever produced.
> Although such a comment may tread on the toes of several other works by the same composer and detract from
> their appreciation more than is right and proper, it nevertheless makes clear the extraordinary impression that
> this new trio has made at its public performance as well
> as in private circles. Such an impression must certainly
> be significant and must make everyone hungry to get to
> know the work itself. We felt like this when we were at
> the public performance of this favourite composition. We

now know it not merely from repeated scrutiny [of the score], which is insufficient, but also from hearing it, and know from experience that it must make a powerful impact and what causes it to do so. The work is not only a rounded whole, with sustained interweaving of themes and the sure mastery of form, which one already knows from the best of the composer's earlier works, but also has as much as anyone could desire of lively excitement, fresh drive, joyful brilliance.[115]

Music for Voices

Mendelssohn's songs, like Beethoven's, have not in recent times been prized as highly as those of Schubert and Schumann. This is partly because, as R. Larry Todd has observed, Mendelssohn "did not fully explore the potential ramifications of the song cycle." Indeed, Todd's appraisal of the songs indicates that he shares what he calls the "conventional wisdom" that "Mendelssohn's solo and duet lieder do not rank among his most significant efforts."[116] In his own time, however, Mendelssohn's lieder were considered by many to be one of the most successful aspects of his output. Their very simplicity, fully in accord with the views of his mentor Goethe, which gave many of them almost the character of folk-song, was seen as a virtue. Eduard Krüger, a trenchant contemporaneous critic of Mendelssohn's sacred music, regarded his songs as "immortal."[117] Wilhelm Heinrich Riehl, too, thought that, notwithstanding Mendelssohn's striving for perfection in large-scale works, it was in his songs that he "showed himself to be most perfect." Shortly after Mendelssohn's death he wrote:

> Mendelssohn had a clear theoretical conception of the nature of the folk-song, indeed, as is well known, he also wrote folk-songs with the intention of copying the style and spirit of the folk-like manner in them. This, in itself, we do not find in the case of any of the preceding great masters. But, what is more, he understood the historical significance of the folk-song; since his was, in general, not only a creative but at the same time also a critical and inquiring mind, this understanding was from the

very start determined by the most significant feature of his artistic character. The folk-song was debased by the cheap imitators of the Viennese School, and became mannered in the hands of the musical Romantics: it was therefore important to him to reach back to its purer original form as this had been passed down to us from the old times. A similar thing had already happened before with the pioneering poets, such as Arnim, Brentano, Uhland, etc., who deliberately transferred the old, simple form and expression of the mediaeval song into their imitations of folk-song; thus in singing Mendelssohn's universally known "Minnelied" or his song "Scheiden," approximately the same mood envelops us as with the aforementioned poetic works. We need not wonder that this decisive turning-point in the history of music occurred later than in literature, since musicians in general emerged much later than poets from the period of naive creativity and sought consciously to take their place in the nation's complete cultural-historical revolution. Thus it came about that through Mendelssohn the German folk-song, in its deeper historical sense, was, as it were, rediscovered, and that in him that mysterious impulse to seek the generative power for all kinds of music in the folk-song, which is a pervasive element in the music of our time, became a conscious deed.[118]

Like Mendelssohn's secular vocal music, his sacred works, with the partial exception of *Elijah*, have largely disappeared from the repertoire. Although he wrote many compositions to religious texts in earlier years, he issued only two publications of sacred music before *St Paul*.[119] Even in the last ten years of his life he published only a handful more, though these included the large-scale Symphony-Cantata *Lobgesang*, the Psalms with Orchestra, and *Elijah*. Many other smaller pieces, however, were performed, and several of those written for Berlin during the 1840s were issued immediately after his death.[120] The Berlin compositions were primarily intended for performance in a liturgical context; others, including Psalms 42, 95 and 114, which he published between 1838 and 1842, were composed with concert performance in mind. The "concert" psalms aroused considerable contemporary interest and enthusiasm, and the *Lobgesang* was immediately received as one of the composer's most important works. But public enthusiasm was not always matched by equivalent critical acclaim. In the period immediately after Mendelssohn's death, an increasing number of German writers questioned whether his sacred music, particularly that intended for liturgical use, was fit for its purpose. Even *Elijah* was quickly subjected to cavilling criticism in Germany.

Despite modern perceptions, shared to some extent by writers sympathetic to the composer, that these works, especially Psalms 42 and 95, are vitiated by "softness and sentimentality" or are even "unpleasantly unctuous" in places,[121] reviews at the time of their publication were overwhelmingly appreciative and do not seem to have attracted criticism of this kind, even from less enthusiastic writers. Macfarren's judgment that Psalm 42 "as a whole, and in all its parts, is a composition of exquisite beauty, comprising passages of the gentlest supplication, the tenderest pathos, and the most exciting grandeur,"[122] is typical of the response of Mendelssohn's contemporaries. At the time of the first performances of Psalm 42 in 1838, for instance, Schumann remarked: "Though Mendelssohn has long been recognized as the most finished, artistic nature of our day, in all styles, whether of church or concert-room, original and of masterly effect in the chorus as in the Lied, yet we believe that in this 42d Psalm he has attained his highest elevation as church composer; yes, the highest elevation that modern church-music has reached at all. The grace, the art of workmanship which such a style demands, is fully displayed here; tenderness and purity in the treatment of details, power and inwardness of the masses, but, above all, what we cannot term other than the intellectuality of the whole delights us, and proves what art is to him, as well as what it is to us through him."[123]

The following year, after the psalm's publication, a reviewer in the *Allgemeine musikalische Zeitung* remarked that in the first chorus "the whole flow of the vocal parts and the manner of accompaniment, particularly the very notable structures of the sections, which can have a more deleterious than beneficial influence on the nature of the overall impression if ignored or treated with a misguided desire for variety by the inexperienced, has the dignity of Handel's time. The faithfully maintained unity of the vocal parts in conjunction with the gradually increasing, though never powerfully growing, or even once again decreasing, orchestration gives the chorus a sterling appeal, without the composer needing to have recourse to any kind of exaggeration." The following soprano solo he characterized as "likewise resembling Handel's manner, as far as is possible for another personality in another era." Then, after describing the subsequent numbers up to the quintet section, he observed: "This extremely effective quintet is the high point of the piece and will be found powerfully moving, even where it is only moderately well performed. Gradually, without any abruptness, the basic tone of the music has approached that of good liturgical music of our time, so that it feels familiar to everyone. We are sure that every unbiased person will agree with this statement." Having discussed the final fugue, noting the feeling among some that it was "too secular," he concluded: "It is certain, on the other hand, that these peculiarities of feeling are only shared by relatively few, and that the great majority feel the stately and forward-moving chorus appealing and effective in its increased power, so that the composition of this Psalm . . . must be designated more impressive than the preceding one [Psalm 115, op. 31], notwithstanding the quantity and justice of the recognition that one received."[124]

For many, Mendelssohn's setting of Psalm 42 remained his finest. Schumann, reviewing the New Year's Day concert of 1840, at which Psalm 114 received its first performance, commented: "He who writes many works successively, in the same style, naturally suggests comparison with himself. And so it was here. Mendelssohn's beautiful older psalm, "As the hart pants" [Psalm 42], was yet fresh in the memory of all. There was some difference of opinion regarding the merits of the two works, but the majority of votes was for the older one. . . . No one entertains any doubt respecting the special beauties of the new Psalm, though I cannot deny that, in regard to freshness of invention (particularly in the latter half), it falls somewhat behind the other, and even reminds us of some things we have already heard by Mendelssohn."[125] The remarks of another reviewer suggest that not everyone in Leipzig shared Schumann's opinion about the relationship between the two psalm settings. This reviewer stated that Psalm 114 was, "in our opinion, in terms of its innermost content, one of the most sublime compositions he has ever written. . . . The conception of the text as well as the realization of the whole work give new proof of the rich mind and great mastery of the celebrated composer." And after a detailed description of the work, he concluded: "The effect is so striking and direct that everyone must immediately be gripped by it; and if it also receives a performance as perfect and beautiful as this one under the composer's direction and with such excellent means, the tremendous applause with which the whole assembly thanked the honoured master is comprehensible and natural."[126]

Psalm 95, first performed in 1841 and published the following year, called forth one of the comments that indicate the reverential attitude of those who were gripped by what Brockhaus and others described as the "Mendelssohn mania" that affected many in Leipzig during his lifetime. A long review by Carl Ferdinand Becker contained the statement that it was "a work by a richly gifted and thoroughly cultivated artist, by a master whose name is firmly established in the annals of the history of art and extends far beyond the borders of Germany; a work by such a coryphaeus of art as *Mendelssohn Bartholdy* can only be *observed*, *never* criticized in the literal sense of this term. Who could imagine that they stand at *such* a high level of artistic cultivation that they can look down from *above* on the achievements of such a significant artist?"[127]

Of all the sacred works Mendelssohn wrote between *St Paul* and *Elijah*, however, it was the Symphony-Cantata *Lobgesang* that seems most powerfully to have seized the attention and roused the admiration of contemporaries. Although generally disparaged (or at least relegated to a relatively insignificant ranking in his output) for much of the twentieth century, it was seen at the time as a work of major importance, and to judge by its publication history and the number of performances it received, it retained that position throughout the nineteenth century. After the première of the *Lobgesang* in the Thomaskirche in Leipzig, as part of the Gutenberg Festival in June 1840, Schumann commented: "The work was enthusiastically received, and its choral numbers especially must be counted among the master's freshest and most charming creations. Every one who has followed the progress of his labours knows what this means, after such great performances as have preceded this. We did not intend to give a detailed description, but we must mention a duet, interrupted by a chorus, "I waited for the Lord," at the conclusion of which a whisper rustled throughout the entire assemblage,—which means more in a church than loud applause in a concert-hall. It was like a glance into a heaven filled with the Madonna eyes of Raphael."[128] Following its performance six months later at the Gewandhaus on 3 December 1840, Schumann, noting that "the composer had in the meanwhile successfully revised the work," expressed his unqualified approval: "All praise for the splendid composition, as it was, and as it now is! We declared it before. Everything that can make people happy and ennoble them—pious feeling, consciousness of power, its freest, most natural expression—may be found here; not to speak of the musical skill of the composition and the imagination with which Mendelssohn worked on this piece, especially in the parts where the chorus predominates."[129]

The *Allgemeine musikalische Zeitung* took the opportunity to look retrospectively at Mendelssohn's contribution to sacred music and at its significance for the present: "Through his oratorio *St Paul*, later through the composition of the 42nd Psalm, not to mention the earlier individual church pieces in a less decided style, Mendelssohn has revealed such an outstanding calling for this genre of music that from now on one receives each new work of this kind with the certain feeling in advance that it will be as deeply felt as it will be masterly in execution. That a composer of our time should turn in this direction, at such an early age, in the full flowering of his capabilities, with the love and enthusiasm that shines forth from Mendelssohn's sacred music, is all the more gratifying, since we normally see that it is mostly veteran artists who choose this genre for preference." And the enthusiastic review concluded with thanks to the "highly revered artist" for a "significant work that stands by the side of his finest and that should be frequently performed in a worthy manner, to his fame and our joy."[130]

The position that the *Lobgesang* came to occupy in England was foreshadowed in reviews at the time of its early performances and by assessments like Macfarren's in 1849. Comparing the work, inevitably, with Beethoven's Ninth Symphony, Macfarren remarked:

> There is also a more earnest, since a decidedly religious,
> character in the composition of Mendelssohn than in
> that of Beethoven, and the three instrumental move-
> ments are more in accordance with, and more decidedly
> a prelude to the song of laudation which they introduce,
> than are the first three movements of Beethoven's sym-
> phony, from the gloomy grandeur and pensive melan-

choly of which the Ode to Joy bursts as a powerful contrast, as the upheaving of a depressed spirit in the
exultant dilation of a contracted heart. The chorale with
which the Lobgesang opens displays at once the solemn
intention and sacred character of the whole, and these
are throughout never lost sight of; but the 'praise' is that
of a great mind, which feels that the pouring out of its
best feelings and its noblest, is the devoutest homage:
thus we find all conventionalities are eschewed completely; no form or style, because it has the name of sacred, is employed to impose a false character of devotion
upon the hearers, and the effect of the whole is grand
and impressive because of its beauty, and not because of
any accepted form of technical treatment.[131]

Mendelssohn's last major sacred work, *Elijah*, was widely seen as his
crowning achievement in the genre of sacred music, and perhaps of his
oeuvre as a whole. Within a year of appearing in print it had been performed as far afield as New York and St Petersburg. Its popularity with
choral societies remained substantial well into the twentieth century, and
it is still performed regularly, though less frequently, in many parts of the
world. Reaction to the oratorio in English-speaking regions was, from the
first, almost overwhelmingly enthusiastic, and almost uncritical. Macfarren's response may stand for many. In his 1849 article he began his survey
of Mendelssohn's compositions with *Elijah*, which he described as "the
most important," stating that it "exhibits all the profound skill of the
accomplished musician, all the brilliant imagination of the enlightened
poet, and all the earnest solemnity of one imbued with the sublime dignity of the subject." He observed of the text that "in its selection, its
disposition into separate movements, not only the greatest skill and judgment, but the highest epic powers are evinced." Among references to
individual features, Macfarren remarked: "Throughout the work, not a
movement, a phrase, a note, is introduced, that is not intended to, and
does not successfully, bear upon and aid in the development of the great
design of the whole. The recurrences in a subsequent portion of the work
to the musical phrase upon which the words of the curse are uttered, in

a place where the effect and the consequence of this awful denunciation are described, and which is then elaborated into an extensive and complicated chorus, is one of the many instances throughout the work in which the musical expression is made in a wonderful manner to bring out, enforce, and even elevate the dramatic interest." He considered the chorus "Thanks be to God" to be "one of the grandest, most powerful and impressive, and in all that imagination can suppose, or criticism describe, most beautiful compositions that enrich the art."

Macfarren concluded his appraisal with great approval: "In this oratorio the most surprising musical effect and the most profound poetical justice go hand-in-hand throughout, in the powerful contrast of character that is everywhere preserved between the different personages of the story: thus we have the majestic, awful dignity of Elijah, which in various phases still manifests itself, whether in his curse, in his resignation, in his command or in his prayer; the pure devotion of Obadiah; the incensed and violent fury of Jezebel; the sufferings of the afflicted people, and their exultant rejoicing on the removal of the curse; the fanatic madness of the priests of Baal, and the beatific serenity of the choir of angels. Volumes might be written in praise of this extraordinary creation, which would leave still volumes more to say, and all would but convey this obvious truth:—the more we understand the greatness of his work, the less can we understand, but the more must we reverence, the greatness of the author."[132]

Although the number of performances *Elijah* received in Germany testifies to widespread appreciation, German critical responses to the work were generally less whole-hearted, more inclined to probe for weaknesses than English ones, especially with regard to the text and its organization. German reviewers seem to have felt a greater obligation to single out individual points for criticism, even when they admired the work as a whole. Otto Lange's review, published in the *Neue Berliner Musikzeitung* less than a month after Mendelssohn's death (judging by the mixture of present and past tenses, it was drafted while he was still alive), is typical in this respect. (Lange's overall estimation of *Elijah* was much higher, however, than his opinion of *St Paul*, which he had characterized in the *Vossische Zeitung* the previous year as "not the outpouring of a truly creative genius")[133] His concluding remarks on the two oratorios are particularly interesting.

Mendelssohn has such a fine intellect, is such a thinking musician that, since he moves freely and independently in the realm of music, he must be accorded the most immediate recognition, often admiration. He is, more than any among the artists of the present day, in control of the forms and laws of art; he has such a quantity of knowledge at his command that, with his taste formed by the works of the greatest masters, he is always able to employ their most beautiful methods and the most correct means. People must judge for themselves, from the insight gained from hearing it in a performance, how this occurs in the present work. From the aesthetic standpoint we adopt a different position. It will not have escaped the gentle reader that we have often referred, in our review, to the dramatic plan that underlies the scenic construction of the material; the introduction to this article specifically dealt with it. We are of the opinion that Mendelssohn recognized that the age of oratorio is really past. It was no longer possible for him to hold strongly to the forms that had served him in *St Paul*. He introduced no chorales in his *Elijah*, and laid no particular stress on the old ecclesiastical form of the fugue. Certainly Bach took the latter course in his *St Matthew*, with a single exception. But we have reason to believe that this was for entirely different reasons. The religious spirit and ecclesiastical-dogmatic consciousness of his times was different. If Mendelssohn retained the Bachian form as a whole in *St Paul*, he was only in that respect a man of his time, since this form is saturated with the spirit of that time, and we have for this reason spoken against the work on another occasion. In *Elijah*, however, he has worked his way out of this consciousness to a far greater independence and freedom, and we believe that *Elijah* would have paved the way for him to a completely new phase of dramatic music. For this reason too we mourn at the tomb of the departed. With him an epoch in art is, if not ended, at least halted in its progress. No-

one could have doubted that he would have been able to
create a romantic opera like *Lorelei;* we shall only say
here, as a well-founded presumption, that he contained
within him the seed of a new high point of dramatic
music that would have overcome the extreme triviality of
contemporary grand opera by means of musical art.[134]

Otto Jahn, in an extended discussion of the oratorio, also approached
the work from a generally favourable but not uncritical standpoint, but
his idea of the work's character and its relationship to *St Paul* was quite
different. The tone of his appraisal is indicated by the first two paragraphs:

> Although it is in any case no easy task to appraise the
> total significance of a large-scale work by a great artist, a
> judgment of *Elijah* is made peculiarly difficult. The grave
> that covers the master, whose work was completed early,
> is still too fresh for pure pleasure in his works not to be
> tainted by mourning over his loss. This is not the tone
> for an unbiased judgment, if the memory of his faithful,
> tireless striving for the highest in art does not make it a
> duty to treat his works in this spirit. To the young man
> we lay a laurel wreath on the coffin in token of what he
> promised; the mature master will only be honoured by
> the attention and seriousness with which we endeavour
> truly to understand his creations, for in this understand-
> ing alone lies the ability to judge what he intended and
> achieved.
>
> What makes the judgment even more difficult in
> many respects is the comparison with *St Paul* that every-
> one feels impelled to make. For then *Elijah* appears even
> in the disadvantageous position of the successor. Through
> its conception and manner of treatment, *St Paul* initiated
> a real advance in sacred music and exercised a decided
> influence on similar efforts in our time. Anyone who ex-
> pects *Elijah* to open up another new field will find him-
> self deceived. To this expectation alone we are not enti-
> tled; but if we ask whether we find that in this work the

master has advanced along the path that he opened up with fresh and vigorous strength, with the same fine feeling for the noble and true, I answer with absolute conviction: Yes. If I look at the oratorio as a whole, I can detect no falling off, it expresses Mendelssohn's individuality clearly and powerfully in conception and invention as well as treatment and execution, the peculiar beauty of his style as well as the little weaknesses of his manner"[135]

Having devoted most of the first three pages to critical scrutiny of the text, Jahn turned to the music. He described the structure of the opening section and estimated that "as a whole, just as in individual features, it is masterly; it is in a single mould and a single mood, which is depicted with a variety of nuances, with the individual motives maintained in the most correct equilibrium, with a progressive enhancement of the deepest truthfulness; it is finely laid out and grandly implemented." The following scene, between Elijah and the Widow, however, he considered to have failed in its object; he felt that, instead of providing relief between the preceding and succeeding scenes, "the episode rather weakens the impression of that which goes before and harms the following." And, referring specifically to the music, he remarked: "Individual features are fine and beautiful, but on the whole I find here rather an external conception of restless passion than internal depth and warmth, the motifs are not grand and significant, the whole presentation somewhat hasty." In the next section he particularly admired the handling of the choruses in which Elijah confronts the priests of Baal, characterizing them as "of great freshness and liveliness, sustained in general in the manner of the choruses of heathens in *St Paul* and some in *Antigone*, without a definite similarity in particulars. In all this an individual expression of an enthusiastically aroused sensuality predominates, which is, however, far removed from effeminacy or luxuriance, appearing serious throughout, indeed, at the same time even dry."

Jahn's extensive survey continued similarly to record his predominant appreciation but significant criticisms of the work, and he concluded: "Generally, nothing much is gained by a mere description, and I leave the purely technical to the professionals, I was concerned with the overall aesthetic appreciation. Where, therefore, I could not agree with the master's intentions I have sought to justify my divergent opinion, as I would have done to him directly if I had been granted this joy. I took it for a pious duty to strive, as far as I could, with honest effort, so that the work he has left us will also truly profit us."[136]

A contemporary reaction, not intended for public dissemination, from a Leipzig acquaintance of Mendelssohn whose appreciation of music was that of an amateur, provides a rather different perspective. After hearing *Elijah* on 3 February 1848 Heinrich Brockhaus wrote in his diary:

> They used his birthday to give his last great work *Elijah*
> its first performance. One cannot straightway form a
> clear idea of such a great, deep work after a single hear-
> ing. In any case it is a rich, beautiful work, worthy of
> Mendelssohn's genius and bringing his musical activity to
> a close in the worthiest manner. Whether the music in
> general shows a waning of power, as some maintain, I do
> not know; I truly rejoiced over much of it and would
> like to consider it as a beautiful sign in our time that some-
> one at the height of his fame should set himself the task
> of creating something like this. That church composers
> as a rule expect too much of their listeners is only too
> certain, and Mendelssohn too has failed to understand
> this moderation in *Elijah*. Composers do not consider
> that the receptivity of the mind has its limits, especially
> in a serious work of art where diversity must necessarily
> be lacking. I regard more than two hours of church mu-
> sic as harmful.

When he heard the oratorio again a couple of months later, however, he confessed that he "was gripped by it much more than the first time.[137]

Among those who adversely criticized *Elijah* at an early stage was Eduard Krüger, whose review, apparently written before Mendelssohn's death, appeared in successive issues of the *Neue Zeitschrift für Musik* in December 1847. Krüger censured the text, as Jahn was to do, though much more strongly, but also found fault with many aspects of the musical treatment, maintaining, for instance, that Mendelssohn failed to make the music express the characters of the various protagonists. Unlike

Lange, he did not see the oratorio as a step towards opera but viewed it rather as a misguided sublimation of what he had once believed was Mendelssohn's true operatic vocation. In 1840 Krüger had declared, referring to Mendelssohn without specifically naming him, "Only a single bard remains to us, of German birth, German outlook, German art, the only rightful heir of the heroes of the previous century. In him lies our hope that music is not yet in a state of collapse: in him there is an independent, new song, full of sensual beauty and intellectual depth, and the pathos of our artistic period, in which he is great, has not yet absorbed the ethos. I do not name him, words fail me to praise him appropriately. May heaven and the muses grant that this beautiful power might be directed from the field of oratorio, in which it is not entirely at home, to that of opera! Who, admittedly, can counsel genius!"[138]

Mendelssohn's engagement with German opera was a key factor in his reputation, which remained unresolved at the time of his death. Few can have expected him to die without composing a mature opera and few doubted that, had he done so, he would have enjoyed widespread success in this field as in others. German operatic expectations were intimately connected with a sense of German national identity, however, and in this respect Mendelssohn's theatrical music had scarcely offered encouragement to those who looked to him for a way forward. His early operas contained nothing distinctively German (except their music), and his later theatrical music was connected with Greek (*Antigone* and *Oedipus*), English (*Ein Sommernachtstraum*) and French (*Athalie*) drama. Only in the secular cantata *Die erste Walpurgisnacht*, which paradoxically aroused relatively little interest at the time, did he tackle a secular text by a classic German author, though the enlightened message of Goethe's poem was hardly in tune with the underlying mood of the 1840s. The author of the entry on Mendelssohn in Brockhaus's *Conversations-Lexikon* in 1846 concluded his article with the statement that *Antigone* and *Oedipus* were "an undertaking which, however excellent the achievements are from the musical point of view and however much we honour the benefit of generating in the public a taste for simplicity in this manner, must be described as of little advantage from the standpoint of the development of national art."[139]

Such issues remained very much alive at the time of Mendelssohn's death, as obituary notices indicate.[140] Perhaps, had he completed it, *Die*

Lorelei would have provided the impetus to national art that many hoped for, but it is highly questionable whether the characteristics suggested by surviving portions would have determined the future of German opera for long. The direction of Mendelssohn's development after 1847 can scarcely be predicted,[141] but perhaps the increasingly nationalistic and anti-Semitic mood of the second half of the century would in any case have militated against Mendelssohn's being seen as an acceptable representative of German opera. Posterity, however, was denied the fascinating prospect of a competition between Mendelssohn and Wagner for hegemony in the theatre.

TEN · Posthumous Reputation

48 · Obituaries and Contemporaneous General Assessments

Mendelssohn's death inevitably called forth many obituaries, and although these were to a large extent seen as occasions for honouring his memory, rather than for sophisticated critiques on the value of his legacy, they provide useful insights into his status around the time of his death. Among German obituaries, that by Gustav Kühne, editor of the Leipzig journal *Europa*, stands out as particularly perceptive. It is dated the day after Mendelssohn's death and reflects the opinion of someone who, though not a member of his intimate circle, had observed his career in Leipzig at first hand. This obituary also has the added interest of Schumann's endorsement; in a list of material jotted down in his memoirs of Mendelssohn, Schumann described it as "the best that was written about Mendelssohn."[1] Kühne wrote:

The rehearsals of Elijah here were suddenly suspended; the nervous illness that befell Mendelssohn soon after his return from his summer travels made the performance of the oratorio uncertain. It was given two days ago in Berlin, it is being rehearsed in Vienna; only in England has he performed it himself. Yesterday on a concert evening—the musical performance was suspended—at twenty minutes past nine his life came to an end; a stroke, the third in a fortnight, paralysed head and heart. Not yet quite 39 years old, he was born on 3 February 1809, his tender nature became a victim of the inexorable force, too soon according to man's expectations, too soon for his work; too soon for a mourning wife, for five flourishing children, for the brother who was with him during the last few days, too soon for the sacred flame of the

most noble artistic enthusiasm, irreplaceable for a movement in music of which he was the purest and truest
leader, for a movement that perhaps finishes for ever
with him.

Mendelssohn was the last bearer of the classical trend
in the romantic movement in music. Growing up in Zelter's school, nourished by the essence of the strict old
classic composers Bach and Handel, his music gladly
kept itself in this earnest culture, even if it inclined to
the fragrant, cloudy heaven of romanticism as it confronts us in [Carl] Maria von Weber's hunting-horn
sounds [*Maria v. Webers Waldhornklängen*]. His inclination is constantly to return to the earnest culture of the
old school, even when he is possessed by Beethoven's
wonderful heaven- and earth-shaking daemon. Mendelssohn's romanticism did not share with Weber's the urge
to derive material and melody from folk sources. His
calmer nature remained far removed from Beethoven's
passionate titanic flight. Mendelssohn's muse was of a
Protestant cast; Old Testament power, chastity, simplicity
and sublimity, being a personal inheritance of his origin
and descent, stamped his oratorios with the strictest seal,
which was only softened by the amiable innocence of his
playful grace illuminating them with all the charm, all
the magic of fresh beauty. And so, a late-comer in his
art, he had the privilege of maintaining his full individuality amid the inheritance of great minds, not through
narrow measuring out and computation, not through calculation and timorous choice, just as little with false mania for esoteric methods that had never been used before,
but wholly true to his nature, full of simplicity and sublimity in his oratorios, full of sweet amiability in his
songs. He has been called strong in the tender; he was
equally tender and temperate in the strong. Falling short
of Weber in romantic richness and Beethoven in stormy
power encompassing both Heaven and Hell, a distinctive
impetus towards the religious regions of music neverthe-

less lead him to true greatness of feeling. Although he failed to equal both those geniuses in invention, he still opened up to us a new sound world which for sublimity finds its like only in Handel and Bach, for amiable innocence perhaps finds its unlooked-for relationship only in Papa Haydn, but which never again appeared in this combination. That, amidst the blustering upsurge of the romantic, he so purely and serenely sustained these two elements of his nature, sublimity and childlike innocence, both of which bound him to the unbending law of natural simplicity, may well really indicate the place of his music at the crossroads between two epochs, as the end of an old period whose works are eternal and as the beginning of a new one, the artistic worth of whose accomplishments are still questionable. Perhaps he had already fulfilled his mission.[2] He did not find his way to opera, his youthful work Die Hochzeit des Camacho remained an isolated attempt and the combination of church style with the fragrance of fairyland, with which he clothed the old Greek tragedy and Shakespeare's Midsummer Night's Dream, still did not, it appears, give him the new operatic style that we now require from the creative muse of German music. The harsh demands of criticism, however, so often overlook necessity in the limitations of a distinctive nature. Mendelssohn's music was revelatory and successful in prayer, with ancient biblical power and richness, and in fairy tale, with its sweet magic. German music of the present day still owes us its great contribution to the poetry of the people's life in the hot impulse of reality; Meyerbeer's eclecticism may well reveal the key to it, but with this ingenuity in all techniques and styles it can scarcely lead to a new blossoming of art. Yet nowhere, perhaps, has criticism been so wide of the mark as in the assertion that Mendelssohn's music may be more the outcome of reflection than of free creative inspiration. Rarely among the inheritance of great treasures of the past has a talent lived so purely in itself, so completely filled with an impulse, so completely satisfied in the unfolding of its nature. It is always the high striving for purity of style, always the technical polish in his creations that has been prized, overlooking all the musical intelligence and the creative instinct, which in him was so pure and deep, so subconscious, chaste and original to a rare degree. Leipzig, to which he almost uninterruptedly devoted the best twelve years of his life, is in the best position to know that we have lost with him a great authority in his art, a representative of the true direction, a virtuoso on his individual instrument, a master of conducting. That we have lost a genuine artistic nature, an original creative genius, could only be overlooked in his compositions if the confused yearning for the monstrous or the refined calculation of the combined senses were exclusively to carry off the palm of victory. Perhaps, in epochs of noisy effect making, genius is to be recognized precisely by its retreating, so as to remain, in its more peaceful effects, all the more faithfully a genuine bearer of divinely inspired art.

Mendelssohn's music has not been taken up by his contemporaries without loud approval, not without the deepest fervour of enthusiasm. Even an artist is seldom celebrated to such an extent, seldom is the talent in the man, and the man in the talent, as greatly loved as in his case. . . . [3] As a man he was only accessible to a few, but to these few he was a rare phenomenon, seeming a miracle in his loving, blissful friendship, a miracle in his effects on the circle of close friends, a miracle of inspiriting power in his effects when a work of art was to be called into being. It is known that old orthodox musicians commanded their troops in the orchestra with sceptre in hand like heroes; Zelter was known as a Blücher[4] with a conducting baton. Mendelssohn had that from the old master, but he had more, he knew how to generate enthusiasm affectionately, how to awaken for the beauties of art, in the smallest details, feeling and understanding, inspiration and perseverance. If anyone were to write the annals of music in Leipzig, Mendelssohn would be the high point in his account.

The key to his being called away so soon may well lie in his early perfection. A precociously mature child, a psyche that hurried forwards in its development at the cost of bodily existence, he was already initiated into all the mysteries of art at an age when others only had a faint glimmer of understanding. Zelter took the boy from Berlin on journeys and ran the risk of making a mere wonder child of him. Already in his fifteenth year the young Felix produced his first formally completed quartet; at seventeen he brought his opera to the stage in Berlin. Academically and artistically Mendelssohn was mature at an early age, as a creative talent he only accomplished his best in his manhood.[5] And since he was taken away so soon his powers were not destined to come to a standstill; he died at the height of his finest creativity.[6] In Paris, where he wrote the Overture to A Midsummer Night's Dream, and in Rome where he wrote several of his romantic scenes and songs, he could still pass for a youth. In Düsseldorf his talent for orchestral conducting developed, and his whole fresh cheerful nature blossomed into sturdy, self-possessed manliness. There he created his St Paul. Leipzig understood how to win him in the year 1835, and if Berlin knew how to enchain him for a short while, and England repeatedly celebrated the old Christian musician in him, Leipzig nevertheless remained, despite isolated dissonances, his home, the place where he was treated best, the most receptive arena for his temperament, which, for all its unyielding desire for independence, was devoted where it found devotion. By his own admission, nowhere in the world did he have an orchestra that, with slender means, worked so well together, or such a drawing together of all forces for the artistic ends for which his talent strove. Mendelssohn did not create the virtuosity of the instrumental music here; it rested on the broad basis of manifold conditions; but it experienced its flowering with its now deceased master, a youthful master who was so old in knowledge and experience and remained so young in his artistic heart and soul.

This art, that was his, has already required several earlier sacrifices. It seems to make a highly excited nervous life a condition for its priests. For Mendelssohn there was the additional factor that the nervous element was, perhaps, a dominant characteristic of his family. A stroke killed his sister Fanny in Berlin at the piano, at the sacred place in her artistic life. This death, last spring, was almost a portent for him. The visit to his home, only a few weeks before his nervous attack, may have had a shattering effect on his excitable nature. Death stole upon him in the midst of the rehearsals for his Elijah, and as he was called away from his fortune as a man, from his harmony as a musician, as he ascended *ad coelestas harmonias revocatus*, his music has become the mantle that he leaves behind.[7]

More conventional and less penetrating, perhaps, but offering a different perspective, strongly conditioned by knowledge of Mendelssohn's family background and of his later activity in Berlin, was the obituary by Ernst Kossak that constituted the entire contents of a black-bordered issue of the *Neue Berliner Musikzeitung* on 10 November 1847.

Those whom the gods love die young—and he died at the peak of his life and work in the midst of well-established activities, far-reaching plans and great artistic conceptions, he died and left us, apart from his past works and his ashes, the most splendid, comforting thought that such a death, which can tear a powerful man from a rich existence, gives the most beautiful evidence of the immortality of the human soul, for Nature, which allows nothing to be lost from her gentle governing hand, only opens to the striving spirit the eternally

shining door of a temple hall to which he has now ascended over clouds and floating mist: to sacrifice on the
secret altar of heavenly art.

But that is the inner power of such a spirit, the power
of its own light, that his personality, shining brightly over-
the ages, still appears to stand before our eyes, like stars
on the horizon, pouring forth its light for many years,
while the thing itself has nevertheless long been shattered
and strewn among the atoms of the universe.

The words of St John the Evangelist: "short and miserable" have commonly characterized the lives of most of
the dead; to the deceased in question much and good
was given! An unusually early development of his genius
made him into a cheerful and fortunate young creative
musician, at an age when the normal boy clung to his
childish games or allowed the first dreams of adolescence
to come into flower; thus, with fewer years, his life became longer than eighty summers that had not been devoted to such gigantic activity. This boon of fate was not
sufficient for him. The most precious jewel of life: he
bore in himself the character of a man surrounded by
the costly gems of his natural gifts. Born under the most
fortunate circumstances, as the grandson of a Platonic
philosopher, the son of a father who valued the material
things in life only insofar as they might help to foster
higher treasures of the spirit, he was able, on coming
into life, to stretch out his hand for all sorts of things
that are unattainable for millions of others. He stretched
it out and chose a strict and serious life dedicated to art.
Armed with the means to make the venal world serviceable, he entered the arena just like a talented poor man
and fought in the foremost ranks for the laurel wreath
that his incorruptible honesty disdained to purchase. This
wonderfully beautiful trait of character can only be seen
as founded on the inner freedom of his being, which,
nourished by studies of classical antiquity, developed an
aristocrat in art and living of a kind that threatens gradu-

ally to disappear from the present-day world. But these modes of thought in the realm of intellect had yet another particular influence on the character of his activity as a musical artist. The strict logic of academic studies lead the young composer, who was committed to purity of content by his sterling teachers Zelter and Berger, and by family resemblance to the philosopher Mendelssohn, to a similar strictness in the area of musical forms. His intrinsic energy served to consecrate everything that left his hands, so that it could not fail to be raised above the level of merely charming sensuality. He possessed an uncommonly high conception of the essence of music and he made it his life's aim to obtain the goal that also floated before Beethoven as the musical artist's ideal. Nature does not, however, give anyone everything; she imparted to the soul of the deceased that addiction to reflection, arising perhaps from the modesty and inner humility that is only characteristic of great spirits, which he felt about his compositions coming so soon after the incomparable works of Beethoven. He too could feel his soul constrained by the godlike power of that genius. Thus a tender breath of melancholy lay on his spirit, which already fluttered more tenderly over the first works of the youth and clustered more thickly about his last works: that affliction of the human soul, to find oneself standing against the mysterious natural barrier to knowledge of the beautiful, the true and the good.

It is redundant to mention his works; for they are inscribed in the annals of all art-loving peoples of Europe, but as well as this last laurel wreath, which we attempt with too weak a hand to press upon the forehead of the deceased, the names of the most celebrated artistic creations may be ranged around his catafalque like banners of mourning. These are his versions of A Midsummer Night's Dream, the Antigone and his oratorios St Paul and Elijah. If in these two latter works his thoughts about the miracles of the Old and New Testaments join hands over his remains in artistic enlightenment, the former musical settings of the most exalted artworks of the ancient and romantic epochs stand at the foot of his bier as everlasting evidence of his all-embracing, deeply poetical spirit. In his art he reconciled the opposing ages with a gentle spirit. However, we do not for that reason pay any less regard to his smaller works. Descending from his symphonic works, in which treasures of astonishing industriousness and rich golden veins of genius reveal themselves to the connoisseur, we discover at the other end of the scale such animation, even of the smallest forms, that, as in the microscopic life of Nature, only the most severely scientifically and aesthetically equipped eye can encompass all the individual parts in their harmoniousness. As lyricist, he grasped the songs of our poets with deep feeling, and if, excepting one juvenile work, he had only just now dedicated himself to the highest artistic form of musical word setting—the grand tragic opera—this is not a charge of idleness, but much more a cause for admiration at his self-restraint, which, before it would sacrifice the highest perspectives to the requirements of a shallow and pleasure-seeking multitude, would rather deprive itself of the final artistic satisfaction. This was what he meant to us as an artist and as a man of culture.

The tears that follow him will serve better than paltry words to show what he meant as a man to his relations, friends and artistic contemporaries. We remain respectfully silent before the sorrow of a stricken family that has lost such a husband and father; we only look about us in the circle of our contemporaries, from whom a teacher, a model, a beloved friend and promoter of the good is torn, and we honour and marvel at this widespread sympathy and love which the living man enjoyed and which accompanies the dead man to the grave.

One consolation has, to some extent, been left to the inner circle of those to whom he gave his love: he has come back to us for ever, for when he was living the requirements of his artistic duties and his exalted, manly striving for freedom often called him away from the place of his birth.[8] He sleeps, next to the remains of a sister who was spiritually like him, in the Hallischen Friedhof, and he has earned this sleep with the indefatigability of his work and this place with the love of his heart. It is only the last flowers of autumn that adorn his grave; his creations bloom around him in the everlasting spring of immortality.[9]

Many English obituaries focused, understandably, on Mendelssohn's local impact, relating anecdotes of his performances and personal life. An obituary in the *Atlas* clearly expressed what was touched upon in many when it remarked: "The personal influence of Mendelssohn on the progress of music, especially in England, cannot be replaced; and that we shall never see him, hear him, or partake again in the enthusiasm which he excited, is our deepest subject of regret. He was the adopted son of England; he repaid our hospitality and friendship by good offices abroad; and was probably the first who opened a regular musical inter-communication between Germany and England. . . . His personal qualities and accomplishments gained him that ascendancy in English musical society which he employed, in the largest sense, for the good of music."[10]

English attitudes towards Mendelssohn's position in the musical pantheon varied. Davison, in the *Times*, observed that at the time of Mendelssohn's first visit to England he "already promised, with small fear of the promise being unfulfilled, to surpass all his contemporaries and equal any of his predecessors," that "at the age of 25, Mendelssohn was already beyond question the greatest living composer," and that his works were, "now that death has invested their author with the order of the classics, beyond the pale of criticism."[11] Chorley evidently felt that he was giving Mendelssohn the highest status when he stated that "the world of imaginative creation has received no such shock" since the death of Sir Walter Scott.[12] In *Fraser's Magazine* Mendelssohn was characterized as "the great and rising genius of the age," but perhaps not yet quite on a level with his greatest predecessors. Others who might have shared that view would probably have agreed, however, that "if he fell short of the greatest aim, he fell nobly," and that "Mendelssohn's genius can only be appreciated

by reference to that of the greatest masters."[13] Among those who unhesitatingly ranked Mendelssohn with the greatest composers was Macfarren.
His more considered appraisal of Mendelssohn's position, published just
over a year after his death, may be seen as a formulation of the orthodoxy
that was to obtain, virtually unchallenged, in England for several decades.

> Felix Mendelssohn Bartholdy may justly be regarded as
> one of those very few among mankind whose genius at
> once separates them from, by its exalting them above the
> world around them, and unites them to, by its sympath-
> ising with, that world which it extends from the limited
> circle of private personal knowledge to the boundless in-
> clusion of all educated men in all place and in all time;
> as one of those men, whose intellectual superiority, while
> it distinguishes them from the narrow sphere of their
> own social connections, identifies them with that broad
> universe of all human intelligence which ever and every-
> where acknowledges the impersonal presence of a master
> mind, in the influence it produces. The death of this
> truly great musician is so recent as to be still a matter of
> keen regret, not only to those who enjoyed the peculiar
> happiness of his personal acquaintance, but to all who
> love the art of which he was, and always will be, so bril-
> liant an ornament. To society the loss of Mendelssohn is
> irreparable, since with him have died his cordial friend-
> ships, his genial and enchanting manners, his marvellous
> facility of musical improvisation, and his surpassing exec-
> utive power on the organ and the pianoforte; to the art
> his loss is even yet more heavy, since by his death we are
> deprived of the works which he would, had he lived,
> have added to the list of masterpieces that constitute the
> imperishable monument of his immortality; the former
> could have been but for a time, and are, therefore, not
> so much to be lamented by his sincerest friends and
> warmest admirers as the latter, which would have been
> for always, are to be deplored by the whole world, pres-
> ent and future. We have a right to regret these uncreated

works, since, as Mendelssohn died in the prime of life, and in the full vigour of his genius, and as his last productions possess, in addition to the freshness and evident spontaneousness of his earlier compositions, that maturity of development which can only result from experience in writing and thinking with the most highly organised mind, there surely died with him the capacity for equal, if not superior, things to those with which, as it is, he has endowed the world. It is true that Mozart and Weber in his own art, and Rafaelle [*sic*] and Byron in poetry and painting, died all at the same age as Mendelssohn, and all of them, like him, when their genius seems to have been at its point of culmination; from which we may infer that there is some connexion between the exercise of the highest powers of imagination and the physical faculties, which renders that age one of peculiar fatality: and it is rather a confirmation than a contradiction of such a suggestion to adduce that Handel and Haydn wrote their greatest works—those upon which entirely rests that reputation which is henceforth identical with the existence of music—after the age at which those great men ceased to write for ever; since we see that the highest power of imagination, in these composers, was not exercised until after that fatal period; they both completed their mission to the world and ceased to write, having exhausted the intellectual fire within them, some years before their death.

It was, perhaps, not in his lifetime, not until now, that we can review the whole of his works collectively, regarding them rather as one chain of ideas that develops the progress and the entirety of his genius than as so many separate compositions, that the world is capable of assigning to Mendelssohn his true rank as a musician; but now that we have before us a complete panorama of his mind in the whole of its productions, we are justified in the impression so long entertained, that his grade is with the highest, and that we own in him the true associate of Bach, Handel, Haydn, Mozart and Beethoven. His claims to this eminence lie in the purely classical character of all his writing, by which is to be understood not merely cold correctness, but irresistible beauty in the highest style of musical expression; and in the striking originality that so obviously manifests itself in all his works as to give them an individuality which, it is not too much to say, is not to be found in the music of any of the great composers with whose names his is here classed, and which, devoid of mannerism, can hardly be attributed to the collected works of any other musician. This assertion is so strong, and includes so much beyond the immediate subject of the present remarks, that it may require some explanation to justify it; and as this individuality forms a most important characteristic of Mendelssohn's genius, it may not be superfluous to enter somewhat at length into its discussion.

A lengthy discussion follows, with Macfarren claiming that the resemblance of thematic and harmonic material between composers did not necessarily indicate lack of originality. He then went on to consider originality of style, asserting that, although the great composers from Bach to Beethoven were dependent on each other for the development of their style, Mendelssohn can be seen, like Purcell, to be more of an innovator.

This long digression is important to the subject, insomuch as it goes to explain the application of a term which is meant to convey the chief idea of Mendelssohn's excellence, and as it may serve to illustrate the position that this composer takes in relation to those who have preceded him. It will be now to demonstrate, so far as the want of musical examples leaves it possible to do, what are the peculiar claims to originality that Mendelssohn's music possesses. First, then, his phraseology is quite his own; but, while it is made up of such particular progressions as make it always recognisable as his, it has the general clearness, fluency and force that associate it

with all our ideas of what is beautiful. This phraseology
is rendered the more powerful and striking by the support of the harmonies which, although not unusual in
themselves, are peculiar in their rhythmical distribution,
and sometimes in their progression and resolution. It is a
favourite practice of Mendelssohn, sometimes to continue
one note through a long succession of chords—sometimes to continue one chord through a long succession
of what can only be described as passing notes, but
which are of such importance as entirely to influence the
effect of the harmony; to select at random two striking
examples, reference may be made to the opening of the
Ottet for stringed instruments, and to a passage in the
chorus, "Ye Spotted Snakes," in the *Midsummer Night's
Dream.*

A mere general remark upon his harmonies will be
perhaps more to the purpose, which is, that he produces
a peculiarly novel effect by the frequent introduction of
the combinations, or, more particularly, the progressions,
of Bach and his era, as the basis and accompaniment of
his own original phraseology, or of less individual modern passages; and it is not only that he employs these ancient progressions, but, entering into the spirit of them,
he extends its exercise beyond even what Bach himself
with all his infinity of contrivance ever practised.

More striking in itself, and far more important to the
art, is his resolution of certain chromatic discords upon a
principle occasionally hinted at in the middle and later
works of Beethoven, but never carried to such an extent
as it is by Mendelssohn in his earlier works; such for instance as the chord of the minor ninth on the tonic to
the chord of the seventh on the dominant, with the progression of the intervals of the seventh and ninth of the
first chord to the third and fifth of the second, and
many others which it would be here tedious to describe.
There is the more merit in these innovations—discover-
ies they would be better named—on account of their be-

ing in direct violation of all pre-existing rules of harmony; and they evince the greatness of his genius as a philosopher no less than as a musician, by showing him capable of penetrating, through the obscurity and prejudice of the schools, to the truth of nature, and by his most successful practice to lay the foundation of a theory, which in intelligence, in usefulness, in comprehension, and in what constitutes true philosophy, surpasses all that had ever before been advanced in musical and (so far as connected with music) acoustical science—a theory which translates the province of music from art to nature, and so dignifies its investigation, in the scale of human study and research, from the learning by rote of the arbitrary trammels of bygone times and schools, to the examination and comprehension of a subject, the principles of which are as deeply rooted as those of perspective or light itself.

Mendelssohn is again remarkable for great originality of construction; and this, while he preserves the general outline, or certainly its chief features, to which in what has been said of Haydn and his influence on the art allusion has already been made, manifests itself in the novelty of detail, with which this classical outline is filled up. The intermezzo or scherzo of Mendelssohn is a form and style of movement entirely his own. To illustrate that his originality was identical with his genius, and not, as was the case with Beethoven, a gradual modification of the style of others, we find an example of this novel conception in his very first published work, the set of pianoforte quartets dedicated to Goethe, that were composed and printed at a very early age, while he was yet in his pupilage to Zelter, whose correspondence respecting him with Goethe contains such highly interesting particulars of the development of his extraordinary mind. Those who are acquainted with Mendelssohn's music will recognise the originality alluded to in the Ottetto for stringed instruments, which, when he produced his symphony in

C minor for the first time in London, he arranged for the orchestra, and introduced in the place of the original minuet and trio; the first of his instrumental movements in his dramatic music for *A Midsummer Night's Dream*; in the third movement of his symphony in A minor, and in the scherzos of both his pianoforte trios;[14] of all which it would be difficult, if not impossible, to point out the happiest example. The ceaseless excitement, not only of continually springing beauties that each flashes upon the hearer before his attention is released from that which precedes, but also of the intrinsic passion of the music itself that characterises these movements, produces an effect more irresistibly captivating than anything that can be compared with it in the whole treasury of the art, and more completely carries one out of oneself, out of the world about one, out of the cares, the thoughts, the very passions of one's inward heart, to identify one's all of consciousness with the feeling it engenders, in a manner that only a work of highest genius can effect—more completely and unanimously unites an audience with the author than perhaps any one course of thought, or habit of thinking, however variously developed, that has found expression in musical composition.

Another brilliant originality of Mendelssohn is the purely poetical overture; the intention of which is to achieve more a musical than a dramatic effect, and to convey an impression far more comprehensive than the cold critic can receive from the notes alone, without the will so far to meet the author in his meaning as to incline his mind to the suggestiveness which constitutes the chief feature of the work. Something to the same purpose had previously been accomplished in that marvellous masterpiece, the Pastoral Symphony of Beethoven, at least in so far as that purpose is to convey the musical expression, without words, of the influence upon the mind of actual things and actual characters; but in the manner of effecting that purport, and in their method of appealing to the sympathy of their hearers, the overtures to *A Midsummer Night's Dream*, the *Isles of Fingal*, and the *Schöne Melusine*, may be said to stand quite alone. Mendelssohn again exhibits an original style in his oratorios, which is manifest in the generally more dramatic character they possess than the previous works of that class, in the effect of contrast to other pieces, and solemn repose in themselves, which he produces by the introduction of his chorales; and more particularly in *Elijah*, in his avoiding all the conventional, and one may almost say, the, in these days, pedantic parade of fugue-writing, which, by long acceptance, had begun to be recognised as an essential and unexceptional part of the constitution of an oratorio; retaining all of contrapuntal elaboration and ingenious and effective imitation that were necessary to show the earnestness of intention by giving solidity of character to the work, to produce the massive and imposing effect that the subject required, and to give that important musical interest to the composition which was to rank it with the grandest things of its class, rejecting all the mere forms of school-learning, that fetter the genius of a composer and encumber the effect of his work.

In lighter music Mendelssohn has originated a great source of delight to all who have true musical feeling, in his songs without words, for the pianoforte, which as elegant, nay more, often highly impassioned and always exquisitely melodious trifles, have nothing to exceed, and scarcely anything to parallel them: their form is quite their own, and their matter wholly their author's.

To the concerto Mendelssohn has given an entirely original character; in the first place, by the omission of the first tutti, which, albeit in a great number of instances of the previous concertos of some of the best writers for their various instruments, the most interesting portion of the composition, and always the most important, as containing the proposition or announcement of the subjects of which the remainder of the movement was constituted, was still always felt to be a somewhat anomalous delay of the commencement of the solo, in which, and in the performer, must rest the chief attention and interest of the audience; and, in the next place, by the joining together of the three movements, reserving the only complete and satisfactory termination of the work until the entire conclusion. This second feature of Mendelssohn's concertos, which belongs also to his symphony in A minor, was partially anticipated by the occasional union of the adagio and rondo in the works of the same class of other composers; but in these instances the slow movement may generally be said to form rather a somewhat extended introduction to the last than an entirely developed self-interesting portion of the composition, as is the case in the concertos of Mendelssohn, and in the separated movements of his predecessors: there is closer example for it in the symphony in C minor, and the Pastoral Symphony of Beethoven, and in several of that composer's chamber works, where the scherzo and the finale, each being in itself complete as a separate movement, are so connected, the one so entirely growing out of the other, that they cannot be detached in performance. This is the sort of connexion that Mendelssohn makes between his different movements; but what Beethoven does with the two last Mendelssohn does with the whole work. To Beethoven may also be traced the idea of opening the concerto with the introduction of the solo player, of which we find examples in his pianoforte concertos in E flat and in G; but only in so far as the idea was to draw at once the attention of the audience to the principal executant, can it be referred to that original; for in the examples alluded to the introductory solo for the pianoforte is purely preludial, and leads to the usual tutti, which is of the length and importance to the rest of the movements as a sort of proem or argument to the whole, as it was and always had been the custom to make it; whereas, in Mendelssohn's concertos the solo instrument at once announces the chief subject of the movement, and so, not only wakens the attention, but also excites the interest of the audience at the very outset.

Before quitting this branch of our subject, particular mention must be made of the *Midsummer Night's Dream* overture; which, as an example of originality, must always be a perfect marvel of the human mind. A careful examination of all its features, and a comparison of them with all that had previously existed in the writings of other composers; must establish the conviction that there is more that is new in this one work than in any other one that has ever been produced. In the first place, it is a complete epitome of its author's style, containing the type of all the peculiarities of idea, character, phrase, harmony, construction, instrumentation, and every particular of outline and detail for which his style is remarkable; in the second place, it presents many novelties, more than are contained in any other one work, of harmonious combination and progression, and of orchestral arrangement and effect; in the last place, the first thought, the idea, the intention of the work, is as wholly novel as the manner in which it is carried out; and to sum up all, these many and daring novelties are not introduced with the speculative hesitation of an uncertain experimentalist, but with the confidence and with the result of one who had gathered them from the study of a lifetime of experience of ages. And yet Mendelssohn was but sixteen when he produced this wonderful masterpiece. Thus does genius leap at once to the long-sought and carefully-digested conclusion of philosophy!

In fine, Mendelssohn wrote in every class of musical composition, and with equal success in all; and, by the peculiar colouring of his mind, no less than by the novelties of form and detail, he imparted to all an original novelty.

The second part of Macfarren's article consists largely of a broad survey of all Mendelssohn's major works (some comments from which are included elsewhere in relation to the reception of individual works), and it concludes:

> Thus, then, it is seen that Mendelssohn wrote in every class of musical composition, and with equal success in all; and by the peculiar colouring of his mind, no less than by the novelties of form and detail he employed, he imparted to all an originality and novelty.
>
> Having at such length descanted on the merits of Mendelssohn, it will be but justice to him and to others, and to the reader, to adduce what have been pronounced to be his faults. A very few words will dismiss them, and so the heaviest portion of the critic's labour will become the lightest of the reader's. It is true that his melodies are often more fragmentary than continuous—that his compositions abound more in detached, though beautiful phrases, than in streaming, unbroken and unquestionable tune; and it is no less true that he is generally less successful in the composition of slow movements than those of a more exciting and animated character; but true as are both these propositions, there are so many brilliant exceptions to each as to make it a matter of question with his enthusiastic admirers whether the peculiarities referred to were not points of design with him, rather than evidence of inability to avoid them. To conclude: whether we regard him as a musician or as a man, as a poet or as a friend, as an artist or as a companion, the world has known no one more to love while living, more to regret now dead, nor more to honour as only a great genius can be honoured, by the pure study and true appreciation of his works, than Felix Mendelssohn Bartholdy.[15]

49 · Critical Consensus in England during the 1850s

The durability, in England, of the view so forcibly expressed here, in the face of a gradually increasing tendency to challenge Mendelssohn's continuing dominance of contemporary music, is suggested by many articles in the English press during the next three decades. As long as Chorley in the *Athenaeum* and Davison in the *Times* and the *Musical World* remained dominant figures in English music journalism, their unbounded admiration of Mendelssohn enjoyed the status of orthodoxy. In 1852 Chorley, discussing Schumann and Wagner (whom he and others in England inconsistently regarded as the leading representatives of the so-called Young Germany), remarked: "Trial after trial, experience after experience, have led to the same results—to convictions increasing in strength, that, as regards composition—its aims, limits, and means—Young Germany is in a fever which, should it last, will superinduce an epilepsy fatal to the life of music." He then poured scorn on the notion that Schumann was "put forth by Young Germany as superior to Mendelssohn."[16]

In America, although Mendelssohn was greatly admired, it was not felt necessary to bolster his position by traducing all his possible rivals. In 1856, for instance, *Dwight's Journal of Music* in Boston directly challenged this tendency in the British press; having reprinted a number of London reviews of Schumann's *Paradise and the Peri*, the journal observed: "Those from the *Musical World*, like the articles in the same journal last year about Richard Wagner, manifest a disposition to find nothing good in any music emanating from certain recent German composers, whom it is pleased to sweep together into one category, called sarcastically the "Music of the Future." Mr Chorley, of the *Athenaeum*, is equally bitter and systematically opposed to whatsoever hails from that quarter. So is the musical critic of the *Times*, and so are most of the musical oracles of England; while at the same time they claim Mendelssohn to themselves, set him up as the model and *ne plus ultra* of a musician, and abuse the Germans for not publishing every MS work or sketch he left behind him, good, bad, or indifferent."[17] Commenting on this article, and its support for Schumann, The *Musical World* took the opportunity to elaborate its view of the antithesis between Mendelssohn's music and that of the Young Germans.

There is one consoling point in all this vain preaching
up of what is vicious in art—or rather, of what has really
no claim to be denominated *art*—among our cousins,
the Yankees. Those critics who are most enthusiastic
about Wagner and Schumann are always either sneering
at or endeavouring to throw cold water upon the greatest
musical genius of his day—the legitimate successor of
Beethoven (although no more like Beethoven than Schumann is like Wagner—resembling Beethoven alone in
that high instinct which made both disdain to pass off
charlatanism for art). We of course allude to Mendelssohn. It is the same in Germany as in America. In Germany, critics who are shallow enough, or mad enough, to
be proselytes of Wagner, are furious against Mendelssohn,
because Mendelssohn while he lived was a beacon to
warn us from the rocks and quicksands that are always at
hand for the unwary. The observation of certain "intelligent Germans" of Mr Dwight's acquaintance that, "given
half the *ideas* found in *Paradise and the Peri*, Mendelssohn, by his consummate treatment, would have produced a wonder of the world," is merely intended to
convey by innuendo that Mendelssohn had no *ideas*, or
at least not so many as Schumann, which is neither more
nor less than preposterous nonsense.[18]

50 · Critical Dissension in Germany during the 1850s

The continuing consensus in England during the 1850s about Mendelssohn's status, therefore, stands in sharp contrast to the situation in Germany. Although a substantial portion of his music retained much of its
popularity with German audiences, performers and some critics, his reputation was quickly subject to more persistent assaults from quarters that
had already been the source of attacks during his lifetime. Some criticisms
were overtly based on racial grounds;[19] but similar motivation also seems

to have played a significant, if covert, role in apparently musical judgments.[20] This may particularly have been the case with Mendelssohn's sacred music, which sparked controversy in the period immediately following his death. Eduard Krüger, expounded his reservations about Mendelssohn, and especially his sacred music, in a review of the posthumously published *Three Psalms*, op. 78 in 1850:

> Looking at the present score fills us with sorrow on account of the departed bard, out of whose legacy the indefatigable publishers have brought it to light. Sorrow on account of the prematurely deceased, who was to many the greatest phenomenon in the art of the present day. To us he was not this: we believe that, at the same time, more gifted people, not merely in natural creative power, but also in a correct estimation of their powers, worked for the benefit of our art. Choosing a wrong path is in itself a blunder that does not happen to the true genius, or more rarely happens to him than to searching, confused talents. If even Mozart and Beethoven hazarded the sacred domain, which did not suit their nature and gifts, they nevertheless either did not tarry in these errors—for they only touched upon that which was foreign but did not cultivate it—or even in their errant ways they have dispensed the sparks of other lights. All this is different with Mendelssohn. His whole direction in ecclesiastical[21] music is an unsuccessful one. Why should we not say openly that Berlin Christianity is not capable of finding any blossom from the tree of life, since this is clearly demonstrated daily?—If he who has grown great in the busy world, been dissected by criticism, and been long estranged from heavenly simplicity, looks into himself one quiet day and feels the vanity of inflated metropolitan arrogance, and the emptiness and lifelessness of stillborn fashionable forms irritate him—and he feels an unfamiliar warmth, a soft, gentle glow of other worlds and bodies, where there is no more criticism and learned stupidity . . . now indeed this is all praiseworthy and mov-

ing, and certainly indispensable for a new holy life. But
is this all immediately creative, formative, reaching up to
new bliss in life through the most powerful beauty? No!
It is hardly the vestibule of vestibules. A quiet self-
forgetting cry of conversion is only a tiny step towards
that which the holy art wants to and ought to do.

Not every one of these words applies directly to Mendelssohn: distantly, however, they apply to him, who
grew great in the bonds of that spirit of the times which
he sought to cast off: but one is aware that the chains
rattle, even if more quietly than with those of rougher
temperaments.—We must admit that his gently pious
songs at least waver closer to nobler creations than the
average contemporary's unecclesiastical productions. Even
where we observe something that is outwardly more
powerful, or artistically purer, richer creations—in respect
of power the veteran F. Schneider stands to the fore, in
respect of melodic fullness the much misunderstood
Löwe—however, they are no nearer to that which Mendelssohn also seeks. They have perhaps displayed a higher
artistic consecration, but have not revealed ecclesiastical,
highly spiritual poetry.

Krüger went on, at considerable length, to claim that the art of his
own day was scarcely equal to expressing the genuinely sacred, but suggested that it was also impossible to achieve this by imitating the older
forms in which he found his ideal of religious beauty. He seems, however,
to have considered that these older models, created, as he saw it, by men
who were filled by the pious spirit of their time, were capable of inspiring
a new religious art, for he wrote: "Only through revivifying the beauty
of more fortunate times will the path along which we may walk to the
holy sanctuary be found. That means no imitation, repetition, relishing
the past and reconstruction: it means rather: Return to truth, penetrate
into the true bright depth of the stream of living water, which today we
only hear roaring in the distance.—Perhaps so that a fulfilled, brightly
peaceful time is granted to our great grandchildren, in which, out of the
blessed simplicity of Eccard[22] and the proud excellence of Handel and

the simmering depths of Sebastian [Bach] a new one will be born, who
will celebrate the new-born evangelical church. There, however, there will
certainly be neither *St Paul* nor *Elijah*, nor Berlin penitential psalms, but
rather a new illuminating word from age-old springs, before which false
sickly humility blanches, and smooth vanity flees weeping."

Krüger then returned to the subject of Mendelssohn's music:

> We have already often tried to show how every exalted
> path was entirely denied, and the broad wealth of heroic
> forms remained unreachable, to the soft, amiable virginal
> feelings of our Mendelssohn. *St Paul* and *Elijah* proved it;
> their fame lasted an hour, their glory was tied to the
> contemporary activity of the amiable bard and has died
> with him.[23] That may well be a bitter truth. Yet it does
> not concern him alone, but also the time, which he
> could not escape. If we would give all his oratorios and
> sacred works for the charming, scented beauty of his
> youthful songs, for the fanciful romanticism of his won-
> derful overtures, we only acknowledge his inner being as
> he himself recognized it in peaceful hours. He stands
> with respect to gifts and capacity at approximately the
> same level as Em[anuel] Geibel.[24] Within these con-
> straints he is beautiful and good, indeed powerful, like
> Geibel, in the pretty miniature painting of this time;
> what lies beyond he could yearn for with anguish but
> not grasp in palpable reality.

At this point Krüger launched into a sharply critical appraisal of *Three
Psalms*, op. 78, in which he twice referred to "rabbinical" declamation,
concluding:

> The result of this consideration is not agreeable. We have
> tarried unwillingly over such negative matters. But it is
> the duty of criticism and history, from time to time, to
> look for a conclusion concerning the great departed, and
> for the sake of his fame to speak the truth.
> If in doing so we have pierced a tender feeling heart,

belonging to the new Berlin religion, then we are sorry
about the heart but not about the religion; for it is necessary to eliminate from the latter what sickly philosophy
has concealed in it, and only then is the new renewed
yet old-original beauty, which sounds and resounds and
ignites an eternal fire like the old prophets, possible. As
long as warm pulsating life is strangled and distilled by
the air pump of fantasizing vanity, there is no living
beauty.—A long time ago, a deep-feeling man—no Berliner—personally reproached me from a true heart, that I
had so critically pulled *Elijah* apart. To him in the first
instance these words are spoken: perhaps they will convince him that these animadversions are uttered not out
of pleasure in negativity, but with the intention of final
and eternal affirmation.[25]

The man referred to in the last paragraph, Wilhem Wauer, took
Krüger's remark as a challenge. His response, which is probably more
representative of the feelings of German musicians and music lovers than
Krüger's views, provides a lively illustration of the polarities of opinion
about Mendelssohn's sacred music in Germany at that time. As it so
clearly reveals the stance of those who revered Mendelssohn's music, and
their perception of his place in the development of mid-nineteenth-
century music, it is included here in full. Beginning pointedly with a
poem by Emanuel Geibel, Wauer wrote:

Having just returned from a journey to Dresden—which,
amid the storms of winter, was extended to three full
days as a result of the sudden postponement of the concert and breakdown of the trains—where we had been
lured by a brilliant performance of Robert Schumann's
Paradise and the Peri, on which occasion all the praise
and all the criticism of this work, which is so rich in
highly poetic beauties as in notable weaknesses, to which
Dr Krüger has devoted his time, swam vividly before our
eyes, we find in no. 1 of this journal a detailed review,
from the pen of the aforementioned critic, of the *Three*

Psalms, op. 78, by Mendelssohn-Bartholdy, which have just appeared in print. Now, indeed, it probably does not require another journal article to rescue the value of Mendelssohn's sacred works from the critical knife even of such a learned reviewer as Dr Krüger; in any case we would have left it to others to throw further light on the ideas expressed in that essay about the artistic direction and the ranking of the pious creations of the deceased master, if the close of the article, which referred to me, had not caused me for once to enter the lists publicly against Herr K., with particular reference to his views about Mendelssohn.

The letter cited by him had the aim of inciting the ingenious author to a worthy discussion of *Elijah*, in that I hoped he would powerfully counter the unprecedentedly superficial, unworthy reviews of this work, demonstrating impudent lack of feeling, which had been published here and there at that time. I did not then know his own article about *Elijah* in the *Neue Zeitschrift für Musik* and therefore had no idea that I had invited an opponent to be an advocate. Herr K.'s statement is therefore not precise, at least it could refer to a reproach about a deed of which I did not yet know anything.— This explanation seemed necessary, for the sake of general understanding.

In any case it is pleasing that for once Herr Dr K. has seriously gone on the record and brought his views into the open. This way it should be easier for those of contrary opinion to find firm ground on which a battle can be fought. As K. very properly remarked, it is indeed a matter of the greatest importance that the world gradually becomes clear about the whole nature of a great departed one, and it may therefore be permissible that a weak champion, who in any case, as Herr K. can already see from the opening of the article, is not a one-sided, exclusive Mendelssohnian, be first in the field, in the expectation that better troops are in readiness to continue the fight with greater force if he himself must retreat with bloody wounds.

The new psalms discussed by Herr K. are not yet known to us, we shall not, therefore, touch upon anything that was said concerning them in particular for the time being, and shall focus on the critic's general observations. K. starts from the point of view that the present day is absolutely incapable of producing any true church music, least of all in the circles of those who have grown up in metropolitan Berlin. For this reason, too, the true spirit of the church could not live in M.'s sacred works. These contain only a shallow reflection of the holy sounds of the good old time, not even sounds springing from a holy heart and life.—If such a certification of impotence for a whole period is already in itself a curious thing, one must already be careful about prejudgments that concern a particular circle, so it is doubly wretched to deny that even in such a disrupted and distracted time individual souls can always be found in whom Christianity, the content of a man's life that reaches out beyond the earthly, has put down roots firmly and extensively enough to be able to find sufficient nourishment and power in itself, so that it will not be led astray by the raging, bewildered cry of the masses. Such people have appeared in every period, and it is precisely these that are the germ for more beautiful universal renewals in the future; and what is to prevent us from believing that our dear departed master was one of these? He may have lived in and with the world, he may not have drawn shyly back from contact with the press of humanity about him, but even Herr K. does not seem to want to deny that he retained a pious and virginal soul. The present writer, to his deep sorrow, did not know the noble departed personally, but what he heard and read about him can only confirm him in his belief. If one were to accept all this it would remain for Herr K. to show in which qualities of Mendelssohn's sacred works their unecclesiasticalness and sickliness lay. Eccard, Bach, Handel appear for Herr K. to be the universal representatives of church music, in the sense that he considers to be orthodox, the only ones who knew how to reproduce the expression of the true and genuine church of their day, as of all times. We freely admit that little or nothing is known about Eccard as man and Christian. Sebastian Bach certainly lived as a true servant of his church, though his whole tendency was that of the so-called pietists, and his immortal works probably do not reveal much of the spirit of the defunct church of that time, but are the effusion of his subjective Christian, warm heart in a form and manner of expression over which people would rightly shake their heads if a modern Christian composer tried to bring them to us anew. Furthermore, Bach did not sink such deep roots in his own time, and it was left to the more recent period to take him more securely to heart.—But let us agree, Herr Dr Krüger, the form is not the main thing, it is the spirit that dwells in it.—But it may only be given to a minority nowadays (and not merely weaklings) to sink themselves into those mysterious depths, in order triumphantly to dig out the rich booty of the spirit, and for this reason we require from our masters new, not antique treasures, old wine in new bottles, the same divinely inspired heart, yet with prayers in new versions.—Handel only threw himself into the realm of oratorio, initially out of ambition, when he could no longer maintain himself in the field of opera. It was a fortunate step; here he achieved great things. It is probably impossible to tell whether he himself was a devoted Christian, though one assumes it from his works. We are happy to accept it; but Handel, like Bach, did not live at a time when Christianity was actively pervasive, at least the stark, cold literalness of their period was a powerful enemy of the spiritual life and Christian ardour, yet we consider their works to represent the most genuine ecclesiastical sounds.

What, therefore, gives us grounds to assume that, through the fault of his time, Mendelssohn could not have been capable of creating the ecclesiastical, the truly pious? It is all the clearer that he wrote out of the impulse of his own heart, he, who must have known only too well that the tendencies of the present day were not conducive to such forms. And yet he devoted his best powers to this genre, and still saw the more elevated as the keystone of his artistic career. In what, therefore, is the lack of dedication, the flatness of the works of our master to be found? Do they lack majesty, dignity, inner richness? There is nothing more to prove, is that not so, Herr Dr Krüger?—It is bad enough for someone whose feeling, conception, negativity is balanced by the feeling, the conception, the affirmation of thousands. Is a composer who chose the whispering of elves, love songs, romantic overtures, Greek tragedies for his music, perhaps inherently incompetent to produce ecclesiastical creations? One or the other! No-one can serve two masters!— Where in Mendelssohn's "religious" works can Herr K. show something undignified, common, frivolous in the portrayal of Christian elements, in the manner of Rossini's *Stabat Mater*? Where does the solemn lack solemnity, the noble nobility, the sublime sublimity, the gentle lack pious tenderness and softness, without weakness? Where does Mendelssohn depict repentance, contrition, sorrow of death in tones of worldly pain? Power and abundance of melody, beautiful, pure, rich construction; where is the deficit of these? Does Herr Dr K., despite his assurance to the contrary, not want to see majesty, greatness where he encounters them? Is it, in sacred works (oratorios are not church music), a sin not to suppress the tender fragrant breath of romanticism, which K. admiringly picks out in our master's songs and overtures, or to depict the solemn, and even the disturbing, in a poetic guise? Are there not therefore moments in *St Paul, Elijah, Lobgesang*, in the three grand psalms such as cannot be discerned by any human eye in the works of the immortals exclusively revered by Herr K.? Are not, for instance, the Motets op. 69 an outpouring of the purest childlike piety that can be imagined? May Christianity and the divine in general only be delivered to mankind in the strictest forms, and does it cease to be Christian and divine with the abandonment of the form? The student from Halle in velvet gown, imbibing Christian wisdom from a Tholuck teacher during a cheerful walk, is just as dear to us as the priest in Talar. But let us take Mendelssohn's oratorios and psalms in the way they are intended, not merely for churches and sacred places (Handel's creations too do not all belong there), let us take them as solemn piety and ardent faith carried out into the world, as missionary sermons in a free, appealing form. What use is it, then, always to conjure up the old again and again, the old which the new master has brought closer to us in a more understandable and accessible manner, without denying the pure source from which he strengthened his youthful power, the old which is reconciled once more with a world alienated from God precisely by this new thing, and which, without the new mediator, would, with few exceptions, long have become distant and alien to the present day. The rest we shall gladly leave to the future, but when Herr K. says that the fame of *St Paul* and *Elijah* has died with their creator, we really do not know through what spectacles he perceives the world about him. It may, therefore, be that Mendelssohn was more gentle and tender than Bach and Handel, for that reason he is also not the Bach or Handel of the eighteenth century; rather, he occupies their place in the nineteenth, just as the founder of a future evangelical church will not be a St Paul or a Luther, but nevertheless a man who in his own way can do something similar. Furthermore, it is interesting to see which master of our time Herr K. would place above Mendelssohn in many respects. Fr[iedrich] Schneider, Loewe,

Hiller, Chopin, Schumann, Gade. We hardly think that all these significant men, the worthy creator of *Das Weltgericht* at their head, would give Herr K. their sincere thanks for this acknowledgment; it is scarcely conceivable that they themselves would believe in such fame.

Schumann and Gade, the two inspired sons of art, the two brilliant stars in the heaven of musical poetry, even they ought for the present to turn in on themselves and quietly wrestle with themselves, so that they might in truth deserve this position. Their most recent works show no advance. Gade's Octet appears to suffer from many deficiencies, Schumann's Adventlied, words by Rückert, is, always excepting great individual beauties, a tedious work, not even rich in flow and verve, with very many forbidden "second progressions." However, we still think very highly of the former for the sake of the excellent compositions of previous years.

So we have more or less touched upon that which initially needed to be said; this little essay is certainly not complete and exhaustive; may the important subject still be discussed from very many sides with serious and thorough consideration of the essence of the matter.

Of the works that have so far been published from Mendelssohn's legacy, *Athalie* and *Lauda Sion*, both beautiful complete works of art, are by far the most significant and substantial. Whether it were beneficial to have published the Sechs Sprüche for eight-part chorus, op. 79, we leave undecided. They are simple, unassuming choral pieces, without particular significance. In the first of them the main theme from *Athalie* is reused, and, indeed, not to the same words, as is the case with a passage from the second of the three psalms reviewed by Herr K., to the words: "Was trübst du dich, meine Seele," etc. (see the master's 42nd psalm). The deceased probably did not intend all these things for general circulation, and we are therefore not clear whether it was a good thing to let such posthumous pieces see the light of day. There are music lovers lacking sufficient piety, who, on the basis of such occasional pieces, belabour their creator despite the legion of his truly imperishable masterpieces.

We close now with the conviction that we shall, in the first place, have succeeded in changing Herr Dr Krüger's opinion just as little as he achieved this result with us; but we wish, as has already been said above, that, as long as it remains necessary because of hostile criticism, our attempt might provide the impetus for the further extension of a dome of reasoned defence to be erected over the green spring forest of Mendelssohn's creations.[26]

Krüger's response to Wauer followed a couple of months later in the same journal. It is unnecessary to reproduce the majority of the text, which generally reiterates points from the earlier article, elaborated with often obscure, quasi-theological arguments; but a few of Krüger's remarks cast further light on aspects of contemporary opinion. At one point Krüger turned to the question of Mendelssohn's character:

It is natural that our opponent thinks here of the personality. Mendelssohn achieved more through personal amiability than through the depth of his works. I advance this opinion without having met him personally, just like my opponent. Personal influence expresses itself as secretively as every higher faculty. No-one but the ego and God sees the innermost aspect of a person. It is the same too with piety. No-one can see this, no-one prove, only sense, feel, imagine. One can see works of art and draw conclusions from them about their origins. Naturally, it is true that all human judgment is deceptive. Therefore, if Leipzig and Berlin worshipped the spiritual prophet in Mendelssohn and the worldly one in Meyerbeer, that is just as deceptive as if an individual disagrees. Truth is not revealed by a majority of votes.[27] The decisive judgment cannot be founded on personal or other external motives, only on deeper scrutiny of the works and the sincere commitment of the heart.

At one point Krüger also touched upon the question of the critical reception of Mendelssohn's works: "How was it a few years ago? All the papers rejoiced over the *Antigone* and its reception by the enlightened public in Berlin, while very quietly a few odd fellows whispered that the thing was damned tedious, but people were cautious. . . . A few years later people said it openly. The censorship, which gave rise to the trivial opinion of the press, is as evident here as anywhere. About the year 1841 a sharp criticism of M's *Walpurgisnacht* could not be published in Leipzig, since several editors rejected it: it wandered therefore to the literary journal in Hamburg and found acknowledgment even among keen admirers of Mendelssohn." And he concluded with a judgment on the future of the composer's reputation: "Mendelssohn's sacred works will have faded away in a generation. Beethoven has been dead for a generation and Mozart for two—no-one calls them outmoded, they dwell among us. Of the soft, virginal Felix the sweet juvenile songs will remain, they are immortal: apart from these probably a few of the excellent instrumental works, not all; of the so-called sacred pieces, little or nothing."[28]

A broader view of Mendelssohn's career and legacy as a whole was taken by Wilhelm Heinrich Riehl.[29] His appraisal provides a particularly thoughtful and informative assessment of the extent of Mendelssohn's influence on German music during his lifetime, and the nature of his popularity.

> About twenty years ago, in the present musical period,
> the romantic school ruled, like an ageing queen who had
> seldom been more aware of her earlier nobility, a musical
> "Young Germany," whose enthusiasm, like that of the literary one, was centred on Paris, began to gain ground;
> Meyerbeer at its head sought to bring new elements to
> the sensitive nature of Weber and Spohr, by means of overexcitement, audacious mixing of styles, and highly original distorted forms that astonished the musical rabble;
> and Rossini's and Bellini's enticing manner resounded

quite at its most sonorous throughout the whole of Germany.

At that time a young man appeared whose endeavour caused a sensation, because it appeared so unusual, who took little notice of Paris and Italy, who occasionally ignored Mozart and Haydn yet consulted all the more diligently what Handel and Bach had written. He revivified in a craftsman-like manner the old forms of these fundamentally powerful yet rough masters and took pains to re-naturalize the old chaste seriousness into music that had become frivolous. He even wanted to smuggle back into the concert hall the old artistic fabric of counterpoint, which the majority of musicians used almost to equate with the lost secret of the mediaeval mason's huts! But he did not merely stick to the pure, boldly intricate forms; he wanted to be a real tone poet, a tone poet in the spirit of the age; and that which the romantics, indeed, which the Young Germans claimed as their own, sounded out even from his classical forms, in a manner often wonderfully exciting, sometimes coquettishly witty, also at times very singular and contradictory.

At this many connoisseurs of art wrinkled their noses and said: "That is certainly a very extraordinary man, what a pity he is 'merely a peculiarity.' " By this they meant that it was only a beautifully flowering tree that stood alone and would bear no fruit.

Now twenty years have passed and we have already buried the man, but not forgotten him—Felix Mendelssohn Bartholdy. About the "peculiarity" there is something to say. It has prevailed, not with this or that person, no, it has become universal, the whole of musical Germany became more or less infected by this Mendelssohnian "peculiarity"; it did not make its way suddenly and by force, it penetrated like a fine, persistent May rain, which is well known to penetrate most deeply. Mendelssohn did not gain what one calls "éclat" with any-individual work, as Meyerbeer had, and yet when he died everyone said that he had been the greatest of living composers. In that respect this musician is unique among artists of our time. What, then, had he chiefly written? What others do not write, because no-one wants to hear them: oratorios and church music, cantatas, symphonies, quartets, sonatas. Very many German musicians compose in the same genres out of an irresistible urge, but also with the painful awareness that such works will be left on the shelf for ever. Mendelssohn was almost the only lucky one who was still permitted to write in these genuine forms of the German spirit, who everywhere brought serious works to performance and publication; in recent years he was truly in command of music and of the public as a brilliant master always should be, yet so seldom can be. He was too clever not to accommodate himself to the whims of the prevailing taste now and then, but he was also too proud ever to have allowed this to be overtly noticeable. He often composed like a true diplomat. In the end, admittedly, he did not need to work diplomatically, for his peculiarity had itself become the prevailing taste, and hundreds, consciously or unconsciously, followed Mendelssohn's path; and now there is hardly a choral society in a small country town that does not think it a point of honour to sing the choruses of Mendelssohn—the "learned" Mendelssohn.

Mendelssohn had become the first master in a long time who once again centralized the musical taste of Germany in a particular direction. A special topography of our German musical life will shortly be opportune. For unfortunately our composers may now be more conveniently grouped entirely externally according to mountain tops and flood plains than according to internal art-historical criteria. Our musical separatism is even greater than the political, for it is far more accidental and arbitrary than that. There is at the present time Viennese, Berlin, Hamburg, Leipzig music; German Music has become a historical term, like German Empire.[30] Since Mendelssohn has died, one can no longer say of any of the younger tone poets that he has a German public. At most a couple of song writers and a few mediocre talents in the frivolous opera style have become popular everywhere. Robert Schumann is fêted as a messiah by the trendsetters in the region of the river Elbe, but the Thuringian woods are already the watershed of this fame. How many people know Schumann's larger works in the south and west of Germany? I am no admirer of Schumann's muse, but just as I wish that it might universally find the correct critical appraisal, I also wish that it might be universally known. Richard Wagner is an artistically extravagant man, but nevertheless a phenomenon of which one must take notice. But how many opera stages, indeed, how many musicians beyond a narrow circle have taken notice, practically, of his creations? Hebbel may pass for a congenial literary manifestation. Almost all large theatres tried his dramas once, not to proclaim adherence to their aesthetic tendencies but because they considered it a point of honour, so to speak, to take literary-historical notice of this idiosyncratic poet. Of such a point of honour next to nothing is known in the musical world. The difficulty of getting to hear a Wagner opera, which has so far existed, has driven the expectation of these works unduly high, far higher than all Wagner's brochures together with the proclamations of his friend Franz Liszt could ever have done.

We have lost all centralization of our musical literature. The state of our poetical literature is golden compared with this pitiful splintering. The Austrian lyricists, a Lenau, Zedlitz Grün, etc. are directly recognized as German poets. Yet it only seems like yesterday that we doubly celebrated these men in the "empire"[31] as the heralds of German spiritual culture for that eastern-border state. A whole series of not unworthy Austrian song composers ranged themselves alongside the aforementioned lyric poets. But with the exception of precisely the most superficial and mannered of them, their names have hardly penetrated to the north; with their songs it will take a good while yet. By the by, we recall the statement which was published some years ago as given out by one of the leading Viennese music publishers, the content of which was that he published only "Austrian music!"

Only Mendelssohn's musical lyric has lastingly established itself in all German lands.

For German opera there are half a dozen stock exchanges. Such as Berlin for the north-east, Hamburg for the north-west, Frankfurt for the south-west, etc. Success in these places firmly fixes the exchange rate of a new work—not for Germany, no, only for the river system, the mountain formation which encloses the other towns that are dependent on the relevant stock exchange. Thus here too we have musical topography. An opera has brilliant success in the whole area of the Frankfurt clay-slate and sandstone area, in the whole region of the Munich chalk area, however, it flops, and *vice versa.* Germany no longer possesses a musical capital. At the end of the eighteenth century Vienna was one, before that for a time Leipzig-Dresden, Hamburg and other towns. Now music becomes ever more narrowly localized. Whoever wants to move musical Germany must look outside his own borders to find the Archimedean point from which he must apply the lever. Meyerbeer sought and found this point in Paris. His success converted a whole series of German opera composers to the belief that they had to be untrue to Germany if they wanted to take musical Germany by storm.

Even in church music, which had already been centralized to the point of paralysis at times, the greatest inconsistency is now apparent. The field in which even the greatest mistress of centralization, the Catholic Church, was unable to centralize, is one in which one might certainly have thought that no man could succeed. Each cantor, each organist, each cathedral choirmaster composes his own masses, Marian hymns, motets, preludes; none of them takes any notice of the others. How could a consensual artistic direction be created there?

And yet Mendelssohn succeeded superlatively in doing this. He set the whole of musical Germany astir, wondering whether he might apply the lever in Germany itself.

However, in Mendelssohn's case, too, this was only possible because of a peculiar social position that he gained in the artistic world. He was the first musician who actually made music for "fine society"—in the best sense of the term. He was not the gnarled, self-contained German burger, like Bach, but a versatile, cultivated, socially adroit, wealthy, exquisitely mannered man, personally known in almost the whole of Germany, in demand in all select circles. What a tremendous contrast with the old musicians of the previous century! Thus Mendelssohn also wrote in the spirit of this cultivated society, which now spread itself evenly and by proxy into all classes. He made the serious forms of the old strict chamber music more elegant, cleaner and more refined, he chastened and bridled the aesthetic slovenliness of modern salon music, he sought to enliven church music with a more subjective aptness of feeling, so one can say that Mendelssohn's chamber music, concert music, pieces for the salon and for the church may all equally well be performed in select social circles. That is the levelling effect of modern culture. One would profane a piece of Bach's church music if one were to perform it at teatime; a piece of Mendelssohn's church music is not thus profaned, rather it lifts and ennobles the tone of the tea party. Mendelssohn is always ingenious, always discriminating in his use of form. At his first appearance it was something quite new to encounter a modern, elegant musician whose work could also be enjoyed by someone with a finely cultivated intellectual and artistic spirit without constantly stumbling over a crude violation of

musical logic or without having to be irritated by unsym-
metrical forms, a musician who wrote songs without
choosing the silliest texts, wrote chamber music without
being tedious, and salon music without being frivolous, a
tone poet of Jewish extraction whose style was free of
Jewish mannerisms,[32] while almost all the favourite
Christian composers of the day employed an exaggerated
Jewish manner.[33] It is the present North German delicacy
and versatility of culture, with its smoothing out of all
rough national characteristics, that found expression in
Mendelssohn's music.

In small and individual aspects of execution Mendelssohn was new and individual, as a whole not; he created
no new categories of musical form, but only reformed
and ingeniously extended the old ones.[34] Here too the
spirit of our modern refined society is reflected. Mendelssohn possessed a sure aesthetic and art-historical knowledge of the character appropriate to each individual category of musical composition and worked accordingly
with the sureness of the finished master. The pig-headed
stubbornness that, boasting here of the right of its subjective genius, breaks the ban of custom and tradition
was alien to him. Beethoven, in the "Dona nobis pacem"
of his *Missa solemnis* wants to show us, theological Germans, by means of that notable trumpet duet, that one
could also supplicate for the peace of God with trumpets
and drums. Berlioz has imitated him in this in his Requiem, in which he uses the big drum to beg the Lord for
peace for the departed. Joseph Haydn, in his childlike
joyfulness composed a Kyrie Eleison to which one could
dance. Of such bold liberties of true and false genius
Mendelssohn knew absolutely nothing. He knew, on the
contrary, that such extravagant or naive things would
scarcely suit an experienced, cultivated man in our civilized society.

In terms of cultural history, therefore, Mendelssohn is
no less a characteristic personality for the present than

Bach was for his time. No other art can show a man who, in his artistic work, stood so much in the middle of the social life of our cultivated circles and who in addition was so comprehended and valued by them as Mendelssohn.

Whereas a hundred years ago people were certainly not of one mind about what they should make of the isolated, profound Bach, we now, forthwith, have a truly universal opinion about Mendelssohn, and it is difficult to say anything further to the point about him that would not already be a generally accepted view.

Mendelssohn's influence must forthwith become a universal one, for the "cultivated society" in which he worked and lived, in whose spirit he created, is the same throughout Germany. Bach, by contrast, in his tough social confinement, also remained confined locally in his work and fame as a composer for a very long time.

Now it is evident in any case with Mendelssohn that much, particularly in his larger works, is painstakingly constructed, that he knew how to compose just as cleverly as Lessing delineated things, and his work very often seems to be inspired by true genius where, however, it is only the result of an extraordinary talent; that he still always fell short of the free genius of a Mozart and Beethoven by that infinitely small fraction that would have to be added to the weight of talent so that it might become genius, but which he never could add. Yet this should not be allowed to infringe on Mendelssohn's greatest glory, namely, the glory of his purifying, reformative work. For this calling he possessed a single fundamental condition, which everyone could envy him. He was the fortunate one who alone succeeded in remaining strict, serious and pure in his creations, and yet—in becoming popular. The advantage of his personal circumstances helped him no less than his giftedness and tenacious determination to fight for and seize this rare fortune. Mendelssohn the musical purifier will be far more painfully missed by the nation than Mendelssohn the creative tone poet. Hardly, for example, had his oratorio *Elijah* become available to wider circles, than societies from all around hastened to rehearse that difficult and, for amateurs, very ungrateful work. Germany may possess one or other master who could write an equally excellent work of this type, but it certainly does not possess another on the strength of whose name alone such music, which has to be honestly studied and yet will only be enjoyed and understood by few, would immediately penetrate into all levels of musical society; with Mendelssohn we have lost the only man who could everywhere blaze a trail for a serious work.

Anyone who wants to give him his just due should make people consider how many thousand he has driven to the study of Handel and Bach and how, for the whole nation, he created through his works a new understanding of these men, who remain a blazing glory for all time and whom we had so long forgotten. Indeed, some who otherwise only wished to hear Parisian or Italian music were once again actually given a desire for German music by Mendelssohn. Thus one clearly sees how much more effectively the direct influence of artistic activity works than any amount of preaching and teaching. For long enough eager judges of art had already fruitlessly drawn attention in words to Bach's and Handel's example; when Mendelssohn set their admonitions in notes he struck home with a single stroke.

Mendelssohn never betrayed his nationality; how very few German masters can stand alongside him in this respect! Very many of them, in fact, write in an unGerman spirit without ever realizing that they are doing so. For of all the arts music is still the one that is commonly practised in the most thoughtless manner. Whereas poetry and visual art allow the deep changing relationships of the whole life of the nation to pour in on them, the work of the majority of composers is deter-

mined by chance or, at best, by a lucky instinct. The result of this is that music, despite its having apparently
become so powerful, has so very little purifying and ennobling effect on the spiritual life of the nation as a
whole. Mendelssohn consciously chose for himself a position of national effectiveness. Many musicians could forgive him everything except this one thing.

In this respect it is a rare quirk of history—or perhaps
even something more—that Mendelssohn should not
have brought another opera to fruition. Formerly it
could be accepted that one carelessly composed an opera
overnight and precisely in this way it could best succeed,
but this has changed. Nowhere but in opera had such a
fundamental penalty to be paid as the interruption, for
half a musical generation, of more profound artistic education, and Mendelssohn, to whom one has conceded
this education so ungrudgingly, who was perhaps
uniquely in a position to release German opera from its
prevalent imperfection,—had to die when he had hardly
finished the first act of an opera.

That restorative tendency by means of which German
historical painting has recently won such significant vic-
tories has also taken root in music with Mendelssohn, indeed, it has become a characteristic feature of present-day
music. Just as Overbeck, Veit and Steinle painted the
biblical stories, about which for a long time people
wanted to know nothing, in the strict old manner, Mendelssohn wrote his oratorios, his church music; but he
did not stop with the ecclesiastical, nor did he cling as
single-mindedly as they did to the old and outmoded,
for which reason his horizons were world-wide, his work
more vital and more appropriate to the times, although
he was also not always successful in mastering completely
the painstakingly created, the manufactured. If an effective historical school establishes itself in our music,—and
we shall wager much that it must and will come in the
near future—then Mendelssohn will be called the fore-

runner of this school. We would like to implore the younger generation beside the grave of the master not to forget that this is the great inheritance which he left to us and also to take care that such an inheritance is brought to light.

Mendelssohn's place in the history of art could be compared to that which is occupied by the Carracci in the history of Italian painting. They too purified the degenerate art, in that they turned back to the study of the old classical masters, in that, sustained at first by theoretical awareness—like Mendelssohn—they created ingenious, well-devised works. One designates the movement which they founded as that of the eclectics. This name could be applied equally well to Mendelssohn, who, with art-historical awareness, also collected and unified into a whole all the merits of earlier schools, which is not only new in its parts but also in its compound. It always signifies a period of overripeness, of fading if it is necessary for the artist to look backwards in order thus to get inspiration for new creations from the study of more fortunate predecessors. Is that now also the situation in the history of music? Does not the excess of playing with form, do not the exaggerations of purely technical effects seem awfully similar to the manifestations of decadent historical painting? The Carracci were unable to stem the incoming tide of corruption; will the Mendelssohnian school be able to do it in the long run?

By taking Handel, Bach and Beethoven as the principal foundations for the further development of modern music, Mendelssohn furthermore gave rise to a major transformation not merely in the end product but also in the common historical point of view. Where possible Mendelssohn effectively ignored precisely those masters who, until then, were almost universally regarded as the genuinely classical ones—Mozart and Haydn, particularly the latter. His whole orientation is also, in fact, an indirect polemic against theirs. That is easy to understand, for that very degeneration of modern music, against which Mendelssohn fought so manfully, was rooted on the one hand in the misunderstanding of Beethoven, but on the other in an insipid shallowness that went back in a straight line to the mechanical imitators of Mozart and Haydn. The latter orientation made itself evident in the [eighteen] twenties in a manner that seems almost precisely similar to the contemporaneous blossoming of "almanach" poetry, Clauren-like novel writing and Raupach-like play writing. It is obvious that this kind of music, which loses itself in the shallows of the most barren triviality, must have been particularly distasteful to a man like Mendelssohn, and if, recently, such silly musical twaddle also decked itself out with the discarded tinsel of German and French neo-romanticism, it was not vanquished, since the philistine is, after all, immortal. Mendelssohn reacted against this in that, by means of Handel, Bach and Beethoven, he wanted to make us forget the Viennese classical school. In this he succeeded beyond measure and one must understand that, despite his classical spirit, he knew better than even the musical Young Germans and Neo-romantics how to put the nice, clear cosiness of Mozart and Haydn out of circulation.

But by this one-sidedness he primarily made himself suffer. For in Mendelssohn we often miss very sorely that which is precisely Mozart's and Haydn's greatest achievement in comparison with the period of Handel and Bach, namely, the harmonic roundness of the total work, the wise economy of the whole, the youthful vitality of inspiration. Mendelssohn's larger works are always plastic and harmonious in all their individual parts, but the plasticity of the whole is lacking in most of them. This comes to the fore most sharply in *Elijah*, where one beauty effectively strikes the other dead, where among so many excellent individual aspects no larger group could be separated out and thus the whole yet again contains a certain monotony of colouring. For that reason Mendelssohn's smaller works, where he could not make this mistake, create a much more immediate impression than his large ones. Already in the excessive spinning out of the theme, to which a one-sided study of Bach and Beethoven easily leads, that lack of wise economy is revealed. The more the music departs from its natural simplicity, the more it becomes a learned composition, the more broadly the theme is spun out. This is even more noticeable in Spohr than in Mendelssohn, and especially in the ageing Spohr. In the old days the themes were short-winded, disjointed; Mozart and Haydn expanded them to concise and precise dimensions that combined brevity and roundness; Beethoven not infrequently even exceeded the bounds of correct proportion in this respect. It is always the sign of incipient degeneration in art when its simple basic forms become excessively extended. And here is the Achilles heel of the otherwise so moderately noble Mendelssohnian technique.

But we shall take another look back at Mendelssohn's reforming mission.

Is it not a national disgrace that the Germans now vie with the Parisians in their superficial opera genres, their fantasies, études and rondos, neglect those sublime forms, the oratorio, sonata, symphony and quartet, which stem from the depth of the German spirit? Mendelssohn was entirely a national master in that he made it his whole life's mission to re-establish respect for these noble forms. And thus it happened that he quite easily fell into a frigid elegance when he occasionally composed "salon music": when, on the other hand, he composed a German song, a piece of church music, a sonata, he always joyfully opened his heart. That should be a lesson and a warning to others.

Mendelssohn did his best to give his larger works the greatest possible perfection, but it is precisely in his smallest ones that he showed himself to be most perfect— in his songs—and this is not his least claim to fame.

Mendelssohn treated the German song, from the artless folk style to the verses of Heine, which though externally toying with a folk-like tone are essentially over-sophisticated, as thoughtfully and nobly as Mozart and Schubert.

The old man Goethe once laid his hand on the boy Mendelssohn, in whom he rejoiced, and the strict old master Cherubini issued to the youth, in weighty words, the accolade for his artistic career: it must have been Mendelssohn the song composer on whom Goethe's hand rested and to whom Cherubini's prophetic praise was uttered. It may seem to us, however, to be an auspicious sign of the times that it should only be in the small song that the most patriotic musical poet of the present day became creative with entirely untrammelled genius.[35]

51 · *Das Judenthum in der Musik*

Riehl's reference to Mendelssohn's freedom from Jewish mannerisms may perhaps have been an oblique response to Wagner's openly racist critique of Mendelssohn in *Das Judenthum in der Musik*,[36] the first substantial attack on Mendelssohn's reputation that openly linked his Jewishness with his artistic standing and ability. Wagner's article was an explicit and extensive exposition of the idea not only that the Jews as a race, regardless of whether they had converted to Christianity, were in some sense disabled from achieving the heights of artistic expression but also that there was a Jewish conspiracy in artistic matters, by which the activities of Jews were to be promoted by any means available, while non-Jews were to be suppressed. The latter attitude lasted well into the twentieth century, finding its culmination in the Nazi horrors of the 1930s and 1940s.

In the first two chapters Wagner expounded his premises in general. In his introduction he considered the transformation of the political and social position of the Jews in the first half of the nineteenth century, coming to the conclusion that "in spite of all speech-making and written manifestations on their behalf, we continue to be repelled by any prospect of actual and practical contact with them." He claimed that "the involuntary repulsion . . . which the person and character of the Jew is thus found to awaken . . . is stronger and more weighty than the zeal which we are prepared to enlist for its effacement"; and he added that people deceived themselves in "continuing to classify as bad manners all frank reference to our natural antipathy to the Jewish character," stating that it was better to bring this into the open and seek to understand the nature of the ill-will "which continues to exist in spite of all our liberal representations." Having next considered how the Jew had progressed from a powerful position in financial matters to domination in cultural ones, Wagner then concluded his introduction:

> We have now to examine more closely the reasons why the particular stage at which its development has now arrived, and the fact of its present basis being inconsistent with any further advance of that which is natural, necessary and truly beautiful has brought the public Art-taste of our time within the Jew's busy fingers. . . .
>
> It is unnecessary to add anything in confirmation of this "Jewification" of modern Art, for it is patent to the eye and proves itself to our senses quite unaided. We should have, moreover, to extend this enquiry a great deal too far were we to desire to undertake to extract the reasons for this manifestation from the various features of our Art-history. That which is to be esteemed as of supreme importance is to test our powers in this struggle for freedom, should emancipation from the oppressions of Judaism present itself to our minds as indispensable. No abstract definition of the manifestation itself will enable us to acquire this force, but an accurate acquaintance with the nature of that involuntary feeling which, asserting itself within us, takes the form of an invariable dislike of the Jew. If we quite frankly avow that feeling its study may be counted upon to reveal what it is that, in the Jew, we so dislike. We can then show a better front of opposition to what we know for certain, and even its

mere discovery will be sure to assist in driving this demon from the field. Only under the protection of a
misty twilight is he at present able to stay there at all;
and it is we, benevolent humanitarians forsooth, who
have, ourselves, cast that twilight round about him,
though only to render his ordinary aspect less distasteful.

In his second section Wagner considered the Jew's characteristics, revealing a repulsive degree of racial loathing. First he considered the Jew's
appearance, noting that it "strikes us as something so unpleasantly incon-
gruous that, involuntarily, we wish to have nothing in common with
him." He considered it inconceivable that the faithful representation of
"the Jew's exterior" could be undertaken in art. "When plastic Art wishes
to represent the Jew, it generally draws its model from imagination; either
discreetly ennobling or leaving out altogether those traits which charac-
terise his presence in ordinary life." He claimed that "no character,
whether antique or modern, hero or lover, can be even thought of as
represented by a Jew without an instant consciousness on our part of the
ludicrous inappropriateness of such a proceeding." From this he drew the
conclusion that "if we hold a man to be exteriorly disqualified by race
for any artistic presentment whatever—that is to say, not merely for any
one in particular but for all without exception—it follows that we should
also regard him as unfit for any artistic pronouncement."

Wagner then turned to the manner in which the Jew expresses himself:
"The speech of the Jew is however of even greater effect upon us—an
effect which constitutes the essential feature to dwell upon in referring to
Jewish influence upon Music. The Jew converses in the tongue of the
people amongst whom he dwells from age to age, but he does this invariably after the manner of a foreigner." Declining to consider whether
the host races were culpable for this situation, since "it is foreign to our
purpose," he proceeded to focus on what he saw as the "aesthetic character" of its consequences. He argued that since "a Jew speaks his modern
European language only as if acquired and not as if he were native to it,"
he is shut out "from all capability of full, independent and characteristic
expression of his ideas." Furthermore, "our entire European civilisation"
has remained "in the position of a foreign tongue to the Jew," and he
has had no part in its development "but at the most, merely looked on,

with feelings cold and even hostile, as is natural to a homeless unfortunate. In such language or in such art the Jew can naturally but echo and imitate, and is perforce debarred from fluent expression and pure creative work." Wagner considered "the mere audible twang of the Jew's speech particularly offensive" and felt that the "hissing, shrill-sounding buzzing and grunting mannerisms of Jewish speech fall at once upon our ear as something strange and disagreeable in kind." For him this was not merely incidental; he insisted that the "exceptional importance of this circumstance" should be recognized: "Hear a Jew speak; every shortcoming in point of human expression has its sting, and the cold indifference of his peculiar 'Gelabber'[37] never rises to any warmth—not even in presence of the stimulation to higher or heated passion. On the other hand, should it happen that we become impelled to such ardour when speaking to a Jew, his incapability of effective response will invariably cause him to give way. Never does the Jew become aroused in merely sentimental expression with us. If ever he becomes excited at all it is on behalf of some special and selfish interest. Either it is his material profit which is in question, or his personal vanity; and, as his excitement has usually a distorting effect upon his speech, it also assumes a ridiculous character not in the least calculated to arouse sympathy for the speaker." He disregarded the fact that many educated Jews of his own generation had grown up with German as their native tongue.

In the next section, dealing with "musical creation," Wagner attempted to show how the Jew was constitutionally incapable of true musical creativity:

> Repulsed therefore in a manner most hurtful to his feel-
> ings by a Society of which he is unable to seize the
> spirit, the educated Jew is driven back to his own race,
> where at all events everything is immeasurably clearer.
> Whether he will or not this is the source from which he
> needs must draw what he requires, but here again he is
> confronted by the dearth of material for
> "What to say"; [was]
> as assistance in the direction of
> "How to speak" [wie]
> is all that it is capable of offering him. The fact is that

the Jews have never had an Art of their own—never a
life replete with art-possibilities. Features of universal human application are not to be found amongst them, the
sum of their resource being the peculiar mode of expression indicated above. One source and one only may be
said to offer itself to the Jewish composer, and that lies
in the solemn musical service dedicated to his Jehovah;
for after all it is to the synagogue that he must look if he
hopes to obtain motives alike comprehensible and of true
folk-character.

Wagner went on to condemn the music of the synagogue, however, as
being in a condition of "the greatest corruption," having stagnated for
thousands of years "without any development or movement of inner life,"
like everything else connected with the Jews in his view. On the other
hand he regarded it as "the merest caricature of Church-song," a horri-
fying and absurd succession of "gurgling, jodeling and babbling sounds
confusive of all trace of sense and spirit."

By a tortuous process of reasoning Wagner then suggested that "the
higher Jew, seeking the satisfaction of his art-needs at their proper source
in the instinctive life of his people," turns vainly to this music for inspiration. He stated that "those melismi and rhythms of the synagogue cap-
tivate the musical fancy of the Jewish composer quite in the same way as
an instinctive familiarity with the melodies and rhythms of our own folk-
song and dance constitutes a nucleus of power for the creators of our
musical works of art; whether vocal or instrumental," but he concluded
that "out of our copious range of folk-song only such material is open
to the musical faculty of perception of the educated Jew as may happen
to strike his fancy as intelligible; but only that can be intelligible to him,
in the sense of being able to be applied artistically, which is found to
present some feature of approach to Jewish musical peculiarities." The
"heart and soul" of the "inner life" of "our" music (that is, German
music), according to Wagner, are inevitably foreign to the Jewish musician, who if he recognized this would not dare "to compete with us in
our art-creation"; but the Jew "is never induced . . . to indulge in any
such deep meditations," and he "listens to our art-productions and their
life-giving inner organism in a merely superficial manner," so that all he

perceives are "exterior resemblances" to what it is in his limited capacity to understand.

The consequence of this in Wagner's opinion is that the Jew "mistakes the exterior of the manifestations in our musical life and art-domain for the real substance of them. Thus it is that his conceptions of them when he ventures upon a reproduction strike us as strange, odd, indifferent, unnatural and distorted; to such a degree that Jewish musical works often produce upon us an impression similar to that which we might expect from a poem of Goethe, if recited before us in the Jewish gibberish." Then, obliquely intimating that he was thinking particularly of the tendency represented in Mendelssohn's music, he wrote:

> In the same way as a confused heap is made of words
> and phrases in this jargon does the Jewish composer
> make a confused heap of the forms and styles of all ages
> and masters. Cheek-by-jowl we meet them in the most
> lovely chaos—formal peculiarities of the various schools
> all huddled together. The intention in these productions
> having merely been to speak, and to do this at all haz-
> ards, and therefore to the exclusion of all consideration
> of any object sufficiently worthy to confer upon the
> speech some value, the only means of rendering such
> babble at all exciting to the ear is continually to change
> the means and mode of expression.
>
> Heartfelt excitement and true passion find their own
> appropriate tongue when, striving to make themselves in-
> telligible, they formulate an utterance. The Jew, however,
> as already described in this connection, has no real pas-
> sion—or, in any case, no passion of a nature to impel
> him to art-creation.
>
> But without such passion there can also be no repose,
> for a genuine and noble stillness is naught else than pas-
> sion which has subsided and become appeased in resigna-
> tion. Where there has been no previous passion we re-
> cognise no calm—but only dullness; the usual contrast to
> which, in Jewish work, is that pungent unrest which is

so noticeable from end to end of it; only ceasing in fact to make way for the aforesaid dullness, which is one as devoid of spirit as of feeling.

All that the Jew's ambition to engage in Art has really yielded must therefore necessarily possess the properties of coldness and indifference, if not even those of triviality and nonsense; so that the period of Judaism in modern music can only be described historically as one of complete unfruitfulness and of a stability fast perishing.

Having now established his premises and demonstrated, as he thought, the inevitable artistic impotence of the Jew, Wagner proceeded to consider overtly how this might relate to two of the most successful musicians of his own day: Mendelssohn and Meyerbeer. Meyerbeer, whose artistic stance was widely seen by German musicians as a betrayal of their inheritance, and whose work was equally detested by Mendelssohn and Schumann, provided Wagner with a relatively easy target for his racially motivated vitriol. (He never mentioned Meyerbeer by name, since he was still alive and occupied an important position in the German musical establishment, but the identity of his victim was apparent to all.) Mendelssohn, however, provided a more difficult target. Not only had he been brought up a Christian and written some of the most admired Christian music of the period; he had also been intimately associated with the cause of German music and was regarded by many as the legitimate successor of the great German masters of earlier times. Wagner's own ambivalence about Mendelssohn's achievements is clearly evident. Although he made many individual disparaging remarks about Mendelssohn, even Wagner could not simply deny his status as a musician of extraordinary natural gifts, exceptional cultivation and high artistic aims; he could, however, undermine it by means of apparently plausible conclusions drawn from specious a priori assumptions that were presented as self-evident truth. As Mendelssohn was dead he addressed the matter directly:

Where is the manifestation by which all the preceding could be rendered clearer—where is one to be found more calculated instantly to convince us—than that presented to us in the works of a composer of Jewish extraction who was endowed by Nature with specific musical gifts to a degree hitherto equalled by few?

Everything which in the course of our enquiry into the antipathy we feel towards the Jewish character gave ground for reflection—whether the contradictions of this character within itself and towards us, or its incapacity, whilst outside our domain, to deal with us on that ground—or, its want of the power even to formulate so much as an earnest desire to further develop the productions which have sprung from us—all these accumulated considerations rise up with the importance of a tragic conflict as we find them exhibited in the nature, life and art-career of the composer who was taken from our midst at such an early age—Felix Mendelssohn-Bartholdy.

By him we have been shown that a Jew may be gifted with the ripest specific talent, he may have acquired the finest and most varied education, he may possess the highest and most finely-tempered sense of honour—and yet, notwithstanding all these advantages, he may remain unable, even in so much as one solitary instance, to bring forth that deep effect upon our hearts and souls which we expect from Art because we know its capability in that direction—because we have experienced it many a time and oft—in fact, whenever a hero of our craft has designed, as it were, to open his mouth to speak to us.

To the critics by profession, who must necessarily have arrived at a similar view, the duty falls of confirming this unquestionable fact by references to individual instances among the Mendelssohnian productions. The general statement, however, will here be made sufficiently clear if we recall that, in hearing a piece by this composer, our attention is only fixed whilst graceful, smooth and artificial figures are in progress. These are brought forward ordered and combined more or less for the entertainment of our fancy; their changes being akin to those of the kaleidoscope. But never do we feel moved at those situations where the figures are intended to express any deep or pithy heart-sensation.[38] At that point even formal productive capacity for Mendelssohn entirely ceased; for which reason wherever, as in oratorio, he approached the Drama, he was obliged to appropriate without scruple any-individual feature which he could gather from this or that predecessor, according to whom he had taken for his model for the time being. In doing so it is to be well observed that, in his expressionless modern speech, he had a marked preference for our old master, Bach, as model. Bach's musical language grew up at that period of our musical history when the universal musical tongue was still struggling for the power of individual and exact expression. The purely formal and pedantic had still so strong a hold upon it that, even in the case of Bach, it was only through the stupendous power of his genius that purely human expression was enabled to break through such an obstacle.

The language of Bach stands to the language of Mozart, and finally to that of Beethoven, in the same relation as did the Egyptian Sphinx to Grecian sculpture; and, in the same way as the Sphinx with human face seems to strive to quit its animal body, so does the noble human figure of Bach seem to strive to quit its ancient periwig.

The luxurious musical taste of our time is subject to an inconceivable and thoughtless confusion; which lies in the fact that we complacently listen, at one and the same time, to discussion of Bach and Beethoven's mode of expression. We actually make ourselves believe that the difference between them was merely an individual and formal one; losing sight of the fact that it really stands for an important landmark in the history of our culture.

The reason of this is, however, obvious enough; for the speech of Beethoven was the musical language of a complete, finished, warm-feeling man, and could neces-

sarily proceed from no other. It was the speech of a music-
-man so perfect that, of irresistible impulse, he had
pressed forward beyond the domain of absolute music,
the limits of which he had measured and extended to
their utmost; and, in doing so, had shown us the way to
the fruition of all arts through music as their only successful extension.

The speech of Bach, on the other hand, can be suita-
bly imitated by any well-equipped musician; even though
it be not in the same sense that Bach employed it. In it
the formal element predominates; the purely human element being not so completely the governing feature that
the

"What to say"

is able to assert itself quite unconditionally, and this for
the reason that it is still too much engaged in the throes
of

"How to speak."

The flimsiness and waywardness of our musical style
has been, in consequence of Mendelssohn's endeavour to
deliver unclear and worthless material in the most agree-
able manner possible, if not actually introduced, at all
events, pushed to its utmost limits. For whilst Beethoven,
the last in the chain of our genuine music-heroes, with
intensest longing and miraculous powers, strove ever for
the clearest and most accurate expression of that which
was otherwise unspeakable, by the sharply-cut plastic
form of his tone-pictures, Mendelssohn dwindles these
trophies in his productions; thus reducing his effects to
the level of dissolving views and of fantastic shadow-
pictures. By such uncertain tints our capricious imaginative powers may be excited, but our pure and manly
longing for clearer artistic insight is scarcely so much as
moved to any hope of fulfilment.

Only when the irksome consciousness of this limita-
tion of power appears to influence the composer's mood,
compelling him to the expression of a soft and melan-

choly resignation, does Mendelssohn present himself to us characteristically; and he does so then in the subjective sense of a refined character which, confronted by the impossible, makes confession of its own impotence.

This, as has been said, constitutes the tragic feature in Mendelssohn's life; and, should we desire to extend our sympathy to any personality within the domain of art, we could not refuse it in a strong measure to him, notwithstanding that its force is likely to be diminished when we reflect that, in his case, the tragic was rather a passive resultant feeling than one leading to active, suffering and enlightening conviction.[39]

Wagner's insincerity is demonstrated by his own recorded comments to and about Mendelssohn. On 8 June 1843 he had written to him, "I am proud to belong to the nation that produced you and your *St Paul*,"[40] and at the same time he wrote to the Saxon theatre intendant Lüttichau that it was "a work that is a testimony to the highest flowering of art. The reflection that it was composed in our times fills us with justifiable pride for the age in which we live."[41] Later, although Wagner made many individual disparaging remarks about Mendelssohn, he again undermined his own thesis with private expressions of his admiration for some of the concert overtures, especially *Die Hebriden*, about which Cosima wrote in 1879, "In the evening we go with Herr R[ubinstein] through the three Mendelssohn overtures, of which the *Hebrides* impresses us as truly masterly," and later the same year Wagner even described it as "a much greater artistic masterpiece" than the "Aryan" Weber's *Oberon* Overture.[42] But Wagner also feared Mendelssohn. The major problem seems to have been that Mendelssohn's achievements and his enormous popularity threatened Wagner's conception of the historical development of music and his own place in it. This is fascinatingly illustrated by an entry in Cosima's diary in 1869, the year Wagner reissued *Das Judenthum* under his own name:

In the evening R. and Richter play Mozart's C Major Symphony as a piano duet, in the course of which R. gets very indignant about the faulty arrangement: "That is just like the Germans—always carrying on about Mo-

zart, and then they produce such editions!" Listening to
the Andante, I found myself thinking of Beethoven, and
I felt as if one might say to him, "Alas, alas, you have
destroyed it, this beautiful world." But in his heart he
built it up again. The gods have ceased their sweet and
blessed playing, and instead of Paradise we have life, with
all its terrible agony and the salvation which flows from
it. There is no returning to Paradise, though there is to
Heaven, and Mendelssohn, who perhaps flattered himself
that he could restore the original state, is merely childish.
With Beethoven musical creation becomes human, Mozart is the world of animal, vegetable, and mineral, the
innocent, naive world, unknowing both in gladness and
sorrow; in the whole panoply Wagner appears as the revelation, as religion. In this history of creation the venera-
ble Bach appears somewhat like the entire planetary
system, before it separated itself from the sun. On such
levels there is, however, no place for the gnat Mendelssohn to vaunt himself.[43]

52 · Changing Critical Perspectives

A few writers overtly followed Wagner in his identification of Mendelssohn's Jewish inheritance as the root cause of his supposed musical weaknesses. In 1852, for instance, Wilhelm von Lenz claimed that "the Hebraic
element detectable in the ideas of Mendelssohn stands in the way of his
works' universal acceptance without distinction of time and place . . . Jews
often advance to the first rank when it is a question of acquiring mechanical abilities . . . the real artist, the composer, is not derivative; it is
his own nature he must express. . . . The music of Mendelssohn echoes
the psalmodic chants of the synagogue, just as the Jewish spirit, as we
have characterized it, plays a part in his thinking."[44] Many others echoed
the insinuations of effeteness in Mendelssohn's music. Joseph Schlüter
referred in 1863 to "the absence of innate vigour, masculine simplicity,
and genuine feeling" in Mendelssohn's music, and although he suggested

that this was not true of all his works, as "unjustly insisted upon by Marx,"[45] he attributed it even to such works as the A major and A minor symphonies, asserting: "The hard trials and acute sorrows which alone could give emotion, pathos, and tragical grandeur to compositions of this kind never fell to the lot of the happy *Felix*—and to counterfeit emotion and raging grief was utterly foreign to his upright, candid nature." In respect of the oratorios, however, Schlüter felt that "Mendelssohn has displayed such a fund of exquisite originality, and such dignity and solemnity (especially in St. Paul) in his treatment of this previously almost neglected branch of composition, that his works may henceforth be regarded as models of modern oratorio composition." But although he admired the "noble choruses" in *Elijah*, he disliked "the somewhat overstrained pietism of some of the solos." He ended his appraisal: "Nevertheless—and we trust without incurring the charge of inconsistency—we are constrained to admit that in the musical world of our day (on which female and *dilettanti* influences are brought to bear in no slight degree) Mendelssohn plays an all too important part. Scarcely a concert takes place without one or even more of Mendelssohn's compositions. Not only do the great models of Bach and Handel seem likely to be cast into the shade by the very composer who has deferred to them in so eminent a degree, but even Schumann—the last musician of historical importance—has had to make way for the favourite of the day." Yet at the very end of his book, after castigating the works of Berlioz, Liszt and Wagner but praising "a considerable number of, for the most part, sterling and admirable musicians" (including Joachim, Brahms, F. David, Volkmann, Rubinstein and Raff), Schlüter concluded: "Are we to believe that the field of art lies fallow and must be ploughed up before it can produce another crop? True, no one among living composers has been able to replace Mendelssohn; and, were *he* still living, we should most certainly never have heard all this talk about new theories in art."[46]

A few years later August Reissmann, a fundamentally sympathetic biographer, also displayed the tendency to provide a critical corrective to what he evidently saw as excessive admiration for Mendelssohn among many musicians and music lovers. He thought that "the school [of composers] that meant to create in his spirit is mostly responsible for people beginning to undervalue his great deserts . . . for it only tried to imitate his manner." Like Schlüter, he compared Mendelssohn and Schumann, observing that the former was "unremittingly concerned to fill and revivify the old forms with the new spirit, but almost entirely with less success than that contemporary fellow worker, Robert Schumann, because, under the influence of training and upbringing, originality and immediacy and power of invention were lost." In line with contemporaneous notions of cultural progress, Reissmann argued that in almost every field Mendelssohn "had a profound effect on the feelings of our time, but really without a higher gain for the development of our art."[47]

While in Germany during the first two decades after his death Mendelssohn's stature was being hotly debated—but his music widely performed—the French paid him little attention either in print or in the concert hall. So long as opera remained the principal focus of French musical life this situation changed little; but as performances of instrumental music became more popular, Mendelssohn's music began to arouse greater interest. His distinctive style of "classical romanticism" seems to have appealed increasingly to French taste and provided an alluring model for many French musicians of the generations of Gounod and Saint-Saëns. This quality in Mendelssohn's music was highlighted by Hypolite Barbedette in 1868: "As he was in his life, so he was in his music. We have said and reiterated sufficiently that Mendelssohn is a passionate artist; but, in love with Bach's precepts, worshipper of rules and of form, he imprisoned the passion with which he was inundated within narrow confines, and his music is the same as his life was, *passionate but contained.*" Barbedette doubted, however, whether Mendelssohn's music, as he was at heart a "puritan,"[48] would ever be really popular in France. He concluded: "Nothing equals the vogue that Mendelssohn enjoys in Germany and England. In Leipzig one speaks of him as of a second Beethoven, as of a Goethe, as of one of the greatest artistic personalities. In London, it was only necessary for him to appear for everyone to rise in acclamation. His person, his music became the object of incredible ovations there, and his works are still played there in preference to all others. In France, it is not long since it has been universally accepted; it was contested for a long time. Mendelssohn was hardly known here, while in Germany he enjoyed a colossal renown; and whatever may be the sympathy that his music inspires nowadays, it is not destined to strike deep roots among us because it does not conform to our differing tendencies."[49]

Barbedette's remarks about Mendelssohn's continuing popularity calls attention to the paradox that in Germany, despite all the manifestations of criticism, Mendelssohn's music still elicited widespread admiration at the end of the 1860s and his continuing high status in the 1870s was emphasised by the publication, between 1874 and 1877, of the Breitkopf und Härtel edition of his collected works. In England, too, his compositions remained central to the repertoire, as Barbedette noted; but whereas critics and public were largely united in their esteem during the 1860s, dissenting critical voices began to be heard with increasing frequency during the last thirty years of the century. Thus Friedrich Niecks felt it necessary to defend Mendelssohn against some of his contemporary critics in 1875,[50] and the changing climate is indicated by comments in the *Musical Standard* in 1877: "It is impossible not to notice that an immense majority hold Mendelssohn in no very high esteem. Many, probably sickened by the mannerisms of his myriad imitators, never can mention his name without a sneer; others deny him his due meed of respect because they believe him to be an overrated man." A writer in the *Musical Times* quoted these comments and responded to them in an article entitled "Is Mendelssohn in Danger?": "All this may be real enough to the writer, but we fancy that he has mistaken a coterie for the great world. At any rate, our experience is very different. Allowing that his popularity has lost whatever it derived from a personal fascination without a parallel in the history of art, Mendelssohn is as much beloved as ever he was by the mass of those to whom music appeals."[51]

In Germany, too, Mendelssohn's music remained popular with the concert-going public in the 1880s, despite the growing tendency of critics, many of whom were enthusiastic Wagnerians, to characterize his music as facile and shallow. In the *Allgemeine deutsche Biographie* in 1885, Gustav von Loeper, who in contrast to many felt that it was in his vocal music that Mendelssohn achieved the true summit of greatness, called him "the first oratorio composer of our century" and argued that in this field "he will live as long as German music exists," remarking: "It is always a festal evening for our societies when one of his larger choral works is performed and a noble enthusiasm aroused by it in all hearts. He will stand alone in this for a long time, for nature rarely succeeds in uniting qualities that are capable of such universal effects in a single person."[52]

One notable shift of emphasis, which gained strength towards the end of the nineteenth century, concerned Mendelssohn's moral character. In his own time and for several decades afterwards his "blameless character" was widely cited as a recommendation for his works. Comments like those of the Reverend H. R. Haweis in 1871, in his phenomenally popular *Music and Morals*, are typical: "In this age of mercenary musical manufacture and art degradation, Mendelssohn towers above his contemporaries like a moral lighthouse in the midst of a dark and troubled sea. His light always shone strong and pure. The winds of heaven were about his head, and the 'Still Small Voice' was in his heart. In a lying generation he was true, and in an adulterous generation he was pure—and not popularity or gain could tempt him to sully the pages of that spotless inspiration with one meretricious effect or one impure association."[53] Frederick Crowest, too, implicitly linked the excellence of Mendelssohn's character with that of his music, asserting in 1874: "Mendelssohn's was a noble nature; spurning all that was base, mean, and insincere; full of fiery energy, yet as simple and lovable as a child's. Let those who wish to become acquainted with it, read his collected letters; and there is for those who desire to know him as a musician, his sublime music."[54]

These opinions remained in circulation for decades (Haweis's book reached a twentieth edition in 1906 and Crowest's was reissued as late as 1926). In the post-Wagnerian, post-Freudian world of the early twentieth century, however, such notions were increasingly derided, and it is much more common in later assessments to find Mendelssohn's irreproachable character and life equated with a perceived lack of depth, or at least emotional detachment, in his music. This connection, which had been insinuated in Mendelssohn's lifetime, for instance by Hirschbach in 1845 and in the appraisal in Brockhaus's *Conversations-Lexicon* in 1846,[55] is echoed in the 1890s by the American writers John K. Paine and Leo R. Lewis: "Mendelssohn's genial and refined nature mirrored itself in his music. Nevertheless, with all the beauty, sweetness, classic form and purity of his music, one thing is missed,—tragic depth and fire. He did not touch the deepest chords of the heart like Beethoven and Bach, perhaps because his existence was not clouded by adversity, or because he arrived without serious struggles at the complete development of his artistic powers."[56]

A process of retrenchment from the frequently asserted mid-nineteenth-century view that Mendelssohn was on a level with the greatest of his predecessors, or at least was surpassed only by the very greatest, is evident in many writings from the end of the nineteenth and the beginning of the twentieth centuries. George Bernard Shaw's celebrated condemnation, in 1889, of Mendelssohn's "kid-glove gentility, his conventional sentimentality, and his despicable oratorio-mongering"[57] condensed into a single striking aphorism the reservations and objections of musicians that had crystalized during the last quarter of the nineteenth century from a host of different causes, few of which were genuinely related to Mendelssohn's music itself. Yet, despite the often severe criticism of Mendelssohn's style or of significant portions of his output, many writers seem to have been reluctant to relegate him to a lower status in the canon of great composers. Thus John S. Dwight could write in the early 1890s that Mendelssohn was "gifted with original creative genius—a genius not so deep and absolute, so elemental, so Titanic as that of Bach and Handel and Beethoven, nor of so celestial a temper as that of Mozart." But at the same time he asserted of the Symphony in A Minor: "After the immortal nine of Beethoven, there is no Symphony more perfect in form than this, of charm more enduring, although we have the great one of 'heavenly length' in C by Schubert, and such noble ones by Schumann." And, attempting to fix Mendelssohn's place in the canon, he wrote: "Four we count above all others in the temple of tone-art and genius:—Bach, Handel, Mozart and Beethoven. Can we fill out a second four without the name of Felix Mendelssohn Bartholdy? Choice may vary as to one or two names in that second quartet; of Schubert and Schumann there can be no question, some may have preference for Haydn, or for Gluck, or Weber, Cherubini, even for Rossini; but when with the other distinctions we take into account that of many-sidedness, all-round musicianship, can any other four compete with Mendelssohn except to his advantage?"[58]

Another American author, Nathan H. Dole, who admired Berlioz, Liszt and Wagner, and showed no particular taste for Mendelssohn's music, observed in 1891: "Mendelssohn is in a certain sense the musician of the unmusical; his 'Songs without Words' appeal to the young Philistines of the conservatories; his 'Elijah' is the masterpiece for religious Philistinism." And he remarked: "It seems indeed rather ludicrous in a recent writer to speak of him as being the last of the musical Titans . . . it may be safely maintained that he had not the spontaneous creative genius of a Bach, a Mozart or a Beethoven." Dole credited Mendelssohn merely with "the distinction of having 'restored the lost art of counterpoint,' and bringing back classic forms at a day when romanticism was compelling men like Meyerbeer and Weber into enchanted, if not dangerous ground." In his chapter on Schumann he observed, "Both have exerted great influence on musical art. But Mendelssohn's was ephemeral, and felt mainly by those of weaker fibre; whereas Schumann's has been felt especially by stronger natures." Nevertheless, he stopped short of questioning Mendelssohn's right to be regarded as a major composer, and concluded his lukewarm assessment with the rather surprising comment: "Though it is somewhat the fashion to sneer at him, it seems safe to predict, that as time goes on his fame will rather increase than diminish."[59]

The centenary of Mendelssohn's birth in 1909 called forth many conventional articles marking the event without any attempt at critical analysis. A number of writers, however, took the opportunity to consider the discrepancy between Mendelssohn's reputation then and half a century earlier. In England Ernest Walker observed that "no one in touch with the inner musical life of the country can deny that for a very large number of the most talented of the younger men and women Mendelssohn hardly exists. . . . A quarter of a century ago concert-goers were familiar with all sorts of works—orchestral, chamber, vocal: where can they be heard now? . . . a great mass of Mendelssohn's music is apparently being simply forgotten by almost everyone." Contrasting the old view with the new, he remarked: "Emotional profundity and technical perfection—these were the qualities his contemporaries acclaimed in him, and now we can concede even the latter only with very many reservations." Although Walker's ostensible purpose was to argue that the disparagement of Mendelssohn was going too far, he seems to have agreed with most of the current criticisms: "It is useless to deny that about a great deal of Mendelssohn's music there is, as one of our chief living critics has said, a 'flavour of stale chocolate': and neither emotionally nor in any other respect is the giant's robe for him." Entirely rejecting the sacred music, Walker argued that only some of the instrumental music—the overtures and a few selected movements from other works—deserved to live; even the Violin Concerto, which remained popular, might not, he suggested, have survived "had there been more great concertos for violinists to play."[60]

It is symptomatic of the level to which Mendelssohn's reputation had sunk in intellectual circles that in the *Spectator*, shortly after this, C. L.

Graves could refer to Walker's article as "probably the best appreciation of Mendelssohn that has appeared in the English press." Yet Graves took a more sympathetic view and advanced the following explanation for the decline in Mendelssohn's reputation:

> While Mendelssohn's fame suffered from the "sixties" on-ward from legitimate competition as the genius of Schu-bert, Schumann and Brahms gained wider recognition in the concert-room, and the tremendous influence of Wag-ner made itself felt on the stage, he gradually became the special aversion of those who base their claim to enlight-enment on the extent of their divergence from the opin-ion of the majority. . . . Along with justifiable criticism there was mixed up a great deal of unwarrantable dispar-agement. This hostility was chiefly shown among the ex-treme Wagnerites . . . and it gradually became so acute in certain circles that to confess to an admiration of Men-delssohn exposed one to the risk of being written down as Early Victorian, *bourgeois*, and altogether "out of movement." This attitude has found copious expression during the last ten years in the Press and in books de-voted to musical criticism.

Graves's recital of the charges these critics levelled against Mendelssohn contains many that are familiar from earlier attacks: his privileged back-ground and systematic education meant that "he had none of the irreg-ularity, angularity, or colossal egotism associated with daemonic genius"; in addition, "his moral excellence, integrity, lovableness, and charm are treated as so many damning proofs of his shortcomings when tried by the test of heroic antinomianism"; and "his all-round musical equipment, his remarkable performances as an organist and pianist, and his skill as a draughtsman, linguist, dancer,—these, according to such critics, are only evidences of a superficial versatility irreconcilable with the true concen-tration of genius."[61] Even among those who were not rabid Wagnerians were many who had absorbed the detractions of Mendelssohn that stemmed directly from Wagner and his circle. Charles Villiers Stanford, probably influenced also by the then current interest in eugenics, seems to have accepted the racial slur propagated by Wagner in 1850. He wrote in 1916: "[Mendelssohn's] music, always finished to the smallest detail, always picturesque when written under inspiring conditions . . . and invariably careful not to outstep the limitations of his genius, does not, as a rule, retain its first appeal in subsequent repetition. His trick . . . was the dangerous one of perpetual and unvaried repetition of phrases and even bars: a habit which probably had its source in his Hebrew blood." He also stated that Mendelssohn "possessed great reverence for his predecessors but no great depth of invention or design in himself."[62] In this and many other cases the propaganda of the Wagnerians, which aimed to leave "no place for the gnat Mendelssohn to vaunt himself,"[63] seems unconsciously to have been absorbed.

Among younger writers Donald Francis Tovey, as a contributor to the *Encyclopaedia Britannica*, took a more positive view of Mendelssohn than many of his contemporaries. In his postscript to the article by Rockstro, reprinted in the eleventh edition (1910–1911), Tovey commented that "in the early Wagner-Liszt reign of terror" Mendelssohn's "was the first reputation to be assassinated."[64] Tovey's appraisal in his own article on Mendelssohn for the next revision of the encyclopaedia was characteristically independent. He considered Mendelssohn's early death to have been, "perhaps, one of the most inopportune events in musical history; inopportune for his reputation . . . ; disastrous for many musicians who hoped to learn from him; and doubly inopportune as making it impossible for him and the pioneers of new musical developments to learn from each other." He even went so far as to imply that Mendelssohn, had he lived, might have countered Wagner's domination of mid-nineteenth-century music: "He would soon have seen the reality of Wagner's new sense of movement, and would have experimented with it. And Mendelssohn's experiments were apt to succeed in the long run." Tovey, however, reflected the prejudice of his generation in condemning "the sentimentality of Mendelssohn's efforts at a religious style," damning the beginning of the Andante religioso of the *Lobgesang* as "the origin of almost all that is sickly in English church music."[65]

During the period between 1890 and 1920 the tide of criticism in Germany largely mirrored that in the English-speaking world, but after the First World War growing critical engagement with radical new trends in European music, represented by such composers as Stravinsky, Bartók and Schoenberg, further depressed Mendelssohn's reputation. Adolf Weissmann, in 1922, looking at the "problem of modern music," mentioned Mendelssohn a couple of times, merely to condemn his compositions as "a weak reflection of eighteenth-century work" and "unexacting neo-classical music."[66] During the period between the two world wars few serious scholars could be found to say much in Mendelssohn's favour, and many dismissed him unceremoniously. Thus, in Gerald Abraham's *A Hundred Years of Music* (1938) he is effectively written out of the history of romantic music; the opening paragraph of the preface, in which Mendelssohn is not mentioned at all, says, "The early eighteen-thirties saw the opening of the careers of a number of composers—Chopin, Liszt, Berlioz, Schumann—who brought a new note into music" and, a few paragraphs later, "The central position of any book on music of the last hundred years must inevitably be occupied by Wagner." Where Mendelssohn is mentioned in the body of the book it is always in negative terms. Discussing how a number of composers reverted to more classical procedures in later life, Abraham remarked: "It is noticeable that of the renegades from romanticism, Mendelssohn—who possessed less musical vitality than any of the others—was first to go." Referring to "compensating values" in the later works of these composers, he commented: "In Mendelssohn's case the compensating elements are pitifully few." Of the Symphony in A Minor Abraham asserted: "As a whole [it] symbolizes only too well the course of its composer's career: the brief touch of inspired romanticism at the beginning followed by a dreary waste of mere sound-manipulation, relieved only by the oasis of the light-handed scherzo, and ending in a blaze of sham triumph."[67] Here Abraham, perhaps taking his cue from Hans von Bülow's often cited comment that Mendelssohn began by being a genius and ended by being a talent, delivered a more damning judgment, since Bülow at least stressed that Mendelssohn was perfect in both phases.[68]

Abraham's judgments were nevertheless an honest reflection of his own musical perceptions and preconceptions. But in Germany during the 1920s and 1930s very different forces were at work. Wagner's claim that artistic impotence was an inevitable consequence of Jewish blood, and that there was a universal Jewish conspiracy in music had been regularly echoed during the second half of the nineteenth century, for instance, in the anti-Semitic writings of Rudolf Friedrich Grau.[69] Even a musicologist as positive about much of Mendelssohn's output as Hans Joachim Moser, writing around 1920, saw evidence of his Jewishness in the fact that "he lisped, was highly strung, very often ill, and died like father and sister of a stroke at an early age." Moser maintained that "the decidedly Jewish element in his music" was evident in "the lack of German weight and profundity," the "unstylistic" imitation of Handelian dotted figures and the use of "dangerously frequent six-eight rhythms," as well as "a shrewd aversion to all music expressive of ambiguous ideas, an all-too-smooth treatment of merely pleasant ideas, carried out with cosmopolitan suavity," and "the notable gift of being able to feel just as good in Bach's style as in Silcher's."[70] Despite his admiration for individual works, Moser concluded that Mendelssohn was "a talent of perhaps the greatest mechanical polish, yet certainly no true genius in our sense."[71]

More remarks along these lines, but infinitely cruder, were published after the rise to power of the Nazis in 1933, and within a short time critical condemnation was reflected in an almost total cessation of public performances of Mendelssohn's music in Germany and Austria; what repeated denigration had never been able to achieve was quickly accomplished by dictatorial decree. Distasteful as it is, a representative example will aptly illustrate the kind of diatribe that accompanied the forcible suppression of Mendelssohn's music in Germany. A couple of extracts from a book by Karl Blessinger, published in Berlin in 1939, illustrate the tone and absurd illogicality of such polemics.

> The history of music in the nineteenth century is not yet written. The enormous bulk of available factual material about this period has not yet been organized from more elevated points of view, and methods of musical scholarship employed until now break down with respect to this problem, since with the traditional approach the whole picture dissolves into a multitude of individual developments, which seem only to have an extremely loose inner connection. If we direct our attention to individualism, which is especially characteristic of the nineteenth century, we still gain nothing decisive by doing so. For we see yet again that in the background a unifying stage management is operating, which from the beginning de-

termines the direction of the development and which
sought, at least, to decide the success or failure of individual people and trends. Although the difficult battle
that individual, especially German, masters were forced
to engage in to establish their worth may initially appear
to the observer as the personal struggle of genius against
an unsympathetic environment, we must ultimately recognize, if we want to look deeper, that it was not this
environment itself, but its secret rulers that so constantly
hindered the rise of these genial masters. Here, however,
we then come up against Judaism directly, which since
the beginning of the century also began to infiltrate into
the development of music as a self-contained power,
partly directly and partly indirectly, and proceeded out-
wards concentrically from various positions so as eventually in 1918 to control almost completely the musical life
not only of Germany but of the world.

It was precisely these different points of departure that
contributed a decisive element to the growth of Jewish
hegemony. Because of the fact that representatives of individual "tendencies" were externally in conflict with one
another the presumption was therefore made that a non-
Jew who opposed one of these tendencies would inevitably fall into the arms of the others. The most tragic case
of this kind is the case of Schumann, who in his celebrated criticism of *Les Huguenots* stood out manfully
against Meyerbeer under the banner of righteousness, but
in the same breath committed himself to Mendelssohn,
who externally represented a tendency other than Meyerbeer, yet precisely like the former worked not for
German music but for the establishment of a Jewish musical hegemony in Germany.

And referring specifically to Mendelssohn, Blessinger wrote:

In discussion of the Jewish question in music one is time
and again confronted with the assertion that Mendels-

sohn, for instance, was nevertheless a great master. Against this it must be stressed that the question of mastery as such is absolutely irrelevant to the matter under consideration here. It is self-evident, objectively considered, that it required the application of mastery and achievement to make it possible for Judaism to conquer and destroy the centuries-old German musical culture in such a short time. Yet only a, so to speak, baseless, i.e., Jewish, science can make this viewpoint the starting point for its judgment. For us, the question of who might have wielded this mastery and what the aims are that it serves must be in the foreground.

The fact now becomes clear that mastery and skill are things that certainly do not necessarily need to be united with creative power. And it is precisely the Jews who took care to acquire every kind of superficial skill from their host peoples, without thereby being in any way creatively gifted in our sense of the term, and we shall see that here too Mendelssohn was no exception; furthermore, it becomes absolutely clear, if one considers the phenomenon of Mendelssohn in connection with his family, that he used his mastery exclusively in the service of pan-Judaism and that his effectiveness, despite apparent harmlessness, decisively furthered the subversion of German musical life.

After sections on Mendelssohn and Bach, Mendelssohn as interpreter, and Mendelssohn as composer, all of which are exclusively negative, Blessinger ended his diatribe:

And if today musicians and music lovers still regret that their favourite compositions, i.e., the Midsummer Night's Dream overture, the Hebrides overture, the Violin Concerto, etc., have disappeared from the programme, we may first counter that it is infinitely more regrettable that highly significant works by German composers, such as the Schumann Violin Concerto, threatened to disappear completely because of Jewish intrigues.[72] And we may, secondly, assert that before the war [1914–1918] the music of Mendelssohn was universally no longer taken seriously in musical circles, that one used to pass it over as a matter of course with a deprecatory shrug of the shoulders, and that only after the fatal November 1918 did this music come into the foreground again. Before the war, apart from the "Songs without Words," in the music portfolios of young ladies, and the chorus "Wer hat dich schöner Wald," Mendelssohn was as good as forgotten. It was the Jews of the post-war period who tried to make him immortal at last. Let us once and for all get rid of this Jewish insinuation that the abandonment of Mendelssohn signifies an impoverishment of our music.[73]

This kind of twaddle stands in sharp contrast to the measured and thoughtful reassessment of Mendelssohn's historical significance and importance that the American musicologist of Hungarian birth, Paul Henry Lang, included in his *Music in Western Civilization* just two years later. While accepting some of the received wisdom about Mendelssohn's position in the canon, Lang's assessment must be counted among the freshest, most objective, and most favourable among important musicologists of his generation. He observed: "There can be no question that in many of Mendelssohn's works there is missing that real depth that opens wide perspectives, the mysticism of the unutterable. A certain sober clarity permeates his music, not the clarity of mood and conviction, but that of the organizing mind. His balanced proportions are the result not of a classic outlook on life but of a remarkable intellect and refined taste. . . . While we cannot help noting the limitations of Mendelssohn's music, largely due to his nature and his social philosophy, his frail figure becomes gigantic if we glance at the musical world around him. What he created is not overwhelming, it does not carry us away; he was not one of the very great, but he was and remains a master, and he has given us much that fills us with quiet enjoyment and admiration." Lang accepted Schumann's dictum that Mendelssohn was "the one who has most clearly recognized the contradictions of the time, and the first to reconcile them,"[74] commenting: "The dual personality of the romanticist is present in Mendelssohn, but it does not lead to internal struggle, sapping the physical and creative strength of the artist. Calm and clarity accompanied him throughout his life; a certain inborn feeling for orderly expression was seldom missing; the two personalities lived together and found expression alternately." Lang, writing almost a hundred years after Mendelssohn's death, was able to take a more detached view of Mendelssohn's place in the development of German music, and, having no direct connection with the period dominated by Mendelssohn's imitators, discerned that "in the hands of his lesser followers this art froze into sentimental academicism; what was brilliant craftsmanship and noble and truly artistic conception became mere formalism accentuated by sentimental pseudo-romanticism."[75]

The period immediately following the end of the Second World War in 1945 was characterized by a steady increase of scholarly engagement with Mendelssohn, resulting partly from a reaction to the Nazi proscription and partly from the interest engendered in 1947 by the hundredth anniversary of Mendelssohn's death. The quantity of biographical and critical studies and new editions of his music that has appeared during the second half of the twentieth century is impressive. Many studies have been published in scholarly journals and collaborative books and as monographs, many more of Mendelssohn's letters have become available in reliable versions (though a complete publication of the surviving letters remains a task for the twenty-first century). A projected complete edition of Mendelssohn's works, which began in 1960 and made available many unpublished early works for the first time, ceased publication in 1977, but work on a new scholarly edition was set on a sound footing again in 1997.[76] Attempts at a serious reappraisal of Mendelssohn and his works in general were given a boost by the publication of Eric Werner's *Mendelssohn*, in 1963; but despite his obvious sympathy, Werner's judgments on a substantial part of Mendelssohn's music frequently reflected older negative opinions, and, as a work of scholarship, the book is vitiated by inaccurate quotation and the absence of adequate referencing. One of the issues tackled in Werner's study—Mendelssohn's relationship to his Jewish origins, its effect on his life and its connection with his work—became a major focus for discussion, especially in the last couple of decades of the twentieth century, and has, inevitably, provoked a degree of controversy. The identification of a Mendelssohn "problem" by Carl Dahlhaus in 1974 focused sharper attention on the vicissitudes of Mendelssohn's reputation and their relationship to changing aesthetic criteria as well as the extra-musical factors that influenced the reception of his work.

In general books of music history many of the old stereotype views have regularly reappeared, freshly packaged but clearly recognizable. The almost unremittingly negative appraisal in *Man and his Music* (1962), by Harman and Mellers, for instance, even mimics Shaw's tone, as well as his prejudice, commenting on the oratorios: "We can take a little Tennysonian honey, so long as we are not simultaneously bullied with a pietistic morality that seems to us irrelevant."[77] In 1984 Leon Plantinga remarked towards the end of his cautious and rather conventional consideration of Mendelssohn that the "very qualities of amenity and regularity" that made his music popular in his own day made it "seem pallid by the end of the century, when the potently expressive musical language of Wagner and the Wagnerians had become the norm." But he concluded, perceptively, with the observation: "In the twentieth century, when all the styles of the nineteenth century seem historical, there are clear signs of a reawakening interest in the work of this extraordinarily gifted composer."[78] During the last two decades of the twentieth century a considerable number of substantial scholars devoted themselves extensively to Mendelssohn studies. Collections of essays (including eleven volumes of *Mendelssohn-Studien* [1972–1999] dealing with the Mendelssohn family in general), publications of conference papers, individual critical studies and biographical studies have offered stimulating and often bold reinterpretations of Mendelssohn's position, both historically and artistically.[79] And as Larry R. Todd pointed out at the end of his article on Mendelssohn for the second edition of *The New Grove Dictionary of Music and Musicians*, (2001) investigation of the still extensive unpublished materials "for the first complete edition of Mendelssohn's music and letters will undoubtedly reveal much new information about this critical figure in 19th-century musical life."[80]

For the listener, Mendelssohn's works have never been so easily or so comprehensively available as they have become through modern recordings; and the growing interest in historical performing practice, sweeping away many of the accretions of later traditions, has played an important part in providing a new aural experience that seeks, however speculatively, to recapture Mendelssohn's own conception of his music. These circumstances create fertile ground for continuing reassessment. The twenty-first century may truly be able to view Mendelssohn's life and work afresh, throwing off the shackles of inherited notions of originality and derivativeness, profundity and shallowness, sentiment and sentimentality.

Notes

The following abbreviations are used for the titles of German music journals:

AmZ   Allgemeine musikalische Zeitung
BamZ   Berliner allgemeine musikalische Zeitung
NBMz   Neue Berliner Musikzeitung
NZfM   Neue Zeitschrift für Musik
WaMZ   Wiener allgemeine Musik-Zeitung

ONE · *The Man*

1 · Appearance and Manner

1. Bennett, *Life*, 179.
2. *Grove's Dictionary* 3rd ed., 3: 418. (Told to Grove by Richard Doyle.)
3. C. Wagner, *Diaries* 2: 247.
4. *Athenaeum* 20 (1847): 1179.
5. Polko, *Reminiscences*, 76–77.
6. Benedict, *Sketch*, 7.
7. Lampadius, *Life*, 250.
8. Devrient, *Recollections*, 2–3.
9. K. Mendelssohn, *Goethe and Mendelssohn*, 3.
10. Devrient, *Recollections*, 64–66.
11. Hiller, *Letters*, 8.
12. Fétis, *Biographie*, 368. Fétis's perception of "haughtiness" may perhaps have had something to do with the unpleasantness that had occurred between them in London in 1829, when Fétis published an article, including a claim that Mendelssohn had spoken disparagingly of Purcell's music at a performance in St Paul's Cathedral, which Mendelssohn felt obliged to deny in print. The article and letter were printed in *Atlas* 4 (1829): 444, 460.
13. Lampadius, *Life*, 213.
14. Ward Jones, *Honeymoon*, 70. See also the editor's note on this reported incident, p. 65 n. 1.
15. Eckardt, *David*, 242.
16. Unpublished journal, Royal Archives, Windsor.
17. Polko, *Reminiscences*, 76–77.

18. *Grove's Dictionary*, 3rd ed., 3: 418 (partly from Moscheles).
19. Lampadius, *Life*, 213.
20. Lampadius, *Life*, 209.
21. Lampadius, *Life*, 249–50.
22. Sheppard, *Charles Auchester*, 32–33.
23. Wasielewsky, *Aus siebzig Jahren*, 60–61.
24. [Mrs (Sarah) Austin], *Fraser's Magazine* (1847): 733.
25. Chorley, *Modern German Music*, 2: 384.

2 · *Character and Personality*

26. Wasielewski, *Aus siebzig Jahren*, 61.
27. *Athenaeum* 20 (1847): 1179.
28. Chorley, *Modern German Music*, 2: 28–29 (footnote).
29. Rockstro, *Mendelssohn*, chap. 16.
30. Schumann, *Erinnerungen*, 76–77.
31. C. Wagner, *Diaries*, 2: 624.
32. C. Wagner, *Diaries*, 2: 627.
33. Wagner, *My Life*, 237–38.
34. For a stimulating discussion of Wagner's obsession with Mendelssohn, and Mendelssohn's aesthetic aims see Botstein, "Aesthetics," in Todd, ed., *Mendelssohn and His World*, 5–42.
35. Schumann, *Erinnerungen*, 32–33.
36. Berlioz, who genuinely admired Mendelssohn's music, was hurt to discover what Mendelssohn had written to his family about him when the *Reisebriefe aus den Jahren 1830 bis 1832* were published in 1861.
37. Macfarren, "Mendelssohn," *Imperial Dictionary*, quoted in Banister, *Macfarren*, 75.
38. Mendelssohn did not normally keep a diary; this was written jointly with Cécile between 29 Mar. and 27 Sept. 1837, partly so that they should have an account of each other's activities during their first separation.
39. Ward Jones, *Honeymoon*, 100–01.
40. See section 14 for the full text of this document.
41. Bruno Hake, "Mendelssohn als Lehrer, mit bisher ungedruckten Briefen Mendelssohns an Wilhelm von Boguslawski," *Deutsche Rundschau* 140 (1909): 453–70. Translated by Susan Gillespie in Todd, ed., *Mendelssohn and His World*, 332.
42. *Grove's Dictionary*, 3rd ed., 3: 418.
43. Moscheles, *Life* 1: 170.
44. Devrient, *Recollections*, 64–70.
45. Devrient, *Recollections*, 79–80.
46. Hiller, *Mendelssohn*, 2.
47. Hiller, *Mendelssohn*, 26.
48. Hiller, *Mendelssohn*, 31.

49. Hensel, *Family* 2: 316. (The duet referred to is the opening number of Spohr's *Faust*, sung by Faust and Mephisopheles in the streets of Mainz at night, after they have emerged from a party.)

50. Gotch, *Mendelssohn*, 46.

51. Gotch, *Mendelssohn*, 67.

52. Gotch, *Mendelssohn*, 71–72.

53. Ward Jones, *Honeymoon*, 96–97.

54. Hiller, *Mendelssohn*, 150–51.

55. Fanny to Klingemann, 1837, in Hensel, *Family* 2: 37.

56. Hiller, *Mendelssohn*, 130.

57. Brockhaus, *Tagebüche*, 1: 429. Several accounts of Mendelssohn's angry impatience with musicians and pupils are included in other chapters.

58. Hiller, *Letters*, 54.

59. Devrient, *Recollections*, 91.

60. Ward Jones, *Honeymoon*, 75.

61. Hiller, *Mendelssohn*, 171–72.

62. Journal, 16 June 1842, 10 Nov. 1847.

63. Schumann, *Erinnerungen*, 60–61.

64. Moscheles, *Life*, 2: 161. Schumann, in his *Erinnerungen*, 34–35, also stated that Mendelssohn never wanted to be seen as director. However, Eismann implausibly transcribed "nie" (never) as "nur" (only).

65. Mendelssohn, *Letters, 1833–1847*, 354.

66. Mendelssohn, *Letters from Italy and Switzerland*, 308.

67. Mendelssohn, *Letters, 1833–1847*, 75.

68. Mendelssohn, *Letters, 1833–1847*, 79.

69. Letter of 31 Jan. 1837, translated by Gillespie in Todd, ed., *Mendelssohn and His World*, 301.

70. A photograph thought by Max Schneider (*Felix Mendelssohn im Bildnis* [Basle, 1953]) to be of Felix Mendelssohn is now known to be of his brother Paul.

71. Nordmann, "Eine Begegnung," 74.

72. Eckardt, *David*, 182–83.

73. Schumann, *Erinnerungen*, 60–61.

74. See, for instance, his letter to G. A. Macfarren of 28 Dec. 1845 concerning the publication of his edition of Handel's *Israel in Egypt*.

75. Schumann, *Erinnerungen*, 26–27.

76. Literally "touch me not" plant; i.e. the Sensitive Plant (*Mimosa pudica*).

77. Kühne, "Felix Mendelssohn-Bartholdy." *Europa* (1847): 758.

3 · *Relationships with Women*

78. C. Wagner, *Diaries*, 1: 131.

79. Todd, ed., *Mendelssohn and His World*, 259ff.

80. Werner, *Mendelssohn*, 247.

81. Werner *Mendelssohn*, 384.

82. Letters to FMB from Louise Bendixen and from James William Davison, Bodleian Library, Oxford, MS MDM d.42 nos. 26 and 160. Actually, most of Davison's letter is an elaborate (serio-comic?) attempt to persuade Mendelssohn to dedicate the English edition of the Lieder op. 57 to the soprano Miss Dolby in such a way that Davison, who wanted to propose to her, could gain credit with her for obtaining the dedication. See also Boyd Alexander, "Felix Mendelssohn Bartholdy and Young Women," *Mendelssohn-Studien* 2 (1975): 71–101.

83. Unpublished letter in the New York Public Library (according to Werner).

84. Unpublished letter of 18 Oct. 1831 quoted in Werner, *Mendelssohn*, 182.

85. Nohl, *Letters*, 414.

86. Nohl, *Letters*, 425.

87. Citron, *Letters*, 279.

88. Hensel, *Family*, 2: 37.

89. Hensel, *Family*, 2: 23.

90. Hiller, *Mendelssohn*, 60–61.

91. Eckardt, *David*, 86–87.

92. Klingemann, *Briefwechsel*, 255–62.

93. MS M.D.M. c. 42: 131–32.

94. Moscheles, *Life*, 2: 165.

95. Holland and Rockstro, *Jenny Lind*, 1: 381.

96. Holland and Rockstro, *Jenny Lind*, 2: 9–10.

97. Werner, *Mendelssohn*, 435–36.

TWO · *Multiplicity of Talent*

4 · *Writing*

1. Schumann, *Erinnerungen*, 32–33, 36–37, 46–47, 50–51, 70–71.

2. Hiller *Mendelssohn*, 23.

3. Schumann, *Erinnerungen*, 60–61.

4. Schumann, *Erinnerungen*, 52–53.

5. Hauptmann, *Letters*, 2: 255–56.

6. Hiller, *Letters*, 169.

7. Schumann, *Erinnerungen*, 54–55.

8. Three of these are printed in Reissmann, *Felix Mendelssohn-Bartholdy*, 319ff.

9. Hiller, *Letters*, 170.

10. R. Larry Todd suggests that Voss was Droysen in *New Grove*, 2nd ed., but in a letter to Klingemann on 20 Feb. 1833 Mendelssohn writes, "I myself could even have made verses by Voss in his comic vein." *Briefwechsel*, 112.

11. *Das Mädchen von Andros* (Berlin, 1826), 3.

12. K. Mendelssohn, *Goethe and Mendelssohn*, 52–53.

13. Schneider, "Vorwort" to *Paphlëis*, 7.

14. See section 9.

15. See section 36.

5 · Editing Music

16. Devrient, *Recollections*, 163.

17. Handel, *Israel in Egypt*, preface.

18. Bodleian Library, Oxford, MS. M.D.M. d.45: 211.

19. K. Mendelssohn, *Goethe and Mendelssohn*, 175.

20. Bodleian Library, Oxford, MS. M.D.M. d.48: 175.

21. K. Mendelssohn, *Goethe and Mendelssohn*, 175–80.

22. Bodleian Library, Oxford, MS. M.D.M. d.48: 236.

23. K. Mendelssohn, *Goethe and Mendelssohn*, 185.

24. Schumann, *Erinnerungen*, 52–53.

6 · Drawing and Painting

25. Hensel, *Family*, 1: 221.

26. Devrient, *Recollections*, 175.

27. Mendelssohn, *Letters, 1833–1847*, 306.

28. Johann Gottlob Samuel Rösel (1768–1843).

29. Rudolf Elvers, trans. Craig Tomlinson, *Mendelssohn: A Life in Letters* (New York, 1986), 25.

30. Most of these are reproduced in David Jenkins and Mark Visocchi, *Mendelssohn in Scotland* (London, 1978).

31. Hensel, *Die Familie*, 1: 257.

32. Mendelssohn, *Letters from Italy*, 16.

33. Mendelssohn, *Letters from Italy*, 153–54.

34. MS MDM c.21 fol. 150, reproduced in *Felix Mendelssohn Bartholdy*, Bodleian Picture Books Special Series No. 3 (Oxford, 1972), no. 16.

35. Mendelssohn, *Letters from Italy*, 219–21.

36. Reproduced as the frontispiece to vol. 2 of John Ruskin, *Works*, The Library Edition, ed. E. T. Cook and Alexander Wedderburn. 39 vols. (London, 1903–1912).

37. *Letters, 1833–1847*, 108.

38. *Letters, 1833–47*, 261.

39. *See Family*, 1: 223

40. This painting, together with the twelve others from this stay in Switzerland, is beautifully reproduced in colour in F. Mendelssohn, *Aquarellenalbum*, ed. M. F. Schneider and C. Hensel (Basel, 1968).

THREE · *Family Background, Childhood and Education*

7 · *Moses Mendelssohn*

1. See section 15.
2. For the text of Friedrich Wilhelm II's patent giving equality with Christians to Daniel Itzig, his children, grandchildren and their spouses see Geiger, *Geschichte* 2: 147–50.
3. [Joseph Mendelssohn], "Moses Mendelssohn's Lebensgeschichte," in G. B. Mendelssohn, ed., *Moses Mendelssohn*, 1: 32.
4. G. B. Mendelssohn, ed., *Moses Mendelssohn*, 1: 53 4

8 · *Abraham, Leah and Fanny Mendelssohn*

5. Hensel, *Family*, 1: 62.
6. Hiller, *Letters*, 2.
7. Johann Peter Kirnberger (1721–1783), composer and theorist, pupil of J. S. Bach.
8. Marx, *Erinnerungen*, 1: 116.
9. Devrient, *Recollections*, 9.
10. Suttermeister, *Eine Reise*, 2nd ed., 299.
11. See Citron, *Letters*.

9 · *The Children's Education*

12. Carl Friedrich Zelter (1758–1832), composer, teacher and conductor of the Berlin Singakademie.
13. Ludwig Berger (1777–1839), composer and pianist.
14. Carl Wilhelm Henning (1784–1867).
15. Johann Gottlob Samuel Rösel (1768–1843).
16. Devrient, *Recollections*, 7–10.
17. Johann Ludwig Casper (1796–1853), medical doctor and writer on medicine, who was also active as a poet and writer of libretti.
18. Johann Daniel Heinrich Stümer, Berlin tenor, engaged at the Royal Opera from 1811 to 1830. He sang the evangelist in Mendelssohn's 1829 revival of Bach's *St Matthew Passion*.
19. Unidentified; probably another tutor, perhaps Rösel's predecessor as drawing master.
20. Unidentified.
21. Autograph letter in the Pierpont Morgan Library, Mary Flageler Catry Music Collection. My translation. Most of the letter is translated in Todd, *Mendelssohn's Musical Education*, 14–15.
22. The autograph manuscript of Felix Mendelssohn's *Paphlëis* was purchased at auction in 1952 by the Düsseldorf Landes- und Staatsbibilothek, and the poem

was published in Basel in 1961, edited and introduced by Ursula Galley, with a foreword by Max F. Schneider.

23. The introduction to the 1961 edition of the poem argues that it dates from autumn 1820 or spring 1821. Paul Mendelssohn later wrote on the paper in which the autograph is wrapped, "Fragment of a comic-heroic poem, entitled Paphlëis, which Felix made about me in around 1820. (Bruckstück aus einem Spott-Heldengedicht, betitelt (Paphlëis) welches Felix etwa um 1820 herum auf mich gemacht hat)." But it seems probable that, in its present form, it may have been written as late as 1823 or 1824. In a letter home from Doberan, written on 3 July 1824, Felix addressed Paul as "o Paphel!", suggesting perhaps that the poem was relatively fresh in their minds. The handwriting in the autograph seems considerably more mature and flowing than that of the letter of 22 March 1820, indicating that even if the poem was written earlier the surviving manuscript is a later fair copy.

24. See, section 4.

25. Each line of the present translation adheres faithfully, in its alternation of dactyls and trochees, to the verse structure of Mendelssohn's original. Mendelssohn's punctuation has been retained, except where it is peculiar to the German language, but since he used punctuation marks and, especially, quotation marks very sporadically and rather haphazardly, they have been supplemented here for the sake of clarity.

26. Devrient, *Recollections*, 2.

27. "Den Classiker Ιάχοψ," Friedrich Jakob's textbook *Elementarbuch der griechischen Sprache*, published in 1807.

28. A nonsense name.

29. This word is difficult to read and its meaning obscure.

30. Mendelssohn miscalculated the stress in this line and ended with two trochees; I have reproduced his error in the translation.

31. This is a nonsense word, but it evidently related to *Kalligraphie*.

32. *Bratäpfelbekränze*, presumably a baked-apple confection with decoration in the form of a garland.

33. The pun on *hören auf* (listen) and the separable verb *aufhören* (cease) in the line "Alle die Nachbarn hören nun auf, doch hören wir nicht auf" cannot be paralleled in English.

34. The meaning of "Schlicker und Masse" in this context is obscure. *Schlicker* is not a normal German word, and though *Masse* can mean bulk, both words were apparently intended to be nonsensical here.

35. Presumably one of the family's female servants. Here and three lines later Mendelssohn stresses the name Amalie (evidently pronounced Amalee) in two different ways: in this line it is ‾ ˘ ‾ and three lines later ˘ ˘ ‾.

36. Devrient, *Recollections*, 16, 19, 20–21
37. Schubring, "Reminiscences," 373ff.

38. This is almost certainly the Friedländer who lived at 44 Rosenthalerstraße, just round the corner from the Neue Promenade, from whose house Paul's companion Pinne is described as coming in *Paphlëis*.
39. Louis Spohr, 1784–1859. His opera *Faust* (1813) had been premièred in Prague in 1816 and was published in vocal score by Peters in 1822. It was not staged in Berlin until 1829.
40. The language of the toast is that of freemasonry; "assistant" is a translation of the German "Geselle" (otherwise translatable as "journeyman"). According to Hensel this event was a rehearsal of the opera that took place on Felix's fifteenth birthday, 3 February 1824. Hensel's version of Zelter's remark differs slightly from Dorn's; it is translated in Hensel, *Family*, 1: 120–21, as follows: "My dear boy, from today you are no longer an apprentice, but an independent member of the brotherhood of musicians [Geselle]. I proclaim you independent in the name of Mozart, in the name of Haydn and old father Bach."
41. Dorn, "Recollections," 397–99
42. Benedict, *Sketch*, 7–9.
43. Moscheles, *Life*, 97–98.
44. Speyer *Wilhelm Speyer*, 83.
45. See section 4.

FOUR · *Religion and Race*

1. Karl Lachmann, editor of the works of G. E. Lessing.
2. P. and C. Mendelssohn, *1830 bis 1847*, 4th ed., 2: 141–42.
3. Brockhaus, *Tagebüche*, 1: 388.
4. Bodleian Library, Oxford, MS. M.D.M. d.43: 17, 51.
5. J. Mendelssohn's note: Nicolai said: the "widow Bernhard"—but Bernhard still lived for a long time after this event.
6. [Joseph Mendelssohn], "Moses Mendelssohn's Lebensgeschichte," 49ff.
7. Hensel, *Family*, 1: 25.

8. The Privilege is printed in Geiger, *Geschichte*, 2: 147–50.
9. In 1769 Lavater challenged Mendelssohn either to embrace Christianity or refute it.

10. [Joseph Mendelssohn], "Moses Mendelssohn's Lebensgeschichte," 43–44.
11. Hensel, *Family*, 1: 79–80.

14 · *Felix Mendelssohn's Faith*

12. Mendelssohn's biblical quotations, from Luther's translation, have been given here in the King James Version of the Bible.
13. "durchleuchtendes Auge." Changed by Pfarrer Wilmsen to "durchschauendes Auge"—literally: through-seeing eye.
14. Wilmsen's amendment: How, in our youth, should we wholeheartedly experience knowledge, or how could we at any time faithfully and unswervingly fulfil our duty?
15. Wilmsen amended "Gras" to "Rohr" (reed).
16. As published in Klingemann's *Briefwechsel*, the passages given here in italics are printed in slightly larger type.
17. Mendelssohn seems to have quoted from memory and to have combined a number of phrases from different verses in this passage.
18. Wilmsen's addition: Through devout participation in the public communal worship of God.
19. Wilmsen's addition: "Let your light shine before men, that they may see your good works, and glorify your Father, which is in Heaven [Matthew 5:16]," says Christ.
20. Wilmsen's addition: So that his soul does not lack the most powerful and noblest sustenance and thus sink ever deeper.
21. Wilmsen amended "Heiden" (heathen) to "Völker" (peoples); the word here in the King James Version is nations.
22. Wilmsen's amended "zeigen" (show) to "andeuten" (indicate).
23. Wilmsen's addition: In any case it is not a matter of the personal presence of Christ in the Communion, but only a question of our absorbing the spirit of Jesus Christ and the image of his love and faith in us, and uniting ourselves with him in the sincerest belief in the reconciliation that he has endowed for us.
24. Wilmsen's addition: religious.
25. Wilmsen's amendment: the proscription [Verordnung].
26. Wilmsen's addition: in the Roman Empire.
27. The document, together with Wilmsen's response, is printed in Klingemann, *Briefwechsel*, 358–62.
28. Schubring studied with F. E. D. Schleiermacher (1768–1834) at the University of Berlin.
29. His compositions were invariably headed L.e.g.G. (Lass es gelingen Gott) or H.D.m. (Hilf Du mir).
30. Op. 35.
31. Schubring, "Reminiscences," 373ff.

Notes to Pages 90–103 · 509

32. Hensel, *Family*, 1: 74–75 (the first two sentences are only found in Werner, *Mendelssohn*, 33).

15 · The Family Name

33. Citron, *Letters*, 66–67.
34. The reference must be to the journey to Paris undertaken by Abraham and Felix in 1825, during which Cherubini endorsed the sixteen-year-old Felix's talent.
35. This, in fact, applied only to his publications and to his public activities; his own seal, which he used throughout his later years, had the Hebrew inscription "Moses the stranger from Dessau."
36. Abraham refers to the time when the family lived in Hamburg under French rule. This statement also lends support to the literalness of Zelter's comment, in a letter to Goethe, that Felix "is a good, handsome boy, happy and obedient. He may be the son of a Jew, but no Jew. The father, with significant sacrifice, has not circumcised his sons and brings them up properly as it should be done." In the original 1834 edition of *Briefwechsel* the reference to circumcision was excised; "seine Söhne nicht beschneiden lassen" became "seine Söhne etwas lernen lassen." The original text was first published in Max Hecker's edition of the correspondence. Leon Botstein, ("Aesthetics," 39–40), perhaps without considering Abraham's letter, suggested that Zelter's comment was intended metaphorically.
37. Bodleian Library, Oxford, MS.M.D.M.b.4, translated in Werner, *Mendelssohn*, 36–38.
38. Translated in Citron, *The Letters of Fanny Hensel*, 68.
39. However, he evidently used Bartholdy as his official name in Munich in 1831 (see section 40. For further discussion of this issue see Sposato, "Creative Writing," 196.

16 · Early Nineteenth-Century Anti-Semitism

40. Gilbert, *Bankiers*, 35, n. 54.
41. Werner, *Mendelssohn*, 28.
42. Botstein, "Aesthetics," 40, n. 40.
43. Institution of the German Federation from 1815 to 1866; based in Frankfurt.
44. *der leugnenden Scham.*
45. Varnhagen von Ense, *Denkwürdigkeiten*, 3: 541–42.
46. Werner, *Mendelssohn*, 40.
47. Todd, ed. *Mendelssohn and His World*, 262.
48. Werner, *Mendelssohn*, 282.
49. The phrase "erst setzen sie sich zehnmal, dann kömmt der Christ," in which the second word is very unclearly written, would literally mean "first they sit down [or: settle themselves] ten times, then might come the Christian."

50. Schumann, *Tagebücher*, 2:122–23.
51. See section 51.

FIVE · *Professional Career*

17 · The Singakademie

1. Partly quoted in Werner, *Mendelssohn*, 179.
2. Commissioned for Munich, with a libretto by Karl Immermann, but abandoned in the summer of 1832.
3. Mendelssohn, *Letters from Italy and Switzerland*, 337–40.
4. Letter of 25 May 1832 in Mendelssohn, *Letters from Italy and Switzerland*, 351–52.
5. Devrient, *Recollections*, 147.
6. Devrient, *Recollections*, 147–48.
7. Klingemann, *Briefwechsel*, 98.
8. Devrient, *Recollections*, 150.
9. Lampadius, *Life*, 32.
10. Klingemann, *Briefwechsel*, 100.
11. Klingemann, *Briefwechsel*, 110.
12. Devrient, *Recollections*, 153.
13. Mendelssohn had, however, directly criticised Devrient for his apparent self-satisfaction earlier in the year. See section 35.
14. A visit to Berlin by Moscheles in October had provided one of the bright spots in this otherwise unpleasant period.
15. Klingemann, *Briefwechsel*, 105–6.
16. Rellstab, *Kritiken*, 217.
17. *AmZ* 35 (1833): 126.
18. (1794–1842) one of Meyerbeer's brothers.
19. Klingemann, *Briefwechsel*, 110.
20. See his letter to Ganz, included in K. Mendelssohn, *Goethe and Mendelssohn*, 187.
21. The year of European revolutions.
22. Klingemann, *Briefwechsel*, 109.

18 · Düsseldorf

23. Klingemann, *Briefwechsel*, 112.
24. In the Bodleian Library, Oxford.
25. Actually 1817.
26. Ries (died 1838) conducted or co-conducted the festivals of 1825, 1826, 1828, 1829, 1830, 1832, 1834 and 1837.
27. Fétis, never averse to relaying a bit of scandal, wrote in his 1838 article on

Mendelssohn, in his *Biographie*, 1st ed., 6: 368: "A kind of rivalry had been established between him and Ries on the occasion of the Rhenish musical festival, because he was going to accept a post of kapellmeister at Düsseldorf that would give the two of them alternatively the duty of conducting these festivals. Unfortunately the consideration proper to distinguished artists was absent from this rivalry. Ries told me of the mortification this affair had caused him." In the 1863 edition (2d ed., 6: 79) the last sentence became: "Unfortunately the consideration proper to distinguished artists was absent from this rivalry. Mendelssohn spoke about the conducting of his competitor in scarcely polite terms, which were reported to the latter. Ries then told me about the mortification caused him by the unseemly language of his young rival."

28. Tr. Madame Decker.

29. It was common practice at this time to divide large orchestras into solo and ripieno groups, the former consisting of one pair of each wind instrument and a single pair of timpani together with the first few desks of string players, and the latter of the whole orchestra, which might contain two or three times the numbers of the solo group. Such a practice was almost universal at music festivals and was also current in Vienna in Beethoven's lifetime, at the Gesellschaft der Musikfreunde for instance, where the Fifth Symphony, among many other works, was performed in this fashion. (See Brown, *Die Neubewertung*.)

30. Woringen's account here glosses over the unpleasantness connected with Mendelssohn's withdrawal from his involvement with the theatre, illuminated below by quotations from his own letters, from a letter from his father, and in Devrient's *Recollections*.

31. See below for Mendelssohn's own comments on the state of music making in Düsseldorf in a letter to Ferdinand Hiller of 14 Mar. 1835.

32. v. W., "Felix Mendelssohn-Bartholdy in Düsseldorf in den Jahren 1833–35," *NBMz* 1, no. 48 (1847): 389–92. This account has not previously been available in English.

33. Mendelssohn, *Letters, 1833–1847*, 18–19.

34. Mendelssohn, *Letters, 1833–1847*, 28.

35. Mendelssohn's draft of "Observations," apparently intended for the directors of the Theatrical Association, dealing with the division of responsibilities between Immermann and himself in relation to the statutes of the association, probably dates from this period. It is preserved among his papers in the Bodleian Library, Oxford (MS M.D.M. c.49: 4).

36. Mendelssohn, *Letters, 1833–1847*, 47–48.

37. Mendelssohn, *Letters, 1833–1847*, 52–55.

38. Devrient, *Recollections*, 186–88.

39. Hensel, *Family* 1: 86–87.

40. Letter of 3 Jan. 1835 in Elvers, *Letters*, 204.

41. Hiller, *Mendelssohn*, 45–47

42. Despite Schleinitz's reputation among the unsympathetic as "Mendelssohn's toady," with the implication that his attachment to Mendelssohn was not based on sound musical judgment, he was apparently no mean musician; as a singer, Ferdinand Hiller described him as "one of the most distinguished of living amateurs" (Hiller, *Mendelssohn*, 152).

43. The former director, Pohlenz, had resigned in 1834.

44. Mendelssohn, *Letters, 1833–1847*, 76–78.

45. *AmZ* 37 (1835): 834.

46. *AmZ* 42 (1840): 26.

47. Lampadius, *Life*, 42–43.

48. See section 30.

49. Mendelssohn, *Letters, 1833–1847*, 82.

50. Loewe, *Selbstbiographie*, 191.

51. Moscheles, *Letters*, 197–98.

52. Hiller, *Mendelssohn*, 157. For the context of this quotation see section 30.

53. Chorley, *Music and Manners*, 3, 95, 103.

54. Schumann, *Music and Musicians*, 1: 364–65.

55. Schumann, *Music and Musicians*, 1: 388.

56. Schumann, *Music and Musicians*, 1: 393.

57. Hauptmann, *Letters* 2: 193.

58. Eckardt, *David*, 136.

59. 22 Aug. 1841, Bodleian Library, Oxford, MS M.D.M. d. 40: 47.

60. Eckardt, *David*, 141.

61. Chorley, *Music and Manners*, 3: 94.

62. The idea was first suggested by David in a letter of 31 May 1839, and Mendelssohn responded to it on 24 July with the comment, "You well know that you can always depend on me any time you need me and my fingers." Eckardt, *David*, 111 and 118.

63. 18 Nov. 1840, in Klingemann, *Briefwechsel*, 251.

64. See also Cooper, "Mendelssohn, David und Bach," 157–79.

65. Reporting on this concert, at which Mendelssohn played viola not only in his Octet, but also in Spohr's Double Quartet in D minor, op. 65, the *Allgemeine musikalische Zeitung* remarked: "Their performance acquired special interest on this occasion by the fact that Kapellmeister *Kalliwoda* and the composer of the Octet, *F. Mendelssohn-Bartholdy*, were so gracious as to undertake the viola parts, at which the public expressed its joy right at the start by loud acclamation. The performance of both pieces was full of spirit and life, in every respect extraordinarily successful as a whole, and the copious applause of the public followed every single movement." *AmZ* 42 (1840): 241.

66. Hiller, *Mendelssohn*, 156–63.

67. Brockhaus, *Tagebüche*, 1: 385.
68. Schumann, *Music and Musicians*, 1: 408.
69. Schumann, *Music and Musicians*, 1: 400.
70. Devrient, *Recollections*, 206–7.

20 · *The Genesis of the Leipzig Conservatorium*

71. Mendelssohn, *Letters, 1833–1847*, 183–88.

21 · *Between Berlin and Leipzig, 1841–1844*

72. D. Brodbeck, "A Winter of Discontent," 2.
73. Mendelssohn, *Letters, 1833–1847*, 203.
74. Mendelssohn, *Letters, 1833–1847*, 209.
75. See Mendelssohn, *Letters, 1833–1847*, 207.
76. Mendelssohn, *Letters, 1833–1847*, 217–19.
77. Klingemann, *Briefwechsel*, 258.
78. Mendelssohn, *Letters, 1833–1847*, 231–32.
79. Mendelssohn, *Letters, 1833–1847*, 233–35.
80. Devrient, *Recollections*, 222.
81. Mendelssohn, *Letters, 1833–1847*, 236–37.
82. Mendelssohn, *Letters, 1833–1847*, 238–39.
83. Mendelssohn, *Letters, 1833–1847*, 243.
84. Mendelssohn, *Letters, 1833–1847*, 247.
85. Devrient, *Recollections*, 234.
86. See section 30.
87. Mendelssohn, *Letters, 1833–1847*, 272.
88. See Mendelssohn, *Letters, 1833–1847*, 273–75.
89. Mendelssohn, *Letters, 1833–1847*, 275–79.
90. Moscheles, *Letters*, 232.
91. Mendelssohn, *Letters, 1833–1847*, 279.
92. Hiller, *Mendelssohn*, 199–200.
93. C. F. Becker, David, Hauptmann, Pohlenz and Schumann had formally been approached by Mendelssohn on 12 Jan. 1843 about teaching in the music school and had accepted. See Bodleian MS. M.D.M. d. 43: 23.
94. Klingemann, *Briefwechsel*, 279.
95. Klingemann, *Briefwechsel*, 280.

22 · *The Establishment of the Leipzig Conservatorium*

96. The preceding sentence was misleadingly translated by Gage as follows: "On one occasion, soon after the founding of the Conservatorium, he sat up the half of a night, in order to mark just high enough the performances of each scholar

at the examination." The German original (p. 144), however, reads: "In der ersten Zeit saß er einmal eine halbe Nacht, um bei der Censurvertheilung für jeden einzelnen Schüler eine passende Bemerkung niederzuschreiben." It seems likely that "Censurvertheilung" refers to the type of report on students' progress preserved in the Bodleian Library collection MS.MDM c.49: 12.

97. Lampadius, *Life*, 120–23.
98. Moscheles, *Letters*, 233.
99. This has been suggested on the basis of a misreading of a passage in Schumann's *Erinnerungen*. See Werner, *Mendelssohn*, 387.
100. Moscheles, *Letters*, 239–40.
101. *Repertorium* 1 (1844): 200–1.
102. Further information about Mendelssohn's involvement with the Conservatorium can be found in section 33.

23 · Generalmusikdirektor in Berlin

103. Bodleian MS. M.D.M. d.44: 22.
104. Mendelssohn, *Letters, 1833–1847*, 304–6.
105. Hensel, *Family*, 2: 217.
106. Hiller, *Mendelssohn*, 214.
107. See Hensel, *Family* 2: 217.
108. Hiller, *Mendelssohn*, 213.
109. Eckardt, *David*, 190.
110. Mendelssohn wrote the passage in parentheses in English.
111. At first Mendelssohn had been told that only strings could be used in the cathedral music.
112. Eckardt, *David*, 195–97.
113. Hensel, *Family*, 2: 237.
114. Hensel, *Family*, 2: 252.
115. See letter of 6 Nov. 1843, Bodleian Library, MS. M.D.M. d.44: 175.
116. Mendelssohn, *Letters, 1833–1847*, 319.
117. Mendelssohn, *Letters, 1833–1847*, 324–25.
118. Grove, *Dictionary*, 3rd ed., 3: 409.
119. Hensel, *Family* 2: 302.
120. See Mendelssohn, *Letters, 1833–1847*, 342–47

24 · The Final Years in Leipzig

121. Wagner reported that Hiller "boasted of having quarrelled with [Mendelssohn]." *My Life*, 295.
122. *Musical World* 21 (1846): 633.
123. Mendelssohn, *Letters, 1833–1847*, 314.
124. *Repertorium* 2 (1845): 313.

125. *Musical World* 50 (1846): 683–84.

126. See Meinaradus, *Jugendleben*, 1: 246.

127. Letters of 21 Dec. 1838 and 29 Jan. 1839, Bodleian Library, MS. M.D.M. d.34 no. 170 and MS. M.D.M. d.35 no. 40.

128. Evidently Conrad Schleinitz. The comment about Mendelssohn being "above all criticism," however, seems to reflect C. F. Becker's 1841 review of Psalm 95.

129. Herrmann Härtel and Carl Friedrich Kistner.

130. *Repertorium* 1 (1844): 199.

131. The German original uses capitals for the personal pronoun here and subsequently (though not consistently throughout, as reflected in this translation) when referring to Mendelssohn. This is normal in German (as in English) only when referring to God.

132. Perhaps an oblique reference to Schumann's review of the Psalm op. 42. See section 47.

133. In another article Hirschbach had made fun of the pretentiousness of the term *Conservatorium*.

134. Conrad Schleinitz.

135. Carl Friedrich Kistner (1797–1844).

136. Presumably David shared Mendelssohn's distaste for Berlioz and had not concealed the fact.

137. Hauptmann was of a retiring and sedentary disposition.

138. The *Signale* was considered "lightweight" music journal at that time.

139. *Repertorium* 2 (1845): 397–403.

140. Meinardus, *Jugendleben*, 246.

141. Brockhaus, *Tagebüche*, 2: 187.

142. Moscheles, *Life*, 2: 162.

SIX · *The Practical Musician*

25 · *Keyboard Playing*

1. Bülow, *Ausgewählte Schriften*, 2: 171. From a review of a performance of Mendelssohn's *Lobgesang* at Crystal Palace under August Manns written for *Signale* 35, no. 64 (1877).

2. Entry for 7 Dec. 1869 in C. Wagner, *Diaries*, 1: 70.

3. Benedict, *Sketch*, 24–25.

4. Reprinted in *Musical Times* 2(1848): 154–55.

5. *Athenaeum* 20 (1847): 1178.

6. Edwards, *Musical Haunts*, 43.

7. Bennett, *Life*, 179.

8. Letter of 10 Aug. 1840 in Mendelssohn, *Letters, 1833–1847*, 188.

9. *AmZ* 20 (1818): 791.

10. Aloys Schmitt (1788–1866). Pianist and composer. Established in Frankfurt from 1816, where he taught Ferdinand Hiller.

11. *AmZ* 24 (1822): 273.

12. *AmZ* 25 (1823): 55.

13. See section 11.

14. Rellstab, *Leben*, 2: chap. 11. Partly reproduced in K. Mendelssohn, *Goethe and Mendelssohn*, 11ff.

15. See *Die Gartenlaube* 1 (1867): 4–8.

16. Moscheles, *Life*, 1: 99–100.

17. *Quarterly Musical Magazine and Review* 7 (1825): 312 (translated "from a German periodical work").

18. See section 36.

19. *BamZ* 4 (1827): 96.

20. *Times*, 1 June 1829.

21. *Athenaeum* 2 (1829): 462.

22. Rollett, *Begegnungen*, 35–6.

23. Hiller, *Mendelssohn*, 17–18.

24. *Revue Musicale* 6 (1832): 59.

25. Devrient, *Recollections*, 157–8.

26. Schindler *Biographie*, 215.

27. Hiller, *Mendelssohn*, 35–36.

28. Chorley, *Modern German Music*, 49–52 (reprinted from his *Music and Manners*).

29. Original footnote: He was particularly pleased with the double diapason, in the swell, observing "how beautiful that *humming* is!" . . .

30. *Musical World* 6 (1838): 8–10.

31. Klingemann, *Briefwechsel*, 222.

32. In German notational convention B-flat, A, C, B-natural.

33. Schumann, *Music and Musicians*, 47–48, 45–46.

34. Bennett, *Life*, 179.

35. Allegro brillant in A, op. 92, composed 23 Mar. 1841.

36. Schumann, *Tagebücher*, 2: 45, 133, 144, 156, 262.

37. *Spectator* 17 (1844): 618–19.

38. *Musical World* 44 (1869): 666.

39. Polko, *Reminiscences*, 87–89.

40. H. C. Colles, retaining Grove's article, more or less entire, in the third edition of the dictionary (1928) observed: "It is retained as a masterly presentation of the view of Mendelssohn accepted when his reputation stood highest" (3: 374).

41. Grove's footnote: The late Dr Charles Graves, Bishop of Limerick.

42. *Grove's Dictionary*, 3rd ed., 3: 418, 422–23.

43. Trans. Susan Gillespie in Todd, *Mendelssohn*, 209, 211.

44. *Grove's Dictionary*, 3rd ed., 3: 423.

45. Moser, *Joachim*, 46.
46. See Brown, *Classical and Romantic*, 415ff.
47. See Cooper, "Mendelssohn, David und Bach," 157–79.
48. 14 Nov. 1840 in Mendelssohn, *Letters, 1833–1847*, 196–98.
49. Hans von Bülow's remark, reported by Grove.
50. Joachim and Moser, *Violinschule*, 3: 228.
51. See above, section 19.
52. *Grove's Dictionary*, 3rd ed., 3: 423.
53. K. Mendelssohn, *Goethe and Mendelssohn*, 11–12.
54. Devrient, *Recollections*, 11–12.
55. Hiller, *Mendelssohn*, 4–5.
56. This clause has been modified from Lady Wallace's version, where it was translated misleadingly as: "This was followed by a stop on the last note, and a pause,"
57. Mendelssohn, *Letters from Italy and Switzerland*, 265–67.
58. Devrient, *Recollections*, 140–41.
59. Polko, *Reminiscences*, 75.
60. *Musical World* 4 (1837): 9.
61. *Spectator* 17 (1844): 547.
62. Rockstro, *Mendelssohn*, 116–17; Holland and Rockstro, *Jenny Lind*, 1: 330.

27 · *Sight-Reading and Musical Memory*

63. Hirsch, *Gallerie*, trans. in *Musical World* 4 (1837): viii. The same passage also occurs in Schilling, *Encyclopaedie*, 655. According to Hirsch the information was derived from the 1833 edition of Brockhaus's *Conversations-Lexicon*, but this edition of Brockhaus does not include an article on Mendelssohn; presumably Hirsch made an error in citing his source, which I have not been able to identify.
64. Grove, *Dictionary*, 3rd ed., 3: 423.
65. Berlioz, *Voyage*, 1: 71.
66. Quoted in Grove, *Dictionary*, 3rd ed., 3: 423.
67. See section 11.
68. *Musical Times* 39 (1898): 226.
69. K. Mendelssohn, *Goethe and Mendelssohn*, 15–16.
70. Moscheles, *Life*, 1: 102.
71. Hiller, *Mendelssohn*, 55.
72. See section 11.
73. Hiller, *Mendelssohn*, 28–29.
74. Müller, *Auld Lang Syne*, 15–16.
75. C. Wagner, *Diaries*, 2: 138.
76. Dorn, "Recollections," *Temple Bar* 34 (1872): 404.

77. See section 9.
78. Letter of 11 Mar. 1823, cited in K. Mendelssohn, *Goethe and Mendelssohn*, 35.
79. Hiller, *Letters*, 4.
80. *BamZ* 4 (1827): 84.
81. Grove, *Dictionary*, 1st ed., 2:264.
82. See Franck, *Erinnerungen*, 3.
83. *AmZ* records occasions in 1836 (38 [1836]: 275) and 1840 (42 [1840]: 241), and Benedict (*Sketch*, 43) referred to another performance in 1843, which is also mentioned in Niels Gade's letter to his parents of 20 Nov. 1843 (see Krautwurst, 154), and in the *NZfM* 20/26 (28 Mar. 1844).
84. Krautwurst, "Mendelssohn als Bratschist" 151–60.
85. Webern, "Erinnerungen," 83.
86. See Spohr, *Selbstbiographie*, 2: 308.
87. *Musical Times* 1 Nov. (1897) quoted in Nichols, *Mendelssohn*,141.

29 · Other Instruments

88. Müller, *Auld Lang Syne*, 19–20.
89. Hiller, *Letters*, 20–1.

30 · Conducting

90. Schumann, *Erinnerungen*, and *Music and Musicians* 1: 374.
91. See below, note 116.
92. Devrient, *Recollections*, 6–7.
93. Schubring, "Reminiscences," 373ff. Reprinted in Todd, *Mendelssohn*, 228, 229.
94. *BamZ* 2 (1825): 365.
95. Devrient, *Recollections,* 58–61.
96. See Woringen's account in section 18.
97. The family's residence outside Hamburg at the time of Felix's birth.
98. Hensel, *Family*, 1: 284–85.
99. Mendelssohn, *Letters, 1833–1847*, 20.
100. Benedict, *Sketch*, 24–5.
101. Lampadius, *Life*, 44.
102. Hiller, *Mendelssohn*, 156–58.
103. Polko, *Reminiscences*, 76–77.
104. See section 19.
105. The Berlin orchestra, which had been run with almost miltiary discipline by Spontini, was subject to fines for misbehaviour.
106. Eckardt, *David*, 156.
107. See Devrient, *Recollections*, 234. (See section 21.)

108. See Eckardt, *David*, 190 (but see section 23).

109. A long article on the controversy, from the *Musical Examiner*, is reprinted in Nichols, *Mendelssohn*, 146–53.

110. *Atlas* 20 (1845): 347.

111. *Spectator* 17 (1844): 466.

112. Hauptmann, *Letters*, 2: 191.

113. Wasieliewski, *Aus siebzig Jahren*, 58–60.

114. See section 33.

115. Meinardus, *Tonkunst*, 212.

116. Wagner, *On Conducting*, 22–24.

117. See above, note 90.

118. See Brown, *Classical and Romantic*, 299ff.

119. *John Bull*, 13 July 1844.

120. Grove, *Dictionary*, 3rd ed., 3: 423.

121. Lampadius, *Life*, 172–76.

SEVEN · *The Teacher*

31 · Charles Edward Horsley

1. Hake, "Mendelssohn als Lehrer," 453–70.

2. See Klingemann, *Briefwechsel*, 112.

3. Camille Marie Stamáty (1811–1870).

4. Grandson of Johann Wolfgang von Goethe.

5. Eduard Franck (1817–1893), who had already begun to study with Mendelssohn in Düsseldorf.

6. Klingemann, *Briefwechsel*, 206.

7. Bennett, *Life*, 41–2.

8. Klingemann, *Briefwechsel*, 202.

9. Mendelssohn first met Hauptmann in 1834. See Hauptmann, *Letters*, 1: 109.

10. K. Mendelssohn, *Goethe and Mendelssohn*, 116–18.

11. K. Mendelssohn, *Goethe and Mendelssohn*, 127–30.

12. Horsley, "Reminiscences," 346.

32 · Emil Naumann

13. Mendelssohn, *Letters, 1833–1847*, 168–71.

14. Charles Horsley.

15. Naumann's footnote: Word for word as immediately written down.

16. Naumann "Erinnerungen," *NBMz* 3(1865): 353–355 and 361–2. The letter referred to in the final sentence is given in Mendelssohn, *Letters, 1833–1847*, 353–54, where it is mistakenly dated March 1845. The final part of Naumann's reminiscences

(pp. 362–63) concerns the music festival at Aachen, which Mendelssohn directed in May 1846.

33 · *The Leipzig Conservatorium (Wasielewski, Rockstro, Meinardus)*

17. A word play on *Leibdiener*, which means valet, literally body servant.
18. Wasielewski, *Aus siebzig Jahren*, 34–36.
19. Rockstro's note: We have already alluded to this, in connexion with his powerful rendering of Beethoven's Concerto in G major, and his own, in G minor.
20. Rockstro's note: No other clef was ever used at the Conservatorium for the soprano part; nor were the students ever permitted to write alto or tenor parts in any other than their true clefs. This wholesome law was absolute in all the classes.
21. Rockstro's note: In July, 1846, the writer enjoyed the privelege of having a Double Quartett tried in this way, the two first-violin parts being played by David and Joachim.
22. Rockstro's note: "Ich bin ein sehr beschäftiger Mann."
23. Rockstro's note: "Dummes Zeug."
24. Rockstro's note: He once gave the writer a theme, consisting simply of three Cs—a dotted quaver; a semiquaver, and a crotchet: and afterwards extemporised upon it himself; using the three Cs as the initial notes of an enchanting little melody, which he worked up into a species of *Lied ohne Worte.*"
25. Rockstro, *Mendelssohn,* 104–13.
26. Stanford, *Pages,* 74–5.
27. Moscheles, *Life,* 2: 171.
28. Bodleian Library, Oxford MS. M.D.M. d. 50: 179. Meinardus's elder brother had already written in 1843 inquiring about the possibility of Ludwig Siegfried's entering the newly founded Conservatorium (MS. M.D.M. d. 44: 136).
29. The German word is *Primaner,* which indicates a pupil in the highest class of a *Gymnasium.*
30. Johann Christoph Gottsched (1700–1766), author, dramatist and critic. He insisted that German literature should be subordinated to the laws of French classicism but was worsted in controversy with the Swiss writers Johann Jakob Bodmer and Johann Jakob Breitinger, who demanded that poetic imagination should not be hampered by artificial rules.
31. Gotthold Ephraim Lessing (1729–1281), author, dramatist and critic. His critical work *Laokoon,* his dramas *Minna von Barnheim* and *Nathan der Weise* (in which the eponymous character is a thinly veiled portrait of his friend Moses Mendelssohn), and other writings gave him an important place in eighteenth-century German literature.
32. The German word *Zerrbild* implies a rather unpleasant caricature or cartoon.
33. Meinardus, *Jugendleben,* 1: viii, 208, 217–45, 256.

34. Schumann, *Erinnerungen*, 38–9, 44–5.

35. Schumann, *Tagebüche*, 2: 81.

36. Reinecke, *Und manche liebe Schatten steigen auf.* Berlin, 1900. Trans. in Todd, *Mendelssohn and His World*, 312. Reinecke studied privately with Mendelssohn in 1843 and was closely associated with Schumann.

37. Meinardus, *Tonkunst*, 212.

34 · Joseph Joachim

38. Moser, *Joachim*, 39–40, 45–6, 67, 73.

EIGHT · *The Composer*

35 · Aesthetics and Aspirations

1. Schumann, *Erinnerungen*, 36–7.

2. See section 18.

3. Turner, "Mendelssohn's Letters", 212 (my translation).

4. Moscheles, *Letters*, 242.

5. Hiller, *Mendelssohn*, 155–6.

6. Klingemann, *Briefwechsel*, 282.

7. Devrient, *Recollections*, 195–6.

8. Schumann, *Erinnerungen*, 42–3.

9. From a conversation with J. C. Lobe originally published by Lobe as "Gespräche mit Feilx Mendelssohn" in *Fliegende Blätter für Musik* 1 (1855): 280–96, in which Mendelssohn's ideas about composition are expounded at considerable length. There is an English translation of the whole article by Susan Gillespie in Todd, *Mendelssohn and His World*. This translation is taken from Marx, *Music of the Nineteenth Century*, 51. Further insight into Mendelssohn's attitude towards techniques of composition is given by Emil Naumann in the passage quoted in section 32.

10. Mendelssohn, *Letters from Italy and Switzerland*, 304.

11. See section 44.

12. See Fink's critique of *St Paul*, section 44.

13. See section 2.

14. Schumann, *Erinnerungen*, 36–37.

15. Devrient, *Recollections*, 113.

16. Eckardt, *David*, 95.

17. Devrient, *Recollections*, 241–42 (with additions from Turner, "Mendelssohn's Letters," 231).

18. Mendelssohn, *Letters, 1833–1847*, 269–70.

19. Mendelssohn, *Letters from Italy and Switzerland*, 123.

20. Hiller, *Letters*, 44.

21. Moscheles, *Letters,* 97.

22. Devrient, *Recollections,* 120–21.

23. Mendelssohn, *Letters, 1833–1847,* 228.

24. Moscheles, *Letters,* 118–20.

25. Hensel, *Family,* 1: 163.

26. Mendelssohn, *Letters, 1833–1847,* 2.

27. Klingemann, *Briefwechsel,* 82–83.

28. Mendelssohn, *Letters, 1833–1847,* 125–26.

NINE · *Critical Reception*

36 · The Early Years, 1818–1829

1. See section.

2. This was probably the fully orchestrated version of his D major string symphony, of which Moscheles heard a performance in Berlin in 1824.

3. *AmZ* 25 (1823): 337, as translated in the *Quarterly Musical Magazine and Review* 5 (1823): 409.

4. K. Mendelssohn, *Goethe and Mendelssohn,* 51–52.

5. *BamZ* 1: (1824): 168–69.

6. *AmZ* 26 (1824): 181–84.

7. *AmZ* 27 (1825): 531–32.

8. Eurer Sonata: familiar plural, i.e., Mendelssohn and Rietz. The use of the familiar plural here and elsewhere gives the review an even more patronizing tone than is apparent in English.

9. *BamZ* 2 (1825): 367–67 (*sic*! actually three pages: there is a printing error in the journal which gives the page that should rightly have been 368 as 366, and the mistaken numbering then continues).

10. Mendelssohn, *Paphlëis,* "Vorwort," 7 (translation from Grove).

11. Schumann, *Erinnerungen,* 64–65.

12. *BamZ* 2 (1825): 365.

13. S. d. K. L. C., "Berlin in 1825," *Caecilia* 4 (1826): 83.

14. *Caecilia* 4 (1826): 85.

15. *AmZ* 29 (1827): 156–57.

16. See section 25.

17. *das englische rohtönige Basshorn.* Presumably the ophecleid part, perhaps played here on an instrument of the serpent family.

18. "Felix Mendelssohn-Bartholdy in Stettin (eingesandt [sent in])," *BamZ* 4 (1827): 83–84.

37 · Die Hochzeit des Camacho

19. Hensel, *Family,* 1:132.

20. His charming liederspiel *Heimkehr aus der Fremde* was written to be privately

performed for his parents' silver wedding celebration in 1829, and he never considered publishing it. It was first publicly performed in 1851 in Leipzig and later the same year in England, translated by H. F. Chorley as *Son and Stranger*.

21. *BamZ* 4 (1827): 141–42.
22. *AmZ* 29 (1827): 410–12.
23. *AmZ* 31 (1829): 353–56.
24. Polko, *Reminiscences*, 217.

38 · Piano Music and Songs, 1825–1829

25. *AmZ* 29 (1827): 122–23.
26. *AmZ* 30 (1828): 63.
27. *AmZ* 29 (1827): 813–15.
28. *Caecilia* 8 (1828): 111.

39 · The Initial Impact of Mendelssohn's Music in England

29. From *AmZ* 25 (1823): 337 (given above in note 3).
30. *Quarterly Musical Magazine and Review* 7 (1825):312. See section 25.
31. *Harmonicon* 7 (1829): 173.
32. *Athenaeum* 2 (1829): 364.
33. *Atlas* 4 (1829): 364.
34. Devrient, *Recollections*, 87.
35. *AmZ* 38 (1836): 337–38.
36. Holland and Rockstro, *Jenny Lind*, 1: 388–89.
37. His visit to Berlin is recorded in Fanny's diary for 31 Aug. 1829. See Citron, *Letters*, 82.
38. *Harmonicon* 8 (1830): 101.

40 · The Years of Widening Recognition, 1831–1836

39. He refers to the secular cantatas for the Dürer festival (April 1828) and for Humboldt (September 1828).
40. K. Mendelssohn, *Goethe and Mendelssohn*, 186–87.
41. Mendelssohn left Munich with a commission for an opera.
42. *AmZ* 34 (1832): 57–58.
43. See section 25.
44. Hiller, *Recollections*, 20.
45. Hiller, *Recollections*, 21.
46. The parts of *Ein Sommernachtstraum* were published in 1832, and parts and a piano duet arrangement of *Die Hebriden* in 1833. *Meerstille* was extensively revised in 1834 before its publication as score and parts in 1835. *Die schöne Melusine*, was published simultaneously in score and parts in 1836.

47. *Harmonicon* 10 (1832): 152.
48. *Athenaeum* 5 (1832): 356
49. See section 17.
50. *AmZ* 35 (1833): 22–23.
51. *Caecilia* 16 (1834): 256–60.
52. *Die Klage hat nicht Grund, wohl aber Gründe.*
53. The works were published only in orchestral parts not in score, at that time. 141–42.
54. *AmZ* 37 (1835): 209–11.

42 · The Concert Overtures

55. *Harmonicon* 10 (1832): 141–42.
56. *Athenaeum* 34 (1832): 326.
57. *AmZ* 35 (1833): 126.
58. *AmZ* 36 (1834): 428–29.
59. The mixed metaphor is Fink's!
60. In 1836 (see the next paragraph), this clause became "by which means the inner world is expanded, and the beauty of the image is made even stronger and more penetrating by translation into another medium."
61. [G. W. Fink] *AmZ* 37 (1835): 295–96.
62. *AmZ* 38(1836): 322–23.
63. *Conversations-Lexicon* (Leipzig: Gebrüder Riechenbach, 1836), 7: 164.

43 · Songs without Words

64. Ward Jones, "Mendelssohn and His English Publishers," in Todd, *Studies*, 240–55.
65. Brockhaus, *Conversations-Lexikon*, 9th ed., 9: 489.
66. Kahlert, "Claviercompositionen," 257–58.

44 · St Paul

67. Brockhaus, *Conversations-Lexikon*, 9th ed., 9: 489.
68. Fink, "Paulus,"*AmZ* 39 (1837): 497–506, 513–30.
69. Ward Jones, *Honeymoon*, 95.
70. Moscheles, *Letters*, 220–21.
71. [Taylor], "The Birmingham Festival," *Spectator* 10 (1837): 899–901.
72. *Musical World* 4 (1837): 9.
73. The journal was filled at that time with reports on the seventh meeting of the British Association for the Advancement of Science.

74. *Athenaeum* 39 (1837): 709.

75. Pearson, "Deutsche Oratorienmusik," *WaMZ* 3 (1843): 123.

76. Fanny, in a letter of 4 Feb. 1836 (Citron, *Letters,* 199), criticized some of the recitatives as having passages that were "too modern."

77. Ds, "Ueber Mendelssohns Paulus," *Caecilia* 19 (1837): 201–16.

78. Many reviews discussed the propriety of setting God's words to Paul on the road to Damascus for a female chorus.

79. Schumann, *Music and Musicians,* 1: 302–11.

80. Fétis, *Biographie,* 1st ed., 6: 368–69.

81. Immaterial comment on the singer Charlotte Weltheim.

82. In contrast, Fanny remarked in her letter of 4 Feb. 1836 that it was in the recitatives that "the strength of the entire work resides."

83. Paris [pseudonym for Jeanette von Haza], "Flüchtige Bemerkungen", *Caecilia* 20 (1838): 135–50

84. Schumann, *Music and Musicians,* 1: 276.

85. *AmZ* 44 (1842): 386.

86. Philokales, "Paulus," *WaMZ* 6 (1846): 565.

46 · General Appraisals during Mendelssohn's Lifetime

87. Hirsch acknowledged the Brockhaus *Conversations-Lexicon* (1833), i.e., the 8th edition, as his source, but Brockhaus did not, in fact, contain an article on Mendelssohn until the 9th edition in 1846.

88. Schilling, *Encyclopädie,* 4: 654–56.

89. Hirsch "Mendelssohn," *Gallerie,* 81.

90. Such as the writer's comment on the reception of *St Paul.* See section 44.

91. See section 26.

92. Anon, "Life of Felix Mendelssohn Bartholdy," *Musical World* 4 (1837): 6–10.

93. See section 18, note 27.

94. Fétis, *Biographie,* 1st ed., 6: 367–69.

95. *Revue musicale* (trans. in *AmZ* 48 (1846): 377).

96. See Federhofer-Königs, "Der unveröffentliche Briefwechsel," 7–94.

97. Untranslatable wordplay: *liebenswürdige als würdige.*

98. Becher, "Über Hektor Berlioz," *WaMZ* 5 (1845): 589–90.

99. Brendel, "Robert Schumann," 149. (Partly translated in Jurgen Thym, "Schumann in Brendel's *NZfM* from 1845 to 1856," in Finson and Todd, *Mendelssohn and Schumann,* 32–33.)

100. The author had stated incorrectly, as in earlier biographical articles, that Mendelssohn was born in Berlin.

101. Brockhaus, *Conversations-Lexikon,* 9th ed., 9: 488–89.

102. *Repertorium* 2 (1845): 391–92.
103. Schumann, *Music and Musicians*, 2: 63–66.
104. The term *mannerism (Manier)* was used pejoratively both in English and German at that time, to indicate the excessive employment of recognizable formulas. In music it was levelled particularly against the later works of Spohr.
105. I.e., natural horns in different keys to increase the available natural notes.
106. A. K. [August Kahlert], *AmZ* 45 (1843): 341–44.
107. *Musical World* 17 (1842): 185–87.
108. Schumann, *Music and Musicians*, 2: 113–15.
109. *AmZ* 47 (1845): 204.
110. *AmZ* 47 (1845): 787.
111. *AmZ* 48 (1846): 873–77.
112. H. H. [Herrmann Hirschbach], *Repertorium*, 2 (1845): 217.
113. Schumann, *Music and Musicians*, 2: 184.
114. Schumann, *On Music and Musicians*, 217.
115. Fink, *AmZ* 42 (1840): 497–99.
116. Todd, "Mendelssohn, Felix," in *New Grove Dictionary of Music and Musicians*, 2nd ed., London, 2001, 16:409.
117. See section 50.
118. Riehl, *Musikaliche Charakterköpfe*, 1: 115–16 (footnote).
119. *Drei Kirchenmusiken*, op. 23 (1830), and Psalm 115, op. 31 (1835).
120. Notably opp. 78 and 79 in 1849 and op. 91 in 1851.
121. Werner, *Mendelssohn*, 347.
122. *Musical World* 24 (1849): 54.
123. Schumann, *Music and Musicians*, 1: 381–82.
124. *AmZ* 41 (1839): 119–23.
125. Schumann, *Music and Musicians*, 1: 400.
126. *AmZ* 42 (1840): 26.
127. *AmZ* 44 (1842): 1.
128. Schumann, *Music and Musicians*, 1: 115.
129. *Neue Zeitschrift für Musik* 13 (1840): 188.
130. *AmZ* 44 (1842): 181, 208.
131. *Musical World* 24 (1849): 54.
132. *Musical World* 24 (1849): 53.
133. Quoted in Hermann Menges, "Auch ein Wort über das Oratorium 'Paulus' von Mendelssohn–Bartholdy. *Berliner musikalische Zeitung* 3, no. 40 (3 Oct. 1846):" n.p. [4].
134. Lange, "Elias," NBMz 1 (1847): 399–400.
135. Jahn, "Ueber F. Mendelssohn Bartholdy's Oratorium Elias," *AmZ* 50 (1848): 113–4.
136. Jahn, "Elias," *AmZ* 50 (1848): 119–21, 143.

137. Brockhaus, *Tagebüche*, 2: 156, 187.

138. Krüger, "Ueber die heutige Oper," *NZfM* 12 (1840): 58–59.

139. Brockhaus, *Conversations-Lexikon*, 9: 489.

140. See section 48, especially Kühne.

141. But see Tovey's comment below, section 52.

TEN · *Posthumous Reputation*

48 · *Obituaries and Contemporaneous General Assessments*

1. Facsimile in Schumann, *Erinnerungen*, 27

2. Schumann made similar remarks, twice, in his *Erinnerungen*: "Did he feel that his mission was fulfilled?" (50/51). "His mission was fulfilled. He himself knew this best of all." (54/55).

3. The whole of the section omitted here is included in section 2.

4. Blücher: general commanding the Prussian forces against Napoleon at Waterloo.

5. K. seems not to have been aware of the early date of the *Midsummer Night's Dream* Overture, as his comment below indicates.

6. K.'s footnote: We hear that Mendelssohn wrote a quartet in the Rhineland during the summer, which, in its passionate impetus is the fieriest product of his muse and will be numbered among his best soul portraits with respect to depth and beauty. A few weeks before his death his friends played it for him. It has not yet been heard in public. An opera is also talked about (perhaps the Lurelei [*sic*], text by Geibel), of which the first act is said to be finished, this too being a work from last summer in the Rhineland. Five new songs of his are being published by Breitkopf und Härtel.

7. K. [(Ferdinand) Gustav Kühne, 1806–1866], "Felix Mendelssohn-Bartholdy," *Europa* (13 Nov. 1847): 757–59.

8. Berlin. The writer evidently forgot that Mendelssohn was born in Hamburg.

9. Kossak, "Felix Mendelssohn-Bartholdy", *NBMz* 1 (1847): 369–72.

10. *Atlas*, reprinted in *Musical Times* 2 (1848): 154.

11. *Times*, 18 Nov. 1847, p. 5.

12. *Athenaeum* 20 (1847: 1178.

13. *Fraser's Magazine* (1847): 737.

14. Footnote: To which we may add the scherzos of his quartets in E flat and E minor, from the last published set, and the Intermezzo of the quintet in A.— Ed. M. W.

15. Macfarren, "Mendelssohn," *Musical World* 24 (1849): 33–37, 56.

49 · *Critical Consensus in England during the 1850s*

16. *Athenaeum*, reproduced in *Musical World* 27 (1852): 821.

17. *Dwight's Journal*, reprinted in *Musical World* 31 (1856): 541.

18. *Musical World* 31(1856): 536–37.

19. See section 51.
20. See Donald Mintz, "1848," 126–48.
21. Krüger used the word *kirchlich*, translated here as ecclesiastical; elsewhere he also used *geistlich*, translated as sacred, and at one point (not included here) contrasted the two. His intention is not entirely clear, however. He clearly did not intend *kirchlich* to mean liturgical, since he evidently regarded the term as applicable to the oratorios. In a later article Krüger defined the terms, obscurely, as follows: "the ecclesiastical [Kirchliche] (in art) is the plastic animated beauty of open truth, the sacred [Geistliche] a reflection of it, a dark-coloured abolition of that bright, light form." *NBMz* 1 (1850): 81.
22. Johannes Eccard (1553–1611) was widely seen in mid-nineteenth-century Germany as a Protestant equivalent to Palestrina, representing the pure *a capella* ideal for nineteenth-century Protestant church music.
23. In Donald Mintz's stimulating article (p. 137) this passage ("ihr Preis ist an den gegenwärtig wirkenden liebenswürdigen Sänger geknüpft gewesen und mit ihm gestorben") is mistranslated as "praise for them was linked to the beloved singers then performing them and died with those singers."
24. The poet who provided the text of Mendelssohn's unfinished opera *Dic Lorelei*.
25. Krüger, "Drei Psalmen," *NBMz* 4 (1850): 3–5.
26. Wauer, "Mendelssohn und Krüger," *NBMz* 4 (1850): 25–27.
27. This seems directly to challenge the Hegelian ideas that were central to Abraham Mendelssohn's way of thinking.
28. Krüger, "Zur Kritik Mendelssohn's," *NBMz* 4 (1850): 81–83.
29. Riehl's article seems to have been originally published shortly after Mendelssohn's death, possibly in the Nassau *Allgemeine Zeitung* or the Augsburg *Allgemeine Zeitung*, for which he wrote between 1847 and 1850. It was reprinted in the first volume of his *Characterköpfe* in 1853, immediately after an article on Bach, with the following introduction: "To this picture of the most honourable German burger and musician of the eighteenth century may be contrasted the phenomenon of a genuine child of the nineteenth, of a man who belonged just as much to the 'cultivated society' as Bach did to the bourgeoisie, who had a rare understanding of Bach, who had strengthened and inspired himself through the study of Bach's works yet who was, from the social point of view, an artistic personality different to the point of contradiction from the old master. The pages on Bach's social characteristics were an obituary—on the hundredth anniversary of his death: the following sketch is likewise an obituary, written under the immediate impact of the death of a significant contemporary:—in November 1847."
30. "das deutche Reich." At the time of Mendelssohn's death the idea of a united German Empire seemed a remote possibility to many; Riehl probably refers obliquely to the demise of the Holy Roman Empire in 1806.

31. "Reich." Riehl's quotation marks.

32. "der nicht jüdelte in seiner Schreibarten." The German verb *jüdeln* has no equivalent in English; it means literally "to speak with a Jewish accent and use Jewish expressions." Compare with Wagner's *Das Judenthum in der Musik*.

33. "jüdelten."

34. See here Lobe's reports of conversations with Mendelssohn about "originality" in Todd, *Mendelssohn and His World*, 187–205.

35. Riehl, *Musikalische Characterköpfe*, 91–116.

51 · Das Judenthum in der Musik

36. *Das Judenthum in der Musik* was first published under the pseudonym K. Freigedank in the *Neue Zeitschrift für Musik* in 1850 and later issued under Wagner's own name in a slightly revised and expanded edition in 1869.

37. Translator's note: A mocking (supposed Hebrew) pronunciation of "Geplapper," meaning babble.

38. Original note: Of the New-Jewish system designed upon the basis of this particular quality of Mendelssohn we speak later.

39. R. Wagner, *Judaism in Music*, 1–39.

40. Oxford, Bodleian Library, MS. M.D.M. d.43: 289.

41. Cited in Werner, *Mendelssohn*, 390.

42. C. Wagner, *Diaries*, 2: 319, 369.

43. C. Wagner, *Diaries*, 1: 120–21.

52 · *Changing Critical Perspectives*

44. Lenz, *Beethoven et ses trois styles*, 1: 39–40.

45. See Marx, *Music of the Nineteenth Century*, 89, for instance, where Marx claimed that Mendelssohn's example caused his contemporaries to flee from "everything indicative of strength of character and decision"; blaming him for encouraging their "undecided and effeminate aspirations."

46. Schlüter, *General History*, 323–34, 327, 348, 350.

47. Reissmann, *Felix Mendelssohn-Bartholdy*, 317, 310, 311.

48. The word *puritain* was often used as synonymous with Protestant.

49. Barbedette, *Mendelssohn Sa vie*, 150–51.

50. Niecks, "On Mendelssohn," *Monthly Musical Record* 5 (1875): 162–64.

51. *Musical Times* 18 (1877): 209.

52. Loeper, "Mendelssohn-Bartholdy," 21:344.

53. Haweis, *Music and Morals*, 90–91.

54. Crowest, *Great Tone Poets*, 315.

55. See sections 46 and 47.

56. Paine and Lewis, "Music in Germany," 592.

57. In a review of 23 February 1889, reprinted in *The Great Composers Reviews and*

Bombardments by Bernard Shaw, ed. Lewis Compton (Berkeley and Los Angeles, 1978), 122.

58. Dwight "Mendelssohn", 424, 431, 436

59. Dole, *Famous Composers*, 2nd ed., 347, 375, 374.

60. *Manchester Guardian*, 3 Feb. 1909, reprinted in Ernest Walker, *Free Thought and the Musician* (Oxford, 1946), 30–34.

61. Graves, *Post-Victorian Music*, 149, 146–48.

62. Stanford, *A History*, 284.

63. See above, note 43.

64. *Encyclopedia Britannica*, 11th ed., 18:124.

65. *Encyclopedia Britannica*, 14th ed., 15:244.

66. Adolf Weissmann *The Problem*, 16, 29.

67. Abraham, *Hundred Years*, 9–10, 70–71.

68. See Graves, *Post-Victorian Music*, 150.

69. *Ursprungen und Zielen unserer Kulturentwicklung* (Origins and aims of our cultural development) (Gütersloh, 1875); and *Die Judenfrage und ihr Geheimnisse* (The Jewish question and its secrets) (Gütersloh, 1881).

70. Phillipp Friedrich Silcher, 1789–1860, a folk-song collector who "also composed some 250 songs modelled after Mozart, Weber and Mendelssohn but folklike in style." (Luise Marratta-Schär, "Silcher, (Phillipp) Friedrich" *New Grove*, 2nd ed.). Moser seems to have thought that Mendelssohn modelled his songs on Silcher's.

71. Moser, *Geschichte*, 2: 153, 164.

72. Joseph Joachim, wholly in the spirit of reverence for Schumann's memory, had advised against the concerto's publication.

73. Blessinger, *Mendelssohn, Meyerbeer, Mahler*, 7, 9, 42.

74. See section 47.

75. Lang, *Music in Western Civilization*, 811.

76. *Leipziger Ausgabe der Werke von Felix Mendelssohn Bartholdy*.

77. Harman and Mellers, *Man and his Music*, 833.

78. Plantinga, *Romantic Music*, 254.

79. Extensive lists of recent scholarship will be found in *New Grove*, *RISM*, and in John Michael Cooper's *Felix Mendelssohn Bartholdy: A Guide to Research* (New York and London, 2001).

80. *New Grove*, 2nd ed., 16: 410.

Bibliography

Abraham, Gerald. *A Hundred Years of Music*. London, 1938.

Banister, Henry Charles. *George Alexander Macfarren*. London, 1891.

Barbedette, Hypolite. *Felix Mendelssohn (Bartholdy): Sa vie et ses ouvres*. Paris, 1868.

Becher, Alfred Julius. "Über Hektor Berlioz." *Wiener allgemeine Musik-Zeitung* 5 (1845): 589–90.

Bendedict, Julius. *Sketch of the Life and Works of Felix Mendelssohn Bartholdy*. 2nd ed. London, 1850.

Bennett, J. R. Sterndale. *The Life of William Sterndale Bennett*. Cambridge, 1907.

Berlioz, Hector. *Voyage musical en Allemagne et en Italie*. 2 vols. Paris, 1844.

Blessinger, Karl M. *Mendelssohn, Meyerbeer, Mahler: Drei Kapitel Judentum in Musik als Schlüssel zur Musikgeschichte des 19. Jahrhunderts*. Berlin, 1939.

Bode, Wilhelm. *Goethes Schauspieler und Musiker*. Berlin, 1912.

Botstein, Leon. "The Aesthetics of Assimilation and Affirmation: Reconstructing the Career of Felix Mendelssohn." In *Mendelssohn and His World*, ed. Todd.

Brendel, Franz. "Robert Schumann mit Rücksicht auf Mendelssohn-Bartholdy und die Entwicklung der modernen Tonkunst überhaupt." *Neue Zeitschrift für Musik* 22 (1845): 149. Partly translated in Jürgen Thym, "Schumann in Brendel's *Neue Zeitschrift für Musik* from 1845 to 1856." In *Mendelssohn and Schumann*, ed. Jon W. Finson and R. Larry Todd. Durham, N. C., 1984.

Brockhaus, Heinrich (publisher). *Allgemeine deutsche Real-Encyclopädie für die gebildeten Stände. Conversations-Lexikon*. 9th ed. Leipzig, 1846.

———. *Aus den Tagebüchern von Heinrich Brockhaus*. 5 vols. Leipzig, 1884.

Brodbeck, David. "A Winter of Discontent: Mendelssohn and the *Berliner Domchor*." In *Mendelssohn Studies*, ed. Todd.

Brown, Clive. *Classical and Romantic Performing Practice*. Oxford, 1999.

———. *Die Neubewertung der Quellen von Beethovens Fünfter Symphonie / A New Appraisal of the Sources of Beethoven's Fifth Symphony*. Wiesbaden: Breitkopf und Härtel, 1996.

Bülow, Hans von. *Ausgewählte Schriften*. Leipzig, 1896.

Chorley, Henry Fothergill. *Modern German Music: Recollections and Criticisms*. 2 vols. London, 1854.

————. *Music and Manners in France and Germany.* 3 vols. London, 1841.

Citron, Marcia J., ed. and trans. *The Letters of Fanny Hensel to Felix Mendelssohn.* New York, 1987.

Cooper, John Michael. "Felix Mendelssohn Bartholdy, Ferdinand David und Johann Sebastian Bach: Mendelssohns Bach-Auffasung im Spiegel der Wiederentdeckung der 'Chaconne.'" In *Mendelssohn-Studien: Beiträge zur neueren deutschen Kultur- und Wirtschaftsgeschichte.* Vol. 10. Berlin, 1997.

Crowest, Frederick. *The Great Tone-Poets: Being Short Memoirs of the Greater Musical Composers.* 1st ed. London, 1874. 5th ed. London, 1885.

Dahlhaus, Carl, ed. *Das Problem Mendelssohn.* Studien zur Musikgeschichte des 19. Jahrhunderts. Vol. 41. Regensburg, 1974.

Dannreuther, Edward. "The Romantic Period." In *The Oxford History of Music*, 2nd ed., vol. 5. Oxford, 1931.

Devrient, Eduard. My Recollections of Felix Mendelssohn-Bartholdy, and His Letters to Me. Trans. Natalia Macfarren. London, 1869. Trans. of *Meine Erinnerungen an Felix Mendelssohn-Bartholdy und seine Briefe an mich.* Leipzig, 1869.

Dole, Nathan H. *A Score of Famous Composers.* 1st ed. New York, 1891; 2nd ed., renamed *Famous Composers.* 2 vols. London, 1903.

Dorn, Heinrich. "Recollections of Felix Mendelssohn and His Friends." *Temple Bar* 34 (1872): 397–99. Translated anonymously from *Aus meinem Leben*, 3: 43–81. Berlin, 1872.

Dwight, John S. "Felix Mendelssohn Bartholdy." In *Famous Composers and Their Works*, ed. John K. Paine, Theodore Thomas and Karl Klauser. Vol. 2. 2nd ed. London, [c. 1895].

Eckardt, Julius. *Ferdinand David und die Familie Mendelssohn Bartholdy: Aus hinterlassenen Briefschaften zusammengestellt.* Leipzig, 1888.

Edwards, Frederick George. *Musical Haunts in London.* London, 1895.

Elvers, Rudolf, ed. *Felix Mendelssohn: A Life in Letters.* Trans. Craig Tomlinson. London, 1986.

Federhofer-Königs, Renate. "Der unveröffentliche Briefwechsel Alfred Julius Becher (1803–1848)—Felix Mendelssohn Bartholdys (1809–1847)." In *Studien zur Musikwissenschaft.* Vol. 41, 1992.

Fétis, François Joseph, *Biographie universelle des musiciens et bibliographie générale de la musique.* 1st ed. Paris and Brussels, 1835–1844. 2nd ed. 1860–1865.

Franck, Richard. *Musikalische und unmusikalische Erinnerungen.* 3 vols. Privately published, 1928.

Geiger, Ludwig. *Geschichte der Juden in Berlin.* Berlin, 1871.

Gilbert, Felix, ed. *Bankiers, Künstler und Gelehrte: Unveroffenlichte Briefe der Familie Mendelssohn aus dem 19. Jahrhundert.* Tübingen, 1975.

Gotch, Rosamund Brunel., ed. *Mendelssohn and His Friends in Kensington: Letters from Fanny and Sophy Horsley Written 1833–36.* London, 1934.

Graves, C. L. *Post-Victorian Music*. London, 1911.

Grove, George. "Mendelssohn-Bartholdy, Jakob Ludwig Felix," reprinted in *Grove's Dictionary of Music and Musicians*. Ed. H. C. Colles. 3rd ed. 3: 374–435. London, 192.

Hake, Bruno. "Mendelssohn als Lehrer, mit bisher ungedruckten Briefen Mendelssohns an Wilhelm von Boguslawski." *Deutsche Rundschau* 140 (1909): 453–70. Trans. Susan Gillespie. In *Mendelssohn and His World*, ed. Todd.

Harman, Alec, and Wilfred Mellers. *Man and His Music*. London, 1962.

Hauptmann, Moritz. *The Letters of a Leipzig Cantor*. 2 vols. Trans. A. D. Coleridge. London, 1892. Trans. of *Briefe von Moritz Hauptmann an Franz Hauser*, ed. Alfred Schöne, Leipzig, 1871, and *Briefe von Moritz Hauptmann an Louis Spohr*, ed. Ferdinand Hiller, Leipzig, 1876.

Haweis, Hugh Reginald. *Music and Morals*. London, 1871. 5th ed. London, 1874.

Hecker, Max, ed. *Briefwechsel zwischen Goethe und Zelter in den Jahren 1799 bis 1832*. Berlin, 1913.

Hensel, Sebastian. *The Mendelssohn Family (1729–1847), from Letters and Journals*. 2 vols. London, 1881. Trans. of *Die Familie Mendelssohn 1729–1847, nach Briefen und Tagebüchern*. 2 vols. Berlin, 1879.

Hiller, Ferdinand. *Mendelssohn. Letters and Recollections*. Trans. M. E. von Glehn. London, 1874. Trans. of *Felix Mendelssohn-Bartholdy: Briefe und Erinnerungen*. Cologne, 1874.

Hirsch, Rudolf. "Mendelssohn Bartholdy, Felix." In *Gallerie lebender Tondichter. Biographisch-kritischer Beitrag*. Güns, 1836.

Hirschbach, Herrmann. See *Musikalisch*.

Holland, Henry Scott, and W. S. Rockstro. *Memoir of Madame Jenny Lind-Goldschmidt*. 2 vols. London, 1891.

Horsley, Charles Edward. "Reminiscences of Mendelssohn by His English Pupil Charles Edward Horsley." *Dwight's Journal of Music* 32 (1872): 345ff., 353ff., 361ff. Reprinted in *Mendelssohn and His World*, ed. Todd, 237–51.

Jahn, Otto. "Ueber F. Mendelssohn Bartholdy's Oratorium Elias." *Allgemeine musikalische Zeitung* 50 (1848): 113–22, 137–43.

Joachim, Joseph, and Andreas Moser. *Violinschule*. 3 vols. Berlin, 1902.

Kahlert, August. "Felix Mendelssohn Bartholdy Claviercompositionen." *Caecilia* 16 (1834): 256–60.

Klingemann, Karl, ed. *Felix Mendelssohn-Bartholdys Briefwechsel mit Legationsrat Karl Klingemann in London*. Essen, 1909.

Kossak, Ernst. "Felix Mendelssohn-Bartholdy Geb. 3. Febr. 1809. Gest. 4. Nov. 1847." *Neue Berliner Musikzeitung* 1 (1847): 369–72.

Krautwurst, Franz. "Felix Mendelssohn Bartholdy als Bratschist." In *Gedenkschrift Hermann Beck*, ed. Hermann Dechant and Wolfgang Sieber. Laaber, 1982.

Krüger, Eduard. "F. Mendelssohn-Bartholdy, Drei Psalmen (2. 43. 22.) Opus 78, No. 6 der nachgelassenen Werke. Leipzig, Brietkopf und Härtel. 2 Thlr. 20 Ng." *Neue Berliner Musikzeitung* 4 (1850): 3–5.

———. "Ueber die heutige Oper" *Neue Zeitschrift für Musik* 12 (1840): 58–59.

———. "Zur Kritik Mendelssohn's." *Neue Berliner Musikzeitung* 4 (1850): 81–83.

Kühne, (Ferdinand) Gustav. "Felix Mendelssohn-Bartholdy." *Europa Chronik der gebildeten Welt* (13 Nov. 1847): 757–59.

Lampadius, Wilhelm Adolf. *Life of Felix Mendelssohn Bartholdy*. Ed. and trans. W. L. Gage. New York, 1865. From *Felix Mendelssohn-Bartholdy: Ein Denkmal für seine Freunde*. Leipzig, 1848.

Lang, Paul Henry. *Music in Western Civilization*. New York, 1941, reissued London, 1965.

Lange, Otto. "Elias, ein Oratorium nach Worten des alten Testaments componiert von Felix Mendelssohn-Bartholdy." *Neue Berliner Musikzeitung* 1 (1847): 397–400.

Lenz, Wilhelm von. *Beethoven et ses trois styles*. Paris, 1855 (original ed. St Petersburg, 1852).

Lobe, Johann Christian. *Die Gartenlaube* 1 (1867): 4–8. See also Susan Gillespie, trans. "Conversations with Felix Mendelssohn." In *Mendelssohn and His World*, ed. Todd. Trans. of "Gespräche mit Felix Mendelssohn." In *Fliegende Blätter für Musik* 1 (1855): 280–96. Leipzig.

Loeper, Gustav von. "Mendelssohn-Bartholdy, Felix." In *Deutsche allgemeine Biographie*. Vol. 21. Leipzig, 1885.

Loewe, Carl. *Selbstbiographie*. Berlin, 1870.

Macfarren, George Alexander. "Mendelssohn Bartholdy, Felix." In *The Imperial Dictionary of Universal Biography . . .* , ed. J. F. Waller. 3 vols. London, [1857–1863].

———. "Mendelssohn." *Musical World* 24 (1849): 33–37, 53–56.

Marx, Adolf Bernhard. *The Music of the Nineteenth Century and Its Culture*. Trans. A. H. Wehran. London, 1855. Trans. of *Die Musik des neunzehnten Jahrhunderts und ihre Pflege: Methode der Musik*. Leipzig, 1855.

Meinardus, Ludwig Siegfried. *Ein Jugendleben*. 2 vols. Gotha, 1874.

———. *Die deutsche Tonkunst im 18. und 19. Jahrundert*. Leipzig, 1888.

Mendelssohn, G. B., ed. *Moses Mendelssohn's gesammelte Schriften*. Leipzig, 1843–1845.

Mendelssohn Bartholdy, Felix. *Briefe aus den Jahren 1833 bis 1847*. Ed. Paul Mendelssohn Bartholdy and Karl Mendelssohn Bartholdy. 4th ed. Leipzig, 1864. 1st ed. Leipzig, 1861. Trans. Lady Wallace. *Letters of Felix Mendelssohn Bartholdy from 1833 to 1847*. London, 1867.

———. *Reisebriefe aus den Jahren 1830 bis 1832*. Ed. Paul Mendelssohn Bartholdy. Leipzig 1861. Trans. Lady Wallace. *Letters from Italy and Switzerland.* 2nd ed. London, 1874. 1st ed. London, 1862.

————. *Briefe aus den Jahren 1830 bis 1847 . . . .* Ed. Paul and Karl Mendelssohn Bartholdy. 4th ed. Leipzig, 1878.

————. *Eine Reise durch Deutschland, Italien und die Schweiz.* Ed. Peter Suttermeister. 2nd ed. Tübingen, 1979.

————. *Letters of Felix Mendelssohn to Ignaz and Charlotte Moscheles.* Trans. and ed. Felix Moscheles. London 1888.

Mendelssohn, Joseph. "Moses Mendelssohn's Lebensgeschichte." In *Moses Mendelssohn's gesammelte Schriften,* ed. G. B. Mendelssohn. Vol. 1.

Mendelssohn Bartholdy, Karl. *Goethe and Mendelssohn.* Trans. M. E. von Glehn. 2nd ed. London, 1874. 1st ed. London, 1872. Trans. of *Goethe und Felix Mendelssohn-Bartholdy.* Leipzig, 1871. The English edition also contains a miscellaneous selection of Mendelssohn's letters; the second edition includes additional letters.

Menges, Hermann. "Auch ein Wort über das Oratorium 'Paulus' von Mendelssohn-Bartholdy." *Berliner musikalische Zeitung* 3, no. 40 (3 October 1846): n. p.

Meyer, J., ed. *Das große Conversations-Lexicon für die gebildeten Stände . . . .* Vol. 21. Hildburghausen, 1852.

Mintz, Donald. "1848, Anti-Semitism, and the Mendelssohn Reception." In *Mendelssohn Studies,* ed. Todd.

Moscheles, Charlotte. *Life of Moscheles, with Selections from His Diaries and Correspondence.* Trans. A. D. Coleridge. 2 vols. London, 1873. Trans. of *Aus Moscheles' Leben: Nach Briefen und Tagebüchern.* 2 vols. Leipzig, 1872–1873.

Moser, Andreas. *Joseph Joachim: A Biography.* Trans. Lilla Durham. London, 1901. Trans. of *Joseph Joachim: Ein Lebensbild.* Berlin, 1898.

Moser, Hans Joachim. *Geschichte der deutschen Musik.* 2 vols. Stuttgart and Berlin, 1920–1924.

Müller, F. Max. *Auld Lang Syne.* New York, 1898.

Musikalisch-kritisches Repertorium aller neuen Erscheinungen im Gebiet der Tonkunst herausgegeben durch einen Verein von Künstlern, redigirt von Herrmann Hirschbach. Erster Jahrgang. Leipzig, F. Whistling, 1844. Later *Repertorium für Musik,* herausgegeben unter Mitwirkung merherer von Herrmann Hirschbach. Zweiter Jahrgang. Leipzig, Gustav Brauns (Commission), 1845.

Naumann, Emil. "Erinnerungen an Felix Mendelssohn-Bartholdy." *Neue Berliner Musikzeitung* 3 (1865): 353–55 and 361–63.

Nichols, Roger. *Mendelssohn Remembered.* London. 1997.

Niecks, Freiedrich. "On Mendelssohn and Some of His Contemporary Critics." *Monthly Musical Record* 5 (1875): 162–64.

Nohl, Ludwig, ed. *Letters of Distinguished Musicians.* Trans. Lady Wallace. London, 1867.

Nordmann, Johannes. "Eine Begegnung mit Richard Wagner in Dresden (1847)." In *Richard Wagner Jahrbuch* 1 (1886): 74.

Paine, John K., and Leo R. Lewis. "Music in Germany." In *Famous Composers and Their Works*, ed. John K. Paine, Theodore Thomas and Karl Klauser. Vol. 3. 2nd ed. London [*c.* 1895].

Pearson (Pierson), Henry Hugh. "Deutsche Oratorienmusik in England." *Wiener allgemeine musikalische Zeitung* 3 (1843): 121–23.

Plantinga, Leon *Romantic Music*. New York and London, 1984.

Polko, Elise. *Reminiscences of Felix Mendelssohn-Bartholdy*. Trans. Lady Wallace. London, 1869. Trans. of *Erinnerungen an Felix Mendelssohn-Bartholdy*. Leipzig, 1868. The English edition includes a selection of Mendelssohn's letters, mostly to English recipients.

Reissmann, August. *Felix Mendelssohn-Bartholdy: Sein Leben und seine Werke*. 2nd ed. Berlin, 1872. 1st ed. Berlin, 1867.

Rellstab, Heinrich Friedrich Ludwig *Kritiken und Erinnerungen*. Berlin, 1861.

———. *Aus meinem Leben*. 2 vols. Berlin, 1861.

Repertorium für Musik. See *Musikalisch*.

Riehl, Wilhelm Heinrich. *Musikalische Charakterköpfe*. 8th ed. 2 vols. Stuttgart, 1899. 1st ed. 3 vols. 1853–1856).

Rockstro, William Smyth. *Mendelssohn*. London, 1884.

Rollett, Hermann. *Begegnungen: Erinnerungsblätter (1819–99)*. Vienna, 1903.

Schilling. Gustav. *Encyclopädie der gesammten musikalischen Wissenschaften*. Stuttgart, 1835–1842.

Schindler, Anton. *Biographie von Ludwig van Beethoven*. Münster, 1840.

Schlüter, Joseph. *A General History of Music*. Trans. Mrs Robert Tubbs. London, 1865. From *Allgemeine geschichte der Musik in ubersichtlicher Darstellung*. Leipzig, 1863.

Schubring, Julius. "Reminiscences of Felix Mendelssohn-Bartholdy. On His 57th Birthday, February 3rd 1866." *Musical World* 31 (12 and 19 May 1866). Translated anonymously from "Erinnerungen an Felix Mendelssohn-Bartholdy." *Daheim* 2 (1866): 373ff. Reprinted in *Mendelssohn and his World*, ed. Todd.

Schumann, Robert. *Erinnerungen an Felix Mendelssohn Bartholdy*. Ed. G. Eismann. Zwickau, 1948.

———. *Music and Musicians: Essays and Criticism*. Trans. Fanny Raymond Ritter. Vol 1. London, 1877. Vol. 2. London, 1880. Trans. of *Gesammelte Schriften über Musik und Musiker*. Leipzig, 1854.

———. *On Music and Musicians*. Trans. Paul Rosenfeld. London, 1947. Trans. of *Gesammelte Schriften*. . . .

———. *Tagebücher, 1836–1854*. Ed. Gerd Nauhaus. 2 vols. Leipzig, 1987.

Schneider, Max. *Felix Mendelssohn im Bildnis*. Basle, 1953.

Sheppard, Elizabeth Sara. *Charles Auchester. A Memorial*. 3 vols. London, 1853.

Speyer, Edward. *Wilhelm Speyer der Liederkomponist, 1790–1878.* Munich, 1925.

Spohr, Louis. *Ludwig Spohr's Selbstbiographie.* Cassel and Göttingen, 1860.

Sposato, Jeffrey S. "Creative Writing: The (Self-) Identification of Mendelssohn as a Jew." *Musical Quarterly* 82 (1998): 196.

Stanford, Charles Villiers. *Pages from an Unwritten Diary.* London, 1914.

Stanford, Charles Villiers, and Cecil Forsyth. *A History of Music.* London, 1916.

Suttermeister, Peter, ed. *Felix Mendelssohn Bartholdy. Eine Reise durch Deutschland, Italien und die Schweiz.* 2nd ed. Tübingen, 1979.

Taylor, Edward. "The Birmingham Festival." *Spectator* 10 (1837): 899–901.

Todd, R. Larry. *Mendelssohn's Musical Education . . . .* Cambridge Studies in Music. Cambridge, 1983.

Todd, R. Larry, ed. *Mendelssohn and His World.* Princeton, 1991.

———. *Mendelssohn Studies.* Cambridge, 1992.

Tovey, Donald Francis. "Mendelssohn-Bartholdy, Jakob Ludwig Felix." *Encyclopaedia Britannica.* 14th ed. London, 1929.

Turner, J. Rigbie. "Mendelssohn's Letters to Eduard Devrient." In *Mendelssohn Studies*, ed. Todd.

Varnhagen von Ense, Carl August. *Denkwürdigkeiten des eigenen Lebens*, ed. Konrad Feilchenfeldt. Vol. 3. Frankfurt am Main, 1987.

Wagner, Cosima. *Cosima Wagner's Diaries.* Ed. Martin Gregor-Dellin and Ditrich Mack. Trans. Geoffrey Skelton. 2 vols. London, 1978 and 1980.

Wagner, Richard. *Judaism in Music.* Trans. Edwin Evans. London, 1910. Trans. of *Das Judenthum in der Musik.* Leipzig, 1869.

———. *My Life.* Ed. Mary Whittall. Trans. Andrew Gray. Cambridge, 1983. Trans. of *Mein Leben.* 2 vols. Munich, 1911.

———. *On Conducting.* Trans. Edward Dannreuther. London, 1887. Trans. of *Ueber das Dirigieren.*

Ward Jones, Peter, ed. and trans. *The Mendelssohns on Honeymoon: The 1837 Diary of Felix and Cécile Mendelssohn Bartholdy, Together with Letters to Their Families.* Oxford, 1997.

Wasielewsky, Wilhelm Joseph von. *Aus siebzig Jahren.* Stuttgart and Leipzig, 1897.

Wauer, Wilhelm. "Felix Mendelssohn-Bartholdy und Dr Eduard Krüger." *Neue Berliner Musikzeitung* 4 (1850): 25–27.

Webern, Emil von. "Felix Mendelssohn Bartholdy. Aus den Erinnerungen des Generalleutnants Karl Emil von Webern." *Die Musik* 12 (1912–1913): 83.

Weissmann, Adolf. *The Problem of Modern Music.* Trans. M. Bozman. London and Toronto, 1925. Trans. of *Die Musik in der Weltkrise.* Stuttgart and Berlin, 1922.

Werner, Eric. *Mendelssohn: A New Image of the Composer and His Age.* Trans. Dika Newlin. London, 1963.

Williams, Ralph Vaughan. *National Music and Other Essays.* London, 1963.

[Woringen, Ferdinand von]. v. W. "Felix Mendelssohn-Bartholdy in Düsseldorf in den Jahren 1833–35." *Neue Berliner Musikzeitung* 1(1847): 389–92.

Index

Abraham, Gerald, 493

Allgemeine musikalische Zeitung (Leipzig): general appraisals of FMB's activity, 121, 348; Gewandhaus concerts, 148; critical stance of, 190, 195; FMB's performing, 204; FMB's instrumental works, 325, 327, 329, 333, 342, 350, 353, 356, 360, 406; *Die Hochzeit des* Camacho, 338, 340; *St Paul*, 363; FMB's sacred works, 412, 415

America, critical opinion, 447–48

Argens, Marquis de, 85–88

Arnim, (Ludwig) Achim von, 411

Arnold, Carl, 80, 332

Athenaeum, The, 345–46, 356, 373, 447

Atlas, The, 201, 346, 436

Auber, Daniel-François-Esprit: *Fra Diavolo*, 140

Austin (née Taylor), Sarah, 9

Bach, Johann Sebastian: *St Matthew Passion*, 40–41, 80, 157, 239, 385; projected *Gesamtausgabe*, 46; *Wohltemperierte Clavier*, 61, 284, 296; motets, 130; as classic composer, 131, 439, 451, 455, 485, 488–89; monument in Leipzig, 151, 174, 192, 216; FMB's performance of, 155, 230; Chromatic Fantasia and Fugue, 157–58, 223; Chaconne, 157–58, 223; Triple Concerto (keyboard), 185; organ works, 211–14, 216–17; FMB's view of, 212, 221; D Minor Concerto (keyboard), 218; Violin Sonata in B Minor, 281; B Minor Mass, 290; impact on FMB, 342, 376, 378, 395, 428–29, 461,

470–72, 481–82, 494, 496; influence of *St Matthew Passion* on FMB's *St Paul*, 363, 368–72, 418; comparison of FMB with, 457, 465, 467, 484, 529; FMB's popularisation of, 468

Bad Doberan, 48 (and fig. 2), 111

Bad Soden am Taunus, 53 (and fig. 10), 278

Baermann, Heinrich, 30

Banck, Karl, 405

Barbedette, Hypolite, 486

Bartholdy (originally Salomon), Jacob Lewin, 104

Bartholemew, William, 342

Bartók, Béla, 492

Becher, Alfred Julius, xxiv, 394–97

Becker, Carl Ferdinand, 175–76, 179, 414

Beer, Heinrich, 121–22

Beethoven, Ludwig van: Piano Sonata op. 106, 19; *Fidelio*, 76; C Major Trio, 122; "Pastoral" Symphony, 126, 442, 444; *Leonore* overture, 126; as classic composer, 131, 347, 409, 439, 448, 460, 481, 489; symphonies in Leipzig, 151–52, 159, 191; FMB's performance of, 155–57, 230–32, 243; Ninth Symphony, 174, 235, 238, 251, 254, 332, 415–16; Piano Trio op. 70/1, 208; Fourth Piano Concerto, 208, 218–19, 349, 444, 521; *Kreutzer* Sonata, 217, 236; FMB's view of, 221, 321; Thirty-two Variations in C Minor, 222; Piano Sonata op. 111, 222; FMB's interpretation of, 222; *Coriolan* Overture, 230; Fifth Piano Concerto, 233, 444; *Egmont*,

Beethoven, Ludwig van (*continued*)
242; Fourth Symphony, 244;
Eighth Symphony, 252–54;
Eroica Symphony, 254; Second
Symphony, 254; comparison
with FMB, 325, 345, 382, 391,
396, 440–42, 449, 466–67, 482,
484, 486, 488; "Adelaide," 361;
impact on FMB, 334, 339, 342,
343–44, 351, 356, 361, 395, 428,
434, 470–72; Choral Fantasia,
352; Violin Concerto, 406; Fifth
Symphony, 444
Bellini, Vincenzo, 460
Bendemann, Eduard, 50, 130
Bendixen, Louise, 29, 504
Benedict, (Sir) Julius, xxiv; recollections
of FMB, 4, 77–78; FMB's musi-
cal qualities, 201, 243
Ben More (Scotland), 49 (and fig. 3), 51
Bennett, (Sir) William Sterndale, xxiv,
155, 183, 262–63; recollections of
FMB, 3, 203; FMB's piano playing, 217
Berger, Ludwig: as FMB's teacher, 62, 76,
204, 301, 325, 327, 434; as composer, 332; FMB's respect for, 337
Berlin: *Singakademie*, 40, 64, 80, 111,
115, 118–22; FMB's professional
activity in, 117–18; FMB's distaste for, 120, 122, 162–64, 167–
68, 245–46, 278, 346; Academy
of Arts, 161–67, 184–85
Berliner allgemeine musikalische Zeitung,
325, 332
Berliner musikalische Zeitung, 195
Berlioz, Hector, xxv, 466, 485, 489, 493;
FMB's opinion of, 13–14, 316–17;
F. Hiller's view of, 26; in Leipzig, 174–75, 188; F. David's view
of, 194; opinion of FMB, 230,
394, 502; reception in Vienna,
392; comparison with FMB, 396–
97
Bernhard, Isaac, 58, 85–86
Bible, FMB's knowledge of, 37
Birmingham Festival (1836), 370–71

Blanchard, Henri, 394
Blessinger, Karl, 494–96
Blume, Heinrich, 340
Blümner, Heinrich, 160, 173
Boguslawski, Wilhelm von, 14, 261
Böhme, August Julius Ferdinand, 176,
179
Botstein, Leon, 109
Brahms, Johannes, 409, 485, 491
Brendel, Franz, xxv; *Neue Zeitschrift für
Musik*, 197; compassion of FMB
and Schumann, 397
Brentano, Clemens, 411
Brockhaus, Heinrich, xxv, 84; impres-
sion of FMB, 22; Mendelssohn
mania, 158, 196–97; *Elijah*, 421
Brunel, Isambard Kingdom, 20–21
Brunel (née Horsley), Mary Elizabeth,
20
Bühnau Grabau, Henriette, 176
Bull, Ole, 22
Bülow, Hans von, 493
Bunsen, Carl Josias von, 161, 183–84
Byron, George Gordon, Lord, 40, 133, 438

Caecilia, 332, 344, 351, 374
Campagnoli, Bartolomeo, 149
Carracci, Annibale and Lodovico, 470
Casper, Johann Ludwig, 63
Chelard, Hippolyte-André-Jean-Baptist,
156
Cherubini, Luigi, 267, 395, 473, 489; *Ali
Baba*, 131, 319–20; Requiem, 131,
140; *Les deux journées* (*Der Was-
serträger*), 140
Chopin, Frédéric François, 209–10, 222,
458, 493; Studies, 284
Chorley, Henry Fothergill, xxv, 436,
447, 524; impressions of FMB,
3, 9–12, 203; Gewandhaus or-
chestra, 151–52; Gewandhaus
repertoire, 155–56; FMB's
piano playing, 210–11; *St Paul*,
373–74
Cologne, 1835 Musical Festival, 243
Crowest, Frederick, 488
Czerny, Carl, 392–93

Dahlhaus, Carl, 499
Dando, Joseph Haydon Bourne, 237
Dante, FMB's translations of sonnets, 39, 133
David, Ferdinand, xxv; FMB's physical stamina, 6; as orchestral leader, 150, 153, 167, 194; as teacher, 175–76, 179, 272, 307; as composer, 195, 485; quartet playing, 237, 282; solo playing, 406
Davison, William Henry, xxvi, 29, 436, 447, 504
Devrient, Eduard Philipp, xxvi, 246; recollections of FMB, 4–5, 15–17, 23, 65, 73–74, 167–69, 226, 313; FMB's opinion of, 14, 18, 120–21, 311; Abraham MB, 61; FMB's education, 62–63; the Singakademie election, 118–21; FMB's conduct in Düsseldorf, 141; FMB's piano playing, 208–9, 224; FMB's conducting, 238–41
Dirichlet (née Mendelssohn Bartholdy), Rebecka (Henriette), 25, 62
Döhler, Theodor (von), 26
Dole, Nathan H., 489
Dorn, Heinrich Ludwig Egmont, xxvi, 230; recollections of FMB, 75–76, 234
Dryden, John, 40
Dussek, Jan Ladislav, 19, 204
Düsseldorf: FMB's painting lessons, 47–48; FMB's engagement in, 115, 123–45; 1833 Lower Rhine Musical Festival, 241–42
Dwight, John Sullivan, 447, 489

Eccard, Johannes, 450, 455
Eichhorn, Johann Albrecht Friedrich, 164, 169, 184
England, FMB's liking for, 346
Ensheim, 59
Ernst, Heinrich Wilhelm, 237

Falkenstein, Johann Paul, Baron von, 160, 162, 176, 185

Fétis, François-Joseph, xxvii, 501; impressions of FMB, 5, 393–94
Fink, Gottfried Wilhelm, xxvii, 314, 353–54, 356–59, 363–70, 409
Franck, Eduard, 130, 236, 262
Franck, Hermann, 37
Fränkel, Rabbi David, 58
Fraser's Magazine, 436
Friedrich II, King of Prussia, 57, 85–88
Friedrich August, King of Saxony, 160, 162–63, 173
Friedrich Wilhelm II, King of Prussia, 88–89
Friedrich Wilhelm III, King of Prussia, 161
Friedrich Wilhelm IV, King of Prussia, 115, 161, 168, 170–73; as crown prince, 128, 130
Freytag, Gustav, xxviii
Fuchs, Aloys, 25

Gade, Niels Wilhelm: as composer, 155, 174, 190, 458; as conductor, 185–86, 248; as FMB's protégé, 195; as teacher, 272, 285; as performer, 287
Gans, Leopold, 237
Gauntlett, Henry John, 211
Geibel, Emanuel, 451–52, 528
Gilbert, Felix, 109
Gluck, Christoph Willibald (von), 155, 230, 489
Goethe, Johann Wolfgang von, 478; FMB's appreciation of, 23–24, 37; FMB's translation of Terence, 40; *Achilleïs*, 65; correspondence with Zelter, 111, 441; FMB's visits to, 223, 230; comparison with FMB, 395, 486; influence on FMB, 410, 422, 473
Goethe, Walter, 262
Goldschmidt, Otto, 33, 284; FMB's piano playing, 222
Gottsched, Johann Christoph, 302
Gounod, Charles-François, 486
Grabau, Henriette. See Bühnau Grabau, Henriette

Grau, Rudolf Friedrich, 493
Graves, Charles Larcom, 491
Grell, Eduard August, 121
Grell, Ludwig, 332
Grenser, Carl August, 153–55
Grosheim, Dr., 344
Grove, (Sir) George, 6, 15, 219–21, 223
Gugel, Heinrich and Rudolf, 204
Gyrowetz, Adalbert, 387

Handel, George Frederick: *Israel in Egypt*, 38, 41–46, 126, 130–31, 157; *Acis and Galatea* and "Dettingen" Te Deum, 40–41; *Samson*, 131; *Messiah*, 131, 157, 182, 385; *Judas Maccabeus*, 131, 225; FMB's performance of, 155; FMB's admiration for, 319; impact on FMB, 342, 353, 363, 369–72, 376–78, 412–13, 428–29, 461, 470–71, 494; as composer, 438–39, 450, 455, 485; sacred works 457; FMB's popularisation of, 468; comparison of FMB with, 489
Handley (née von Schauroth), Delphine, 28–30
Harman, Alec, 499
Harmonicon, The, 345, 347–48, 350, 355, 360
Härtel, Hermann, 156
Hauptmann, Moritz, xxvii; on FMB's letters, 38; as teacher, 175–76, 179, 269, 272, 285, 307; reputation in Leipzig, 195; on FMB's conducting, 248; FMB's opinion of, 263–64, 270–71
Haweis, Hugh Reginald, 488
Haydn, Franz Joseph: *The Seasons*, 130, 232–33; FMB's performance of, 131, 155; as model for composition, 282, 471; as classic composer, 347, 438–39, 441, 461, 470, 472; *The Creation*, 363; comparison with FMB, 382, 489, 466; influence on FMB, 429
Haza, Jeanette von, 381

Hebbel, Friedrich, 463
Hegel, Georg Wilhelm Friedrich, 74
Heinke, Henry, 203
Henning, Carl Wilhelm, 62
Hensel (née Mendelssohn Bartholdy), Fanny (Cécilia), 29–30, 111, 118, 182–83; death of, 53, 432; relationship with FMB, 61–62; musical abilities, 79; religious faith, 90–92; the family name, 105, 108; *Ein Sommernachtstraum* première, 181; piano playing, 222; FMB's revisions, 313; FMB's artistic agenda, 320–21
Hensel, Sebastian, xxvii; *Die Familie Mendelssohn*, 76, 184, 337
Herz, Henri, 321, 392
Heyse, Carl Wilhelm Ludwig, 39–40, 60, 62, 64, 68–69, 111, 139
Hildebrandt, Theodor, 50, 130, 271–72
Hiller, Ferdinand, xxvii–xxviii, 134, 155, 230, 235, 272, 458; recollections of FMB, 5, 19, 21–24, 26, 237, 312, 349; FMB's feelings for Cécile, 30–31; FMB's writings, 39; Lea MB, 60–61; Leipzig Gewandhaus orchestra, 151; Leipzig quartet concerts, 157; *Ein Sommernachtstraum* première, 181; estrangement from FMB, 185; FMB's piano playing, 208, 221–22, 224–25; Twenty-four Studies, 232; FMB's conducting, 244–45
Hirsch, Rudolf, 389–90, 392–93
Hirschbach, Herrmann, xxviii, 399, 488; Leipzig Conservatorium, 179; Leipzig music, 187–96; FMB's Violin Concerto, 407–8
Homberg, Herz, 59
Homer, FMB's knowledge of, 37
Horsley, Charles Edward, xxviii, 263–66
Horsley, Elizabeth Hutchins (Mrs. Horsley), 20
Horsley, Francis Arabella (Fanny). See Thompson (née Horsley), Frances Arabella,
Horsley, John, 15

DATE